HERITAGE OF BRITAIN

HERITAGE OF BRITAIN

Great Moments in the Story
of an Island Race

Published by
THE READER'S DIGEST ASSOCIATION LIMITED
London   New York   Montreal   Sydney   Cape Town

Dawn of the island's story

For nearly a quarter of a million years nomad hunters struggle for survival in an untamed land before farmers from the Continent set Britain on the road to civilisation

The story of mankind in Britain goes back a quarter of a million years to a time when men's whole lives were a bitter struggle against gnawing hunger or unexpected death. Slowly, through the aeons of time, they learnt to master new skills, and began the long struggle to control their environment. It was the beginning of the epic journey to civilisation.

In the late Ice Age, when Britain was still joined by land to Europe, bands of hunter nomads roamed what is now southern England. At first they possessed only primitive flint axes like those found at Swanscombe in Kent. Slowly, they evolved finer and more effective hunting weapons. But still, during the worst times when ice, snow and blizzards swept the land, their shelters were caves like Kent's Cavern in Devon (pp. 14–15).

Between 4000 and 3000 BC, groups of primitive farmers arrived in Britain, this time by sea, for Britain had become an island. They began to sweep away the island's mantle of virgin forest, to grow grain and raise their cattle, sheep and pigs. At last man was not wholly dependent on nature. He was beginning to control his own food supply.

Now that some men could grow and store more than they needed to eat, others could set up specialist industries like the flint mines of Grime's Graves in Norfolk (pp. 16–17); and, as men settled and population grew, there was leisure to ponder the mysteries of life and build impressive, complex monuments, such as Stonehenge (pp. 18–19).

The Metal Age produced a race of wealthy chieftains in Britain. Adorned in their finery of gold and amber, they were buried in great mounds like the Bush Barrow near Stonehenge (pp. 20–21).

About 600 BC iron began to replace bronze as the metal for tools and weapons. An exuberant and beautiful art developed (pp. 22–23) under the patronage of chieftains. These were the fierce warriors who confronted Julius Caesar when he invaded England in 55 BC.

ACHIEVEMENT OF THE FIRST BRITONS

For more than 1000 years, the building and re-building of the awe-inspiring sanctuary at Stonehenge on Salisbury Plain reflected the development and progress of early man in Britain. Recent surveys and excavations have shown that the great monument was more than a religious meeting place. It may have been a gigantic observatory, the result of early man's strong determination to learn more about the mysterious forces which affected his everyday life. Mastery of the movements of the heavens would enable him to anticipate the seasons' changes – a tremendous break-through in a predominantly agricultural age. Stonehenge survives as a reminder of this brilliant ingenuity and determination to conquer the unknown.

Men battle for survival in an age of ice and snow

AN ICE-AGE HOME
Kent's Cavern, a series of winding, narrow passages and great chambers, reaches more than 300 ft into a limestone hill near Torquay in Devon. Festoons of stalactites hang from the roof. Here, 40,000 years ago, Old Stone Age people sheltered. They used tools of flint, antler and bone (right).

Forty thousand years ago, Britain was in the last stages of the Ice Age. A great ice-sheet covered the north. Small groups of hunters roamed the arctic wastes to the south. Sometimes the blizzards and bitter winds drove these people – and often their animal prey – into the shelter of caves. Kent's Cavern, near Torquay, is one such refuge.

To this complex of narrow passages and vast chambers of limestone came generations of highly skilled hunters for more than 20,000 years. They possessed a sophisticated arsenal. They had spears and spear-throwers, long shafts which effectively increased the length of a man's arm so that he could throw spears greater distances. They also used bone harpoons and weapons with fine flint cutting edges set in wooden handles.

Hunter and hunted
Often, after a kill, the hunters dragged their quarry back to the cave. The bones left on the cave floor over passing centuries provide evidence of the generations who had found a refuge in these caves.

Remains of mammoths, woolly rhinoceroses, cave bears, horses, hyenas, red deer and reindeer have been discovered. They date from the last spell of intense cold, which began about 17,000 years ago.

A fragment of human jaw with three teeth in place was also unearthed. The teeth differ from those of a man of today only in their degree of wear and freedom from disease. They were worn down by the tough food of the hunters.

THE HUNTERS AND THEIR KILL *The hunters of the Old Stone Age were skilled at organising group expeditions to hunt the great beasts of the Ice Age. Their survival depended on their courage and skill. At Kent's Cavern, hunters prepare to skin and joint a dead cave bear, using flint tools. Animals' warm skins gave the hunters comfort in an inhospitable world.*

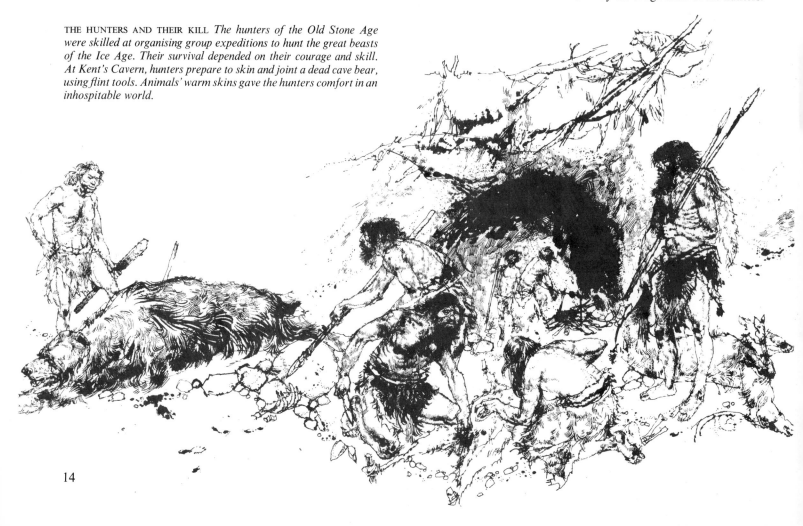

THE FIRST KNOWN BRITON

When Britain was still joined to the Continent 250,000 years ago, the first known inhabitant lived in the valley where the Kent town of Swanscombe now stands. He and his tribe shared the forests with the prehistoric animals that meant two things to them: meat and danger. There were straight-tusked elephants, gigantic cattle called aurochs, two species of fearsome rhinoceroses, horses and red deer.

The gravel pit where Swanscombe man's only remains – the skull bones (below) – were found.

Moving in for a kill, Swanscombe hunters trap a deer.

Armed only with wooden spears, the Swanscombe hunters tracked their prey in the forests of oak, elm and viburnum. After a kill, they skinned and butchered the animal on the spot using hand-held flint axes, skilfully chipped to give cutting edges. Flints were so plentiful and easily chipped that, once used, they were often simply thrown away.

Swanscombe man probably had beetling brows and a massive jaw. Only three of his skull bones have survived, but experts believe that he was not very different from men of today. His brain was much the same size.

His life was precarious. Disease and hunting accidents must have taken a heavy toll. The bones which have been found belong to someone who died young – probably aged only 20–25.

The most tantalising question about Swanscombe man is whether he understood the secret of fire. Pieces of charcoal and fire-shattered flints have been found with his bones and tools, but they may have been the result of forest fires.

These early Britons made clothes of fur and skin, sewn together with bone needles. They also knew how to use and control fire.

Their elaborate tools, their skill in tracking and killing their prey, and the speed with which they adapted to the changes of the Ice Age suggest a highly developed people. The inhabitants of Kent's Cavern were just that – the first Modern Men to live in Britain. They belonged to the *Homo sapiens sapiens* group, which includes all present-day people. Their sophisticated culture ushered in the final phase of the Old Stone Age.

During the Ice Age, the sea level constantly changed, and Britain was periodically joined to the Continent. The hunters spent much of their time on the move, following their prey as it migrated with the seasons. But arctic Britain was inhospitable, the edge of the habitable world. It attracted few hunters, and there were probably fewer than 2000 people in Britain south of the ice-sheet. Traces of them have been found in caves in the Mendips, in South Wales and Derbyshire.

BRITAIN'S FIRST ART *A Stone Age hunter scratched this horse on bone at Creswell Crags in Derbyshire, almost 40,000 years ago.*

The hunters had to devote most of their energy to survival. Yet they possessed a high degree of artistic skill. This can be seen in many of the articles they used. The carefully made barbed harpoons and spear-throwers reveal a people who took pleasure in functional design.

The so-called ceremonial staff from Gough's Cave at Cheddar in Somerset is a fine example of their craftsmanship. The patiently whittled antler rod, 6½ in. long with a hole at one end, was perhaps an arrow-straightener.

Life after death

The hunters adorned themselves with strings of animal teeth and mollusc shells. They had a reverence for the dead, and almost certainly believed in life after death.

This deep-rooted belief has been revealed by a discovery at Paviland Cave in the Gower peninsula of South Wales. There the early Britons buried one of their young men with great care. The corpse, that of a tall man aged about 25, with the head missing, was laid out and covered with powdered red ochre. Stones were set at each end, and around were placed an ivory bracelet, ivory rods, perforated shells and an elephant's skull, probably for his use in the afterlife. Was this burial a special case – honours afforded to a man of high status – or was it perhaps a sacrifice to the gods? Whatever the motives, these relics show that the creative powers of these Britons were directed beyond the needs of sheer subsistence.

Britain in the harsh grip of the Ice Age

About 1 million years ago, the climate of the Northern Hemisphere began to deteriorate. In Europe and Asia the Ice Age had begun.

But the Ice Age was not a continuous period of ice and snow. Four major phases of intense cold, the glaciations, were separated by three warmer periods. It was during the second of these that Swanscombe man lived.

At the height of a glaciation, Britain was uninhabitable, with an ice-sheet up to 1000 ft thick in the north. During the second glaciation it reached the Thames Valley.

South of the ice, glaciers gouged out the valleys. Biting winds swept the frozen ground where only dwarf pines and lichens could grow. This tundra was the home of reindeer, woolly rhinoceroses, cave bears and mammoths. It was during the last glaciation that Modern Men lived at Kent's Cavern.

As it became warmer, the ice retreated northwards. Grasses and sedges, and later pine and birch forest, replaced the tundra.

During the first and third of these warmer periods, the climate was hotter than today. Hippopotamuses and rhinoceroses roamed the forests of firethorn and oak.

EXTINCT BEASTS *The mammoth and woolly rhinoceroses of the tundra died out when the weather grew warmer and the forests took over.*

BRITAIN BECOMES AN ISLAND *About 8000 BC, as the ice retreated, water flooded from the North Sea across the land-bridge and into the Channel. The gateway from the Continent was closed.*

Skilled miners create Britain's first industry

A PREHISTORIC PITHEAD

Local superstition has named this site, near Thetford in Norfolk, Grime's Graves – the digging place of the devil ('Grim'). But in reality it was one of the first industrial sites in Britain. More than 4500 years ago, men of the New Stone Age mined for flint there. The chalk figure of a woman (right) was perhaps a fertility symbol worshipped by the miners.

UNDERGROUND
Men at work in the flint mines. Equipped with only simple tools – picks and axes – these prehistoric miners excavated 10,000 cu. ft of earth and stone from one of the mines' many shafts and galleries.

Perhaps the greatest break-through in the story of the British islands took place gradually over 1000 years of history. After more than 200,000 years, in which the inhabitants of Britain had lived by hunting and gathering wild plants and fruits, a new way of life slowly evolved.

The new age came about because of a great wave of migration from the Continent about 3500 BC. The migrants were Britain's first farmers. They forged primitive agricultural settlements out of the untamed wilderness of their new country.

Over centuries their knowledge and experience spread throughout the country as farming slowly supplanted hunting as the principal source of food. Agriculture, however, needed new and different implements with which to tend the fields. This need led to the creation of Britain's first industry – flint mining.

The flints which were dug out of the ground were chipped and polished into the tools of the new age – axes for felling trees, primitive farming implements and weapons for defence. They represent a significant step in the evolution of organised life, the beginning of the long process of turning England into pasture and arable land, and helping to create a society where trade flourished.

An underground maze

Of the 17 flint mines which have been found in southern England, the most remarkable is Grime's Graves, near Thetford in Norfolk, a 93 acre area of intensive mining which was being worked over 4500 years ago.

Since the best flint lay buried 40 ft below the surface under thick layers of sand, clay and chalk, the miners had to sink deep shafts to reach it. No fewer than 600 shafts were dug at Grime's Graves, varying in depth from shallow open-cast workings 10–15 ft deep to astonishing pits 40 ft deep and over 40 ft wide. The complex system of tunnels and galleries followed the thin flint seams and formed an elaborate underground maze.

These gigantic workings were all excavated with the most primitive of tools. All the miners had to dig with were picks made of deer antlers, or polished flint axe-heads fitted into wooden handles.

Wooden shovels were probably used to clear away surface sand and clay, and the flint was raised to the surface in wicker or skin baskets attached to ropes. These were brought up from deep, dark chambers lit by torches or chalk lamps fuelled by animal fat.

Now and then things went wrong. One shaft which failed to find a good vein of flint was turned into an underground shrine, possibly to placate the gods of fertility who were believed to watch over production.

Close to the entrance to one of the galleries, chalk blocks were piled to form a pedestal. On top of this was placed a chalk figure of a pregnant woman. Near by stood a chalk phallus

16

and carved chalk spheres. Towards the centre of the shaft, another pedestal, this time of flint, bore seven of the antler picks and a small chalk cup, possibly for making offerings to the gods.

The miners were also traders whose wares were peddled over a wide distance along the upland ridgeways which connected the scattered farming communities. The rough stone was not cut to its final shape until it reached the customer, who would grind and polish his tool to a smooth surface.

The rough pieces of stone were exchanged for corn, skins, pottery or other necessities of life. Some flint travelled great distances. Tools of Welsh stone have been found as far east as Essex.

Considerable skill and ingenuity marked these early mining exploits. Grime's Graves is proof that, even at this early stage of history, full-time craftsmen-specialists already existed. The beginnings of industry and of trade had come to Britain.

TECHNOLOGY IN STONE

In the absence of detailed records, stone tools provide valuable clues to the development of technology in prehistoric Britain. Some 300,000 years separate the crude 'choppers' of the early hunters from the finely shaped arrow-heads which were fashioned by farmers modern enough to practise metal-casting.

Chipped core of flint, shaped c. 300,000 BC.

Swanscombe man's hand-axe, c. 250,000 BC.

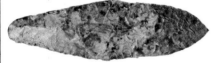

A Wiltshire farmer's flint dagger, c. 2000 BC.

Polished stone battle-axe, c. 2000 BC.

Flint arrow-head, made c. 1800 BC.

A new society takes root on the fertile downs

No one will ever know why the first farmers embarked on the dangerous journey to Britain, but their arrival in the south of England brought about one of the greatest of all changes in the history of the island.

In 4000 BC, Britain was still populated by men who hunted their food and ate wild fruit and roots – just as their ancestors had done for at least 200,000 years. But by 3000 BC, self-sufficient farming communities had spread to most parts of the country.

The farmers brought with them in their small boats not only the seeds of barley and of wheat, but sheep and cattle. They brought new types of stone tools including sickles.

With their flint axes, they hacked out clearings in the thick woods, which covered most of the country. The logs and underbrush were burnt and the seeds sown into the ash-enriched earth. In southern Britain, the well-drained chalk and limestone hills proved to be exceptionally fertile.

But these first farmers were mainly dependent for their daily livelihood on their herds of sheep and cattle, whose need for grazing helped to replace forest with grassland. Because their animals needed a constant supply of fresh grazing-land, the first farmers were semi-nomadic, moving on when grazing was exhausted.

Life on the land

Life was scarcely easier for them than for the hunting people they were supplanting. Clearing the land, breaking the soil, sowing and reaping was in many ways a more arduous form of existence. Crops and animals were prey to natural disasters such as bad weather or outbreaks of disease. But, for the first time, the food supply was at least partially under human control.

In good years, enough grain could be grown to last through a lean winter. In the autumn, cattle could be butchered to provide meat for many weeks. Clothing made from their hides gave admirable protection against the winter cold. So the farmers persisted, and the hunter-gatherer bands gradually disappeared or were absorbed into their numbers.

The tools of the new farmers were extremely primitive. Digging sticks were used for planting and hoeing. Later, knowledge of the ard – a crude plough pulled by men or oxen – reached Britain from the Continent. Sickles and various other cutting tools and scrapers, made from fine flint blades and mounted in bone or wood handles, were also used. Axes served to help build timber and thatch huts.

To store grain, and perhaps milk, the farmers needed containers. The art of pottery making was thus brought to Britain. At first, the dishes that were made were plain and undecorated. But by about 3300 BC decorations had begun to be scratched on the clay.

As food supplies became more abundant, the farming societies grew rapidly. Across the inhabited world, herding and agriculture helped to increase the population to many times what it had been in the hunting and gathering era of about 8000 BC. The same area of land could support many more farmers than hunters. And, as farming techniques improved, a more settled life became possible.

An increasingly large and complex society soon began to construct its first full-scale monuments. On several hilltops in southern Britain, such as Windmill Hill in Wiltshire and Hembury in Devon, large earthwork enclosures were erected. Around them were dug a series of ditches, which in places were bridged by solid causeways.

An elaborate society

These causewayed camps were certainly not inhabited all the year round. They may have served as tribal gathering places for barter, feasting or worship. There, scattered communities could reaffirm their rules and relationships with each other.

During the same period, a definable social structure began to emerge in Britain. The top rung of the ladder was occupied by prominent men and their families, who received burials of marked splendour.

Whole communities might work together to build their tombs – long earthen mounds or barrows from 30 to 100 yds long. Beneath each, several people were buried and their high status was commemorated by the white chalk, which shone for years before grass grew again on these mounds. These honoured dead headed a now quite elaborate society. The basis had been laid for the dramatic cultural developments of the next 1000 years.

FARMERS' ART *Earthenware pots fashioned by the early farmers who settled in Wiltshire. The first pots were plain and dish-like.*

The mystery of Britain's Stone Age masterpiece

A STONE AGE CATHEDRAL
Dawn at Stonehenge, Britain's greatest prehistoric monument. The ruins of this unique sanctuary have aroused the awe of visitors for centuries. The Normans acclaimed it one of the wonders of Britain. Archaeologists now believe that the stone circle was built about 4–5000 years ago. But its precise purpose still remains a mystery.

High on the windswept downs of Wiltshire are the ruins of one of Britain's first and in some ways most impressive cathedrals. Over a span of nearly 1000 years, generations of prehistoric men toiled at the building of the great stone circles of Stonehenge.

But the reason for their long years of activity, the inspiration that drove them to build and rebuild this massive monument, has never been discovered. In all its stark grandeur, Stonehenge remains one of the greatest mysteries in the story of man.

The first steps

Work began at Stonehenge sometime after 3000 BC, when primitive farming communities living on the Wiltshire downs excavated a circular ditch with a 6 ft high wall of chalk inside, enclosing a circular area more than 280 ft across. Just inside, a circle of 65 pits was dug. They probably resulted from religious ceremonies, and were discovered in the 17th century. Some of the pits have since been found to contain cremated human bones.

Around 600 years passed before the next stage of building at Stonehenge began. About 2200 BC, at least 80 bluestones, each weighing up to 4 tons, were set up in a double circle.

These stones originated in the Prescelly Mountains in Dyfed, more than 150 miles away. Some experts believe that they were carried to southern England by ice and flood

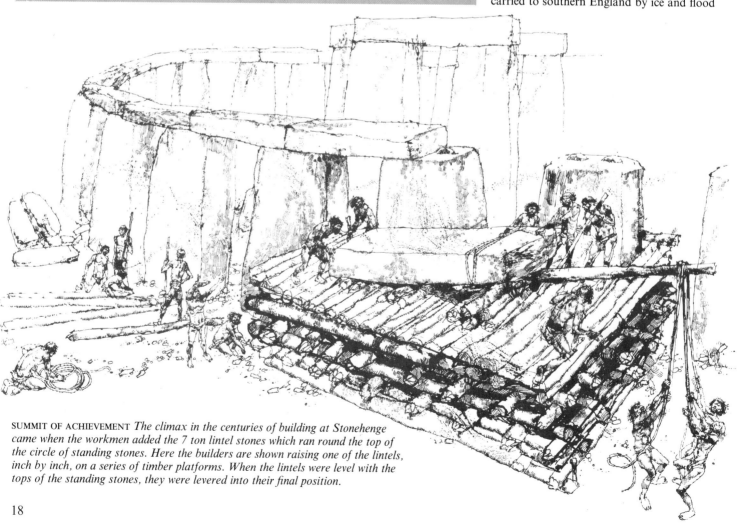

SUMMIT OF ACHIEVEMENT *The climax in the centuries of building at Stonehenge came when the workmen added the 7 ton lintel stones which ran round the top of the circle of standing stones. Here the builders are shown raising one of the lintels, inch by inch, on a series of timber platforms. When the lintels were level with the tops of the standing stones, they were levered into their final position.*

waters during an Ice Age. Others consider that the builders themselves may have brought them on rafts by sea and river to the Avon Valley, and then dragged them overland to Stonehenge.

Even before this second version of Stonehenge was completed, it was replaced by a grand new design. The bluestones were apparently taken down and stockpiled near by. Great sarsen stones – blocks of sandstone found on the Marlborough Downs – were loaded on to sledges and dragged the 20 miles to the site over rollers of logs.

The task was enormous. Recent experiments have shown that 200 men would have been needed to move the largest stone even on level ground. When the stones finally reached the site, the work of erection began. The outer circle, about 100 ft in diameter, was composed of 30 upright stones, each weighing about 25 tons. Its 30 lintels weighed about 7 tons each.

For the uprights, foundation pits would have been dug with one side sloping. Then, each stone was probably dragged out on rollers until its base projected above the bottom of the pit. By levering the other end up, the stone could be slid into the hole.

The next stage was to raise it into a vertical position by levering from an adjacent timber stack and by hauling. When all the uprights were in position, work on the lintels could begin. It is probable that they were raised inch by inch on a stack of timber and finally slid sideways on to the top of the standing stones.

Culminating achievement

As the last lintel fell into place, the building of Stonehenge reached its climax, the highest achievement of prehistoric people in Europe. A few years later the bluestones were finally placed to form the 'inner sanctum' of the Stonehenge that stands today.

The monument was now complete, about 1000 years after the digging of the first ditch. Clearly it fulfilled a major role in the life of the inhabitants of the Salisbury Plain. But the nature of that role is shrouded in mystery.

The mathematical accuracy of the stones' positioning has led some experts to suggest that Stonehenge was designed as an elaborate observatory. Priests could have used its stones in relation to the rising and setting sun to measure time – and then to plot the times to sow crops, to slaughter cattle and to perform other necessary acts of the farming year. The observatory could also have helped them to predict eclipses of the sun and moon – events regarded with superstitious awe.

But the prime motive for these centuries of dedicated activity must have been religious. Even in the first years of its long life, Stonehenge was a place of mystery – a temple dedicated to the unknown power which governs the sun and moon, the wheeling galaxies of the night sky and all the miraculous workings of life on earth.

Lasting memorials to prehistoric genius

The new way of life brought to Britain by immigrant farmers had led to enormous social changes. Closely knit, settled communities had grown up, ruled by prominent families. These had led, about 3000–2500 BC, to the building of great hill-top camps as meeting places, and to the construction of collective tombs for men of wealth and power. The next 500 years saw the creation of Britain's first monumental architecture.

Men began building huge earthwork enclosures, or henges, at Avebury, Durrington Walls and Marden, all in Wiltshire. At Avebury, one of the largest henges in Britain, the outer bank has a diameter of 1400 ft. The henge at Durrington is 1600 ft across.

The henges acted as religious centres for large areas and they were used for over 500 years. They were rather like medieval cathedrals. Both resulted from enormous communal effort and centralised organisation motivated by religious aspirations.

The exuberance and vision of the same farming people also led to the building of Silbury Hill, in Wiltshire, the largest man-made structure in prehistoric Europe. Earth and layers of chalk blocks were piled up to a height of 130 ft. But excavations over many years have revealed no clue to its purpose.

By this time, society had become sufficiently organised to supply the immense labour force necessary for these great projects. Agriculture had reached a stage where men could be spared from the fields for long stretches. This had been achieved in a mere 1500 years – the time since the introduction of farming.

Britain's first scientists

Some experts believe that late in this period Britain produced its first scientists – men capable of undertaking extended periods of observation of the sun, the moon and the stars. They used their knowledge to construct stone circles in which the stones were meticulously placed, to form gigantic mathematical instruments. These arrangements may have been used for the measurement of time, and to predict phases of the moon and even eclipses.

Britain's first scientists belonged to farming communities, with a way of life determined by the seasons. In Britain, with its uncertain climate, their accurate methods of dating the seasons must have been particularly valuable. At Stonehenge their technical skill and deep religious instincts created a monument that remains one of the wonders of the world.

WORK OF GENERATIONS *Silbury Hill, in Wiltshire, was the largest man-made structure in prehistoric Europe. It covers 5½ acres.*

STONE AGE SANCTUARY *At Avebury, Wiltshire, Europe's largest stone circle lies within a henge, a circular ditch and bank enclosing 28 acres.*

BURIAL PLACE *This 'dolmen' or tomb of great stones at Llanglydwen in Dyfed was once covered by a great mound of earth.*

MOUNTAIN MONUMENT *Rimmed by mountains in the Lake District, Castlerigg stone circle, formed of 38 stones, is 100–110 ft across.*

A warrior chieftain takes his treasures to the grave

MONUMENT TO A BRONZE AGE CHIEF
On Normanton Down, near Stonehenge, Wessex tribesmen erected this round barrow over the remains of their leader about 3500 years ago. The rich ornaments and weapons buried with him, such as this gold belt hook (right), suggest that he was a man of great importance. But the outstanding symbol of the chieftain's power was his mace (below), headed with polished stone and decorated with carved bone.

The barrows that dot the downlands of southern Britain are an enduring legacy of an age when the first organised societies were formed in Britain. The rulers of these early societies were invested with a power and grandeur that their subjects believed would continue even after death itself. This was the motive that prompted the lavish burial ceremonies that produced the downland barrows.

One such ceremony took place about 1650 BC, when a group of tribesmen carried the body of their ruler across Salisbury Plain to a sacred burial ground within sight of Stonehenge. When they reached the appointed place, the mourners laid their dead chieftain – a tall, stout man – on his back, with his head towards the south. He was regally dressed, and splendidly armed as befitting a leader and a warrior. The care taken over this no doubt indicated the status his people believed he would hold in the next world.

The possessions buried with him in the Bush Barrow were products of a new form of society – one which created an aristocracy commanding technical skills never seen before in Britain. The chieftain's followers did not rely on brittle, blunt-edged stone tools, nor on the primitive metal implements of their predecessors. Their smiths worked the copper, tin and gold of Britain into ornaments of great beauty – fit for the use of a king.

Ornaments for a king

Two daggers were placed at the chief's right side. One was made of copper, with a blade nearly 10 in. long, and one of bronze, with a blade nearly 1 ft in length. Both had wooden handles, and both were sheathed. The pommel of the smaller one was decorated with thousands of tiny gold pins arranged in intricate patterns – a work of delicate and skilful craftsmanship.

A hook of gold adorned his belt. Just above the chief's left shoulder, in a position convenient for a right-handed grip, the tribesmen laid his bronze-headed axe. A knife, also of bronze, rested in his hand, and above his head lay an object made of wood, metal rivets and bronze – probably a shield.

Not far away, again on his right-hand side, was reverently placed what must have been the chieftain's symbol of office – a wooden staff, decorated with finely wrought ivory and topped with a large polished stone: his ceremonial mace. Only one other example has been found – a macehead made of stone, decorated with gold bosses, from a royal burial in Dorset.

When the funeral itself was over, the mourners turned their attention to the final

A ROYAL FUNERAL *On a sacred plain within sight of Stonehenge, a Wessex chieftain is buried in full regalia. His followers provided him with the finest luxuries of the Bronze Age. At his side they laid daggers of copper and bronze, and his ceremonial mace. A breastplate and belt hook, both of gold, adorned his body. With his bronze battle-axe at the ready and his shield above his head, the chief would be fully equipped for the afterlife.*

The age of metal transforms life in Britain

Two hundred years before the people of Wessex buried their chieftain in the Bush Barrow, the first metal-using races came to Britain. They brought with them knives and axeheads made of copper, and gold jewellery. More importantly, they brought the knowledge needed to extract these metals, to make useful alloys and to fashion them. The Metal Age had begun in Britain, and now the island's valuable tin, copper and gold ores could be worked into useful tools and beautiful ornaments.

Copper produced by smelting ore is soft enough to be hammered into shape, but hard enough to take a cutting edge. And so it was an obvious starting-point for the prehistoric smiths. They soon discovered that by adding a small amount of tin it was possible to make a much harder alloy – bronze.

Tools made of bronze would make a sharper point and cut much more cleanly than copper or flint. Unlike stone, bronze tools could be recast if they broke, re-straightened if they bent, and sharpened over and over again.

To begin with, copper and tin – and therefore bronze – must have been rare in Britain. But gradually the knowledge and use of the new material spread, as the copper ore supplies of Ireland, Wales and northern England were opened up, and tin from Cornwall became more accessible.

At first, bronze seems to have been used for luxury goods only. Bronze beads and even small knives, found in the early graves, were status symbols, rather than practical tools. Tools for everyday use were still made of flint.

A few centuries later, more effective daggers were made, together with flat bronze axes. These were the weapons buried with the Wessex chieftain in the Bush Barrow.

In the early stages, the objects were cast by pouring the molten metal into open moulds of stone or clay. Then they were hammered or trimmed into final shape. But as supplies of bronze increased, so did the range of products and the technical skill of the smiths.

Another new metal

Fostered by contacts with metal-working on the Continent, British trade and production in bronze reached its peak in the 8th century BC. But during the next two centuries, knowledge of an even better metal was beginning to spread to the island. It was iron – abundant, widespread and much more durable.

Producing iron tools involved an elaborate process of high-temperature smelting, reheating and forging – a process which remained unknown to generations of British bronzesmiths. The secrets of iron-making were gradually carried across Europe from the eastern Mediterranean.

From about 500 BC, British warriors, like their Continental neighbours, were equipped with iron stabbing swords and, occasionally, iron-fitted chariots. But these people knew more than fighting. They were Celts – as famous for their delight in decoration as they were notorious for their ferocity. They hammered their iron not only into weapons, but into the finest art of prehistoric Britain.

rites. Over the body they raised a 25 ft high bowl-shaped mound of earth and chalk, which served both to protect the corpse of their chief and to commemorate the position he had enjoyed during his lifetime.

The dead ruler was a member of the Wessex people, warrior aristocrats with contacts as far afield as Brittany, Ireland and Northern Europe. Their lands were inhabited by farmers and traders whose traditions and way of life dated back several centuries, and by more recent immigrants with a rudimentary knowledge of metal-working.

Wealth and power

The Wessex people brought the rich metal resources of Britain under their control, and founded a culture of exceptional wealth and power. Their prosperity was founded on a network of far-flung trading connections. Goods were exchanged with the inhabitants of Ireland, Scandinavia, Brittany and central Europe, and they perhaps even made trading agreements with the people of the eastern Mediterranean.

Their homeland on the Wiltshire Downs was ideally situated for trade. Northwards lay the shores of the Bristol Channel, from which boats crossed to Ireland. Southwards, they were within easy reach of the English Channel and Continental trade routes.

In this way the Wessex chieftains could exchange the grain, wool and hides produced by their peasant subjects for the precious metals of Ireland, Cornwall, Wales and northern England. And these goods, in turn, would be traded for the luxuries of all Europe. In addition to wealth, trade brought them increased knowledge and power.

Their brilliant organisational abilities, their exceptional technical skills and, above all, their mastery of metal, made the Wessex people the master craftsmen of their age.

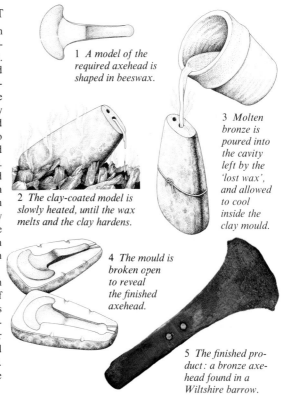

THE EXUBERANT ARTS OF A WARRIOR PEOPLE

Like the Celtic character, Celtic art was energetic, exuberant and explosive, and yet at the same time full of humour.

The Celts, a warrior people, spread across much of Europe by the 5th and 4th centuries BC. Many established themselves in well-defended hill-forts in the south and west of England. Often highly complex constructions, the hill-forts were protected by a system of multiple ditches and ramparts. Within these virtually impregnable hill-top fortresses the members of a tribe and their animals lived.

By about 200 BC, an essentially British style of Celtic art began to appear under Continental influence. Individual 'schools' of artists, working under the patronage of wealthy chieftains, developed their own distinctive styles.

When Julius Caesar came to Britain in 55 BC, British craftsmen were lavishing their skills on objects used to display wealth and status – weapons, shields, helmets and horse trappings. Specialists worked full-time to pro-duce magnificent products for the wealthy and excelled in metalwork, particularly iron and bronze. Even articles for everyday use, such as pots, weaving-combs and spindlewhorls, were enlivened with simple elegant patterns.

The artists took their inspiration from nature, often repeating the gentle curves of the rolling hills in rounded, flowing patterns. A straight line or a sharp angle was almost unknown in the richly embossed and usually abstract designs.

Behind it all lay the suspicion of humour. sometimes called the 'Cheshire cat' style. After a short gaze almost any design will dissolve into the shape of a human face. Sometimes you see the whole, sometimes just the grin.

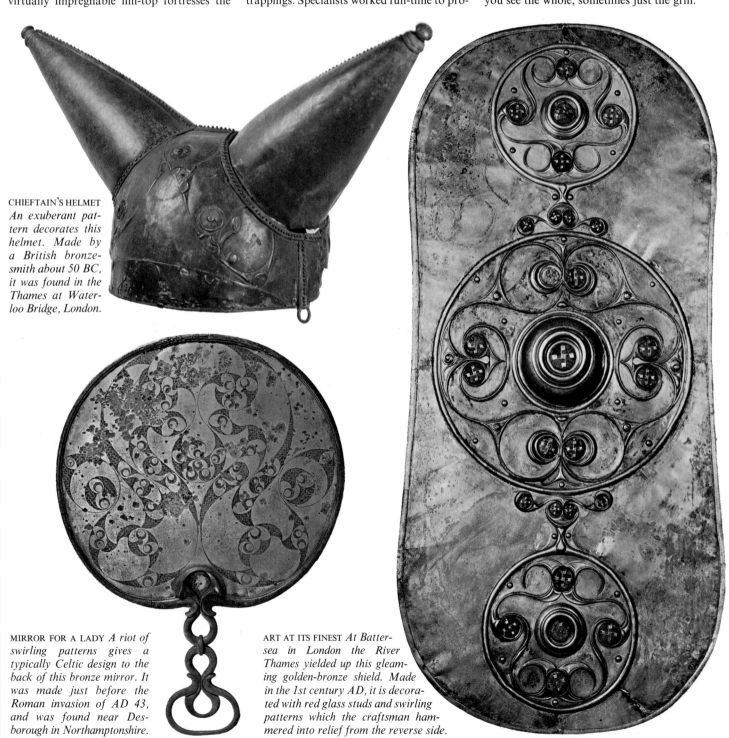

CHIEFTAIN'S HELMET *An exuberant pattern decorates this helmet. Made by a British bronze-smith about 50 BC, it was found in the Thames at Waterloo Bridge, London.*

MIRROR FOR A LADY *A riot of swirling patterns gives a typically Celtic design to the back of this bronze mirror. It was made just before the Roman invasion of AD 43, and was found near Desborough in Northamptonshire.*

ART AT ITS FINEST *At Battersea in London the River Thames yielded up this gleaming golden-bronze shield. Made in the 1st century AD, it is decorated with red glass studs and swirling patterns which the craftsman hammered into relief from the reverse side.*

CELTIC ARCHITECTS IN TIME OF WAR

About 2000 years ago, as the legions pushed the Roman Empire northwards, the whole of Celtic Europe was on the move in their path. A chieftain and his supporters, probably about 50 people in all, sailed to Shetland from the Orkneys in search of a safe place for a farmstead. They took over the Iron Age farming community which lived in round stone houses protected by a circular wall on the lake island of Clickhimin.

The newcomers then set about building a broch – a communal farmhouse within a massive stone tower. For, in that time when danger was always near, they found that the island site alone was not enough for their protection.

It was an enormous task. The outside of the broch was 65 ft in diameter and it stood 40–50 ft high. Large quantities of building stone, ferried from the mainland, were needed. It was stockpiled in the yard, the builders living in temporary huts near by.

The main entrance, at ground level, was a 17 ft long passage through the wall, opening into the central courtyard. A solid wooden door, with a guard-room just beyond it, made the entrance virtually impregnable.

The central courtyard, about 33 ft across, was surrounded by tiers of timber rooms. These were two or three storeys high, and they backed on to the inside of the tower wall.

A staircase, built into the thickness of the wall, led from the first floor to the top of the tower. Two small rooms inside the wall at ground level provided storage space, or perhaps additional living-rooms.

The work of the community was done on the ground floor. There was a central stone-lined hearth in the courtyard, and jobs such as smithing, corn-grinding and weaving were done in the rooms around it. These also housed the cattle in winter. The people themselves lived and slept in the upper storeys.

The Clickhimin community prospered. From the safety of their fortress home, the tribesmen traded skins, wool, hides, corn and slaves for iron and bronze weapons and goods from the south.

Over 500 brochs like that at Clickhimin are known in Scotland. The Celtic architects put all the emphasis on strength and security, and the brochs must have been among the strongest fortresses in all prehistoric Europe.

But, by about AD 150, the Romans had defeated the tribes of central Scotland, and the main threat to the broch people was over. The great defensive farmsteads were no longer needed.

The best preserved of all the brochs built by the Celts stands on a lonely headland on Mousa, one of the Shetland Islands. Its walls are 43 ft high.

Celtic tribesmen built Clickhimin broch in Shetland about 2000 years ago. Their ingenuity and skill combined to produce an elaborate, circular farmhouse within a massive, defensive wall. This was a safe, strong home in a time of constant warfare, and its inhabitants prospered in its shelter.

MAGNIFICENT TRAPPINGS *This bronze mask, showing a brilliantly stylised horse, may have decorated a chariot. It came from the tribal centre of the Brigantes at Stanwick, Yorkshire.*

A CELTIC IMAGE *Excavations at Gloucester uncovered this superb head of a man, carved in limestone in the 1st century AD. The protruding eyes and nose and the heavy locks of hair suggest a Celtic god. The tapering shape of the face was much admired by the Celts.*

JEWELLER'S ARTISTRY *A Celtic craftsman made this gold torc, or collar, about 50 BC. He put a coin of the time inside one of the terminals. The torc, fashioned from eight strands of twisted wire, was found at Snettisham, Norfolk.*

Britain prospers under Rome's rule

*The Roman conquerors bring to Britain all the benefits
of their civilisation – superb roads, well-planned cities,
luxurious villas – and 300 years of peace*

The march of civilisation from Rome made its first, hesitant steps in ancient Britain in 55 BC. The ambitious general Julius Caesar landed with an army and began to explore this uncharted isle of the north. Caesar found a misty, fertile land, partly cultivated and filled with warring tribes. His pen recorded for history his first glimpse of this strange country: 'The population is exceedingly large and the cattle very numerous. Tin is found inland and small quantities of iron near the coast. There is timber of every kind, except beech. Most of the tribes of the interior do not grow corn, but live on milk and meat and wear skins. All the Britons dye their bodies with woad, which makes them a blue colour, and this gives them a terrifying appearance in battle.'

Caesar's curiosity about this strange race was not satisfied by his first brief visit. He made a second expedition the following year. It was constantly harassed, but eventually the British submitted. Caesar gladly accepted tribute and sailed back to Roman Gaul (pp. 28–29).

But Caesar never reached the heart of the island, and it was not until AD 43 that the invasion of Britain began in earnest. Then the disciplined legions gathered the stubborn islanders into the Roman Empire. The invasion was planned as a triumph for the Emperor Claudius. From the south-east, the Roman army fanned out, conquering the British in fierce battles around their fortified hill towns such as Maiden Castle in Dorset (pp. 30–31).

Within four years a frontier had been established from Lincoln to Exeter. To the west, constant troubles with the British tribes lured the legions out on punitive expeditions. And there was a brutal lesson to be learnt before the virile people of the south-east were fully absorbed into the empire. In AD 60 a rebellion broke out, led by a widowed queen, Boudicca. Great areas of the new province were devastated (pp. 32–33).

But the rebellion was quickly smashed. The *pax romana* – the peace of

MEMORIAL TO THE POWER OF ROME

Hadrian's Wall, stretching relentlessly across the moors, valleys and crags of northern England, is the most impressive and lasting legacy of Rome in Britain. The Emperor Hadrian began the wall in AD 122, and its 73 mile length from the Tyne to the Solway was completed in eight years. This feat of military engineering kept the northern barbarians at bay.

The construction of the wall was a turning point in Rome's policy towards its empire. Hadrian decided that further expansion would serve no purpose. He was determined to create a world of stability and peace within the existing frontiers. In Britain he succeeded. Behind the protecting wall, Roman civilisation flourished for more than 250 years.

JULIUS CAESAR *In 55 BC, Julius Caesar, Rome's most famous military commander, led his army across the Channel to Britain. A year later he returned, but failed to make a lasting conquest.*

CLAUDIUS AND VESPASIAN *The unmilitary Claudius (left) ordered the conquest of Britain in AD 43. During the campaign he visited Britain for 16 days, but he left the fighting to able commanders such as the young Vespasian (right), who was also to become emperor.*

HADRIAN *This Roman coin was minted to commemorate Hadrian's visit to Britannia in AD 122. He ordered a great wall to be built to defend the northern frontier.*

SEVERUS AND CONSTANTINE *In AD 208 Septimius Severus and his son Caracalla (left) brought the Imperial court to York and drove the barbarians back across Hadrian's Wall. In York, nearly 100 years later, Constantine (right) was proclaimed emperor.*

Rome which reached across the world – had come to Britain. With peace came unity, law and order, majestic buildings, roads, trade and – for the fortunate few – a luxurious way of life that was not to be surpassed for 1900 years.

At Fishbourne, near Chichester, a huge palace was built about AD 75 and fitted out in sumptuous style, with baths, gardens and mosaic floors by a team of expert craftsmen who perhaps came from Rome itself (pp. 34–35).

The 2nd century was a time of unprecedented prosperity and expansion. Everywhere the villa owners were improving their estates and properties, many of them adding the comforts of central heating and simple mosaic floors. In the growing towns trade flourished. As British tastes became more Romanised, local artists and craftsmen augmented the flood of imported goods.

At York, the most northerly city of the empire grew up. It was really two cities: the fortress from which the army patrolled the northern frontier, and a bustling civilian centre. And in AD 208 the city played host to a great soldier and ruler. Emperor Septimius Severus brought his family and the Imperial court there. Severus was determined to subdue the savage tribesmen who were harrying the northern frontier. For more than two years he led his vast empire from York, and died there in AD 211 (pp. 36–37).

Severus was not the only emperor to visit York. More than 80 years earlier, in AD 122, Hadrian came there during his tour of the empire's borders. He began Hadrian's Wall – a defensive frontier which stretches from sea to sea across the 'neck' of Britain. For more than 250 years it marked the boundary with the tribal lands to the north (pp. 38–39).

But Hadrian's Wall was also the frontier of the empire. There the advance of Rome stopped. Beyond it lay primitive peoples waiting and watching for their moment to seize upon the treasures of Roman civilisation.

Enemies from all sides

The great wall and the courageous campaigns of Severus did much to stabilise the northern frontier. But late in the 3rd century the coasts of the island were ravaged by Saxon pirates. To meet this danger, a system of forts was built along the east coast – the Saxon Shore. To the first forts at Brancaster and Reculver, eight more were added to extend the system.

But as the power of Rome ebbed, generals fought each other for the emperor's throne. They drained the army in Britain of men desperately needed for defence against the increasing boldness of the barbarians – the Picts, Scots, Franks and Saxons. By 410 the army had virtually withdrawn from the island, and the Emperor Honorius wrote to the towns of Britain telling them to look after their own defence. The promising land which had tempted Caesar more than 450 years earlier was now left to the barbarian hordes.

During the next decades the cities which had brought the ease and order of Rome to the remote northern island withered away. Many were totally abandoned for centuries. In Britain it was soon as if the splendour of Roman civilisation had never been.

But something remained. Lost beneath a protective layer of earth and vegetation, superb mosaic floors and busts of emperors, gods and goddesses lay undamaged for centuries. Fifteen hundred years later archaeologists were to uncover these riches of Roman civilisation – a reminder of the achievements of Britain's era as a province in the great empire (pp. 40–41).

There was another still more potent legacy. Among the many religions brought to Britain by the Romans, one faith took so firm a hold on the hearts of the inhabitants that it survived the deluge. Retreating before the pagan invaders, Britain's first Christians withdrew into the mountains and remote valleys of the west. There they clung to the faith which was to unite the kingdoms of Anglo-Saxon Britain 250 years later.

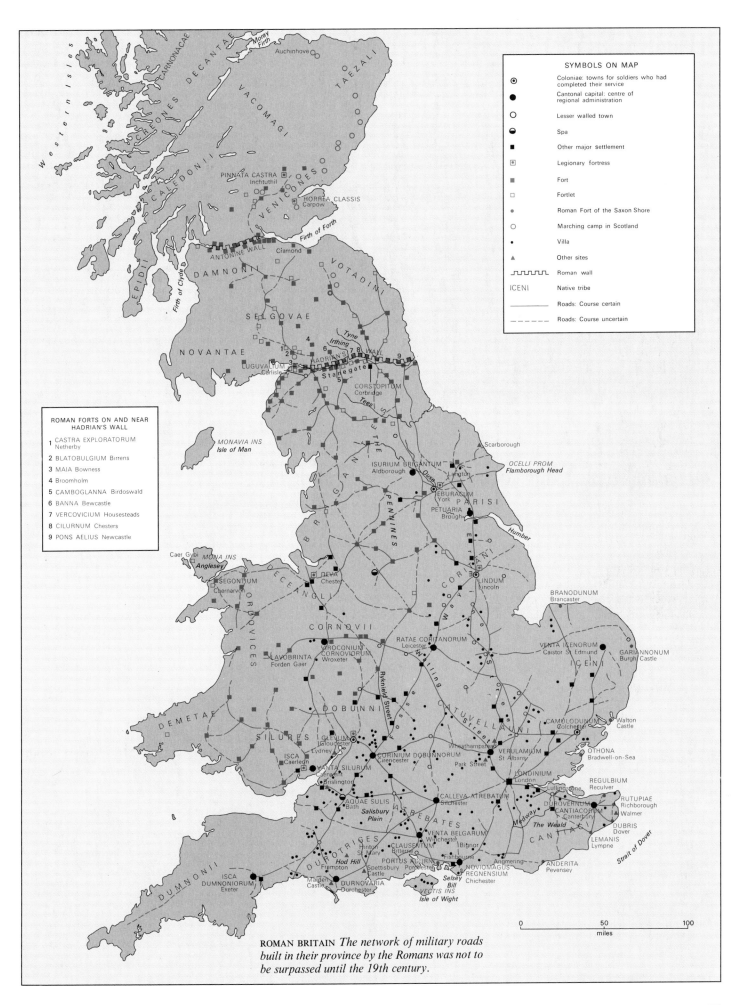

SYMBOLS ON MAP

⊙ Coloniae: towns for soldiers who had completed their service

● Cantonal capital: centre of regional administration

○ Lesser walled town

◑ Spa

■ Other major settlement

⊡ Legionary fortress

▪ Fort

□ Fortlet

• Roman Fort of the Saxon Shore

○ Marching camp in Scotland

· Villa

▲ Other sites

⊓⊔⊓⊔ Roman wall

ICENI Native tribe

——————— Roads: Course certain

- - - - - - - Roads: Course uncertain

ROMAN FORTS ON AND NEAR
HADRIAN'S WALL

1 CASTRA EXPLORATORUM
Netherby

2 BLATOBULGIUM Birrens

3 MAIA Bowness

4 Broomholm

5 CAMBOGLANNA Birdoswald

6 BANNA Bewcastle

7 VERCOVICIUM Housesteads

8 CILURNUM Chesters

9 PONS AELIUS Newcastle

Western Isles

CARNONACAE

CREONES

DECANTAE

Moray Firth

Auchinhove

TAEZALI

VACOMAGI

CALEDONII

VENICONES

PINNATA CASTRA
Inchtuthil

HORREA CLASSIS
Carpow

EPIDII

Firth of Forth

DAMNONII

ANTONINE WALL

Cramond

VOTADINI

Firth of Clyde

SELGOVAE

Tyne

Irthing

NOVANTAE

4

6

7 8 WALL

9

1

2

LUGUVALIUM
Carlisle

3

HADRIAN'S

Stanegate

5

CORSTOPITUM
Corbridge

Tees

MONAVIA INS
Isle of Man

Scarborough

ISURIUM BRIGANTUM
Aldborough

Ouse

Langton

OCELLI PROM
Flamborough Head

EBURACUM
York

PARISI

PETUARIA
Brough

Humber

B
R
I
G
A
N
T
E
S

THE PENNINES

Caer Gybi

MONA INS
Anglesey

DECEANGLI

SEGONTIUM
Caernarvon

O
R
D
O
V
I
C
E
S

DEVA
Chester

CORNOVII

LAVOBRINTA
Forden Gaer

VIROCONIUM
CORNOVIORUM
Wroxeter

RATAE CORITANORUM
Leicester

LINDUM
Lincoln

BRANODUNUM
Brancaster

VENTA ICENORUM
Caistor St Edmund

GARIANNONUM
Burgh Castle

ICENI

C
O
R
I
T
A
N
I

F
o
s
s
e

W
a
y

DEMETAE

DOBUNNI

Ryknield Street

Watling Street

CATUVELLAUNI

CAMULODUNUM
Colchester

Walton Castle

SILURES

GLEVUM
Gloucester

Lydney

Fosse Way

Watling Street

Wheathampstead

VERULAMIUM
St Albans

Park Street

OTHONA
Bradwell-on-Sea

ISCA
Caerleon

VENTA SILURUM
Caerwent

Brislington

CORINIUM DOBUNNORUM
Cirencester

LONDINIUM
London

Lullingstone

REGULBIUM
Reculver

RUTUPIAE
Richborough

Walmer

AQUAE SULIS
Bath

Salisbury Plain

ATREBATES

CALLEVA ATREBATUM
Silchester

DUROVERNUM
CANTIACORUM
Canterbury

The Weald

Medway

CANTII

DUBRIS
Dover

LEMANIS
Lympne

Strait of Dover

DUROTRIGES

Hinton
St Mary

CLAUSENTUM
Bitterne

VENTA BELGARUM
Winchester

Bignor

PORTUS ADURNI
Portchester

Fishbourne

Angmering

ANDERITA
Pevensey

Hod Hill

Frampton

Spettisbury
Castle

NOVIOMAGUS
REGNENSIUM
Chichester

Selsey
Bill

ISCA
DUMNONIORUM
Exeter

Maiden
Castle

DURNOVARIA
Dorchester

VECTIS INS
Isle of Wight

DUMNONII

0   50   100

miles

ROMAN BRITAIN *The network of military roads
built in their province by the Romans was not to
be surpassed until the 19th century.*

Julius Caesar comes and sees - but fails to conquer

THE BEACH WHERE CAESAR LANDED
Caesar and his army struggled for a foothold near Walmer, in Kent, in 55 BC. The shelving shingle beach was their first obstacle. The legionaries, each staggering under 88 lb. of equipment, waded through deep water in the face of British resistance.

About 9 a.m. on August 26, 55 BC, a fleet of warships appeared off the Kent coast. On the clifftops thousands of British charioteers, stone-slingers and spearmen watched grimly as the Roman fleet pitched and rolled in the Channel swell.

A force of 10,000 Romans was approaching the island's shore, under the command of Julius Caesar. At 46, he was already in control of the newly won territory of Gaul – and ambitious for even higher office.

He needed an audacious gesture to further his popularity with the Roman Senate and people. And he knew that the idea of Roman legions landing in the remote and fabulous island would win him fame in Rome.

Mysterious island

The Romans knew little of Britain. It was reported to be rich. There was talk of gold and pearl fishing. Its slaves were highly valued, and it exported tin and copper.

Apart from that it was a place of mystery, the centre of the Druidic religion which the Romans had met in Gaul. But, more practically, it provided a refuge for Caesar's enemies.

The invasion force set sail from Gessoriacum (Boulogne) in Gaul at midnight. But confronted by the cliffs bristling with British warriors, Caesar chose to bide his time. Eventually, he chose his spot, a shelving beach probably near what is now Walmer.

The Britons had followed the Roman fleet along the shore and were waiting on the beach – footsoldiers armed with swords, spears and slings, and charioteers. The Britons watched as the first Roman soldiers, weighed down by their armour, began to wade ashore.

The clamouring defenders dashed into the sea to hurl themselves on the advancing soldiers, or to throw volleys of spears at the struggling enemy. Roman morale wavered. As Caesar himself wrote, his men were totally unused to this kind of warfare – 'with the result that they did not show the same alacrity and enthusiasm as they did on dry land'.

The situation was now critical, but suddenly the standard-bearer of the Tenth Legion jumped overboard bearing the Roman eagle aloft. No legionary would let his standard fall into the hands of an enemy. The troops lost their hesitation and rushed after him.

The brilliant commander

For the Romans, the main problem was lack of mobility in the face of an enemy which commanded the beach and could easily regroup. Caesar ordered his scout ships to rush with reinforcements to any point where help was needed. Gradually and painfully the Romans gained a foothold on dry land. Finally, they charged, totally shattering British resistance. But they were robbed of final success, for the cavalry, so essential for the rout of a broken enemy, had been delayed in the crossing. The long day ended in uncertainty.

Nightfall brought near disaster. A sudden gale combined with unusually high tides wrecked many of Caesar's transport ships anchored offshore, and damaged his warships which were beached on the shingle.

Caesar had taken a calculated risk when he had set out for Britain. It was dangerously late for campaigning in the wet northern climate. He had brought no winter supplies, so the loss of his ships made his plight desperate.

Next morning Caesar set about the task of

ROMAN BEACH-HEAD *Fierce British resistance dismayed the invaders, but they were rallied by the standard-bearer of the Tenth Legion.*

saving his expedition. Craftsmen began salvaging what ships they could, while forage parties were sent out in search of corn.

The British responded with attacks on the forage parties, and on Caesar's camp. But they were no match for disciplined legionaries.

One night in mid-September, Caesar and his men slipped away to Gaul. He had come, and seen – but not conquered.

Caesar did not like to leave a job unfinished. He spent the winter months planning. He now knew that the British were capable of combining in the face of an invader. He had also learnt what kind of resistance he could expect.

By July of the following year, 54 BC, he was ready with a massive force – about 800 vessels laden with men, horses and equipment.

Caesar's triumph

But this time the Roman landing was unopposed. After establishing a base camp, Caesar's army broke out of Kent, taking the battle north of the Thames into Hertfordshire, the territory of the Catuvellauni. Eventually, Caesar succeeded in capturing the principal Catuvellauni stronghold (possibly the earthwork still surviving at Wheathampstead). The war-lord Cassivelaunus, who had temporarily united the British, was forced to come to terms, and agreed to pay tribute.

Caesar now felt that he had achieved enough. His own ambitions lay closer to Rome. Once again he withdrew his forces in September – and this time he did not return.

It was the last Britain was to see of the Roman legions for nearly a century. Caesar, his honour and curiosity satisfied, won his 'Triumph' – public recognition in Rome of a major victory. For him, at least, Britain had served its purpose.

The lure of the misty off-shore isle

The fierce tribesmen who had made Caesar's two visits to Britain so precarious were to enjoy almost a century of independence. The Catuvellauni stopped paying tribute to Rome. But peaceful trade between Britain and the Continent flourished, and the Romans saw no need of a permanent conquest.

Yet the lure of the unconquered islands beyond the frontiers of civilisation remained. The poet Horace called Britons 'the remotest inhabitants in the world'.

The more prosperous Britons were not so keen on being remote. They developed a taste for Roman luxuries such as wine, oil and delicacies like *garum*, a kind of fish-paste, as well as glass and pottery.

Relations with Rome varied from tribe to tribe. But, on the whole, peaceful relations were maintained. In AD 16, when some Roman soldiers were shipwrecked in eastern England, they were immediately returned to the Continent in safety.

Troublesome island

Emperor Augustus thought of conquering Britain, encouraged by the pleas of rival British tribal leaders who were threatened by the rising power of the Catuvellauni under their king, Cunobelinus – Shakespeare's 'Cymbeline'. But pressures elsewhere in the empire prevented any positive action.

The mad Emperor Caligula, in AD 41, actually assembled an invasion force at Boulogne in Gaul, but changed his mind.

That same year, Caligula was assassinated and Cunobelinus died. While the old king had lived, Rome had been happy with the growing trade links and friendly relations he had established. But now the Catuvellauni had once again, as in Julius Caesar's day, become a menace to Rome's northern frontier, Gaul.

Gallic trouble-makers fled to their fellow tribesmen across the Channel and used Britain as a base. In addition, Britain was the training centre for the fanatically anti-Roman Druid priests. The island had become a menace to the peace of the Roman Empire. The new emperor, Claudius, decided to bring the troublesome island under his imperial sway.

VICTIM OF WAR *Caesar's campaigns of conquest were paid for in human suffering. This Roman statue shows the death of a hostile tribesman.*

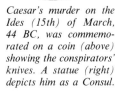

Heroism in defeat as Britons make their last stand

SIEGE COMMANDER *The conqueror of Maiden Castle was Vespasian, a soldier, who in AD 69 became Roman Emperor. He made his military reputation in the conquest of Britain.*

DEFENDERS' STRONGHOLD

Defending their island against the Roman conquest, the British made a fierce stand at Maiden Castle, near Dorchester. Archaeologists have uncovered grim evidence of the skeletons of horribly mutilated bodies buried in shallow graves after the battle.

Rising from the green Dorset hills 2 miles from Dorchester stands the ancient fortress of Maiden Castle, the scene of one of the fiercest battles of the Roman conquest of Britain. The fall of this massive bastion in AD 44 was the death-blow to British resistance in south-west Britain.

The task of subjugating the south-western tribes had been given to Vespasian, a brilliant and vigorous general who, 25 years later, was to become Emperor of Rome. Vespasian was only 33 when the invasion of Britain began. He came from a humble family – his father had been a tax collector in Asia. But he was already making a name for himself as a soldier, and he had recently distinguished himself in a decisive battle on the River Medway in Kent by outflanking the British.

His task was formidable. The British tribesmen wisely chose to avoid set battles, confining themselves to skirmishes against parties foraging for corn, or ambushes on small patrols. The tribesmen preferred to dig in on the hillforts, many of which had been tribal centres for over 500 years. These forts were surrounded by lines of deep ditches, the earth

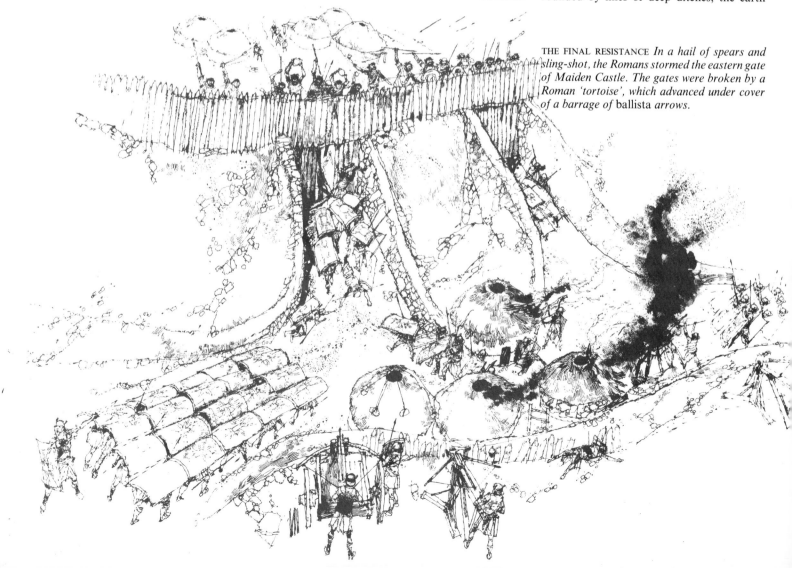

THE FINAL RESISTANCE *In a hail of spears and sling-shot, the Romans stormed the eastern gate of Maiden Castle. The gates were broken by a Roman 'tortoise', which advanced under cover of a barrage of* ballista *arrows.*

from which was built up into ramparts up to 45 ft high. Ramparts swept inwards towards gateways which, in turn, were protected in front by ramparts topped with fighting platforms. Maiden Castle had as many as seven lines of defence before its West Gate.

Vespasian and his Second Augustan Legion first established a supply base at the head of Chichester harbour, in the territory of the friendly local king, Tiberius Claudius Cogidubnus. From here he took the Isle of Wight, which offered little or no resistance. Then he began the systematic reduction of the tribes, moving relentlessly across the land, with a supply fleet in constant support.

One by one he mopped up pockets of resistance. The historian Suetonius says that he fought 30 battles, subdued two powerful tribes and captured 20 *oppida*, or fortified towns.

Slaughter by the sword

But the greatest trial of Roman strength came at Maiden Castle, a massive fortress half a mile long, with ramparts towering 125 ft above the surrounding fields, and topped with wooden stockades. The ramparts were manned by fierce Durotriges, a tribe adept at sling warfare, who left behind them after the battle an ammunition dump of 22,000 sling-stones.

The Roman answer to stones was *ballistae*, spring guns of wood, animal hair and gut that fired deadly metal arrows with a range three times that of a British sling-shot. Under a barrage, the defenders retreated until they were among their families and livestock in the inner defences. And the Romans advanced in *testudo*, the close 'tortoise' of legionaries sheltering under their interlocked shields, relentlessly cutting down anything that stood in their path. They reached some circular huts in the courtyard before the gates, which they set alight. Then, as the smoke billowed about, they stormed the gates.

The Romans must have been aroused to fury by the resistance of the British, for in a confusion of savagery, they hacked down the defending warriors, their womenfolk, their children and the old.

Archaeologists have uncovered the grim result of this battle, a series of hastily dug shallow graves near the scene of the fight – 23 men and 11 women buried amid the ashes of the burnt huts. The bodies had been bundled in carelessly, though the necessary food and drink for their journey into death were placed in most of the graves.

But the skeletons are a fearful testimony of the ferocity of the battle – mutilated limbs, and skulls with gaping sword slashes. One skull had no fewer than nine savage wounds, and one skeleton had the head of a *ballista* bolt still embedded in its backbone.

The conquerors built a town at Dorchester, and there the survivors of the massacre were re-settled. It was 300 years before anyone built again on the hill at Maiden Castle.

The Romans return to conquer Britain

When Claudius replaced his mad nephew Caligula as ruler of the Roman Empire in AD 41, he inherited a shambles. He had to restore public confidence and, above all, he had to show the legions that had made him emperor that he could act decisively.

The conquest of Britain served all his political aims. By enlarging the empire, rather than restoring order in an existing part of it, he would be entitled to a triumph – a sure way to please the Roman citizenry. Also, the death of Cunobelinus, king of the Catuvellauni tribe, had created unrest which threatened Gaul.

Claudius, aged over 50, was anxious for military honour. In August AD 43, an invasion force, four legions and auxiliaries numbering over 40,000 men, landed unopposed on the Kent coast – possibly at Richborough. In command was Aulus Plautius, who was to be Britain's first military governor.

His objective was Camulodunum, modern Colchester, now the Catuvellaunian capital. By arrangement, Claudius remained in Rome waiting for the message which would bring him to Britain to complete the campaign.

Plautius advanced through Kent to the Medway, where the British first opposed him. He then had to fight his way to the Thames, where he halted and sent the arranged message to Claudius.

Claudius left the luxury of his palace in Rome immediately and set sail for Marseilles. The contemporary historian Suetonius says that he was nearly wrecked on the way. From Marseilles he travelled for 13 days by carriage and litter through France to Boulogne.

He brought with him two warlike novelties for the British – an elephant corps, and 12 camels.

Claudius joined his army on September 5.

VICTORS' ARROGANCE *Roman stone-carvers often chose to depict scenes showing the victory of their legionaries over British tribesmen.*

Two days later he led the attack on the British. The battle may have been fought on Brentwood Hill, between London and Colchester, with a marsh on one flank and a dense thicket of hawthorn on the other.

Now Claudius's military menagerie came into its own. The elephants easily penetrated the hawthorn bushes. The smell of the alien camels maddened the native horses and threw the British charioteers into confusion.

In the ensuing rout 4700 Britons were killed and 8000 were taken prisoner. The Romans lost only 380 dead with 600 wounded. Colchester fell, and Caractacus – the outstanding British warrior – had to flee for his life.

Claudius triumphant

Claudius spent only 16 days in Britain. He received the submission of the conquered tribes and hurried back to Rome to claim his triumph. The Senate awarded him the title of Britannicus because, in the words of an inscription still in Rome, 'without any mishap, he received in unconditional surrender, eleven conquered British kings'.

Plautius now completed his task unhindered by the imperial court. With the Twentieth Legion in reserve at Colchester, the remaining three fanned out and occupied the land behind the frontier Claudius had laid down – a line from Lincoln to the south Devon coast. The new defences were served by the 190 mile Fosse Way, Britain's first military frontier road. Along it were forts manned by detachments of troops.

Beyond this line were the wild unconquered tribesmen. But within the new frontiers the process of ruling – and civilising – the islanders could now begin.

A woman inspires the British to revolt against Roman might

RELIC OF REBELLION

The carving on this tombstone of a Roman officer, Longinus, shows him trampling a defeated Briton with his horse – an expression of the arrogance which was a cause of Boudicca's uprising. When Boudicca's furious mob sacked Colchester 11 years after Longinus's burial, they defaced his tomb and threw down its headstone.

Rome nearly lost Britain, its new imperial possession, in AD 60. Only 17 years after the invasion, in one of the bloodiest episodes in the island's history, the subject Britons rose against their new masters.

The revolt was against Roman injustice and corruption. Its tragic heroine, Boudicca, was a formidable woman, according to the Roman historian Dio Cassius: 'In appearance terrifying, in the glance of her eye most fierce, and her voice was harsh; a great mass of the tawniest hair fell to her hips.'

Unfair extortion of tax money and massive redistribution of land to Roman veterans had already angered the British. But the revolt finally centred around Boudicca herself.

Her husband, the Roman vassal-king Prasutagus of the Iceni, a tribe living in East Anglia, had willed his estates jointly to Boudicca and Emperor Nero. In this way he hoped to circumvent the law by which the lands of vassal kings without sons passed directly to Rome. But when he died, Roman officials not only seized his domains, but took the lands of Icenian nobles as well. Roman legionaries then sacked the royal palace, flogged Boudicca and raped her two daughters.

The Iceni exploded in rebellion at the outrage, and the uprising quickly spread to other tribes in south-east England. The rebels' timing was perfect. A large part of the occupying army under the command of the province's governor, Suetonius Paulinus, was occupied in massacring the Druids in North Wales, two weeks' march away from East Anglia.

Tacitus, the historian, noted in surprise that the British did not object to a woman as a leader. Her streaming hair acted as a banner to the horde following her war chariot.

Their first target was Colchester (Camulodunum), a city settled by Roman veterans, who were hated for their arrogance. The unwalled town was overwhelmed in two days, and Boudicca began to exact a terrible revenge.

Blood and fire

The last defenders took refuge in a temple built in honour of the Roman Emperor Claudius. There they were slaughtered to a man and the temple was burnt down.

Paulinus, who by now was marching his legions back from North Wales, rode ahead with a detachment of cavalry, and found London in a state of panic.

The governor made the agonising decision to abandon London to its fate. The evidence of Boudicca's wrath on the undefended town is a thick layer of ashes which lies under the soil of much of the present-day City of London.

The same fate awaited Verulamium (St Albans) – the next centre to fall. Modern excavations have revealed the burnt-out remains of a row of timber-built shops. The flames must have engulfed the entire block in a matter of minutes.

Tacitus estimated that 70,000 people died in

ANTI-ROMAN FURY *Enraged by insults to their queen, Boudicca, the Icenian tribe rose against Roman rule in AD 60. They sacked London and Colchester, and burnt St Albans (below).*

these bloody episodes. He records: 'The barbarians would have no capturing, no selling, nor any kind of traffic usual in war. They would have nothing but killing, by sword, cross, gibbet or fire.'

But Boudicca had over-extended her resources. Food supplies had been neglected, and her undisciplined followers were beginning to break up into plundering bands. The Roman Legions from Wales were now within striking distance of the British.

The two forces met in the south Midlands. Paulinus drew up his force of about 17,000 men in a defile with his flanks protected on three sides by woods, and an incline in front up which the British would have to charge. The British warriors outnumbered the Romans three to one. But they were hampered by their families whom they had brought with them – an undisciplined horde of over 100,000 people.

The final defeat

It was Roman discipline that won the day. The British were annihilated; 80,000 were slain. Boudicca escaped to the woods, where it is believed she poisoned herself.

There was a short period of vengeance on the Iceni, but in Rome Emperor Nero supported a policy of conciliation towards the vanquished tribesmen. Instead of continued reprisals there was pardon and reform.

Boudicca had won a posthumous victory. In the aftermath of her moment of triumph, a system of justice and order was established which was to last for over three centuries.

Bringing the 'Pax Romana' to Britain

Before Britain became a province of the Roman Empire, it was split into warring tribes. But the Romans established a system of law and order which gave the island its first taste of national unity, and opened up communications so that trade could flourish. Under Rome, Britain was, to enjoy three centuries of unprecedented peace and prosperity.

Romans encouraged their subject nations to adopt their ways. The historian Tacitus records how the conquerors tamed the wild Britons. He reported: 'In place of distaste for the Latin language came a passion to command it. In the same way, our national dress came into favour, and the toga was everywhere to be seen. And so the Britons were gradually led on to the amenities that make vice agreeable – arcades, baths and sumptuous banquets. They spoke of such novelties as "civilisation", when they were only a feature of enslavement.'

Rome comes to Britain

Though the essence of Roman civilisation was racial toleration, it was also firmly based on a class society. There were Roman citizens and there were slaves. But it was always possible for non-Italians to gain the privilege of Roman citizenship by merit, influence or service to Rome.

It was in the towns, the centres of Roman influence and administration, their civilisation had its main impact. Ordered streets, with shops and temples and a central forum, sprang up with amazing speed. The estimate of 70,000 dead in London, St Albans and Colchester during Boudicca's rising, only 17 years after the invasion of Claudius, gives

some idea of how quickly these new towns had grown.

With equal speed and efficiency, the Romans constructed their network of over 6000 miles of roads. Not until the turnpike roads of the late 18th century was a comparable attempt made at road-building. By the end of the first century, a traveller could journey from Colchester to Constantinople as fast as at any time before the reign of Queen Victoria.

Trade flourished under the protection of the Roman legions, not only within the island, but between Britain and the rest of Europe. Amphorae (large jars) of wine and oil were shipped from the Mediterranean in bulk, ceramics and glass from Germany, France and even Egypt. Local enterprises flourished. Potteries sprang up everywhere. Their products were on sale in the market towns, together with the work of other native craftsmen working in metal, wood and leather.

If Tacitus was right in regarding this civilisation as 'enslavement', it was a form of slavery which provided a good life for many Britons.

ROMAN LUXURY *Pottery figures from a child's grave at Colchester show diners reclining in the Roman manner. The standing man is reading to the diners from a scroll.*

A palace proclaims the power and luxury of Rome

The building of a Roman palace at Fishbourne in Sussex must have amazed the British. Only 30 years before, when Claudius established Roman rule in the island, they had witnessed the brute strength of their conquerors. Now the British were to see another side of their rulers – elegance and luxury on a scale far beyond their imaginations.

Nothing like the new palace had been seen before in Britain. There had been a stone-built country house on the site during the reign of the Emperor Nero (AD 54–68). But the builders and craftsmen who were called in about AD 75 had orders to construct a palace fit for a king.

'King and Legate'

Nobody can be certain who was the owner of the Fishbourne Palace, but the most likely answer is Tiberius Claudius Cogidubnus, a powerful ally of Rome. He was a king of the Regni, a tribe which occupied present-day Hampshire and Sussex. The Regni had allowed their territory to be used as a base for Vespasian's advance into western England.

The contemporary Roman historian Tacitus wrote that Cogidubnus 'maintained his unswerving loyalty (to Rome) down to our own time', and that his loyalty had been rewarded by the gift of estates. An inscription found in 1723 in Chichester, a mile from Fishbourne, describes him as 'King and Legate to the Emperor'. These titles would have made him eligible for a seat in the Roman Senate.

The palace was built to impress – but by its luxury and ostentation not by its military strength. A visitor approached it from the east along the Chichester road, which led directly to the columned front of a monumental entrance hall 80 ft wide and over 110 ft long. At the far end of the hall there was a pool with a fountain. Beyond this again was a large formal garden 270 ft across, enclosed by the four wings of the palace.

The entrance hall was well lit by windows and the walls were painted in bright, simple

THE BOY ON A DOLPHIN

The finest of the many superb mosaic floors found at Fishbourne Palace shows a winged boy playfully riding on a dolphin (above). The marble head of a boy (right), possibly represents the son of the palace's owner. The statue is of continental workmanship and dates from the 1st century AD.

ROMAN MAGNIFICENCE *The huge Roman palace at Fishbourne near Chichester was built c. AD 75, probably to house a native king protected by Rome. The columned entrance (centre), ornate courtyard and the audience chamber and offices (back wing) were intended to overawe and impress British subjects.*

LASTING MEMORIAL TO THE ROMANS

The Romans brought with them to Britain one form of art which they had made very much their own – the mosaic. Mosaic floors, made of fragments of hard stone, were designed to last – and they have proved the most enduring of all the works of Roman Britain. Many beautiful floors have survived almost intact, while buildings of brick and stone which surrounded them have crumbled away leaving little trace.

Mosaic floors were used to decorate town houses, country villas and to pave bath-houses. In Britain the wide range of local stones contributed to the fine colour and rich variety of the mosaics.

The construction of a fine mosaic, using thousands of small fragments of carefully selected material, was a long and complicated work. Only the richest people could afford this elegant luxury, and the presence of fine mosaic floors is a sure

The spirit of autumn, from a floor mosaic in the city of Corinium, now Cirencester. This fine mosaic was made in the 2nd century.

sign that a town house or villa was owned by a man of high status. Mosaics in towns became common from AD 150–200 onwards. Most of the mosaics in towns and villas date from the 4th century, when town life flourished and villa life was at its most luxurious.

Gradually, British craftsmen learnt the art from their Roman masters. Some of their mosaics portray animals and flowers, as well as a host of the gods and goddesses which the Romans introduced to Britain. They provide a fascinating glimpse of life in Roman Britain.

This elaborate scallop-shell design comes from a 2nd-century floor mosaic in a Roman house at Verulamium, now St Albans, Hertfordshire.

colours. The overwhelming effect of grandeur was given by the sheer scale of the interior.

Directly opposite the entrance hall, and at a slightly higher level, stood the vaulted audience chamber reached from the garden by a flight of steps leading to a columned porch.

This west wing seems to have been the official part of the building, and the two large rooms on either side of the audience chamber may have been dining-rooms.

The north wing lay largely hidden behind a colonnade. It was a series of suites of rooms looking inwards on to two separate private courtyards. Its luxury suggests it was intended for honoured guests. Less spacious suites in the east wing may have been for minor officials.

The south wing of the house was probably the private living quarters of the owner and his family. It had two colonnades, one looking over the main garden, the other south over a garden which sloped down to the sea.

Evidently, the owner valued scenery and solitude; but equally he liked luxury, for his wing was convenient to the bath suite with its hot, tepid and cold baths and plunges. Strangely enough, the palace was not centrally heated. Perhaps the architect who designed it was not used to building for an English climate.

The palace covered over 230,000 sq. ft, an area roughly five times that of Canterbury Cathedral. Glass was brought from Egypt, pottery from Germany and France, marble from Turkey, Greece, Italy and Spain. Stone

came from the Weald of Kent, Selsey Bill, the Isle of Wight and Gloucestershire. Much of the building material passed through the busy harbour at Fishbourne.

Gardens of splendour

Tons of locally produced iron nails, roof tiles and vast quantities of oak were used. But perhaps the most staggering aspect of the palace was not so much the grandeur of its plan, but the immense trouble taken over its interior.

Almost all of its 80 or so rooms were floored with mosaics – the earliest found in Britain. Most of them were in traditional Roman patterns, occasionally featuring sea creatures. Many were of exceptional quality – as fine as any of the elaborate floors to be seen in the houses of Imperial Rome.

The gardens were no less magnificent. With their bubbling fountains fed from a header tank through underground ceramic pipes, their statues and their formal hedge-lined paths, they rivalled those in Rome itself.

Some time towards the end of the first century, the owner of Fishbourne Palace died and the house was divided into smaller units. Nearly 200 years later, when further alterations were in progress, the palace was destroyed by fire. Careless workmen may have started the blaze; or perhaps the palace was one of the first victims of Saxon pirate-marauders. But enough has survived to give a picture of the palace which symbolised the luxury of Rome.

The leisurely life of a prosperous ruling class

The luxurious way of life which was introduced to Britain at Fishbourne spread to other splendid villas in many parts of Britain. It was a way of life far removed from the customs of the native tribesmen-peasants – an expression of the supreme power of the Romanised ruling classes.

Most of the great villas reached their peak of comfort and artistic elegance during the first half of the 4th century. About 700 villas have been discovered in Britain. Although most of these were relatively modest farm houses, a minority were clearly the luxurious mansions of successful and wealthy people.

They incorporated such comforts as very large warm baths, and reception rooms with under-floor central heating. One villa, at Bignor in Sussex, had a summer drawing-room, facing south with a fountain playing in its centre, and another equally splendid living-room with central heating for the winter. Both chambers had mosaic floors depicting scenes from Roman mythology and walls painted with imitation marble.

All the larger villas were self-sufficient, with adjoining buildings for slaves and ranges of barns for the animals. They were surrounded by great estates of well-cultivated fields, and these lands were the source of most of the corn, fruit and vegetables which were offered for sale in the market towns.

Inside, the villas were furnished with statues, armchairs of wood or wicker-work, bronze chests, ornamental tables and comfortable couches with cushions covered with bright woven cloth. These were the hallmarks of the luxurious life Rome imported to Britain.

A BRITON AT WORK *This bronze statuette of a Romano-British ploughman and his oxen was discovered at Piercebridge, County Durham.*

FARM TOOLS *Farmers had iron implements such as this ploughshare (left) and a two-pronged hoe (right), which were used in cultivation.*

A northern city becomes the heart of the Roman Empire

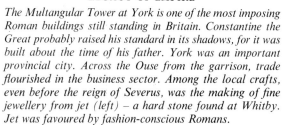

LEGACY OF EMPIRE
The Multangular Tower at York is one of the most imposing Roman buildings still standing in Britain. Constantine the Great probably raised his standard in its shadows, for it was built about the time of his father. York was an important provincial city. Across the Ouse from the garrison, trade flourished in the business sector. Among the local crafts, even before the reign of Severus, was the making of fine jewellery from jet (left) – a hard stone found at Whitby. Jet was favoured by fashion-conscious Romans.

THE EMPEROR'S LAST JOURNEY *The body of Septimius Severus is borne in state to his grave outside the walls of York. Hard campaigning against northern tribes had hastened his death.*

From the northern regions of Britain in the second century of Roman rule came a desperate threat to the African-born emperor, Septimius Severus. In AD 208 Severus marched with his army and his court to York. For two years this garrison town became the heart of his sprawling empire, while Severus subdued the rebellious tribes.

Fight for survival

Severus was a usurper. He seized the throne in AD 193 by a daring, forced march on Rome from his African province after the murder of Emperor Pertinax. But only three years later he was challenged by a new contender – Clodius Albinus, governor of Britain. Albinus sailed to Gaul to press his claims, draining the island of its defensive troops. The two claimants clashed at Lyons in France. Severus won the day. Albinus committed suicide and left his rival undisputed emperor.

But the price was heavy. Northern Britain had been left to the mercy of the Brigantes, a plundering tribe from the Pennines. Other tribes had poured over Hadrian's Wall. Anarchy spread. The task of ending the chaos and saving Britain for the Roman Empire was to occupy much of the rest of Severus's life.

At first, while he returned to Rome to ensure his power, Severus sent generals to pacify the restless province. But after ten years it was still not under control. By AD 208 Severus was 50 years old, and in failing health. But he was a keen soldier and could not resist the lure of the empire's most testing battlefield – the hills of North Britain. He descended on York with his wife and two sons, Caracalla and Geta.

York was a major frontier city of the empire. It was in two parts. North of the Ouse lay the fortress; to the south a cosmopolitan town with shops, law courts and forum.

A splendid palace was built for Severus. From there, in two summers, Severus marched to subdue the defiant tribes north of Hadrian's

BREAD AND CIRCUSES

Generations of Roman emperors believed that the best way to preserve the loyalty of their far-flung subjects was to provide them with 'panem et circenses' – bread and circuses. Even in Britain, one of the most remote provinces of the empire, there was a constant succession of popular entertainments.

A stage mask found at Caerleon, Gwent.

Most Roman cities had amphitheatres outside the walls. They were used for plays and pantomimes. In the arenas inside the cities, sporting events and real tragedies were played out. Men and animals were torn or hacked to death in gladiatorial clashes which drew cheering, bloodthirsty crowds. Many pots made in Roman Britain show gladiators fighting, and depict tales of their feats.

Gladiators locked in combat, on a vase c. AD 200.

Rome's civilisation takes root in British soil

Where the legions came and conquered, the Romans built towns. They were to stamp the order of Rome on barbarian Britain.

To the towns came lawyers and tax collectors. They bound the people of the empire into the legal and fiscal network of Rome.

Roman towns were built to a chessboard pattern. They often began as collections of soldiers' families and traders beside fortresses. Streets carved the towns into blocks, and at the centre was the forum – the town square. Along one side of the forum stood the basilica, or town hall, and the other sides were lined with shops and colonnades.

Benefits of Roman life

In the basilica the taxmen, administrators and the local council met, and legal disputes were settled by Roman justice. The language of the law was Latin.

In the streets behind the forum the industrial market was established where potters, blacksmiths, tile-makers, carpenters and weavers all worked. There were also bakeries and laundries, and in the bigger towns and cities slaves were used to deliver goods.

To the forum, farmers from the villas and estates outside the towns brought grain, meat, butter, cheese, milk and eggs to sell. Their cries mingled with those of traders selling wines, textiles from northern Italy, red Samian pottery from Gaul, glass-ware, leather boots and medicines of the East. The loose exchange of corn and crops for fish and skins had been replaced by Europe's first common market.

The main public buildings of the Roman towns were built of stone and a form of mortar resembling concrete. The bigger ones had their own courtyards and baths. On social occasions local dignitaries met to dine on oysters, salmon, poultry, game and fruit.

Most houses had access to running water, piped from wells through the town by skilled plumbers. All were served by main drains. More prosperous citizens were able to afford their own central heating, supplied by a hot-air hypocaust.

Fashion played an important part in the lives of women in Roman Britain. While men conducted business in the forum, their wives frequently met at the hairdressers' salons.

Chalk was used to whiten the face and arms, red ochre to colour lips and cheeks, and powdered ash for eyebrows. In Rome the writer Martial knew of one woman who had false teeth, a wig and false eyebrows. No doubt such fashions also reached Britain.

But the Romans also brought a deeper culture to Britain. The first schools opened in British cities soon after the invasion. By AD 300 there were probably schools flourishing in the major towns.

Tutors gave lessons in elegant salons. Here, the descendants of the old tribal chiefs studied Latin, literature and art. Tacitus noted that young Britons showed 'an enthusiastic desire' for learning. In the space of a few generations the island and its people had been transformed.

Wall. In two ruthless campaigns he drove the Caledonians as far as the Moray Firth. Though he failed to conquer them completely, his action gave time for the legions to restore the Wall. His fighting spirit contributed to the peace of Britain for the next 200 years.

It also hastened the end of his life. The ailing emperor's return to York was marked by an omen of doom. The contemporary Roman writer Spartianus recalls that as Severus was borne by litter to the town, black sacrificial animals escaped from the Temple of Bellona – Goddess of War – and followed him to the gates of his palace. It was Severus's last journey. He died that winter at York, and was buried outside the city wall.

It had been the old emperor's wish that his two sons, Caracalla and Geta, should rule jointly after his death. They hastened back to Rome. Within a few months Caracalla had murdered Geta, and had slain thousands of his supporters. But his bloody reign was ended in its turn by an assassin in AD 217.

The Imperial spotlight fell once again on York nearly 100 years later. In AD 306 another emperor, Constantius, died in York and was succeeded by his son – Constantine the Great. Constantine took two decisions which assured him of a lasting place in history. Firstly, he made his capital in the eastern city which took his name – Constantinople.

His other decision was even more momentous. In AD 313 he became the first emperor to permit Christianity – a turning-point for the civilised world.

CENTRES OF CIVILISATION

The splendid Roman bath at Aquae Sulis – modern-day Bath – was rediscovered in the 19th century.

Every town of any substance in Britain had its public baths – the clubs and community centres of Roman civilisation.

Some baths, like the famous ones at Bath, were built over warm, natural springs, containing many valuable salts. The Romans recognised their health-giving properties and established the first resort town there – Aquae Sulis.

In other towns the waters and steam rooms were heated by the hypocaust, which carried hot air through ducts from a central furnace.

Roman Britons went to their baths in the afternoons. They could play games or sports in the courtyards, gossip in the steam rooms, or tone up with a cold plunge and massage.

Flasks of body oil and strigils – back-scrapers – were provided for their use. Separate sessions were held for men and women. There was a small admission charge, but soldiers and children were often allowed in free.

This iron strigil, a body-scraper used by bathers to remove oil, was found at Walbrook in London.

A glass flask which held oil for anointing the body. Also found at Walbrook in London.

A great wall marks the limits of Rome's Empire

WORLD RULER *This 2nd-century bronze head of Hadrian was found in the Thames at London Bridge, probably hurled there by Saxon raiders.*

ORDERED BY AN EMPEROR

The great wall which Emperor Hadrian ordered to be built across northern Britain more than 18 centuries ago. This section at Housesteads shows how the engineers designed it to take advantage of hills and slopes which would be difficult for an enemy to storm.

FRONTIER DUTY *The legionary fort at Housesteads as it probably looked when still under construction. The soldiers are living in leather tents until their barrack blocks are built. Beyond the west gate a squad of troops marches along the military road that linked forts and milecastles spaced along the wall. An ox cart ambles through the gate with supplies, while sentries on the ramparts keep watch for attackers.*

One of the most impressive monuments of the might of Rome is Hadrian's Wall, stretching across the neck of northern England. It is also one of the world's most effective fortifications – for it played a vital role in providing Britain with nearly 300 years of peace.

During the first 70 years of the Roman occupation of Britain, this, the wildest frontier of the empire, was ravaged by tribesmen from the north and threatened from the south by the restless Brigantes of Yorkshire.

The master builder

Into this turmoil in the year AD 122 stepped Emperor Hadrian. He was a man of new ideas. And the greatest of these was to see that the mighty empire could expand no further.

Until Hadrian, the driving force of Rome had carried its civilisation ever further forward into the untamed areas of the world. With Hadrian came an age of containment. He turned the legionaries into defenders – and it was in Britain that he met the greatest test of his policy which changed the history of the Roman Empire.

He decided to build a wall to 'separate the barbarians from the Romans'. It was a mammoth task, one of the greatest ever undertaken by Roman power. But it took only seven years.

Altogether, at least 8500 men were employed to build the wall. They worked in 'centuries', groups of 80 men, piling the stones 15 ft high. Every Roman mile (1620 yds) they built a milecastle, and in between two watch towers. And 16 large forts, about 5 miles apart, were built to house the garrison.

Each group worked on a 40 yd section, then moved on. The great barrier crept across the hills, taking advantage of every major slope and craggy outcrop of rock.

This was a dangerous and lonely posting for the legions. The climate was cold. The work was hard. It is probable that the soldier builders had to down tools to fight off the wild raiders, who must have resented this unnatural barrier across land they held to be their own. Possibly it was this opposition that forced the Romans to cut the thickness of the wall from 10 ft to 8 ft to speed the work.

The men quarried more than 27 million cu. ft of stone, and dug a ditch 9 ft deep and 27 ft wide along the north side of the wall. But at its western end, nearly half its 80 Roman miles, the wall was built of turves because there was no suitable stone available. When the wall was finished, a great ditch known as the *vallum* was dug on the south side, perhaps because the Romans could not even be sure of the loyalty of the tribes in their rear, such as the Brigantes.

Abandoned to the wind

For 250 years Hadrian's sturdy fortification served its purpose well. But its success depended on the constant manning of garrisons with loyal and well-disciplined men. But in the 4th century the forces were no longer available.

Generals feuding for the Imperial throne drained away troops. Others were ordered away to fight Goths, Vandals and Huns battering on borders much nearer to Rome. In AD 407, the last effective Roman forces left Britain for the Continent.

No final, glorious battle decided the fate of the wall. It was simply abandoned to the wind, rain, wild flowers and the barbarian. After nearly 350 years of peace and civilisation, Roman Britain had finally come to an end.

THE GREAT BARBARIAN CONSPIRACY

Roman Britain faced its greatest challenge in AD 367, when barbarians assailed it from north, east and west. Acting in unison, Picts poured over Hadrian's Wall, Saxons landed on the North Sea coast, and the Irish swooped down on the western seaboard.

The military commander of Roman Britain was apparently taken prisoner. The Count of the Saxon Shore, charged with keeping the sea raiders at bay, was defeated and presumably killed. Plunderers swarmed unchecked.

Emperor Valentian sent a Spaniard, Count Theodosius, to deal with the situation. He landed with fresh troops in 368. The invaders, laden with loot, were no match for them. Theodosius liberated London, proclaimed amnesty for soldiers who had deserted and spent the winter pulling the army together. As a morale-booster, he set up a mint so that his legionaries would be paid regularly. In the spring, the great advance northwards began.

Marauders were flushed from their lairs, legionary strongpoints were retaken and shore defences revitalised. Naval patrols watched the Irish. In two years Theodosius restored peace.

When Theodosius left Britain it seemed the barbarian plot had failed. But the peace he left behind was a fragile one. The decline of the empire was now a fact, and nothing could prevent its eventual fall.

LIBERATOR *Theodosius watches as reinforcements arrive at Rutupiae – Richborough on Thanet, Kent.*

Fight for survival as Roman power crumbles

The Roman way of life in Britain did not end overnight. It withered away gradually under the pitiless onslaught of invaders and the draining of resources as the legions were withdrawn for Continental campaigns.

But the barbarian invasion of 367 marked a turning point. From then on life in the province sank towards the chaos of the Dark Ages. Forty years later Britain ceased to be part of the Roman world.

During 300 years of Roman rule, the Britons had become accustomed, at least in the south-east, to prosperity and peace. Great villas, or farming estates, worked by an ample supply of peasants and slaves, produced food for the flourishing cities.

But things were changing. The central government in Rome was now weak. Barbarian attacks were increasingly strong and more frequent. And above all, the powerful army had aspirations of its own. The men not involved in frontier duties were free to indulge in the activities of victorious troops in conquered lands, the most attractive being the acquisition of booty. In 383 and again in 406, British commanders took their troops to the Continent, to pillage and to bid for the Imperial throne. Each episode ended in disaster.

A brief respite came in 396–8 when Stilicho, a Vandal-born general of brilliance, reorganised British defences. But in 401, Stilicho and his army left Britain to defend Italy, the heart of the empire itself.

By 407 matters had reached crisis point. Three times in 25 years Britain had been depleted of its army. Confidence had never fully returned after 367. Now the morale of the country was in tatters. Villas were abandoned; their fields reverted to scrub. The country-dwellers fled to the safety of the walled cities. But trade on which city life depended rapidly declined with the slump in agriculture and growing hazards of travel.

In 410 the Saxons raided the coasts once more. The Britons seized the opportunity to break away from Rome, establishing their own administration as best they could. Centralised government had evidently broken down completely. In the death agony of Roman Britain, the towns wrote to Emperor Honorius asking for help, only to be told that from now on they must look after their own defences. Britain was on its own.

BARBARIANS *A carved Pictish stone slab found at Aberlemno in Angus, shows Pict fighting men on foot and horseback.*

ROME'S RULE ENDS – BUT A RICH LEGACY SURVIVES

As Roman civilisation collapsed under the successive blows of barbarian hordes, its splendid buildings were devastated and all their riches laid waste.

In the towns, abandoned by fleeing citizens, trees and bushes pushed their way through the pavements and dislodged the columns and pediments of forums and temples. In many of the villas which had carried luxurious Roman living to the remotest corner of the empire, cattle were stabled in the magnificent tiled bathrooms and formal chambers. Within a few generations the civilisation which had brought Britain one of the longest and most settled periods in its history was buried beneath rubble and scrub.

But many of its finest creations proved miraculously immune to the ravages of time. Hundreds of years later, marvellous works of art and architecture were unearthed from the layers of earth and undergrowth. Intricately patterned mosaics, fresco paintings, relief sculptures and busts to unknown gods in magnificent temples had been preserved.

Some of the great wealth of Roman art came to light by patient archaeological research, others by pure chance. It was workmen digging a drain who discovered Fishbourne Palace, near Chichester, with its rich mosaic floors; and in Suffolk a ploughman turned up the Mildenhall Treasure, one of the finest hoards of Roman silver ever found. It was apparently buried by a rich family before they took flight from the barbarian invaders.

Much of the decorative work of the early period of Roman occupation was done by foreign craftsmen and artists. They were brought in to embellish the villas which sprung up in south-east Britain after the Claudian invasion. Soon, British craftsmen learnt the newly imported skills and established flourishing schools of mosaic work, glass and pottery manufacture, sculpture, painting and metal work.

Nothing inspired the Roman artists and sculptors as much as the many gods and goddesses they brought with them from Imperial Rome, and these figures and busts are among the most fascinating and beautiful pieces of Roman art in Britain.

Gods of the empire

The Romans also adopted many of the Celtic gods, some interchangeable with their own. Mars, the Roman God of war, corresponded closely with the Celtic deities Belatucadrus and Calumus. Throughout the north of England Roman soldiers built shrines to Celtic gods, no doubt seeking the protection of these powerful local deities in their campaigns against the fierce neighbouring tribesmen.

Some of these shrines were complex buildings filled with treasures such as the splendid

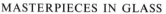

MASTERPIECES IN GLASS

Glass-blowing, which was invented about the 1st century, transformed the use of glass from a luxury only the rich could afford into a thriving industry, which supplied glass vessels and medallions for practical and decorative use. Much of the early glass came from the Rhineland; other objects from as far away as Egypt. Many pieces, some of them with fragile handles or intricate designs, survived in the ruins of Roman Britain.

CHRISTIAN HOUSEHOLD *The Romans introduced Christianity to Britain during the 3rd century, and it spread quickly. These paintings, found in* Lullingstone Villa, are of the sacred monogram, made from the first two Greek letters of Christ's name, and of a man praying.

temple, built on a hilltop above Lydney, to Nodens, a hunter-god of the Forest of Dean. Nodens's temple, decorated with mosaic panels and filled with religious ornaments and sculpture, was made up of a nave and a series of chapels and aisles. The outbuildings included public baths, shops and a hostelry for pilgrims to the shrine.

The Romans also imported gods which they had adopted from other parts of their empire. A Persian god, Mithras, became the object of a thriving cult in Britain and temples to him were built throughout the island. A sculpture unearthed in London shows the god as a handsome youth with long curly hair, and other portrayals depict him slaying a bull, symbolising the conquest of nature. His followers too, many of them rich merchants, were expected to show their willingness to conquer the wild elements in human nature. The cult involved severe physical and mental tests.

The most lasting legacy
Among the strange cults the Romans brought to Britain was the primitive faith which was eventually to triumph and lead to a new civilisation. Introduced to Britain in the 3rd century, Christianity flourished under the Romans and inspired its own art, the finest examples of which were found in the Roman villa at Lullingstone in Kent.

As the barbarians advanced on their trail of pillage and destruction the Christians fled to the hills, where they fostered and kept alive their faith. And there, in the remoter reaches of the country, Christianity grew, to become the greatest legacy of Roman civilisation.

THE MILDENHALL TREASURE

During the last troubled years of Roman rule in Britain, in the late 4th and early 5th centuries, Saxon raids from the Continent became ever more menacing. A wealthy family living at Mildenhall in Suffolk panicked – and buried their hoard of silver treasure for safety. They were never to recover it.

Nearly 16 centuries later, during the Second World War, a ploughman working at Mildenhall set his plough 4 in. deeper than was usual. He struck an object – and found a hoard of encrusted objects which he gave to his employer. Believing them to be made of lead or pewter, the farmer left them, neglected, in his home. But in 1946 an inquest declared the find to be treasure trove and their true value came to light.

The Mildenhall Treasure is probably the most important collection of Roman works of art ever to be found in Britain. It consists of 34 pieces of highly ornamented silverware, priceless in value. When cleaned, the pieces were found to be in an almost perfect state of preservation, made of the finest-quality silver. The bulk of the collection dates from the 4th century, but some could be as early as the 2nd, indicating that the family heirlooms were collected over several generations.

The centrepiece of the hoard, which was found 30 yds from the remains of a 4th-century Roman building, is a magnificent dish, nearly 2 ft in diameter and weighing 18¼ lb. A relief shows the head of Oceanus, god of the sea, in the centre, with other gods and sea monsters surrounding him. Other pieces of the treasure include dishes, goblets, a fine bowl with a lid and eight spoons, five of which are of the kind that may have been used as christening gifts.

Most of the treasures were either made in Rome or in Gaul; but some items, like a fluted bowl, were probably worked in Britain.

The Mildenhall Treasure is a magnificent reminder of the high state of Roman culture in Britain, and an intriguing sidelight on the history of the troubled times when it was so hurriedly buried by its wealthy Romano-British owners.

A bowl and cover, engraved with wild animals, from the Mildenhall Treasure, one of the most important collections of Roman silver found in Britain.

A FAMILY OF GODS *Throughout much of Roman history, Roman religion allowed considerable freedom of worship, and the Romans imported to Britain many different gods from all over their empire. The many statues they left behind show their variety – a Jupiter (left), a Sphinx and a Lar, or simple household god. A head of Mithras (right) was found at the Walbrook Temple to Mithras in London. It had been made in Italy of marble and was buried in London by the god's followers, with other cult objects, during a period of persecution by Christians.*

Invaders forge a united nation

Waves of land-hungry warriors come to Britain, first as raiders, then as settlers who build the villages of England and slowly create a realm united by the Christian faith

With the Anglo-Saxon invasions of the 5th century, a new era opened in British history. It lasted for six centuries and ended in apparent disaster at the Battle of Hastings in 1066. Yet during this time, these newcomers of West Germanic stock – Angles, Saxons, Jutes and Frisians – created the pattern of villages that was to endure to modern times.

The Anglo-Saxons came from areas outside the Roman Empire, from the coastline which stretches from Jutland to the mouth of the Rhine. They brought an alien way of life with them, and their settlement was not unopposed or easy. The native British, now more Celtic than Roman, were still capable of putting up stout resistance.

Various ancient hill-forts became the bases of British war leaders for their campaigns against the invaders. One of these, Cadbury Castle in Somerset (pp. 46–47), holds a mystery that remains unsolved. According to legend, it was the home of Arthur, the heroic leader of the Britons in their struggle.

For a time the British managed to halt the tide of settlement and conquest. But, by the late 6th century, the Anglo-Saxons had resumed the offensive. After victory at the Battle of Dyrham in 577, they were well poised to overrun all of Britain to the borders of Wales, Devon and Cornwall. They also advanced into the lowlands of the north-west, and as far as the Firth of Forth and modern Edinburgh in the north-east.

After about 600, the Saxons in Britain were organised into several small kingdoms. In the early days Northumbria, formed by the merging of two

A SYMBOL OF SAXON FAITH

The Anglo-Saxons first came to Britain as pagan raiders about AD 400. Three centuries later they had peopled and tamed much of England. It was they who began the clearing of Britain's ancient forests in earnest. They cleared far more than the Romano-Britons before them.

During these centuries, the Saxons embraced Christianity. And, although still divided into many kingdoms, they established a united Church. It was to be the inspiration of their finest works of art, such as this 10th-century ivory depicting the Crucifixion (inset). Their faith also inspired works of architecture. The tower of Sompting church in West Sussex has survived for 1000 years as evidence of their skill. It is similar to towers built in the Rhinelands in the same period. The use of Roman bricks at Sompting shows how Saxon England grew out of the ruins of Roman Britain. The village of Sompting, with its church, was among hundreds of settlements founded by the Saxons. These communities, and the well-tended fields which surrounded them, were the lasting legacy of the Anglo-Saxons.

PLOUGHING AND SOWING *The Anglo-Saxons were, above all things, a farming people. These pictures, from a Saxon calendar made in the 11th century, are a rare contemporary record of Saxon life. A man ploughs in the month of January. His plough, drawn by four oxen, has a blade to cut the sod in front of the share, and a wheel for control. The Saxons brought this type of heavy plough from the Continent. It was a boon in the lowlands of the English Midlands, where the Saxons prospered.*

CUTTING WOOD *The Saxons relied on wood. It was their only fuel and their main building material. Carts and wagons, and all manner of tools and utensils were made of wood. The Romans, and the Celts before them, had made little inroad into the forests of Britain. It was the Saxons who began the long process of turning woods and marshes into fields, making slow but lasting changes in the landscape. The Saxon artist showed men cutting wood in February.*

RAKING, DIGGING AND SOWING *March was one of the busiest months of the Saxon year. After winter frosts, the soil was ready for final digging and sowing. The peasant was required to work up to three days a week in unpaid service to his lord at this time of year. He was expected to 'lie at his lord's fold as often as it falls his lot', and to plough and plant 5 acres a week at his own expense. The rest of the time he could look to his own livelihood.*

SHEEP TENDING *Every Saxon farmer – lord and peasant alike – owned sheep. And Saxon wool gained a high reputation for its quality. This rich heritage was to become the foundation of English wealth in the Middle Ages. In May, the lambing season nearly over, shepherds and their seasonal helpers had to be constantly on the lookout for the wild beasts – wolves and foxes – which preyed on their flocks.*

kingdoms in the north – Deira and Bernicia – was the most powerful. The East Angles of Norfolk and Suffolk formed a somewhat isolated kingdom. In the south-east, Kent, Sussex and Essex were among the earliest kingdoms.

The formation of the two most important of these early kingdoms, Mercia and Wessex, was slower and more complicated. It was not until the second quarter of the 7th century that the Mercians, led by their pagan and war-loving ruler, Penda, built up a powerful military confederation over the Midlands. Wessex was an earlier creation. But, like Mercia, it was not until late in the 7th century that it achieved the power its founders sought.

All these kingdoms were converted to Christianity in the course of the 7th century. The missionary zeal of St Augustine (pp. 48–49), who was sent by Pope Gregory the Great, brought the people of the south-east into the Church, in direct contact with Rome. Meanwhile, St Aidan, from St Columba's island monastery of Iona in Scotland, helped St Oswald of Northumbria to convert his people, following Celtic practices. Representatives of those favouring Roman and Celtic customs met to resolve their differences at Whitby in 663–4, at the great synod called by King Oswy of Northumbria. After that, all the kingdoms turned to Rome for inspiration and guidance. In this way, unification of the kingdoms through Christianity was achieved about 300 years before political unity.

For the Anglo-Saxons, the rich lands of England had been worth fighting for. Their careful agriculture brought wealth. The treasures found at Sutton Hoo in East Anglia (pp. 50–51) show the wealth attained by a Saxon king.

The threat from across the North Sea

Generation by generation over the succeeding centuries, the divided kingdoms of Saxon England moved towards unity. Mercia came close to achieving it under King Offa.

But national unity was not to be won by English effort alone. It took a new, external threat to force unity upon England. After 800, the heathen Vikings – notably the Danes – were an ever-increasing menace.

Northumbria, the Christian stronghold of the north, suffered severely. After the sacking of the monastery of Lindisfarne (pp. 52–53) the Christian torch, lit by St Oswald, came close to being extinguished.

It fell to another kingdom to take up the struggle against the menace. The hour produced the man – Alfred, ruler of Wessex (pp. 54–55). By an all-out military effort, he and his successors were able first to contain and finally to reconquer the lands that had fallen under Scandinavian control.

The Anglo-Saxons were not totally concerned with war. They were primarily a farming people. But during the 8th century, their vigour and vitality began to manifest itself in town life. London flourished.

The Church was powerful under both Celtic and Roman churchmen. St Dunstan of Canterbury inspired the foundation of many monasteries in the 10th century, which were to have a lasting effect on religious and social life.

Scholarship also flourished. Monks such as Bede produced works in Latin. But authors also wrote in Anglo-Saxon – the beginnings of the English language. The epic poem 'Beowulf', telling a great warrior's story and more than 3000 lines in length, was composed in the 8th century.

Learning was encouraged by kings such as Alfred, who assembled a notable group of scholars. They translated many works from Latin, and books 'most needful for men to know' were made accessible to the English in their own language. The *Anglo-Saxon Chronicle* also took shape at this time.

But, despite Alfred's victories, Scandinavian influence was long-lasting, and in the late 10th and early 11th centuries a fresh move brought the Danes success. From 1016 to 1042 a Christian Danish dynasty ruled England.

The Anglo-Saxons now produced their last king of the direct Saxon line – Edward the Confessor. Under his rule art flourished, carrying on a long tradition of Anglo-Saxon craftsmanship (pp. 58–59). And his own contribution was the creation of Westminster Abbey (pp. 56–57), a towering monument to the Christianity the Anglo-Saxons had come to treasure.

On Edward's death in early 1066, the throne passed to his brother-in-law, Harold, Earl of Wessex, the strongest man in the kingdom. But, as the *Anglo-Saxon Chronicle* recorded, he 'met little quiet in it as long as he ruled the realm'. In 1066 England was wealthy and potentially powerful. Its throne was a rich temptation to any warrior. William of Normandy played for high stakes when he landed on the Sussex shore that autumn.

ANGLO-SAXON BRITAIN *Saxon settlement in Britain began in the 5th century. It was another 500 years before the Saxon kingdoms were welded into the united kingdom of England.*

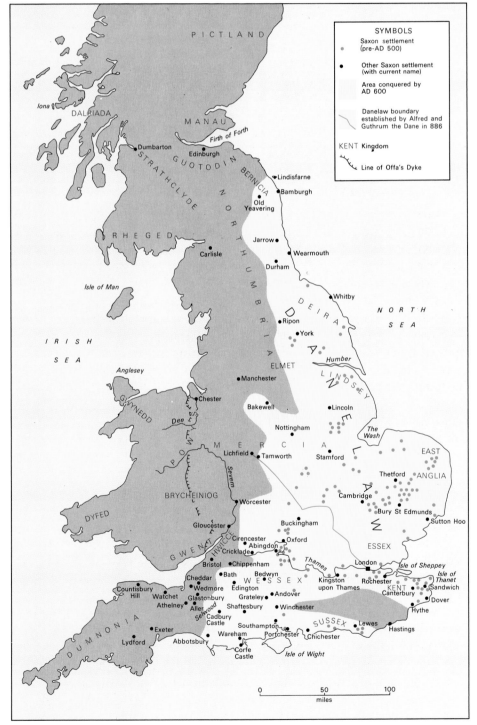

REAPING *Everyone in Saxon England knew the importance of a good harvest. Here, three peasants cut corn with sickles; a fourth binds it into sheaves. Three more harvesters load sheaves on to a cart. The great Saxon estates, the* vills, *were arranged so that they included woods, meadows, arable land and common-land grazing. The strips of cultivated field were allotted to the lord, peasants and tenants, so that every man had some good land and some less fertile.*

HUNTING WITH THE FALCON *Young birds and animals were hunted at their fattest and most succulent in October. Hunting with falcons and hawks reached England from the Continent in the mid-9th century. The sport soon became popular with the nobility, and laws governing it were strictly enforced. Pheasants, partridges, quails, ducks, teals, woodcocks, hares and rabbits abounded in the countryside.*

THE WARM FIRE OF WINTER *In November, the harvest gathered in and the farm animals safely in the byre, the Saxon peasant could relax. Some animals would be killed and their meat salted to preserve it. But after the twelve days of Christmas festivities, Anglo-Saxon peasant's fare was monotonous – bread and porridge, with occasional milk, fish and cheese and, rarely, salt meat and dried fruit.*

THRESHING AND WINNOWING *Work out of doors was shunned in December. In the barn, the peasants would carefully beat out the corn to separate the grains from the ears. Then came the job of sifting the corn to get rid of the chaff. After that, the precious corn was bagged for storage, ready to be taken to the mill.*

45

A hilltop fortress keeps its age-old secret

WAS THIS CAMELOT?

Cadbury Castle, Somerset, viewed from the air. In recent years, archaeologists have been at work on the site, trying to discover whether this pre-Roman hill-fort was the head-quarters of Arthur, the legendary hero of British resistance to the Saxons.

Above the Somerset village of South Cadbury, close to the Dorset border, stands an ancient hill-fort which has become the subject of the most romantic mystery in British history. For a tradition which reaches back for at least 500 years links this quiet spot with the legendary castle of Camelot and its ruler, King Arthur.

Cadbury Castle, as the fort is named, was originally built by the Iron Age inhabitants of the area. It is constructed to a pattern found in many places in southern Britain, crowning a 500 ft hill whose sides are covered with massive banks and ditches, designed to discourage an enemy from storming the 18-acre enclosure at the summit.

But it was not strong enough to defy the Romans. When Vespasian led his legions in the conquest of south-western Britain, he took the fortress by storm. During the four centuries of Roman rule it fell into decay but, as the Romans withdrew, Cadbury was re-occupied by the Britons of the area for defence against both the pagan Anglo-Saxon invaders and the many rival British kingdoms.

From this era of bloody war and sudden death dates a mystery which has never been solved. According to the Tudor historian and chronicler John Leland: 'At . . . South Cadbury standeth Camelot, sometime a famous town or castle . . . The people can tell nothing there but that they have heard say that Arthur much resorted to Camelot.'

Was Cadbury the home of Arthur? Did this great British war-leader in fact exist? A medieval story-teller, Geoffrey of Monmouth, wrote of Arthur, his battles and of his magic sword. Other writers added the romance of the Round Table, the ill-starred love of Lancelot and Guinevere, and the magician Merlin.

But these legends were not of their own creation. They drew upon older sources – the ancient memories of the Celtic peoples of Wales, Cornwall and Brittany – which originated in the Dark Ages of the 5th to 9th centuries. Then, the British ancestors of these Celts were engaged in a long and bitter struggle to preserve their homeland from the Anglo-Saxon invaders.

Arthur the war lord

Most historians today agree that Arthur existed, though he was probably not a king. He may have been leader of a band of highly mobile men. This would account for his ability to move swiftly through Britain to win the dozen victories associated with his name.

The monk Nennius, writing in the 9th century to extol the Welsh, described Arthur as *dux bellorum* (battle chief) in his *History of the Britons*. At Mount Badon, probably near Swindon, he won his greatest victory over the Saxons. In that battle, Nennius recorded, 960 men fell 'in one onslaught of Arthur's'. The triumph was so overwhelming that the Saxons made no further encroachments on

AS IT WAS *The British chief who reoccupied Cadbury in the 5th century rebuilt much of its defences. The most striking features of his improvements were a timber gate-tower, built about 470, and a great hall.*

the scene of major rebuilding operations at exactly the period when Arthur must have lived.

The man who ordered the rebuilding of Cadbury was clearly an exceptionally powerful British chief. He was strong enough to raid far-off Saxon settlements in search of slaves and booty, for early Saxon ornaments have been found at Cadbury.

The castle also fits the Arthurian legend because of its geographical location and the size and scale of its defences. On the present archaeological evidence, Cadbury gives the best idea of what Arthur's base must have been like, with its great feasting hall.

Modern legend

Despite all the accumulated evidence of modern archaeology, the mystery of South Cadbury may never be solved. Even at Cadbury today, archaeological fact merges into legend. A local tradition claims that Arthur sleeps beneath the hill, and will rise again when his country calls.

Arthur's reputation was not confined to Britain. Writing about 1170, the chronicler Alanus de Insulis recorded: 'What place is there within the bounds of the empire of Christendom to which the winged praise of Arthur the Briton has not extended? The peoples of the east speak of him as do those of the west, though separated by the breadth of the whole earth.'

A land threatened by invaders from all sides

After the Romans withdrew from Britain in the 5th century AD, the Britons faced many enemies. Although Germanic pirates had been raiding the east coast for some generations, it seemed to the British that their island was chiefly threatened by Picts from the north and by Scots from Ireland. So their rulers followed the example the Romans had set and hired German princes and their war-bands to fight off the Picts.

Unwittingly the British themselves had taken the first step that was to lead to their doom. German warriors were established from the Vale of York to Southampton Water.

These tribesmen brought their families with them and were given land to till in return for military defence. But only 50 years after they arrived, the policy began to break down. The newcomers had come to realise the weakness of their employers. No doubt there was pressure from land-hungry fellow-tribesmen on the Continent as well. A series of revolts began.

Saxon triumph

The British kingdoms did their best to hold out against this pressure – especially in the west. But their alliance was broken by defeats at Dyrham in Gloucestershire in AD 577 and at Chester in 616. By the late 7th century, most of England was under the rule of Angle or Saxon kings.

The native British, however, were not expelled or exterminated. Though some fled to the far marches of Wales, the west and the north, historians now believe that much of the English settlement was peaceful – a slow take-over of the decaying Romano-British villages and estates. Both Celtic Briton and Germanic Saxon had a part in the making of England.

British territory for the next 50 years. But it was at this point Arthur passed into legend. According to the Celts, he never died but was merely sleeping. One day he would wake again to drive the Saxons into the sea. As late as 1113, when a group of French monks laughed at this story in Cornwall, the local people were so angered that they attacked them.

Arthur's fortress

Other legends told of Arthur's lavish court at Camelot. Many sites have been suggested for this fabulous palace. Cadbury is perhaps the most probable. It was never the spectacular building chronicled by the medieval romancers, but there is no doubt that it was

---

'THE ONCE AND FUTURE KING'

One of the first authors to collect many of the myths and legends surrounding the heroic figure of Arthur, King of the Britons (left), was Geoffrey of Monmouth. In his *History of the Kings of Britain*, written in the 1130's, the reign of Arthur was the highlight. According to Geoffrey, Arthur was crowned as King of the Britons at the age of 15 and led his people to triumphs over both the Saxons and the Picts. These were won with the aid of the king's magic sword, which Geoffrey called Caliburn but later writers renamed Excalibur.

Arthur went on to conquer Ireland, Iceland, the Orkneys, Norway and Gaul. But his treacherous nephew Mordred allied himself with the Saxons against his uncle. Arthur and Mordred eventually met in battle. Though Mordred was slain, Arthur himself received a deadly wound and was carried away to the Isle of Avalon in the far west and rested there until it healed.

Many other writers added more stories to the legend. These included the tragic love of Lancelot and Guinevere, the quest for the Holy Grail, and the legend of the Round Table. But on one fable they all agreed: Arthur would return in a time of trouble when his people called upon him. He was, in truth, 'the once and future king'.

A medieval illustration shows Arthur's Round Table in all its glory as Galahad, the purest knight of all, is introduced to membership.

ARTIST'S RECORD *In this 11th-century illustration of Noah's ark, a monk based his work on the longboats used by the Saxon invaders.*

Faith and war in an age of kings

Inspired by William the Conqueror, a line of strong-willed monarchs, ruling by the sword, slowly forge a nation from the disunited peoples of England

On a cold October morning in 1066, England was dragged into a new world. As a result of the Norman victory at Hastings (pp. 64–65), a small and isolated island became part of the European continent. The British gained from Europe new ideas in war, government, religion and art. They were to contribute ideas of their own. But first the island was to be subjected to an alien military rule. It was just under 300 years before Normans and Anglo-Saxons began thinking of themselves as Englishmen.

In his 21 year reign, William the Conqueror demonstrated all the contrasts of medieval England. Though he was extremely religious, William nevertheless subjected England to a baptism of fire. It was he who taught the English that peace rested on violence – on revenge ruthlessly visited on all who dared to defy the will of the king.

Vast stone castles such as the Tower of London (pp. 66–67) helped to consolidate William's might. Great cathedrals and abbeys, such as, Ely, Peterborough and Durham (pp. 70–71), stood out as citadels of Norman Christianity, commanded by harsh, uncompromising prelates, in the heart of a hostile land.

But William's abilities were not inherited by his heir, William Rufus. For 13 years this monarch presided over a nation torn by aristocratic quarrels and trampled down by foreign mercenaries. Many of his subjects must have heard with unconcealed relief of the death of Rufus in the New Forest in August 1100 (pp. 68–69), and of the accession of Henry I to the throne.

THE KING IS CROWNED

The line of kings planted on the English throne by William, Duke of Normandy, ruled by the sword. And they had another power at their command – the teaching of the Church that a king's authority came directly from God. The mystic ritual of the coronation service played a vital part in establishing this belief. This illustration of an English coronation, dating from the turn of the 13th century, shows the king seated, surrounded by his archbishops and bishops, while nobles and courtiers look on. The same ritual has continued to the present day. The coronation chair (inset) was first used by Edward II in 1308. Since then, every ruler of England – with the exceptions of Edward V and Edward VIII – has been crowned on it.

STRUGGLE *In the Middle Ages nobles constantly struggled with their royal overlords. Only a strong king could keep such men in their place. Here, John of Gaunt, the mightiest baron of his day, feasts with his retainers.*

CHIVALRY *A clash at a tournament. The code of chivalry dominated court life in medieval England. Edward III even re-founded King Arthur's legendary Round Table for his nobles.*

GUILDS *A master oversees a mason (right) and a carpenter (left). An apprenticeship could last as long as ten years.*

Henry's dour and stern manner won him few friends in his day. But his dictatorial rule, though hated by his barons, brought peace to English homes. His one failure had nothing to do with politics. His inability to sire more than one legitimate son brought danger. For stability depended on a peaceful succession, and in the Middle Ages even healthy men were likely to be struck down in the prime of their lives. Just such a fate intervened on November 25, 1120, when Henry's heir, the 17-year-old Prince William, was drowned crossing the Channel in the *White Ship* (pp. 72–73).

This calamity brought upon England nearly two decades of anarchy. For the succession was disputed by Stephen, Henry I's nephew, and Matilda, Henry's daughter. Their struggle lasted for 19 years – the 'dark winter', in which it was said that 'God and his saints slept'.

Kings, nobles and Church struggle for power

But Henry II, who succeeded Stephen in 1153, was a remarkable king. He gave his country an administrative system which was the envy of Europe. Henry's quick mind and tireless energy enabled him to rule an empire which covered two-thirds of France, as well as England and Ireland.

Henry usually acted on instinct, dealing rapidly with problems as they arose, outwitting his enemies by speed of action. But occasionally his instinct betrayed him. A few hasty words spoken to a group of knights at Christmas 1170 involved him in a crisis which was sensational even in a violent age – the murder of Archbishop Becket in Canterbury Cathedral (pp. 74–75).

England's next king, Richard I (the Lionheart), had little in common with his father. He took after his mother, the glamorous and passionate Eleanor of Aquitaine. Richard's triumphs on the Third Crusade (pp. 76–77) brought fame and renown to English arms. But his country paid a heavy price for this pursuit of chivalry. And Richard's brother, John, though reviled by posterity, was far more effective a king than his brother. He built on the work of his father to give England the firm government it needed. But like his father, John, too, had to face the bitter and lasting opposition of the Church. This, combined with the hostility of his barons, brought him down. In June 1215, John was forced to put his seal to Magna Carta at Runnymede (pp. 80–81). There, he signed away many of the powers so painfully won and maintained by his ancestors.

The downfall of John was above all the work of the Church, which was now equal to the strongest of kings. Its dominance was expressed in the first great Gothic cathedrals of England. Canterbury was rebuilt in pure French style from the money given by pilgrims to the shrine of Thomas Becket. Wells Cathedral (pp. 82–83) illustrated that English architects could adapt the new style to their own English tastes. And another significant event in this enlightened age was the foundation and slow development of England's first university at Oxford (pp. 78–79).

John's dark reign gave way in 1216 to the long and gloomy rule of his young son, Henry III. Though Henry's intentions were good, his unworldliness and incompetence exasperated his subjects. The expense and shame of a succession of calamitous foreign wars brought the king to his knees in 1258.

In that year, the barons embarked on a bold experiment in constitutional government. Summoned by a brilliant adventurer, Simon de Montfort, England's first Parliament (pp. 84–85) assembled in 1265. But this experiment was short-lived, for Henry's son, the able Edward I, soon restored royal power. Edward's ambition was to fulfil the dream of his ancestors by uniting the whole of the British Isles under his rule. Wales was conquered and English power there buttressed by a line of castles – buildings which rank with Hadrian's Wall among the most effective fortifications ever built in these islands (pp. 86–87). But even the mighty Edward met his match in Robert Bruce and his hosts of patriotic Scots.

Where Edward I had failed, his wretched son, Edward II, could scarcely be expected to succeed. At the Battle of Bannockburn in 1314 (pp. 88–89), Edward led his troops to England's most humiliating defeat since the Battle of Hastings. Hounded from his throne by his rebellious subjects and his estranged wife, he met a miserable death in Berkeley Castle in 1327.

Edward III was only 15 when he was called upon to rule over the ruins of his father's kingdom. But it was he who bound the nation together and led it in an enterprise which his successors carried on for more than a century – the struggle for their rights in the fields of France.

In June 1340 a great naval victory at Sluys laid the foundations of English sea power. At Crécy in 1346 (pp. 90–91) and Poitiers, ten years later, the proud armies of France were humbled by a handful of English longbowmen.

Even as Edward's armies were winning glory in France, his country was being devastated by the monstrous ravages of plague. In 1348–9 rats brought the Black Death to English shores (pp. 92–93). More than one-third of the population died in torment. The resulting unrest came to a head under the boy-king Richard II. In the Peasants' Revolt of 1381 (pp. 94–95), the serfs of Kent rose in rebellion, marched on London and confronted the king at Smithfield. Only Richard's presence of mind saved his throne. But in 1399 he lost his throne and a year later his life, when he was secretly put to death at Pontefract Castle. Despite the troubles of Richard's reign, English culture rose to new heights in the work of a new generation of English poets. Chief among them was Geoffrey Chaucer (pp. 96–97).

The reign of Henry IV was a period of reconstruction after the unity of England had been shattered by Richard II and his enemies. The great barons of the north, led by the Percy family, were crushed at Shrewsbury (pp. 98–99), and the foundations laid for England's campaigns of conquest under Henry's son. At Agincourt in 1415 (pp. 100–1), Henry V repeated the achievements of his great-grandfather, Edward III, by destroying a French army vastly superior to his own. The crown of France itself was soon within Henry's grasp. But he died prematurely in 1422 and his son, Henry VI, was not the man to fulfil his father's dreams. His inability to govern lost the English their empire in France and unleashed upon them the horrors of civil war. The Wars of the Roses (pp. 104–5), a struggle between the rival houses of Lancaster and York, were to convulse the realm for 30 years.

The need for a strong king

Henry redeemed himself, in the eyes of posterity at least, by his generous patronage of the arts. Two great educational foundations – Eton and King's College, Cambridge (pp. 102–3) – owe their existence to him. But these achievements mattered little to his people, who rejoiced when he was finally overthrown by Edward IV, the Yorkist claimant to the throne.

Edward tried to bring back strong rule to England. He encouraged the arts as well. In the houses of prosperous merchants and educated noblemen could be found the first books printed by William Caxton (pp. 106–7). But in a land torn by civil war, it would take more than the financial genius of Edward IV to restore the peace. His able but ruthless brother, Richard III, reopened old wounds when he seized the throne. Only after his death at Bosworth in 1485 (pp. 108–9) could the crown be restored to its former lustre, under a new dynasty.

In the Middle Ages, Englishmen came to believe that only the rule of strong kings could save them from anarchy. They were to have a full measure of such rule under the Tudors.

RELIGION *Monks worked on menial tasks, but the orders they belonged to controlled vast riches. The Cistercians were so wealthy that in 1198 they raised one-third of the ransom of 150,000 silver marks that Leopold of Austria demanded for the release of Richard I.*

TRADE *The cloth industry was medieval England's most important trade. In this miniature, painted in 1482, dyers dip cloth into heated cauldrons of red dye. Women, too, were employed in the textile trade – a 'spinster' was originally a single woman who earned her living by spinning yarn.*

SERFS *Peasants till the fields supervised by an overseer. Those working on the land were often bound to it for life. But in England the Black Death of the 1340's helped to end the system.*

Saxon and Norman meet to decide England's fate

BATTLEFIELD FOR A NATION
Nine centuries ago on this peaceful field at Telham Hill, East Sussex, the sound of clashing arms rang out as Norman and English soldiers met in battle to decide the fate of England. At the end of the battle, King Harold was dead and the English army routed.

As dawn broke on October 14, 1066, a thin column of men wound their way out of Hastings towards nearby Telham Hill. They were the soldiers of the last conquering army ever to set foot in England. Their commander, William, Duke of Normandy, had for years cast covetous eyes across the English Channel and awaited patiently the moment to strike at his island neighbour. Now, his moment had come.

On the summit of a neighbouring hill lay the camp of the defending English army, led by King Harold. At any other time these strong-limbed Saxon warriors would have been formidable enemies, but on that morning they were exhausted and disorganised. Three weeks earlier they had defeated Harold Hardrada, the King of Norway, in a pitched battle at Stamford Bridge in north Yorkshire. Then on the news of the Norman invasion they had marched 250 miles south. Such was the speed of their march that many of Harold's archers and infantrymen had fallen behind through sheer exhaustion.

A moment's cool calculation would have persuaded Harold that it was a mistake to rush headlong into battle. He could have held off, fortified London and left Duke William to fritter away his supplies and his energy in laying waste southern England. But no English leader of those days could risk the dishonour of appearing to stand by while English villages were ravaged. The invader had to be hurled back, not starved into retreat.

Preparing for battle
While the English recovered from the march, the Normans listened to their duke. 'Now is the time for you to show your strength,' he told them. 'You are fighting not only for victory but for survival.'

King Harold had hoped to take the Normans by surprise. But the English were slow to prepare for action, and by 9.00 a.m. they had still not lined up ready for battle. It was William who had the advantage of surprise.

First, the Norman archers advanced to within bow-shot and opened fire. Then, placing a bag of holy relics round his neck, the Norman commander led his army of horsemen and infantry in three groups down Telham Hill and up the slope towards the English position. The English foot soldiers hurriedly assembled and formed a wall of shields to resist the enemy advance. As the Norman light infantry came within 70 ft of the English ranks they let loose a hail of javelins.

Then the two armies clashed, and the English battle-axes sang through the air, biting deep into Norman bone. In the fierce hand-to-hand struggle, two of Harold's brothers were among the first to fall. But the English shield-wall held firm and the Norman attack wavered. The Breton troops on the left of the Norman line turned and fled. Then, a rumour flew through the Norman ranks that William himself had been killed, and his half-brother, Odo, Bishop of Bayeux, desperately tried to halt the flight of the invaders. Harold was on the point of gaining a spectacular victory.

'I shall yet be victorious'
Instead of making a disciplined advance, however, the English allowed their enthusiasm to get the better of them. They swarmed down the hill on foot in full pursuit of the Norman horsemen. It was a fatal mistake. Drawn up in ordered ranks, the English infantry were more than a match for William's cavalry. But once they broke ranks, the Norman knights had only to turn and cut their assailants to pieces.

Seizing his opportunity, William raised his helmet in the air. 'Look at me! I am still alive, and by the grace of God I shall yet be victorious.' His followers took heart and charged the English once again. This time their attack was irresistible. Alarming gaps were carved in the English ranks, and no reinforcements could be found to fill them.

Finally, four Norman knights broke through to where Harold and the élite corps of his army were gathered. The king desperately tried to fight them off, but he could not parry four thrusts simultaneously. One knight struck Harold to the ground with his lance. Two others hewed at his prostrate body, and the fourth cut off the king's head.

As the news of Harold's death spread through their ranks, the already demoralised English gave up the fight. Thousands fled from the field in disarray to take refuge in the surrounding woods. Many more were butchered where they stood. A small band rallied near where Harold had fallen and fought a hopeless rearguard action against their pursuers.

Hastings need not have been the end for Saxon England, but the Saxon nobles could

COMETS AND CATASTROPHES

During the Middle Ages, man's faith in the Christian religion was unshakeable. Therefore, natural phenomena in the skies such as comets and eclipses were often looked upon as divine intervention and greeted with awe and terror. The appearance in 1066 of Halley's Comet, named after the 17th-century astronomer who charted its orbit, had exactly that effect. It was regarded as a sign that God was about to punish King Harold for breaking an oath which he had sworn to William of Normandy some years before, when he was shipwrecked in France, promising to support the duke's claim to the English throne. By accepting the throne himself in January 1066, Harold had broken his word and thus, it was believed, faced divine vengeance. And to many, the outcome of the Battle of Hastings, in which Harold was killed and Saxon England fell to William and his Norman invaders, seemed to justify their forebodings of disaster.

A photograph of Halley's Comet, during its most recent appearance in 1910. This was the sight that so frightened the English in 1066.

In this detail from the Bayeux Tapestry, a court astrologer warns King Harold that the comet will bring disaster in its wake.

not agree who was to be king. Edgar, the next in line to the throne, was only nine years old. While the Saxons disputed, William advanced cautiously, capturing Dover and Canterbury. Then the Saxon forces at Winchester – the stronghold where the royal treasure was kept – surrendered. With the whole of south-east England in his hands, William conferred with the Saxon leaders at Berkhampstead. There, according to an 11th-century edition of the Anglo-Saxon Chronicle, 'he was met by Bishop Aldred (the Archbishop of York), Prince Edgar, Earl Edwin, Earl Morcar and all the best men from London ... they gave him hostages and swore oaths of fealty and he promised to be a gracious lord to them'. England's fate was decided – the Normans had come to stay.

A KING FALLS *A new interpretation of the Bayeux Tapestry has shattered the myth of Harold's death. It is now known that Harold is to the right of the Norman horseman (centre) falling beneath the hooves as he defends himself with an axe. Above him is the inscription* Harold Rex Interfectus Est *('King Harold is killed'). Previously it was thought that the man with an arrow in his eye, to the horseman's left, was the king. The myth was originated by the Norman Abbot of Bourgeil, who mistook the figures while writing on the battle 30 years later. But it is now known that medieval artists always showed death by a falling or prostrate figure.*

William I: Rule by fear, fire and the sword

William the Conqueror won his throne by force and he defended it by force. Any opposition to his rule was brutally crushed. Not only the English suffered, for the king also dealt harshly with Normans who showed too much ambition or independence of mind.

William was justly proud of having conquered England. He lost no opportunity of displaying his power, especially when he wanted to impress foreign ambassadors with his importance. During his reign he made a point of solemnly wearing his crown in public to receive the veneration of his subjects.

Instant obedience to the Norman king

William's appearance suited his personality. He was tall, broad and thick-set, and was noted for his moroseness. His voice was harsh, and his manner of speaking clipped and concise. He spoke as if he expected – and required – instant obedience.

He practised a strict piety and was an enthusiastic founder of churches and monasteries. Indeed, at the end of his life he feared that the brutality he had displayed during his career, would deprive him of salvation. On his death-bed he confessed that he had 'subjugated England by slaughter and by persecuting it beyond endurance'.

Almost with his last breath, he added: 'I have cruelly oppressed my subjects, unjustly disinherited them, and killed large numbers of them by famine and violence. May God forgive me for my sins.'

In spiritual and humane terms they were sins indeed, but as conqueror and king they had been the basis of his success in establishing his rule over England.

FACE OF THE CONQUEROR *A stone sculpture of William I, England's first Norman king. He treated the English harshly and only repented of his deeds on his death-bed.*

The Tower–a fortress to subdue capital and kingdom

BUILT BY THE CONQUEROR
For nearly 1000 years, the Tower has played a key role in Britain's history. Built by William I to overawe London, it has been fortress, royal residence, prison, place of execution, armoury and a home for the crown jewels. The White Tower (above) is its oldest part.

castles were not built of stone, however. They consisted of a ditch and an earthwork rampart (the 'bailey') topped by a wooden palisade. In the centre was a tall mound (the 'motte') with a wooden keep – the last refuge of the garrison. They were cheap and quick to build, and easy to repair.

But in places of special importance, William built stone keeps. The first of these was begun at Exeter in 1068, after the town's citizens had twice rebelled. William paced out the site himself. Another was built at Colchester.

Building the White Tower
But the most impressive stone keep of all was the White Tower of the Tower of London, so-called because its walls were originally whitewashed. London was the largest and wealthiest city in the land. Its citizens – numbering some 30,000 – had resisted the Normans for some weeks after Hastings, and William needed more than a primitive wooden castle to overawe them. Within the city walls, he built Baynard's castle (on the Embankment). Then, to the east of the city, just outside the walls, arose the White Tower.

It was typical of an age of warlike bishops that the architect William chose to build the White Tower was a churchman. Gandulf, Bishop of Rochester, had won a reputation as a military architect by building a fortress-like tower beside his cathedral.

Apart from its windows, the White Tower looks much the same today as it did when it was built to Gandulf's design. It was extremely large by the standards of the day, for it had to house not only a strong Norman garrison, but occasionally the king and his bustling court with its crowds of clerks and servants.

The Tower was four storeys high. The ground floor was given over entirely to store-

PLACE OF WORSHIP *The stern severity of the Chapel of St John in the Tower was a fitting place of worship for the Norman garrison.*

The Tower of London is the enduring symbol of the Norman Conquest. Its sturdy grey mass of stone stands out across the River Thames as a monument to the last successful invasion in Britain's history.

When William, Duke of Normandy, embarked on his conquest of England in 1066, he already had vast experience of warfare. For generations his ancestors had fought to retain their hold on the duchy of Normandy, and to expand into the neighbouring provinces.

They had learnt that a district could be conquered by force, but then lost as soon as an army withdrew. William knew that a few carefully placed castles, designed to be manned

by small garrisons, could hold a nation in thrall. His first action on landing in England was to build a wooden castle – the parts for which he had brought across the Channel – at his landing place.

A network of castles to crush resistance
In the years following the Conquest, Norman castles sprang up in every place where William feared the slightest opposition from his new subjects. As he moved northwards in 1068, William built castles at Warwick and Nottingham. On his return march to London he ordered castles to be constructed at Lincoln, Cambridge and Huntingdon. Most of these

A ROYAL STRONGHOLD *The Tower of London is seen in all its late medieval glory in this 15th-century manuscript. Many kings – including William Rufus, Henry I, Henry III and Edward I – improved on the Conqueror's work, to make the Tower the most powerful fortress in Europe.*

The mailed fist of the Normans rules England

Even after William the Conqueror's decisive victory at Hastings, it seemed that final triumph was a long way off. London still held out. William must have known that if resistance continued, his communications with Normandy were vulnerable and his sources of supply uncertain.

But at this crucial moment Saxon England's leaders surrendered to William. On Christmas Day 1066 he was crowned King of England.

It was not until 1068 that the Conqueror faced his first real challenge. It came from the north. In January, a Norman army was massacred in Durham. A few weeks later, the Normans fled from York, leaving it to be occupied by the rebels. This was the most serious defeat suffered by the Normans in England. Yet such was the English leaders' indecision that at the news of the Conqueror's approach the rebellion collapsed.

In the heart of the Fens

The last men to resist the Norman oppressors held out in the fens of East Anglia. There, a Lincolnshire thegn (lord), Hereward the Wake, brought together refugees from every part of England, and at the end of 1070 launched a campaign against the Normans.

The Isle of Ely, Hereward's chief refuge, was protected on all sides by treacherous and uncharted marshes. But from the early summer of 1071 the isle was continuously besieged by William's army. Faced with starvation, the defenders' morale crumbled, and within a few weeks the king was master of Ely. Only Hereward himself escaped.

William's suppression of English resistance was brutal. The north was punished for rebellion by being laid waste with fire and sword. But the Conqueror achieved his object. Norman rule was to be permanent.

rooms, enabling the garrison to withstand a long siege. The entrance was on the first floor and was approached across a broad moat. On the upper floors the king and his officials lived when they stayed in London.

The first stage of the building was finished in 1078. But in 1091, when the Tower was 'by tempest and wind sore shaken', William Rufus, the Conqueror's son, had it strengthened. Henry I, Henry III and Edward I added further improvements. By 1307 there had been built around the Norman fortress a series of gateways, ramparts and towers that made the Tower of London one of the largest and most invulnerable strongholds in Europe.

Long after the Norman conquerors had won acceptance, the shadow of the Tower still loomed over England's history. It became the destination of the ruler's enemies – and the site of many executions. To most Englishmen the Tower was a place of misery and dread.

'In truth there is no sadder spot on the earth,' wrote the 19th-century historian, Thomas Babington Macaulay. 'Thither have been carried, through successive ages, by the rude hands of gaolers, without one mourner following, the bleeding relics of men who had been the captains of armies, the leaders of parties, the oracles of senates, and the ornaments of courts.'

A RECORD OF WEALTH

Domesday Book is the record of the great national survey ordered by William I in 1085, to discover the true wealth and probable future wealth of England. Royal officials journeyed throughout the land, detailing the property owned by everyone from the king downwards.

The survey was carried out quickly but with such thoroughness that, according to a chronicler, 'not even one ox, or one cow or pig escaped notice'. When the information had been gathered, returns were submitted for individual 'hundreds' – subdivisions of counties.

The two volumes of Domesday Book cover most of England. London, however, was omitted, together with the far north, which had not been conquered when the survey was made. The original volumes were first of all kept at Winchester, and later brought to Westminster.

A copy of Domesday Book. It was written by French clerks who were accurate and speedy.

SAXON HERO *A 19th-century illustration of Hereward the Wake, who led Saxon resistance to the Norman conquerors. He held out in the fens of Lincolnshire for a year.*

The huntsman king meets a mysterious death

DEATH IN THE NEW FOREST
William Rufus met his death in 1100 where this tree now stands, near Minstead. He was killed by an arrow while hunting – but whether it was fired deliberately remains a mystery.

The last year of William Rufus's reign was a time of strange portents, omens of murder and whispers of treason. Tortured minds imagined they had seen devils in the New Forest and wells flowing with blood on the Berkshire Downs.

But William Rufus was not a superstitious man. He laughed aloud when such omens were reported to him. Even when a monk arrived at his court and predicted that the king was about to die, William did no more than giggle to his courtiers: 'He is a monk and dreams for money. Give him 100 shillings.' It was August 1, 1100, and William's last night on earth.

Omens of disaster

That night at Brockenhurst, where William was staying in preparation for hunting in the New Forest, the king had a nightmare. He dreamt that he was being bled by his private surgeon, and that the blood gushed up to the ceiling and shut out the light of the sun. Waking in terror, he called his chamberlains and ordered them to stand guard over his bed while he slept, and to keep a candle burning in his chamber. But, despite these precautions, William was unable to sleep. He rose at dawn, dressed and announced his intention of going hunting. His attendants protested. They regarded dreams and omens as serious matters,

and urged the king to devote the morning to business. William grudgingly postponed the hunt until the afternoon.

That afternoon, William Rufus rode out of Brockenhurst into the New Forest. With him were his usual host of flatterers and sycophants, chief among them a French noble, called Walter Tirel. Tirel was a soldier of fortune, drawn to England by tales of Rufus's extravagant court, who had swiftly won the king's favour.

William liked to hunt with the crossbow. It was less accurate than the traditional English longbow, but easier to shoot from the saddle. On that afternoon he had six bolts, newly forged by a local smith. Two of these he gave to Tirel. 'Here, have these,' he said, 'it is only right that the sharpest bolts should go to the sharpest shot among us.'

As the laughing party of courtiers rode out of Brockenhurst, a monk stood in their path. He carried a message from the Abbot of Gloucester, warning the king of a dream in which one of his monks had been told that England was shortly to have a new king. William guffawed and rode on. 'Is it not strange that such a wise old abbot should write me such trifles when I have so many other things to attend to?' he asked Tirel. 'Does he think that I am like the English, who abandon all their plans whenever they hear of the snoring dreams of some old hag?'

The fatal moment

The party now divided, but William and Tirel stayed together and rode westwards through the forest. At the far end of a clearing, a stag moved in front of a clump of bushes. The king took aim and shot his bolt. The beast was hit but only wounded. As it fled, William turned his horse after it and Tirel followed him. The stag ran directly into the setting sun and William could scarcely see to aim a second shot. He shielded his eyes with his hands and spurred on his horse. Then came a high-pitched twang and a bolt struck the king in his side, just below the heart. He slumped in the saddle and groped at his side in a vain attempt to break off the shaft. Then he fell to the ground. Tirel rode up and dismounted. The king was unable to speak and was plainly

MURDER OR ACCIDENT? *William Rufus falls in this Victorian illustration. The fatal arrow was believed to have been shot by Walter Tirel, a courtier, who fled to France. Some said Tirel had quarrelled with William, others that he was part of a plot; but Tirel claimed his innocence.*

dying. Tirel remounted his horse and galloped away from the scene.

Did Walter Tirel, who had never sworn allegiance to the king, kill him in the New Forest on August 2, 1100? Tirel was the only man known to have been in the vicinity when the king died. With one accord his contemporaries accused him of the deed.

Some men thought that it was an accident. Perhaps Tirel had himself been aiming at the stag and struck the king in error. But others hinted darkly of a plot. Walter Tirel was a fine shot, and it seemed unlikely that his bolt would have gone so far astray. He had quarrelled with the king the previous night. William had boasted that he would invade France and celebrate Christmas at Poitiers. Tirel's patriotic pride had been offended and he had poured scorn on the idea. It seemed that the quarrel had been made up. But did Tirel's temper fail him? Or were there other conspirators waiting for the king in the forest that fading August evening – perhaps in the employ of William's ambitious young brother, Henry? Henry was certainly quick to take advantage of his brother's death. Instead of pursuing Tirel, he hastened to Winchester and seized the treasury. It is one of the deepest mysteries that English history holds.

SPORT OF KINGS

A peasant hunts with the poor man's longbow.

Hunting was the favourite pastime of the Norman kings of England, and they went to great lengths to indulge their pleasure. By the end of the 12th century, one-third of England had been set aside as royal forest – a term which at that time meant simply an area devoted to hunting. The New Forest, created by William the Conqueror, was one of the earliest. Deer and wild boar were preserved for the king's sport alone, but his barons and abbots were allowed to hunt lesser game, such as hare and fox.

Penalties for poaching in Norman times were savage. The man killing this deer risked execution if his crime were ever to be discovered.

William II: 'Wanton, lascivious and corrupt'

UNLOVED IN LIFE *This early 14th-century illumination – the first-known portrait of William Rufus – depicts the king's violent end. But William's death was never avenged, for his corrupt, aggressive and blasphemous life had won him the hatred and enmity of his people.*

The King of England for 13 years after the death of the Conqueror, William Rufus – so-called because of his flame-red hair – was unfortunate in his choice of enemies. In addition to the traditional enemies of the Norman kings – their over-mighty barons – he also took on the Church. And though William had the upper hand in this quarrel, it was the Church who had the last word, for it was by churchmen that the chronicles of medieval England were written. 'A wicked, avaricious, evil-living man,' wrote one. 'Wanton, lascivious and corrupt,' agreed another. And the Church had much to complain about in William's reign. Anselm, Archbishop of Canterbury, was forced to spend most of the reign in exile, while the king plundered churches and stole their lands.

From love to hatred

William's worst mistake was that he recklessly threw away the popularity he had enjoyed when he first became king. In 1087, one of William's barons, Odo of Bayeux, rebelled against his accession, but the people of England flocked to support their new king. In return, William made sweeping promises of reform and good government – but, as soon as the danger had passed, he conveniently forgot all his handsome words. And when Archbishop Lanfranc, Anselm's predecessor, rebuked him, William responded angrily: 'Who can be expected to keep all his promises?' In 1093, William fell ill. At death's door, he accepted Anselm as archbishop and again promised to reform. But on his recovery he once more broke his word.

The stern unbending moralists of the day were disgusted by the frivolity of William's court. His generosity to his favourites drew a great number of ambitious, self-seeking young men, many of them foreigners, whose behaviour the English considered offensive and unmanly. But a graver charge levelled against the king was that the sycophants who came to his court were allowed to ride roughshod over all others. Although he held several Church offices, William's chief minister, the notorious Rannulf Flambard, mercilessly extorted money from the Church. But the most unpopular men at William's court were his mercenary soldiers. When the news of the king's approach reached any English village, the populace would leave their homes and take to the forests rather than submit to their brutality.

A man of contrasts

The Norman kings were men of striking contrasts, and none more so than William Rufus. For however much his contemporaries blackened his reputation, they could not deny that he had some redeeming features. Even as he confiscated the wealth of the Church with one hand, he returned it with the other in the form of lavish religious foundations. Despite his faults, Rannulf Flambard was an efficient administrator – and he paid for the building of the choir of Durham Cathedral. William placed his mercenaries and courtiers above the law, but where others were concerned he enforced justice. In his day, the law was obeyed by every man in England – except for the king and his immediate followers.

Above all, William Rufus regarded his father, the great Conqueror, with an almost superstitious reverence and constantly emulated him. He was perhaps the cleverest of the Norman kings, yet his character remained elusive, a tissue of paradoxes. He had only himself to blame if few men mourned him.

A FORTRESS CHURCH STANDS GUARD ON THE BORDER

MASSIVE GRANDEUR *Durham Cathedral is England's greatest masterpiece of early-Norman architecture. It was begun in 1093 as a shrine for St Cuthbert, the most famous saint of the north. This view of the aisle shows the ribbed vaulting of the massive roof. The earliest of its kind in Europe and the only one in England, the roof was considered a construction miracle in its day.*

WRITER'S TRIBUTE *Situated on a hill above the River Wear, few cathedrals have a more impressive setting than Durham. Sir Walter Scott paid it tribute on a bridge-stone (above).*

Sir Walter Scott's description of Durham Cathedral was 'half church of God, half castle 'gainst the Scot'. The words of the 19th-century novelist aptly describe the magnificent building that soars above the River Wear and dwarfs even the castle beside it.

Durham Cathedral was built in an age when both the faith and the mortal bodies of Christians were in constant danger from the ravages of the heathen. In 875 the monks of Lindisfarne, off the Northumbrian coast, were driven by the Danes from their island sanctuary. They took with them their most precious relic, the body of their 7th-century bishop, St Cuthbert. In 999, a year of grim foreboding when many men awaited the end of the world, they settled at Durham – and found prosperity and peace.

Built around a shrine

A century later, in 1093, the first Norman bishop, William of St Carileph, began to build a cathedral around the shrine of the saint. By 1133, enough of the construction work was finished to give St Cuthbert's body a resting place in safety at the heart of one of the strongest citadels of the Church. It still retains the air of a fortress. In medieval times, lit only by flickering candles, it must have had the appearance of a gloomy cave.

Strength and simplicity are the keynotes of

Durham's style. The massive pillars, for all their ornate carved decoration, are emphatically structural. They look as though they could support the world itself.

These pillars and the round arches between them are solidly Norman. But above, the arches forming the vaulted roof of the nave are pointed, a device developed by the 12th-century masons of Durham to bring greater height and light to the upper parts of the structure. This is the first appearance in Europe of the pointed arch – the feature that was to be the secret of the world's greatest works of architecture during the next four centuries. Durham is not only the triumphant climax of the Norman style, but also the first hint of the Gothic.

Influences from the East

Soon, St Cuthbert's shrine became the most popular in the north of England. Though only men were admitted to the tomb itself (women being forbidden to cross the strip of black marble in front of the font), pilgrims of both sexes flocked to Durham – and pilgrims meant profit for the Church.

As the money flowed in, so the cathedral grew – notably to the west, where the lovely Galilee Chapel was built in 1175. At that time it was lovelier still, its 12 broad arches supported only on marble columns. The stone shafts are 15th-century reinforcements.

There is something curiously Islamic about those arches. Their zigzag ornamentation, always described as typically Norman, is really Moorish in origin, brought back to England by early Crusaders. This exquisite chapel was chosen as the final resting place of the Venerable Bede, the 7th-century scholar who became the father of English history. The fame of Bede's *Ecclesiastical History of the English*

ISLAMIC ARCHES *The Galilee Chapel, built in 1175, shows the Moorish influence brought back by early Crusaders. It houses the tomb of the Venerable Bede.*

SAINT'S BLESSING *A 12th-century portrait of St Cuthbert painted on the Galilee Chapel's wall.*

People had won worldwide renown for the northern church. In displaying his sacred tomb, Durham reinforced its claim as the citadel of the Holy Church in the north.

The work of enhancing Durham's stern grandeur continued in the following centuries, even though its bishops were busy with other concerns. They had authority over the Palatinate of Durham, which extended from the Tees to the Tyne and also included other lands far to the north on the Scottish border. Within these boundaries the bishop was responsible for administration, justice, coinage, supervision of markets and levying troops. Soldier-bishops, such as Anthony Bek and Thomas of Hatfield, who both led armies against the Scots, were more common than architect-bishops.

Nevertheless, Durham Cathedral did grow and did change. In the 1230's, Bishop Richard le Poore, who had already built one cathedral at Salisbury, enlarged the East End, adding the Chapel of the Nine Altars, where the more

ornate Gothic style contrasts strikingly with the simplicity of the original Norman building.

The 14th century brought new riches, with the gift of the great screen behind the High Altar which is encrusted with more than 100 gilded and painted alabaster figures. In this last great age of Durham's building, twin towers were set up at the West End and a central spire was raised to dominate the city.

But in 1429 the spire was struck by lightning, charring the wooden belfry and irreparably damaging the stonework. The monks of Durham were apparently too poor to pay for the necessary rebuilding and resorted to sending one of their number out into the world to beg for money, armed with a silver-gilt crucifix and a piece of cloth in which the body of St Cuthbert had been wrapped.

Presumably these relics failed to stir the people of the palatinate to pious generosity, for nothing was done until 1455, by which time the whole structure was in danger of collapse. Even then work proceeded slowly; and it was 1499 before the great tower was finished. After four centuries of building, Durham was complete.

Survival through the ages

With this achievement, the era of medieval building closed. A less constructive age was dawning. On December 31, 1540, the monastery was dissolved and its treasures were confiscated – a catastrophe for which even the opening of St Cuthbert's tomb and the discovery of his body 'incorrupt, with his face bare and his beard as it had been a fortnight's growth', must have been poor compensation. Four hundred years of tradition were destroyed. More disasters were to follow. In 1650, 4000 Scottish soldiers, captured by Oliver Cromwell after the Battle of Dunbar and imprisoned in the cathedral, burnt the choir stalls for fuel.

And yet, miraculously, Durham has survived. Firm on its river-girt rock, it seems to breathe indestructibility and confidence, honouring its God, sheltering its saints – and keeping the Scots in their place.

Few examples of Norman metalworkers' art have survived which can compare with this 12th-century sanctuary knocker. The grotesque and frightening face once had coloured enamel eyes.

Shipwreck sets England on the road to civil war

But for the pride of a 17-year-old prince, England might have been spared 19 years of bloody civil war – years during which, as the chroniclers said, 'God and his saints slept'. A Norman prince had to grow to manhood quickly, and William of England, grandson of the mighty Conqueror, was no exception. Although just turned 17, he had won his spurs at the side of his father, Henry I, during bitter fighting and tortuous diplomacy in Normandy. He had faced death in battle, though his chin was not yet darkened by a beard. Broad shouldered and quick with a jest, he was as great a favourite with the ladies as he was popular with the soldiers. As heir to the crown, he was courted by the young nobility of the nation and by any man with a name or fortune to make.

Such was the prince who, on November 25, 1120, refused to share a ship with his father for the voyage back to England from Barfleur in Normandy. England's name was feared and respected throughout Europe, and the young prince had played his part in making it so. It was beneath his dignity to have to take only the second place on a voyage. So he bade his father farewell and ordered the *White Ship* to be prepared ready for sea.

A voyage doomed to disaster

The *White Ship* was the finest vessel in England of its time – large, stoutly built and recently re-equipped. But the ships of those days were still perilously small and flimsy. Each week brought new tidings of ships lost in the Channel, dashed against submerged rocks or carried away by strong currents. Men avoided the sea whenever possible. Very few of them could swim for more than a few yards, and a disaster at sea meant certain death for most of

THE LINE OF DISASTER

A contemporary illuminated 'family tree' shows how the sinking of the White Ship *off the Normandy coast in November 1120 changed history. The manuscript, at the British Museum, includes Henry I (top) and the line to his son William, who drowned in the disaster. After that, the tree shows Matilda, Stephen and Henry II.*

DISASTER IN THE CHANNEL *As the* White Ship *struck a hidden rock, panic broke out on board. Prince William and a handful of companions managed to escape in a small boat. But the prince ordered it to return to rescue his sister and it was swamped by other passengers trying to clamber on board.*

the passengers. Men confessed their sins and prepared for death before even the shortest of sea voyages.

The crew of the *White Ship* – who had spent the evening in drunken revelry – promised the young prince that they would quickly overtake the king's party and arrive first in Southampton. It was already dark before they ran down the beach, singing and laughing, and launched the ship from the shore. With the prince, embarked all those who paid court to him as a rising star. There were several of Henry's illegitimate children, a nephew of the German emperor, earls and barons, important churchmen and civil servants on board.

Aground on the rocks

The *White Ship* sped out into the Channel, its drunken crew steering an erratic course towards England. But the night concealed the hazards of the Normandy coast. As the passengers retired to their beds, the ship struck a submerged rock. It shuddered violently. The timbers of the side broke, and the vessel began to list heavily. With cries of panic the passengers rushed on deck and tried to help the sailors to free the ship with boat-hooks. Others seized oars, in a desperate attempt to row the ship off the rocks before its hull was crushed by the pounding sea.

The first thought of William's attendants was for the prince's safety. A small boat was quickly launched and William, with a few companions, boarded it. The shore was only a few hundred yards away, and the royal party might have escaped safely. But at that moment an illegitimate sister of the prince cried out to him not to leave her to her death. Prince William took pity on her, and ordered the

sailors to row back. The *White Ship* was now sinking rapidly, its timbers breaking up under the pounding waves. Many people were clinging to pieces of wood in the bitterly cold water and, as the prince's boat came into view, the panic grew. They all struggled to climb on board or hold on to the sides. The boat swayed from side to side and finally capsized.

For days afterwards, richly dressed bodies were washed up on the Normandy coast. Few of the victims were ever identified; most were never found. A butcher from Rouen, the humblest of the ship's passengers, was the only one who survived.

'No ship ever brought such misery to England,' proclaimed a chronicler, 'none was ever so notorious in the history of the world.' The absence of an heir threatened to destroy the whole fabric of Norman monarchy. For with the death of Henry's only legitimate son, no man could be sure that the law of the realm would not die with him.

An oath to secure the succession

Henry I had 22 children, 20 of whom were bastards. William's death left only Henry's daughter, Matilda, to represent the direct line of the Norman kings. Anxious to secure her succession, Henry made his barons swear an oath in 1121 that they would support her.

But they did so reluctantly, since they were unwilling to accept the prospect of a woman on the throne. And when Henry died in December 1135, they rallied to the support of the first claimant to arrive in England from Normandy – Stephen, Henry's nephew. The citizens of London declared him their king. And in January, his election as king was confirmed by Pope Innocent III.

Henry I: A king sees his hopes shatter

Henry I, the youngest son of William the Conqueror, shared his father's practical, down-to-earth attitudes; he had all the qualities of greed and ruthlessness that characterised the Norman kings of England. He was brusque and plain-speaking. He ate and drank in plenty. He slept heavily and snored loudly. In addition to his two legitimate children, he had 20 illegitimate ones.

Despite his gross manners, in politics Henry was the subtlest of his family. He preferred to gain his ends by negotiation, persuasion and diplomacy, rather than by brute force. By such methods he won Normandy from his brother, Robert, at the beginning of his reign in 1086, and made England a power to be reckoned with on the European continent.

Keeping the peace

Like his father, Henry spent much of his time dealing with rebellions by his barons. He preferred diplomacy, but this had often to be discarded for suppression. Henry was at all times intensely suspicious, constantly in fear of plots and treason. He suspected his closest servants of planning his death. He regularly changed the position of his bed, and armed guards stood at every door of his chamber. His sword always hung beside his bed.

Not all Henry's enemies were rebellious barons. The longest and most bitter struggle of his reign was with Anselm, the saintly Archbishop of Canterbury. Henry insisted on controlling the Church himself, for bishops at that time were powerful and wealthy men, and he demanded the right to appoint his friends to important Church posts. But it was not until 1107, after seven years of intrigue and diplomacy, that he got his way.

Search for an heir

But Henry's most serious problem remained unsolved. Although his mistresses bore him innumerable sons, his wife bore him only one before her death in 1120. When that son was drowned in the *White Ship* in the same year, Henry was left without a male heir. Legend has it that after the disaster he never smiled again; he may well have realised that the hopes of his dynasty had foundered with the ship. He married again within eight weeks of the disaster, but his second wife, Adelaide, daughter of Godfrey VII, Count of Lorraine, failed to produce a male heir.

This lack of a son was the direct cause of the civil wars that were to follow Henry's death. No one, in the Middle Ages, could feel secure until a new king had come to the throne and renewed all the old laws. On December 1, 1135, Henry died after a meal of lampreys, his favourite sea-food. The anarchy that followed lasted for 19 bitter years.

NINETEEN LONG WINTERS

Quick action by Stephen (left) in seizing the throne saved England from the haughty, tactless and grasping Matilda. It did not ensure that the rule of law which his uncle, Henry I, had upheld would be maintained. Though Stephen was kind and generous, he lacked the ruthlessness necessary in a medieval ruler. There was, as the *Peterborough Chronicle* recorded, 'treason soon in the land, for every man that could forthwith robbed another'. Stephen's uncertain rule lasted from 1135 to 1154. It went down in history as the 'nineteen long winters when God and his saints slept'. The rule of law that Henry I had striven so hard to establish seemed doomed to perish in these years of anarchy, pillage and destruction.

Stephen was not entirely to blame. Matilda landed in England determined to take the crown. To gain support, he gave away royal lands and relaxed his uncle's tight rein. But such weakness lost him the respect of his feudal lords and inspired a series of civil wars. It was a price that a stronger man might not have been forced to pay. But it secured Stephen the throne and, by a treaty of settlement, the succession passed peacefully to the greatest of medieval English monarchs, Matilda's son, Henry II.

A scene from the 12th-century illuminated Bury Bible depicts the siege of a walled town during the breakdown of law and order in the unsettled 19-year reign of King Stephen.

The clash that led to murder in the cathedral

WHERE BECKET FELL

Today, a plaque marks the spot in Canterbury Cathedral where, on December 29, 1170, Archbishop Thomas Becket paid with his life for his opposition to Henry II. He was put to death by four of Henry's impetuous courtiers, who had taken at face value their king's angry demands to be rid of 'this miserable priest' who 'insults me to my face'.

As the year 1170 closed, a conflict which had been dividing England for six years reached its climax. The Archbishop of Canterbury, Henry II's erstwhile friend Thomas Becket, had defied the king's demands to control the power of the Church.

These demands were far-reaching. Henry had forbidden the clergy to exercise their time-honoured right of appeal to Rome as the final authority in matters concerning the Church; he had diverted the papal tax known as 'Peter's Pence' – it was used for the building of St Peter's in Rome – to his own purposes. Finally, he had gone as far as ordering the priests of England to take an oath against the pope.

Becket had held out against this pressure. He went into exile and took refuge in the abbey of Pontigny in France. At the beginning of December, however, he had met the king in Normandy and agreed to be reconciled. But on his return to Canterbury, Becket publicly excommunicated his enemies from the pulpit of the cathedral on Christmas Day 1170.

Henry's patience was exhausted. The Archbishop of York and the Bishops of London and Salisbury hastened to him, to report that Becket was determined to discipline those churchmen who had supported the crown. In a moment of exasperation, Henry railed at the 'idle cowards of my court who stand by while this miserable priest insults me to my face'. These hasty words were to inspire a deed which shocked the whole of Christendom.

Four knights, Reginald FitzUrse, William de Tracy, Hugh Mauclerk, and Richard le Breton – took the king at his word. To rid him of this troublemaker would surely be a great service to the realm. They hastily left the royal court, which at that time was in Normandy, and set sail for England. There, they planned to arrest the archbishop and imprison him to await the king's pleasure. Or, if this was impossible, they would kill him.

The final quarrel

At 4 p.m. on December 29, 1170, the knights reached Canterbury. A bustling crowd of onlookers had gathered outside the cathedral, drawn by news of Becket's latest defiance of the king, and by sinister rumours of violence and murder. FitzUrse ordered his retainers to guard the gates of the cathedral precinct. He and his three companions then entered the great courtyard and demanded that the monks take them to the archbishop.

Thomas Becket was in his study next to the great hall. Reginald FitzUrse was the first to speak: 'We have a message for you from the king. He commands that you and your followers shall leave his realm. After your insolence there can be no peace between you.' The knights menacingly approached the archbishop. Voices were raised and finally they strode out, shouting 'To arms! To arms!' On this signal, their followers outside the gates swarmed into the courtyard, replying with the cry 'King's men!'

From his study, Becket heard the sound of splintering wood and the muffled shouts of the king's soldiers. His clerks pleaded with him to take refuge in the cathedral, and almost dragged him out through the cloisters and into the north-west transept.

But Becket refused to be hurried. He was proud of his dignity as primate of England, and would not save himself by flight. As the monks tried to bolt the cathedral door he stopped them, crying: 'The Church of God is not a fortress. Open it!'

'I am no traitor'

Seconds later, the knights burst through the doors. 'Where is Thomas Becket, traitor to his king and kingdom?' demanded FitzUrse. From the steps leading to the High Altar Becket replied: 'I am here, no traitor but a priest of God and an archbishop.'

A sword glinted in the candlelight, and the archbishop reeled as a blow struck him in the shoulder. FitzUrse raised his axe and struck at his head. Another of the knights, William de Tracy, stepped forward and dealt Becket such a blow that his sword broke in two with its force. As soldiers ran jubilantly out into the cloister, Hugh Mauclerk placed his foot on the dead man's neck and scattered his brains on the floor with the point of his sword. 'Here,' he cried, 'is one traitor who will not rise again.'

But Becket had the final word. An eyewitness to the tragedy, William fitzStephen, wrote that 'the sun's gaze was averted, its rays hidden from the earth and the day veiled in darkness...a terrible storm cloud overhung the firmament, the rain fell suddenly and swiftly and the thunder rolled round the Heavens. After this, the sky turned a deep red in token of the blood which had been shed and in horror at the outrage.'

This was the stuff of legend. Within three years Becket had been canonised by Pope Alexander III, and his tomb had become a shrine for pilgrims from all over Europe. Henry himself was forced to do public penance – being whipped in Canterbury Cathedral on the site of Becket's murder. But this did not stop him in his purpose. He succeeded in bringing the English Church under royal control – a position which his successors never lost.

Becket had failed in his great struggle. His martyrdom had been in vain. But for 360 years his memory lived on. Then Henry VIII had the shrine destroyed. But even this action could not destroy the legend of a man of God who perished for his beliefs.

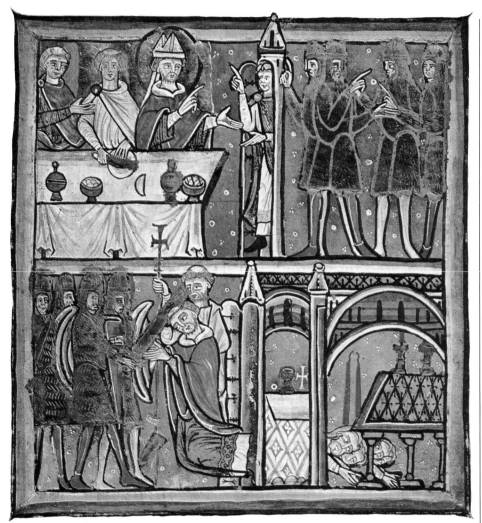

A medieval illumination tells the story of the events leading up to and following Becket's death. At the top, the knights overhear the king and plot to kill the archbishop. Below, Becket is murdered and pilgrims are seen praying at his tomb.

Henry II: Rebuilding after the anarchy

Henry II, the man whose hasty words led to the death of Thomas Becket, had inherited a kingdom shattered by two decades of civil war, and a discredited and despised crown. His consuming aim was to re-establish royal power and prestige, and his achievements made him one of the most successful rulers of medieval England.

Henry recognised that he had to ensure that his subjects lived in peace and security if he was to keep their loyalty. To do this, he introduced trial by jury, a turning point in English history. For the first time, the king's justice was made available to all – high or low-born. A brilliant administrator, Henry also built up a large professional civil service to make sure that his policies were effectively carried out.

Might of the crown

Henry was determined to make his crown the one power in the land. The over-mighty barons, who had terrorised England under the weak Stephen, were soon brought to heel. Only the Church, under the obstinate leadership of Thomas Becket, held out in refusing to meet Henry's demands. In particular, the king was determined to take some of the powers that the Church courts possessed. All men, he argued, should be equal before the law – the king's law. This was what Becket refused to yield him – and the subsequent quarrel was to lead to the archbishop's martyrdom.

Henry's other failure was within his own family. He married Eleanor of Aquitaine for her wealth; but then he unceremoniously deserted her for the charms of a beautiful mistress, Rosamund Clifford. Eleanor never forgave him, and she passed her hatred on to their four sons – Richard, Henry, Geoffrey and John. And the king's last years were tormented by the rebellions that his children fostered against him. In 1183, Henry and Geoffrey joined the nobles of Aquitaine in a rising against their father and their brother, Richard. No sooner had Henry II dealt with this than Richard himself turned against him and eventually joined with the French king to wage war against his father.

Alone and friendless, the ageing Henry was forced to beg for peace. Stricken with fever, he met Richard and Philip of France and agreed to all their terms. But it was not Richard's treachery that broke his father's heart. For he learnt from Philip that his favourite son, John, had also conspired against him. 'Enough,' he cried, 'now let things go as they may. I care no more for myself or for the world!' Two days later he died on July 6, 1189.

Henry's proud spirit had been broken and many of his achievements shattered. But his greatest work survived – the rule of law – as his gift to future generations.

CULT OF A MARTYRED SAINT

No single deed shocked medieval Christendom more than the murder of the saintly Archbishop Thomas Becket in his cathedral at Canterbury, in December 1170. Immediately, Becket was acclaimed as a martyr, and within three years Pope Alexander III had canonised him. In 1174, Henry II himself visited the tomb to do penance

Pilgrims confer outside the walls of Canterbury in this 15th-century illustration. St Thomas's tomb attracted thousands from all over Europe.

for the deed his hasty words had inspired. From then on, the shrine of St Thomas was one of the greatest centres of pilgrimage in the Christian world. Kings, princes, nobles, merchants, priests and peasants journeyed there, all anxious to see one of the miracles said to occur at the shrine. Such a journey was immortalised 300 years later by England's greatest medieval poet, Geoffrey Chaucer, in his *Canterbury Tales*.

Becket's fame spread still further. In the Holy Land, an order of Christian knights was founded in his memory. Even in the remoteness of Iceland a long poem, 'Thomas Saga Erkibyskups' (The Saga of Archbishop Thomas), was written telling the story of his life. Relics, too, were in great demand. Among the chief 'miracle-workers' on sale were phials supposed to contain drops of the martyred Becket's blood, collected by his faithful monks from beneath the High Altar immediately after his death.

But in the 1530's, when England broke with the Roman Catholic Church, Henry VIII ordered the shrine to be destroyed, and confiscated all the rich gifts which had been lavished on it over the centuries. The memory of St Thomas, however, he could not destroy. It still lives on in the Canterbury of today.

England's king leads an army to the Holy Land

THE 'LIONHEART'S' MEMORIAL

Within weeks of Richard I's coronation as king, he planned his first Crusade to the Holy Land. For Richard, war was to become a way of life. It is as a warrior that he is remembered, as this contemporary tile from Chertsey Abbey shows. But Richard's campaigns were an expensive burden for his people, and a source of growing discontent. He once remarked that he would sell London if he could find a buyer.

NO QUARTER *Richard imposed harsh surrender terms after the fall of Acre. The king gave the infidel Muslims no quarter; he regarded their lives as forfeit, and on August 20, 1191, watched (on the balcony, left) as 2700 of them were being put to the sword.*

For 200 years, the fervent Christianity that dominated medieval Europe inspired a great military movement – the Crusades to the Holy Land. Under the red cross of the Crusaders, monarchs and nobles – and, on occasion, peasants and children – marched to rescue the 'Holy Places' of Christendom from the hands of the infidel Muslims.

The Crusades started in 1095, when knights from Europe first set sail for Palestine. They captured Jerusalem and set up four Crusader kingdoms, building vast fortresses, such as Krak des Chevaliers in Syria, to secure their hold on their new possessions.

But Crusader rule was not to last. The Muslims rallied and, by 1189, the Crusaders were close to being driven out of the sacred land they had given so much to conquer. Jerusalem had fallen to the armies of the Muslim leader, Saladin, and only two cities in the whole of Palestine remained in Christian hands.

It was at this decisive moment, within weeks of his coronation as King of England, that Richard I drew up his plans to intervene. Nowhere in Europe did the romantic fascination of men with the Holy Land have a stronger pull than in England. Now Richard launched an expedition to Palestine. He left England in December 1189 and on June 6, 1191, he landed in Palestine.

The first task was to recapture the great fortified port of Acre, an essential base for the Crusaders if they were to avoid being driven into the sea. When Richard arrived, their siege had been going on for two years. But a man who had won the reputation of 'the first soldier of Europe' and boasted the proud nickname of 'Lionheart', was not willing to brook delay. He immediately took command and, by the first week of July, it was clear that the city could hold out no longer. On July 12, Acre surrendered to the triumphant Crusaders.

But the fall of Acre was only the first stage in the battle for the Holy Land. Both sides – Christian and Muslim – realised that the decisive conflict was still to come.

Leaving garrison in Acre, Richard marched the Crusader army south along the coast, hoping to be able to turn inland towards Jerusalem. But Saladin barred the Crusaders' path, and the Christians' high hopes soon gave way to despair. The desert sun beat down pitilessly on the heavily armoured knights; many of the recent arrivals perished from sunstroke or malaria. Stragglers were swept up by squads of Muslim horsemen.

Battle on the plain

By early September, it was clear that the Muslims intended to force a battle. This took place on a narrow plain north of the town of Arsuf, some 2 miles from the sea and bounded on both sides by forest.

Richard drew up his army with bowmen in the front and the cavalry behind them. The Knights Templar, so dreaded by the Muslims that prisoners were never ransomed, but always beheaded, were on the right flank. Now Richard and his troops waited for the Muslim assault. When it came, the Crusaders held their ground, and eventually their adversaries began to tire. But Richard refused to order a counterattack. The Christian army was to wait until the full force of the Muslim attack had been spent. The Knights Templar, however, lacked the

Richard I: Champion of Christendom's cause

Richard I, the Crusader king, was the least English of all England's monarchs. He spent no more than six months in his native country during his ten-year reign. These were unhappy years for England – years of destructive conflict between those who governed in Richard's absence; years of crushing taxation as the absent king drew on English wealth to finance his ambitious enterprises abroad.

Richard's brilliant victories in Palestine did something to compensate England for the unrest that followed his departure. But he had all the hot-tempered and impetuous characteristics of his family. During his Crusade, he quarrelled with Duke Leopold of Austria, who never forgave him for throwing the Hapsburg standard into the moat at Acre.

This last dispute had far-reaching consequences. On his return to Europe in 1192, Richard was shipwrecked on the Adriatic coast and forced to travel disguised as a common soldier through Leopold's territories. But he was recognised and arrested at an inn near Vienna. Leopold cast him into prison and demanded a ransom of 150,000 silver marks.

The king's brother, John, took advantage of his capture to raise rebellion. And Richard's loyal subjects faced the bill for his ransom. The money was raised in a few months, but Richard stayed no more than two months in the land that had bought his freedom. The rest of his reign was spent campaigning to defend his lands in France, until he was killed by an arrow fired from the castle of Chalus on April 6, 1199.

CHRISTIANITY'S CHAMPIONS

The example set by Richard I in 'taking the Cross' was soon followed by many of his nobles. Enthusiasm for the Crusade was whipped up by preachers and minstrels and many volunteers came forward; those men who refused to follow their king were often presented with a distaff and some wool, implying that they were no better than women. The pope, for his part, offered the Crusaders indulgences, absolving them from their sins.

Though the Crusaders failed to liberate the Holy Land, their expeditions produced a lasting legacy. For they gained from the Arabs some of the secrets in science and mathematics that the West had lost during the Dark Ages, after the fall of the Roman Empire.

The Crusader John de Holcombe's tomb, in Dorchester Abbey, Oxfordshire, is a fine example of medieval craftsmanship.

---

king's patience and decided to force his hand. Two of them charged towards the enemy, to be followed by others. Then suddenly the whole body of the Christian cavalry spurred their horses forward.

Suppressing his anger at this disobedience, Richard took personal command of the assault. The Muslims wavered, then broke ranks and fled. Saladin's reputation for invincibility was shattered.

This was the high point of Richard's Crusade. The road to Jerusalem was open, and the Crusaders jubilantly advanced towards their goal. But 12 miles from the city the army was halted – not by their foes but by quarrels between its commanders. Philip Augustus, who had already returned from Palestine to France after quarrelling with the imperious Richard, had attacked Normandy. In England, Richard's brother, John, ambitious for supreme power, was plotting against him.

On receiving this news, Richard had no choice but to order a retreat back to the coast. Realising that the disunity of his forces made military victory impossible, he began negotiations with the Muslim leaders, Saladin and Safadin. These came to nothing and once more Richard advanced on Jerusalem. This time, he led an advance party to within sight of the city walls. But again quarrels forced the Crusaders to retreat. Finally, a treaty was agreed between the Christian and Muslim leaders, which gave the Crusaders a strip of land along the coast of Palestine. They were also ceded the ports of Acre and Jaffa, and pilgrims were to be allowed to visit Jerusalem. The peace was to last three years.

Richard had failed to fulfil his dream. No English king would liberate Jerusalem – nor would one again go on Crusade. The city was to remain in Muslim hands until the First World War, more than seven centuries later.

ABSENTEE KING *Richard spent only six months of his reign in England. After his return from the Crusades he fought in France, where he met his death in action.*

On a Thames-side meadow England's freedom is born

BIRTHPLACE OF LIBERTY
No name is more closely linked to the tradition of English freedom than Runnymede in Berkshire. There, in 1215, the barons and churchmen of England forced their reluctant king, John, to seal the first charter promising liberty to his subjects.

A ROMANTIC VIEW *John, his barons, and Archbishop Langton confer in this Victorian illustration of their meeting at Runnymede, while an official prepares to seal the charter. It had taken civil war to force John to agree to its demands.*

Step by step in the spring and summer of 1215, an all-powerful feudal monarch was driven to grant his subjects rights and liberties which set his country on the path to constitutional government. John, ruler of all England, had, by the severity of his rule, driven the barons of feudal England to forget their long-standing quarrels and unite in the struggle against him. Such men had their own particular grudges against John, and their motives were suspect in the eyes of the people. But it was John's misfortune that their cause was joined by a man of outstanding reputation, Stephen Langton, Archbishop of Canterbury. In the great events that were to follow, his voice was to prove decisive.

Revolt was a part of life in medieval England. There were always nobles who felt aggrieved at their exclusion from royal favours, which were too few to go round. But John's rule was more bitterly resented than most of his predecessors, for reasons for which the king was not entirely to blame.

An enormous debt and expensive wars in an age of inflation compelled him to exact from the barons far heavier payments than his predecessors had demanded. And his sense of royal duty induced him to temper justice in favour of women, children and the poor – often at the expense of the rich.

Nor had the Church reason to love John. For six years, from 1207–13, Langton had been forced to live abroad in exile until, at last, the king recognised him as Archbishop of Canterbury. During that time John attacked the Church without mercy, confiscated part of its wealth and forced seven English bishops to flee to the Continent.

There was thus a powerful and widespread opposition in the making when, in 1213, the king left England to campaign in France. His absence gave the barons time to plan their moves carefully, and the disastrous outcome of his wars against Philip Augustus, King of France, provided them with their opportunity.

But the Great Charter – Magna Carta – which the reluctant John was forced to seal on the banks of the Thames at Runnymede in June 1215, was nearly never presented to the king at all. At first, John had been prepared to listen and compromise, but soon his ungovernable temper got the better of him. In May 1215, he hysterically rejected the rebellious demands of the barons, shouting at their messenger: 'Take away your absurd, impertinent piece of paper and trouble me no longer.' Civil war was the result.

This war began disastrously for John's opponents. They laid siege to Northampton, but were forced to abandon it after 15 days. Meanwhile, the king had not been idle. He sent fast riders to the barons who had not yet joined the revolt, offering them favours and promising to mend his ways if they would join him. At this moment, the rebels seemed to be facing total defeat.

London – the key to success

Then they made a decision that was to change the fate of their campaign – and the course of English history. They marched on London. The king's French mercenaries, commanded by the Earl of Salisbury, hurried to reach the capital first, but they arrived too late. Early on the morning of May 17, the rebel barons stood before the walls of the city. The majority of Londoners were loyal to the king, for he had recently granted them a charter of liberty. But while they were at Mass, a small body of wealthy citizens, who sympathised with the rebels, opened the gates. By the time Mass was over, the city had fallen.

Overnight, John's cause was lost. Once London had fallen, the uncommitted nobles flocked to join the rebellion. Unrest spread over the entire country. The men of Devon rose; in Northampton, mobs looted the homes of suspected royalists. By the beginning of June an invincible force had gathered in London to confront the king. Moreover, Philip Augustus, King of France, had promised to send the rebels aid.

John realised that he had to yield if he was to keep his throne. Even the most loyal of his nobles, chief among them the wise William Marshal and the able administrator Hubert de Burgh, urged him to make concessions. He moved his headquarters to Windsor Castle, where he could feel secure behind the stout walls of the keep. The barons set up their camp at Staines, their forces controlling the London road and protected from attack by the marshes of the Thames.

Between Windsor and Staines, in the water meadows of Runnymede, the two sides met. John's fate had already been resolved before the walls of London, so there was little room for argument. Each baron received the royal kiss of peace, and took food and drink with the king to cement their new-found friendship. John then solemnly set his seal upon the great charter – Magna Carta.

Foundation stone of English liberty

Later generations of Englishmen came to regard Magna Carta as the foundation stone of English liberty. But, alone among the great documents of human freedom, it has no sweeping statement of principle, no general declaration of the rights of all men. The barons who drew up much of the document were hard, practical men, with no time for theories. Most of its clauses – 'headings which the barons seek and the lord king grants' – recited their specific complaints against the lawless behaviour of King John, and ended with a promise that it would not be repeated.

But indiscriminately mixed with these detailed and specific complaints were principles of law, which in future ages were to be regarded as the backbone of English liberties. John was not to levy unauthorised taxes or fine men excessive amounts for trivial offences. His officers could no longer seize crops without paying for them. Knights were not to be forced to serve the king overseas. The Church could not be oppressed, nor its wealth confiscated. And, most important of all, 'to no one will we sell, deny or delay right or justice'.

These clauses were largely the work of Stephen Langton. It was his great achievement, in persuading the barons to insert clauses benefiting others, to expand a purely baronial agreement into a great national charter touching all classes of the realm.

Throughout its length, Magna Carta insisted that the king could not be above the law. In the future, he must govern his subjects according to its terms and not according to his own whim. If a monarch were to break the terms of the charter, his subjects would be released from their obligations to obey him and could legally bring about his overthrow.

But the most important thing about Magna Carta was not what it said, but the fact that it was granted at all. Wrested from the hands of an unwilling monarch, it marked the point at which the feudal monarchy of England was forced for the first time to recognise the limits of royal power. Every medieval king of England up to the time of Edward IV confirmed the charter. And long after its detailed provisions were forgotten, the spirit of Magna Carta was to guide the development of the English constitution. As a 13th-century chronicler wrote: 'The barons stood against the king for the liberty of the Church and realm.'

THE RULE OF LAW *King John stamped the royal seal (above) on Magna Carta (left) on June 15, 1215. Its terms were a precedent cited time and again by opponents of royal power in centuries to come.*

John: A king trapped by his ambition

Until John (right) succeeded to the throne of England in 1199, few, if any, took him seriously. Even when he tried to overthrow his brother Richard I while he was on Crusade in Palestine, the latter did not punish him. 'Think no more of it, John,' he said. 'You are only a child who has been led astray.'

In May 1199, John finally came to the throne. He immediately indulged his taste for luxury and display. He feasted regularly and dressed magnificently. He took frequent baths – a most unusual practice in those days – and even possessed a dressing gown. But the long years of waiting had soured his mind, and he came to the throne with a powerful inferiority complex. No English king ever had so strong a desire to assert his authority. Nor was there one who was so untrusting.

A royal failure

If John had managed to win success, no doubt opposition to him would never have materialised. But he discovered that his power was weaker than that of his great father, Henry II. Philip Augustus, King of France, was the ablest monarch in Europe; he won Normandy from John in a few months. Pope Innocent III held half of Europe in his power; John was no match for him. Stephen Langton, Archbishop of Canterbury and chief architect of Magna Carta, was the most formidable bishop ever to challenge an English king.

The king's mailed fist

Thwarted by these powerful enemies, John's response was to turn on his barons, who felt the full weight of his rule. He constantly bullied and threatened them, menacing their lands and taking their eldest sons hostage for good behaviour.

Even the remotest of John's subjects could not feel safe. The king was perpetually on the move – appearing without warning to punish or browbeat some unsuspecting victim. His secretive ways and his suspicious nature finally drove many of his nobles to join together in rebellion. Men who had fought against each other for decades were now united by hatred of John. All the grievances of England against John and his predecessors were visited on him in a few short months. Out of this hatred Magna Carta was born.

John survived the granting of the charter by only a year. In October 1216, while campaigning against rebels in the Midlands, he died of fever at Newark. He was buried in Worcester Cathedral, where his body still lies.

TWO CENTURIES OF GENIUS DEVOTED TO GOD'S GLORY

PAGEANT IN STONE *Nearly 400 statues are fitted into niches on the West Front of Wells Cathedral. The original concept of this cavalcade of angels, bishops and kings was that of Bishop Jocelin Trotman, who died in 1242; his grand plan was completed 40 years later.*

There is something comfortable about Wells; no greater contrast could be imagined than that between the citadel church of Durham on its crag above the dark River Wear and this graceful West Country cathedral, breathing harmony and composure. Wells gives the impression of a place which avoided the violent episodes of our history.

Built to honour God

There was a Norman cathedral at Wells but, about 1180, Bishop Reginald de Bohun, who conceived the grand design of the present building, decided to start on a new site. 'The honour due to God should not be tarnished by the squalor of His house,' he said.

The result was a building full of space, air and light, with the typical ribbed vaults and pointed arches of the new Gothic style of building, vastly different from the dark, fortress-like Norman churches with their round arches and massive pillars.

Building began about 1185, and was largely completed by Bishop Jocelin Trotman after Reginald became Archbishop of Canterbury. Jocelin's work was hindered by a quarrel with King John which forced him to spend five years in exile, but the accession of Henry III brought an upward turn to the fortunes of the bishop and his cathedral. Henry gave 60 oaks 'from our woods at Cheddar for the work of the church at Wells', and also made an annual donation to the building fund.

Bishop Jocelin's greatest project was a West Front designed to display nearly 400 statues – the richest sculpture gallery in England. Conceived by Jocelin as a magnificent array of religious and lay figures united into one vast panorama, it was not completed until 1282 – 40 years after the bishop's death.

His successors were faithful to his great inspiration, and every niche of the vast design was eventually filled with a statue. Most of them were more than life size, depicting angels, apostles, prophets, saints, bishops, kings, noblemen and ladies. They were laboriously carved and hoisted into the seven tiers of niches carefully prepared for them.

Above the central doorway is a representation of the coronation of the Virgin Mary. Soaring above that again is Christ in glory. The holy figures are flanked by a cavalcade of statues paying their devotions. Although this wonderful façade has not escaped the ravages of time and the Reformation, it remains a unique survival of medieval piety.

A style dominated by simplicity

The central tower was built in the 1300's, and the western towers were added in the late 14th and early 15th centuries; but they were intended from the start, and their architects plainly conceived them as developments in the mood of the original building. The result is a single harmonious unity, the most perfect example of the simplicity that characterises early-English cathedral architecture.

From the outside, the great church possesses infinite tranquillity; but within there is unexpected drama. The moment the visitor passes through the west door he is struck by the effect of the great arch of the crossing which stands immediately ahead. Here the two sides of the cathedral converge halfway to the roof, intersect, and then – magically – continue, snaking upward to form another, inverted, arch above. On each side of the intersection are two huge eye-like roundels. The motif is repeated at the entry to each transept.

These marvellous arches were not a part of the original plan. The buttresses were improvised to solve a crisis in about 1340, when the walls began to crack under the weight of the new central tower.

The nave itself has its splendours – the piers at once massive and delicate, each consisting of 24 clustered shafts. The details are of incom-

DESIGN REVOLUTION *The inverted arches of the nave were a brilliant innovation, designed when the church began to collapse in 1340.*

TIME-WORN STEPS *The Prior's Staircase, worn down by the tread of generations of the faithful, was built in the early 14th century.*

GLORY OF WELLS *The vaulted roof of the 14th-century Chapter House is one of the greatest architectural triumphs of the cathedral.*

parable craftsmanship and originality. The capitals of the columns were each individually carved by craftsmen who possessed a ready sense of humour as well as skill. Some are even devoted to the theme of toothache.

Beyond the crossing, the contrast is complete. Comparative simplicity gives way to flamboyance, with stone tracery climbing over every available inch of wall to tangle its tendrils in a fantasy of net-vaulting in the roof. This eastern end was subjected to a major rebuilding in the mid-14th century and it is late-Gothic architecture at its best. Most of the craftsmen who built our cathedrals are anonymous, but it is known that the man responsible for all this brilliance in carved stone was the local master-mason, William Joye. He also designed the serenely beautiful central tower and the airy Lady Chapel.

This octagonal chapel was originally conceived as a separate building. Its tall, five-light windows are fine examples of late-Gothic tracery, and all but one of them are filled with fragments of early-14th-century glass.

Unspoilt by time
The pictures in these windows have disappeared, but the rich kaleidoscope of colours – ruby, ultramarine, golden-brown, olive green and white – is immensely satisfying. When it was decided to join the Lady Chapel to the cathedral, Joye created a linking building of great beauty, using slender shafts of marble to enhance the sense of spaciousness.

Yet still the best is to come. The Chapter House is approached by a breathtaking flight of broad stone steps which curve up to a double-arched doorway of miraculous delicacy. Within is one of the most beautiful rooms to be found anywhere. Each wall of the octagonal chamber is pierced by an enormous

and intricate window. From the central pier of Purbeck marble spring the 32 ribs of the vault. A stone bench running right round the wall could seat the 50 canons who, generation after generation, have met here to discuss the affairs of the cathedral. Here, perhaps more than anywhere else, one feels the spirit of Wells – the quiet serenity that soothes and refreshes all who visit this lovely place.

This feeling of serenity spreads outwards from the great cathedral. For Wells inhabits its own little island of peace. All the neighbouring buildings are of the same mellow, golden stone – the Chain Bridge and the gate houses, the gigantic cloister, the moated Bishop's Palace, and the fascinating Vicars' Close, the only complete medieval street left in Britain. All are charming in themselves, and together, in the shadow of the cathedral itself, they form a single unspoilt unity – a little enclosed world of lawns and water and mellowed stone in which the Middle Ages last for ever.

SCENES FROM COUNTRY LIFE

In the 13th century, England had a native school of sculptors whose skill and ingenuity has never been surpassed. These medieval stone-carvers were working for the glory of God, not for their own fame, and it was rare for them to leave behind even a record of their names. But their carvings in such cathedrals as Wells form an enduring memorial.

Two styles of sculpture are superbly represented at Wells: the spiritual figures in their niches on the West Front, and the equally effective but far more worldly carvings which decorate the capitals and columns inside the cathedral. These interior sculptures are not only marvels of skill; they also capture for eternity the vigorous life of England in the Middle Ages, when the vast majority of the population lived in villages, and even the largest city, London, had only 60,000 inhabitants.

Some of the carvings seem to echo the ancient theme of fertility and harvest; rich foliage entwines round bunches of grapes and other fruits. Other sculptures depict scenes from daily life in Somerset. A farmer wakes up to discover a fox making off with his goose. Four carvings tell the story of two men being caught stealing fruit. A cobbler eternally mends shoes while, near by, a poor woman who cannot afford shoes pulls a thorn from her foot.

FIRST AID *A carved capital in the nave shows a barefooted peasant woman pausing to pull out a thorn which has got stuck in her foot.*

STOP THIEF! *An angry farmer belabours a bearded robber caught stealing fruit from his orchard.*

People and peers meet in Britain's first Parliament

THE BIRTHPLACE OF PARLIAMENT

Westminster Hall, near the House of Commons, is the oldest-surviving part of the great royal palace of Westminster. It was the scene of the historic assembly of Henry III's barons and bishops in 1265 when England's first Parliament was called.

Englishmen have long been sustained by a belief in the sturdy independence of the English character. This belief has been demonstrated time and again throughout their history in demands for the protection of their liberties. But it was in the creation of Parliament – one of the greatest gifts that Britain has given to the world – that a new force was given to England's own struggle for freedom and liberty.

It was under Henry III that, for the first time, this force made itself felt in English history. On a March morning in 1265, a historic assembly gathered together in the dim light of Westminster Hall. The bishops, abbots and barons of England had met to draw up terms of peace between Henry III and his subjects, who had rebelled at his incompetence and extravagance.

There was nothing new in such a meeting.

A similar assembly had forced Henry's father, King John, to agree to Magna Carta 50 years before. But on this day in 1265, a new force shared the stage with these hereditary rulers. Seated in the hall were two knights from each shire, and two leading citizens from each of the most important towns of the realm. In the presence of this imposing body – England's first Parliament – Henry swore to mend his ways and reform his government.

This astounding achievement – the single-handed creation of Parliament – was the work of one man, Simon de Montfort. Simon was a French adventurer who, 30 years before, had arrived penniless at Henry III's court. He soon won the king's friendship, married Henry's sister, and became one of the most powerful nobles in the kingdom. But with success, Simon became arrogant. He tried to impose his will on the king, and finally the two men

quarrelled. Simon then turned to his fellow barons who, under his leadership, drew up the Provisions of Oxford and forced a council upon Henry to control the affairs of the kingdom he had failed to rule.

But the upstart Simon was almost equally distrusted by his new allies. To bolster his power, he determined to bring into the government men of the rising middle classes – the 'Commons' of England. Knights from the shires and prosperous merchants from the towns were in any case becoming a force which no king or baron could afford to ignore. Their support had become indispensable.

A power to rival the throne

Now, as the Parliament deliberated in the king's own palace, Simon had reached the summit of success. A subject had challenged the might of his monarch and won. But the victory was to be short-lived. His main ally, Gilbert de Clare, Earl of Gloucester, now regarded Simon's use of power with increasing distaste. Joining the royal cause, Clare freed the king's son, Edward, from Simon's captivity at Hereford. Edward cut off Simon's force behind the Severn, and at the Battle of Evesham in August 1265 killed Simon and most of his followers.

But the Parliament that Simon had created lived on. From the small beginnings that he had witnessed in Westminster Hall was to grow a mighty power, which would help to depose a king within the course of the following century.

Paradoxically, Parliament owed its survival to the statesmanlike qualities of Simon's most bitter enemy, Henry's son and successor, Edward I. In 1275, Edward called his first Parliament, and others followed at regular intervals throughout his reign.

Edward realised that in his efforts to bring peace to England after bitter years of civil war, he could use Parliament as a symbol of national unity. King, Lords and Commons collaborated to reform the outdated laws of England, and Edward consulted his Parliaments on all the great issues of state. Moreover, to fulfil his dream of uniting Britain under one rule, Edward needed money – and Parliament was the quickest and most efficient body through which to raise the taxes he needed to wage war in Wales and Scotland.

Parliament, however, had yet to assert its independence. This great stride forward started in the 14th century – a century of war in which the rulers of England needed vast taxes to support their ambitious attempts to conquer France. The never-ending demands for grants and subsidies put a powerful weapon into Parliament's hands, and it was not slow to use it. Taxes were voted only after the king had promised to remedy grievances. And by the 1350's, the Commons were pressing Edward III to agree to their demands to control the principal source of royal revenue – the *maletot*, a tax on wool.

This tax was of vital importance. By this time the wealth of England was largely vested in the curly fleeces of the sheep that grazed on vast acres of land throughout the kingdom. In 1360, Edward finally gave way; he agreed that the *maletot* should not be levied without the consent of Parliament. The Commons had won the first battle to control taxation.

With this advance, the Commons soon grew bolder. In 1376, they even tried to put Edward's corrupt ministers on trial. And 24 years later, they played a leading part in forcing his grandson, Richard II, to abdicate.

The Parliaments of Henry IV proved to be even more aggressive than their predecessors. The king was forced to alter his policies and cut down his extravagance. Only the renewed onset of the popular war with France saved the Lancastrian monarchy from a major conflict.

But when the war with France ended in defeat in the 1440's, the old bitterness returned. Parliament's position was strengthened further by the Wars of the Roses, when its members were wooed by the rival contenders for the throne – the Houses of York and Lancaster.

Power of Parliament

At first the strong Tudor monarchs, successors to York and Lancaster, controlled generally docile Parliaments. But by the end of Elizabeth I's reign, Parliament was beginning to assert itself again. In the most turbulent session, that of 1601, taxes to meet the cost of the queen's unpopular Irish wars were granted only after prolonged and acrimonious debate. And the Commons' protests against government grants of monopolies of goods and services were stilled only when the queen promised to curb them herself. Parliament was now an integral part of English life – and, as the Stuarts were to discover when they tried to do without it – it was indispensable.

Henry III: His rule led to civil war

Henry III was a man of mediocre abilities. The tragedy of his reign was that he possessed a burning ambition and an exalted idea of his own grandeur.

Henry longed to be the dominant figure on the European stage. His eyes turned particularly towards France, where he dreamt of reviving the French empire his father, John, had lost. He married a French wife, Eleanor of Provence, in 1236 and filled his court full of her friends and relations. But his barons were uninterested in Henry's ambitions, and resented the taxes they paid to finance his wars.

In 1254, Henry embarked on the crowning folly of his reign – the attempted conquest of Sicily, the crown of which had been offered to his son, Edmund, by the pope. In four years his kingdom was bankrupt, and his power had been wrested from his hands by his nobles.

In 1258, led by the idealistic Simon de Montfort, Earl of Leicester, the nobles set up a committee of 24 barons, which governed the country for almost two years. Others toured England unearthing evidence of corruption and misgovernment.

Henry's attempt at a counter-stroke failed miserably, when his army was routed at Lewes in 1264. Yet slowly the barons' enthusiasm waned. They turned against de Montfort – especially after his creation of Parliament – and gradually deserted him.

Finally, Henry gathered enough support to strike back at the hated earl who had once been his closest friend. On August 4, 1265, Simon was slain at the Battle of Evesham. England had learnt that it could not do without a king, even though that king was deluded and incompetent.

A KING AND HIS PARLIAMENT *This 16th-century illustration is the earliest-known portrayal of Parliament in its medieval infancy. Edward I presides, flanked by the kings of Scotland (left) and Wales (right). Edward made great use of Parliament to reform English law.*

UNWISE KING *Henry III's effigy from his tomb in Westminster Abbey. He ruled England for 54 turbulent years. Though a sincere man, his political folly turned his subjects against him.*

Eight mighty fortresses to hold a turbulent kingdom

PROUD HARLECH — A MASTERPIECE IN STONE
Edward I ordered Harlech Castle to be built in 1283 as part of his plans to subdue the fiery Welsh. The defences of this clifftop fortress were designed to withstand any weapon that the ingenuity of medieval man could bring to bear.

An anonymous chronicler wrote 'the kingdom of Wales has been overthrown', after one of his country's greatest princes, Rhys ap Tewdr, had been killed in a Norman ambush in 1093. The Normans had crushed England almost overnight; now the end for Wales seemed near. Yet this turbulent principality managed to preserve its independence until Edward I's invasion of 1282.

Many factors combined to delay the progress of subjugation. Chief among them were the terrain and the weather. The Berwyn Mountains stood in the path of Henry II's determined invasion in 1165, and the incessant rain of the principality soon doused the ardour of Norman chivalry. The Welsh princes, too, soon became adept at using English quarrels to their own advantage. Under a strong king, they would make vague promises of obedience, but under a weak one they intrigued with rebel barons to win concessions.

This form of diplomacy the Welsh understood well, for their own land was divided into many kingdoms. And, paradoxically, it was the achievement of unity under the proud and ambitious Llywelyn ap Gruffydd, ruler of Gwynedd, that brought upon them an invasion they could not resist.

The last leader

In 1277, after Llywelyn had refused to pay him homage, Edward I launched his armies into Wales. The traditional Welsh tactics of guerrilla warfare availed them little when confronted by a leader of Edward's genius. The proud Llywelyn was humbled and forced to

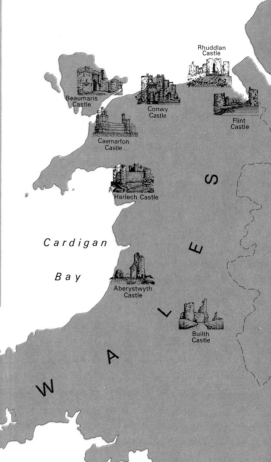

CHAIN OF COMMAND The chain of eight massive stone strongholds constructed in the 25 years after 1277 were Edward I's ultimate weapons against the threat of a Welsh uprising. They were also his ultimate memorial, for they still stand. Most of the castles were carefully sited so that they could be provisioned from the sea by the English.

Workers from all over England were recruited to help build Edward I's castles in Wales.

THE IMPREGNABLE CASTLE

The building of invincible castles was an art that the English learnt on their Crusades to the Holy Land. The principle they brought back was the concentric idea – that, within the main enclosure of a castle, second and third lines of defence should be provided. If the enemy captured the outer wall, the rest of the fortress could still hold out.

It was this form of castle that Edward I built in Wales. His castles combined an outer curtain of massive walls and towers with a complex barbican protecting the gatehouse of the inner ring of defence. The old square towers were replaced by round ones, which had few blind spots and which deflected boulders more easily.

The main weapon these castles had to face before the invention of cannon was the siege engine – the siege catapult, a form of giant crossbow on wheels, and the trebuchet, a lever device operated by men pulling on ropes, which could launch stones of a quarter of a ton.

make peace. But he could not face the loss of the power he had laboured so long to build up and, urged on by his brother, Dafydd, he rose in revolt in March 1282. Eight months later, Llywelyn was killed in a skirmish near Builth. He became known to the Welsh as *ein elyw olaf* (our last leader), for Wales was then annexed to England.

Edward was determined to hold what he had so painstakingly won. He made his young son Prince of Wales to please his Welsh subjects in 1301. But his main task was to build impregnable fortresses so that never again would Norman rule be threatened.

A chain of castles
In the space of 25 years Edward I built a vast chain of castles in Wales – the greatest feat of royal building in British history. The strongholds of Harlech, Caernarfon, Conwy, Beaumaris, Flint, Rhuddlan, Builth and Aberystwyth embodied all the lessons that military architects had learnt over the centuries. They were erected in fulfilment of Edward's vow to enforce law and order upon the Welsh. And in their massive strength they were a tribute to the people he had just conquered; only the finest castles in the world

could withstand the courage and cunning of this wild warrior race.

The master of the king's works in Wales came from Savoy, Master James of St George d'Esperance, Europe's most renowned military architect. James had been with Edward in Gascony and Scotland, and he was paid the exceptionally high salary of three shillings a day. Under him worked an army of officials, clerks, masons and labourers. The scale of the enterprise – the total cost was estimated at £80,000 – brought one of Europe's wealthiest kings to the verge of bankruptcy.

A report sent to London in 1296 gives a glimpse of the operations at Caernarfon. Some 400 skilled masons were continuously at work, and 1000 unskilled labourers assisted them in making the mortar and lime. There were also 200 carters, 30 smiths and carpenters and a guard of 30 men. Great stone blocks were brought to Caernarfon by sea; 30 boats and 160 wagons were needed to keep the builders supplied. Only a few miles away, the same feverish activity could be seen at Beaumaris.

Such was the rivalry between the castle-builders, that they even diverted royal money in the effort to complete their work first. At the beginning of 1296, a royal ship carrying the wages for the masons at Caernarfon was intercepted by the men working at Beaumaris. The workers at Caernarfon complained to the king of the sharp practices of their rivals. The moat had been begun, the walls were 24 ft high and 15 ft thick, but the work was behind schedule. Would not Edward help them by sending more money and materials? But the calls on the royal purse were many and pressing; in the event, Beaumaris was ready for a garrison in the summer of 1298, more than a year before Caernarfon.

Maintaining the conquest
The medieval art of castle-building reached its highest point in these lonely outposts of English power on the northern coast of Wales. Edward's castles were built to withstand any siege weapon that medieval man could bring to bear – the ram, the bore, the catapult and the mine. But, more important, the whole structure was designed to make any attack both difficult and dangerous. Each wall, each tower, each gateway was built with this in view. And later they were further refined.

Vast as they were, Edward's castles were designed so that they could be defended by a small force. The great fortresses of Harlech, Conwy and Caernarfon were each normally manned by only 30 to 60 men. They served their purpose well. Edward had fought a bitter war to bring the Welsh under his rule, but never again would that rule be seriously threatened. No longer would a sudden rising like that of 1294–5 take the English off their guard. For, as James of St George wrote to his master: 'You know well that Welshmen will be Welshmen even if they appear to be pacified.'

Edward I: He fought to rule a united Britain

CROWNING A KING *The coronation of Edward I. His dream was to unite the three countries of Britain under his rule.*

Edward I was the most formidable king to rule medieval England. In his long reign he achieved more than any king since the Conqueror. He transformed the law of England, and made his crown the richest and most powerful in Europe.

Edward's success was chiefly due to his ability to pick his subordinates. In Robert Burnell, his Chancellor, he had an assistant of conspicuous ability and undoubted loyalty. Under Burnell there worked a talented corps of royal civil servants. Edward knew the value of such men, and rewarded them with high salaries in their lifetimes and Masses in the royal chapel after their deaths.

Other kings before him had shown Edward's energy; others had displayed his political skill. But Edward also had extraordinary good luck. Nicholas Trevet, a close friend of the king, believed that Edward's life was charmed and his enterprises favoured by God. This luck stood by him on the battlefield, and in his complex dealings with Wales and Scotland.

Edward's over-riding ambition was to unite Britain under one rule, concluding the conquest that William I had begun more than two centuries before. His great-grandfather, Henry II, had invaded Ireland and won the region around Dublin known as 'the Pale'; and his father, Henry III, had made a tenuous claim to the overlordship of Scotland.

Edward first turned his attention to Wales. His success there was given permanence by the enduring strength of the castles he built. Next he marched into Scotland, taking advantage of the internal disputes among the Scots in the 1290's. But the Scots found a war leader of equal genius in Robert Bruce, and the ageing Edward was repeatedly frustrated in his attempts to hold the lands he had won in battle. In July 1307, he was leading his army in a last great campaign when he died just south of the border – leaving his mission to a son who was ill-equipped for the task.

Robert Bruce triumphs in Scotland's day of victory

CAUSE OF THE BATTLE

In 1314 the hard-pressed English garrison at Stirling Castle anxiously waited for their king to drive off the Scots under Robert Bruce. Edward II's determination to relieve Stirling led to his complete defeat at Bannockburn, within sight of the castle walls.

The great stone castle of Stirling stands on a rock overlooking the marshy plain of Bannockburn, guarding the principal crossing of the River Forth. On Midsummer's Day, 1314, English eyes looked anxiously across the plain from the castle walls, hoping to see the approaching banners of the English army. For its commander, Sir Philip Mowbray, had agreed to surrender it to the Scots under Robert Bruce unless an English army appeared before sunset on that day.

Seven years had passed since the death of Edward I, who had brought most of Scotland under his rule. Edward's last wish had been that his bones be carried at the head of the army that was to make the conquest secure. But Edward II had ignored the request and allowed the Scots, under Robert Bruce, to win back almost all they had lost. Now Stirling was the last strongpoint in English hands.

Only hours before the castle was due to surrender, Edward arrived on the banks of the Bannock, 3 miles south of the castle. With him was an enormous army of some 15,000 to 20,000 men. North of the Bannock, across the old Roman road leading to the Highlands, stood the Scottish army. Early in the evening, Mowbray rode into Edward's camp and urged him not to attack. The agreement had already

DISASTER AT BANNOCKBURN *A 15th-century illustration of the Battle of Bannockburn (right). Beneath the walls of Stirling Castle the grim struggle for the mastery of Scotland was brought to its conclusion. The rashness of Edward II was the crucial factor in his army's crushing defeat at the hands of Robert Bruce (above). For Bruce, his victory meant complete independence for Scotland, and also established him firmly as king. The pope recognised him as King of Scots in 1323 and five years later the English made formal peace. Bruce died in 1329 at the age of 53; his dying wish was that his heart be taken for burial in the Holy Land.*

been honoured and the castle relieved. To advance was to risk defeat, and honour would then compel Mowbray to give up the castle to the Scots in accordance with his bargain.

The impetuous Edward resolved to fight. He had little choice. For he had much cavalry, and it was composed of noblemen eager to display their valour and their skill. Many of them were from northern counties and were only partially under the control of a king for whom they had little respect. A cavalry unit led by Sir Humphrey Bohun was despatched to reconnoitre the Scottish position. At the summit of a hill, Bohun encountered Robert Bruce and charged him with a lance. Bruce felled Bohun with a battle-axe and the rest of the English party retreated. Demoralised by this unfortunate incident, the English army made camp for the night.

Disaster on the banks of the Bannock

The next morning the fateful encounter took place. The same incautious enthusiasm that had made Edward reject Mowbray's advice the day before now led him into a fatal blunder. The Scots held the higher ground and the English were exhausted by their march. But when the 24-year-old Earl of Gloucester implored him to wait, Edward taunted him with treachery. 'I shall show you,' replied Gloucester, 'that I am neither a traitor nor a liar.' He mounted his horse and flung his cavalry on the tight phalanx of Scottish pikemen. The horses were impaled by the pikes, and the English charge disintegrated into a fierce hand-to-hand battle. Gloucester's rash advance blocked the English archers' line of fire, and they found themselves shooting into their own men's backs. The English infantry was thrown into hopeless confusion.

Victory for the Scots

Then, suddenly, a host of Scottish irregulars swarmed down a hill behind the Scots, and the English, mistaking them for reinforcements, fell back in retreat. 'On them, on them,' cried the Scots, 'they fail!' The English fled in disorder towards the marshes and the Bannock, where many hundreds were killed.

Edward himself rode hard for Stirling Castle. But Mowbray refused to admit him to safety and prepared to hand over the castle to the Scots. Pursued by the vengeful Scots cavalry, Edward then turned east and reached Dunbar to board a ship and sail for England. Other fugitives were not so lucky. The Earl of Hereford and 1600 men were captured at Bothwell Castle. Robert Baston, a monk whom Edward had brought with him to record his victory in verse, was also taken prisoner and forced by his Scottish captors to rhyme the story of their triumph. And the Privy Seal of England, which was with Hereford's party, fell into Scottish hands – a symbol of the completeness of the Scots' victory. One day had secured the independence of Scotland.

Edward II: Fated to lose both throne and life

Edward II came to the throne of England in 1307. He was 23 years old, 'fair of body and of great strength', witty in conversation, and engaged to a beautiful French princess. Yet his life as king was devoid of noble purpose or ambition and, in the end, his stubborn folly delivered him into the murderous hands of his enemies.

In the whole span of the Middle Ages, only three English kings were deposed by violence – Edward II, Richard II and Henry VI. All three had in common a failing which largely contributed to their fate. They all had a taste for incompetent favourites who were loathed and despised by the nobles and people alike. But Edward's choice of favourite was the worst of all. His infatuation with a young French knight, the grasping and effeminate Piers Gaveston, brought him both unpopularity and rebellion.

In the last years of his reign, Edward I had banished Gaveston from his court. But after the old king's death, Edward II's first action was to recall Gaveston from exile and make him Earl of Cornwall. The French upstart was the most favoured and powerful subject in the kingdom. His pride, said a contemporary chronicler, 'would have been unforgivable in a king's son'. Sure of Edward's favour, he deliberately insulted the barons and gave them nicknames to amuse his royal friend and master. The Earl of Warwick became the 'Black Hound of Arden', the Earl of Lancaster, 'Churl', the Earl of Lincoln, 'Burstbelly' and the Earl of Gloucester 'Horeson'.

Edward II had too little sense to realise that the great landowners, traditionally the king's closest advisers, would deeply resent the intrusion of a foreign upstart. So outraged did the barons – and the queen he scorned – become with Edward's infatuation, that in 1308 they forced the king to banish Gaveston. But the unrepentant king recalled him to court a year later. The result was immediate civil war.

The barons now forced Edward to agree to the appointment of Lords Ordainers – a council of nobles led by the king's cousin, Thomas, Earl of Lancaster, to oversee the government of the kingdom. Their first

DOOMED KING
Edward II struggled with his barons throughout his reign. His life ended in deposition and murder.

action was to demand that Gaveston be sentenced to perpetual banishment. But he defied the Ordainers and returned from exile again in 1311.

This time, Gaveston was not to escape. The Ordainers promised him safe conduct to France if he surrendered and, trusting in their word, he did so. But, as he was being taken south from Scarborough Castle, he fell into the hands of his bitterest enemy, the Earl of Warwick. After being led through the streets of Warwick, he was taken to Blacklow Hill, outside the town, and executed.

Edward's reputation did not recover after Gaveston's death. His rustic tastes – singing and dancing, swimming and rowing – were too unbecoming in a monarch. And the shattering defeat at Bannockburn discredited him in the most important task of his reign, the protection of the north and the subjection of Scotland.

The king's chief hope was that the barons would fall out amongst themselves. In 1322 this hope was realised, when a moderate party among the Ordainers, led by the Earl of Pembroke, became so disgusted with Lancaster's incompetence that they joined the king. Lancaster launched a rebellion to regain his lost power, but this ended in his defeat and execution at Pontefract. But Edward lacked the personality to command loyalty. He immediately showered on Hugh le Despenser the favours he had given Gaveston.

A gruesome death

That was the prelude to disaster. Edward's queen, Isabella, now turned finally against him. She sailed home to France on the pretext of negotiating with her brother, Charles IV. There, she became the mistress of the exiled Roger Mortimer and in the autumn an army led by the queen and her lover overran the kingdom. Edward was captured and imprisoned in Berkeley Castle in the custody of Lord Berkeley and Sir John Maltravers. There he was murdered by means which have never been discovered. Rumours spoke of an agonising death accompanied by tortures – intricate enough not to leave a mark on his body.

Such a dreadful death of the Lord's anointed king led to pious calls for Edward's canonisation. They went unheeded. 'Keeping in prison, villainous and opprobrious death cause not a martyr,' wrote a monk, 'but if the holiness of life before be correspondent.'

But the queen and Mortimer were not long to survive their triumph. For Edward's son, the young Edward III, was resolved to revenge himself on his father's murderers. In October 1333, he struck. Mortimer was arrested at Nottingham Castle and, three weeks later, executed. Queen Isabella, whose pleas to 'have pity on gentle Mortimer', were rejected by her son, was sent to a nunnery. Edward II had enjoyed a posthumous revenge.

A handful of longbowmen crush the flower of France

VICTORY FOR THE INVADERS *The Battle of Crécy in 1346 was a triumph for the invading armies of Edward III. But shortage of food and supplies forced Edward to retreat to the coast and so he could not follow up his great victory.*

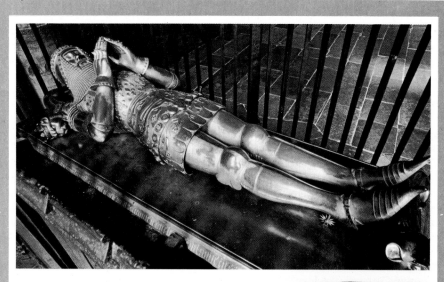

HERO OF AN AGE OF CHIVALRY

Edward III's eldest son, Edward, the Black Prince, characterised the age of chivalry in the 14th century. He won his spurs on the battlefield of Crécy when he was only 16 years old. And 10 years later he scored another victory against the French at Poitiers. A magnificent effigy of the prince (above) and his battle-scarred shield (right) can be seen at Canterbury Cathedral, where he was buried in 1376. Edward won the name Black Prince because of the black armour he wore at Crécy in 1346. His courage and dash made him a popular hero, but he did not live to inherit the throne. The long years of war took their toll on his health. He died aged 46 – a year before his father followed him to the grave.

The Hundred Years' War between England and France was a war against odds for the English, who were always outnumbered by their enemy. But this fact did not stop them winning victory after victory in the field. The first of these came on the afternoon of August 26, 1346, when the vast unwieldy mass of the French army marched towards Crécy, 32 miles south of Boulogne.

Although it had been hastily recruited, this 40,000-strong host was one of the largest armies ever raised in France. The enemy force, the invading troops of Edward III, was scarcely one-third the size. Shortly after 4 p.m. the French army arrived at the rising ground east of Crécy, and stared in disbelief at the well-drawn lines of the English gathered on the hillside opposite them.

For the French this was a rude shock. They had believed the English to be several miles away, and King Philip had not intended to fight that day. He decided not to attack until the light of morning, when the famished and exhausted English soldiers would be hard put to resist the shock of his cavalry.

But the proud nobility of France were not accustomed to disciplined waiting. They had already divided amongst themselves the prisoners they would take. One would have the King of England, another the Earl of Northampton. As Philip's staff officers rode along the marching columns ordering the army to halt, they found confusion everywhere. Units had been parted from their commanders. Foreign mercenaries could not understand what was being shouted at them. Worse still, a number of French knights disobeyed the order to halt and pressed forward, propelling their reluctant crossbowmen – Genoese mercenaries from Italy – before them.

A rain of arrows

This spectacle of disorder was watched in silence by the waiting English ranks. In front stood the longbowmen, drawn up in wedge-like formations, their arrows implanted in the ground before them. They held their fire. By 6 p.m. the French had reached a point 150 yds away – within range of the deadly English longbow. Edward watched from his command post in a windmill. Then a sharp command rang out. The longbowmen fired, and for a few moments the sky was darkened by a rain of arrows speeding into the French line. The Genoese crossbowmen fell in vast numbers beneath the deadly rain. As the chronicler Froissart recounted, the longbowmen 'shot their arrows with such force and quickness that it seemed as if it snowed'.

Then, from the middle of the English line, three cannons spat fire, and hurled enormous stone balls at the oncoming French. Never before had cannon been used on a battlefield. The Genoese crossbowmen had never seen, never expected, such a thing. They turned to flee, but found their path blocked by the French cavalry.

A battle now raged within the French army itself. King Philip shouted in fury 'kill me these scoundrels, for they stop up our road without reason'. His brother, the Duc d'Alençon, ordered his horsemen to cut down the panic-stricken Genoese, but, as they moved to do so, the heavily armoured French infantry, in a desperate lunge to reach the front, trampled the Genoese underfoot. Chaos rapidly spread in the French ranks as all remaining order was lost.

All the while there was no relief from the shower of English arrows. As each bowman used his last arrow, he rushed forward to remove another from the body of a fallen

enemy. At length, the French men-at-arms waded forward through the carnage to engage the English in hand-to-hand battle.

The brunt of the French troops' charge was borne by the young Prince of Wales, known as the Black Prince. His guardian, Godfrey Harcourt, pleaded with the king to commit his reserves and protect his heir. But Edward needed to keep his reserves intact while he

REVOLUTION IN WAR

By 1357 – after two great victories at Crécy and Poitiers – Englishmen were confident of their military superiority over their French adversaries. Nothing contributed more to that confidence than the development of the longbow. Its range was accurate up to 250 yds, and its rate of fire was much quicker than that of the conventional crossbow. The lumbering cavalry which had previously dominated the battlefield was helpless against it.

The longbow also brought about the decline of the feudal chivalry which placed a premium on exploits of personal bravery. The chain mail worn by noblemen afforded little protection against its arrows. As the nobles of France found, to take the offensive against skilled archers was to court disaster.

Longbowmen at target practice. Their weapons were to be the mainstay of English armies for the following 200 years, and won the famous victories of Crécy, Poitiers and Agincourt.

waited for the outcome of a powerful counter-attack, which the Earl of Arundel had just launched on the other flank. 'Is the prince dead or injured?' he asked. The answer was no. 'Then let the lad win his spurs alone, for if God wills it, this day shall be his.' And so it was. The Black Prince held off assault after assault, and at the end of the day the slaughter in front of his division was greater than anywhere else. This feat was not accomplished without some danger. At the height of the battle the prince was thrown to the ground by his foes. But he was rescued by an officer who covered him with the banner of Wales.

By nightfall, over 10,000 Frenchmen had perished. Among the dead were many of the greatest knights and nobles of feudal France. Edward was less than pleased at the slaughter of the French barons and knights, as he would have preferred to capture them alive and receive a ransom for their release. But in an age in which courage was deeply revered, no death was more widely mourned and admired than that of Philip's ally, the blind King of Bohemia. At the climax of the battle he ordered his knights to lead his horse forward in a fatal charge so that he might strike a blow with his own hands.

When night came, Philip found that he was left with fewer than 60 knights. He had been slightly wounded and his horse had been shot from under him. One of the knights put Philip on another horse and forced him to leave the battlefield, explaining to the king that there would be another day for revenge against the English foe. But for the crown of France, Crécy was 'a mournful day indeed'.

A triumph for English arms

Crécy made a hero of Edward III; his judgment and control had been faultless. It established his son, the Black Prince, as the ideal knight of Europe's age of chivalry. But above all it proved the superiority of English tactics – the combination of longbowmen and dismounted men-at-arms over the outdated crossbow and the cavalry charge. Ten years later, this superiority was re-emphasised when the French were again overwhelmingly defeated at Poitiers. Amongst those captured on this proud day for English arms was John II, King of France, who was carried captive to England. He was eventually ransomed for 3 million gold crowns.

But Edward III could not translate military triumph into territorial empire. Like the Romans when confronted with the might of Hannibal, the French adopted guerrilla tactics to wear their enemy down. In this they succeeded, for in 1360 Edward III agreed to the Treaty of Brétigny, which forced him to abandon his ambitions to the crown of France.

However, the dream of complete conquest was not dead in English hearts. It was left to Edward's great-grandson, Henry V, to try to bring the dream to fulfilment.

Edward III: A warrior king's Age of Chivalry

In a century of deep discord between king and subject – Edward's predecessor and successor were both deposed – Edward III was loved and respected by his people. He gave to a knightly society the opportunity to prove itself at arms. Under Edward II the barons had expended their energies in rebellion against the crown; under Edward III they used them in its service.

The pomp and pageantry of chivalry flourished under Edward as never before. The new chivalry reached its peak in 1348 when the king, flushed with his victories in France, proclaimed the new Order of the Garter, which took its name from the occasion when Edward stooped to pick up the garter of the Countess of Salisbury, and rebuked his laughing courtiers with the words, 'Honi soit qui mal y pense' – 'Evil to him who evil thinks'.

Edward pursued his ambition to be King of France for three decades. Lords and squires delighted in the chance to prove their courage and to make a fortune from prisoners' ransoms. Financiers grew rich from contracts for loans and supplies. Nor was war simply the sport of kings. The skill and endurance of the common men who wielded the longbows and manned the ships were plain to see. Edward was vain, ostentatious and extravagant – but these were the very qualities which his people admired.

WAR KING *Edward III at prayer. He is seen in armour with the arms of England and France quartered on his surcoat.*

England's agony – the Black Death claims one in three

BURIAL-PLACE FOR THE VICTIMS
St Mary's Church, Ashwell, Hertfordshire, where victims of the Black Death lie buried. An inscription carved on the church tower reads: 'Miserable, wild, distracted, the dregs of the people alone survive.' A legend says that if the burial site – a grassed-over pit in the background – is disturbed, the plague will re-emerge.

THE TOLL MOUNTS *Grave-diggers work feverishly as the ravages of the Black Death increase. The plague started in China in 1333 and it slowly spread along the trade routes to Europe. In 1348 it reached England; by the time it died down a year later, one-third of the population had perished.*

Life in the Middle Ages was a battle for survival for the majority of Englishmen. Sickness, disease and death were a constant threat. In the mid-14th century, the average Englishman could expect to live only to the age of 38 years. Nor was medical science advanced enough to offer much hope of improving this situation. Such doctors as there were based their knowledge on ancient Greek textbooks, chief among them those written by Aristotle, Hippocrates and Galen. But these concentrated on theory rather than practice, and the only treatment for disease was a variety of herbal remedies. Surgery was primitive and hygiene almost unknown.

Thus, in times of trial and peril, men looked to God and the Church rather than to science for aid and assistance. But, as the terrible plague of the Black Death swept through England in 1348, God seemed to have deserted the English. The poet William Langland wrote that priests 'had no power these pestilences to lette, for God is def now a days'.

Cargoes of germs

Towards the end of June in that fateful year, two merchant ships arrived in the small Dorset harbour of Melcombe (present-day Weymouth), carrying the seeds of disaster in their cargo. For they brought from the Continent the germs of bubonic plague – the Black Death – which had ravaged the population of Europe.

The English knew the plague was spreading towards them, but their primitive medical science was no barrier to the advance of the most virulent epidemic in Western history. The disease, carried by flea-infested black rats, thrived and spread rapidly in every direction, striking Southampton, Exeter, the Midlands and London within weeks.

Everywhere its symptoms inspired terror in men's hearts. Horrible swellings of the glands, the size of grapefruits, appeared without warning and, as the whole body slowly turned black, the swellings festered for four or five

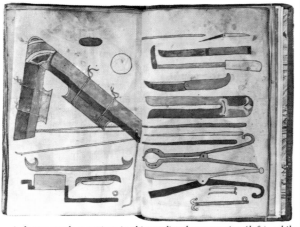
days before death released the victim from his sufferings. Ignorant and frightened men asserted that the disease was carried in a great black cloud, or that it was spread by travelling Jews who poisoned the wells.

Violence and crime increased in the towns; resentment against the clergy and the rich erupted into ugly riots. Men grew sceptical of the Christian argument that all things were just in God's mysterious creation, and the frail fabric of medieval society began to break down.

By January 1349 the epidemic had London in its grip. Edward III dissolved Parliament and the court left London in haste for the countryside, where there was less risk of infection. The rich fled to their country houses, the bishops to their summer palaces.

The Abbot of Westminster was among the first to flee, but his flight failed to save him; he was one of the first to die, and 27 of his monks followed him to the grave. Three successive Archbishops of Canterbury died in the space of 12 months. London's cemeteries were too small to take the hundreds of dead who

arrived every day. For many years after the plague an inscription could be seen on the site of the Spittle Croft cemetery: 'This churchyard was consecrated in the year of Our Lord 1349 when the Great Plague was raging; wherein were buried more than fifty thousand of the dead whose souls God have mercy upon.'

The plague created social problems. Men were afraid to travel and consequently little food reached the towns, adding starvation to the sufferings of those whose poverty made escape impossible. Many Englishmen, in any case, had their resistance to the disease lowered by previous years of famine.

Consequences of the plague

The burial of the dead aroused bitter illfeeling. The Church insisted that only consecrated churchyards could be used, while the people were convinced that even beneath the ground bodies were a source of infection. At Winchester, a burial service was disturbed by a mob who demanded that the victims be buried outside the town walls.

In the countryside, too, the population was halved in some places. Landowners' profits fell sharply as labourers who knew that they were in short supply demanded two or three times their usual wages. In vain, the government tried to intervene, issuing the Statute of Labourers, a measure which laid down that wages should be fixed at pre-plague rates. It also tried to control prices. But the policy failed in both these aims, and during the next 30 years peasant unrest built up, eventually to explode in the Peasants' Revolt of 1381. Recruitment to the armies of Edward III suffered grievously. Priests could not be found to say Mass in poor parishes.

The destruction of one-third of England's population of 3 million, and the laying waste of over 1000 villages, was a disaster unparalleled in modern times. 'Truly,' remarked one chronicler, 'no sin of man could be so awful as to deserve such a punishment of God.'

London – the breeding ground for pestilence

On the eve of the Black Death, 60,000 people were crammed into medieval London. Filth accumulated in the streets and armies of rats bred in dark alleys. Sewage was flung into streets designed with a central channel to carry it to the nearest stream. Householders were required by law to clean the patches in front of their houses, and 'scavengers' were appointed to rake up the rubbish. At times the stream which flowed past the Fleet prison was so choked with garbage and human excrement, that no water could penetrate to the prison moat. And seven years after the plague, Edward III was still complaining that rubbish on the waters of the Thames obstructed the passage of the royal barge.

The squalor of the city did much to explain the rapid strides made by the plague in London. Not only did Londoners live among diseasecarrying rats; but they also suffered from malnutrition, which weakened their resistance to disease. Rich citizens had orchards and vegetable gardens; the rest depended on food brought from the countryside, which placed a heavy strain on the primitive agricultural system and road network. In times of nationwide famine, it was always the poor of London who suffered the first pangs of hunger. The city's three slaughterhouses – St Nicholas Shambles, Walbrooke and East Cheap – prepared cattle for the butchers in indescribably filthy conditions. During the plague they were thought to be so great a source of infection that they were moved out to Knightsbridge.

Punishing the profiteers

Meat was often putrid by the time it reached the family table. Milk, produced in cramped dairies on the south bank of the Thames, was a luxury. Numerous officials, armed with sheets of regulations, fought a constant war against dishonest food sellers. Sellers of putrid ale were put in the stocks. In 1319, a butcher from West Ham was caught in the act of selling meat from diseased cattle. He was put in a pillory and the carcasses burnt under him – but history does not record whether he survived this treatment. Fraudulent bakers appeared before the courts at each session.

It was small wonder that the wealthy merchants, nobility and clergy preferred to live outside the city walls, building their houses by the Thames and enjoying the luxury of private latrines jutting over the river. The first fashionable suburb of London was Fleet Street, where Edward III's third son, John of Gaunt, built his Savoy Palace. The Archbishop of Canterbury had his country estate at Lambeth, and the Abbot of Westminster had his in Hampstead. But the city of London itself, a contemporary chronicler remarked, was 'no place for the decent sort of men'.

The peasants of England rise to demand new rights

CLASH AT SMITHFIELD *In a medieval illustration, Richard II watches as William Walworth, Lord Mayor of London, stabs Wat Tyler in the shoulder. Tyler's quick wits had won him the leadership of the Peasants' Revolt. Without him, it swiftly collapsed.*

CAUSE OF REVOLT

Groats minted under Richard II can now be seen in the British Museum. These coins make up the tax Richard demanded from every citizen of the land in 1380. The attempt to collect it sparked off the Peasants' Revolt.

On Friday June 15, 1381, a cavalcade of some 200 courtiers and soldiers escorted Richard II out of the north gate of Westminster Abbey, riding towards Smithfield. For three days Richard's capital had been sacked and looted by several thousand enraged peasants from Essex and Kent. These peasants had risen spontaneously in rebellion, and now demanded that the king listen to their grievances. They would no longer submit to the yoke of serfdom. They demanded the repeal of the unjust laws which held down their wages. Most of all, they would not pay the grinding taxes needed for the king's futile wars in France.

The revolt begins

Trouble had started a year before, when Richard's government had imposed a new poll (head) tax on his subjects. Its burden fell heaviest on the poor, and the first attempt to collect it was a disaster. In the spring of 1381, a force of commissioners was sent out to collect the balance of the tax, and this was the spark that fired the Peasants' Revolt.

The first rising took place in Essex. When the tax-collectors arrived at Brentwood the villagers declared that 'they would have no dealings with them nor pay them a penny'. Violence soon broke out and swiftly spread to Kent. Gangs of peasants waylaid the commissioners, burnt down manor houses and

destroyed the charters which bound them to their masters. Soon, towns were falling to the rebels and on June 10 they sacked the Archbishop's palace at Canterbury.

Little resistance could be offered. Most of the army was in France, Wales and Scotland. John of Gaunt, the king's all-powerful uncle, was himself in Edinburgh negotiating with the Scottish king.

Many of the citizens of London itself sympathised with the rebels and they easily won entrance. Within hours of their arrival, the Savoy Palace in the Strand, residence of the hated John of Gaunt, lay in ashes. The equally unpopular Archbishop of Canterbury, Simon of Sudbury, together with Robert Hales, the royal treasurer, had been dragged from sanctuary in the Tower chapel. Sudbury pleaded in vain with the rebels, and the unmoved peasants killed him on Tower Hill.

The peasants, however, claimed that they had not risen against their monarch. Their rallying cry was 'King Richard and his true commons'. It was his corrupt ministers, not the king, who had to be hunted down and killed. But even so, the 14-year-old king was taking his life in his hands in riding to meet the rebels at Smithfield.

From the Tower battlements, Richard had watched, impotent, as the flames of the Savoy reddened the sky. For the first time this frail boy had asserted himself against his tutors and advisers, and had agreed to discuss his subjects' grievances.

Smithfield lay outside the walls of London – a large open space, which, even then, served as London's cattle market. There, Richard found the insurgents drawn up in ranks. He took up his station opposite them and called on their leader to come forward. A discharged soldier from Maidstone, Wat Tyler, whose ready tongue had earned him the revolt's leadership, rode forward with a single companion.

Flushed with the success of the revolt, Tyler was in no mood to compromise with his king. He demanded the abolition of serfdom, the hunting laws and bishoprics, and the confiscation of Church property. 'Let no man be the lord of another,' Tyler shouted, 'but all should be equal under the king.' But Richard stalled before these extreme demands and Tyler began to grow abusive.

Then, one of the king's attendants cried out that he recognised Tyler as 'the greatest thief and robber in all Kent'. The rebel leader turned to his companion and ordered him to strike down the heckler. The companion hesitated, however, and Tyler himself rode in among the royal retinue, sword in hand. But

his way was barred by the Lord Mayor of London, William Walworth.

A scuffle followed. Tyler stabbed at the mayor, but in vain, for Walworth was wearing mail beneath his cloak. Drawing his own sword, the mayor stabbed the rebel leader in the shoulder while a royal squire rode forward and ran him through. Mortally wounded, Tyler turned his horse towards the ranks of the peasants, crying out, 'Treachery!' Then he fell to the ground in full view of the assembled crowd.

'Sirs, will you shoot your king?'

For a few moments it seemed as if none of the royal party would escape alive. Then, just as the peasants were drawing their bows to avenge their dead leader, Richard suddenly rode out towards them, his hand raised, and cried: 'Sirs, will you shoot your king? I will be your chief and captain and you shall have from me all that you ask for.' Followed by the insurgents, Richard then rode off towards Clerkenwell fields, while the mayor galloped back into the city to raise a rescue force.

For nearly an hour, Richard talked against time with the roughest of his subjects. Chief among them was John Ball, a half-mad excommunicated priest from Kent, whom the rebels had released from the archbishop's prison at Canterbury. At Blackheath he had preached to them of social equality and political revolution, taking as his text:

Whan Adam delved, and Eve span,
Who was thanne a gentilman?

But at last the king saw the mayor's forces advancing towards the rebels and slowly encircling them. Richard called a halt to the debate and declared the meeting dissolved.

Gradually, the peasants dispersed – but this was by no means the end of the revolt. Many villages around London were plundered and destroyed. In Cambridge, Corpus Christi College was gutted. Parchments, charters and priceless documents were burnt by the mob in Market Square, as an old woman, Margery Starre, cried: 'Away with the learning of the clerks, away with it !' But with the crushing of the revolt in London, the government could move to quell the rebels in the rest of the kingdom. By the end of the year, Richard's proud boast on the morrow of Smithfield had come true: 'Let us rejoice and praise God, for I have this day recovered my lost heritage.'

POWER BEHIND THE THRONE

During Richard II's boyhood, England was virtually ruled by the king's uncle, John of Gaunt, Duke of Lancaster (below). Gaunt was a brilliant administrator, but Richard himself resented such domination. Gaunt's power, however, made him indispensable. His death in 1399 brought about the king's fall. For Richard had exiled Gaunt's son, Henry Bolingbroke, who now claimed his father's lands which Richard had confiscated. Refused this, he deposed the king and seized the throne.

Richard II: The tragic reign of a boy king

Richard II was a child for the first eight years of his reign, and by temperament he remained a child all his life. Richard's coronation was a magnificent spectacle of pomp and ceremony, but behind the pageantry England was ruled by a parliamentary council, dominated by the king's uncle, the powerful John of Gaunt. He had seized control during Edward III's illness and continued to dominate the land during Richard's minority.

Richard, in theory Lord of all England, chafed at the restrictions imposed upon him. A physical weakling, he found it impossible to live up to the standards that his father, the Black Prince, had set. Yet he was taught that he must do so to fulfil the divinity which 'doth hedge in a king'. The conflict in Richard's character was resolved only during the Peasants' Revolt, the supreme moment of Richard's life.

It was not until he reached the age of 18 in 1385 that Richard freed himself from his tutors. But the effect of this long period of frustration on his character was disastrous. For the rest of his life he reacted with hysterical passion when anyone tried to argue with him, or control his policies.

A royal misfit

Richard liked to move in a small circle of friends. To outsiders he was moody and suspicious, especially after the death of his first wife, Anne of Bohemia, in 1394, which removed the last restraint on his self-control. When the Earl of Arundel arrived late for the funeral at Westminster Abbey, Richard assaulted him. The king's arrogant bearing grew ever stronger throughout the rest of his life.

These failings of character brought Richard into conflict with the nobility and with Parliament. In 1386, Parliament deprived Richard of much of his power by appointing a commission to control the government. But Richard refused to accept defeat and mustered a small army, which was routed at Radcot Bridge in December 1387. A new Parliament, called the 'Merciless Parliament', met in 1389 and convicted several of Richard's friends of 'treason'; two of them were hanged, drawn and quartered, and others of them were beheaded.

Richard recovered control by promising to be more conciliatory in the future. But he never forgot how he had been treated, and nine years later he began to take his revenge. His enemies were exiled, executed or imprisoned, and their estates confiscated. Among them was the Earl of Arundel, the man Richard had attacked four years before.

Rebellion and overthrow

So confident was Richard that in 1399, when John of Gaunt died, he seized his lands and then left the kingdom to lead his armies in a campaign in Ireland. This was the moment for which the king's many enemies had been waiting. In June, Henry Bolingbroke, John of Gaunt's son, returned from exile in France. He landed on the Humber and rapidly collected an army to march against the king. Among his chief supporters were the Earl of Northumberland, head of the powerful Percy family, and Ralph Neville, Earl of Westmorland. With frightening suddenness, Richard's power disintegrated in his hands. His few friends betrayed him, and he took refuge in Conwy Castle with a force of only 100 men.

Even the walls of Conwy could not protect him, and within a few weeks Richard surrendered himself into the hands of his rival. In September a deed of abdication was extracted from the once-proud king, and Henry placed the crown on his own head. The rest of Richard's life was spent in a solitary dungeon deep in Pontefract Castle. There, in 1400, he was either starved or smothered to death by his gaoler – an obscure end to England's most eccentric monarch. The absolute monarchy he had tried to create perished with him.

FORCED ABDICATION *Richard II hands his crown and sceptre to his cousin, Henry Bolingbroke, in this 15th-century illustration. Richard overcame one threat to his throne in the Peasants' Revolt. But he could not resist his rebellious nobles when they rose against him in 1399.*

A POET'S ACHIEVEMENT – TO CATCH THE SPIRIT OF HIS AGE

The title 'Father of English Poetry' belongs by tradition to a 14th-century Londoner who wrote poetry in the intervals of a busy public career. For over 500 years, Geoffrey Chaucer – courtier, diplomat, civil servant and poet – has held a unique place in the minds of his countrymen. It was he who first gave literary expression to the English sense of humour in his masterpiece *The Canterbury Tales*. This work, written in the late 1380's, is a timeless comedy of medieval life and manners and mixes bawdy farce, gentle satire and shrewd observation of human beings. In its rich profusion of characters drawn from life, this poem gives a unique insight into the medieval world.

First poet of English

Chaucer's poetic genius, flowering in the springtime of English culture, raised the native tongue to a dignity and importance that hitherto only such languages as French and Latin had enjoyed. He established through his art the distinctive strengths and beauties of English – its music, economy, its flexible ease and its blend of vigour and delicacy. These qualities appear in such lines as the opening of the Prologue to *The Canterbury Tales*:

> *Whanne that Aprille with his shoures sote*
> *The droghte of Marche hath perced to*
> *   the rote . . .*
> *And smale fowles maken melodye,*
> *That slepen al the night with open ye . . .*
> *Than longen folk to goon on pilgrimages.*

In modern translation:

> *When April with its sweet showers*
> *has pierced the drought of March to*
> *   the root . . .*
> *and small birds make melody,*
> *that sleep all night with open eye . . .*
> *then folk long to go on pilgrimages.*

Chaucer's presence fills the pages of *The Canterbury Tales*, giving the reader an intimate sense of a kindly, shrewd and penetrating mind. Yet little is known of Chaucer's private life. He was born about 1340, the son of a London wine merchant. Before he was 20 he accompanied Edward III to the French wars, where he was captured and ransomed.

On his return to England, Chaucer became a valet in the royal household, and was the

PLUMP POET *A portrait of Chaucer from an early edition of* The Canterbury Tales. *In it the Host of the inn describes Chaucer as being 'elvish' in appearance, absent-minded and tending to middle-aged stoutness – 'he in the waist is shaped as well as I'.*

particular favourite of Edward's second and third sons, Lionel, Duke of Clarence, and John of Gaunt, Duke of Lancaster. Soon, Chaucer was sent on diplomatic missions to Italy, Flanders and France. At home, he served, apparently with distinction, under both Richard II and his supplanter, Henry IV. He held such mundane but lucrative and necessary offices as Clerk of the Works and Comptroller of the Customs and Subsidy of Wools, Skins and Tanned Hides in the Port of London. He died in 1400 and was the first of England's poets to be buried in Westminster Abbey.

A lover of life

Chaucer married Philippa Roet, a lady of the court, but passages in some of his works suggest that he discovered little happiness in marriage. When he was about 40 he was threatened with a law suit concerning his alleged abduction of a woman called Cecilia Champaigne. He had a son, 'Little Lewis', possibly an illegitimate child, for whose benefit he prepared a treatise on the astrolabe, an instrument used in medieval astronomy.

The few personal glimpses we have of Chaucer are supplied by the poet himself in his own works. It is clear that he loved flowers, particularly the common daisy, and was deeply attracted to women. The jolly Host in *The Canterbury Tales* describes the poet as 'elvish' in appearance and tending to corpulence – 'he in the waist is shaped as well as I'.

What matters most for posterity is that Chaucer was a great lover of life, and that he could describe the world he knew and enjoyed so well in language unsurpassed for richness and rhythm. A worldly man himself, Chaucer's poetic vision of life was worldly too. The people he writes about are real people, economically described in telling detail. That is why the characters of *The Canterbury Tales* – like

---

PIONEERS OF A NEW LANGUAGE

The language which was to express some of the world's greatest literature was born in England in the 14th century. While Chaucer was turning the everyday speech of London into the language of poetry, two other writers were using the common tongue for a more uplifting purpose. John Wyclif and William Langland forged the language into a weapon in their struggle against the Roman Catholic Church and its popes.

In medieval England, Latin was the language of the Church and the Bible. It was spoken and written exclusively by scholars and churchmen. But when John Wyclif inspired a group of fellow-scholars to make the first complete translation of the Bible into English in 1382, he was not merely championing his native tongue.

To Wyclif, Latin was the symbol of Church authority, as distinct from the authority of God. By replacing Latin with the English language, he sought to create a national Church which could speak directly to the common people. Although a scholar and a priest, Wyclif attacked enforced confessions, penances and indulgences – the system by which priests took money for pardoning sins. He even proposed that the Church should do without popes and bishops.

Another reformer who chose the English language for his attack on the princely rulers of Church and state was William Langland, a clerk and poet, who wrote 'Vision of Piers Plowman'. He tried to show simple souls the way to salvation.

REBEL PRIEST *Wyclif was called a heretic because he wanted all men to read the Bible. But he was protected by powerful nobles.*

VISIONARY *A page from a manuscript of William Langland's 'Vision of Piers Plowman', written about 1362. This manuscript dates from 1427 and is kept in the Bodleian Library, Oxford.*

TOUGH SEADOG *The ship's captain who made the pilgrimage had much to repent of. Chaucer tells how he stole wine from foreign traders and was merciless with prisoners. 'If, when he fought, the enemy vessel sank, he sent his prisoners home; they walked the plank.'*

GENTLE LADY *According to Chaucer, the well-bred prioress showed every sign of enjoying her pleasant life. She was remote from the troubles and bustle of the world with her lapdogs and her cultivated manners. But she was very likeable – 'all sentiment and tender heart'.*

PILGRIM'S WARNING *The canon's yeoman had grown thin and shabby in the service of a cleric who practised witchcraft and alchemy. The yeoman warned his fellow-travellers against trying to turn base metal into gold: it led to 'empty moneybags and addled brains'.*

Whatever the flavour of the tales – ribald or tragic, heroic or ironic – the men and women who tell them spring from the printed page. These portraits are as true to life as the poet can make them: the Nun who had such a zest for courtliness that she would 'her upper lip wipe so clean, that not a trace of grease was to be seen'; or the Pardoner, with his false relics – pigs' bones and the like – with which he imposes on the poor and makes 'monkeys of the priest and congregation'.

Imagination and realism

Such merry realism contrasts with the moving lyricism of others of *The Canterbury Tales*. Not until Shakespeare reached maturity does any other English writer display so rare a blend of imaginative and realistic gifts. Chaucer's eye was almost as keen as Shakespeare's. It had the same dispassionate clarity, the same wonderfully unfailing sharpness for observation of detail.

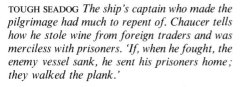

JOLLY HYPOCRITE *The friar was a pleasant, easy-going fellow. He never imposed harsh penances on sinners who came for confession. He was no stranger to innkeepers and was good company to all – except those who could not contribute to his needs.*

MONEY-GRABBER *The steward or reeve of the poem was a successful guardian of his lord's lands and wealth. He was even more successful in lining his own pocket. But a lifetime of terrorising tenants and peasants had left him 'old and choleric and thin'.*

the Miller with a wart at the tip of his nose, on which 'stood a tuft of hairs red as the bristles of a sow's ears' – and other poems are instantly recognisable, even today. Their outlook may be moulded by the Middle Ages, but in their greed, lust, cynicism, generosity and goodness they are timeless.

Chaucer's genius as the first English poet with the power to create a vivid world of fiction emerged in his poem *Troilus and Criseyde*, a moving study of young love blighted by infidelity, set against the background of the Trojan Wars. In its narrative, drive and the directness of its dialogue it resembles a novel, written long before that literary form was even thought of.

But the work for which Chaucer is most famous – and justly so – is his account of that magnificent cavalcade of medieval personali-

ties, *The Canterbury Tales*. The story tells how some 30 pilgrims make the journey from London to the shrine of Archbishop Thomas Becket at Canterbury. As they go, each of them tells a tale. The travellers include the Merchant, the Knight, the Miller, the Nun, the Pardoner, the Franklin, the Squire, and the Wife of Bath.

Chaucer's characters provide an engaging cross-section of contemporary life. Although the poet moved in court circles, he chose his personages from the middle and poorer classes. The coarse, the proud, the sanctimonious and the over-hearty – they are all there, and their creator pokes good-humoured fun at almost all of them, gently exposing their weaknesses and idiosyncrasies but never stripping them of their dignity as human beings. The procession that moves across Chaucer's pages is as bright as the figures on a medieval manuscript.

Only two of the stories told on the road to Canterbury appear to have been drawn entirely from Chaucer's imagination. The rest were traditional tales or free adaptations from the works of other writers. But the credit for the realistic characterisation in the tales and the depth of philosophical thought that underpins the poem, belongs to Chaucer alone.

He did not live to complete *The Canterbury Tales*. His pilgrims arrive at their destination, but do not make the return journey to London. We never learn which of them wins the free meal at the Tabard Inn in Southwark, which the Host promised would be the reward for the teller of the best tale with the 'fullest measure of good morality and general pleasure'.

The Host's decision, in any case, would not have been easy. With such rich profusion, every tale adds munificently to our own heritage of pleasure.

Proud lords of the north fight to overthrow their king

STRONGHOLD OF THE MASTERS OF THE NORTH

Alnwick Castle, Northumberland, was the principal stronghold of the Percies. From its grim fortifications this proud family built up an almost-independent empire through war and diplomacy. At its height, their rule covered much of northern England.

In the Middle Ages, a man's place in life was largely determined by his birth. Moving between their enormous castles, leading private armies and administering the affairs of vast provinces, the nobles of northern England were often little less than kings; and sometimes even more so.

Of these families, destined by birth to play their part in the bloodstained politics of medieval power, none was stronger or more ambitious than the Percy family of Northumberland – described by Shakespeare as the 'proud Percies'. In their great pride, they overthrew one monarch and placed another on the throne, though they paid for this with the life of their greatest son, the brilliant Henry Percy, nicknamed Hotspur, on the bloody field of Shrewsbury.

Many things helped the Percies in their rise to wealth and fame. Among them were the threat the Scots constantly posed on the northern border, and the distance separating their domains from London. But most important was the native shrewdness of their race. High office brought the Percies the opportunity to enrich themselves, and they grasped it greedily. Such was the family that fought a private war with the crown of Scotland at its own expense, and once had the crown of England £52,000 in its debt.

The ablest and most arrogant members of the family were Hotspur and his uncle, Thomas Percy, Earl of Worcester. Both took a leading part in the rebellion that deposed Richard II, and placed Henry IV on the throne in 1399. With his courtly manners and explosive temper, Hotspur was idolised by his contemporaries. His reputation reached a peak in September 1402, when he crushed the Scots at Homildon Hill in Northumberland, capturing 80 noblemen. But, after his victory over the Scots, Hotspur complained that Henry IV had failed to repay the money the

INTRIGUE FOR POWER *Richard II (mounted, centre) surrenders to Bolingbroke in 1399. In front of him stands Henry Percy, Earl of Northumberland, whose decision to join the rebels ensured the success of their cause. But three years later, he and his family turned against the king.*

THE NORTH'S MASTERS *The Percies dominated the north in medieval times. Their castles and the major battles they fought are shown (left).*

Percies had spent fighting the campaign. So he refused to hand over the Earl of Douglas, most powerful of the nobles captured at Homildon, arguing that if Henry could not settle his debts, then Hotspur was entitled to receive the earl's ransom.

The two men quarrelled and Hotspur, with his father, the Earl of Northumberland, and his uncle, rose in rebellion. The Percies denounced as a usurper the king whom they had helped to the throne and announced that Richard II had not died at Pontefract, but was still alive. Negotiations were swiftly opened with the rebellious Welsh forces of Owain Glyndwr.

Hotspur's plan was to recruit fighting men from Cheshire and North Wales – regions where loyalty to Richard II's memory remained strong – and then march on Shrewsbury, where Henry IV's son, Prince Hal, was camped. Having seized the prince, Hotspur would wait for the forces his father was mustering in the north and for his Welsh allies under Glyndwr. The united armies would then advance to confront the king. But the king and his able Scottish lieutenant, George Dunbar, led his forces in a rapid march north, and managed to reach Shrewsbury a few hours ahead of the Percies. The fate of Henry's crown, the dynasty he was trying to establish, and the fortunes of the mightiest of his subjects were now to be decided in a single day's violent conflict.

A fight to the finish

Even though Henry had thwarted his original plan, Hotspur resolved to give immediate battle. On Saturday July 21, 1403, the king received the Percies' last defiant challenge. 'We do intend to prove with our own hands personally against thee, Henry, Duke of Lancaster, unjustly presuming and named King of England, without right of title, but only of thy guile.'

The two armies now prepared for action. Hotspur had stationed his troops on high ground, and the king's forces had to charge up a hill to get to grips with them. As the 16-year-old Prince of Wales charged up the slope, he and his men faced a hail of arrows from the Percy archers. For the first time, English troops had to face the weapon with which they had wrought such havoc on the battlefields of France. But Henry's men were undeterred and soon came to close quarters with their enemy.

The fighting lasted until nightfall. The armies were evenly matched, but at the end of the day Hotspur's cause was lost and he himself lay dead upon the field.

Nor did the other members of Hotspur's family escape. His uncle was beheaded two days later, and the old earl, Hotspur's father, had no choice but to throw himself on the king's mercy. It was to be many years before the north would see a Percy ruling again in the proud manner of his ancestors.

Henry IV: The usurper king's uneasy reign

KING BY THE GRACE OF GOD *Henry IV's seizure of the throne from his cousin receives the blessing of the Church in this contemporary illustration of his coronation in 1399. Henry looked forward to a long and successful reign, but it was short and constantly troubled by revolt.*

When Henry IV forced his cousin, the 32-year-old Richard II, to abdicate in 1399 and took his place on the English throne, the wealth of the Duchy of Lancaster and the power of the Plantagenets were united in a single pair of highly capable hands. The events of 1399 ought to have made the English monarchy unchallengeable. Instead they ushered in a period of turbulence and rebellion, of royal bankruptcy and constant crisis.

Henry should have found it easy to win recognition for his new authority. According to the chronicler Adam of Usk, he had rescued England from a ruler whose crimes included 'perjuries, sacrileges ... exactions from his subjects and cowardice'. But within a few months of his accession, Henry faced threats on every side. In Wales, he had to deal with a formidable national rebellion under the leadership of Owain Glyndwr. In the north, the mighty Percies turned against him. Despite the fact that the two nations were supposedly at peace, the French launched murderous raids on the south coast and landed troops in Wales. Henry's success in parrying each of these threats to his crown was striking evidence of his force of character and political skill.

Worn down by the cares of office

But the king was not to enjoy his victory for long. Although only 32 when he came to the throne, Henry's constant cares made him prematurely old. Once handsome and active, he became ill-tempered and lost much of his intellectual drive.

In 1405, Henry was further weakened by a mild stroke, which his contemporaries thought to be leprosy, God's punishment for ordering the execution of Archbishop Scrope

for treason. For much of the rest of his reign, he was forced to look on as a bitter struggle for power raged about him. One faction, led by the king's younger son, Thomas, and by Thomas Arundel, the aristocratic Archbishop of Canterbury, dominated the government for almost five years. In 1410, however, they were edged out of power by Prince Hal, the young Prince of Wales, and his friends. Only when Henry's half-brother, Henry Beaufort, Bishop of Winchester, tactlessly suggested he should abdicate did the king emerge from his retirement to take personal command of affairs and dismiss the prince from the council.

Henry's energy was entirely taken up by threats to his crown. But although violence was the dominant theme of Henry's reign, the king had a degree of sensibility and refinement which was wholly absent in those around him. He was fond of music in an age when English music was pre-eminent in Europe. He patronised the poets Chaucer and Gower, doubling the former's pension, and invited Christine de Pisan, the first professional authoress in the world, to visit England after reading her poetry. Before his accession, he had been to Danzig, Venice and the Holy Land.

Pained by constant illness, Henry finally collapsed in the early spring of 1413, after an exhausting session of Parliament. His last words were a curious epitaph for such a harsh realist. He begged forgiveness for his usurption of the crown, and told his assembled household that, had he lived, he would have led a Crusade. According to Shakespeare, it had been prophesied that Henry would die in Jerusalem – but in fact he died at the early age of 46 in the Jerusalem Chamber at Westminster Abbey, in March 1413.

'Cry God for Harry, England and St George'

ENGLAND'S IMMORTAL HERO

Henry V's overwhelming victory over the might of France at Agincourt made him the hero of his people – and his reputation as a leader increased after his early death, at the age of 35. This stone relief of the king in full armour is in Westminster Abbey.

England's long struggle for the mastery of France lasted for more than a century, but only once did the English come close to complete success. In 1415 Henry V, who, as legend had it, had been a wastrel as Prince of Wales, launched his country once again into a gigantic gamble – with the final conquest of its rich and powerful neighbour as the prize. Henry had a united island behind him in this cause. Parliament and the Church agreed willingly to extra taxation. Volunteers flocked to the colours, for war meant a chance of adventure, ransom and plunder.

Clash to decide the fate of France

The struggle came to a head on October 25, 1415, when the English and French armies clashed on the field of Agincourt. The night before the battle was stormy, as the two opposing forces camped on the open ground by the forest of Agincourt, 20 miles inland from Boulogne. The French army, numbering according to some accounts as many as 50,000 men under the Constable d'Albret, lay between the English and the coast, blocking their line of march towards Calais and their winter quarters. The French were in high spirits. Their laughing and shouting disturbed the quiet of the night, and drink flowed in abun-

dance. The French commanders were playing dice – the stakes being the English prisoners they confidently expected to capture on the field the next day.

But a grim silence hung over the English tents. Henry's negotiations with the French had failed, and the king knew that he had to defeat them or face captivity and perhaps even death. The weakness of the English army – it was barely 4000 strong – gave little cause for hope. Its men were hungry, and many were suffering from dysentery contracted at the siege of Harfleur. One of its leaders, Sir Walter Hungerford, gloomily confided that he wished he could have 10,000 of the best archers in England with him. A contemporary chronicle reported that Henry angrily replied: 'You are wrong. I do not need a single extra man, for my hope is in God, and if my cause is just I shall prevail whatever the size of my following.' This was the origin of Shakespeare's 'a little touch of Harry in the night'.

Agincourt had been chosen with care by the French. Their army included large contingents of cavalry, and the flat, narrow plain, bounded on either side by thick woodland, was ideal cavalry country. But the French had forgotten the rain. By the morning, the ploughed fields that separated the two armies had become a

HENRY V *Only premature death deprived the cleverest and most ambitious of the Lancastrian kings from winning the throne of France.*

muddy marsh. Rising at dawn, Henry heard Mass and then made his final plans for the battle. Knowing how heavily he was outnumbered, he and his subordinate commanders, the Duke of York and Lord Canoys, decided to concentrate almost all their men to hold the open ground between the woodlands, and so prevent the French from outflanking the English line. Only a tiny reserve was left to secure the camp in the rear. Henry also took great care over the placing of the archers. They were ordered to provide themselves with 6 ft wooden stakes, which they could dig into the ground as a defence against the French cavalry. Now all the English could do was wait.

CLASH ON THE BATTLEFIELD *English cavalry, pikemen and archers throw the French into confusion in this 15th-century miniature of Agincourt. The French chose the battlefield because it seemed to be ideal cavalry country. But mud and England's bowmen upset their calculations.*

Henry V: A captain of genius wins France

Few kings of England have been as idolised both in their lifetimes and by posterity as Henry V. In England's long struggle to win France, Henry came within an ace of achieving the ambitions of his ancestors. Only his death at the age of 35 cheated him of triumph.

Henry's path was eased by the disordered state of France after 40 years of corrupt government and civil war. His ambitions began modestly, but they became ever greater as each attack he made met with less and less resistance. When he first struck at Normandy in 1415, Henry had only a speedy raid in mind. But, for the second time in a century, a vastly superior French army was shattered by a small force of English longbowmen.

After his victory at Agincourt, Henry went on in 1417 to attack Normandy. Then, in 1419, the powerful Duke of Burgundy recognised Henry as King of France. Within a few months, the whole country was under English control. Fine generalship and shrewd diplomacy had brought Henry to unequalled heights of power. But dysentery struck Henry down on August 31, 1422, leaving a baby son – Henry VI – to succeed him. Two months later the French king followed Henry to the grave. If Henry V had lived a few weeks longer, he might have been King of France. But his son was to lose all he had gained.

Meanwhile, the French had arranged themselves in three lines. After a long pause, in which each side waited for the other to attack, the first French line of heavily armoured infantry advanced. But the impetus of their charge was broken by the mud before they had even crossed half the distance to the English line. Henry ordered his archers to shoot. The devastating flights of arrows that had slaughtered French men-at-arms at Crécy and Poitiers again caused appalling casualties. By the time the surviving French finally reached the English position, they were exhausted.

A desperate hand-to-hand struggle followed. The French attacked fiercely with swords, while the English archers dropped their bows and resisted with axes. Soon, confusion was spreading among the French, who slowly fell back. But this retreat embroiled them with their second line which had by then been ordered forward. A wall of bodies built up, from the top of which the English slaughtered their foes in hundreds.

The carnage lasted for two hours before the third and final French line – the cavalry – hurled itself on the English. This attack caught Henry's forces unawares. For a moment, there seemed the danger of a breakthrough, and behind the English lines were several hundred French prisoners, many of high rank, not yet disarmed. Henry was forced to make a rapid and ruthless decision. While he faced the final French assault, 200 archers were ordered to kill the prisoners. But as the hapless captives were butchered, the fate of the battle was decided. Almost as soon as it reached the English archers the cavalry attack collapsed, and the French horsemen turned and fled.

Towards the French throne

The rain, the longbow and their own heavy equipment had broken France's feudal chivalry. The French had lost 7000 men, among them the finest of their nobility. Their country was left defenceless and leaderless in the face of England's ambitious 28-year-old king. In contrast, the English had lost under 100, and the only lord to fall was the Duke of York.

A one-sided struggle continued for the next four years. The French now had not only to contend with an invader. Their old insane king, Charles VI, had to watch helplessly as the two great families of Armagnac and Burgundy added civil war to his country's other miseries. Finally, in 1420, it was agreed that Henry should marry Katherine de Valois and be formally recognised as heir and regent of France. On May 21, the treaty confirming this was ceremoniously signed in the cathedral at Troyes. Henry used the seal of his great-grandfather, Edward III, for the ceremony. But he had far outshone Edward's achievements, for he had brought England to one of the highest points of success in its long history.

AGE OF ARMOUR

By the beginning of the 15th century, old-fashioned chain mail had been replaced by plate armour (above). This armour was complex and difficult to forge; its great centres were Milan in Italy and Augsburg and Nuremberg in Germany. But at Agincourt, even the new armour was found to be vulnerable to the deadly power and accuracy of the longbow. Armour, however, continued to be worn in battle until guns and gunpowder finally put an end to its usefulness in the 16th century.

A SOARING MONUMENT TO ENGLAND'S AGE OF FAITH

TOWERING PINNACLES *Henry VI expressed his piety and love of learning by building King's College Chapel, seen here from the River Cam.*

In his 50 years of disastrous rule, Henry VI left only one tangible legacy – the buildings which expressed his own qualities of Christian faith and devotion to learning. The chapels he called into being at King's College, Cambridge, and at Eton College embody the highest ideals of medieval Christendom. In them the Gothic style, which had dominated Europe for four centuries, had its last flowering.

Only the east end of Eton College Chapel was completed, and plans for an enormous nave were eventually abandoned. But the work at King's College was carried through by Henry and two of his Tudor successors to perfection. The chapel is almost 100 yds long. Its great length and astonishing height serve to emphasise the soaring aspirations of Gothic architecture. The eye is led upward to the exuberant fan-vaulting, and then towards the great east window and the high altar. The effect is undeniably beautiful, and deeply impressive.

The work of two dynasties

Henry was only 19 when he gave orders for the beginning of the work at King's College in 1440. He paid frequent visits to the site and supervised the progress of the building. The provision of adequate labour and materials for his great works at Eton and King's was probably the only matter over which he exercised royal authority. While Yorkists and Lancastrians vied for the crown, Henry was issuing letters patent for the conscription of labourers to work on these two projects.

King's College Chapel was too enormous to be finished in Henry's lifetime, but he left in his will meticulous instructions for its completion, even including methods to be used to discipline 'any mason or other labourer who shall be found unprofitable or of any such ill demeanour whereby the works shall be

A KING'S LEGACY *Henry VI is remembered best for two glorious buildings which he created at Cambridge and Eton. In this view towards the east window of King's College Chapel his ideas are carried out to perfection. The fan-vaulting is a masterpiece of the late-Gothic style.*

hindered'. Hindered they unfortunately were, owing to the disturbed times. The chapel was not completed until 90 years later, during the reign of Henry VIII. Yet, throughout these nine decades, the original inspiration was zealously preserved. King's is all of a piece, an ordered whole in a sense that is unique among medieval buildings; and it has survived the centuries unmarred – even in such details as its brilliantly coloured windows and carved ornaments.

A building of inspiring beauty

Seen from the river, the twin west towers soar heavenwards, the great west window scarcely contained between them. This is perhaps one of the best known and best loved of English views.

The inside of the vast building is even more breathtaking than its exterior. It is a marvel of spaciousness and light. The long, narrow nave and choir are incredibly high and crowned by superb fan-vaulting.

This incomparable roof is the work of two masons, John Wastell and Henry Semerk. In 1513 they were commissioned to create 'a good, sure and sufficient vault for the great church... after the best handling and form of good workmanship according to a plan'. They did their work well. The vault is an artistic and technical masterpiece.

The great roof runs the full length of the building, for the nave is separated from the choir by a carved wooden screen. This screen is a perfect match for the stonework. Its richly detailed carvings, by an unknown French or Italian craftsman, are among the finest woodwork in Europe. The repeated cyphers of AB and HR show that they were made between 1533 and 1536, when Henry VIII was married to Anne Boleyn. Apart from this woodwork and the brilliance of the glowing windows, the decoration of the church is simple. A few boldly carved designs are repeated again and again, providing an impression of confidence and cohesion.

By a startling irony the chapel, which was to express the piety of its founder, is stamped in all its details with the insignia of the more worldly Henry VIII. These dramatic carvings express the aspirations of the Royal House of Tudor – the rose and crown of their dynasty, the portcullis, the strange royal beasts and the fleur-de-lis, signifying the Tudors' claim to the throne of France.

King's College Chapel is quite as big as many Gothic cathedrals. In a sense, it is as impressively beautiful as any of them. Yet its mood is different. The clue lies in these secular carvings and the tell-tale initials of Henry VIII and the queen he married in violation of the old laws of Christendom. King's College Chapel fulfils its founder's aims as an intensely religious building; but it also evokes a later mood in which piety was allied with a new spirit of patriotism.

A VANISHED ART

The soaring windows of King's College Chapel mark the swan song of an ancient craft.

Depicting biblical stories in coloured glass was a medieval way of teaching Christian stories to the illiterate. To the minds of simple people they seemed to have a magic power – for the passing clouds and the movement of the sun across the sky made the stiff figures of saints pulse with apparent life and movement.

All over England, religious buildings, from great abbeys and cathedrals to remote parish churches, were enriched with these testimonies of faith. But stained-glass windows were to prove the most vulnerable of all the creations of the Middle Ages. When England became Protestant, mobs stormed the churches smashing 'graven images', which they believed had no place there. Within a few years much of the work of five centuries of glass-making was destroyed.

By good fortune, King's College Chapel escaped unscathed. The multi-coloured windows have survived unharmed to this day, the most impressive survival of stained glass in Britain, and a brilliant testimony to a vanished art.

TELLING A STORY *Unlettered peasants learnt their Bible from the pictures in stained-glass windows.*

A KING'S AMBITION

Henry VI's idea when he founded Eton College in 1440 and King's College, Cambridge, the same year was that the scholars of Eton should be transferred to King's 'when sufficiently imbued with the rudiments of grammar'.

Seen from the Thames or across the playing fields, Eton College Chapel soars as imposingly as King's. If Henry had had his way it would have been only the choir of an immense church. But his ambitious plans languished after he was deposed and eventually murdered.

The wall-paintings in the chapel were the work of two English artists, William Baker and a man called Gilbert, and were finished by 1488. They were whitewashed over by the college barber in 1560, rediscovered in 1847 and covered again by Victorian Gothic stalls. Workmen destroyed the upper row in the process. Only in 1923 were the paintings finally revealed and, after expert restoration, they can be seen for what they are – the finest 15th-century murals in Britain.

HIDDEN ART *The Eton murals are visible in all their splendour after being lost for centuries.*

ETON THROUGH THE EYES OF AN ARTIST *The 18th-century Italian artist Canaletto found inspiration in the English scene. He painted this view of Eton College Chapel from across the River Thames.*

Two families fight for the throne in 30 years of war

SYMBOL OF CIVIL WAR

This helmet, now to be seen in the Victoria and Albert Museum, once protected the head of an English infantryman on the bloody battlefields of the Wars of the Roses. In that turbulent age, thousands of common soldiers perished as kings and mighty barons fought for power in a struggle that was to last for 30 years.

THE FATEFUL CHOICE *In a 19th-century illustration from Shakespeare's* Henry VI, *English nobles choose sides by plucking white and red roses – the badges of York and Lancaster.*

For 30 years, from the middle of the 15th century, England was torn by a vicious and violent struggle between rival claimants to the throne. The source of this conflict lay in the deep bitterness of dynastic rivalry. From the sons of Edward III had sprung two great families, the houses of York and Lancaster. Each family believed that it had a legitimate claim to the throne. Each found support among the barons and nobles of the nation, who were greedy for wealth and power.

But open conflict did not break out until the 1450's. By that time, the once profitable Hundred Years' War with France had ended in defeat and disaster and the English economy lay stagnant. The incomes of the barons fell, while their appetite for extravagant display never ceased to increase. And, where once strong kings had dominated their subjects, the weak and feeble-minded Henry VI was a figure no man could fear. This pathetic member of the House of Lancaster seemed an easy prey to greedy Yorkist eyes. His crown and his royal gold glinted in invitation to his enemies. But there were few battles in these years of civil

GREAT PEER, GREAT QUEEN *Two of the chief figures of the wars – the Earl of Warwick (left) and Henry's queen, Margaret of Anjou.*

strife – scarcely half a dozen in three decades. The clash came far above the heads of ordinary people, in the palaces of southern England and the grim castles of the north and west.

There, dominating men and women pitted themselves against their rivals in contests of willpower and ingenuity. There was the Earl of Suffolk, Henry VI's grasping and corrupt minister, and the most influential man in the court. His impeachment and murder in 1450

removed a strong minister, and thus was a decisive step on the road to open conflict. There was Margaret of Anjou, Henry's hated French queen, who led her troops into battle herself, and whose resourcefulness and determination almost saved her husband's throne. Above them all towered the figure of Richard Neville, Earl of Warwick, known as 'the Kingmaker'. Warwick was the subtlest as well as the most unscrupulous politician of 15th-century England. For 20 years the mightiest supporter of the Yorkist cause, he was to change sides dramatically in a desperate bid to preserve his personal power.

York and Lancaster

Until the 1450's, the energies of England's great families had been spent in the French wars. But when the Hundred Years' War ended in final defeat, the nobles transferred their ambitions, passions and quarrels from the soil of France to that of England itself. The seeds of the conflict that was to set father against son for 30 years were sown in Parliament. There, in 1450, was voiced the demand that Richard, Duke of York, wealthiest man in England after his cousin the king, and a champion of reform, should be recognised as heir to the throne. When three years later Henry VI suffered his first attack of insanity, his subjects rejoiced as Richard succeeded in making himself regent. But he did so in the face of relentless opposition from the queen, and her friends among the corrupt ministers of the court. As soon as the king recovered his sanity, she released her supporters from prison and banished York from the court.

Richard turned to force. But the first Battle of St Albans in May 1455 was inconclusive. It was not until the war of 1459–61 that intrigue gave way to open conflict. In two decisive battles, at Wakefield and St Albans, the Yorkists were defeated and Richard of York was himself numbered among the dead. Margaret of Anjou had his head crowned with a paper crown, and then had it placed above the gates of York to mark her triumph.

This was the queen's victory, and it was the queen who threw it away. Her own arrogance lost her whatever support she had once enjoyed. Moreover, Richard's son, Edward,

BLOODY DEFEAT *At Tewkesbury in 1471, the Yorkists (left) crush their Lancastrian enemies. A scene from a contemporary manuscript.*

BATTLE *During the years of civil war, battles were few in number.*

SCOTLAND

* Lancastrian victory
* Yorkist victory

Hexham 1464

ENGLAND

Towton 1461

Wakefield 1460

Blore Heath 1459

Bosworth 1485

WALES

Ludford 1459

Mortimers Cross 1461

Edgcote 1469

Northampton 1460

Tewkesbury 1471

St. Albans 1455 1461

Barnet 1471

0   50   100 miles

took up his father's cause. The Lancastrians met defeat in their turn, and when Edward seated himself upon the throne in Westminster Hall on March 4, 1461, there were few who regretted the passing of the red rose of Lancaster. The old king, Henry VI, remained at large, a wandering fugitive with a small band of attendants, for a few years longer. But his cause was irrevocably lost. Even the mighty Earl of Warwick could not remake a king whom he had once unmade, and his attempt at Barnet (1471) to do so led to his own death. But the campaign was not over.

The final reckoning

Lancastrian hopes now rested not on Henry, but on his redoubtable queen and her young son, the 17-year-old Prince Edward, who both landed at Weymouth from France on the day of Warwick's defeat.

Undeterred by the news of Barnet, the queen at once started recruiting a new army, and soon was on the march towards Gloucester, where she planned to cross the River Severn to join forces with the Welsh levies of Jasper Tudor, Earl of Pembroke. But Gloucester held out for the Yorkist cause, and Edward IV hurried to its relief. Margaret now decided to cross the river to meet her allies at Tewkesbury, where Edward's pursuing army caught up and attacked her.

The clash between the two armies was for a time indecisive, but in the end the Lancastrians suffered a crushing defeat, largely through the inactivity of one of their leaders, Lord Wenlock. He failed to order his troops forward to support the forces of the Duke of Somerset. Wenlock had already changed sides twice in the course of the wars, and might well have been planning to do so again. But he did not live to receive the rewards of his treachery, for Somerset himself beat out Lord Wenlock's brains with a battle-axe. All was now lost, and the panic-stricken Lancastrian soldiers began to throw down their arms. Many were slaughtered trying to cross the river.

The Yorkists offered no quarter – not even to the highest. For Prince Edward, too, met his end at Tewkesbury. According to some accounts, he perished on the battlefield, crying in vain for mercy to his treacherous brother-in-law, Clarence. But more probably, he was betrayed to the Yorkists by his hosts in a house where he had taken refuge. His death, and the murder of his father in the Tower of London three weeks later, seemed to end Lancastrian hopes of ruling England.

But this was not to be the end of the story. In 1485, the seemingly triumphant Yorkists were challenged by the last of the Lancastrian line, the young Prince Henry Tudor. And with the death of Richard III, the last of the Plantagenets, on Bosworth Field, there came to the throne a new dynasty which was to reunite a divided land and lead it back to greatness – the House of Tudor.

Henry VI: His kingdom was 'not of this world'

'The king is but a natural fool, and no man to be ruling this land.' From the lips of a farm labourer, John Merfield, in the marketplace of Brightling in Sussex one summer afternoon in 1450, came this condemnation of his royal master, Henry VI. Merfield paid a heavy price for his indiscretion, for he was found guilty of high treason and put to death. But future events were to show how much truth there was in his words. Early in the autumn of 1453, the 32-year-old Henry suffered the first attack of the insanity which was to dog the rest of his life. The first fit lasted only 16 months. But it dramatically confirmed a fact which had been long suspected by the king's councillors – that he was incapable of controlling the government of his kingdom.

A man set apart from his age

The truth was that Henry had never behaved as a king was expected to do. 'His sole delight was to immerse himself day and night in the law of God,' recorded his chaplain. Henry's councillors constantly complained of the long hours he passed in prayer, when pressing matters of state required his attention.

Henry's childlike simplicity had its attractive side. But his reign was disastrous. He wanted his nobles to live in peace with one another, but he did not command them to do so on his authority as their king. He preached feebly at them, and then resigned himself to events.

Even his Tudor descendants never suggested that Henry was an impressive monarch. But they claimed that miracles had occurred at his tomb, and tried to have him canonised as a saint. Certainly his kingdom was 'not of this world'.

SAINTLY KING *Henry VI was no man to control England's turbulent nobility. He helplessly watched his country slide into the civil war that was to cost him his throne.*

Caxton's vision brings Britain into a new age

PRESENTED AT COURT *A contemporary manuscript shows Edward IV receiving* Dictes and Sayenges of the Phylosophers *from his brother-in-law, Earl Rivers, who translated it into English from the French. Caxton printed the book on his press at Westminster.*

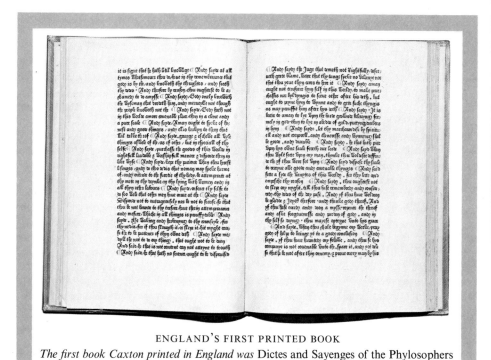

ENGLAND'S FIRST PRINTED BOOK
The first book Caxton printed in England was Dictes and Sayenges of the Phylosophers *in 1477. It is now in the British Museum. Caxton was originally driven to learn printing by the time-consuming tedium of copying out translations in longhand.*

The book which Edward IV accepted from a kneeling courtier, in a simple ceremony in November 1477, was a milestone in British history. The king's brother-in-law, Anthony Woodville, Earl Rivers, presented him with a copy of *Dictes and Sayenges of the Phylosophers*, which the earl had himself translated from the original French. What made the occasion so special was not the book's contents, but that it was the first book to be printed in England.

A man of vision
The man who brought this revolutionary invention to England was William Caxton, a rich wool merchant. Caxton had become a printer almost by accident. In 1469 he started to translate a French history of Troy, but found copying in longhand so tedious that his 'pen became worn, his hand weary, his eye dimmed'. With typical energy and determination, he decided, at the age of 48, to learn the newly developed craft of printing.

Before this time, books had been produced by hand. Specially trained scribes laboured for months and sometimes years to make beautiful illuminated manuscripts. Most of these dedicated men worked in monasteries, so the works they produced were largely concerned with religion – lives of the saints and

works of devotion. Almost all such books were written in Latin.

But this process was not only long and arduous – it was also extremely expensive. Only the fortunate few could afford the luxury of a library. Books were so valuable, and so few in number, that even in the universities they were kept chained to the shelves.

A German, Johann Gutenberg, had set up the first printing press in Europe in the city of Mainz in about 1440, and by the time Caxton decided to learn printing most of the larger German cities had their own presses. It was to Cologne that Caxton went to learn his craft between 1470 and 1472.

Being a rich man, Caxton could afford to establish his own press at Bruges in 1474. A year later, he published his first book, *The Recuyell of the Historyes of Troye* – the one which he had found so difficult to copy a few years before. This was followed by another translation, *The Game and Playe of the Chesse*, which appeared in 1476.

Caxton now resolved to give up the wool trade and devote himself to full-time printing, writing and publishing. Towards the end of 1476, he returned to England and set up his press in a building near Westminster Abbey. Since he was both a shrewd businessman and a conscientious scholar, Caxton had a double

reason for going into business – to make money and to spread knowledge.

The book presented to the king was only the first of nearly 100 titles he printed at Westminster between 1476 and his death in 1491. Caxton catered for all tastes. His customers were aristocrats, clergymen, students, middle-class landowners and merchants. Books on chivalry and romance, manners and morality, history, philosophy and religion, were all available for a few pence. Among them was an encyclopedia, *The Myrrour of the World*, the first illustrated book to be printed in England. Maintaining a high standard of accuracy and clarity, Caxton also printed nearly all existing English literature, including the first great English poem, Chaucer's *Canterbury Tales*, and Sir Thomas Malory's *Morte d'Arthur*, the story of Arthur and the legendary quest for the Holy Grail. He also published many more translations from abroad. These included great works from the past, such as those of the Roman author Cicero, and Aesop's fables.

One language for the nation
One of Caxton's main problems was to decide how to establish a standard form of English which he could use in his books. He had no dictionaries to guide him. Latin was still the language of the educated. There were as many dialects spoken as there were regions of England. Caxton wrote of the difficulties he faced in his preface to a translation of Virgil's *Aeneid*: 'Certayn marchauntes were in a shippe in Tamyse and for lacke of wynde thei taryed

This model of Caxton's first hand-press was made in 1812. It is now in the Science Museum. From Caxton's press grew the printing industry of today.

atte Forlond (the North Foreland in Kent) and wente to lande for to refreshe them; And one of theym . . . cam in-to an hows and axed for mete; and specyally he axyed after eggys; and the goode wyf answerde that she coude speke no Frenshe . . . And theene at laste another sayd that he wolde haue "eyren" then the goode wyf sayd that she vnderstod hym wel. Loo, what sholde a man in thyse dayes now wryte, "egges" or "eyren"?'

Caxton chose to use the English of the court and capital. And in a century, largely due to his efforts, this became the accepted written word of England.

Caxton established a long-standing link with the Church because ecclesiastics were the most literate section of the community, and therefore potential buyers of books. One of Caxton's earliest pieces of work was a poster advertising the *Sarum Ordinale*, a church service handbook.

Not merely a printer, Caxton continued to pursue his own scholarly work with great vigour. In 1481 he began the massive task of translating and modernising an earlier Latin version of a work called *The Polychronicon*, completing it in the astonishing time of 18 months with 800 pages of about 400 words each, with a final supplementary section. In all, it consisted of 340,000 words.

Like so many inventions, printing came into being because it was needed. By the mid-15th century, books were in such demand that their production could no longer be left to monks and scholars laboriously copying manuscripts in longhand. And the invention spread with surprising speed – from the Rhine Valley to every European country, including Russia, by the end of the century. By 1500, more than 1700 presses had produced more than 40,000 editions.

When Caxton died towards the end of 1491, his printing business was continued by Wynkyn

de Worde, his manager and foreman. De Worde remained at Westminster for a few years. Then, he moved to St Bride's, Fleet Street, where there were good business prospects among the many ecclesiastics who had settled between St Paul's and Temple Bar.

If Caxton's emphasis was on quality, de Worde's was on quantity: not without good reason is he known as 'the father of Fleet Street'. Unlike Caxton, de Worde was solely dependent on printing for his livelihood, and books came thick and fast from his press.

By the time he died in 1535, de Worde had printed 800 items, almost half of them for use in grammar schools.

Power of the press

Some of the printing practices of the day were irresponsible. Inaccuracy was common, and often deliberate. One picture block might be made to serve several purposes, appearing over several captions and illustrating different subjects, even being printed several times in one book.

In the Middle Ages the printed word made possible the religious pamphlets of the Reformation, and provided the materials for the wide-ranging scholarship of the Renaissance. The medieval court which witnessed the presentation of Caxton's book could not know of the occasion's far-reaching consequences for Britain. The invention of printing was as shattering in its impact on the medieval world as the invention of gunpowder. Printing brought new ideas flooding into the long-isolated kingdom in an explosion of knowledge seldom paralleled in human history. It was to remove scholarship from the restraining hands of the monks, and assist in the liberation of mankind. In that process of liberation, Caxton's successors in London, Oxford and Cambridge played a significant part.

Edward IV: A youth wins the throne for York

In a snowstorm on Easter Sunday 1461, Edward, Duke of York, defeated Henry VI at Towton. Three months later he was crowned king. He was just 19 years old.

Edward was well equipped to meet the challenge of bringing order to a country which for six years had been torn by civil war. He was nearly 6 ft tall, and his striking good looks gave him the physical presence of a king. And he also possessed administrative skill. From the start, Edward declared his intention of reforming the royal finances so that he could avoid raising unpopular taxes. He reorganised the government, repressed disorder and supported English merchants overseas.

Yet within eight years of his coronation, Edward was a fugitive. Supremely confident in his own ability, he had tried to manage without the support of his most powerful subject, his uncle, the Earl of Warwick, known as 'the Kingmaker'. In 1469, Warwick allied himself with the exiled Henry VI, and forced his nephew to flee the kingdom.

But a year later Edward returned. Two brilliant victories at Barnet and Tewkesbury in 1471 shattered the Lancastrian armies. Warwick himself was killed and the luckless Henry put to death in the Tower. Edward was now free to complete his reforms.

In his later years, Edward's nature was coarsened by the wars and the betrayals he had experienced. Nevertheless, when he died of a fever in 1483, he had earned a place among England's notable statesmen and soldier kings. His great misfortune was that he died before his sons were old enough to rule the country in his place.

ROYAL REFORMER *Edward IV established the House of York on the throne by deposing his Lancastrian rival, Henry VI. His aim was to end the disorder brought by civil war.*

'Treason! Treason!'–Richard falls fighting at Bosworth

WHERE A ROYAL DYNASTY FELL
Nearly five centuries ago, Bosworth Field, outside Market Bosworth in Leicestershire, rang with the clash of steel as two English armies battled for the throne. Fighting bravely after being betrayed by his allies, the last Plantagenet, Richard III, perished. By the end of the day a new dynasty, the House of Tudor, had won the throne. Its monarchs were to unite their divided realm and lead it to greatness over the next century.

On the green fields outside the village of Market Bosworth, some 10 miles from Leicester, two armies clashed on an August day in 1485. The battle was to close an epoch in English history and bring to power the brilliant Tudor dynasty.

The dawn of August 22, 1485, found the 10,000-strong army of Richard III camped in a strong position on the summit of Ambien Hill. The bulk of Richard's forces occupied the centre and took their commands from the king himself. In front of them stood a large body of archers under the Duke of Norfolk, and behind them the private army of Henry Percy, Earl of Northumberland.

Plotting by the leaders

This imposing array, it seemed, could scarcely fail to vanquish Henry Tudor's army, gathered on the plain below. Was not Henry's hurriedly collected force only half the size of Richard's? Was not the king one of the boldest and most skilled commanders of the day?

But treason was in the air. Invasion had been threatening ever since Richard had ascended his brother's throne. When Henry Tudor landed at Milford Haven on August 7, the army at his back was scarcely 2000 strong, and the majority of his troops were convicted French felons, persuaded to enlist by the bribe of a free pardon. Only two English noblemen – Henry's uncle, Jasper Tudor, and the Earl of Oxford – rallied to the rebel cause.

For months, however, Henry's agents had been sounding out possible sympathisers and re-awakening the ashes of Lancastrian loyalty. Rhys ap Thomas, the Welsh leader who had sworn to Richard that the usurper would only reach England over his dead body, had already gone over to Henry, taking with him the recruits he had raised for the Yorkist cause. Richard was now tormented by one question: how far could his nobles be trusted?

This especially applied to the third army on the field that August morning. It was the 3000-strong host of Lord Stanley and his brother, Sir William. Lord Stanley was the steward of Richard's household, and a great man in his native Lancashire.

When Henry Tudor landed in Wales to claim the throne, Stanley had been absent

MEN OF VALOUR *Yorkists and Lancastrians clash in the Wars of the Roses. These bloody years saw the emergence of men of determined courage and ruthless ability. Such a man was Richard III (right), who, through his loyalty and generalship, helped his brother, Edward, to the throne. But Richard's reputation was blasted by his seizure of the crown after Edward's death in 1483 and the death of the princes in the Tower. King for only two years, he perished as he had lived, in violence at Bosworth Field in 1485.*

THE MYSTERY OF THE PRINCES IN THE TOWER

Of all the black deeds that have stained the name of the Tower of London, none is more infamous than the murder of Edward IV's young children in 1483. The elder boy, the 12-year-old Edward, was brought to the Tower in May, while he was still king. In June his 10-year-old brother, Richard, was taken from sanctuary in Westminster Abbey and carried off to join him. Gradually, the princes' lives became shrouded in secrecy. For some weeks inquisitive visitors to the Tower caught glimpses of the brothers as they played together in the garden. But by the end of the summer they had been confined in an inner room. Only the occasional fleeting appearance of a boyish face at a barred window confirmed that they were still alive. A doctor who attended them reported that they lived in constant fear. Then silence fell.

By the autumn the news leaked out that the princes were dead. Contemporary chroniclers hinted that the boys may have been murdered, though without suggesting who was responsible. But in 1485, Henry VII formally accused Richard of 'shedding infants' blood', and Tudor historians tried to substantiate this charge, aiming to strengthen the new dynasty. Sir Thomas More claimed that Sir James Tyrell, an ambitious crony of Richard's, had later confessed to having arranged for the princes to be suffocated on Richard's orders, and this is the story that has passed into legend – and Shakespeare.

Henry VII had as good a reason as Richard to eliminate all rivals to the throne; but the princes died in the autumn of 1483, while Henry was in exile on the Continent and far from ready to make his bid for power. So suspicion points inexorably at Richard; yet decisive evidence of his guilt has never been found. The most perplexing mystery in the history of England remains unsolved to this day.

A Victorian picture of Edward IV's sons in the Tower. Richard III's reputation has never recovered from the charge that he murdered them.

Richard III: The reign of the last Plantagenet

No king in English history has been the source of more mystery and controversy than Richard III. For many, Richard will always be the hunchbacked 'wicked uncle' of legend, who had his two nephews murdered in his greedy quest for the throne.

But for others, Richard is the most defamed man in history – an energetic and inventive politician, whose evil reputation was foisted on him by his Tudor successor, Henry VII, to justify his own seizure of the throne.

Sir Thomas More, who wrote a hostile biography of Richard 30 years after the king's death, claimed that he was a sinister figure from the moment of his birth. He wrote that Richard had been born 'feet forward, also not untoothed'. And from More, too, stemmed the description of Richard that was later made famous by Shakespeare – 'little of stature, ill-featured of limbs, crookbacked, his left shoulder higher than his right, hard-favoured of visage'. But though Richard was sickly and undersized as a child, and a sad contrast to his tall and handsome brothers, there is no evidence that he was the misshapen figure depicted by More.

Survival in a turbulent age

As a boy, Richard was well schooled in the sudden shifts of fortune that his turbulent century heaped upon the noble and powerful. Before he was ten, he had been a Lancastrian prisoner, had lost his father in battle and been a fugitive in Flanders with his mother. Finally, in March 1461 he saw the triumph of his family, when his brother Edward became king.

While Edward IV was on the throne, Richard's future was assured. The king showered lands and titles on his young brother and, from the age of 17, Richard was at Edward's side in every crisis. He shared the Yorkist command at the victories of Barnet and Tewkesbury. Then, at the age of only 18, he was sent to subdue the northern borderlands, and brought them under firm control.

Richard's greatest concern was that England should have a strong and orderly government. And when Edward IV died in April 1483, leaving the crown to his 12-year-old son, Richard feared a new civil war, with powerful noblemen vying for control of the realm through the boy king. His response was to seize the throne himself, ruthlessly crushing all resistance, and imprisoning little Edward and his 10-year-old brother Richard in the Tower. There, before the end of the year, the boys perished.

But Richard's crown was not secure, and he survived his nephews by only two years. On Bosworth Field his reign ended, as it had begun, with violence. Two days later Richard's body was flung into an unmarked grave.

---

from court. Richard's first act was to summon him to help repel the invaders. But Stanley wavered, opening secret negotiations with both sides. Richard's reaction was to arrest Stanley's eldest son, Lord Strange, and hold him hostage. But as the king surveyed his troops on the eve of the battle, he could only gaze anxiously at Stanley's camp and wonder on which side those 3000 retainers would fight.

The trumpets of the Tudor army sounded while Richard was still making his final plans for the battle. A large body of rebels advanced rapidly on the royal archers under Norfolk. After several minutes of savage fighting, Norfolk's line showed signs of breaking and the king, who had watched the engagement from the top of Ambien Hill, sent in a small force of reserves. The rebels fell back, but in the confusion Norfolk was reported slain. Disorder spread through the royal ranks and the king's commanders looked anxiously to their master for further reinforcements.

Richard sent a messenger ordering Stanley to join him. Stanley refused; he had decided not to intervene until he could see which side was winning. The king angrily ordered the execution of Stanley's son, but then realised that this would resolve any doubts in Stanley's mind and instantly countermanded the order.

Richard then called on Northumberland, whose forces were massed immediately behind him. The true weakness of the king's position suddenly became clear as Northumberland's reply was read out by a messenger. The earl would stay where he was until he saw what Stanley had decided.

The last charge

In desperation, Richard gathered his own personal retainers and men-at-arms together and pointed out the lonely figure of Henry Tudor at the other side of the battlefield. They would charge across the field in front of the massed immobile forces of the Stanleys and snatch a spectacular victory from the very hands of the usurping prince.

The royal cavalcade galloped swiftly across Sir William Stanley's front. Now Sir William saw that his moment had come. He entered the battle on Henry Tudor's side, and as the royal force reached the Welsh prince's personal guard, it found itself trapped by a grim alliance of the king's rival and his treacherous friends. Defeat was inevitable.

Fighting with a savage bravery to which even his enemies paid tribute, Richard fell within a few yards of his adversary, his body scarred by wounds. His last shouts were: 'Treason! Treason! Treason!'

Sir William Stanley dismounted and plucked the crown from the dead king's head to place it on that of Henry Tudor. As for Richard, his naked body was thrown over a horse and carried from the field.

The dawn of an age of adventure

After long years of civil war, England unites as a new dynasty – the brilliant House of Tudor – leads the way to future glory

In 1485, when the Tudor dynasty came to power, England was divided and bankrupt after 30 years of civil war. The country counted for little on the Continent, whether in diplomacy, commerce or war. But the spirit which had once won the English an empire in France was not dead. In just over a century, the brilliant Tudors directed it into new fields to revitalise their kingdom and make it the envy of the world.

The transformation of medieval anarchy into efficient government was no easy task. It owed much to the fact that three of the five Tudor monarchs were rulers of extraordinary ability, and much also to their continuing good luck. Their abilities showed themselves in their astute choice of servants and policies; their luck in the fact that they lived to an advanced age and left obvious heirs to succeed them.

Yet, when the first Tudor, Henry VII, fought his way to the throne at Bosworth Field, few Englishmen realised that an age of civil war, royal incompetence and bankruptcy was over. They saw no reason why another powerful baron should not seize the throne by force, just as Henry and others before him had done. But Henry soon proved to be one of England's most astute rulers. He quickly made his position at home unchallengeable.

Propaganda was the key to Henry's success. In order to be strong, the Tudors had to appear strong. Magnificent displays of wealth and power (pp. 114–15) were more than a way of life. They were instruments of state. So long as Englishmen thought that their king could defeat any rebellion, they were unlikely to join one. Henry VII at once grasped this point. And he easily disposed of the last Yorkist claimants to the throne – two impostors called Lambert Simnel and Perkin Warbeck.

Henry was active in other fields as well. He made a profitable trade agreement with Spain and by such encouragement of trade, and his patronage of explorers such as Cabot (pp. 116–17), he opened up a new chapter in England's history. The new wealth and the new spirit of confidence and

THE TUDORS AND THE WORLD

Hans Holbein, court painter to Henry VIII, depicted two emissaries sent from France to his master's court in his painting 'The Ambassadors'. They are surrounded by objects symbolising the 'new learning' of the Renaissance – including an astrolabe, a hymn book by Martin Luther, and a globe marked with the latest voyages of discovery. Under the Tudors, England ended its long isolation from the Continent. The inquiring spirit of the Renaissance, with its self-confident belief in the ability of man to achieve all his aims, soon established itself. The impact of such men as Holbein and his friend the Dutch scholar Erasmus, who also visited Britain, inspired a culture which became the envy of the world under Henry VIII and his daughter, Elizabeth.

111

END OF AN ERA *By Tudor times, the monasteries, once the powerhouses of the Christian faith, had fallen into decay. Members of religious orders were criticised for their corruption – as in this picture of a monk drinking.*

RELIGIOUS EXILES *The followers of the new Protestant religion found themselves persecuted when Henry VIII's daughter, the Catholic Mary, came to the throne. Many – like the Duchess of Suffolk and her family (above) – were forced to flee into exile.*

HARD TIMES *A woodcut from* The Sorrowful Lamentation of the Pedlars, *published in the mid-16th century, bemoans the harshness of the times and the decay of trade. When Elizabeth came to the throne, thousands of labourers had been forced off the land by enclosures which were turning cultivated fields into pastures for sheep. A new Poor Law brought help to the ill and aged, but poverty was seen as a vice. The thousands of 'sturdy beggars' roaming the land were harshly treated. A persistent beggar could be sentenced to be whipped 'until his or her body be bloody', and the law even laid down that such offenders could be put to death.*

peace produced a new style of architecture. The rich could build for comfort, instead of for protection. The domestic intimacy of the house built by the Comptons at Compton Wynyates (pp. 118–19) was a striking contrast to the grimly turreted castles of medieval England.

Henry VII's son and heir lacked only one of his father's qualities – the habit of careful economy. But he had no need of it, for his father's wisdom had provided him with an enormous personal fortune and a realm blessed by ever-increasing prosperity. Henry VIII believed in display as a mark of power, and this was amply shown at the Field of the Cloth of Gold in 1520 (pp. 120–1). There, Henry met Francis I of France and their meeting was formal recognition that England had won back her status as a great power.

A tyrant king and his ministers

But to begin with, Henry left the hard business of policy-making to his astutely chosen ministers. Cardinal Thomas Wolsey, the first of these, was a supremely skilled politician, who enjoyed almost absolute power. His vanity, however, was to bring about his fall (pp. 124–5). It showed itself in the building of Hampton Court (pp. 122–3), a residence which threatened to outshine even the king's own palace.

Wolsey's successor, Thomas Cromwell, was if anything even more efficient. And his tasks were even more complex and demanding. First, he had to free Henry from his first wife, Catharine of Aragon, to enable him to marry Anne Boleyn (pp. 126–7). To achieve his master's 'Great Matter', Cromwell let nothing stand in his path. When all else failed, he broke his country's links with the Roman Catholic Church, an enterprise which abruptly altered the whole course of English history. In men such as the saintly Sir Thomas More (pp. 128–9), the English Reformation claimed some of the nation's finest figures as its victims. It overturned institutions as long established as the monasteries (pp. 130–1), and it rode roughshod over the popular indignation expressed by the rebels of the Pilgrimage of Grace.

Even Cromwell was not immune from the revolutionary power he had unleashed. In 1540 he fell foul of Henry and perished on the block. For, in the dark years of Henry's last decade, no one was safe. The men and women who lived through these years of tyranny were painted for posterity by the first great artist to work in England, Hans Holbein (pp. 132–3).

Golden age for England

Henry's tyranny, his six marriages and the Reformation itself stemmed from one over-riding concern. He feared that the Tudor achievement would crumble without a male heir. During the short reign of his sickly son, Edward VI, these premonitions were to be fulfilled. The kingdom was dominated by nobles who attempted to exploit the tensions caused by religious upheaval. Edward encouraged extreme Protestantism, but his sister, Mary, the next in line to the throne, was a devout Catholic. So, when Edward died, the ambitious Duke of Northumberland tried to place Lady Jane Grey on the throne. Her tragic rule was to last only nine days (pp. 134–5).

Though Mary came to the throne with popular support, she soon lost the love of her people. Try as she might, Protestantism had put down roots too firm to be stamped out. Mary found that she could not restore the monasteries, as their lands were now divided among thousands of small landowners. Her persecutions and burnings, especially of the Oxford Martyrs – Latimer, Ridley and Cranmer – only added to the national mood of discontent (pp. 136–7). Latimer proved to be a better prophet of the future than the bigoted queen, when he shouted from amidst the flames: 'We shall this day light such a candle . . . in England as I trust shall never be put out.' When Mary died childless in November 1558, she left behind a nation united in hatred of her and her principles.

Had Mary produced an heir, popular revulsion against Tudor rule might have led to the downfall of the dynasty. But her sister, Elizabeth, was quick to establish her popularity. Her coronation in 1559 (pp. 138–9) was a magnificent curtain-raiser to the achievements that were to follow. Elizabeth had all the dictatorial instincts of her family, but she also had qualities which none of them had enjoyed. She was subtle when they were brutal. Above all, she understood her people as no other Tudor had done. She knew that they must be guided and cajoled, not bullied and coerced. For four decades, the magic of Elizabeth's personality stamped every feature of English life. The men and women who played their part in this dazzling period of English history were given immortality in the tiny jewel-like portraits of Nicholas Hilliard (pp. 140–1).

But Elizabeth, too, faced many grave problems. And none was more intractable than that posed by her Catholic cousin, Mary, Queen of Scots. Having lost her throne after the murder of her husband, Darnley (pp. 142–3), Mary fled as an unwelcome exile to England. There, she was the focus of every conspiracy against Elizabeth's rule. For 19 years, Mary was kept in prison. Finally, Elizabeth was forced to have her executed (pp. 144–5).

'The lords and masters of the sea'

Elizabethan England, however, had a self-confidence that could afford to ignore the stresses of politics. On the oceans, a hardy breed of sea-faring adventurers pushed the frontiers of exploration outwards. Their pioneering voyages were crowned by Drake's circumnavigation of the world (pp. 146–7). 'The sea is full of English ships,' a Spanish official complained, 'for the English have become the lords and masters of the sea and care for no man else.' At home, this spirit of confidence and wealth found expression in houses of unparalleled flamboyance, such as Longleat (pp. 148–9).

When the crisis of Elizabeth's reign came in the 1580's, this self-confidence stood England in good stead. The simmering rivalry with Spain broke into open war in 1585. Three years of preparation by the Spanish culminated in the launching of the mighty Armada in 1588 to invade Britain. But, in one of the most remarkable victories in English history, the Spanish fleet was scattered by the genius of Elizabeth's sea-dogs (pp. 150–3).

This was the glorious climax of the Elizabethan age. It was the achievement not only of England's famous captains but of the common soldiers and sailors who shouted their love for the Virgin Queen at her great review at Tilbury. 'God send me such a company again, if need is,' the commander of the fleet, Lord Howard of Effingham, remarked. In the world of poetry and drama this feeling of confidence was matched by William Shakespeare (pp. 154–5), who gave his country and the world plays without rival.

The last years of Elizabeth's reign were clouded by personal and political troubles. She had long outlived the friends and councillors of her youth, and now she became infatuated with a young favourite, the Earl of Essex. But in 1601 he raised a revolt against her and she had no choice but to order his execution (pp. 156–7). For two more years she lived on – a monument to an age that had passed beyond recall. In Parliament, new voices were being raised, making demands with which she had little sympathy. Yet she never lost her hold on the hearts of her people. 'This I count above all,' she told the House of Commons, 'that I have reigned with your loves.' And in her achievements she had amply fulfilled the hopes with which her illustrious grandfather, Henry VII, had come to the throne 118 years earlier.

HIGH LIFE *Hunting in the royal park at Nonesuch, Surrey. The rich suffered little from the economic depression of the time.*

A HOPELESS CAUSE *Such was the patriotism of Elizabeth's England that appeals by Jesuit priests such as Edmund Campion (left) to overthrow the heretic queen met with little success. Campion went to the stake at Tyburn in 1581.*

FROM AMERICA *The merchant-venturers of Elizabethan England brought many strange things back to their homeland. Among them was the potato plant, which, according to tradition, was discovered by Sir Walter Raleigh in Virginia in the 1580's.*

NEW LEARNING *Pupils under instruction, in a contemporary woodcut. Tudor England saw a vast expansion in education. Edward VI encouraged the foundation of grammar schools, and under Elizabeth, his sister, Rugby and Harrow were established. But teaching was still centred on the classics, and modern languages and history were not studied.*

THE PEACOCK AGE

Life in Tudor England was governed by a rigid social system, which was held to follow God's divine laws. As there was a hierarchy in Heaven, from the Almighty down through the Seraphim and Cherubim to the lesser angels, so there was an order of authority and status on earth, from kings and queens through the social scales of gentleman, merchant and burgess to yeoman and lastly 'artificer and labourer'. Sir Thomas Elyot, author of a book on etiquette, warned that 'where order lacketh, there all thing is odious and uncomely'.

At the nerve centre of the political and artistic life of the nation lay the magnificence of the court. Henry VIII and Elizabeth were at pains to establish an impression of God-like monarchy. The court, with its pomp, ceremony and ostentation, became the centre of power and prestige, the lode-star for every artist, musician or actor hungry for fame. The landed gentry sent their children to court to acquire finesse.

The degrees of society were mirrored by its clothes. 'As for their outward show,' said Sir Thomas Smith, a prominent politician, 'a gentleman...must go like a gentleman, a yeoman like a yeoman, and a rascal like a rascal.' Fashions in clothes changed rapidly and only the very wealthy could afford to follow them. A damask gown could cost £81, and brocade was 10s 8d a yard, while a clergyman's salary might be less than £10 a year.

More than any other individual, Elizabeth herself summed up in her person the spirit of the age. Moving in splendour from one royal residence to another, her extravagant white gowns attesting to the virginity that had become a symbol of her power, she was supremely aware of her position as head of Church and state – God's chosen deputy on earth.

MAN OF FASHION *Tudor etiquette stipulated that people had to dress according to their station in life. There were complaints that 'players and cutpurses' dressed like gentlemen. Here Richard Sackville, Earl of Dorset, wears the padded doublet, embroidered breeches, high, starched ruff and extravagant silk hose that were fashionable at court. Men's clothes often outshone women's.*

FAMILY MEALS *Tudor children were dressed as miniature adults, in the elaborate brocades and starched ruffs of their parents. They were brought up with strict discipline to assume their destined place in society. In this painting, Lord Cobham's family sit at table, eating dessert, with the family pets, a parrot and a monkey. Elizabethan dessert generally consisted of fruit – here apples, pears and grapes – nuts and wine.*

TUDOR BEAUTY *Eliza-beth Vernon comb-ing her hair, in a sumptuously em-broidered court dress. Elizabe-than fashions became so ex-travagant and changed so rapidly that the writer Fynes Moryson accused his countrymen of 'becoming more sump-tuous than the proudest Persians'.*

COUNTRY SCENES *Elaborate tapes-tries and embroidery enhanced the ostentatious display of Tudor life. A bed belonging to the Earl of Dorset, in which Queen Elizabeth slept, had cloth-of-gold hangings said to have cost £8000. A detail from the Bradford table carpet (above) and an embroidered cush-ion from the late 16th century (left) depict country scenes. Em-broidered rugs and carpets were frequently used as table coverings.*

COURT MUSIC *At every level of society, people in Tudor England loved music, and under Henry VIII, a composer himself, the court came to be its leading patron. Here, in an illustration from Henry's own psalter, musicians are seen playing a pipe and tabor (drum), harp and virginal.*

A ROYAL MUSICIAN *Henry VIII created a fashion at court for composing musical tunes and setting verses to them. Although music was considered an essential part of an upper-class education, performances were only given in private. If a gentleman plays 'in a common audience', Sir Thomas Elyot wrote in his book on etiquette, 'it impairs his estimation, the people forgetting reverence when they behold him in the similitude of a common servant or minstrel'.*

115

A flag and a cross – and Britain's empire begins

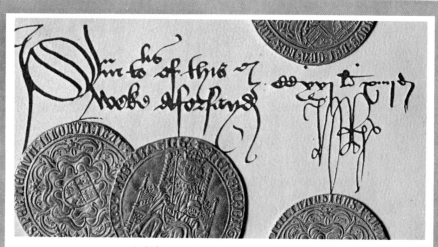

A £10 REWARD FROM THE KING

Cabot was paid £10 by Henry VII after his first voyage to North America in May 1497. The payment 'to hym that founde the new isle of New-Found Land' was entered in the king's personal accounts book, now in the Public Records Office in London.

In May 1497, five years after Christopher Columbus discovered the New World, a small ship, the *Mathew*, sailed west out of Bristol. Its captain, a Venetian named John Cabot, had arrived in England a few years before in search of support for voyages of exploration.

Cabot believed like Columbus that the route to the spice-rich islands of Asia lay westwards, and Columbus's discoveries seemed to confirm this theory. For when the Genoese explorer made his landfall, he was convinced that he had reached some barbaric islands off the coast of Asia. He did not realise that he had reached a new continent.

Across the Atlantic
Cabot promised his patron, Henry VII, that he would find new ocean routes to Cipangu (Japan) and Cathay (China). Henry, prepared to do anything that might further his nation's prosperity, had already considered enlisting Columbus himself in England's commercial interests. When Cabot appeared with his own promises, and with the resources of Bristol's experienced seamen behind him, Henry took up this offer. He granted Cabot and his sons a licence to travel north, east or west across the Atlantic Ocean.

Because of her shipping industry, Bristol had been one of England's richest towns for over 300 years. She exported leather and cloth to Europe. Fish, coal and iron were sent up the River Severn to the Midlands. Into Bristol came wine and silks from the Continent, tin

from Cornwall and fish from Iceland. Cabot had no difficulty in persuading Bristol's merchants to back his search for new riches.

So Cabot, with his one ship and 20 men, left Bristol in the early summer. He sailed to the south-western corner of Ireland, and then headed due west across the Atlantic. He made

land after 35 days – the first seafarer to cross the northern Atlantic since the Vikings in the early 11th century. But the details of his landing in the first English venture to North America are vague. No written account of the voyage survives. Cabot himself called the land that he sighted 'New-Found Land'; but it may have been Nova Scotia, somewhat to the south of Newfoundland.

Rewarded by the king
Having planted the royal standard and a crucifix, Cabot explored the coast for a month, noting the great forests of trees suitable for masts, and the 'infinite quantity of fish' in the sea. He then sailed for home and, having made a remarkably quick return passage in 15 days, he was back in Bristol by August 6, 1497.

Cabot believed that he had discovered the northern coasts of Asia, and promised that, by sailing further to the south-west, he would be able to reach China and the 'Spice Islands'. No one doubted him, and he received a hero's welcome. In London he was dubbed 'The Great Admiral', wore fine silk clothes and was followed everywhere by an admiring throng. Henry VII rewarded his daring in a more practical manner, giving him £10, a pension of £20 a year, and – most welcome of all – an assurance of a bigger fleet for a second voyage in the spring.

In May of the following year, Cabot sailed again, this time with five ships. He reached the east coast of Greenland in early June and named it Labrador's Land. As he sailed along the coast, looking for a passage, the cold grew intense and the icebergs bigger. On June 11 the crews refused to go on and Cabot had to put

following the death of Jane Seymour in 1537. Nine continental candidates were seriously considered, and five of them agreed to sit for Holbein. In 1538 he travelled to Brussels to paint Princess Christina of Denmark, Duchess of Milan, a 16-year-old widow with a 'singular good countenance'. But Thomas Cromwell urged the claims of a German princess, Anne of Cleves. Cromwell assured the king that her beauty exceeded that of Princess Christina 'as the golden sun excelleth the silvery moon'.

Painting the 'Flanders mare'

Both Anne and her sister Amelia were available, and Holbein painted them both. Henry chose Anne, but when he saw her in the flesh he was disappointed. He exclaimed: 'I am ashamed that men have so praised her as they have done – and I like her not.'

Luckily, Holbein suffered no disgrace from this episode. Possibly the king recognised, in fairness to the artist, that no portrait could convey some of the more annoying qualities of the 'Flanders mare' – her inability to speak English, her dowdy taste in clothes, and her lack of interest in music and the other arts.

During the next four years Holbein was kept busy painting the king, his successive queens and the anxious courtiers. He also turned his hand to the painting of miniatures, which were to inspire Tudor England's second great court artist, Nicholas Hilliard.

Holbein was only 46 when he died of the plague in London. But in 12 eventful years he had given Britain an art form which was to become one of its greatest assets – the tradition of beautiful and profound portraits.

KING'S PAINTER *Holbein's superb mastery of the portrait reached its peak with his studies of Henry VIII. This portrait was painted in 1536, the year Holbein was made King's Painter. The cool glance, raised eyebrows and tight mouth reveal a man in love with power.*

ENGLAND'S HOPE *As Henry Tudor's reign drew to a close, the people of England looked to the sole male heir, young Prince Edward. In this touching portrait Holbein captured the pathos of an innocent child fated to inherit problems far beyond his understanding.*

THE 'FLANDERS MARE' *In the search for a new bride for the king, Holbein was sent to Germany to paint Anne of Cleves. His picture decided the king in her favour. But, on seeing his bride, Henry disgustedly called her a 'Flanders mare'. He divorced her within months of marriage.*

The tragic reign of England's nine-day queen

AN INTRIGUER'S EPITAPH

England's nine-day queen, Lady Jane Grey, went to the block because of the passion for power of her scheming father-in-law, John Dudley, Duke of Northumberland. He made this elaborate carving in his cell in the Tower of London. Dudley sought but failed to secure a pardon by renouncing the Protestant faith. 'A living dog is better than a dead lion,' he said.

In January 1553, Edward VI entered the last stage of the disease that was to end his short reign six months later. As the young king lay dying of tuberculosis, the Duke of Northumberland, Lord President of the Council, was busy spinning the threads of a complex plot, designed to secure for the future the position he now held as England's regent and power behind the throne.

His intrigue centred on a 15-year-old girl, Lady Jane Grey. Northumberland planned to make her England's next sovereign, and to rule through her as he had ruled through Edward. Such was the background to the briefest and most pathetic reign in English history.

Puppet on the throne

Ambitious, hard and unloved, Northumberland calculated his procedure with meticulous care. He selected a candidate for the throne who was a devout Protestant – the grand-daughter of Henry VIII's sister. She was admirably suited to appeal to all Englishmen who feared that the recognised heir, Mary Tudor, would overturn the Reformation and return England to Rome. The links between Jane's family and his own had been cemented through a series of carefully arranged weddings culminating in Jane's marriage to his own son, Lord Guildford Dudley.

Finally, in June 1553, he persuaded the dying Edward VI to sign a will bequeathing his crown to Jane. The stage was set; now the duke need only move the players.

From the moment that Northumberland's choice fell upon her, Lady Jane was no more than a puppet. Her private life and her own personality receded into the shadows.

Yet had her fortune been less harsh, Jane would have been a considerable figure in her own right. Her character was far from weak. She was highly educated and zealously religious; gentle, but with a touch of real authority; innocent in an unaffected way, but no fool. With her grace and delicate beauty, she might have been an ornament to her age. But, instead, she was made the martyr to the iron self-will of a burningly ambitious man.

Edward VI died at last on July 6. Northumberland and his colleagues in the Privy Council kept his death a secret for four days while final preparations were made. Then they proclaimed Lady Jane as queen. At first she insisted that Mary was the 'rightful heir' and, according to contemporary accounts, fainted when the council told her that she was Edward's chosen successor. But she later submitted to what she thought was God's will. For greater security she was taken to the royal residence in the Tower of London. She was rowed down the river from Syon House on July 10. It was to be her first and last state journey.

A nine-day reign

At first, Jane had behind her the whole power of the state, carefully gathered by Northumberland into his own grasping hands. Her rival, Mary, the elder daughter of Henry VIII and the legitimate heir to the throne, had only narrowly escaped capture and imprisonment by the duke's forces, and seemed to have no other weapon than her own resolution. But this was to carry her through to victory.

When Jane was proclaimed queen, Mary fled with a handful of supporters to East Anglia. There she issued a stern order to the Privy Council, reminding them that her succession had long ago been confirmed by Act of Parliament, and insisting on their loyalty.

Claiming that Mary's support was confined to 'a few lewd, base people', Northumberland and his fellow-plotters prepared to send an army against her. The duke took command himself, although he was filled with doubt at leaving the source of his power in the hands of men he barely trusted. His parting words to the council echoed his profound suspicion. 'If you mean deceit,' he thundered, 'God will revenge the same.'

The duke had much to trouble him. 'The

TRAGEDY IN THE TOWER *A pathetic incident in Lady Jane Grey's last seconds on the scaffold is shown in this Victorian painting (top). After tying a handkerchief over her eyes, Jane (portrait above) searched with her hands for the block.*

people press to see us,' he wrote as he marched northwards, 'but no one sayeth God speed us.'

Every day came news of growing support for Mary. Noblemen and gentry rushed to join her. Royal ships and soldiers deserted to her cause. One by one, towns all over the country declared their allegiance to her. And as soon as Northumberland marched away from London, his own colleagues on the Privy Council started to look to their own safety.

Within days of his departure, the plot had fallen apart. The council left the Tower and proclaimed Mary as queen. Even Jane's own father, the Duke of Suffolk, turned against his

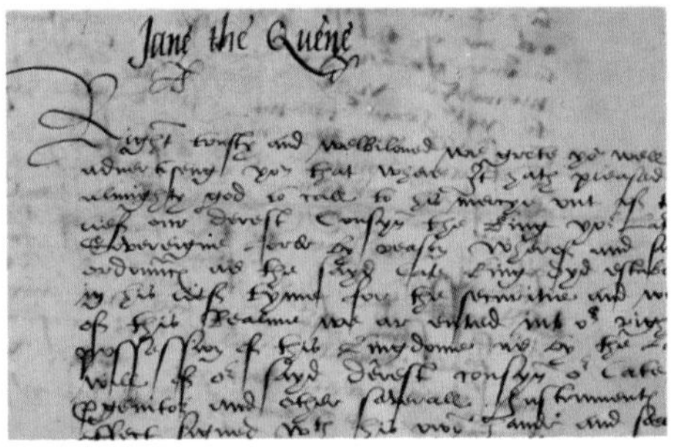

QUEEN'S LETTER *Jane demands support from the Marquess of Northampton against the 'untrewe dayme of Lady Mary, bastard daughter to our great Uncle Henry the eight'. But few nobles rallied to her cause.*

daughter. On July 19, he recognised Mary and put Jane under arrest. Five days later, Northumberland, now in Cambridge, conceded defeat. His great gamble had failed and his spirit was broken. He gave himself up and was imprisoned in the Tower.

London greeted Mary's victory with wild joy. 'For my time,' wrote an eyewitness, 'I never saw the like. The bonfires were without number, and what with the shouting and crying of the people, and ringing of bells, there could no one man hear what another said.' It was a triumph for Mary – a triumph too for the principles of orderly succession which Northumberland had sought to overthrow.

Living on borrowed time

At first Mary proved merciful in her victory. True, she could not let Northumberland live: he and two of his closest followers were executed in August. But Jane and her husband, though sentenced to death, were spared, until in January 1554 Mary was given cause to reverse her generous and compassionate decision.

In that month she found herself facing a popular rebellion, threatening not only her personal safety but that of her dynasty too.

The hot-headed Sir Thomas Wyatt raised the standard of revolt in Kent and marched on London at the head of 4000 men. His action showed his contempt for Mary's decision to marry a Catholic foreigner – Philip of Spain. In agreeing to this match she had thrown away the support of patriots, and she was obliged to take Wyatt's threat very seriously.

Innocent on the block

A succession of misfortunes and bad judgments eventually led to disaster for Wyatt. But those luckless innocents in the Tower, Jane and her husband, fell victim to his gamble.

Five days after Wyatt's rebellion had been crushed, the young couple were taken out of their prison and beheaded. The 16-year-old Jane met her death with astounding courage and composure. She rejected the offer of a reprieve if she denounced the Protestant faith. And, as she was taken to the block, she recited the 51st Psalm: 'Have mercy upon me, O God, after thy great goodness.' On the scaffold, she denied that she had ever desired the crown and said she perished 'a true Christian woman'.

Beautiful, learned, obedient – above all, firm in her devotion to the Protestant faith – Jane had been a pawn in other men's hands. Her life and her death were forfeits in a vicious power-game of dynasty and religion.

Edward VI: A boy-king governed by his elders

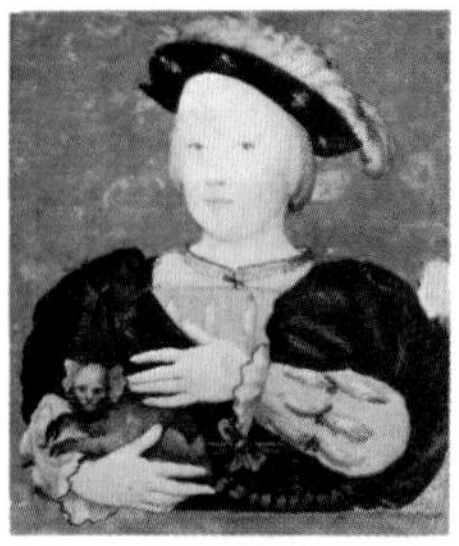

Henry VIII's only legitimate son was born to his third wife, Jane Seymour, on October 12, 1537. Within two weeks, the queen was dead. For the first six years of his life, the young Prince Edward (right) was brought up 'among the women'.

Then, in 1544, his education was entrusted to two of the leading scholars of the day, Richard Cox and John Cheke. Edward emerged from their hands, learned, precocious and devoutly Protestant.

The old king died in January 1547, and his 10-year-old son was crowned on February 20 in an atmosphere of rejoicing. But the child-king had no real authority, for his power was held by others. First it was grasped by Edward's maternal uncle, Edward Seymour, Duke of Somerset, who had himself declared Lord Protector. Somerset was charitable towards the poor, but arrogant and overbearing to the rich and powerful. The leading nobles conspired to dislodge him in 1549, and three years later he was beheaded. His place was taken by John Dudley, Duke of Northumberland, a man skilled at ingratiating himself with the king, but greedy and ambitious for himself and his kinsmen as well.

By now the young king was beginning to form a personality of his own. But he had always been a sickly child and in January 1553, at the age of 15, he developed tuberculosis. By May Edward was now beyond any treatment that his doctors could give. And when the end came in July, the Swiss Protestant theologian John Calvin lamented: 'By the death of one youth, the whole nation has been bereaved of the best of fathers.'

PRAYERS FOR THE PEOPLE

The English *Book of Common Prayer* (title page below) was published in 1549. The literary masterpiece of its day, the book was largely written by Thomas Cranmer, Archbishop of Canterbury. His main aims were to end the superstitions which he believed had crept into church services, to have one standardised form of prayer and to have the prayers in English, not Latin, 'to the end that the congregation may thereby be edified'. The book's prose was soon common reading for both rich and poor.

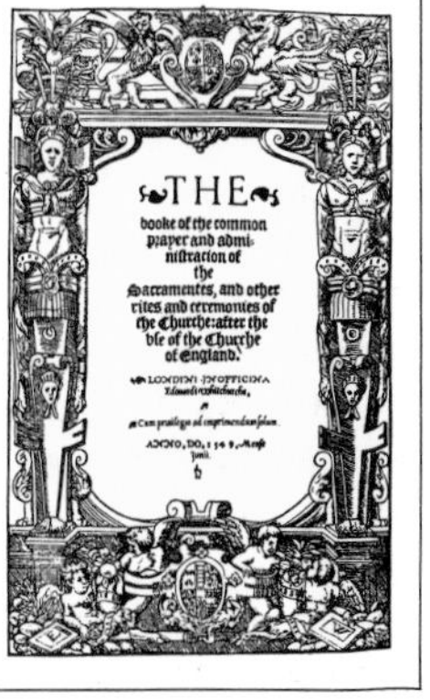

A CONTEMPORARY RECORD

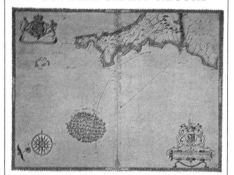

In the first of a contemporary series of charts showing the Armada's progress, the Spanish fleet is seen off Cornwall. English and Spanish scout ships are also shown.

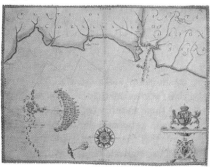

The English fleet sails out of Plymouth harbour in two squadrons. The plan was to menace the Armada from the rear. By this time, the Spanish had taken up their battle formation – a perfect crescent shape – which was designed to protect the weaker vessels in the fleet.

A skirmish off Portland Bill (left) was the first clash between the fleets. It temporarily breaks both their formations, then the Armada manages to reform and sets off up the Channel. The English, now in four squadrons, follow in close pursuit.

Driven from Calais by English fireships, the now disorganised Armada flees into the North Sea to start its disastrous voyage home. Spain lost 50 ships and 20,000 soldiers and sailors.

INVINCIBLE SAILOR *Francis Drake, Vice-Admiral of the English fleet, led the attack as the Armada sailed up the Channel.*

the purpose. Seven other ships were also prepared and, at midnight on July 28, were sent on the flood tide into the heart of the Spanish fleet.

The first two were intercepted, but the rest sailed on. The Spanish captains, terrified lest these blazing apparitions might explode, panicked. They cut their anchor cables and made for the open sea. The fireships drifted harmlessly to burn themselves out on the shore. But they had done their work; the close formation of the Armada had been broken.

The sun rose to reveal the Spanish ships scattered for miles along the coast. Howard at once brought the whole of his fleet into the attack. He and his squadron wasted time capturing a galleon which, in the night's panic, had run aground. But his subordinates –

Drake, Hawkins and Frobisher – kept their heads and attacked the heart of the Armada. The Spanish were running out of ammunition and the English were able to batter away unmolested with their cannon at short range. The proud warships of the Armada, riddled with holes, began to sink lower into the water. Three galleons were put out of action, many more were crippled and hundreds of Spanish sailors killed or wounded.

On the following morning, the Armada stood on the verge of destruction. To the windward lay the English fleet, to leeward the treacherous shoals of the Dutch coast. 'It was,' wrote one Spaniard, 'the most fearful day in all the world, for the whole company lost all hope of success and looked only for death.' Even if the English did nothing, it seemed that the Armada must be driven to destruction on the shore.

Then, quite suddenly, the Armada was reprieved by the weather. The wind swung round to the south-west and the battered Spanish were able to sail unhindered into the North Sea. At a council-of-war on board their flagship, the Spanish admirals agreed that if the wind changed again they would return, but as long as it stayed in its present quarter they would sail north. For three days the English fleet followed the Armada northwards. Then on August 2, off the coast of Scotland, the wind changed again to north-west. The English lost contact and turned for home.

With the new wind the Armada might have renewed its threat. But it was a spent force, with no choice but to limp home. Driven headlong by the wind which had saved them

a lamp[...]
conseq[...]
where, [...]

Give[...]
that co[...]
compa[...]
made [...]
attract[...]
denoun[...]
embitte[...]
imitato[...]
our fea[...]

A frien[...]
But fr[...]
was sm[...]
tial pa[...]
noblem[...]
a compa[...]
Men', i[...]
entitled[...]
1599 he[...]
called [...]
already[...]
ford's la[...]

Shake[...]
him as [...]
He was[...]
nature',[...]
17th-cen[...]
'handso[...]
'a very r[...]

Poems a[...]
Many re[...]
but refer[...]
Sonnets,[...]
mission [...]
puzzling[...]
man (pr[...]
his sens[...]
became [...]

Shake[...]
life in L[...]
to his W[...]
faded in[...]
marriage[...]
Susanna[...]
named l[...]
devoted [...]
age of 11[...]
or 11, p[...]
introduc[...]
death asi[...]
as can b[...]

Shakes[...]
extent co[...]
changing[...]
but it als[...]
ment. He[...]
into expe[...]
range of s[...]
of langua[...]

During [...]
speare's c[...]
be divide[...]

FIRE IN THE NIGHT *The death-blow to the Armada came when the English sent fireships into the Spanish fleet as it lay anchored off Calais. Though Medina Sidonia did not lose a single ship, the effect of the attack was disastrous. His commanders panicked and fled in confusion.*

earlier, ship after ship foundered as the battered Armada sailed northwards.

Medina Sidonia issued sensible orders to his fleet, still more than 100 ships strong. They were to steer a course 30 miles north of Cape Wrath on the north-western tip of Scotland and keep well west of Ireland.

Those who followed his advice reached home. But others, desperately short of food and water, disobeyed and steered for Ireland in the hope of picking up supplies. Some 25 ships foundered on the rocky crags of western Ireland. Some Spaniards were drowned escaping from the wrecks while hundreds struggled ashore, only to be rounded up and slaughtered. The Lord Deputy of Ireland had sent out the order that all captives be put to death.

Doomed from the start
The great Armada had been humiliated. Spain had lost 50 ships and 20,000 men. On hearing the news, Philip II shut himself up in his magnificent palace, the Escorial, and gave himself up to prayer. Only his confessor dared to approach him. Medina Sidonia retired to his country estate.

Philip's navy was far from destroyed. Within a few years, it was stronger than ever. But the blow to Spanish prestige in Europe was irreparable. The invasion plan was misbegotten and doomed from the start. But what the world noted was that the mightiest empire on earth had been dealt a crushing blow by a small Protestant nation.

TREASURE FROM THE SEA
Pursued by the English and scattered by the winds, the defeated Armada sought a route home round Scotland and Ireland. The Spanish ships were carrying huge quantities of treasure: gold coin to pay the men, richly wrought religious objects, silver tableware, personal jewellery, charms and talismens. At least 25 of these floating treasure-ships were wrecked on the Irish coast, and for over three centuries their cargoes lay buried beneath the waves. But in June 1967 a carefully planned diving expedition off the coast of Ireland by a young Belgian diver, Robert Stenuit, began to bring to light the riches that had been lost to the sea.

Two finds from the wreck of the Girona, *a jewel in the shape of a salamander (above), carried as a charm against fire, and a relic box.*

Victors whose efforts were unrewarded

As the Spanish Armada vanished into the mists of the North Sea, the fleet that had defeated it put back into port. But the fate of the victors was almost as pitiable as that of the enemy they had vanquished.

As soon as the fleet got back to shore, disease swept through the ships. Lord Howard of Effingham implored the help of Lord Burghley, the queen's principal minister: 'Sickness (plague) and mortality begin wonderfully to grow amongst us,' he wrote.

Howard searched for lodgings for his men. But his search turned up nothing better than barns and outhouses. The Spanish had killed 100 men at the most; disease carried away thousands of Elizabeth's sailors.

Anxious to save money, the government ordered rapid demobilisation. Men who expected full pay were fobbed off with a small advance. Hawkins, the Treasurer of the Navy, bitterly accused Burghley of saving the pay of those who had died, though they left families behind them. Hawkins and Drake set up a fund, known as the 'Chatham Chest', to provide relief for the distressed sailors. This was an unprecedented act of private charity. But disentangling his official accounts, finding money from nowhere, and doing his best for the men proved too much for Hawkins. He asked to be relieved from his post: 'God, I trust, will deliver me of it ere it be long, for there is no other Hell.'

Elizabeth's broken promise
In the end, Howard paid off some of the men with treasure taken from a captured Spanish galleon, promising to repay the queen from his own purse if she objected. 'It were pitiful,' he explained, 'to have men starve after such a service.' And he appealed to Elizabeth's self-interest: 'If such men should not be cared for better than to let them starve and die miserably, we should very hardly get men to serve.'

Elizabeth had indeed previously pledged herself to pay for victory with hard cash. In her famous Tilbury speech, she had held out the promise of a rich reward to strengthen her people's fighting spirit: 'I know already for your towardness you deserve rewards and crowns, and we do assure you, in the word of a prince, they shall be duly paid you.'

But 'the word of a prince' proved fickle in this case. Elizabeth may well have regretted her apparent ingratitude. But she was the unwilling prisoner of her empty coffers. The cost of mobilising the entire English fleet to fight the Armada had almost bankrupted her treasury. Even during the battle, food and ammunition had run short. The real culprits were reluctant taxpayers and corrupt officials, who between them squeezed both the monarch and the forgotten heroes of 1588.

A weeping queen sends her favourite to the block

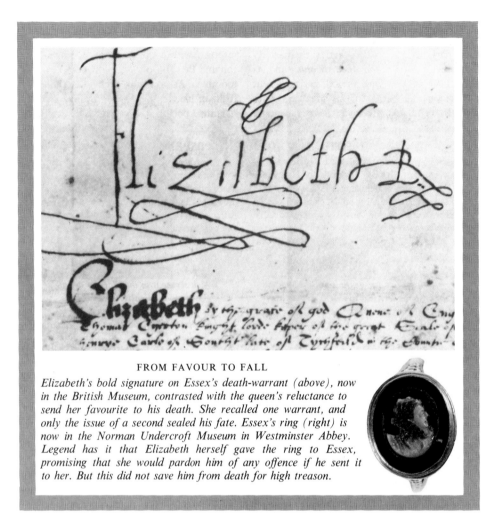

FROM FAVOUR TO FALL

Elizabeth's bold signature on Essex's death-warrant (above), now in the British Museum, contrasted with the queen's reluctance to send her favourite to his death. She recalled one warrant, and only the issue of a second sealed his fate. Essex's ring (right) is now in the Norman Undercroft Museum in Westminster Abbey. Legend has it that Elizabeth herself gave the ring to Essex, promising that she would pardon him of any offence if he sent it to her. But this did not save him from death for high treason.

A t 10.30 a.m. on the morning of Sunday, February 8, 1601, Robert Devereux, the 2nd Earl of Essex, had all England at his mercy. He had several hundred swordsmen supporting him – romantic young knights who had fought beside him in his campaigns abroad, fiery Welsh squires from the Devereux estates on the Marches, disillusioned noblemen who felt that Queen Elizabeth had not rewarded them sufficiently. And the earl had only to turn left out of Essex House and lead his private army down the Strand towards the palace of Whitehall to menace the defenceless Queen Elizabeth and her loyal courtiers.

But Essex turned right – away from Whitehall and towards the city of London – and his chance was gone. He hoped to gather extra swordsmen there and to persuade the crowds who flocked to hear the Sunday sermon at St Paul's to respond to his appeal to purge the queen's government of its evil elements. He miscalculated. While he was trying to muster support in the city, Elizabeth's own forces had time to gather. By the time the earl finally turned to march on Whitehall it was clear that he would have to fight.

This miscalculation was typical of Robert Devereux's entire career. He was the supreme popular idol in the closing years of Elizabeth's reign. But he had no competition, for the heroic generation of Elizabethans had come to an end. And the loss of the queen's favour had forced him into revolt.

Romance with a queen

Much of Essex's appeal lay in the qualities that were to bring about his fall – his rashness and his impetuosity. Elizabeth herself was entranced by his dashing, madcap personality. His short temper, his flaring eyes, his unpredictable sulks, his inability to conceal his emotions – all this captivated her. She was 34 years older than Essex, and she felt able to forgive his boyish inconsistency.

For 12 years from 1587 a flirtatious romance between them pursued its explosive course. Elizabeth entrusted the young earl with a succession of responsible tasks – military commands in France and Ireland, naval commands against Cadiz and the Azores.

But Essex owed these favours to more than the power of a young man to entrance an ageing woman. His stepfather, the Earl of Leicester, used his influence at court to win Essex favour. There soon gathered round him a group of able and calculating men, chief among whom were the brothers Anthony and Francis Bacon. Both the Bacons were politicians of formidable talent and ambition.

'For the Queen! For the Queen!'

But Essex needed money as well as power. For the earl's extravagance far outran his income, and his only other sources of funds were the tax-farming offices given him by Elizabeth herself. And, given as a sign of favour, they could easily be withdrawn.

Essex, too, was unequal to the tasks Elizabeth gave him. Though he blustered and sulked his way out of many situations, in 1599 he went too far. He deserted the army he was leading in Ireland, returned secretly to court and broke into the queen's bedchamber. There, he accused his rivals, Walter Raleigh

DESTROYED BY FOLLY *Robert Devereux, Earl of Essex, painted in 1596 when he was 29 years old. Tall and handsome, Essex had an irresistible appeal for women. The ageing queen was so obsessed by him that, when they first met in 1587, she refused to let him out of her sight. Their romance lasted for 12 years.*

and Robert Cecil, of treason, claiming that they were being paid by Spain to ruin England. He was placed under house arrest.

Released at the end of 1600, Essex amplified his accusations. And they became his battle-cry on February 8, 1601, when in his impetuous revolt he tried to rally support in the city of London. 'For the Queen! For the Queen!' he shouted. 'A plot is laid against my life!'

Essex had no evidence for his cries. They sprang from jealousy, from his disappointed hopes – and from fear of bankruptcy, for the queen had at last cut off his income. London's Sunday church-goers ignored the earl's fevered shouts. His followers sheathed their swords and vanished. At the foot of Ludgate Hill his depleted and dispirited band was routed by a band of loyal militia.

A fortnight later Essex was executed. But whenever his name was mentioned in the remaining 25 months of her life, the queen was seen to weep.

SERVANTS OF THE QUEEN

No family in England gave more loyal service to Elizabeth I than the Cecils. William Cecil (above left), later Lord Burghley, was one of England's greatest statesmen. Elizabeth appointed him Secretary of State in 1558. 'This judgment I have of you,' she said, 'that you will not be corrupted by any manner of gifts.' Burghley lived up to this trust, and remained Elizabeth's faithful servant until his death in 1598. His son, Robert (above right), served the queen from 1591, but his quarrel with her favourite, Essex, kept him from high office until 1596. Robert continued his family's tradition of dedicated service under Elizabeth's successor, James I. He died in 1612.

Twilight years of the 'Virgin Queen'

Sir Walter Raleigh's graceful epitaph to Queen Elizabeth I was 'a lady whom time had surprised'. It seemed impossible to her contemporaries that 'Gloriana', the 'Virgin Queen', should age, let alone die. But after the defeat of the Armada in 1588 Elizabeth went into a sharper decline than her subjects realised or than she would admit.

In her sixties, the queen tried to hide her age with cosmetics, and one sharp-eyed courtier noted how she was 'continuously painted not only all over her face, but on her neck and breasts also, and that the same was in some places near half an inch thick'. The French ambassador described her face as 'very aged, long and thin. Her teeth are very yellow and unequal.... Many of them are missing so that one cannot understand her easily when she speaks quickly'. Her famous mane of red hair was a wig.

Elizabeth's infatuation with the Earl of Essex was similar to the deceit she tried to create with her beauty box. It was an attempt to escape backwards from reality to a world she had outlived. Hatton, Leicester, Burghley, her closest friends and advisers, had died, leaving her to cope with problems she could not solve. Inflation soared, so that by 1600 her royal income was worth half of what it had been when she came to the throne. The war against Spain and the campaign against the Irish rebels dragged on, draining her exchequer so that she died £400,000 in debt.

To rule 'with your loves'

And there was a new independent tone in the voice of the Parliament she approached for extra money. When, a frail old woman, she staggered under the weight of her ceremonial robes to open the Parliament of 1601, MPs ostentatiously stood back, and few saluted her with the customary 'God Save Your Majesty'. They were incensed by the financial privileges she had granted to favourites like Essex and Raleigh, and they made their anger felt.

But Elizabeth, unlike her successors James and Charles Stuart, knew when to give way graciously. Promising to reform the abuses the Commons had so bitterly attacked, she summoned them to Whitehall to make their peace with her. And on November 30, 1601, in the crowded Council Chamber, Elizabeth won back the hearts of her subjects.

'Though God hath raised me high,' she told them, 'yet this I count the glory of my crown, that I have reigned with your loves. It is not my desire to live or reign longer than my life and reign shall be for your good. And though you have had, and may have, many mightier and wiser princes sitting in this seat, yet you never have had, nor shall have, any that will love you better.'

Death in the chill morning

This 'Golden Speech' was a masterstroke. It was remembered through the next century of civil war and revolution as the model of a monarch's relationship with the nation – caring, considerate and involving obligations on both sides. It was Elizabeth's last address to her people, but the glory of her reign was not yet over. Within days came the news of the defeat of the Irish rebels. Six months later, an English squadron captured a Portuguese treasure-ship in an action that recalled the heroic days of Drake and his raids on the Spanish Main. Both in the character of the queen and the exploits of the nation, Elizabethan England remained brilliant to the very last.

Unwilling to acknowledge the imminence of her death, Elizabeth shunned any talk of her successor and delayed making her choice until the very last. But in the end a waiting messenger was sent galloping north by her last chief minister, Robert Cecil, to tell James Stuart that he would have the throne that his mother Mary, Queen of Scots, had died trying to ascend. Between the cold dark hours of 2 a.m. and 3 a.m. of March 24, 1603, Queen Elizabeth quietly turned her face to the wall and passed peacefully away, 'mildly like a lamb, easily like a ripe apple from the tree', in the words of her chaplain.

LAST JOURNEY *A contemporary painting of Elizabeth I's funeral procession, the coffin surmounted by an effigy of the queen dressed in full regalia, on its way to Westminster Abbey on April 28, 1603. Thousands of Londoners lined the streets in a moving demonstration of popular grief at the passing of their beloved sovereign.*

Years of strife and bloodshed

*Too obstinate to accept the guidance of Parliament,
two Stuart kings divide the nation and set it on the road
to eight years of bitter and destructive civil war*

In 1603 a new dynasty, the House of Stuart, came to the throne at a fateful moment in England's history. It was the Stuarts' misfortune that they misunderstood the time itself and the character, beliefs and ambitions of the people they were called upon to rule.

The first Stuart, James I, boasted that he was 'an old, experienced king, needing no lessons'. But he and his son, Charles I, both found that their subjects meant to instruct them. Both of these kings obstinately believed in their 'Divine Right' to rule as they chose. Their subjects, however, had followed a different path, for previous monarchs had consulted their people in Parliament. The refusal of the Stuarts to understand this tradition of parliamentary liberty could have only one result – civil war.

In that war, the people emerged victorious. But, though they executed Charles I in 1649, they could find no satisfactory alternative to take the place of a monarch. And so, in 1660, the Stuarts returned.

As James I rode southwards from Scotland to claim his new throne in 1603, no such forebodings crossed his mind. He was supremely self-confident of his ability to rule England as he had ruled Scotland. The king was an intellectual in an age which had little time for subtlety. He also had little understanding of English history. His proposals for the toleration of Catholics were tactlessly presented to an unwilling Parliament, and swept away by the anti-Catholic hysteria which followed the discovery of the Gunpowder Plot to blow up the king in 1605 (pp. 162–3). What James lacked

CLIMAX OF REVOLUTION

On January 30, 1649, Charles I was executed outside Whitehall Palace. On his way to the scaffold, he passed through the Banqueting House, whose ceiling (inset) had been painted by Rubens 15 years before to glorify the Stuart monarchy. This detail shows Charles's father, James I, being received into Heaven.

Like his father, Charles believed that he could impose his will on his subjects. But, as an opponent said, 'No one was wise who permanently opposed himself to the people of England'. And when monarchy was restored in 1660 this vital lesson had been learnt. No English king could afford to be despotic. Subjects would always remember that, having overthrown one king, they could overthrow another.

TWO KINGDOMS *James I's seal shows the united arms of his two kingdoms, Scotland and England. But the English refused to pass a formal Act of Union, and it was to be another century before Parliament brought it about.*

KING AND CHURCH *James listens to a sermon in St Paul's churchyard. He was an ardent supporter of the Church of England, seeing it as a vital part of the system of government he was determined to defend. 'No bishop, no king,' he said. Opponents of the Church, such as the Puritans, were the first to feel his power.*

END OF AN ERA *By making friends with Spain, James ended a tradition which his people regarded as natural to Englishmen. Here, he welcomes back his son, Charles, from an abortive attempt to wed the King of Spain's daughter.*

was common sense, the supreme virtue of Elizabeth's wily counsellor, Robert Cecil, who also served James as chief minister. After Cecil's death in 1612, James abandoned all his policies. The one legacy Cecil left behind was Hatfield House (pp. 164–5), the incomparable work of wealth, taste and dynastic pride which he had built in Hertfordshire.

A king who divided the nation

One of James's first quarrels with his subjects concerned foreign policy. He had come to his inheritance penniless, and his extravagance soon brought the crown of England close to bankruptcy. His over-riding concern was to avoid the expense of foreign wars and so he made peace with Spain, reversing a policy which Englishmen had come to regard as a way of life.

There was, however, another reason for this clash of wills. The Puritans of England were prospering, and they wished to prosper further by destroying the Spanish monopoly of trade with the Americas. This, too, James resisted, and in 1618 the Puritans found their martyr in Sir Walter Raleigh (pp. 166–7), executed ostensibly for treason, but in fact at the behest of Spain.

Isolated from the real world by the flattery of his favourites, James was able to indulge his conceit. He was convinced that he could settle the bitter religious strife that was dividing his kingdom by imposing a compromise. But in 1617 James published a *Book of Sports*, which allowed certain games to be played on Sunday. For the Puritans, already harassed by zealous high-Church bishops, this was the final proof that James had turned his face against true religion. Three years later, the *Mayflower* set sail with its first cargo of Puritan exiles (pp. 168–9). The Pilgrim Fathers were bound for a new world, where they could worship freely.

At home, the question of government was setting king and people on a collision course. The first of the confrontations which were to lead England to civil war came when the House of Commons asserted its strength by impeaching the Lord Chancellor, Francis Bacon, in 1621.

Bacon was the most talented and original thinker who ever served a Stuart monarch. He combined a long and distinguished career in the government service with a leading place in the world of science and letters. His works, together with those of his contemporary, the biologist William Harvey, constitute the most enduring contribution of the age to the progress of scientific thought and discovery (pp. 170–1).

'So good a man, so bad a king'

When James finally died unlamented in 1625, it was thought that Charles would be a great improvement on his father. He was serious-minded and conscientious – a vast change from the ribald and drunken James. The new king, however, had inherited two characteristics from his father – an attachment to the same favourite, Buckingham, and an obstinate belief in his God-given right to rule unchallenged. These were to lead him to disaster.

In 1628 the House of Commons forced Charles to agree to the demands of the Petition of Right, which struck at the whole basis of Stuart monarchy. Its immediate effect was to arouse all Charles's inbred hatred of Parliament. The next year he set out on the ruinous course of 11 years of personal rule.

Charles began this experiment without Buckingham, who had met his death in 1628, assassinated by a deranged army officer. To replace him, Charles chose a group of serious-minded, efficient ministers – chief among them Thomas Wentworth, Earl of Strafford, and Archbishop Laud. The policy they were to follow they christened 'Thorough'. An enlightened king would rule, without fear or favour, for the benefit of all his subjects.

But finance was the king's undoing. Charles's legal advisers found ingenious methods of raising money without resort to Parliament, including an ancient levy called Ship Money. In one of the great constitutional cases in English history, a Buckinghamshire squire, John Hampden, challenged its legality in 1637 (pp. 172–3). The judges found for the king by a narrow margin – but nevertheless Charles's prestige suffered a terrible blow. Voices were now publicly raised against the court and, in an atmosphere of anger and distrust, England awaited the challenge that was to bring the king's rule down.

Ironically, this came not from England but from Scotland – the kingdom James I had left with such high hopes 36 years before. In May 1639, an army assembled to resist Laud's attempts to make the Church of England the official church of Scotland. Revolt broke out, and Charles realised that he had no choice but to recall Parliament.

Charles in private life was a different person from Charles the obstinate king. He had a real love of beauty. He aspired to create a Renaissance monarchy, adorned by noble buildings and fine paintings. From Italy and Holland, Charles brought a magnificent collection of paintings. And he persuaded Van Dyck, the greatest artist of the day, to settle in England, where he captured the grace and elegance of the Stuart court (pp. 178–9). He commissioned Rubens, who spent a year at his court, to paint the ceiling of the Banqueting House in Whitehall. This was Inigo Jones's first perfectly proportioned Classical building, but Jones's masterpiece was Wilton House in Wiltshire (pp. 176–7), built for the rich and powerful Herbert family.

'This is a time of shaking'

The Long Parliament, which was to outlive Charles, met in 1640. Instead of voting the king the taxes he needed, it began its work by putting Strafford, the pillar on which Charles's rule depended, on trial for his life (pp. 174–5). Charles had given his word that Strafford would 'in no wise suffer' for his loyal service to the crown. But the king's word was not equal to the pressure of a hostile Parliament, and he signed the death warrant. It was an action he regretted for the rest of his life. Laud was imprisoned in the Tower. Two extreme views had met head on; the result was civil war.

Charles had the advantage when the war began in 1642. But he failed to press this home, notably after the Battle of Edgehill (pp. 180–1). By 1645 Oliver Cromwell's New Model Army was in the field, and at the Battle of Naseby (pp. 182–3) the Royalist cause was shattered.

Parliament had won the war. What was it to do with the king it had defeated? Charles's stubborn refusal to accept peace terms, his treachery and duplicity, caused passions to flare still higher. In 1649 Cromwell and his followers were driven to try him and execute him (pp. 184–7).

To abolish monarchy was one thing; to find another form of government was a more difficult business. By 1653, when he dismissed the 'Rump Parliament' (pp. 188–9), Cromwell had become king in all but name. For the next five years, his army imposed a severe Puritan rule on the country.

But the rule of the army depended on Cromwell's strength and genius. When he died in 1658, it was clear that he had given England neither a permanent, stable form of government, nor the liberty for which the civil war had been fought. From that disillusionment, it was a short step to the restoration of the Stuarts in 1660.

The English Revolution was over. But it had left a legacy. The Puritan tradition had found its noblest voices in the writers John Bunyan and John Milton (pp. 190–1). And absolute monarchy had received a decisive check. Englishmen had made it plain that they would not be ruled by a despot.

UNPOPULAR MINISTER *The Duke of Buckingham on his death-bed after his assassination in 1628. First minister to both James and Charles I, he was arrogant and tactless.*

STUART DISPLAY *A float from the Lord Mayor's Show. Pomp, pageantry, display and splendour were actively encouraged by the Stuarts. But such ostentation was opposed by the Puritans, who saw it as offensive in the sight of God.*

FINAL CRISIS *Inspired by religious zeal, Scottish Calvinists sign the 'Solemn League and Covenant' in 1638. The Covenanters swore to resist Charles's attempts to impose Anglican ritual, and their success precipitated civil war.*

WORD WAR *King and Parliament found philosophers to support them. Thomas Hobbes (right) produced his defence of absolute monarchy in his* Leviathan *of 1651.*

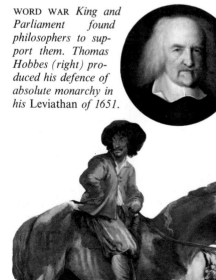

A LESSON LEARNT *Charles II flees after defeat at Worcester in 1651. His exile taught him to abandon the Divine Right theory for which his father died.*

'Remember ... remember the fifth of November'

FAWKES'S 'LANTHORN'
With this lantern, Guy Fawkes planned to kindle the gunpowder and wood the Gunpowder Plotters had stored under the Houses of Parliament in 1605. It was found in the cellar where Fawkes was arrested by the Earl of Suffolk and his men, and is now in the Ashmolean Museum, Oxford.

Seldom have a handful of men come so close to changing the course of history as did those who took part in the Gunpowder Plot of 1605. These young men, inspired by a fierce belief in the Roman Catholic faith, knew that their great plan would involve the deaths of over 300 Protestant leaders, including the king; and they had no compassion for these men. But they showed weakness over the inevitable killing of a handful of Roman Catholics – and it was this weakness which betrayed them in the last tense days before the plot reached its climax.

Deep in the cellars

At 11 p.m. on the dark night of November 4, 1605, a stately figure plodded through the maze of cellars and basements directly under the House of Lords, in the Palace of Westminster. It was the Earl of Suffolk, Lord Chamberlain of the King's Household, with two of his henchmen in close attendance.

Suffolk was there on the orders of the Privy Council, which had received an anonymous warning that violence was planned against James I when he came to open Parliament the next day. The chamberlain had been ordered to search one cellar in particular – one rented by a Catholic courtier, Thomas Percy.

Percy had a surprisingly large stock of coal and firewood there. And it was difficult for the council to see why he had ordered the skulking dark-haired manservant, who went by the name of John Johnson, to mount a 24 hour guard on his winter fuel supply.

As soon as Johnson opened the cellar door he was seized and overpowered. The coal and wood were thrown aside. Hidden beneath them were 36 barrels of gunpowder, connected to a slow fuse. In one corner was a dark lantern. Johnson was taken straight to the Tower, and on the rack confessed his real name – Guido (Guy) Fawkes.

Fawkes is the only Gunpowder Plotter whose name has passed into British folklore. But he was only a subordinate, brought over from Flanders where he had been serving with the Spanish army, because of his professional skill with explosives. He was called in by Thomas Winter, and behind Winter stood his cousin, Robert Catesby, the originator and leader of the plot.

Catesby and Winter were both well-born Catholics. By 1605 they were impoverished and desperate – a situation they blamed on the anti-Catholic laws. They had already tried to mend their fortunes by joining one madcap scheme – the Earl of Essex's rebellion against Queen Elizabeth in 1601 – only to suffer crush-

ENTER FAWKES *Guy Fawkes makes his way into the cellar rented by the plotters under the House of Lords. He stood guard over 'fuel' stocks·for 24 hours under the false name of John Johnson.*

THE GUNPOWDER PLOTTERS *The Gunpowder Plotters confer in this contemporary illustration. Fawkes (third from right) was recruited in Flanders by another plotter, Thomas Winter. He had been serving there as an explosives expert with the Spanish army. He was hanged, drawn and quartered.*

Bates • Robert Winter • Christopher Wright • Iohn Wright • Thomas Percy • Guido Fawkes • Robert Catesby • Thomas Winter

ing fines. They had then approached James in Scotland with a proposal for religious toleration for their faith.

But James's half-promises meant little once he had achieved his ambition of succeeding to the English throne. In 1604 he reimposed the anti-Catholic laws. A desperate blow seemed the only answer.

The plotters thought that if they blew up the House of Lords when the king was opening the new session of Parliament, they would eliminate him, the Prince of Wales and all the leading ministers. They then hoped to seize the next heir, the five-year-old Prince Charles, and raise a general revolt. Governing in the young prince's name, they would reconvert England to Catholicism.

Betrayed by kindness

All was prepared by the end of 1604. Fawkes had arrived from Flanders, and Thomas Percy, who had been drawn into the plot at an early stage, had used his court connections to rent a cellar under the House of Lords.

But the meeting of Parliament that had been planned for February 1605 was postponed until the autumn, and discovery became an increasing risk. Catesby's persuasive tongue steadily won over more followers, until by November at least 13 men were in the secret.

It was in the last days of their long wait that the plotters made their fatal mistake, that of showing pity. They tried to save friends and relatives among the peerage, for Catholics could still sit in the House of Lords.

On October 26, one of these peers, Lord Mounteagle, received an anonymous letter of warning: 'Retire yourself into the country for ... they shall receive a terrible blow this Parliament and yet they shall not see who hurts them.' Mounteagle passed the letter to the Privy Council. Lord Suffolk was despatched to search the cellars.

A dismal fate

On the news that all was discovered, Catesby and Winter, with seven companions, took horse and rode hard for the Midlands. But a posse led by the Sheriff of Worcestershire tracked them down to Holbeach House in Staffordshire.

On the morning of November 8, the sheriff stormed the house, and four of the conspirators were killed. Among them was Robert Catesby, who crawled across the blood-stained floor to kiss a picture of the Virgin Mary before he died. Winter, his brother, Robert, and five others were brought back to London to stand trial with Fawkes. They were sentenced to be hanged, drawn and quartered.

To the last, they refused to repent. The tragedy was that, instead of helping the Catholics of England, the Gunpowder Plot nearly destroyed them. It was to be more than 200 years before Catholics would re-establish their good name and secure full legal toleration.

James I: Blinded by his own wisdom

On April 3, 1603, James VI of Scotland took leave of his subjects and started the long journey south to England. Scotland was a poor and barren land, and James had long envied his cousin, Queen Elizabeth, for the wealth and splendour of her court.

Now he would be able to indulge his passion for hunts, palaces and pageantry. His extravagant wife, Anne of Denmark, too, would have all she desired. The new king's first act on arriving at York was to write to the Privy Council demanding money.

As James drew nearer his new capital, the warmth of his reception went to his head like the rich wine of which he was so fond. 'The people of all sorts rode, ran, nay flew, to meet me,' he later wrote. But in truth, James's new subjects were expressing not so much joy at his arrival, as relief that the succession had been settled peacefully.

'The wisest fool'

Physically, James I, as he now styled himself, did not look the part of a king. His strong Scots accent was thickened by a deformity of the tongue, which was too large for his mouth, making him dribble and 'drink very uncomely'.

He was coarse and profane in his humour. When his bishops said that 'undoubtedly His Majesty spoke by the special assistance of God's spirit', a cynic added: 'the spirit was rather foul-mouthed.'

If James had been a more successful ruler, his lack of manners would not have mattered. But, though he announced that he was 'an experienced king, needing no lessons', his overweening self-confidence blinded him to some lessons that he did need.

James was an intelligent man who had read and thought deeply on questions of religion and government. His published works included a defence of absolute monarchy, a treatise on witchcraft, and even an attack on smoking tobacco. But in dealing with politicians, churchmen and Parliament, he combined pedantry with such ineptitude that the Spanish Ambassador, Count Gondomar, labelled him 'the wisest fool in Christendom'.

For the first seven years of his reign, James was saved from the consequences of his blunders by his principal minister, Robert Cecil, Earl of Salisbury, who tried to carry the Elizabethan ideal of good government into a new age. But James was not interested in government – least of all when it involved working with a critical Parliament. 'I am surprised,' he darkly muttered, 'that my ancestors should have allowed such an institution to come into existence.'

After Cecil's death in 1612, the men James preferred to trust were young courtiers whose sole claim to advancement was their physical beauty. The first of these was Robert Carr, Earl of Somerset. By 1616, however, Carr had

KING AND THINKER *James I was widely read and thoughtful. But, as ruler of England, he introduced policies that alienated his people.*

IN FAVOUR *Robert Carr, Earl of Somerset (left) and George Villiers, Duke of Buckingham were two of James's favourites, with nothing to commend them but good looks.*

been outshone by a new and brighter star, George Villiers, Duke of Buckingham.

James was now rapidly growing senile. He worshipped his 'sweet Steenie gossip' and lavished wealth upon him. Faced with mounting criticism of Buckingham, he wept, saying: 'Christ had his John and I have my George.' Buckingham, for his part, was James's 'most humble Slave and dogge'.

Buckingham, however, had enough wit not to rely on an obviously failing monarch. He cultivated the shy heir to the throne, the young Prince Charles, and the two men allied to force their views on the old king. With a last flash of intelligence, James told Charles, after he and Buckingham had pressed for the impeachment of Lionel Cranfield, Earl of Middlesex, the Lord Treasurer: 'You will live to have your bellyful of impeachments.' For the dying king realised that, by encouraging Parliament to attack royal ministers, his foolhardy son was opening the way for an attack on the crown itself.

MONUMENT TO AN AGE – BUILT BY A KING'S FIRST MINISTER

Hatfield is the Cecils; the Cecils are Hatfield. No great country house has seen more of our history in the making. The Cecil who built this magnificent palace was chief minister to James I. And Hatfield has served his family ever since – a house in which every room has been, at one time or another, a council chamber, and every passage a corridor of power.

In medieval times the manor of Hatfield belonged to the bishops of Ely, and in the 15th century an imposing palace was built there. One wing of this house, containing the banqueting hall, still stands 100 yds away from the later 17th-century building. It is perhaps the finest remaining example of English medieval brickwork.

But few bishops were to enjoy Hatfield. Henry VIII seized it and used it as a country home for his children. It was here that Edward VI and his sisters Mary and Elizabeth grew up, remote from the terrible events at their father's court. Here, too, under an oak tree, Elizabeth was told of her accession to the throne.

It was Elizabeth who made the Cecils, although it was not until after her death that they came to Hatfield as its owners. In a sense, though, the great dynasty began here. For the young queen's first official action, performed in the Great Hall at Hatfield, was to appoint William Cecil her chief Secretary of State.

'This judgement I have of you,' she said, 'that you will not be corrupted with any manner of gifts, and that you will be faithful to the

state.' Her words were almost prophetic. For 40 years the devoted and wily courtier stood at the queen's right hand. And when he died, in 1598, he left a son, Robert, well able to take up the reins of government.

Robert Cecil, small and slightly deformed, was ridiculed by many about the court, but he was respected by both Elizabeth and her Stuart successor, James I, as a shrewd, calculating statesman. James heaped honours on him, made him Earl of Salisbury and left him in almost complete control of affairs of state.

Exchange with a monarch

In 1607 the king took a fancy to Cecil's fine house at Theobalds and offered to exchange it for Hatfield. As soon as Cecil took possession of his new domain, he determined to build a magnificent house which would suitably proclaim his power and wealth, and which would stand as a monument to all that was best in Jacobean taste and craftsmanship.

Cecil personally supervised the building of his masterpiece and used the vast power of his office to obtain the very best men and materials. Stone was brought from France and marble for statues from Italy. Timber was hewn on the vast estate, and millions of red bricks were made on the site by a master bricklayer named Jerome Taulcote.

The man charged with turning Cecil's ideas and designs into reality was Robert Lyminge, described as a 'surveyor' in surviving documents. Cecil, suffering frequent bouts of

JACOBEAN ELEGANCE *The South Front has changed little since its completion in 1611. Robert Cecil achieved its symmetry without using an architect. He himself worked on the plans with his clerk of works, Thomas Wilson, and his surveyor, Robert Lyminge. Cecil spent £40,000 on his magnificent house at Hatfield, but never lived to see it completed.*

illness, and perhaps fearing that he might not live to see the house completed, drove Lyminge on at breakneck pace. Notes and sketches were sent back and forth between master and servant by special messenger.

Lyminge had the best workmen money and influence could buy. There was Maximilian Colt, the Flemish sculptor who had created Queen Elizabeth's tomb in Westminster Abbey; a Frenchman, referred to by the English as 'Lewis Dolphin', made painted glass for the chapel; another Frenchman, Solomon de Caux, devised the complex system of waterworks and fountains; and a score of other master craftsmen came to Hatfield from Flanders, France and Italy.

Supreme achievement

Robert Cecil spent the colossal sum of £40,000 on his new house, which was completed in the incredibly brief period of five years. The date of completion, 1611, is triumphantly proclaimed in stone above the south porch.

In its essentials the house which was finished in that year has remained unchanged for three and a half centuries. It is the supreme achievement of Jacobean architecture and, in a deeper sense, it is also the final flowering of the Tudor style. The features which had been familiar parts of great English houses for the previous century are incorporated in this building with what now appears to be a kind of valedictory

---

ENGLAND'S FIRST BOTANIST

Among the craftsmen brought in by Robert Cecil to beautify Hatfield was John Tradescant. Described then as a gardener, he was really one of Britain's first great botanists.

Cecil set Tradescant on the course which was to enrich the gardens of England for succeeding ages. He sent him to hunt for rare plants and trees in distant countries. Tradescant's later employers, the Duke of Buckingham and James I, gave him the same encouragement. He brought back many rare flowers, a whole group of which were called 'Tradescantia', by the botanist Linnaeus. He toured Europe and America, and was the first to study Russian flora. In 1620 he was on a ship sent to harry Barbary pirates, but he forgot corsairs when he saw Morocco's flowers. A contemporary described him as 'a lover of all nature's varieties', and his collection of specimens included animals as well as flowers.

BOTANIST'S SKETCHBOOK *A detailed sketch (above) of a rare plum by Tradescant (left), the botanist who introduced many plants to Hatfield's gardens.*

workings of an old tradition; but the tradition is interpreted with an extravagance never before seen in England.

The Long Gallery more than fulfils its name – for it is 60 yds in length, although less than 7 yds wide. The great length is relieved by two magnificent fireplaces and, despite the extraordinary proportions, the room is very beautiful and even feels comfortable.

A lasting monument
The gardens were equally novel and extravagant. John Tradescant was commissioned to roam through half the countries of Europe in search of new flowers and shrubs. The Queen of France sent 500 fruit trees, and a vineyard was planted with 20,000 vines supplied by the wife of the French ambassador.

Visiting the mature gardens 50 years later, John Aubrey, the diarist, was deeply impressed. He wrote that the valley of Hatfield was now so beautiful that it must eclipse the Vale of Tempe, the mythological fields of perfection that were believed to be below Mount Olympus.

Sadly, it was not given to Robert Cecil to enjoy the splendour of his new creations. He slept for only eight nights in his house. The man whom Elizabeth had called her 'little elf' was stronger in wisdom and grasp of great affairs than in body. The burdens of serving an incompetent and ungrateful king were too much for his frail form, and he died at Marlborough in May 1612, aged 49.

Little of Robert Cecil's life work survived him; the men who managed the realm in his stead during the following 16 years were chosen for their charm and good looks rather than the Cecil qualities of dogged skill and high dedication. But the house he had built at Hatfield was a more lasting monument. If bricks and mortar can express an ideal, it has proved a powerful spokesman for the aspirations of his family. Its pervasive influence must surely have played a part in leading so many generations of Cecils to carry forward the family tradition – 'faithful to the state' – as the young Elizabeth had so wisely foretold.

MEDIEVAL MAGNIFICENCE *The lifetime of Robert Cecil straddled both the Tudor and Jacobean ages. But his nostalgia for the style of the Middle Ages is reflected in the Marble Hall, with its minstrels' gallery and carved screens. It takes its name from the chequered marble floor.*

GRAND STAIRCASE *The best available craftsmen were brought in by Cecil to beautify Hatfield House. There, they were given a free hand. The individualism of their work is reflected in the elaborate detail of this staircase with its richly carved pillars, lions and cherubs.*

ROYAL EXCHANGE *James I granted Hatfield to Robert Cecil in this Act of Parliament of 1607. He took Cecil's house at Theobalds in exchange.*

splendour; and there is little sign of the careful Classicism which was to dominate architecture during the next two centuries. Clearly, Robert Cecil had no wish to achieve the plain lines of perfect proportion; he was as little bound by the Classical forms as his contemporary William Shakespeare was in drama. He apparently relished intricate geometric patterns, rich materials and, above all, individual carvings made by craftsmen who felt free to express their own moods and fantasies, however grotesque or whimsical.

Hatfield's noblest rooms – the vast hall and the Long Gallery – seem almost self-consciously old-fashioned. Perhaps Cecil conceived them in a mood of nostalgia; for it was in such rooms that the affairs of England had been conducted during the long years of his father's greatness. In this mood of respect for the fruitful past, the builders of Hatfield created a fitting background for the incomparable collection of Tudor treasures, especially the portraits and personal relics of two queens – the Queen of England whom Robert Cecil's father had served so loyally, and the Queen of Scotland whose death he had felt obliged to encompass.

The Great Hall and Long Gallery are re-

The tragedy of the hero who outlived his age

FALLEN FAVOURITE *Writer, explorer and Elizabeth I's favourite, Raleigh fell from favour under James I. Many pleaded with the king to release him, but the king was deaf to such pleas.*

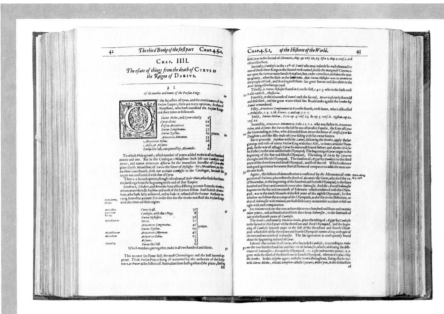

WRITTEN IN THE TOWER

While imprisoned in the Tower of London, Raleigh began writing his History of the World, *as well as studying chemistry and mathematics. But he only completed the first volume, covering the period from the Creation to 168 BC, and James I banned the book as an attack on royal authority. The book is now in the British Museum.*

FATAL DESTINY *Sir Walter Raleigh prepares to meet his fate in 1618 with the stoicism of the Romans he so admired. Ever since his condemnation for treason in 1603, he had lived on borrowed time, knowing that one false move would give James I the chance to send him to the scaffold.*

On the night of December 9, 1603, Sir Walter Raleigh sat writing in a cell in Winchester Castle:

Give me my scallop shell of quiet,
My staff of Faith to walk upon,
My scrip of joy, immortal diet . . .
And thus I'll take my pilgrimage.

The next morning Raleigh was to be executed on a trumped-up charge of treason. James I, new to the throne of England, had allowed himself to be panicked into condemning Elizabeth's former favourite to death.

Raleigh's arrogance had made him the most unpopular man in England before his trial. Mobs attacked his coach as it travelled to and from the prison. But the spirit with which he conducted his defence at his trial turned the people in his favour.

Reprieved but imprisoned

So, at the last minute, James had qualms. He was basically a merciful man, and he did not want to start off his reign by executing a popular hero. On the very morning of the execution, the sentence was suspended and Raleigh conveyed to the Tower instead.

But James's mercy was double-edged, for Raleigh was to live under the threat of execution for another 15 years. However, life in the Tower could have been worse. For he was allowed to live as unrestricted a life as was possible in such a prison.

Meanwhile, the outside world did not lose interest in this illustrious prisoner. Soon crowds were gathering daily on the riverside to watch him pace the battlements. James's wife, Anne, went to see Raleigh and was captivated by him. So was her brother, the King of Denmark, who pleaded in vain for his release. The young Henry, Prince of Wales, was another disciple. 'Who but my father would shut up such a bird?' he exclaimed.

But, as the years passed, the prospect of Raleigh's release faded. Perhaps the bitterest blow was the knowledge that the king's young favourite, Robert Carr, Earl of Somerset, now enjoyed the beauty of Raleigh's cherished home at Sherborne in Dorset, which the doting James I had given to him.

At last Raleigh found the key to his prison door in his dreams of *El Dorado*, a legendary gold mine which he insisted lay at the source of the Orinoco River in South America. By 1616, James was in desperate need of money, and in that year Raleigh was at last released on parole – to search for gold to save the crown from bankruptcy.

Release on parole

But the terms of release were hedged about with conditions. Raleigh had lived all his active life in a world in which England and Spain were bitter and bloody enemies. Now he came out into the daylight of a changed world. Spain was an ally which had to be placated – and the Orinoco lay in Spanish territory. He promised James that he could avoid conflict, and the king replied with a warning that any clash with the Spanish would cost Raleigh his head.

But at 66 Raleigh was an old man. He had already had two strokes, and the voice which had commanded instant obedience as captain of the old Queen's guard was now weak and faltering. When he reached the Orinoco in November 1617, he had to delegate command of the expedition inland to his eldest son, Wat, and his faithful lieutenant, Lawrence Keymis. They promptly sacked the town of San Thomé and Wat was killed. In grief and disappointment, Raleigh sailed home to his own death.

Once again James I faced the dilemma he had side-stepped 15 years before. He ordered a hearing before the Privy Council. No one wanted Raleigh to die; everyone knew he must. Even the Attorney-General, presenting the crown's case, said: 'Sir Walter Raleigh...hath been as a star at which the world gazed; but stars may fall – nay, they must fall when they trouble the sphere wherein they abide.'

Raleigh had a week to prepare for execution, and he made the most of it. He was a classical figure and would make a classic death. He had studied the stoicism of the Romans, and had admired the easy, smiling wit with which the Tudors' victims had suffered.

James I had tried to divert public attention from the execution by fixing it for Lord Mayor's Day. But that morning a huge crowd greeted Raleigh as he left the Gatehouse. Dressed in sombre black, he mounted the scaffold and invited the onlookers to join him in prayer. As he knelt at the block he was asked if he would not prefer to face the east and the rising sun. He replied: 'The matter is not great which way we turn our faces, so our hearts be right.'

The executioner raised the severed head in silence, without shouting the usual formula: 'Behold the head of a traitor! God save the King!' Instead, a voice called out: 'We have not such another head in England.'

An adventurer grows old in the Tower

Dark, magnetically attractive to women and dramatically handsome, Walter Raleigh began his meteoric rise to fame in 1581, when, as a young gallant, he came to court at Greenwich, where he took the fancy of Elizabeth I. According to legend, he spread his cloak upon a muddy path for the queen to walk over on the occasion of their first meeting. His gallantry won him royal favour and soon appointments and lands were showered on him. The high point was reached in 1586, when he became Captain of the Guard. But Raleigh's self-centred arrogance left him without friends, and the queen's infatuation did the rest. In 1587 it was said that Raleigh was 'the best hated man of the world in court, city and country'.

Raleigh spent his new wealth like water. Over five years he spent £40,000 (£1 million today) in trying to establish a colony in his American possessions. Raleigh christened his settlements Virginia in honour of the queen, but his venture failed. All he had to show for it were potatoes and tobacco, both of which he helped popularise in England.

According to legend, once, in these years of favour, Raleigh had taken Queen Elizabeth's diamond ring and carved on the window pane: 'Fain would I climb, yet I fear to fall.' Taking back the ring, she had written: 'If thy heart fail thee, climb not at all.'

Raleigh had climbed high, but when the feared fall came in 1592, it was abrupt and painful. In that year, the queen discovered that he had been carrying on an intrigue with Bess Throckmorton, one of her Maids of Honour. She clapped him into prison, then banished him from court.

Raleigh kept busy enough in his enforced retirement. Much of the time he spent at his fine castle at Sherborne in Dorset, the estate which he saw as the basis of a great family dynasty. He wrote poetry, pursued his mathematical studies and discussed philosophy with the playwright Christopher Marlowe. But his main interest was still exploration. The Orinoco River, in what is today Venezuela, had come to dominate his thoughts. He sent an expedition there in 1594, and followed the next year. He sailed 400 miles up the river in an open boat, vainly seeking the fabulous gold mines of *El Dorado* (the golden land).

A tragic survival

The old glory was never to be fully recaptured. Though Raleigh and the ageing queen were reconciled in 1597, there was to be no place for him under a new king and a new dynasty. Robert Cecil, Elizabeth's Secretary of State, had persuaded James I that Raleigh was an atheist, a republican, a warmonger and a rake. From the moment of Elizabeth's death he was closely watched. In 1603, bewildered at his fall from power, Raleigh was trapped into talking treason against the new king. He was accused of plotting with Spain, tried and sentenced to death. His reprieve in 1603 gave him 15 more years of life. But the Elizabethan world in which he played so great a part had perished with the queen herself.

TOWARDS EL DORADO *On his way to seek the fabled riches of El Dorado in 1595, Raleigh captured the Spanish settlement of St Joseph, Trinidad. But he never found El Dorado; he ran out of supplies while sailing up the Orinoco River and was compelled to turn back to the coast.*

The Pilgrim Fathers sail in search of freedom

SHIP OF LIBERTY

This scale model of the Mayflower, *made early this century, can be seen in the Science Museum, London. The original* Mayflower, *which took the Pilgrim Fathers on their perilous voyage across the Atlantic, weighed only 180 tons, and was only 90 ft long.*

James I had been on the throne only a few months when he told the Puritans that, unless they conformed to the Church of England, he would 'harry them out of the land'. In 1608 a small group of pilgrims took refuge in Holland from threatened persecution, but even there they did not find the freedom they desired. And 12 years later, lured by the prospect of a free life in the new colony of Virginia, a few of them negotiated with a London merchant company, and prepared for a 3000 mile journey to the New World.

The 'Mayflower' sets sail

With their scanty resources they bought a small ship, the *Speedwell*, and crossed from Holland to Southampton. There the *Mayflower*, a square-rigged sailing ship chartered for the Atlantic crossing, awaited them. And there the pilgrims' troubles began.

The merchants insisted that for the first seven years in the New World the pilgrims should work for them; but the Puritans were determined to work their own farms and refused to sign the contract. No longer able to get advances from the merchants, they were forced to meet immediate expenses by selling

£60 worth of precious supplies. As a result, the founding fathers of the New World set out on their great adventure 'scarce having any butter, or oil, not a sole to mend a shoe, not every man a sword to his side'.

The two ships set sail on August 15, 1620, but they were forced to put back into port on two occasions, when the *Speedwell* sprang leaks. Finally, on September 16, the *Mayflower*, crammed with the *Speedwell's* passengers, set out from Plymouth alone. Her 101 passengers were divided into 35 Puritan 'Saints' and 66 'Strangers' – men driven, not by religious zeal, but by hardship, to leave a land which was then in the grip of poverty and famine.

The *Mayflower* was to be the pilgrims' home for more than two months. Only 90 ft long and 25 ft wide, she was a small vessel for so many passengers. Most of them had to sleep on the bare deck, without beds or hammocks, and protected by no more than a leaky canvas cover. Others had to content themselves with sleeping in the ship's longboat.

After a few days the *Mayflower* ran into stormy seas. One of the main beams amidships was bowed and cracked. Fortunately the passengers were able to mend it and the voyage continued. Despite sea-sickness, overcrowded cabins and violent winds, the pilgrims remained cheerful throughout the voyage, singing psalms and praying, confident that God would deliver them into safety.

Citizens of the New World

Only one sailor and one servant boy died on the voyage. One child was born in mid-Atlantic and appropriately christened Oceanus; and when the ship was in sight of land another

boy was born – and given the name of Peregrine, which means Pilgrim. Oceanus was to die in infancy, but Peregrine lived to be 83, one of the first citizens of the New World.

Winter had already fallen when, on November 21, the *Mayflower* dropped anchor, not on Virginia's sunny, fertile shores as intended, but on the desolate northern wastes of Cape Cod. The crew spent half a day trying to turn south towards Virginia, but adverse winds and heavy breakers drove them back on Cape Cod. After a few days the pilgrims reluctantly decided to stay there. Attempts were made to venture inland, but finally they agreed to settle on the coast at a site they named Plymouth. On Christmas Day, 1620, they began building their new homes.

The weather had already played a decisive part in guiding the pilgrims to their new home. Now its menace was to drive them to an act of even greater significance in shaping the history of the New World. Without adequate provisions, and faced by months of winter in an unknown land, their chief need was to maintain unity and prevent demoralisation.

To silence the 'discontents and murmurings amongst some, and mutinous speeches in others', they improvised a system of government – and in their search for unanimity, they chose a method which allowed every man – whether master or servant, 'Saint' or 'Stranger' – an equal voice.

The result was the 'Mayflower Compact', the foundation stone of American government. This read: 'Having undertaken for the Glory of God, and the Advancement of the Christian Faith . . . a voyage to plant the first colony in the northern parts of Virginia,' 41 men, masters and servants agreed to 'covenant and combine ourselves together into a civil Body Politick . . . and by Virtue herof do enact, constitute, and frame such just and equal Laws, Ordinances, Acts, Constitutions, and Offices, from time to time, as shall be thought most meet and convenient for the general Good of the Colony.'

Struggle for survival

John Carver, a 'Saint', was chosen governor, the first popularly elected governor in English colonial history. The seed of American democracy had been sown by citizens, who had the audacity to believe that they could survive on their own.

But in the months to come the pilgrims' faith and resolution was to be sorely tested. As the severe winter set in, the settlers were overwhelmed by an illness which apparently combined scurvy, caused by their starvation diet, with pneumonia, caused by inadequate shelter – for they were living on meagre rations in dugouts, made of rough logs with turf roofs. Every few days throughout the long winter, the shivering survivors gathered around the shallow graves of their fellow adventurers. By spring their numbers had been reduced to a total of 51 men, women and children.

But still their troubles were not over. In April the *Mayflower* set sail for England, cutting off any prospect of escape, and in the same month their elected leader, John Carver, died. In his place, the colonists elected a remarkable Yorkshireman, William Bradford, whose leadership and practical gifts were ideally suited to a pioneer community. Bradford was re-elected 30 times before his death in 1657, and he found time in old age to write the classic *History of Plymouth Plantation*.

Under his guidance, the pilgrims won the friendship of the local Indians, and devoted every hour of the day to the task of reclaiming land and harvesting the fruits of their wild country. From the Indians they learnt how to plant corn, trap animals for their furs and tap maple trees for their sugary syrup.

In the summer, the first wedding in the colony took place between two Pilgrims who had lost husband and wife in the winter. By November the settlers were ready to celebrate the first anniversary of their landing. With 90 Indian braves as their guests, they sat down to what was to prove to be the first Thanksgiving Dinner – a feast of venison, wild goose, eel pie, lobster, corn bread and wild fruits, washed down by new-made wine.

These were the richly deserved fruits of their labours. In adjusting to the harvests of a new hemisphere, the pilgrims were already showing their will to become Americans.

THE PILGRIMS EMBARK *A Victorian painting shows a group of pilgrims leaving to join the* Mayflower, *under a banner reading 'Freedom of Worship'. Led by a minister, friends and well-wishers pray for the voyagers' safety.*

A new Bible to unite the nation

In commanding 54 scholars in 1604 to make a new translation of the Bible, James I launched a work which was to be both the inspiration and the bane of his kingdom.

The scholars worked in groups at Oxford, Cambridge and Westminster. By 1611 they were able to present the king with the fruits of their labours – describing the Holy Writ as 'that inestimable treasure which excelleth all the riches of the earth'.

The king knew well that such treasures are potent stuff. He hoped that his new translation, produced in fertile co-operation by Puritan ministers and Anglican bishops, would become a source of national unity.

But, ironically, the new Bible was not a source of peace. Its immediate impact was to encourage individual conscience and individual judgment. Charles I remarked that 'people are governed by the pulpit more than the Sword'. In their long Sabbath hours of compulsory church attendance, the subjects of James I and Charles I were inevitably influenced by the lesson that earthly powers and crowns cannot prevail against the armies of righteousness: 'How are the mighty fallen, and the weapons of war perished.'

Yet, despite its potent role in the drift to civil war, the success of the 'Good Book' was enduring. For at least four centuries it was to remain by far the most widely read and deeply loved work in the English language.

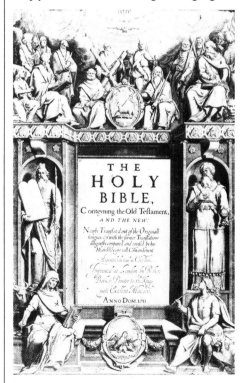

PEOPLE'S BIBLE *The frontispiece of the 1611 King James's Bible. Its translators tried to use popular language, employing only a vocabulary based on words in everyday use.*

THE GENIUS WHO DISCOVERED THE SECRETS OF THE HEART

ROYAL DEMONSTRATION *As physician to Charles I, Harvey could have settled into the easy life of a courtier, but he continued with his experiments, carefully testing and then re-testing his theories. He is shown here demonstrating his theory of the circulation of the blood to the king.*

MEDICAL GENIUS *William Harvey, a 17th-century physician, discovered the circulation of the blood.*

In the 17th century it was not only political ideas which were overthrown, but also the long-established concepts of philosophy and science. This second revolution was launched by Francis Bacon, but the man of science who turned theory into practice was another Englishman, William Harvey.

Harvey was one of those great men so totally immersed in their own work that they seem to stand apart from political and historical events. Yet he was the child of his time, born into the adventurous world of the Renaissance, when traditional knowledge and inherited beliefs were being challenged.

At the centre of this intellectual ferment was the University of Padua in Italy, where the Polish astronomer Copernicus had evolved his startling theory that the earth was not the centre of the universe, but revolved around the sun. It was there that Harvey received in 1602 his diploma as Doctor of Medicine and returned to England and the London College of Physicians.

Discovering nature's secrets

To the public, he appeared simply as a highly successful doctor, especially when, in 1626, he became personal physician to Charles I. But all the while in London and Oxford he was conducting a series of private experiments using modern scientific methods; and he had chosen as his subject the function of the key organ of the human anatomy, the heart.

Harvey was a reticent man who throughout his life shunned controversy. When less-enlightened critics attacked his theory, which he published in 1628, he showed great reluctance to defend himself. But slowly through the next decades his great discovery gained a hold wherever scientists were engaged in the study of human anatomy. He had opened a

HARVEY REMEMBERED *After Cromwell became Lord Protector, Harvey concentrated on teaching at the Royal College of Physicians. Still treasured there are the pointer he used at lectures, his Padua University diploma, and the first edition of his book on the circulation of the blood.*

closed door in the understanding of the body and made possible the advances of modern medicine and surgery.

In Harvey's time the movement of blood was believed to be irregular in direction and speed. Some of it was believed to come from the liver. Also, it was thought to pass directly from the right to the left ventricle of the heart. Above all, there was no notion of the heart as a mechanical device, a muscular pump which controlled the flow of the blood.

Harvey hit upon this idea, and calculated that, at the normal pulse rate of 70 beats a minute, the heart pumped more than 50 gallons of blood an hour. Since that amount of blood weighs three times as much as a man, he reasoned that the blood must continually be re-circulated.

Earlier scientists had noticed little flaps on the veins. Harvey correctly identified them as one-way valves which prevent the blood from going backwards. By tying a tourniquet around a bare arm, and watching how the blood reacted, he proved that the blood passed from the heart along the arteries and returned through the veins.

As a result of such experiments, Harvey was able to overthrow most of the existing ideas about the circulation of the blood. He was never satisfied with his findings until he had checked his ideas by experiment.

A life of quiet dedication

Unlike his great contemporary, Bacon, who was for a period his patient, Harvey did not concern himself with the underlying philosophical problems of the scientific method. He was a practical man, but his lifework – a demonstration of deduction backed by experiment – was the first clear example of the scientific method which Bacon had foreshadowed.

Dr Harvey lived a life of quiet dedication, as a physician and as a scientist, and contemporary records provide few glimpses of his private life. Aubrey, the diarist, records that 'he did delight to be in the darke and told me he could then best contemplate'.

Another characteristic glimpse of him records his presence at the Battle of Edgehill in 1642, where he was supposed to be acting as tutor to Prince Charles, the 12-year-old heir to the throne, and his 9-year-old brother, Prince James. Undisturbed by gunfire and apparently unconcerned at the events which marked the beginning of the Civil War, Harvey spent the battle sitting under a hedge engrossed in a book – while his two young charges narrowly escaped capture or death.

But, despite appearances, Harvey's concentration was not limited to book-learning. His contribution to the heritage of science lay in his resolution to seek for truth by studying the wider 'book' of all created things. In doing so, he became the first of the long line of British experimental scientists who have contributed so much to world knowledge.

A PROPHET OF LEARNING AND THE SCIENTIFIC REVOLUTION

THEORIST OF SCIENCE *Detail of a portrait of Francis Bacon, whose theories laid the foundations of the modern scientific method.*

For hundreds of years, science and superstition went hand in hand. In medieval times, alchemists laboured in their laboratories, on tasks such as seeking an 'elixir' which would give its possessor eternal life, or the 'philosopher's stone', which would turn base metals into gold. In the course of their vain experiments they made many discoveries, but they were unable to realise the importance of what they had achieved. Firstly, they were bound by preconceived traditions, and secondly they lacked any sense of method. And without method, any systematic scientific advance was impossible.

So matters stood until an Englishman of genius, Francis Bacon, took things in hand. Bacon was not a practical scientist; he made no discoveries of his own. But his breadth of vision was such that his work illuminated the entire world of science and philosophy. Shrewd and sceptical, he overthrew the tyranny of ancient scholarship, smashed the intellectual idols of antiquity, and encouraged those interested in the secrets of nature to co-operate in establishing a new spirit of rational inquiry.

Born in 1561 in London, Bacon had a mind of extraordinary diversity. He was essayist, politician, legal authority, philosopher and, in the end, Lord Chancellor. It has even been said that he was the real author of Shakespeare's works. He thought of himself as a man who was over-awed neither by the old, nor by the new, and a hater of every kind of affectation: 'So I thought my nature had a kind of familiarity and relation with Truth,' he wrote on one famous occasion.

Bacon's dedication to this pursuit of truth, and his training as a lawyer, equipped him for his task as the prophet of the new age of science. He proceeded by applying the laws of evidence and burden of proof to scientific theory.

He isolated science from the muddled theories of medieval scholars and called for a truly scientific explanation of nature. And in doing so he pointed the way to the modern approach to scientific method – the process of experiment and observation leading to the laws of science.

Establishing 'scientific method'

Previously, what men regarded as knowledge was what had been handed down to them from ancient authorities such as Aristotle. Bacon's 'scientific method' was simple and revolutionary. First, the scientist, by observation, forms a hypothesis. Then he tests this hypothesis by repeated experiments. And if the experiments are successful he can claim that his hypothesis is a true fact. Knowledge thus becomes as Bacon wrote 'the fruit of experience. Man . . . is the servant and interpreter of nature'.

Unfortunately, Bacon's career failed to match his intellectual gifts. Though he eventually reached the highest office in the land as Lord Chancellor, this reward only came after years of humiliation and intrigue. To gain his ends he betrayed his friends, frequently dishonoured himself and, in the end, was indicted for taking bribes and removed from office.

Disgraced and disappointed, Bacon admitted that he would have done better to have remained faithful to his philosophical curiosity. He wrote that he knew that he was 'by inward calling to be fitter to hold a book than to play a part'. And so he retired to his lavish London house, with its 100 servants, and devoted his last years to the study of philosophy.

Bacon died at the age of 65, following his one recorded attempt to conduct a scientific experiment. It had occurred to him that meat might be preserved in ice instead of salt, and after stuffing a chicken carcass with snow, he caught a chill from which he died a few days later.

Bacon was disappointed with his own achievements. But he recognised that he had rung 'the bell which called the wits together'. And his dream of a meeting of great minds in the service of science and philosophy was fulfilled 34 years later, when the Royal Society was founded. He had laid the foundation for the great scientific revolution that was to change the face of the world.

In the name of 'justice' a commoner defies his king

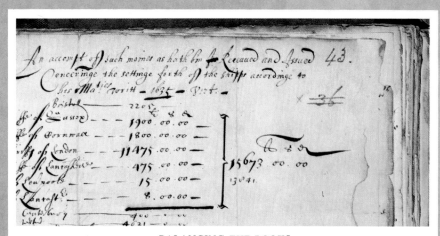

BALANCING THE BOOKS

A fragment of the royal accounts, now at the Public Records Office, London. It shows the large revenue that Charles I raised without the consent of Parliament by levying the tax of Ship Money in the 1630's. London was made to pay £11,475 and Bristol £2205.

Some of the greatest freedoms that Englishmen possess have been won as the direct result of one man's determination to stand up for his rights. Such a man was John Hampden, who in 1636 challenged the personal rule of Charles I by refusing to pay a tax known as Ship Money.

Hampden was a rich Buckinghamshire squire who had served in Parliament. He was a man of pleasant and cheerful disposition and had long been an opponent of unlimited royal power. In 1627 he spent a year in prison for refusing to contribute to a 'forced loan' for the king's war in France. Two years later, when the chief critic of Charles I, Sir John Eliot, was placed in the Tower, Hampden looked after his children. Eliot, a sick man, died in captivity, and Hampden never forgave the king. Ship Money was his opportunity for revenge.

The two flaws in the king's case

In the past this tax, which was for emergencies only, had been levied on coastal towns for the maintenance of the Royal Navy. In the 1630's the navy had been allowed to run down and there was no money to re-equip it. At this time piracy was a nagging threat to English merchant shipping.

In levying Ship Money to meet this situation, Charles appeared to have right and necessity on his side. But his case contained two weaknesses: he extended the tax to inland places and he acted in defiance of the recently accepted Petition of Right, which had declared non-Parliamentary taxation to be illegal. And Hampden was just the man to take up the

TAX TO BUILD A NAVY *Ship Money provided the funds to equip the Royal Navy with magnificent ships such as the* Sovereign of the Seas *(above). Launched in 1637, it was England's first 100-gun battleship. John Hampden (left) refused to pay the tax in 1636. His trial in the next year attracted nationwide publicity, and proved to be the opening shot in the campaign which was to lead to civil war between king and Parliament. In this war Hampden was to die.*

PETITION OF RIGHT

In February 1628, Parliament challenged Charles's bid to win supreme power with four demands. Taxation was not to be levied without Parliament's consent; no one was to be gaoled without trial; no troops to be billeted on private households; martial law to be abolished.

Together, these demands formed the Petition of Right. The king declared that the Petition of Right would 'dissolve the foundation of our monarchy'. But both Houses of Parliament voted in its favour and he was forced to give his assent. However, the agreement broke down within a year. It was finally wrecked by the Opposition leader, Sir John Eliot, who led a revolt against a royal command to adjourn the Commons for a week. Charles was outraged by this presumption. His response was to dissolve Parliament and rule without it for 11 years.

In this 19th-century painting, Members of Parliament prevent the Speaker from carrying out the king's demand to dissolve the 1629 Parliament. But Charles had his way, and ruled without it.

challenge. In 1637 he was summoned before the Court of Exchequer, charged with failure to pay Ship Money of 20 shillings on his lands at Stoke Mandeville, Bucks.

The sum was small, but the issues raised were of profound importance. The king's policies were on trial. As one of the judges said, this was 'one of the greatest cases that ever came in judgment'.

So an air of expectant uncertainty hung about the courtroom on November 6, 1637, as Oliver St John, a virtually unknown constitutional lawyer, rose to defend Hampden. With a brilliant display of learning and logic he rested his defence on two arguments.

First, if subjects were taxable at the royal pleasure, then all property was at the whim and mercy of the king. Secondly, although piracy had been vexatious, it was not an emergency. If the king needed money, the proper course was to call on Parliament.

A deadly blow to one-man rule

St John spoke for two days. The Solicitor-General took four days to answer him. Then followed a battery of legal experts, each meticulously combing the past for precedents to support their pleas.

Hampden's refusal to pay his 20 shillings amounted to a challenge to the king to prove that he had the right to govern England without recourse to its long-established Parliament. In the end, the king's lawyers were unable to establish this right to the full satisfaction of the court, even though Hampden was ordered to pay his tax by a narrow majority of seven judges out of 12. And the five judges who gave their verdicts against the Crown dealt a blow to absolute monarchy from which it was never to recover.

As a result of the case, Hampden emerged as a public figure. Despite paying the fine the judges imposed, his struggle for principle had passed into history. When, three years later, Charles was finally forced to recall Parliament, its members made a hero of Hampden.

When war broke out, Hampden took up arms in defence of his principles. He was wounded in the shoulder during an insignificant skirmish in a cornfield at Chalgrove, near Oxford, in June 1643. Charles I offered to send a surgeon to help him, but it was too late. He died six days later, leaving moderate men on both sides with an acute sense of the wastefulness of war. A contemporary wrote: 'The loss of Colonel Hampden goeth near the heart of every man that loves the good of his king and country. The memory of him will more and more be had in honour and esteem.'

This last prophecy was fulfilled. Long after Hampden's death, the philosopher Edmund Burke put the question: 'Would twenty shillings have ruined Mr Hampden's fortune?' and gave a famous answer: 'No, but the payment of half twenty shillings on the principle it was demanded, would have made him a slave.'

Charles I: 'So good a man, so bad a king'

The young Charles I – unlike his father – was sober, dignified, handsome and courteous. It was said that he had never violated a woman, struck a man, or spoken an evil word. He lacked his father's intellectual grip and knowledge, but at first he appealed to a generation sickened by James I's vulgarity.

Charles was a small man – in some paintings he almost disappears into his riding boots; but he had a deeply rooted sense of his own dignity and importance. His delicate frame and feminine face were elongated by a pointed beard. His melancholy air almost seemed to mark him out for tragedy.

A sickly child, not in the direct line of succession, Charles was raised in seclusion until his brother Henry's death in 1612. He worshipped Henry and his sister Elizabeth who were both personally attractive.

When Henry died and Elizabeth married a German prince in 1613, Charles's transformation into heir apparent did not bolster his self-confidence, especially since James persisted in calling him 'baby Charles'. He over-compensated with pride and rigidity and he instinctively ignored unwelcome advice. His natural shyness and reserve were accentuated by a slight stammer.

Charles's awkwardness with people threw him heavily on those he could trust – men such

THE KING RULES

Charles I hated Parliaments. 'They are of the nature of cats,' he said, 'they ever grow cursed with age.' In 1629 he had done with them. For the next 11 years he carried out a policy which was to become known as 'Thorough'.

Under 'Thorough', the king and his ministers strove with single-minded determination to work for the benefit of all the subjects in the state. A divided nation, they believed, could be united by a benevolent dictatorship.

Charles relied on Thomas Wentworth, Earl of Strafford, and William Laud, who was made Archbishop of Canterbury in 1633, to see this policy through. Both men, however, aroused the country's hatred. Strafford was nicknamed 'Black Tom the Tyrant' because of his brutal rule in Ireland. But it was Laud, the High Church enemy of Puritanism, who brought the monarchy down. His decision in 1637 to impose the English Prayer Book on Scotland led to war with the Scots. Charles's attempts to suppress the rebellion had failed; his army was so weak that he did not dare to cross the border. In 1640 he had to recall Parliament.

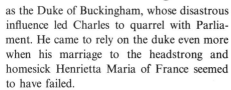

Archbishop Laud, one of Charles I's ministers, whose tactlessness helped to bring down his master.

as the Duke of Buckingham, whose disastrous influence led Charles to quarrel with Parliament. He came to rely on the duke even more when his marriage to the headstrong and homesick Henrietta Maria of France seemed to have failed.

James I had originally hoped to arrange a diplomatic marriage between Charles and the Spanish *Infanta* (Crown Princess). His plans had been frustrated, but the young Charles had not forgotten the languid, sensual beauty of the Hapsburg princess. She was very different from his bride, a gawky 16-year-old with buck teeth and enormous eyes, who burst into tears at the first sight of her husband.

Personal incompatibility was compounded by religious differences. Henrietta Maria was a devout Catholic. She refused even to attend her husband's Protestant coronation service, and insisted on having her own priests.

For two years Charles and Henrietta Maria lived virtually separate lives, while Charles continued to rely on Buckingham for affection and support. But this prop was removed when Buckingham was assassinated in 1628. His death left the king with no friends, only servants. In his despair, Charles turned to his young wife, but her advice was just as ill-founded as the policies of the dead favourite. Coming from the autocratic court of France, she encouraged Charles's despotism.

Charles believed that Parliament's demands for reform would lead to revolution. In 1629 he abandoned parliamentary government. His belief in the 'Divine Right of Kings' was one of the few things he inherited from his father, coupled with a lofty view of the powers and the privileges of the Church.

From peace to civil war

Government without Parliament seemed to him not only natural but right. And by 1635 his attitude seemed to have been justified. England was at peace; the government's accounts had been balanced; one of his leading parliamentary opponents, Sir John Eliot, had died in the Tower, and another, Sir Thomas Wentworth, had been transformed under the new title of Earl of Strafford into his most loyal servant. Public prosperity was crowned by domestic happiness; he and his queen had achieved perfect harmony.

But this calm was not to last. In 1639 revolt in Scotland forced Charles to recall Parliament the next year. The king and his people were soon at loggerheads again. This time, however, the result was civil war.

Charles fought for seven years for his throne. But in 1649 he lost both the crown and his life. To the end, he was a man of principle. He refused to sacrifice his beliefs to keep his crown. And through his death, he paved the way for an eventual restoration of the Stuarts to the throne in 1660.

Supreme sacrifice—a minister dies to save his king

THE ULTIMATE SANCTION
The able and ruthless Earl of Strafford was executed in 1641, falling victim to a vengeful Parliament after seven years as Charles I's minister. He was the last holder of high office to fall victim to this axe and block, now to be seen in the Tower of London.

No event in the melancholy reign of Charles I so disturbed the king's conscience as the death of his most faithful servant, the Earl of Strafford, in 1641.

From 1633 to 1640 Strafford was the king's deputy in Ireland. There, riding rough-shod over the liberties of the people and the rights of property, he imposed the royal policy of 'Thorough' – royal rule without Parliament – with single-minded devotion and brutality.

In 1640, bankrupt and at war with his Scottish subjects, Charles was at last driven to recall Parliament after 11 years of absolute rule. To support him in his emergency he turned to Strafford, promising him that if he did his king this service he 'should not suffer in his person, honour or fortune'. It was a promise that Charles was forced to break. On November 10, Strafford arrived in London. Six months later he was dead, executed by an Act of Parliament.

The fall of Strafford is one of the most tragic stories in English history. An opponent of Charles's first minister, the Duke of Buckingham, in the 1620's, he had been imprisoned, like Hampden, in 1627. In the next year he was one of the most prominent voices in the parliamentary fight to force Charles to agree to the Petition of Right.

Lynchpin of the crown

But once Charles had accepted the Petition, Strafford decided that his duty was to support the crown. 'The authority of a king,' he said, 'is the keystone which closeth up the arch of order and government.'

Strafford thus brought upon himself all the odium of a turncoat. By 1640 his callous rule in Ireland had made him the most hated man in the kingdom. His very presence – his ravaged, parchment face suffused with the blood of rising anger, his body twisted by gout over his walking stick – inspired horror. Queen Henrietta Maria knew well of his loyalty to her husband, but she could not help recoiling from what she thought to be the smell of blood and mud about him.

When Parliament met in November 1640, after 11 years in which its pent-up anger had had no outlet, Strafford was the first object of attack. The members began proceedings to impeach him for 'high misdemeanours', for destroying the rule of law in Ireland. On the same day that the proceedings were started, Strafford went to the House of Lords to 'look my accusers in the face'. He was forbidden to speak, arrested and removed to the Tower.

'Thus he whose greatness in the morning owned a power over two kingdoms,' wrote a chronicler, 'in the evening straitened his person betwixt two walls.'

On his way to the Tower, the crowds cried out, 'What is the matter?' 'A small matter, I warrant you,' Strafford replied. What harm could come to him, he asked in a tender letter

END OF A DILEMMA *The Earl of Strafford (left) was Charles I's most devoted servant. 'The authority of a king,' he said, 'is the keystone which closeth up the arch of order and government.' But his devotion and efficiency aroused the anger of Parliament, and in 1641 it passed a Bill of Attainder which condemned him to death. Charles was in a dilemma. He had promised Strafford his protection, but to fulfil this promise would jeopardise his throne. Realising the king's difficulty, Strafford freed him from his promise and gave his life for the royal cause. He was executed (above) on Tower Hill on May 12, 1641.*

to his wife, when there was 'nothing capital' in the charge against him? Did he not have the confidence and the protection of his sovereign?

Strafford's trial opened in Westminster Hall on March 22, 1641. Not just Strafford, but the whole balance of power between the king and the Commons was at stake. The most damning accusation made against Strafford was Sir Henry Vane's unswerving testimony that he had advised the king to use the Irish army against his opponents in England, to 'reduce *this* kingdom'. But of that there was no proof and, by April 10, impeachment had failed.

Parliament was concerned, however, not with justice, but with political necessity. Strafford was the symbol of absolute monarchy, the enemy of the peace of the country. In Parliament's eyes his death was imperative. And so the House of Commons introduced a Bill of Attainder which, regardless of whether Strafford were guilty of a crime, simply declared it to be the will of Parliament that he should die.

On April 13, his head shrunk between his shoulders, his long grey beard making him look older than his years, Strafford made a last, two-hour speech in his defence. 'These gentlemen tell me they speak in defence of the Commonweal against my arbitrary laws; give me leave to say that I speak in the defence of the Commonweal against their arbitrary treason.' It was an heroic effort, but it failed. The Commons passed the Bill condemning him by a vote of 204 to 59.

King Charles now relied on the House of Lords not to condemn one of their own order for carrying out the orders of the king. But popular clamour raged against Strafford and, as mob violence grew, the Lords gave way.

A selfless sacrifice

Strafford's life now lay with the king. Without his assent the Bill of Attainder was not law. Charles had never taken to Strafford; like Queen Henrietta Maria he could not understand Strafford's rough manners. Yet, no man had rendered him such unstinting service.

In conscience, therefore, Charles could not break his word and give his assent to the Bill. Yet to refuse was to imperil the monarchy. To spare the king, Strafford, selfless to the end, wrote him a letter from the Tower, releasing the king from his promise: 'To set Your Majesty's conscience at liberty, I do most humbly beseech Your Majesty (for preventing of evils which may happen by Your refusal) to pass this bill.'

So, on May 12, 1641, before a crowd of 200,000 at Tower Hill, Strafford, in his last great service to the crown, surrendered his life. For the rest of his life the memory of that scene haunted Charles I. When, eight years later, he came to the same end on the scaffold, almost his last words were, 'An unjust sentence that I suffered for to take effect is punished now by an unjust sentence upon me'.

A nation prepares for bitter civil war

As he put his signature to the Bill which sent Strafford to his death, King Charles murmured tearfully, 'My Lord of Strafford's condition is happier than mine'. Yet the first signs were that Strafford's death was a blood sacrifice which might bring peace and happiness to the nation. Charles gave his assent to a number of reforming Bills, including one that abolished the Court of Star Chamber, and another that ended non-parliamentary taxation. At last, Parliament and the king seemed to have come to a settlement.

Moderate men, however, were alarmed when Parliament forced the king to agree that he would never dissolve it without its consent. Such an assault on the royal power rekindled Charles's hatred of Parliament. For the moment that hatred was impotent. Civil war was impossible because the king did not have command of an army.

Then, in November 1640, news reached London of an event which was to transform the situation. Ireland, released from Strafford's grip, had risen in rebellion. The king hoped that his quarrel with Parliament would be swallowed up in a loyalist reaction against the Irish rebels, that 'these ill news from Ireland may hinder some of these follies in England'.

But to put down the Irish uprising Charles needed to raise an army. And the Commons, who had long since learnt not to trust their king, insisted that unless he changed his councillors they would raise their own army to conquer Ireland. They also demanded a veto on army appointments.

Suddenly there was a spontaneous rally to the king. Throughout 1641 Charles cleverly exploited the new mood. He appealed as the anointed defender of the Established Church against those who wanted to do away with bishops and impose bleak Puritanism. There gathered around the king a party of 'constitutional Royalists', led in the Lords by Lord Digby and in the Commons by Edward Hyde, the future Earl of Clarendon. Hyde had voted for Strafford's death, but when the Church was attacked he turned to support the king. At the same time, Charles began to build up a small military force in London.

'The birds have flown'

Then, in January, Charles destroyed the goodwill which he was winning by one of the hasty acts which were so characteristic of him. With a small body of officers he marched into the Commons to arrest five Parliamentary leaders. But they had already fled. Declaring that 'the birds have flown', Charles retired in confusion. In fear for his safety, he now fled from London with the queen.

Charles's withdrawal to the north had the effect of dividing the nation into Royalists and Parliamentarians. By August, the king had secured enough supporters to strike. At Nottingham on August 22, 1642, he raised his standard. That was a symbolic and ancient summons to his subjects to come to his aid, but it was traditionally the symbol of a rebel proclaiming resistance to the government. Thus, it boded ill for Royalists that the anxious man who raised his standard behind a ruined castle, remote from the capital, was their king. But Englishmen had now to settle with their consciences on whose side they stood.

RAISING THE STANDARD *Having failed to arrest five of his leading enemies in Parliament, Charles fled from London with his queen and raised his standard at Nottingham. Here, he greets his followers. This was a crucial decision; from then on England was divided by civil war.*

AN ARCHITECT CAPTURES THE GLORY OF THE STUART SUNSET

Charles I's self-declared aim was to create the most civilised court in Europe, and during his 24 year reign he collected 1400 paintings and 400 pieces of sculpture. He patronised and encouraged the leading artists of his day, and in Inigo Jones the king had in his service the finest architect of the age.

It was Jones who transformed English architecture on Classical lines, creating a style whose influence was to last for nearly 300 years. Among his masterpieces are the Banqueting House at Whitehall, the Queen's House at Greenwich and St Paul's Church, Covent Garden.

Monument to an age

But the supreme monument to the Stuart age and to the vision of Inigo Jones is Wilton House, Salisbury. One of the king's chief nobles, Philip Herbert, Earl of Pembroke and Montgomery, turned Wilton into a house which rivalled the best the king could achieve. And Charles was not slow to show his admiration for the house. The diarist John Aubrey wrote that the king 'did love Wilton above all places; and came thither every Sommer'.

It is not surprising that Wilton House stood so high in the monarch's affections. The spirit of the carefree – and slightly unreal – 1630's is expressed in the graceful beauty of the principal rooms, which were created to the basic design of Inigo Jones.

The first Wilton House, on whose foundations Inigo Jones achieved his greatest triumph, was erected by William Herbert, grandfather of Philip, in the 1540's. It stood on the site of a great abbey which shared the fate of so many monastic buildings during Henry VIII's Reformation.

William Herbert was a soldier of fortune who had made his name in continental wars, and returned home to serve his king and to marry the sister of Henry VIII's sixth wife, Catharine Parr. The Tudor house of the powerful Herberts witnessed the first performance of Shakespeare's *As You Like It*, and it was there that the poet Sir Philip Sidney wrote his pastoral romance 'Arcadia'.

Only the tower in the centre of the East Front survives unchanged from William Herbert's great house. It was the fourth earl, Philip Herbert, who pulled down the south

block of the Tudor mansion, substituting for it a façade and a set of rooms that have no rival in the history of English architecture.

The king took an interest in the developments at Wilton, and Queen Henrietta Maria urged Inigo Jones, who was then Surveyor of the Royal Works, to submit designs. In the 1630's Jones was at the height of his fame, and most of the leading courtiers were competing for his services.

An artistic triumph

Jones was busy with the Queen's House at Greenwich, but found time to draw up a rough plan for Wilton and to instruct his French assistant, Isaac de Caux, to implement it. In 1635 the work was begun, the earl supervising every stage with frequent assistance from his royal visitors. Charles and his vivacious queen would stroll through the uncompleted state rooms, advising their host on points of detail.

According to a surviving drawing by de Caux of the South Front, the original idea was for a house twice the size of the present one. But the outbreak of the Civil War brought the building programme at Wilton to a halt.

The earl was uncertain which side to join. He was the king's friend and Lord Chamberlain, but all his sympathies lay with the Parliamentarians. Finally he threw in his lot with Parliament. The upheaval meant that

THE KING'S CHOICE *The South Front of Wilton House near Salisbury was rebuilt to the designs of Inigo Jones. The great beauty of the place and the hospitality of the Herbert family brought many famous people to* Wilton. John Aubrey, the diarist, recorded: 'Wilton House was like a college, there were so many learned and ingeniose persons.' Charles I, whom Jones served as surveyor, loved the house 'above all places'.

only the proposed east wing was built. But, strangely, this mutilation of the original plan produced an artistic triumph. De Caux's elevation of the east wing was brilliantly altered, probably by Inigo Jones himself. Towers at each end gave symmetry to the whole composition, and one of de Caux's great venetian windows became the central feature.

In 1647, like some divine retribution for his betrayal of the king, Philip saw his new house largely destroyed by fire. Undaunted, he immediately began the rebuilding. Inigo Jones, who was by now 75 years old, set to work on the magnificent state rooms which are still the chief of Wilton's glories. Neither he nor his patron lived to see them completed.

The work was continued by Jones's nephew and assistant, John Webb, who finished the task in 1653. The conception and designs are virtually all Jones's own, planned and executed with an exuberance belied by the house's restrained exterior. Jones once wrote that 'outwardly every wise man carries a gravity, yet inwardly has his imagination set on fire and sometimes licentiously flies out'.

Wilton embodies this philosophy to perfection. Outside all is harmony and restraint, but within the seven state rooms architects and decorators created an atmosphere of exuberant richness, largely in white and gold.

Most splendid of all is the Double Cube Room which is 60 ft long, 30 ft high and 30 ft wide. This glittering apartment is impressive without being intimidating; it has the feeling of a comfortable *salon* rather than a stately audience chamber. Carved and gilded fruit and flowers festoon the walls, and the lavish decoration is taken up into the moulded and painted ceiling. Equally ornate are the doors and the Italian marble fireplace.

Scarcely less impressive is the Single Cube Room, all the dimensions of which are 30 ft.

The smaller chambers – such as the Hunting Room and the Corner Room – are more intimate, though they, too, glow with sumptuous colours and rich fabrics.

In all the state rooms Jones's decorations have a weight and solidity, a feeling of essential Englishness about them. The English furniture makers, William Kent and Thomas Chippendale, working in the Double Cube Room, a century after it was built, brilliantly adapted their work to his style.

Two men of genius

Inigo Jones had another collaborator whose contribution to Wilton was far greater than that of Webb or de Caux. Sir Anthony van Dyck had painted his superb series of portraits of the Herberts between 1634 and 1636; and the Double Cube Room was specifically designed for these pictures, culminating in the family group that dominates the west wall. Nearly 20 ft wide, it is the largest family group painted by Van Dyck. There are few rooms anywhere in which paintings on canvas combine so effortlessly with gilding and plasterwork to form a single satisfying whole.

These two men of genius combined to make Wilton one of the most beautiful places in Britain; they also gave a lasting expression to the briefly sunlit episode when the ill-starred king and queen 'came thither every Sommer'.

STATELY COMFORT *For all its splendour, the Double Cube Room at Wilton House is still a room to be lived in. After a fire in 1647, it was redesigned to hold Van Dyck's portraits of the Herberts and the king's family. Its classical proportions were a triumph for the masterly Inigo Jones.*

BRITAIN'S FIRST ARCHITECT

Born in 1573, Inigo Jones spent most of his long life providing a graceful background for the Stuart court. He was kept busy designing court entertainments as well as the works of architecture which gave him lasting fame.

The ruinous extravagance of these entertainments made the architect deeply unpopular with the Puritans. At the end of the siege of Basing House in October 1645, he was stripped naked by Oliver Cromwell's troopers and carried away wrapped in a blanket.

When Jones died two years after the execution of Charles I, it was said that the cause of death was 'grief for the fatal calamity of his master'. But he had lived long enough to provide Britain with a body of buildings which satisfied his own high standards – 'solid, proportionable, masculine and unaffected'.

Inigo Jones (above) spent much time working on masques. He designed elaborate stage sets and costumes, such as this Fiery Spirit (right).

A MEMORIAL TO THE GRACE OF A DOOMED GENERATION

The romantic image of Charles I and his court created by Anthony van Dyck is one of the most enduring in the history of art. In a series of breathtaking canvases, Van Dyck succeeded in immortalising and glamorising for ever the supporters of a lost cause, the valiant cavaliers and their ladies.

In the years he spent in Britain – the nine years of his mature genius – Van Dyck made a double contribution to the artistic heritage of his adopted land. He gave Britain the finest court portraits of any period and any country; and he introduced a new style of painting, a style which was to influence more than two centuries of English portraiture.

Chosen by the king

Van Dyck came from the Spanish Netherlands, that part of Europe now known as Belgium. He entered the studio of the great northern master, Peter Paul Rubens, and quickly became his most brilliant pupil. In 1621, at the age of 22, he was attracted to the service of the English crown and sent by James I to Italy to complete his training.

The English court then lost track of him until 1629, when Charles I bought one of his paintings. Three years later, Van Dyck was induced to settle in England and enter the royal service on unprecedented terms – a knighthood and an annual pension of £200. Apart from visits to his native Flanders in 1634 and 1640, Van Dyck lived in England until his death in 1641.

Almost overnight, the new artist at Whitehall revolutionised the style of portrait painting. Elizabethan paintings had enclosed the sitter in a tiny box, with little more than a carpet, chair and curtains as props. The effect was one of frozen immobility. Van Dyck's paintings opened up vistas into the beyond.

Models for the future

For the first time in English history, the picture frame became an open window through which the eye passed into a natural world governed by the rules of perspective.

Van Dyck's figures are always apparently in the act of moving or about to move. They stand elegantly in the midst of twilight landscapes, or walk through shadowy groves.

No painter was more successful in transforming his sitters into the heroes and heroines which they imagined themselves to be. By this imaginative sensitivity to his subject's secret aspirations, Van Dyck was a purveyor of ideals. In his lifetime, this rare skill naturally endeared him to his patrons. After his death they and their successors looked to other artists to give them something of the Van Dyck magic. His great works became the models which all aspiring portraitists knew they must emulate. He had established a tradition of fine portraiture which lasted for two centuries as one of the glories of British art. As a court artist, Van Dyck's first duty was

SORROWFUL KING *Van Dyck painted this triple portrait of Charles I for the sculptor Bernini, who used it as a guide when carving a bust of the king. Later writers fostered a legend that Bernini gazed at the painting and said: 'Something evil will befall this man; he carries misfortune in his face.' But Van Dyck himself would never have accepted this romantic interpretation of his work.*

CHILDREN APART *The confident royal manner is already apparent in five of Charles's children, painted in 1637. From the left, Mary, James, in girlish clothing, Charles, heir to the throne, stroking a pet almost as tall as himself, and Elizabeth playing with Anne, the baby of the family.*

BORN TO RULE *There is a hint of melancholy in all Van Dyck's representations of the king. In this huge canvas, 12 ft high, he broke away from the older tradition of formal portraits and transformed his royal subject into a heroic knight of legend, the unchallenged master of all he surveyed.*

QUEEN OF LOVE *Henrietta Maria and her husband reigned over a world of masques, pageants and banquets which celebrated the ideals of courtly love and beauty. Their happy marriage provided a touching theme for Van Dyck.*

to present an acceptable view of his chief patron, the king. The image he created of Charles I was undoubtedly his master stroke, for it was not a work of mere flattery but rather an evocation of all that Charles wished to be. In reality, the limitations of Charles's own complex character – and the unhappy nature of the age itself – prevented him from realising his aspirations. Perhaps only in Van Dyck's canvases could he fulfil his ambitions as the ideal ruler of an ideal realm.

Later generations have seen in Van Dyck's renderings of Charles I's face the look of a man who foresaw his fate. At the time, however, the sad grandeur of the royal pose, with the heavy-lidded eyes and far-away look, were merely expressions of calm spiritual contemplation. Van Dyck presents a king who was dignified and solitary, with a touch of shadowed melancholy, then the most fashionable of

moods. But no suggestion of defeat or failure was intended – certainly no premonition of impending doom. Painted long before the civil war, the royal portraits were deliberate assertions of absolute power.

Van Dyck depicts him as the Lord's anointed in robes of state, as the ideal gentleman, elegantly leaning on his walking stick in a forest glade, as a Knight of the Garter, as the pious protector of the Church of England, and as a warrior on horseback.

Yet in all these aspects of the king, Van Dyck gave the royal face one consistent representation: elegant, refined and slightly disdainful. Above all, the expression conveyed an aura of intense spirituality, an appropriate mood for the divinely appointed ruler who was answerable to God alone.

The artist's genius touched Queen Henrietta Maria with the same divine radiance. Like her

husband, she was short; but you would not know it from Van Dyck's portraits. Sometimes she appears in the role of a love goddess, reforming a licentious court by the example of courtly love. Sometimes, in shimmering satin and pearls, she is the ideal lady of chivalry, a perfect spouse for Charles in his role as the gallant knight.

A world of make-believe

Henrietta Maria is also presented as the ideal mother, a fitting parent for the innocent royal children who grace Van Dyck's family portraits. These solemn infants are endowed with an artful artlessness and, like their parents, are set apart from ordinary mortals.

The world of Charles I and his queen was almost make-believe, a stage on which the principal actors played their parts behind masks. Van Dyck's genius conferred immortality on an exquisite and ideal world that never really existed. All too soon the masks were to be stripped away.

Even in matters of painting, Cromwell, the man of the future, was at odds with the court. He instructed the artist Peter Lely: 'I desire you would use your skill to paint my picture truly like me and not flatter me at all but remark all these roughnesses, pimples, warts and everything as you see me.'

Confident and invincible as Charles appears in his great horseback portrait, Cromwell – with his 'roughnesses, pimples, warts' – was fated to triumph. But nothing has been able to obliterate Van Dyck's dream world in which the melancholy king and his lovely queen reign for ever. The artist died in the year before the outbreak of war. It was fitting that he should not live to see his dreams shattered.

Edgehill—Cavaliers and Roundheads blunder into war

BATTLE HONOURS *Both sides claimed that they had won victory at the Battle of Edgehill. Charles himself had these medals of honour struck for the leaders of the Royalist army.*

WHERE THEY FIRST CLASHED

The peaceful setting of Edgehill in the Cotswolds was the scene of the first major battle of the Civil War in 1642. For the king, Edgehill was a lost opportunity. Thanks to the brilliance of his cavalry, commanded by his nephew, Prince Rupert, Charles had the better of the day. Had he pursued his advantage, he might have captured London. But instead he delayed and gave Parliament a chance to reorganise.

Edgehill, a sandstone ridge situated in the Cotswolds halfway between Birmingham and Oxford, commands one of the loveliest views in England. A rolling landscape of green fields and scattered copses unfolds to the Avon Valley. There, on a frosty October morning in 1642, the Royalist Cavaliers looked down upon the Parliamentary Roundheads in the valley, and prepared to fight the first pitched battle between Englishmen since the Battle of Bosworth Field more than a century and a half before.

The armies were about evenly matched: Parliament's 2000 cavalry and 11,000 foot against the king's 3000 cavalry and 9000 foot. For Charles I this first clash of the Civil War was critical: he needed to get his army past the Parliamentary forces, led by the inexperienced Earl of Essex, in order to advance on the Parliamentary stronghold of London.

The sunny morning dragged by. Neither side, it seemed, wanted to strike the first blow. Clothed in a black velvet coat with an ermine lining, Charles rode out among his troops and addressed them in characteristically stoical fashion: 'Come life or death, your King will bear you company, and ever keep this field, this place, and this day's service in his grateful remembrance.'

The battle begins

The signal for the fighting to begin came when Charles moved his cavalry halfway down the slope, and a nameless Roundhead gunner at last took it upon himself to fire the first shot – a shot that was to echo down English history. He sighted the king on Knowle Hill, took aim and fired. The cannon-ball fell short, but Charles reacted just as one of his forbears would have responded to a gauntlet thrown down at his feet. The Royalist army was given the signal to advance. In the centre, Sir Jacob Astley, the silver-haired veteran officer of the infantry, uttered a short prayer: 'O Lord, thou knowest how busy I must be this day. If I forget thee, do not thou forget me.'

At about 1 o'clock in the afternoon, a rumble of cannon signified that the Civil War had really begun. The cannonade lasted for about an hour, but did little damage. Then, on the right, Prince Rupert, the 23-year-old nephew of the king, and commander of the

NO TURNING BACK *King and Parliamentary leaders confront each other in this idealised engraving of the Battle of Edgehill. Seven bitter years of civil war were to follow this first action.*

Royalist cavalry, led the first of those brilliant charges which were, over the next three years, to establish him as the finest captain of horse in English history.

His troops trotted down the gentle descent for about a mile, jumped a narrow stream and then, breaking into a canter, headed straight for the Parliamentary cavalry. The sight of Rupert's force galloping towards them was too much for Essex's untrained horsemen. They turned and fled. And as Rupert's men gave chase down the road to Warwick, stragglers spread the news of Parliament's defeat.

'I fear them not!'

The reports were premature. The Cavaliers had made a fatal mistake, for their reserve cavalry, instead of staying to give cover to the infantry, had followed Rupert's charge and joined in the pursuit. No Royalist horsemen remained on the field to guard the infantry, guns and standard of the king.

Now Sir William Balfour, the commander of the Parliamentary reserves, and the most experienced soldier at Edgehill, seized his opportunity. Under cover of hedges, he led his reserve cavalry up the hill. Then, smashing through a brigade of the king's infantry, he reached the Royalist guns and tried to spike them with his own hands. The attempt failed, due to a shortage of nails, but he managed to kill the gunners and, by cutting the traces, to immobilise the guns.

When another brigade succumbed, the Royalist infantry was in danger of being swept away. Some of Balfour's troops came within yards of a spectacular prize: they stumbled across a party escorting the 12-year-old heir to the throne, Prince Charles, and his 9-year-old

brother James (later James II). Prince Charles drew a pistol and prepared to lead a charge. 'I fear them not!' he cried. But the boys were persuaded to ride off in haste.

At the centre of the king's own lifeguard, Sir Edward Verney, the Earl Marshal and bearer of the royal standard, fought hand to hand to save the sacred symbol of martial monarchy. But he was struck down, and the standard was snatched from his lifeless hand. Lord Lindsey, the Royalist infantry commander, whom Astley had replaced after a quarrel on the eve of the battle, was badly wounded and taken prisoner.

Balfour appeared to have won the day for the Roundheads. But once again the tide of battle turned. Prince Rupert, who had managed to arrest the impetuous chase of his men, arrived back on the battlefield just before dusk with half his cavalry. The Roundheads drew back, the royal standard was recovered and the shooting died away.

The action had been fierce. It had also been undisciplined. In the Parliamentary camp that night, the captured Lindsey, embittered towards the young royal favourite, Prince Rupert, vowed never to fight in the field with boys again. The next morning he died.

Missed opportunity

As night fell, and marauders moved in to strip the dead, men on both sides pondered the blunders that had been made in this first major engagement of the Civil War.

The man who learnt his lessons best was a Roundhead officer who had arrived late on the field of battle to find both sides in dispirited disorder. There, he discovered his destiny: to remodel the Parliamentary army and turn it into an invincible fighting force. His name was Oliver Cromwell. And the New Model Army he created was to bring him supreme power.

Each army lost about 2500 men, over half of them through desertion, and each side claimed the victory. The king had the better of the day; the road to London now lay open and undefended. Charles, however, shaken by the carnage he had seen – Verney dead, his young cousin, Prince d'Aubigny, mortally wounded, and 60 of his own footguard strewn in a heap around him – ignored Rupert's advice to press on to the capital. Instead, he fell back to Oxford. By the time he decided to advance on London, the Parliamentarians had found time to prepare. On November 4 Charles reached Reading, but it was another nine days before he reached the outskirts of London – Turnham Green. This was to be as close as he would get to recapturing his capital. There he was confronted by the 24,000-strong 'Trained Bands' of the City of London. A swift blow might have produced decisive results, but instead he decided to retreat. By a disastrous failure of nerve and foresight, Charles had squandered his best opportunity to win the war and save his crown.

Prince Rupert: Scourge of the king's enemies

'Clad in scarlet, very richly laid with silver lace, mounted upon a very gallant black barbary horse,' Prince Rupert of the Rhine, nephew of Charles I, was the most glamorous soldier of the English Civil War. A talented engraver and a competent scientist, he was above all an outstanding military commander, renowned for the lightning speed of his cavalry charges.

When the 23-year-old prince arrived in England from his Bohemian homeland in 1642, he was already a veteran of the Dutch and Swedish wars. He quickly established himself as the darling of the court. Charles appointed him General of the Horse. Rupert armed his men lightly and used them as shock troops, drilled to charge at a gallop rather than a trot, to keep their swords in their hands and to continue charging under heavy fire.

The Royalist cavalry remained undefeated until the Battle of Marston Moor in 1644. And Rupert's personal qualities – frankness and generosity, pride and spirit, speed of decision – won him the affection and loyalty of his troops. After the relief of Newark and York in 1644, the Duke of Newcastle hailed him as 'the Redeemer of the North and the Saviour of the Crown'.

But, in the end, the north was not to be redeemed or the crown saved. Against Cromwell's well-disciplined Ironsides, Rupert's tactics proved defective.

'Though the King's troops prevailed in the charge, and routed those they charged,' wrote the Earl of Clarendon, 'they seldom rallied themselves in order, nor could they be brought again to make a second charge.' It was the less romantic, but more methodical, Oliver Cromwell, who emerged as the greatest military leader of the age.

SOLDIER PRINCE *The impetuous and dashing Prince Rupert was a brilliant exponent of the cavalry charge at full gallop and under heavy fire.*

AMATEURS AT WAR

Edgehill was the first battle to be fought between Englishmen since the Wars of the Roses nearly 200 years before. At the beginning of the Civil War both sides were short of men and guns. More important, both lacked capable commanders. Most of the leaders at Edgehill were inexperienced soldiers who had won their positions by raising regiments of cavalry and infantry. As a mark of their independence, they took their own colours (below) into battle. It was not until Oliver Cromwell emerged as a leader of genius and cool common sense that an efficient army was organised.

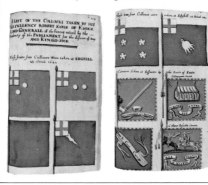

TRIUMPHANT RETURN *Charles II lands at Dover on the way to claim his crown after years of exile and poverty in Europe. He entered London on his 30th birthday. The diarist John Evelyn wrote that such joy had not been seen 'since the return of the Jews from Babylonian captivity'.*

Charles II: The rule of a 'merry monarch'

CAVALIER KING *Charles's mistresses were the talk of England. He also loved the arts, which flourished under his patronage.*

taking his cue from this, Charles – now at Breda in the Netherlands – wrote home that he too wished for and would be guided by a 'Free Parliament'.

Elections were held, and Parliament met. When Monck's cousin, William Morrice, moved that 'the constitution of England lay in King, Lords and Commons', his proposal was passed unanimously. Charles Stuart was invited to return forthwith to rule his country. His new subjects ran riot with their wild rejoicing, ringing the church bells and drinking the health of their monarch on bended knee – though the great diarist Samuel Pepys noted with some distaste that this last gesture seemed excessively slavish.

The king's mercy
Within a month Charles had arrived home. On May 29, his 30th birthday, he reached Blackheath on the outskirts of London, where the Lord Mayor and some 120,000 Londoners were waiting to lead him in procession through his capital. The diarist John Evelyn witnessed the king's entry into London – 'the ways strewed with flowers, the bells ringing, the streets hung with tapestry, fountains running with wine, trumpets, music and myriads of people. It was the Lord's doing.'

Though his Parliament was in the mood for revenge against the Republicans, Charles insisted that only the regicides – the men

actually instrumental in beheading his father 11 years previously – should pay for the hardships and injustices that the Royalists had suffered. The rotting corpse of Cromwell was dug up from its grave, to be hanged at Tyburn and then butchered and reinterred in the criminal pit. But apart from this the watchwords of the Stuart Restoration were to be mercy and reconciliation.

The great Parliamentary army was disbanded peacefully. The Church of England was re-established with little more acrimony than was inevitable in an age of deep religious faith. Men were allowed to keep property that they had purchased legitimately, no matter where their loyalties had lain in the past. And many other past actions and deeds were absolved by an Act of Indemnity and Oblivion. By the end of 1660, Englishmen could justly pride themselves on the accomplishment of a miracle – the bloodless restoration of a monarchy that had once been toppled with such violence and ferocity.

Charles continued to enjoy himself. 'He hates the very sight or thought of business,' wrote the diarist Samuel Pepys. But this was less than fair. The king proved himself capable of decisive and difficult action in his 25 years as ruler. He simply believed that pleasure was as important as work, and he distributed his time accordingly. It was a balance no other king of England has rivalled.

Few women could resist Charles II. 'His complexion is somewhat dark,' wrote a friend in 1660, 'but much enlightened by his eyes which are quick and sparkling . . . His hair, which he hath in great plenty, is of a shining black, not frizzled, but so naturally curling into great rings that it is a very comely ornament.' And Charles made no secret of his enslavement to what he described as 'a fantastical gentleman called Cupid'. He kept both court and country occupied with gossip about his latest love affairs.

Charles enjoyed being known as the 'merry monarch'; sculling alone down a river to clamber over a mistress's wall; dallying openly with the actress Nell Gwynne and bestowing a dukedom on the first of their two sons; gambling at the race course; sleighing, hunting, hawking and taking the helm to race his yachts up and down the Channel.

A plausible estimate of the number of mistresses Charles enjoyed even before he became king runs to 17, and Charles himself acknowledged 14 illegitimate children.

But he had no children by his wife, Catherine of Braganza, the sad and neglected victim of a diplomatic marriage of convenience, and this lack of a legitimate heir was to form the major constitutional issue of Charles's reign – the choice of his successor. For James, Duke of York, his brother and heir, was a Catholic, unacceptable to the Protestant majority of the nation, and the king risked everything to stand by him. In this he showed his great courage. For all his dallying, Charles had learnt the lesson of his father's reign: as he said, he was 'determined not to go on my travels again'.

'Lord have mercy upon us!' The plague sweeps England

On June 7, 1665, the famous diarist Samuel Pepys noticed with dismay that a number of houses in Drury Lane had been marked with red crosses on the doors, and the words 'Lord have mercy upon us'. These were the first signs of the plague Pepys had seen. 'It put me into an ill conception of myself,' he wrote, 'so that I was forced to buy some tobacco to smell and chew – which took away the apprehension.'

The crosses and inscriptions were the grim evidence that the plague had come to London, and the tobacco that Pepys hastened to buy – in the belief that it was an effective protection against infection – was no defence against the ravages of this dreaded disease. Before the Great Plague had run its course at the end of the year, at least 70,000 people had perished in London alone.

The first recorded case of this epidemic had occurred in November 1664, only yards from where Pepys saw the signs that the plague was gaining hold. Carried by rat fleas, the disease first showed itself as a small black blotch or lump on the victim's body. Fever and delirium followed, accompanied by agonising pain. Death or recovery took place within a few days. But in the squalid conditions of Restoration London, there were few who recovered.

The epidemic spread swiftly in the warm

VILLAGE OF DEATH

The Derbyshire village of Eyam as it is today, with a page from the church's register listing the plague victims. The list includes Katherine Mompesson, the wife of the vicar who urged his people to stay in the village so as not to spread the disease. Only one woman tried to escape, but she was driven back by neighbouring villagers.

ANATOMISTS AT WORK *Two surgeons dissect the body of a plague victim, seeking in vain the cause of the disease which killed thousands of Londoners in 1665.*

weather. It was soon carried from London to other cities, including Norwich, Southampton, Portsmouth and, most dramatically, to the Derbyshire village of Eyam.

Eyam's ordeal by plague began just as London was emerging from the worst ravages. In September 1665 the local tailor, Edward Cooper, took delivery of a box of old clothes and patterns. Within two days the servant who unpacked the box was taken ill; four days later he was dead. Cooper himself died a fortnight later; before the end of the month there had been 26 more deaths in the village. By the time the ordeal ended, in October 1666, only 33 of Eyam's 350 inhabitants were alive. The rest had fallen victim to the plague.

MEDICINE AND DEATH *A doctor protects himself against the plague (right) by wearing a mask filled with spices which were believed to purify the air. But medicine could do little for the plague victims, who were hastily buried at night in mass graves (above). The labourers who carried out this gruesome task toured the streets, crying: 'Bring out your dead!'*

The reason for this appalling death-toll was an extraordinary but heroic decision by the village vicar, William Mompesson. Usually people would flee from the places where plague had struck, thus spreading it further. But Mompesson managed to persuade his fellow-villagers to deny themselves this path to safety. He knew that if the people of Eyam fled, they would carry the infection to others; and so he urged them to act as true Christians and remain.

A boundary line was marked out with stakes around the village. Within its limits the villagers settled in to meet their fate, living on food left at the boundary by men from neighbouring villages. For months, Eyam knew only pain, death and the grim struggle for survival. By mid-summer only one man, Marshall Howe, was strong enough to dig graves for the victims. And as his reward for this gruesome task, he claimed all the possessions of those he buried. Yet only one person tried to escape from the village.

Disease of the poor

The Great Plague had struck England after 30 years of relative immunity from the disease, and at the time men blamed the visitation on infected bales of merchandise shipped into London from the Middle East. But the truth was that the Black Death – the outbreak of plague which had decimated the subjects of Edward III just over three centuries earlier – had never entirely disappeared from England.

The disease was rooted in the squalid slums of the 'Liberties' – the shanty towns outside London's city wall – St Giles, Cripplegate, Whitechapel, Stepney, Westminster and Lambeth. It was likely to spread whenever large crowds gathered together. Thus the coronations of both James I and Charles I, and the accompanying festivities that drew tens of thousands into the capital, led to two terrible epidemics in 1603 and 1625.

Some 30,000 died after James's accession, and as many deaths provided a grisly memorial to Charles's first months as king. But the 1665 outbreak, bringing so many deaths after so long a period of immunity, came as a sudden and frightening shock. The pious were not slow to interpret it as God's judgment on the flagrant immorality of Charles II.

The plague was always the disease of the poor. Though it inconvenienced the upper classes, they were far less severely hit. Despite his fears, Samuel Pepys remained in London throughout the worst part of the epidemic – though he packed his wife off to the country and took advantage of her absence to pursue several love affairs. And even though scarcely a day passed without his noting some sign or sight of the plague's effects in London, Pepys's year was far from being ruined by the disaster. On December 31, 1665, he noted with satisfaction: 'I have never lived so merrily as I have done this plague time.'

A battle between superstition and science

KING'S EVIL *A broadsheet shows Charles II laying his hands on a victim of scrofula – tuberculosis of the bones and lymphatic glands – which was thought at the time to be a skin disease. It was known as the 'King's Evil', because people believed that the king's touch could cure it.*

The Great Plague of 1665 laid bare the inadequacy of 17th-century medical science. The standard treatment for sufferers was an old herbal remedy – sage, rue, buttercup root, angelica root, snake root and saffron, infused in malaga. Not surprisingly, this had little effect in combating the disease and its cause remained unknown until the 19th century.

But some progress did come out of the tragedy. The physician Thomas Sydenham brought a new precision to the art of healing. The medieval practice of bleeding a patient was still the common remedy for any ailment, from a headache to a fever, and it was still administered by barbers – hence the red (blood) and white (bandage) of the traditional barber's pole. This ferocious treatment killed as often as it cured. But Sydenham argued that the symptoms of disease should be examined more carefully before this drastic treatment was indiscriminately applied. From his own studies he was able to show that measles and small-pox, for example, were different ailments and so required different treatments.

Surgeons and scientists

Sydenham's most important success came in the treatment of smallpox. He pioneered a method of cooling the patient's fever. Sydenham was the first surgeon to introduce opium into medical practice, and he also helped to popularise the use of quinine for malaria and iron for the treatment of anaemia. He also led the way in describing scarlet fever and in explaining the nature of hysteria and St Vitus's dance.

These were valuable and methodical advances, but the old superstitions and beliefs still lingered on. Sydenham's work won him

more recognition abroad than in England. His arguments only antagonised his colleagues, and the College of Physicians would not elect him to membership. According to one of his friends, Andrew Browne, Sydenham 'died with accusation hanging over his head that he was an impostor and an assassin of humanity'. Richard Wiseman, Charles II's own surgeon, believed that his master's touch could cure the skin disease of scrofula – the 'King's Evil'. But Wiseman – himself a barber surgeon – was also reluctant to wield his scalpel, and examined factors such as the relative healthiness of the air in different localities. He discovered that patients thrived in Hampstead; but an invalid who improved in Knightsbridge was observed to relapse in Holborn.

Towards the truth

Religion and morality were hopelessly mixed up with true medicine. Rickets, the most prevalent disease of the age, was blamed on 'a soft and debauched way of living' – the very opposite of the truth, since it was caused by poor, not excessive, food. Human character and health were still explained in terms of the balance within the body of the four 'humours' – the sanguine, the phlegmatic, the choleric and the melancholic. Medical treatment was often varied according to the dominant 'humour' of each particular patient. Thus a short-tempered, choleric man who had constipation was prescribed rhubarb, while a melancholic patient was given sennapods for the same complaint.

But for all its essentially medieval beliefs, the reign of Charles II marked the era when medicine and surgery became established as serious sciences in their own right.

A spark from a baker's oven sets London ablaze

WEAPONS AGAINST THE FIRE

London's only defence against the fire of 1666 was the simple equipment provided by private citizens. The hand-squirt (top) held no more than 2 pints of water; with the leather fire helmet (left) and bucket (right), it can be seen today in the London Museum.

LONDON IN FLAMES *A contemporary painting by Jan Wyck shows Londoners taking to the Thames to save themselves and their possessions from the Great Fire. The Tower (right) stands unscathed, but old St Paul's (centre) blazes.*

An observer of the Great Fire of London in 1666 wrote that: 'You would have thought for five days that it had been Doomsday from the fire, the cries and howling of the people. My gardens were covered with ashes of paper, linens and plasterwork blown there by the tempest.' And he lived 6 miles from the city in what was then the country village of Kensington.

The fire started at about midnight on Saturday, September 1, in the oven of the king's baker, Thomas Farriner, in Pudding Lane. According to Farriner's own statement, he had checked the oven before retiring to bed that evening; but a few hours later he and his family were awoken by smoke and fumes, 'and, rising, did find the fire coming upstairs'. They escaped through a window to the next-door house. But the housemaid was too frightened of heights to use this route. She became the fire's first victim.

It was a dry autumn, and a strong east wind was blowing. Pudding Lane contained several warehouses packed with pitch, tar and cordage. The flames soon began to spread. At 3 a.m. on that fateful morning the Lord Mayor, Sir Thomas Bludworth, was called out to the blaze, but he dismissed it as insignificant and went back to bed. His folly caused a fatal delay in the organisation of the fire-fighting force.

Four hours later some 300 houses had already been burnt down, according to the diarist Samuel Pepys. Pepys went out to take a look at the spectacle: 'Down to the waterside and there saw a lamentable fire. Everybody endeavouring to remove their goods, and flinging into the River or bringing them into lighters that lay off. Poor people staying in their houses as long as till the very fire touched them, and then running into boats or clambering from one pair of stair by the water-side to another. And the poor pigeons were loath to leave their houses, but hovered about the windows and balconies till they were burned and fell down.'

The city burns

Pepys noted that no one was making any effort to fight the fire: everyone was anxious only to save their possessions and run. The Lord Mayor, called out again at 10 a.m., was still unhelpful. He was asked to check the fire's raging progress by ordering the demolition of houses to create fire-breaks. But his response was merely: 'Who shall pay the charge of rebuilding the houses?'

So Pepys took matters into his own hands. As a government official, he went straight to the king at Whitehall. Charles issued an instruction that the mayor should 'spare no houses but pull down before the fire every way'.

At last some strong action was to be taken. But by now the blaze was a mile long, consuming Fish Street Hill, Canning Street, Gracechurch Street, Lombard Street, Cornhill and Fenchurch Street. There was no stopping it. As darkness fell, Pepys watched from across the river: 'And saw the fire grow; and, as it grew darker, appeared more and more; and in corners and upon steeples, and between churches and houses, as far as we could see up the hill of the City, in a most horrid, malicious, bloody flame. We stayed till, it being darkish, we saw the fire as only one entire arch of fire from this side to the other side of the bridge, and in a bow up the hill for an arch of above a mile long: it made me weep to see it.'

On Tuesday the flames licked up into the tower of the old St Paul's Cathedral. The roof came cascading down into the aisles – a torrent of molten lead. The Tower of London was saved only because the houses round about it had by now been blown up.

Following Charles's orders, the same drastic measures were now being taken to stop the westward advance of the blaze at the Inner Temple. There the king himself and his brother James, Duke of York, were directly in charge of operations. The royal brothers organised bucket chains and worked fearlessly among the flames, commanding, reproving and, on occasions, rewarding their men's efforts from bags of guineas at their sides. 'All that is left of the city and suburbs,' wrote one

At the time of Charles II's Restoration in 1660, London was still very much a country town. On May Days, milkmaids danced in the Strand, and in July 1671 a mad cow ran amok in Whitehall. For, although the metropolis knew its traffic jams – Samuel Pepys was kept fuming for half an hour in his coach on successive days by hold-ups in Exchange Street – open green fields were always within walking distance. One favourite pastime of 17th-century Londoners was to saunter through the meadows to the surrounding villages – the cherry orchards of Rotherhithe, the cake-shops of Islington, and the woods of Vauxhall, loud with the song of nightingales in summer. With his wife out of London, the diarist Samuel Pepys drove out to the greenery of Highgate with Mary, the girl from The Harp and Ball – 'pretty and innocent and had what pleasure I would with her'.

observer, 'is acknowledged to be wholly due to the King and the Duke of York.' And the role played by Charles II in fighting the fire was celebrated by John Dryden, the leading poet and dramatist of the day:

Now day appears and with the day the King,
Whose early care had robbed him of his rest;
Far off the cracks of falling houses ring
And shrieks of subjects pierce his tender
breast.

By the time the fire had burnt itself out on Thursday, September 6, it had consumed four-fifths of the area inside the City walls. Eighty-nine churches – including St Paul's – had been destroyed, and 13,200 houses. A north-countryman said that the capital reminded him of his native fells – a desolate expanse, marked only by odd heaps of blackened stone.

Rebuilding from the ruins

More than 100,000 Londoners had been made homeless: they were camping out on Moorfields, where Charles rode among them to calm the rumours that England's enemies – the Dutch or the Jesuits – had deliberately started the fire.

But such rumours soon spread from London across England. The Oxford diarist Anthony Wood recorded: 'This fire did soe much affrighten the nation that all townes stood upon their owne defence day and night, and particularly Oxon... Three days after the fire began, a butcher driving certaine oxen over Carfax cried to his beasts when he was under the window "hiup! hiup!". Which, some taking for "fire!" run out of the church . . . with the semblance of death in their faces, some saying that they smelled smoke, others pitch etc... and could not be reconciled to their error a long while.'

Out of the destruction some good was to

come. Charles II and his surveyor, Christopher Wren, saw the catastrophe as a chance to create a totally new, stone-built metropolis. But shortage of money, and obstruction from citizens intent on rebuilding on the sites of their old properties, meant that Wren did not have the free hand he wished for. Yet the architect did stamp his character on the capital in a fashion that endured until the Blitz of 1940: gracefully proportioned houses, memorably statuesque churches, and his crowning glory – the great dome-topped cathedral of St Paul's.

DIARIST OF GENIUS

The life of Restoration London still lives today in the pages of the world's most famous diary, kept by a civil servant, Samuel Pepys (below). Born in 1633, Pepys served Charles II as a high-ranking official at the Navy Board. He was conscientious and efficient in his work – a superior once called him 'the right hand of the Navy'. Yet Pepys still found time to create a unique record of his age, mirroring all its foibles and eccentricities.

Pepys kept his diaries from 1660 to 1669, when failing sight made him abandon the task. Because he never meant the record to be published, Pepys wrote frankly, using a shorthand code devised by Thomas Shelton in 1641. After the diarist's death in 1703, the diaries were stored in the library of his old college, Magdalene, in Cambridge. They were not discovered until 1819. The Rev. John Smith deciphered them after working for three years, and they were published in 1825. Since then, the diaries have won a worldwide readership.

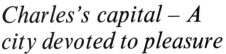

Taverns and lunatics

The River Thames was the dominant natural feature of Stuart London. It was the main highway of the capital, a bustling mass of barges and boats manned by watermen who made up a sturdy and independent fraternity some 2000 strong.

For fear of them, no second bridge could be built across the river to relieve the congested thoroughfare between the houses on London Bridge. And when hackney carriages became fashionable after the Restoration, the watermen successfully petitioned the king to limit this land-based method of plying for hire. Charles called the watermen his 'nursery of seamen', useful recruits for the navy – in contrast to the hackney coachmen, who simply blocked up the streets, transporting the fat and lazy.

Metropolitan tastes in entertainment were catered for by the naked lunatics on show at Bedlam, the moth-eaten lions kept in the Tower, and the countless taverns. The Trumpet, The Sugar Loaf and The Old Horse at Lambeth marsh, where Pepys made love to the wives of his subordinates at the Navy Board, were – along with hundreds more – the haunts of thousands of Londoners. For those who preferred to pay for their pleasures, there were flourishing brothels in such areas as Drury Lane and Moorfields.

But the old city was bursting at the seams. Noblemen became speculative builders, leasing off the simple yet elegant houses they erected on their London estates at profitable rents. The Earl of Southampton laid out Bloomsbury Square, while the Earl of St Albans accelerated the fashionable trend outside the city by developing St James's Square, the beginning of the West End. The London of today was slowly starting to take shape.

WREN'S MONUMENT RISES FROM THE ASHES OF LONDON

Britain's only Classical cathedral, St Paul's, is also the only one conceived and completed by one man within his own lifetime. Christopher Wren was 43 when he laid the foundation stone; he was 79 when the building was completed.

For those 36 years the cathedral was his whole life. Every detail was made to his specifications, every stone shaped and laid under his supervision.

In its grandeur and sheer architectural brilliance St Paul's is a towering monument to Wren's genius. But the continuation of the work from year to year, and its final triumphant vindication of his original vision, demonstrate Wren's other characteristic qualities – his subtlety as a diplomat, his skill as a politician and his fierce determination.

Destined for greatness
Wren was born in 1632, the son of the Dean of Windsor. Even from the start he seemed destined for greatness. At 21 he was described by the diarist John Evelyn as 'that miracle of youth'.

At 29 he became Professor of Astronomy at Oxford, and was a founder-member of the Royal Society, where Sir Isaac Newton claimed he was 'one of the greatest geometers of our time'. Casually, in his early thirties, he

AN ARCHITECT'S SKYLINE *London's skyline (below) painted by the Italian artist Canaletto was punctuated by Wren's spires, steeples and towers. Wren (right) designed 51 churches and many royal palaces and public buildings – including Chelsea Hospital. But his greatest ambition was to give London a dome to rival Michelangelo's dome of St Peter's, Rome. The dome of St Paul's fulfilled this dream.*

turned his attention to architecture, when he was commissioned to design the Sheldonian Theatre at Oxford. There, he discovered the vocation which was to dominate his life.

Inspired by a visit to Paris, he returned to England in 1666 to submit a plan for a noble Classical dome to complete the restoration of old St Paul's Cathedral, ravaged by Cromwell's soldiers. But only ten days after Charles II approved Wren's plans, the Great Fire wrecked London, and the old cathedral. Wren's plans seemed to have been wrecked, too. But he soon realised he was being given the chance of a lifetime. He submitted a plan for a totally new city of piazzas and avenues to rival Paris, but he had a cool reception.

At last, in 1668, Wren received the message he had been waiting for – an invitation to give London an entirely new cathedral. The dean told him: 'You are so absolutely and indispensably necessary to us that we can do nothing, resolve on nothing without you.'

But one thing was still lacking – money. Wren knew that the great work he had in mind would cost hundreds of thousands of pounds, the equivalent of millions in modern money. In the meantime he was appointed Surveyor of the King's Works at £320 a year.

It was only in 1670 that Parliament gave Wren the means to start work – a tax on coal coming into London. At first it yielded only £5000 a year. But it was enough to make a start.

Rising from the ashes
Wren produced a design for a new St Paul's so much to Charles II's liking that a model was built, 18 ft long and at a cost of £600. Two days later Wren was knighted.

But the model appalled church officials. They were horrified at the huge dome and the Classical design for the building, with no recognisable choir or nave, and no spire. Wren, who was as a rule quite imperturbable, wept openly when they turned down his schemes. But he was too wily a diplomat to surrender. He drew a design with a puny dome and spindly steeple, calculated to satisfy the demands of his unimaginative clients.

On June 21, 1675, work began. Wren asked a man to fetch a flat stone to serve as reference point for all the cathedral measurements. The man returned with a broken slab from an old tomb. It was inscribed with the word 'RESURGAM' – 'I shall rise again'.

Wren subtly adapted the plans so that the building in process came to look more and more like the rejected grand model, and less like the absurd official design. When money ran out, he got himself elected an MP and persuaded Parliament to treble the coal tax.

CITY'S CROWN *St Paul's dome still towers 365 ft above the skyline of the present-day city of London. The diameter of the dome is 112 ft, and it weighs 64,000 tons. Inside the outer dome is a brick cone which supports the lantern and cross – a landmark for Londoners.*

CLASSICAL MAGNIFICENCE *It was 20 years after the first stones were laid before Wren turned his attention to the interior of St Paul's. The picture shows the nave from the west, with the high altar in the background. Wren achieved a remarkable impression of radiant light.*

And other problems arose. The site had to be cleared. By January 1676, 753 cart-loads of rubbish had been carried away, and the carting went on for many more months. Work was painfully slow. Stone had to be brought by ship from the Portland quarries in Dorset. The enormous blocks were transferred into barges for the Thames journey, and finally dragged up to the cathedral.

The crowning glory

At last on December 5, 1697, the choir was opened for the first Sunday service held in the new cathedral. The dome, however, was still not begun. But all who saw Wren's drawings realised that London was to be crowned with a supreme work of architecture.

Eventually, tarred cloths were put up in April 1708 'to cover the workmen in hot and wet weather upon the Leading ye Roofe of the Dome'. For the next two years Londoners remained in ignorance of the work which was shrouded in the tangled jungle of scaffolding enclosing the whole cathedral. The first they saw of Wren's visionary building was the huge gold cross gleaming above the building works. When the scaffolding came down, the magnificent dome was at last revealed, crowning the

skyline of towers and spires and steeples which Wren had created.

The old architect was not strong enough to lay the last stone of the building in 1710. His son, Christopher, stood in for him. At the end of 1711 Parliament at last declared St Paul's to be complete. Wren's life work was done. He retired to his riverside house near the great palace he had been rebuilding for William of Orange at Hampton Court.

On February 25, 1723, few people noticed as a frail old man in a rich brown periwig and buff coat with gold frogging, was helped up the steps of St Paul's by his coachman. The 91-year-old architect was paying a visit to his supreme achievement.

For a long time he sat beneath the dome, watching the early spring sunlight play upon the stonework which had fulfilled his life's greatest ambition. Then he turned and hobbled slowly away.

It was his last visit. That afternoon he died peacefully and a few days later he was buried in the crypt of St Paul's. The Latin inscription carved on his black marble tomb expressed his own confidence: *Lector, monumentum requiris, circumspice* – 'Reader, you seek my memorial, look around you'.

MASTER CARVER

To add the final touches of magnificence to St Paul's, Wren assembled a team of master craftsmen – the Frenchman Jean Tijou, who made the cathedral's wrought-iron screens, the Danish sculptor Caius Gabriel Cibber, and Grinling Gibbons, the great woodcarver.

Born in Holland of British parents, Gibbons came to England when he was about 19, and worked first as a ship's carver in Deptford. There, in a 'poor solitary thatched cottage', he was 'discovered' by John Evelyn, the diarist. Evelyn introduced Gibbons to Charles II, who soon recognised his talents and appointed him his Master Carver and Sculptor.

Wren chose Gibbons to work on St Paul's, and the result was the beautiful, intricate carving of the choir stalls, an unparalleled example of the woodcarver's art. This detail (above) from one of the choir stalls shows Gibbon's mastery of his craft and his ability to capture the beauty of fruit and flowers in his carvings.

A trickster's witch-hunt plunges England into panic

NATION IN TERROR

A fictitious plot invented by Titus Oates reduced London to a state of hysteria in 1678. Houses were barricaded against an expected Catholic uprising. Even women carried pistols for protection. Catholic books and relics were publicly burnt. Priests were hunted down and the prisons were filled with suspects turned in by informers. And 30,000 innocent Catholics fled London to escape the mob. Oates's improbable tales gave licence to a host of rogues and adventurers, who took every opportunity to profit from the panic. The tiles (above), now in the Victoria and Albert Museum, London, show how completely an artist of the time had accepted the story that Oates had concocted.

For five years from 1678, the England of Charles II was whipped into a panic so intense that it almost provoked a revolution. The words of one man brought about the execution of some 35 victims, and the pitiless persecution of hundreds of others.

The man behind this panic was Dr Titus Oates, one of history's most successful confidence tricksters. And the field that he chose for his operations was that of religion – still the most volatile powder-keg of all.

The centrepiece to the whole story was Oates's allegation that the pope had commissioned the Jesuits to assassinate Charles II, massacre the English Protestants and overthrow the legitimate English government. After Charles had been killed – by shooting, stabbing or poisoning – his Catholic brother James, Duke of York, was to be set upon the throne. By this means the Church of Rome would again be supreme in England.

This so-called plot existed only in the mind of Oates. It was the scurrilous invention of a callous liar. Oates had been expelled from both school and university, though he had then gone on to take holy orders and practise as an Anglican vicar. In 1675 he had hastily signed up as chaplain aboard the frigate *Adventurer,* in order to escape a charge of perjury. But he soon lost his chaplaincy and, returning to London, mixed with notoriously low company.

Then suddenly, in 1677, he announced his conversion to Catholicism, and went off to Spain and France to study with the Jesuits.

His new course foundered within months. Expelled as an undesirable from the Jesuit school at St Omer in France, he returned to England again, burning with frustration and resentment. Here he took up with an old acquaintance, Israel Tonge – a fanatical, half-mad vicar, filled with hatred for the Jesuits, and the ideal partner for Oates. Between them, this disreputable pair of cranks concocted their wild story of a Popish Plot, and found the ear of the government.

Suiting the mood of the times

Oates hardly cut a trustworthy figure. According to a contemporary, the Jesuit historian John Warner, he had 'the speech of the gutter, and a strident and sing-song voice, so that he seemed to wail rather than to speak'. When he finally secured an audience with the king, Charles saw through him immediately, catching him out on two points of fact. Oates claimed to have met John of Austria, whom he described as tall and fair, but Charles knew that John was short and dark. Oates also claimed he had seen Père La Chaise, the French king's personal confessor, paying out £10,000 for Charles's assassination, in a particular house in Paris. Charles knew from his own days of exile in Paris that the alleged house did not exist.

But though Oates was motivated only by his own malice and self-seeking ambition, he was assisted in his efforts by the political climate of the day. Ardent Protestant politicians took up the fears of a Popish Plot to advance their own party cause. And the plot was given credibility by two strange coincidences. Among the many people Oates had wildly accused of conspiracy was Edward Coleman, a secretary of James, Duke of York. And Coleman, an over-enthusiastic Catholic, had secretly written letters to Catholics on the Continent – including Père La Chaise. This action was imprudent, but not criminal, for

INNOCENT VICTIM *One of the victims of the Popish Plot was the Duke of York's secretary, Edward Coleman. A contemporary woodcut shows him being dragged to execution.*

JUST PENALTY *Oates was pilloried for the fraud which almost altered history.*

the letters said nothing about murder or rebellion. Yet the very fact of writing to such a man provided apparent corroboration for Oates's talk of a plot.

Under questioning, Coleman was urged to save his life by denouncing his fellow-conspirators. Pitifully, he cried that enough was known to condemn him, but he did not know enough to be saved. He was only too accurate.

Then, on October 17, 1678, Sir Edmund Berry Godfrey, the magistrate before whom Oates had first sworn the truth of his accusations, was discovered dead in a ditch at the foot of Primrose Hill, transfixed by his own sword. His murderers were never caught.

Godfrey's murder was the spark that ignited the powder-keg. Loyal Protestants had no doubt that the unlucky magistrate was the victim of Popish assassins. He became a martyr, and his corpse lay in state for two days while thousands filed past, swearing vengeance on his Jesuit murderers.

An enterprising cutler manufactured special 'Godfrey' daggers engraved 'remember the murder of Edmund Godfrey', to be used as protection. He sold 3000 of them in one day to his eager customers.

Hysteria now gripped London. A massacre was expected daily. The streets echoed to the tramp of militia patrolling by day and night. In such an atmosphere, ever wilder accusations were eagerly believed.

A pack of informers even more disreputable than Oates and Tonge sprang up to feed the national panic. Oates himself appeared before Parliament, where he shamelessly accused Charles's Catholic queen, Catherine of Braganza, of treason.

Revealed in his true colours

The panic persisted for months, and its rumbling aftermath was still being felt at the end of 1681. Before it subsided, many innocent Catholics had been packed off to prison to stand trial for their lives. Among those who were eventually executed were men as notable as Oliver Plunket, the Catholic Archbishop of Armagh and Primate of Ireland; and William Howard, Viscount Stafford. Twenty-one men were condemned by one judge alone, the infamous and brutal Chief Justice Scroggs.

Finally, England came to its senses and saw through Oates and his tissue of lies. In June 1684, James, Duke of York, secured a massive £100,000 damages for the libels that Titus Oates had circulated about him. Once he became king, James had further revenge, when his one-time accuser was whipped twice through the streets of London. Oates received over 3000 lashes on that bloody and painful journey in May 1685 – though Catholics thought it small compensation for the blood his perjury had shed. And Oates spent the last 20 years of his life in disreputable obscurity, hounded by poverty, debt and a dismal succession of petty scandals and intrigues.

Battle to 'exclude' the heir to the throne

The hysterical frenzy roused by the Popish Plot led to an event unprecedented in British history before or since. An attempt was made legally to exclude James, Duke of York, Charles II's brother and the heir to the throne, from the succession. For James was the country's leading Roman Catholic, accused by all those who joined in Titus Oates's murderous denunciations.

By the late 1670's, Charles II's over-enthusiastic friendship with Catholic France had produced a deep discontent in England. Another source of dissatisfaction was that a general election had not been held since 1660. The time was ripe for a challenge to the policies of Charles and his ministers.

An alliance of Protestant nonconformists, low churchmen and strict Parliamentary constitutionalists battled ever more fiercely to get a general election called. But when Titus Oates started whipping up Protestant emotions with his tales of popish conspiracy, their line of attack changed. Within weeks of James's secretary, Edward Coleman, being detected in correspondence with foreign Catholics, the Protestant party was proposing that Parliament should ban James from his brother's presence.

It was but a short step to seek the complete exclusion of James from the succession to the throne. This threat stirred Charles into action. He dissolved Parliament in January 1679, and in the next two years summoned and dissolved no fewer than four more Parliaments, in a vain attempt to secure an assembly that would support his brother. But with every fresh election, the Protestant opposition, led by the astute and unscrupulous Earl of Shaftesbury, made more progress.

Charles now found himself virtually deserted. Even two of his mistresses, Louise de Kéroualle and Nell Gwynne, took Shaftes-bury's side. But the desertion that pained Charles the most was that of his illegitimate son, the Duke of Monmouth, who hoped to be legitimised and become heir to the throne in James's place. In the end, however, the king triumphed. He refused to desert his brother, telling Shaftesbury 'I have the law and reason on my side'. The earl was now forced to choose between admitting his defeat or starting a rebellion on behalf of his own candidate for the succession, Monmouth.

The memories of the civil war were too fresh and too painful for such drastic action. Shaftesbury's plans were shattered and he was forced to flee the country. But the episode saw for the first time the emergence of definite political factions – the pro-Parliament, anti-Papist Whigs, and the monarchist, High Church Tories. Britain was launched on the road to her modern party system.

THE FIRST WHIG

One of Britain's first political parties, the Whig Party, was founded by Lord Shaftesbury (below), much of whose political life was devoted to challenging the power of the monarchy. But his career was a source of little pride to later Whigs. He began the Civil War as a Royalist, but finished as one of Cromwell's most trusted servants. After the Restoration he served Charles II. But his hatred of James, the king's brother and heir, and his anti-Catholic views, made him a natural ally for Titus Oates. When the plot collapsed, he was indicted for treason. He fled to take refuge in Protestant Holland, where he died at the age of 61 after only a year in exile.

PROTESTANT PROPAGANDA *A contemporary print shows the anti-Catholic demonstration organised by the Whig leader, the Earl of Shaftesbury, in the City of London on November 17, 1679. In the procession, demonstrators disguised as Jesuits, armed with knives, cardinals and the pope are shown pursuing the first 'victim' of the popish plotters, Sir Edmund Berry Godfrey.*

GREAT MINDS UNITE AND MODERN SCIENCE IS BORN

The restoration of the Stuart monarchy brought not only a deliverance from the moral restraints of the Puritan era, but also a new intellectual freedom. It was a golden age of philosophical and scientific study. Nor were learned pursuits restricted to scholars working in obscure corners at Oxford and Cambridge; patronage, encouragement and genuine interest came from the highest circles. The Royal Society, which symbolised the new spirit of inquiry, was formally constituted with the consent of Charles II only six months after he came to the throne in 1660.

The inspiration of the society came from Francis Bacon who had stressed the importance of experimental science, and the rejection of the ancient traditions which had bedevilled research and progress.

In the *New Atlantis*, he had put forward the idea of a Utopian College, consisting of men who were committed to 'the Knowledge of causes and the secret motion of things; and the enlarging of the bounds of Human Empire, to the effecting of all things possible'. Bacon's arguments were so persuasive that although he never succeeded in putting into practice what he preached, the next generation were infected by his enthusiasm.

In the 1640's a devoted band of Baconians met regularly at Oxford in the rooms of John Wilkins, Warden of Wadham College, for discussion and experimentation. Wilkins was determined to free science from the often ludicrous conventions of Classical philosophers. He wrote that it was 'a superstitious, a lazie opinion to think Aristotle's work the bounds and limits of human invention'. It was this revolutionary attitude to the past which later prompted the Royal Society to choose as its motto *Nullius in verba*, which can be freely translated: 'We do not take anyone's word for it.'

Among the first members of the group were some of the men who were to transform the age: Christopher Wren, still in his twenties but already Oxford professor of astronomy, and Robert Boyle, who was beginning his experiments on the properties of air. On November 28, 1660, they moved to London to form themselves into a permanent society.

The king was deeply interested in the group from the start. He provided the members with objects for discussion: 'His Majestie has sent a small piece of glasse...which though strock with a hamer at the oval end would not breake, but breaking the taile or small part with your hand...the whole would crumble to dust.'

A unique meeting place

The diarist and a founder-member of the Royal Society, John Evelyn, recorded another meeting 'to whiche his Majestie has sente that wonderfull horn of the fish, which struck a dangerous hole in the keele of a ship, in the India sea, which being broake off with the violence of the fish, left in the timber, preserv'd it from foundring'.

In 1662 the king granted the society its first charter as the Royal Society of London for the Promotion of Natural Knowledge. He also presented it with a mace, and provided it with a permanent home at Chelsea and an annual supply of venison for its St Andrew's Day feast.

Where royalty led, others followed. The

OFFICIAL EXPERIMENTER *Robert Hooke, who was the Royal Society's first 'experimenter', used his own microscopes to discover vegetable cells.*

Royal Society became a unique meeting place of the worlds of fashion, politics and scholarship. There was scarcely a great Englishman of the age who was not a member – the dissolute Duke of Buckingham, the dashing general and cousin of the king, Prince Rupert, who himself used to conduct chemical experiments, Samuel Pepys, Christopher Wren, the Earl of Sandwich, the poet John Dryden and the

---

CREATED BY ROYAL PRIDE

The Royal Observatory owes its existence to a royal boast, and a royal fit of pique.

At a palace reception Charles II, stung by some remarks on maritime navigation made by a French visitor, publicly proclaimed that his astronomers could produce accurate tables describing the movements of the heavenly bodies.

But when he ordered the Royal Society to make good his boast, he was annoyed when it reported that it was impossible without a well-equipped observatory, of a kind that Britain did not possess. The king responded by ordering Christopher Wren to build an observatory close to the Palace of Greenwich, which was being rebuilt at the time. In 1675 a building, more beautiful than useful, was erected, and the first Astronomer Royal, John Flamsteed, was appointed at a salary of £100 a year.

The second Astronomer Royal was Edmond Halley, already famous for predicting the orbit of the comet which bears his name. He held the post from 1721 until his death in 1742.

The Octagon Room at the Royal Observatory, Greenwich, was designed by Christopher Wren. It was in this room, through painstaking study of the world's latitudes, that 'Greenwich Mean Time' was established.

towering genius of science, Isaac Newton. Nothing was barred from discussion; every aspect of pure and applied science, technical innovation and philosophical speculation might be explored. Samuel Pepys watched a hen stagger round the floor apparently inebriated with 'Florentine poison', and gazed upon a human foetus preserved in 'spirits of salt'. In March 1667 the transfusion of blood from a sheep to a dog was demonstrated.

Curiosities from Europe

In July 1668 the society considered various archaeological finds, discovered while foundations were being dug for a fort at Sheerness. A letter from Germany, read in April 1680, described a large quantity of hair 'an Inch in length, exceeding thick, and somewhat harsh and reddish', which had been observed growing on a corpse. The supply of interesting items presented to the members of the society was as endless as their curiosity was boundless.

The activities of the society were not confined to idle speculation. The government made frequent use of the services of this unique gathering of great minds. The Royal Society made recommendations on the sanitation system for the new city of London, and the implementation of these recommendations was in part responsible for the gradual stamping out of the plague.

Forum for great minds

But the Royal Society's greatest contribution to the world of science was in providing a forum for the sympathetic discussion of new theories, inventions and discoveries made by the great geniuses of the age. Robert Boyle set the world of chemistry on new lines by exploding the old theory of the four basic elements (earth, air, fire and water) and postulating that all matter is composed of indestructible atoms. Sir William Petty, one of the first practical economists, demonstrated the usefulness of statistics, and Edmond Halley was the first astronomer to make a serious study of the heavenly bodies visible from the Southern Hemisphere. In 1682 he observed the comet since named after him.

It was Halley who suggested to Newton that he should bring together his scientific findings in one book. The result, published with the sanction of the Royal Society, was Newton's *Principia*, probably the greatest step forward in the history of science.

By supporting scientific publications like the *Principia*, and by publishing its own discussions, the Royal Society became the living embodiment of Bacon's revolutionary vision – a community of men dedicated to extending human understanding. It succeeded brilliantly – unleashing a new spirit of inquiry which has lasted into modern days. For Englishmen in the last part of the 17th century, it seemed the world was full of secrets waiting to be unlocked, and that they held the key.

HENRY PURCELL'S TUNES CAPTIVATE STUART LONDON

Under the organ in Westminster Abbey lie the remains of one of the greatest and most original of English composers. For many years he had played there, and no more fitting burial place could be found. An inscription reads: 'Here lyes HENRY PURCELL Esqr. Who left this Life and is gone to the Blessed Place Where only his harmony can be exceeded.'

Purcell was a Londoner. He was born there in 1659 and he died there a short 36 years later. Much of his music was directly connected with the life of the capital. He was an honoured figure both at Westminster Abbey and at court, where the king kept his own choristers and musicians – the Chapel Royal. But his fame also reached out into the streets of London where thousands of people knew the songs and dance tunes he composed for the theatre.

Purcell's father was a Gentleman of the Chapel Royal and master of the choirboys at Westminster Abbey. Purcell became a Chapel Royal chorister at the age of six.

At the age of 15, he had become official music copier at Westminster Abbey under the famous organist and composer John Blow. When Purcell was 21, Blow resigned in his favour. Two years later Purcell was also appointed organist to the Chapel Royal.

Purcell's masterpiece, 'Dido and Aeneas', written about 1689, was the first true English opera. Composed for the pupils of a 'School for Young Gentlewomen' in Chelsea, it was deliberately simple, yet reached new heights of musical and dramatic expression.

Other stage works, like 'Dioclesian' and 'The Fairy Queen', were plays with incidental music which won him far greater success. In 'King Arthur' he collaborated with the poet John Dryden. The famous song 'Fairest Isle' is from this work.

Among Purcell's best-loved songs was 'Lilliburlero', which inspired the soldiers who rallied to William III during his Glorious Revolution of 1688. In 20 years of composition he also wrote over 50 dramatic works, 80 religious works and a mass of incidental music and songs.

'Tears from all'

William III's wife, Queen Mary, was the monarch he liked best, and when she died, in February 1695, Purcell wrote a march and two anthems, including the famous 'Thou Knowest, Lord', for her funeral. 'I appeal to all that were present,' wrote one mourner, 'whether they ever heard anything so rapturously fine and Solemn! . . . which drew tears from all.'

Tears were shed again in the abbey nine months later when 'Thou Knowest, Lord' was played at Purcell's own funeral on November 26. His early death, probably from tuberculosis, robbed England of a supreme musical talent.

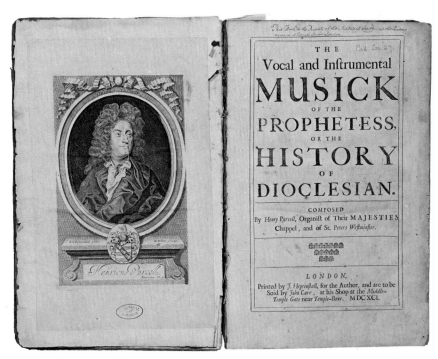

PUBLISHED PURCELL *The only stage work of Purcell's to be published during his lifetime was 'Dioclesian'. Despite the fact that the composer notated every copy sold by hand, the work made a loss. One of the few remaining portraits of the composer appears in the score.*

Rebellion, defeat and a king's bloody revenge

MASSACRE ON THE MOORS
The Duke of Monmouth's ambitions to the throne came to a bloody end at Sedgemoor, Somerset, in 1685. During a night attack on James II's army, his men became bogged down in a massive ditch and they were slaughtered where they stood by government troops.

In July 1685 vengeful government troopers were scouring the west of England. They sought remnants of those rebels who had risen against their lawful sovereign, James II, and had been cut to pieces at the Battle of Sedgemoor a few days before.

One such patrol found a man cringing miserably in a ditch. He did not resist, but trembled abjectly as his captors searched him. In his pockets they found all that he had to eat – a handful of peas snatched as he had fled from the battlefield. Suddenly they realised the importance of their capture. The man that pleaded for his life before them was none other than James, Duke of Monmouth, the leader of the revolt.

For Monmouth, Sedgemoor was the bitter culmination to a lifetime of thwarted ambition. A fortnight before the battle, Monmouth had proclaimed himself King of England, Wales, Scotland, France and Ireland. But now he stood revealed for something far less glorious – the inadequate victim of other men's ambitions and his own conceit.

Charles II, Monmouth's father, deserved much of the blame for his son's fate. Monmouth was the first and most favoured of his illegitimate sons, fathered when Charles was an 18-year-old exile in Holland. There was a rumour that a 'Black Box' contained proof of a marriage between Charles and Monmouth's mother, Lucy Walter, a prostitute. Charles denied any such marriage, but he did not deny his love for his handsome son, whom he brought proudly to England after the Restoration in 1660. He showered the boy with favours and titles, and married him to a wealthy heiress, Anne, Countess of Buccleuch.

Gamble for the throne

But Monmouth was scarcely worthy of these royal indulgences. He was headstrong, vain and ambitious. Pampered by the king, he began to attract interest as a possible heir to the throne. Politicians such as the Earl of Shaftesbury were working to exclude Charles's Catholic brother, James, from the succession. They encouraged the Protestant Monmouth to see himself as a future King of England. Monmouth lent himself willingly to such schemes, deceived by his own ambition and by his father's affection.

But Charles had no intention of altering the succession in Monmouth's favour. He sent his son into exile in Holland, and there he remained until his father died and James II came to the throne in February 1685.

Monmouth and his fellow exiles saw this as their opportunity. In the spring, they laid their plans for an invasion of England which, they hoped, would be met by a popular rising. On June 11, 1685, Monmouth and 82 followers

PROTESTANT HOPE *The Duke of Monmouth, illegitimate son of Charles II, was a Protestant and a good soldier, but little else.*

NIGHT RAID *The Battle of Sedgemoor was a short affair. Monmouth's men were hoping to surprise the royal troops by attacking at 1 a.m. But they were seen by a sentry, and in less than four hours the rebels had lost 1000 men and another 500 of them had been captured.*

TERROR OF THE 'BLOODY ASSIZE'

The notorious 'Bloody Assize' of Judge Jeffreys was seen at its worst during the trial of the ageing Dame Alice Lisle. She was accused of sheltering John Hickes, a minister who had fought for Monmouth at the Battle of Sedgemoor. Dame Alice, the widow of one of Cromwell's followers, did not deny that she had hidden Hickes at her home near Ringwood, Hampshire. But she claimed that she knew nothing of his support for Monmouth, and thought that Hickes, a well-known Dissenter, was a victim of government persecution. But at her trial at Winchester Assizes in 1685, Judge Jeffreys insisted she must have known that Hickes was a traitor. Despite his browbeating of witnesses, the judge could find no one who could prove that Dame Alice was lying. The jury were reluctant to convict her on the scant evidence, but Judge Jeffreys terrorised them into finding her guilty and ordered her to be burnt alive. She appealed to James II, who substituted beheading for burning. Dame Alice was executed on September 2.

Judge Jeffreys browbeats a witness during the trial of the nonconformist preacher Richard Baxter in 1685. At 40, Jeffreys was the youngest-ever – and most brutal – Lord Chancellor of England.

landed at Lyme Regis, a small port in Dorset. The gentry of Lyme – whose fears had been roused as, playing at bowls, they saw the rebels' three ships drop anchor in Lyme Bay – fled in horror from the town. But the humbler townsfolk, including many prisoners the rebels released from the town gaol, flocked to join the invader's banner. Within 12 hours, some 1500 men had rallied to Monmouth's call. Popular resentment against James II's Catholicism ran deep in this corner of England, and Monmouth's hopes of a spontaneous rebellion seemed about to be fulfilled.

But soon things started to go wrong. Not long after the landing, Monmouth's most trusted and experienced comrade, Heywood Dare, was shot in a brawl over a looted horse. The loss of such a leader was a poor start for the enterprise.

Nevertheless, for a fortnight the rebels cause flourished. Their army marched triumphantly through the West Country, gathering strength at every step. When he set up camp outside Bristol at the end of June, Monmouth had about 7000 armed men.

But while Monmouth debated his next move, the government was not idle. Parliament voted James £400,000 to suppress the rebellion, and formally declared Monmouth a traitor. Royal forces, led by Lord Feversham and John Churchill, converged on the rebels.

Under this mounting pressure, Monmouth began to panic. His motley army of peasants was no match for the king's seasoned regiments. He withdrew from Bristol and his forces diminished in numbers as his frightened followers lost heart. Monmouth decided to risk all in a last desperate gamble.

On the night of July 5, the rebels launched an attack on the royalist encampment at Sedgemoor, near Bridgwater in Somerset. At first the royal army was caught by surprise – Feversham was in bed as the battle began. But luck was not on the rebels' side. A muddled order sent both their infantry and cavalry forces into a marshy ditch where, hopelessly entangled, they were massacred by the disciplined volleys of the royal regulars. By dawn the cause was lost, and Monmouth deserted his followers and fled from the battlefield.

A terrible retribution

Monmouth's foolhardy enterprise had a tragic sequel. Monmouth himself was executed on July 15, suffering terribly from the blunt axe wielded by his unskilful executioner. Those of his followers who survived the carnage of Sedgemoor were delivered up to the brutal Judge Jeffreys. In his notorious Bloody Assize Jeffreys ordered the execution of over 300 of the rebels. More than 1000 of them were transported to the colonies and countless others flogged or imprisoned.

But the appalling savagery of this retribution discredited James and his government. The self-seeking Monmouth was soon seen as a noble martyr for the Protestant cause. When, three years later, William of Orange made his own bid for the English throne, these were the memories that helped him to success.

James II: His obstinacy cost him his throne

The last of the Stuart kings, James II was short-sighted, arrogant and obstinate. 'This king,' wrote the French ambassador, 'is neither so self-controlled nor so great a man as has been supposed. He has all the faults of his father Charles I, but he has less sense, and he behaves more haughtily in public.'

James swiftly threw away his initial popularity. He made his subjects nervous. He increased the standing army from 6000 to 30,000 men, keeping 13,000 men at arms on Hounslow Heath to overawe the capital. When ministers – such as Lord Halifax – gave him advice he did not like, he sacked them as disloyal. Worst of all, his ardent Catholicism led him to embark on a campaign to make it the dominant religion in his kingdom. By his policies, he alienated the very men who had been his strongest supporters.

Piety was one explanation for his blundering. Mental degeneration caused by syphilis was more likely, for James – his religious fanaticism notwithstanding – was a greedy and indiscriminating womaniser.

England tolerated 'Squire James' and his clumsiness until his Italian wife, Mary of Modena, produced a son, who replaced the Protestant Mary as heir to the throne. Soon revolution broke out. But even when James was at the mercy of Mary's husband, William of Orange, in November 1688 he might have saved his throne, had he been prepared to agree to terms. Many Englishmen were unwilling to see an anointed king deposed. Compromise, however, had never been James's style, and he went into exile. If he could not have all, he preferred nothing.

PROUD AND FOOLISH *James II was the last Stuart king to rule Britain. His obstinate refusal to compromise cost him his throne in 1688.*

A VISIONARY TRANSFORMS MAN'S VIEW OF THE UNIVERSE

When Isaac Newton was born prematurely on Christmas Day 1642 he was so small that his mother could have put him into a quart pot. For weeks after his birth he was not expected to live, and throughout infancy he had to wear a support around his neck to keep his head from lolling forward on to his shoulders.

A solitary child, endowed with a genius which only intensified his loneliness, he grew up believing that he was destined for future greatness. The date of his birth and the miracle of his survival seemed to him portentous. He came to feel that he had special access to the mind of the Almighty, and that in the mystical raptures of his private meditations the deepest secrets of the universe had been imparted to him alone.

Birth of science

Newton lived in an age in which 'science' can properly be said to have been born. The founding of the Royal Society, by Charles II in 1662, gave official support for the first time to scientific investigation in Britain. But while men of talent and enthusiasm abounded, it took Newton to make the crucial step from the vague theories of 'natural philosophy' to the hard mathematical laws and principles on which modern science is based.

While his contemporaries and the judgment of posterity have concurred in recognising Newton's genius, he himself said: 'If I have seen further, it is by standing on the shoulders of giants.' He considered the groundwork for his great discoveries had already been done by the great Italian, Galileo Galilei, who died the year he was born, and Johannes Kepler, who had died 12 years previously.

Both had made remarkable progress towards understanding the laws which govern the universe. But it was left to Newton, in his three fundamental Laws of Motion, to weld their discoveries together into a coherent whole.

At home in Woolsthorpe, a small village in Lincolnshire, Newton was expected to follow a farming career in the footsteps of his father, who had died before he was born. When his mother re-married, he was put into the care of his grandmother for the rest of his childhood. A delicate boy, he grew into a man to whom secrecy and solitude were second nature. He never married, had few intimate friendships and, though he remained a dutiful son, he formed few close emotional ties.

His academic record at King's School, Grantham, 7 miles away, was unspectacular. But he did show an aptitude for building models of all kinds. He made a water clock, a working model of a windmill and several sundials, displaying a skill at precision handiwork which later stood him in good stead.

In 1661, aged 19, he went to Trinity College, Cambridge, graduating without special distinction in 1665. But at Cambridge he met Isaac Burrow, Lucasian Professor of Mathematics, who took him on to help him prepare his book called *Optical Lectures*. Burrow recognised the first signs of Newton's outstanding talents, and wrote of him as 'a man of quite exceptional ability and skill'.

But it was when he was aged 23 and 24 that Newton's mind was to exert its exceptional power in a way never after repeated. The foundations for all his later thinking, all his major intuitions, were laid during these two extraordinarily fertile, creative years.

When the Great Plague of 1665 threatened Cambridge, Newton was forced to return to his parent's home in Woolsthorpe. Intellectually isolated, he embarked on an astonishing period of sustained mental activity. There is no doubt that Newton did possess superhuman powers of concentration. He was able to hold before his mind philosophical problems that would have exhausted a lesser intellect. 'I keep the subject constantly before me,' he wrote, 'and wait till the first dawnings open little by little into the full light.'

During 1665 and 1666 he calculated the basis for differential and integral calculus, the method which mathematicians have used ever since for solving complex problems. He deduced for the first time the nature and behaviour of light, and the law of gravitation. Legend has it that this discovery came to him as he sat watching an apple fall to the ground beside him in his mother's orchard.

The laws of the universe

Newton acknowledged himself the debt to those two years. 'In those days,' he wrote, 'I was in the prime of my age for invention, and minded mathematics and invention more than at any time since.' But although, by a brilliant combination of intellect and intuition, he had delved further than any scientist into the laws of the universe, he did not publish his findings, but kept them strictly to himself.

He returned to Cambridge in 1667 at the age of 25. His great creative burst was over, and the rest of his life was devoted to consolidating and expanding his ideas.

In 1669 Burrow resigned his post as Lucasian Professor in Newton's favour. Newton was feverishly engaged at the time on experiments into the nature of light. But his first major work came to the attention of the Royal Society only by hearsay. During his experiments, Newton had perfected the first reflecting telescope. The society heard about it, and begged to see it. Newton sent it to them in December 1671 and followed it in the February of 1672 with a paper outlining his optical theories.

Pondering the properties of light, Newton had deduced that all the colours of the spectrum combine to produce 'white' light. But if the blue light, for example, is separated out from the spectrum, it remains blue, even when refracted through a prism.

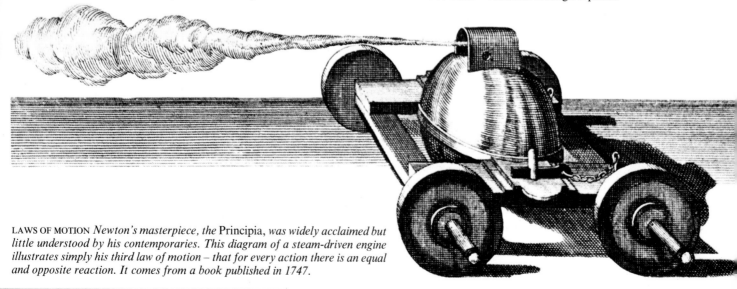

LAWS OF MOTION *Newton's masterpiece, the* Principia, *was widely acclaimed but little understood by his contemporaries. This diagram of a steam-driven engine illustrates simply his third law of motion – that for every action there is an equal and opposite reaction. It comes from a book published in 1747.*

GENIUS OF SCIENCE *Isaac Newton in his eighties.*

REFLECTING THE STARS *Newton's reflecting telescope, the prototype of all modern models, was made entirely by himself. It is preserved by the Royal Society.*

EXPERIMENTS WITH LIGHT *Newton planned an experiment into the properties of light in this sketch from his notebook. He later published a book called* Opticks.

SCHOLAR'S HAVEN *Newton's study in Woolsthorpe Manor, where he evolved most of his theories. He went there during the plague in 1665.*

Newton's optical discoveries led him into a fierce controversy with Robert Hooke, the Secretary of the Royal Society. Thereafter he was reluctant to expose himself to criticism again. His theories on the idea of universal gravitation, in consequence, only came to the attention of the world by accident.

In the late summer of 1684 Edmond Halley, the astronomer who gave his name to Halley's comet, came to Cambridge to ask Newton a question which baffled Royal Society members. What, he asked, would be the orbit of a planet if it was attracted to the sun by a force obeying an inverse square law? Without hesitating, Newton replied 'An ellipse'.

A contemporary account continues the meeting: 'Struck with joy and amazement, Halley asked him how he knew it? "Why," saith he, "I have calculated it".'

Alchemy and the mint

But when Halley asked him to produce his calculation, Newton hunted vaguely around and said he could not find it. He did, however, promise Halley written proof. This promise bore fruit in the shape of perhaps the greatest scientific treatise the world had yet produced, *Philosophia Naturalis Principia Mathematica* – Mathematical Principles of Natural Philosophy, commonly known as the *Principia*.

Published in 1687 in Latin, the *Principia* was so dense and original that few of Newton's contemporaries were capable of grasping it. But for the next 250 years any other work done on the subject was only an enlargement of Newton's principles. Under his system, apples fell and planets rotated in accordance with unchanging laws. His three famous laws of motion formed the basis for all modern astronomy and physics.

The publication of the *Principia* left Newton, at 45, exhausted, once more deep in the public controversy he hated, and with his life's scientific work effectively over.

The remaining 40 years of his life was a slow emergence from the solitary struggle of discovery into the world of public affairs. But his nervous system was badly overstrained, and from 1693–4 he suffered a severe mental breakdown. He became convinced that all his friends had let him down and deceived him. One of his lifelong associations was with Charles Montagu, later Lord Halifax, whom he had first met at Cambridge. Montagu had become a very influential man, and was doing his utmost to find Newton a good position. Yet at the beginning of 1692 Newton was writing: 'Being convinced that Mr Montagu is false to me, I have done with him.' And another friend wrote: 'There is a man lost and so to speak dead for research, so I believe . . .'

Gradually he recovered. In 1697 Montagu obtained for him the position of Warden of the Mint, in London. The job could have been a mere sinecure, but Newton, with his usual enthusiasm, chose a complete overhaul of the British monetary system.

Public duties aside, he continued to scribble away at a study which had long fascinated him – on the occult.

It is hard to reconcile the worldly pompous official of these years with the rapt mystical hermit of earlier years. But Newton's life had always been a mass of contradictions. The man whose powers of logic had exposed the superstitious fantasies of generations had been secretly obsessed with the occult.

Ocean of truth

He wrote more than a million words on alchemy, and his library contained many books by the Rosicrucians, a secret brotherhood which believed in the magical side of alchemy, and mixed religion, disembodied spirits and chemistry.

In 1703, after the death of his old rival, Robert Hooke, Newton, to his delight, was finally made President of the Royal Society. He was knighted by Queen Anne in 1705, the first man of science to be so honoured. He ruled Britain's scientific world like a despot.

Long after his powers of sustained scientific thought had vanished, his interest in alchemy remained. It was as if the great man of science secretly rejoiced at the thought that beyond the world of science and scientific laws there existed an incalculable power, a mysterious force defying rational thought.

Before his death in 1727, at the age of 85, he told his nephew: 'I do not know what I may appear to the world, but to myself I seem to have been only like a boy, playing on the seashore . . . whilst the great ocean of truth lay all undiscovered before me.'

The 'Protestant wind' brings a glorious revolution

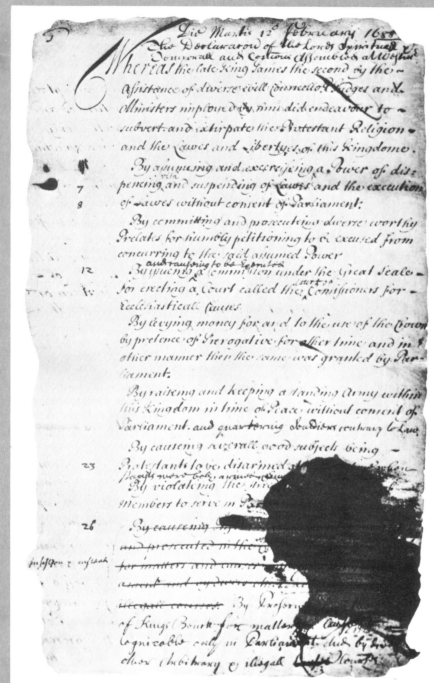

DOCUMENT OF REVOLUTION

One of the foundation stones of the British constitution is the Declaration of Rights, drawn up in 1689 after the last Stuart king, James II, had been deposed. The Declaration listed his misdeeds, including 'raising and keeping an Army within this Kingdom in time of peace and quartering soldiers contrary to the law'. William and Mary had to agree to the new curbs on their power contained in the Declaration – now in the Record Office of the House of Lords – before being given the throne. A Bill based on the Declaration was passed into law as the Bill of Rights in Parliament in 1689, although William made it clear that he resented the move as an undesirable limitation of his power. Lord Halifax, a leading Whig politician, said: 'The king had great jealousy at being governed.'

Early on the morning of November 5, 1688, Simon Jansen Hartevelt, captain of the Dutch ship *Den Briel*, cautiously edged his vessel into the harbour of Torbay in Devon. The navigation buoys round all Channel ports had been removed by order of James II, and Hartevelt's first attempt to gain the harbour had failed. But this time he was successful, and by noon 300 more Dutch ships had dropped anchor beside him.

On board the *Den Briel* was William of Orange, nephew and son-in-law of James. The other ships carried his army of more than 12,000 Dutch and British troops. High on a masthead flew a banner proclaiming 'The liberty of England and the Protestant religion'.

William was a Protestant prince who had married an English wife – Mary, the daughter of James II. He had come to England to restore liberty and to safeguard the Protestant succession. Privately, he hoped to win the throne.

His achievement became known as the Glorious Revolution – a bloodless revolution which established the foundations of England's constitutional monarchy.

Waiting in the wings

Unlike the Duke of Monmouth, whose invasion three years before had ended in ignominious failure, William had made careful preparations to ensure his success. Most important of these was the fact that he had waited for an invitation from powerful men before venturing to set foot in England.

William had refused to be drawn into over-hasty action. So long as his wife remained heir to the throne, he could afford to wait for the Catholic James's death. For three years this hope sustained the English, too. James's policies were hated – but he was ageing. Then, in June 1688, came an event which shattered every Protestant's hopes. James's Italian wife, Mary of Modena, gave birth to a son. The boy

BLOODLESS COUP *A contemporary painting shows William of Orange landing from his fleet at Torbay on November 5, 1688. He then led his army to Exeter, where he waited for the political situation to become clearer and for leading politicians to join him. For William wanted his invasion to be bloodless and popular and had no intention of fighting a savage battle for the crown.*

William and Mary: A new role for monarchy

William of Orange and his attractive wife, Mary, accepted the English throne on terms which transformed the role of monarchy. Mary won the hearts of her people, but William's own part in the transformation won him little thanks. Only twice in the rest of his reign did he enjoy something like popularity with the English nation: after Mary's death in 1694; and in 1697, when he won peace with France. But, otherwise, this brave soldier and masterly statesman was unloved.

The English resented being dragged by William out of their isolation and into the struggle which dominated their foreign king's life – the need to save his beloved Holland from France. And William hardly went out of his way to coax and cultivate his subjects. He heaped wealth on his Dutch cronies and regarded the majority of British politicians as rogues or fools. Even in peacetime he left the country for months on end.

Had she lived, Mary might have taught her husband how to see his rule over the British as something more than a bleak necessity. For she had the charm, the friendliness, the natural touch, which he so painfully lacked.

After Mary's death from smallpox, William cared for little except his single-minded crusade against Louis XIV of France. Physically, he had never been robust. Now he degenerated alarmingly. At 45 he was already an old man, his lungs tortured by asthma and bronchitis. Little wonder that William began drinking heavily to make life bearable. And when he died in 1702, few Englishmen mourned him.

was baptised into the Roman Catholic faith, and the pope was named godfather.

Appalled at the prospect of a continuing Catholic dynasty, seven of England's most notable Protestant politicians decided that the time had come for action. On June 30 they sent William a letter, reviewing the new situation, and ending: 'We, who subscribe this, will not fail to attend your Highness upon your landing.' It was an invitation to invasion. When at last William's powerful fleet set sail, the 'Protestant wind' – blowing from the east – sped it towards the Devon coast, while James's own navy was penned helplessly in the Thames estuary. Nor could James afford to disperse his army along the coasts. And so the landing on November 5 was accomplished without the slightest resistance.

William was no ordinary rebel. He had brought with him not just a band of personal followers, but a strong, disciplined, professional army. Five days after the landing, he marched his force in procession through the city of Exeter, in a manner calculated to encourage his supporters and overawe his opponents. First came 300 cavalry, then a squad of olive-skinned soldiers from the Dutch colony of Surinam, and then a unit of Lapland troops. Thousands more soldiers followed, and at the rear came 21 huge cannon, each one hauled by 16 horses.

The popular welcome expected by William was slow in coming. The people of the West Country had not forgotten the vengeance exacted by Judge Jeffreys the last time they supported a usurper. But as William moved nearer London, his numbers began to swell – and the importance of those who now flocked to his standard more than made up for their tardy conversion to the Protestant cause.

Among them, the most notable were Prince George of Denmark, husband of the king's younger daughter Anne, and – an even greater prize – John Churchill, James's most experienced general. As such desertions increased, James II's remaining supporters became confused and demoralised. James himself was shattered by the defection of two of his own children, Mary and Anne.

A peaceful revolution

Despairing of his cause, the king made arrangements to smuggle his infant son to France, and then decided that he too must flee to safety. As he fled by barge from London, James threw the Great Seal, the symbol of his sovereignty, into the Thames, so that no one could summon a Parliament in his name. And in the driving rain of a late December day, James slipped away unhindered to France.

Even in his last defiant gesture James had been unsuccessful. Five months later the seal was found by a fisherman.

James's flight was all that William needed. In February 1689, William's wife, Mary, returned to her English homeland. Parliament then formally offered the crown to both husband and wife as joint sovereigns. It was a solemn and momentous occasion, for Parliament did not make its offer as a humble suppliant, but as an equal partner in government.

In return for their crown, William and Mary subscribed to a Declaration of Rights drawn up by Parliament – a second Magna Carta, setting out the personal and political rights of all Englishmen. And, as William made his speech of acceptance, a new era in the history of the English constitution began.

DUAL MONARCHY *William and Mary ruled together. He was reserved, with a chilling manner, while she was high spirited and romantic.*

215

Butchery in the glens leaves a legacy of hate

VALLEY OF DEATH

Glencoe, in the Highlands of Scotland, was described by the historian Thomas Babington Macaulay as a 'sad and awful place'. It was desolate, the land was infertile and the weather often rough. But for the rebellious MacDonalds, the towering hills made it a secure hide-out until 1692. Then they were tricked into billeting soldiers in their cottages – and were massacred by their hereditary enemies, the Campbells, just before dawn on a February morning as 'a proper vindication of public justice'.

In the spring and summer of 1691, the Highlands of Scotland were on the point of rebelling against English rule. The Scots still maintained a stubborn loyalty to the exiled Stuart king, James II, deposed in 1688 because of his pro-Catholic policies. To forestall open rebellion, the new king, William III, ordered that every clan must swear an oath of allegiance to him before New Year's Day, 1692. Failure would be punished by savage and brutal reprisals.

Faced with this threat, all the clan chiefs gave way – even such a wild, bloodthirsty tribe of cattle raiders as the MacDonalds of Glencoe.

The MacDonalds' tragedy was that they left their gesture of loyalty too late, even though this was not deliberate.

Their aged chief, MacIain MacDonald, had spared no effort to meet the deadline. On December 29, 1691, he rode through a snowstorm to take the oath at Fort William.

Built near the town of Inverlochy and named after the new king, Fort William was a forbidding strongpoint built to overawe the rebellious Scots. Its governor was a soldier, Colonel John Hill. But when MacIain presented himself before Hill to perform his distasteful duty, the governor announced that he had no power to administer the oath. It must be sworn before a civil official, the Sheriff at Inveraray.

MacIain was appalled. Before him lay a journey of 60 miles to Inveraray – hard enough in good weather, impossible in the storm that was now raging as they talked. And time was running out.

MacIain did not reach Inveraray until January 2. There another disappointment met him: the Sheriff was away, staying with his family over Hogmanay. In mounting anxiety, MacIain awaited his return. Then, at last, on January 6, the Sheriff received him. He shook his head at the long delay, and only when he saw the chief break unashamedly into tears did he relent and allow the oath of loyalty to be taken.

Treachery in the glens

Those six days were to mean the death sentence for the MacDonalds of Glencoe. For, ever since July 1689, when clans loyal to James had wiped out government troops at Killiecrankie, in Perthshire, King William and his Scottish administrators had been anxious to teach the Highlanders a lesson. Old MacIain MacDonald led a clan that was small and unpopular. The king's callous and canny advisers knew that brutal action against the clan would not lead to a general rising. So when the chief's belated oath was considered by the clerks to the Privy Council in Edinburgh, they refused to accept it.

'If MacIain of Glencoe and that tribe can be well separated from the rest,' William wrote, 'it will be a proper vindication of public justice to extirpate that sect of thieves.'

Late in the bitter month of January, 120 red-coated soldiers were dispatched to Glencoe. They were billeted in the tiny crofters' cottages of the valley on the pretext that Fort William had no room for them. The soldiers were mainly Campbells, under Captain Campbell of Glenlyon – bitter enemies of the MacDonalds. Yet they were accepted trustingly in Glencoe, for there was a hallowed Highland understanding that when hospitality has been offered and accepted, even the fiercest feud between guest and host must be laid aside.

After a fortnight of feasting and fraternisation came the execution order. The stark message was passed down from the regimental colonel to Captain Campbell of Glenlyon: 'You are hereby ordered to fall upon the rebels the MacDonalds of Glencoe and put all to the sword under 70. You are to have special care that the old fox (MacIain) and his sons do not escape your hands.'

After dark on February 12 the secret message was carried down the glen. Soldiers were called out into the snow from the cottage firesides to hear their instructions. They were to give no hint of their design until the appointed hour – 5 o'clock on the following morning.

At a few seconds after 5 a.m. the first cries rang out in the frosty air of the dark glen. The

TRAGEDY IN THE GLEN *A Victorian picture shows survivors of the massacre huddling in the snow as their homes blaze. The troops had been told to wipe out the MacDonalds, but many of them escaped. This was because the soldiers disobeyed orders and used muskets instead of swords on their victims. The gunfire awoke many clansmen who had time to run off to the hills.*

first man to die was Duncan Rankin, who lived near the chief's house. Fleeing from the soldiers, he was shot as he stumbled across the river. Soon came the turn of the 'old fox' himself. Ordering his men to MacIain's door, Lieutenant John Lindsay knocked and told a servant that the troops were leaving and wanted to thank the chief for his hospitality. MacIain awakened, climbed out of bed and told his wife to dress.

Soldiers immediately ran into the house, and shots rang out in the darkness. MacIain, hit in body and head, collapsed. He was still wearing his nightshirt, though he had pulled on his trousers. The Campbells stripped his wife naked and tore the rings from her fingers. Down the glen others were at work, bayoneting MacDonalds as they slept.

A child clung to the Campbell commander's knees and begged for mercy. The reply was a pistol shot at point-blank range. When the soldiers tired of using their weapons, they took to fire-raising. In one cottage alone, it was reported, 14 people burnt to death.

Even when facing their doom, the MacDonalds showed their courage. 'If I am to be killed by you,' said one villager, 'I would rather it were not beneath my own roof.' 'I've eaten your meat,' replied a soldier, 'I'll do you the favour and kill you without.' And this villager escaped his fate. As the soldiers closed in on him, he flung his plaid over their heads and fled into the snow.

The massacre was soon over. As the sacked cottages blazed, many MacDonalds heard the din, roused themselves and slipped away unseen. But for the weaker ones this freedom was short-lived. Naked in the snow, they died from exposure, as William III's Scottish Secretary of State, Lord Stair, had intended.

Legacy of hatred

Stair had callously set a midwinter deadline to the oath-swearing. He argued that this was 'the only season in which we are sure the Highlanders cannot escape and carry their wives, bairns and cattle to the hills . . . This is the proper time to maul them in the long winter nights'.

According to legend, not all the soldiers took eagerly to their task. One soldier, sickened by the order to kill a woman and her child hiding in the snow, slew an animal and showed his bloodstained sword to his officer as proof of his obedience.

As a systematic massacre, Glencoe was a failure. Both MacIain's sons escaped, and only 38 butchered bodies were found in the glen – less than one-tenth of MacIain's clan.

But as a symbol of William's cold-blooded and unscrupulous attitude towards his Scottish subjects, it had an enduring effect. No other single event did so much to strengthen Highland loyalty to the exiled James II and his descendants. It was this loyalty among the clans that was to lead to two later episodes in Scotland's tragic and heroic story, the Stuart rebellions of 1715 and 1745.

England and Scotland – from enmity to union

The Scottish Jacobites nursed a deep hatred for England, and the Dutch king, William III, in particular. They had accepted William and Mary as their king and queen in April 1689, more from disappointment at James's craven flight than out of any enthusiasm for the new joint monarchs. They responded warmly when James began fighting to win back his throne.

'Sold for English gold'

The Glencoe massacre and other examples of brutal government aroused undying bitterness in the Highland clans, and even led them to put aside their own differences to unite against their oppressors. But there was resentment, too, among the people of such cities as Edinburgh at England's economic power, and the harsh trading embargoes she imposed against the Scots. Two years after William's death, the Scottish Parliament passed an Act of Security, which prohibited an English monarch from ruling Scotland unless equal trading, political and religious rights were guaranteed. Ominously, it also provided for an independent Scottish army to be raised.

War between the two countries seemed a real possibility. But the English knew how to divide the Scots and rule them. The Lowlanders could be bought and the Highlanders starved into wretched compliance. An almost total union was agreed – on the basis of concessions to the Lowland townspeople. Sixteen Scottish peers and 45 MPs were to sit at Westminster. And although the Scots lost their own Parliament, they retained their own legal system.

The deal, ratified in the Act of Union of 1707, meant that Scotland had, in effect, traded her loyalty to the exiled King James for commercial equality.

The Highland clansmen, still unswervingly loyal to James, were disgusted. 'We are bought and sold for English gold,' they sang.

UNION ACCOMPLISHED *Queen Anne receives the Act of Union from the Duke of Queensberry. Its signing formally united England and Scotland.*

The first Churchill humbles the might of France

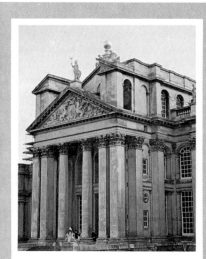

A SOLDIER'S REWARD

Blenheim Palace in Oxfordshire was built by order of Queen Anne and paid for by the nation as a reward to John Churchill, Duke of Marlborough, for his victories over France. The original design was by Vanbrugh.

COMPLETE VICTORY *Marlborough's triumph at Blenheim established his reputation as the finest general in the world. The night before the battle, Marlborough (above) spent much of the time in prayer. At dawn he received Holy Communion. A Dutch tapestry (right) – now at Blenheim Palace – shows the duke on a white horse directing the battle from a hilltop. The battle lasted about eight hours and the French were routed. Their losses were enormous – 26,000 dead and 15,000 captured. The victory meant that the ambitious Louis XIV of France was forced to abandon his plans to dominate Europe, and the shadow that had hung over the Continent for three decades was lifted. But peace was not to be made until April 1713.*

By the beginning of the 18th century, England's lengthy quarrel with Louis XIV was reaching its climax. For 30 years the might of France had threatened the peace of Europe. But on August 13, 1704, English troops fighting at the south German village of Blenheim won their greatest victory since Agincourt, 300 years before. And their commander, John Churchill, Duke of Marlborough, shattered the legend of French military invincibility.

A new phase of war had started as soon as Queen Anne came to the throne in 1702. At first, England's ally the Netherlands had been the centre of the war, but by 1704 French interest had shifted to a greater prize – Vienna, capital of England's other ally, Austria.

Marching halfway across Europe

The Duke of Marlborough knew that the fall of Vienna would fatally weaken the alliance. Resisting Dutch demands that he stay and defend the Netherlands, he decided on a bold stroke that would take his army halfway across Europe to challenge the French on the Danube.

On this 600 mile, three-month-long march, Marlborough's main care was for the welfare of his 40,000 men – a motley collection of English, Dutch, German and Danish soldiers. He arranged a faultless supply system, even ensuring that every man was issued with new boots before the force entered hostile Bavaria. The Allied army thus reached the new theatre of war in peak fighting condition.

At Münster, on the Danube, Marlborough's troops were joined by a smaller Allied force under Prince Eugene of Savoy and prepared to block the path of the French and Bavarian army marching on Vienna. The Allies now had some 52,000 men – 9000 of them British. Their two commanders, the duke and the prince, were both skilled and experienced generals, confident of each other, and ideally suited to be partners in battle.

Marshal Tallard, the French commander, had no wish to join battle with Marlborough, and decided to take up a position so strong that it would deter an Allied attack. He drew up his 54,000 troops along the western bank of the River Nebel, about 6 miles from Münster. Protected by the Nebel and the Danube, and by the fortified village of Blenheim, he assumed that no enemy would be foolhardy enough to risk a battle.

But Tallard had reckoned without the cool daring of Marlborough and Eugene. Tallard's troops were not concentrated for the battle, and this left a fatal weakness in the French centre. Moreover, they were positioned too far back from the banks of the Nebel, giving room for the Allied army to regroup after crossing the river.

As the sun broke through the morning mist on August 13, the astonished French awoke to see the entire Allied army facing them, and preparing to cross the river.

Marlborough had to hold off his attack until Prince Eugene's force had reached its station on the wing. For five hours, 90 French guns poured a relentless fire on the waiting

Allied troops. Marlborough himself narrowly escaped being cut down by a cannon-ball as he rode on a tour of inspection. At last, all was ready, and at noon Marlborough gave the signal to advance.

The French commander in Blenheim, the Marquis de Clérambault, panicked immediately. He summoned up 18 battalions of reserves, thus trebling his original fighting strength. The result was that Blenheim became so overcrowded that his soldiers could hardly move. Rather than try to take the village, Marlborough simply left a contingent of his troops to encircle it, hemming in its 12,000 defenders and raining a damaging fire on them.

'A Glorious Victory'

The main fighting took place outside Blenheim. Here Marlborough showed his mastery of the combined cavalry and infantry action, drawing them up in alternate lines so that each supported the other.

Unable to match this, the French began to weaken and lose formation. Tallard failed to give either direction or inspiration to his men. At 5 p.m. the last triumphant scene of the battle was played out under Marlborough's unfailing direction. The Allied cavalry began to trot forward in close formation, their horses' strides lengthening into a gallop as they thundered towards the French cavalry lines.

The weight and impetus of the charge, and the bloody effect of the flashing Allied swords, was too much for the weary French. Soon they turned and galloped off in full flight.

The day was Marlborough's. Among the 15,000 prisoners taken by the Allies was Tallard himself, who was captured on his way to Blenheim village and brought to Marl-

THE QUEEN AND THE DUCHESS

The friendship of Queen Anne and Sarah Churchill, Duchess of Marlborough, was one of the most celebrated in British history. It started in childhood when the shy, poorly educated and plain Anne met the dominating, witty and beautiful Sarah.

When Sarah married John Churchill, Anne said that she would content herself with 'that little corner' of Sarah's heart which she hoped still remained unoccupied. But Sarah's great fault was her arrogance. Later, she was furious when she found Anne had a new favourite.

The two women quarrelled bitterly and Sarah even described Anne as a 'praying, godly idiot'. The friendship of Mrs Morley and Mrs Freeman – as the queen and duchess signed themselves in their intimate correspondence – came to an end in 1709. And with Sarah's fall from favour, her husband, too, lost his power.

Anne (left) and Sarah (right). Through their friendship the Whigs controlled the government.

---

borough. Still mounted on horseback, the duke took out an old tavern bill, and on the back scrawled a message to his wife Sarah: 'I have not time to say more, but to beg you will give my duty to the Queen, and let her know her Army has had a Glorious Victory.'

As Marlborough wrote, 12,000 panic-stricken men were still surrounded in the village of Blenheim. General Clérambault had not the courage to face the annihilation that confronted his troops – nor the disgrace that would greet any surrender. He mounted his horse, galloped through his infantry and plunged into the Danube and drowned.

The French losses at the Battle of Blenheim were catastrophic: four out of every five troops were killed or taken prisoner, compared with one in every five of the Allies.

When he heard the news of his army's defeat, the French king, Louis XIV, was so shocked that he issued an edict forbidding all mention of the battle.

It was eight days before the news of Blenheim reached England. One gallant officer, Colonel Parke, rode day and night until he reached London. Within a few minutes of his arrival, the cannon of the Tower boomed, the bells were set ringing and every citizen was on the streets. Englishmen had just cause for celebration. For, as the sun set on the field of Blenheim, it was said, the glory of their greatest enemy, Louis XIV, departed.

Anne: The sad story of the last ruling Stuart

It was sadly appropriate that Queen Anne – the last Stuart to rule Britain – was born in 1665, the year of the Great Plague. Her life was to be overshadowed by tragedy and constant ill-health.

Anne's great sorrow was her inability to bear living children, and 17 pregnancies in 16 years left her with no heir and a shattered constitution. By the time she succeeded her brother-in-law, William III, at the age of 37, she was a permanent invalid suffering frequent and agonising pain.

Although Anne's husband, Prince George of Denmark, was devoted to her, the person she felt closest to was Sarah Jennings, a former childhood playmate who had married John Churchill, the soldier who was to lead Anne's armies to great continental victories.

In many ways, the two women were opposites. Anne was quiet and withdrawn, with only average looks, while Sarah was a dominating woman of dazzling beauty. The friendship lasted for more than 30 years, although in later years Sarah found the queen a bore. She once said, after seeing Anne: 'It was extremely tedious to be so much where there could be no manner of conversation.' Eventually, the two women quarrelled and their relationship came to an end.

Anne was petty, argumentative, and had little education or intellect. Yet it was her very limitations that proved her strength and endeared her to her subjects. She echoed their dislike of France and their suspicion of Catholics. Even her personal characteristics – her greed, gout and fondness for hunting and gambling – were reassuringly commonplace after the dark foreign charm of the previous Stuart monarchs.

Establishing the succession

Anne's devotion to duty was formidable. For 14 years she dragged her sick body to endless council meetings, straining her afflicted eyes over state papers and striving to calm the bitter quarrels between Whig and Tory.

The last years of Anne's reign were preoccupied with the question of succession. Her Catholic half-brother, James, the 'Old Pretender', was a constant threat, although in 1701 Parliament had decreed that the throne should pass to the nearest Protestant heir – the House of Hanover.

Because she detested her Hanoverian cousins, Anne refused to let them set foot in England. But in the final days of her life she did ensure the peaceful Hanoverian succession, by sending an emissary to the future George I and assuring him of her friendship. She played a vital part in securing a peaceful change of dynasty – and so helped her country to avoid the agony of civil war.

A nation united under the Georges

*A German dynasty, the House of Hanover,
comes to the throne to preside over decades of growing
prosperity crowned by triumph in war*

In 1714 Queen Anne, the last Stuart monarch to rule Britain, died. A new dynasty came to the throne – an obscure family from the far-away Electorate of Hanover in Germany. The following year, George, Elector of Hanover, was crowned king, as George I. He could not even speak English, but he had been chosen by Parliament as the nearest Protestant heir to the childless Anne. His selection marked a turning point in British constitutional history. For the Hanoverians were strangers in a foreign land, and they had to rely on the guidance of their ministers and Parliaments more than any British monarch had ever done before.

The country the Hanoverians were called upon to rule was unrivalled in Europe in terms of power and prestige. The long years of war with Louis XIV of France had ended in triumph a year earlier. The Hanoverians were to bring to their new kingdom the blessing of a long-lasting peace. For a generation, under the leadership of Sir Robert Walpole, Britain deliberately set out to avoid conflict. His own clearly stated preference was for 'jaw, jaw, not war, war'. In 26 years of peace and prosperity Britain's economic strength reached new heights. And when the test of European war came again, this strength enabled Britain to triumph in the Seven Years' War.

During the entire period, however, the Stuarts and their supporters, the Jacobites, never gave up hope of winning back the throne. Prince James Edward Stuart, whose birth in 1688 had precipitated the Glorious Revolution, landed on December 22, 1715, at Peterhead in Scotland, from exile in

LONDON'S MEETING PLACE

The crowds who gathered on a summer evening in St James's Park (left) embodied the democratic spirit of early-18th-century London. In 1731 a Frenchman commented: 'St James's Park is the public walk of London and open to all. It is a strange sight to see the flower of the nobility and the first ladies of the court mingling in confusion with the vilest populace.'

In this painting, modestly dressed gentlefolk are seen drinking milk fresh from the grazing cows, while opulent aristocrats stroll beneath the trees of the Mall. Kilted Scots and lounging grenadiers supply a rougher note. In the distance rise the newly completed twin towers of Westminster Abbey. Even today St James's Park (inset) preserves much of this rural calm.

221

THE CUP THAT CHEERS *Tea first reached Britain in the 1650's, and tea-drinking had become a popular social habit by the early 18th century. Though all classes drank tea – it cost about a penny a cup in tea-houses – it was the aristocracy who brought its consumption in the home to a fine art. The taking of afternoon tea was soon to become a British ritual.*

CHURCHMEN *English bishops were reputed to be worldly and neglectful of their duties. Many preferred London life to their own dioceses. Bishop Hoadly (right) visited his diocese of Bangor three times in six years. Though a skilled theologian, most people knew him better as a famous glutton.*

CLERICAL CORRUPTION *Parish priests were more often hunting or drinking than preaching. In this satire by Hogarth, a short-sighted vicar reads to a slumbering congregation, while his clerk leers at a parishioner.*

France. His allies included high-placed Catholics and members of the Tory Party. But in February of the following year, after his generals had lost battles at Preston in England and Sheriffmuir in Scotland, James fled back to France. By April the rising had been completely suppressed (pp. 226–7).

The 1715 rebellion broke the Tory stranglehold on British politics which had dominated life during the last years of Anne's reign. The association of many high-ranking Tories with the Jacobites branded them as traitors and rebels in the eyes of George I and his successors. The Whigs took power and held it. For the following 50 years, they carved up all the offices of government, great and small, among themselves.

Prosperity in an era of peace

Political stability was reflected in the sophistication achieved in the arts. The city of Bath (pp. 228–9) was a temple to Georgian elegance. It had been visited by Queen Anne in 1702 and fashionable society soon followed her there. But the uncrowned king of Bath was Richard 'Beau' Nash, known as 'the Arbiter of Elegance'. Nash not only transformed the primitive amenities of this spa town, which had existed since Roman times, but laid down rules of etiquette which brooked no disobedience. Where Bath led, the rest of polite society followed (pp. 224–5). And Bath's architecture, too, was transformed by the work of a father and son of genius – the two Woods.

But this veneer of elegance did not conceal corruption and scandal in public life. Sir Robert Walpole (pp. 230–1), a country squire who rose to become Britain's first Prime Minister, came to prominence in the wake of a famous financial scandal, the South Sea Bubble crisis of 1720–1.

The South Sea Company had offered to take over the National Debt; its failure caused a catastrophic financial crisis. Walpole's bluff common sense – and his outstanding grasp of finance – extricated the country from threatening disaster. His twin aims of prosperity at home and peace abroad were to dominate British politics for the next 20 years. His dominance was such that his enemies gave him the title of Prime Minister. They meant it as a term of abuse, but the office was soon to pass into the British way of life.

The London over which Walpole presided was rapidly expanding, prosperous and uninhibited. The life of its citizens was captured in all its detail by William Hogarth (pp. 232–3), an engraver who soon became the most popular artist of the day. Satire was the language of the age, and Hogarth's most famous works revealed his biting wit. But they also showed compassion. He aimed, in his own words, 'both to entertain and to improve the mind', and portrayed harlots, rakes and the gin-drinking poor as unfortunate victims of their environment rather than as sinners. For, despite the prosperity fostered by Walpole during his period of power, Britain was still a nation of violent social contrasts.

A wealth of artistic talent and achievement

Hogarth was only one of the brilliant artistic talents of Georgian London. Writers such as Defoe and Fielding were producing their greatest works at this time. But the literary giant of the mid-18th century was Dr Samuel Johnson. His greatest work was his *Dictionary*, published in 1755. Even in this, Johnson's famous wit did not desert him; he described a lexicographer as: 'A writer of dictionaries, a harmless drudge.'

Johnson's friendship with James Boswell, a Scotsman 30 years younger than himself, was immortalised by the latter in one of the greatest biographies of English literature – *The Life of Samuel Johnson*. Boswell captured Johnson's dominance of London's literary life with such lively accuracy and wit that it is now impossible to think of one without the other (p. 236).

Music, too, flourished under the Hanoverians. The German-born composer George Frederick Handel made his home in London. His musical output was prodigious, including many operas for the London stage and a series of great biblical oratorios, culminating in the 'Messiah'. It was George II who brought the audience to its feet for the 'Hallelujah Chorus' at the first London performance in 1743. This tradition still survives today (p. 237).

While the arts flourished at home, the drive for empire went forward overseas. Walpole had to abandon his principle of peace in 1739 when London's merchants, avid for trade, forced him into a war against Spain, in order to open up the Spanish empire to their ships. He resigned three years later. But another politician, William Pitt, was to achieve as much success abroad as Walpole had done at home. The Spanish war was a prelude to almost a quarter of a century's struggle for worldwide dominance with Bourbon France.

In 1745, however, a sudden threat struck much nearer home. While most of the British army was engaged against France on the Continent, the Stuarts seized their last chance to win back the British throne. In July, Prince Charles Edward Stuart – 'Bonnie Prince Charlie' – landed in Scotland from France, in an attempt to win the throne for his father (pp. 234–5).

The handsome and courageous 25-year-old prince caught the imagination of the Highland clans, who were quick to rally to his standard. He found the British government completely unprepared. They were forced to recall their troops from the Continent to oppose him. By the end of October, however, Charles had captured Edinburgh and was ready to march into England.

Wars with France to win two empires

He got as far as Derby, only 130 miles from London. But he found no local support, the French failed him and his own troops were dwindling. Forced to withdraw to Scotland, the British army finally cornered his ill-fed and exhausted soldiers on the bleak moor of Culloden on April 16, 1746. The battle went against the prince, and after five months as a fugitive he escaped to France. The Jacobite threat had ended. And France made peace in 1748.

But this peace was to be short-lasting. In 1756 war with France broke out again. On this occasion, action was not confined to Europe but, more importantly, spread to the colonies. In India, Robert Clive made sure that the British would be masters of the sub-continent by winning the Battle of Plassey in 1757. And in Canada, where French and English had lived at dagger-point for 80 years, British dominance was assured by the capture of Quebec by the brilliant James Wolfe (pp. 238–9).

Britain's wealth and power was also expressed in stone. The landed aristocracy used their wealth to leave an indelible mark on the face of Britain with their magnificent houses, surrounded by landscape gardens which ensured perfect 'vistas' in every direction.

Stowe (pp. 240–1), in Buckinghamshire, was perfected by Lord Temple, his architect Robert Adam, and Capability Brown, the greatest landscape gardener of the day. It was the crowning glory of the age of the first two Georges, which came to an end in 1760. In that year, flushed with victory in war, enriched by trade and the wealth of empire, Britain stood on the brink of her greatest achievements yet as a world power. And the quiet confidence of the British people that their country would achieve still greater triumphs was best expressed in a letter by the contemporary diarist Horace Walpole. 'It really looks,' he wrote, 'as if we intended to finish the conquest of the world next campaign.'

ENGLAND'S PRIDE *The land was the source of wealth in the early 18th century. Though rich aristocrats were concentrating land and power within their own hands, the characteristic rural figure was still the squire, seen here in caricature. Disdaining fancy ways, the squire was a bluff farming man, rough-mannered and English to the core.*

AGRICULTURAL REVOLUTION *More than half England's inhabitants still lived off the land in the 1760's. Great strides in agriculture enabled farmers to feed the growing population. The first major innovator was Jethro Tull (top). He mechanised sowing with his seed-drill (above), which he built from parts of an organ soundboard.*

CHILDREN OF A NEW AGE *A free-ranging spirit of scientific inquiry laid the foundations for a revolution which was soon to change the face of Britain. Scientific inventions were now catching the popular imagination as never before. In this painting by Joseph Wright of Derby, a group of adults and children are examining an orrery, the intricate and often beautiful instrument which showed the movement of the planets.*

223

AGE OF VITALITY

The pleasures and pastimes of 18th-century life were as exuberant as the people themselves. At Bath, 'Beau' Nash was attempting to teach the fashionable to put aside their swords and riding boots.

The upper classes were eccentric, individual, sentimental, dramatic and tearful. They were emotional about their friends, cruel about their enemies – and above all they loved to gossip. And the age was rich in great eccentrics about whom gossip revolved.

Much time and trouble was spent on appearance, despite the difficulties of poor sanitation and the absence of baths. The British army in George II's reign used 65,000 tons of flour for powdering wigs every year. Etiquette was immensely important. Books like *The Dancing Master* gave instructions on 'How to take off your Hat and replace it'.

In town, public executions drew such excited crowds that they added a new phrase to the language – 'gala day', which is a corruption of 'gallows day'. The upper classes amused themselves with fighting duels, boxing, gaming, drinking and laying bets. When a passer-by fell down opposite Brook's Club in St James's, bets were laid as to whether he was alive or not – and those who said he was dead objected to the use of restoratives because it would interfere with the outcome of the bet. In the country they hunted and went shooting.

The poor in the country danced jigs and struggled to wrest a living from the land. In town they drank gin, as in Hogarth's famous cartoon 'Gin Alley', where the victims are shown 'drunk for a penny, dead drunk for 2d'.

Drink was one of the few pursuits that knew no class barriers. An astonished French visitor noted the British habit of solemnly sitting down to get drunk after dinner, and added that there was 'not an Englishman who is not supremely happy at this particular moment'.

POPULAR ENTERTAINMENT *The two loves of highwayman Macheath (centre)—Lucy Locket (left) and Polly Peachum (right)—plead for his life, in a scene from John Gay's famous work 'The Beggar's Opera'.*

ENGLISHMAN'S SPORT *The cartoonist Rowlandson drew this picture of a hunt meet. Fox-hunting, rather than older forms of the chase like stag-hunting, was now the popular pastime of country landowners.*

PLEASURE GARDENS *The upper classes, often in disguise, mingled with the common people at Vauxhall Gardens, strolling, drinking, gossiping and listening to the music. On the left side, in this aquatint by Rowlandson, Samuel Johnson and James Boswell sit drinking and chatting to Johnson's friend and benefactor, Mrs Thrale, and the playwright Oliver Goldsmith. Dr Johnson so loved the life of the capital that he said: 'When a man is tired of London he is tired of life; for there is in London all that life can afford.'*

SPECTACLE *Acrobats at open-air fairs were wildly popular.*

DANCING BEARS *The booths at Smithfield or Bartholomew Fair drew crowds with such attractions as puppet-shows, rope-dancers, tumblers, dancing bears, dogs and monkeys, or 'A little Farey Woman, from Italy, being Two Foot Two Inches high'.*

STREET HAWKERS *Many poor traders sold their wares on the street, from muffins to patent medicine, from 'scissors to grind' to live lobsters. Here a man and woman sell mops.*

VILLAGE DANCING *In the 18th century, the spread of land enclosure was gradually driving country folk, deprived of their livelihood, into the towns to find work. But village life still flourished. Here villagers, including a girl with a doll, watch a couple dancing outside an ale-house.*

'A HOT PUDDING, A PUDDING, A HOT PUDDING' *London streets were filled with the deafening noise of drums and flutes, penny-whistles and street-criers calling their wares. Foreigners were despised: they were abused, cheated and swindled, and even sometimes physically assaulted.*

TOWN DANCING *Under the rule of 'Beau' Nash, Bath became the hub of fashionable life. People went there to drink the waters for their health. They attended balls or drank tea in the Pump Room, carefully observing the unwritten code of conduct and dress. Here dancers try out the elegant steps of the minuet, a dance imported from the court of the French kings in Versailles.*

The Stuarts return– in a revolt bound to fail

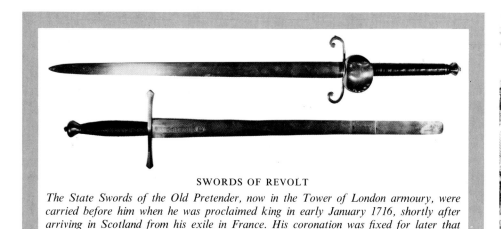

SWORDS OF REVOLT

The State Swords of the Old Pretender, now in the Tower of London armoury, were carried before him when he was proclaimed king in early January 1716, shortly after arriving in Scotland from his exile in France. His coronation was fixed for later that month at the Palace of Scone near Perth, but it never took place.

At Braemar on September 6, 1715, as the Stuart standard was being raised by the Earl of Mar to open his rebellion against the crown, the gilt knob which topped it was dislodged and fell to the ground. It was a disturbing omen for the rebels, hoping to topple Britain's new German king, and to restore Prince James Edward Stuart to the crown of his ancestors.

This Stuart prince – the son of England's last Catholic monarch, James II – was not the sort of man to inspire passionate devotion or win popular support. Like his opponent George I, James was more effective as a symbol than as a person. He had been brought up as an exile in France, and was now in his twenties. He was a colourless, cold character, pessimistic and subject to bouts of ill-health. His strongest personal trait was also his weakest political point, for he clung obstinately to his Catholic faith at a time when it was clear that no Catholic would ever rule England. Much of the blame for his attitude must go to his devout, almost bigoted Catholic mother, Mary of Modena. James was convinced that the justice of his claim was enough to guarantee his success.

The Jacobite dream

In this delusion James was encouraged by a bevy of ill-chosen courtiers, for their ambitions depended on his own. Inside this band of exiles, isolated at the court of the French king, Louis XIV, the hunger for future power spawned intrigue and back-biting. The Jacobites had dreams and ambitions, but no plans.

The death of England's Queen Anne in August 1714 seemed to change all this, and bring a sudden dawn of new possibilities, new personalities, and new initiatives. George I

was not loved in England. His succession was greeted with dismay. The election of January 1715 was marked by a wave of riots. Mobs ran wild in many towns, smashing windows and burning buildings, apparently in sympathy for the Stuarts. The Whig government was in disarray. Fearful of rebellion, it took a harsh repressive line which was more effective in aggravating hostility than in preventing it.

While the Whigs tried to grapple with the confusion, their opponents the Tories saw a chance to exploit it, for many of them believed that their own beliefs and political interests would be better served by a Stuart restoration. Their leader was Henry St John, Viscount Bolingbroke, a man of unrivalled talent among the Tories. His plan was to wait until discontent in England reached fever pitch, and

OLD PRETENDER *James Edward Stuart spent only six weeks on British soil before returning to his long life of exile in France.*

then execute a well-organised coup which would bring the Stuarts back to the throne.

But Bolingbroke was ill-served by his fellow Jacobites. Like James, they wanted action at all costs. Bolingbroke said of James: 'He was a man who expected every moment to set sail for England or Scotland, but who did not very well know for which.'

The Jacobites thought an immediate revolt in Scotland would be enough to spark off an English rising, and sweep James on to the throne in a wave of spontaneous enthusiasm. These muddlers like Ormonde, Middleton and Mar – 'those busy bees that buzz all day about me', as Bolingbroke later contemptuously described them – won the willing ear of James in France. Bolingbroke, alarmed for his own safety, fled to Paris in March 1715. Amid confusion, intrigue and indiscretion, the plans for action went ahead.

The exiles were utterly out of touch with reality in England. To rely on an automatic rising there was sheer folly, for the government was now recovering its sense of purpose and becoming daily more resolute. The English army was loyal and experienced, and the people themselves were calming down.

So blundering and unreliable were James's courtiers, that the English ambassador in France was able to discover the plot and warn his government. Finally, the keystone of the

ROYAL REVOLUTIONARY *A contemporary engraving shows the Old Pretender landing on Scottish soil at Peterhead three days before Christmas 1715. The Scots were not impressed by the sight of the young Stuart prince. One wrote: 'If he was disappointed with us, we were tenfold more so in him.'*

George I: A foreign king who spoke no English

'This is a very odd country' – such was the verdict of George I, Elector of Hanover, on the day after he arrived in England to take up his crown in August 1714.

England may well have seemed odd to a 55-year-old German prince, whose life had been a comfortable round of autocratic rule and keen soldiering in a small German state. But odder still was the way in which he came to be King of England. He was brought to the throne by an Act of Parliament, which had ignored the better claims of more than 50 other candidates to ensure a Protestant succession. A contemporary wrote: 'Fortune that made him king added nothing to his happiness, only prejudiced his honesty and shortened his days.'

And England's judgment on George was no less blunt than his on his new kingdom. The two mistresses he brought with him were nicknamed 'the Elephant' and 'the Maypole', in witness to their contrasting figures. His strange duo of Turkish servants became 'Mustafa and Mehemet'. His advisers, with their 'cacophonous, outlandish German names', were deeply resented.

Throughout his reign, George remained unmistakably a foreigner, happiest when visiting his Hanoverian home. He never mastered his new language, and had to talk to his ministers in French and Latin. Yet he took his royal duties seriously, especially where foreign policy was concerned. Unpopular as a man, he was an effective figurehead and a magnet for national loyalty against the troublesome background of Jacobite rebellion.

Jacobite scheme abruptly collapsed when Louis XIV died in August. With his death hope of French support for an invasion vanished.

Too little and too late

Such was the bleak background against which Mar left France to raise that ominous standard in Scotland on September 6. He had no difficulty in winning the Highlands to the Jacobite cause, for there loyalty to the exiled Stuarts had remained firm. But in every other respect the whole strategy of the rebellion went wildly astray.

Only in the north of England was there any popular response to the call for revolt; and even this was confined to a few half-hearted and badly led men who were easily dealt with by the government. As one rebel wrote: 'That party, who are never right hearty for the Cause till they are mellow over a bottle or two demonstrated that they did not care for venturing their carcases further than the tavern.'

On November 13 came the first real test for Mar's Scottish army – it was a test it did not surmount. At Sheriffmuir, near Perth, Mar's 10,000 men met a much smaller loyalist force commanded by the Duke of Argyll. Though the fighting itself was inconclusive, the result was a Jacobite defeat. For Mar was forced to retreat into the city of Perth, there to remain helpless and inactive while Argyll's army was swollen by reinforcements.

On December 22, James arrived in Scotland, landing at Peterhead in a fishing boat. He was ill with a fever, and cut a depressing figure for a leader. 'For me,' he said to his comrades, 'it is no new thing to be unfortunate, since my whole life from my cradle has been a constant series of misfortunes.'

James was both too late and too gloomy to revive his dispirited followers in Perth. In February 1716, the ruthless General Cadogan took over the command of the English army. The Jacobites lost their nerve and retreated into the Highlands, disfiguring their cause with pointless atrocities, and gradually disintegrating. Their enterprise was doomed. James, Mar and other leaders took ship for France and safety. But their followers were not so fortunate. By April the revolt had been crushed. Two rebel leaders were executed, others lost their estates and titles and some were exiled – all of them victims of the folly of the prince for whom they had risked so much.

FIRST HANOVERIAN *George I suffered from chronic shyness. He hated all ceremony that made him the centre of attention.*

GEORGIAN ELEGANCE CREATES A CITY MADE FOR PLEASURE

From 1702 onwards, the old Roman city of Bath underwent a meteoric rise to become the most fashionable and popular leisure resort in Georgian England. For over 50 years Bath reigned as the unchallenged summer capital of aristocratic society, dictating modes of dress, behaviour and good taste. Men and women of fashion and wit flocked to the town to take its famous waters, to gossip, to match-make, to see – and be seen.

The town, in its turn, put on a new face in keeping with its important new role. Almost completely rebuilt in the 18th century, it became famous for its early town planning, with its beautiful crescents and terraces and its superbly restrained and graceful public buildings. No other 18th-century city can equal its unity of architectural design.

Two factors combined to give Bath its special social appeal. The first was the hot mineral springs which gush out 250,000 gallons of water a day, heated to a constant 49°C. (120°F.). The second was the personality of one man – Richard 'Beau' Nash, a gambler who became Bath's uncrowned 'king'.

Ruled by one man

Born in Swansea of a poor middle-class family, Nash was a failed scholar, soldier and lawyer who excelled in only one area – the organisation of social ceremonies. He first became aide-de-camp to the then Master of Ceremonies, a Captain Webster, and when Webster was killed in a duel over a game of cards, Nash was his natural successor. He began a reign that transformed Bath from a provincial town into a fashionable centre unequalled in England.

Nash began by dressing the part, adopting an exaggerated elegance which soon earned him the nickname Beau. Instead of the popular white wigs of the times, he wore a black one topped with a jewelled cream beaver hat set at a rakish angle. His coat, decorated with braid and lace, was left open to show his embroidered waistcoat and ruffled shirt.

But those who dismissed Beau Nash as a mere fop were soon surprised. Nash showed his practical mind by supervising the paving, lighting and cleaning of the streets, punishing the insolence of sedan chair-carriers and driving beggars and thieves out of the city.

He also encouraged the wealthy men of Bath to put up new buildings, and himself initiated the building of the Pump Room, overlooking the King's Bath, where the company could assemble to gossip, and the Assembly Rooms, with a large, handsome ballroom and adjoining card room.

In both these buildings his word was law. He laid down a rigidly enforced code of be-haviour. He ridiculed the wearing of riding boots at fashionable gatherings, often asking the offender if he had 'forgot his horse'. Even royalty quailed before his frown – Princess Amelia, daughter of George II, was curtly refused one more dance after Nash had decreed the music should stop.

His twice-weekly balls in the Assembly Rooms were imitated throughout the country. The playwright Oliver Goldsmith wrote of them: 'The order, the decorum, the measured pomp, that distinguished the festivities of Bath were the pride and boast of the nation.'

Nash also forbade the wearing of swords. Bath became famous as the 'swordless city', prompting Richard Sheridan to write in *The Rivals*, a play set in the city: 'A sword seen in the streets of Bath would raise as great an alarm as a mad dog.'

The visitors' daily routine was a regimented one, beginning with bathing between 6 a.m. and 9 a.m. and followed by a general assembly in the Pump Room for gossip, three glasses of warm water and music. A public breakfast usually followed before the visitors returned in a sedan chair to their lodgings to change for a service in the abbey.

A late lunch, then another visit to the Pump Room and perhaps a walk filled in the afternoon, while evenings were spent at a ball, the theatre or the gambling table.

Two architects of genius

Under Nash's reign, Bath grew so prosperous that young men flocked there to seek their fortune. Some, like Ralph Allen, a Cornishman, and John Wood, a Yorkshireman, helped to change the face of Bath. Allen devised a way of exploiting the rich stone quarries outside Bath: Wood, and later his son, used the golden stone to cover Bath and its encircling hills in a succession of fine Palladian buildings.

Wood built for Allen his great mansion of Prior Park, a magnificent collonaded building set in terraces and landscaped gardens and made of Bath stone; built partly as an advertisement for the stone which was not then highly regarded.

In 1725 Wood devised a grand plan to develop the city in two parts, each with a central circus for sports, a royal forum for assemblies and an assortment of squares. The scheme was too ambitious for the corporation, and Wood set about building as much as he could privately. In 1727 he moved permanently to Bath, and lived there until his death 27 years later.

Queen Square, which took six years to build, was a perfect example of Wood's concept of a planned layout, with all the houses constructed of the same stone and built in the same proportions. He built a grand palace façade on the north side, with simpler houses on the south. On the slope at the east the houses followed a gently climbing pattern, and on the west were three large separate houses.

Wood then built a series of houses and buildings along what he termed 'parades', where the owners could walk and look out to views of the city or the countryside. He died, however, before he could finish his greatest project, the Circus, and it was left to his son, John Wood the Younger, to complete it. He faithfully followed his father's blue-print, right down to the exact number of magnificent coupled columns on the houses – 324 pairs in all. It was finally completed in 1765.

The young John Wood also contributed a pioneering architectural innovation to Bath – and to Britain. West of the Circus, he built an

CITY OF BEAUTY *An early-19th-century engraving shows Bath's spectacular beauty. The creation of this Georgian city was largely the work of two architects, John Wood the Elder and his son. They gave the city such masterpieces as the Circus, the Assembly Rooms and the Royal Crescent. Among other great 18th-century architects to work in the city was Robert Adam.*

incomparable ring of houses, facing on to a paved centre and overlooking the common. This was the Royal Crescent – the first to be built in the world.

So popular was the style of architecture created by the Woods that soon half a dozen other architects adopted the Palladian style and the use of golden Bath stone. Others such as the fashionable London architect Robert Adam, who designed the charming Pulteney Bridge inspired by Florence's Ponte Vecchio, brought new, complementary styles to the city.

Beau Nash, whose reign in Bath had inspired its new elegant look, died in 1761 at the age of 87 before many of its famous buildings were completed. The city whose life he had ruled for so long did not forget him. He was given a lavish funeral and a handsome memorial in the abbey. Goldsmith wrote: 'The whole kingdom became more refined by lessons originally derived from him.'

Bath continued as a popular resort throughout the rest of the century although its position of dominance was no longer unchallenged. Cheltenham and then Brighton rose to become rival centres. But although the world of fashion passed, it left behind in Bath an enduring monument to a unique age of elegance.

FOCAL POINT *The Pump Room, centre of life in Bath, was built immediately over the Roman reservoir into which gush the curing springs. Here people assembled to drink the waters.*

ITALIAN INFLUENCE *Pulteney Bridge was designed by Robert Adam in 1771, after the style of the Ponte Vecchio in Florence. It carries a broad carriageway with shops on either side, and was named after William Pulteney, an influential statesman, who became Earl of Bath.*

INSPIRED BY ROME *The superb Circus, planned by the elder Wood and completed by his son in 1765, has 30 houses built round a paved open space – inspired by the Colosseum in Rome.*

PALLADIAN MASTERPIECE *The Royal Crescent, often called the 'finest crescent in Europe', was built by John Wood the Younger between 1767 and 1775. The design was deeply influenced by the Classical style of imperial Rome and ancient Greece. It represented the summit of architectural achievement in Bath's hey-day as the fashionable haunt of the rich and powerful in the 18th century.*

MEETING PLACE *The Assembly Rooms, opened in 1771, were designed by John Wood the Younger. Here society met to breakfast, make new acquaintances and hear music or lectures. It was also the scene of magnificent balls.*

An English squire becomes the first Prime Minister

WALPOLE'S BIRTHPLACE
Sir Robert Walpole, a country squire and reckless spender, was born at Houghton Hall, Norfolk, which had been in his family for generations. At his death, he left debts of almost £40,000. But he saw little evidence of wealth during a childhood plagued by ill-health. His father only gave him 2s 6d pocket money a year.

Sir Robert Walpole, for 21 years the leader of England's government, was a politician of such overwhelming stature that he has become famous as 'the first Prime Minister'. The title itself was unknown in Walpole's lifetime, but this brilliant man forged the reality of the office from the turbulent stream of parliamentary politics. The title is a tribute to qualities of statesmanship and character that have rarely been equalled in England's history.

Throughout his life, Walpole was driven on by an inexhaustible personal dynamism, a thrusting urge for individual power. Yet for all his immense ambition and his exceptional talents and energy, he never lost touch with the feelings of the common people. Physically he was large and ungainly, given to enormous meals and long bouts of drinking. Many of his bills still survive and they show that in one year alone he spent at least £1500 on wines, equivalent to nearly £15,000 today. He also had a weakness for chocolates, which he bought by the hundredweight. He paid more for them than he did for his three footmen in a year. His other pleasures were equally gross: he was lecherous, coarse, fond of vulgar display, bewitched by money and extravagant possessions, inordinately proud of himself. In an age of fixed rank and hierarchy, he was a self-made man, and he basked in his success.

At his home, Houghton Hall in Norfolk, Walpole boasted that 'he always talked bawdy, because in that all men could join'. It was said that throughout his life he looked first at his bailiff's reports on hunting and local news from his Norfolk estate, before turning to his official correspondence.

But mentally, Walpole was the reverse of crude. He had a powerful, incisive intellect, and an enormous capacity for hard work. An acute judge of character, he had a deep power of insight into other people's minds and emotions. This served him well – especially in his valuable friendship with George II's wife, Queen Caroline.

'All those men have their price'
In the 18th century, political conditions encouraged the lowest standards of behaviour: a man might make both career and fortune if he were only unprincipled enough. And Walpole knew precisely how to exploit this lust for easy power and money. He himself remarked of his followers, 'All those men have their price'. And, when his skill as a parliamentarian was not enough to win all the support he needed, he did not hesitate to bribe – though rarely with straight cash.

Walpole himself was not immune to the temptations of money. In 1720 he had succumbed, with thousands of others, to the speculative craze of the notorious South Sea Bubble. He made 1000 per cent profit on his investment. And because he was less compromised by the scandal than many in the government, Walpole managed to wriggle clear when the bubble burst, with his public prestige intact. And this dubious episode proved the turning-point in his career. For Walpole was one of the few men free enough – or so the public believed – from the taint of corruption to take on, at the age of 45, the vacant government posts of Chancellor of the Exchequer and First Lord of the Treasury. From these two offices, Walpole was to create a Prime Minister's supremacy.

Until 1742, Walpole remained a giant on the political stage, effortlessly out-topping all rivals. His luck in 1721 was to find an England which had been raised, by his predecessors over the past two decades, to a new height of security and prestige in Europe. On this solid foundation, Walpole was able to construct his own policies of peace and prosperity. By upbringing a country squire, he treated England much like his own estate – fostering her wealth, avoiding the disruption and expense of war. His proud boast to Queen Caroline in 1734, a year of European turmoil, was, 'Madam, there are 50,000 men slain this year in Europe, and not one Englishman'.

'This dance it will no further go'
But so ruthless and arrogant was Walpole behind his bluff façade, and so shameless was his love of power and wealth that he soon became the most hated man in England. A mixed opposition of Tories and rebel Whigs had sought his scalp for years without success. Then, suddenly, in 1733, Walpole gave a hostage to fortune.

At this time, governments raised most of their revenue by taxing land. As a landowner himself, Walpole had long hoped to relieve his fellow squires of this burden. Instead he planned to rely on raising the taxes on the goods which everyone bought. And, because the existing customs duties at the ports yielded such a poor return – a third of them were evaded by massive smuggling – 'inland duties' seemed the answer.

Walpole's Excise Scheme of 1733 was designed to bring this strategy to fruition. By putting two major imports, tobacco and wine, straight into 'Bonded' warehouses, freeing them from customs, but subjecting them to a stiff excise if taken out for home consumption, Walpole could raise enough money to justify abolishing direct taxation outright.

On March 14, 1733, Walpole fired the first shot in what he was confident would be a triumphant battle. For years the government's majority had been cast-iron. The arguments for the Tobacco Bill seemed unanswerable.

But the Opposition was not interested in argument – only in emotion, prejudice and political advantage. For months, their pamphleteers and cartoonists, and their brilliant journal, *The Craftsman*, had carried on a publicity campaign of genius. The rumour had been fostered that Walpole was bent on taxing every necessity of life.

The Opposition's bogy-man was the excise

officer. To prevent evasion, local excise officers needed the power of search to ensure that no dutiable goods had slipped through the net. It proved easier than Walpole had imagined to convince his countrymen that this fore-shadowed a terrifying abuse of government authority. No man's house or goods would be safe. Trade would die. A vast bureaucracy would overturn the constitution.

Fired by this scurrilous but persuasive campaign, the people reacted with fear and fury. As Parliament debated the scheme, it was showered with petitions and protests – especially from London and other ports. Vicious cartoons were on display everywhere. The streets of London were decorated with posters, depicting such popular themes as the 'Vampire Excise' sucking greedily at the people's blood.

The mob ruled the streets, and even Walpole himself was manhandled. But though he was contemptuous of the clamour, his majorities gradually dwindled. At the end of four weeks,

he was left with the choice of abandoning the plan or losing power. Calling his supporters together, he told them, 'with a sort of un-pleased smile', that 'This dance it will no further go'. Walpole had acknowledged defeat.

Walpole's retreat, however, was planned and masterly. Though he had to shelve his cherished scheme and had the humiliation of seeing himself burnt in effigy, he recovered his majority and remained in office.

War – the final blow
But, in 1739, popular fervour forced Walpole to declare war on Spain. For Walpole, war spelt personal defeat: it was the collapse of all he had striven for. As he observed bitterly to the Duke of Newcastle, who led the anti-Spanish party in the cabinet, 'It is your war, and I wish you well of it'.

Walpole was no wartime leader, and in February 1742 he resigned. His era had passed; but it had been unmistakably his own.

BRITAIN'S COLOSSUS *A satirical engraving of the time quoted from Shakespeare's* Julius Caesar *to describe Sir Robert Walpole: 'Why man, he doth bestride the narrow world like a Colossus; and we petty men walk under his huge legs and peep about to find ourselves dishonourable graves.'*

George II: A king who knew his proper place

DOMINATED KING *When George II came to the throne he was expected to dismiss Walpole. His forceful wife, Queen Caroline, changed his mind.*

As far as most Englishmen were concerned, George II was not much of an improve-ment on his father. He, too, was born in Hanover, often absent there, and by no means fluent in English. Ribald placards posted on his palace of St James's testified to popular opinion: 'Lost or strayed out of this house, a man who left a wife and six children on the parish: whoever will give tidings of him shall receive four shillings and sixpence.'

A dapper little man, with a red face and bulging eyes, he had a Germanic passion for method. Business or pleasure – all had to con-form to a strict routine, and he was often to be found outside his mistress's room, watch in hand, waiting for the hour of nine to strike.

Yet George did have some qualities which set him well above his father. George I had thought three hours a good day's work, but George II was a hard worker, with a pheno-menal memory, an eye for detail and an insight into European affairs. Most of all, he had in Queen Caroline a wife of lively intelli-gence and forceful character, who remained the power behind the throne until her death. According to Walpole, the king was 'for all his personal bravery as great a political coward as ever wore a crown and as much afraid to lose it'.

While Walpole and Caroline ruled, George himself took a back seat in government. Later, when forced to be more independent, George showed himself to be a man of quick temper and foul tongue. William Pitt the Elder in particular often aroused his anger. George never forgave him for his description of Hanover as 'that despicable Electorate'. The king hated to be ruled by the decisions of 'that d—d House of Commons'. But, quarrelsome and obstinate though he seemed, George played by the rules of the day. His saving virtue was that – as when he called the hated Pitt to high office – he knew 'when to sacrifice his private inclination to public interest'.

A COCKNEY REVEALS THE HEART OF GEORGIAN LONDON

In the mid-18th century London was a sprawling metropolis: crowded, disorderly, vigorous and often violent. Its vitality and wealth attracted talented men from all over the country. Its 600,000 people lived in extremes of sordid poverty and fabulous wealth.

This was the London in which William Hogarth was born and lived. Its glories and its miseries inspired him to paint – as no other artist had ever done before – a complete picture of his age. Sometimes satirical, sometimes tender, his incisive mind swept aside the polished veneer of Georgian life to express the full-bloodedness of the times and the passion and turbulence which lay underneath.

Born in Smithfield Market in 1697, Hogarth rarely left the city he so brilliantly portrayed. His training came not from study abroad but from his apprenticeship to a silver engraver at the age of 15. By the time he was 20 he owned his own business. At 24 he had won full recognition. This success came from satirical engravings he made for sale at a shilling a copy.

Hogarth's wit was also appreciated by fashionable society, but it saw him more as a caricaturist than an artist. Hogarth, though, was determined to be taken seriously. He enrolled at an art school to learn oil painting. But this came to an abrupt end when he eloped with Jane, the beautiful 20-year-old daughter of his teacher, Sir James Thornhill.

With a wife to support, Hogarth turned to painting small 'conversation pieces' – informal family groups, which were then the vogue. He also found inspiration in the theatrical productions of his day. A scene from *The Beggar's Opera*, a lively work about pimps,

SELF PORTRAIT *Hogarth painted himself surrounded by cultural works by Shakespeare, Swift and Milton – and his pet dog, Pug.*

SOCIAL DRAMA *Hogarth won popularity and fame with his moral dramas – the series of paintings which exposed the follies of his time. In 'Marriage à la Mode', a dissolute noble and a rich girl contract a loveless marriage. It ends with her suicide (above) after the death of her husband and lover.*

prostitutes and thieves which had enraptured London, and his portrait of one of the great actors of the day – 'David Garrick as Richard III' – won him great success.

This interest in the theatre inspired him with an idea which was to give rise to some of his most brilliant works. He decided to present London life in dramatic terms, using his art to make 'scenes' and tell stories.

Hogarth had hit upon an art form which would take full advantage of his curiously varied qualities – his simple moral sense, his affectionate but deeply sceptical attitude to his fellow Londoners, and his ribald wit. In addition, his artistic skill was now at its peak and his four great 'morality plays', each in six or eight scenes, reveal his complete mastery of colour and form and his fantastic powers of invention. Each little detail of these crowded pictures contributes to the whole – and helps in the telling of their sad and sardonic stories.

The first, 'A Harlot's Progress', warned of the perils that could befall a young girl coming to London, her corruption by society and her eventual downfall. In 'A Rake's Progress' Hogarth turned to the themes of extravagance and dissipation. 'Marriage à la Mode,' probably his greatest achievement, attacked the evils of an arranged marriage, while 'Election', based on an actual election in Oxfordshire in 1754, vividly portrayed the debased state of English political life.

An artistic tradition

Pugnacious and combative by nature, Hogarth always felt that he had been denied his due honour as a serious artist. Ironically, this sense of injury probably helped to intensify his gifts as a satirist.

In 1754 he painted a self-portrait in which he included the works of Shakespeare, Swift and Milton – a demonstration of his literary tastes and his claim to rank with the great. But, characteristically, he showed he was not quite serious by including a handsome portrait of his dog, Pug.

Critical of London though he may have been, Hogarth was an intensely loyal man. His critical sense stemmed from a genuine desire to reform the city he loved, and he spent endless time and money managing various charities, particularly orphanages and hospitals.

His patriotism also expressed itself in his wish to establish English art and English artists in a world which assumed that only foreigners could paint. His own work, so firmly founded in the everyday reality of English life, proved once and for all that the English scene can be the stuff of artistic genius.

In this aggressive self-confidence, he laid the foundations for a national school of British art. In the next generation the great work was carried forward by Sir Joshua Reynolds, with the foundation of the Royal Academy, and by the triumphant and wholly English genius of George Stubbs and Thomas Gainsborough.

PAINTING FOR PLEASURE *The glowing oil painting 'The Shrimp Girl' was in Hogarth's studio when he died. Painted for his own pleasure, it reveals his humanity. After his death in 1764, his wife showed the picture to visitors with the comment: 'There's flesh and blood for you.'*

SATIRICAL ART *Hogarth's 'Chairing the Member' lampooned the election system. His fortune was based on the sale of the engravings he made of his pictures. An engraving cost a shilling a copy.*

So near but yet so far – the tragedy of the '45

GATHERING OF THE CLANS

Some 700 Cameron clansmen, the nucleus of an army which was to sweep to within 130 miles of London, rallied to Bonnie Prince Charlie's standard on August 19, 1745. A monument on the banks of Loch Shiel, in Glenfinnan, commemorates their gathering.

HIGHLANDERS' DEFEAT *Nine months after he landed in Scotland to claim the throne of Britain, Bonnie Prince Charlie, seen above in a detail from a contemporary portrait, was decisively defeated by a Hanoverian army on Culloden Moor on April 16, 1746. It was a one-sided battle. The Highlanders were out-numbered two to one, and an early artillery barrage decimated their ranks. Then the High-land charge, previously the terror of English troops, was broken by specially developed new tactics. A vivid impression (detail below) was painted shortly after the battle by David Morier.*

Charles Edward Louis Philip Casimir Stuart, 25-year-old son and heir of the Old Pretender, crossed the River Esk into England on November 8, 1745. Largely on his own eager initiative, he had embarked on a venture which was viewed with grave misgivings by some of his advisers, and with uneasiness by the army of 5000 Highlanders who were accompanying him so far from their native glens.

Yet the prince's confidence was understandable. The fiasco of his father's failure lay 30 years behind, and 'Bonnie Prince Charlie' was a figure of a quite different stamp from the moody and uninspiring James. He was a leader in reality as well as name, a brave fighter and a tireless soldier.

In the months that had already passed since his landing in the Hebrides on July 25, the prince had achieved wonders that augured well for the success of his expedition. He had arrived with only a handful of companions, with little money and few arms. But the clansmen flocked to Charles's standard, raised in Glenfinnan on August 19, 1745.

Marching south towards England
In this month, Charles's men marched southwards to Perth and Edinburgh, where Charles was proclaimed king. The English were not idle, however. Under General 'Johnny' Cope, a force of some 3000 men was massing east of Edinburgh to deal with Charles and his followers. But when the two armies clashed at Prestonpans on September 21, the Highlanders' charge was more than the English could face. 'The panic terror of the English surpassed all imagination,' wrote a participant. 'They threw down their arms that they might run with more speed.'

It was in this moment of national danger, that the actors at the Drury Lane Theatre, in London, added a new song to their programme on September 28. It was 'God Save the King'. For, when Charles crossed the border, only a hastily assembled force under General Wade obstructed his path south. Easily skirting round Wade and his men, Charles took the road to London.

At first all went well. There was surprisingly little panic as the Jacobites advanced. One observer described them as 'those shabby, scabby, scratchy, lowly, shitten rebels'. Many, however, of the well-to-do went to earth with their silver as news came in that Preston had been taken on November 27, Manchester on November 29, and Derby on December 4.

From Derby to London was a mere 130 miles, and the capital was briefly seized by intense terror on the 'black Friday' after Derby's fall. George II himself had the royal yacht made ready to take him to the Continent. But the prince's success was more apparent than real. Neither the expected French invasion, nor spontaneous Jacobite risings in England had taken place – no more than 300 Englishmen had enlisted with Charles. Wade's army was now a formidable force in Charles's rear; the ruthless Duke of Cumberland, recalled from Flanders, was in Staffordshire with 8000 men.

Retreat and disaster
Each step south now took the rebels further from their base, further from any reinforcements. To go beyond Derby was to invite destruction. Even as Londoners panicked, a Jacobite council of war recommended retreat, and Charles, in anguish, had to agree. On December 20 his army recrossed the border with Cumberland's troops in hot pursuit.

Back in the Highlands, the prince restored his numbers and his side's morale with local victories over government garrisons. But this was no permanent answer. The Jacobites were weary, demoralised, unpaid and facing an army almost twice their size.

On April 16, Charles decided to attack Cumberland's men on Culloden Moor. The plan was daring but ill-advised, for Cumberland had devised a new tactic to cope with the Highland charge. Instead of attacking the Scotsman in front of him, each Redcoat soldier bayoneted the exposed side of the Scotsman to the right. The English lost only 76 men to the 1200 of the Highlanders.

The clans never recovered from this bloody battle. Within 20 years the old clan system was dead, and Jacobitism had evaporated into a mere romantic dream.

Royal fugitive – with a price on his head

After the terrible day of slaughter at Culloden in April 1746, Prince Charles Edward fled westwards with a small band of followers. For the next five months he was to roam through the Highlands and islands. By horse, by boat, but chiefly on foot, he passed from one helping hand to another, with a price of £30,000 on his head.

First came ten dismal weeks in the Hebrides, flitting from island to island and back again, a naval patrol at his heels. There were nights spent at sea, others in the open fields. Exposure and privation made him 'ill-coloured, and overrun with the scab'.

By July, Charles was back on the mainland. In the next two months his desperate search for safety took him north as far as Glen Affric, south to Ben Alder. His cheerless shelters – byres, caves, woods, mountaintops – pepper the Highlands. He must have walked hundreds of miles, but he bore his trials gallantly, whistling the Highland airs which, like his Gaelic phrases and his whisky bottle, endeared him to the clans.

These remained superlatively loyal, scorning the huge reward and risking life itself to preserve their beloved leader. At last, on September 19, Charles boarded a French ship to sail to safety. The 14 months of his great adventure were over. He lived for another 42 years, but slowly degenerated into a rambling drunkard. As he himself said: 'I should have died with my men at Culloden.'

ROMANTIC PRINCE
Bonnie Prince Charlie had the natural stamp of a romantic hero. He possessed not only good looks, but a personal charm and magnetism which his father had completely lacked. He was athletic, a golfer and an expert with the crossbow. He played the violin well and loved dancing. The Battle of Culloden Moor was a crushing military defeat, but it failed to destroy the legend of the dashing prince who had come so close to winning the throne for the Stuarts.

The romance was strengthened by the reign of terror conducted by the 'Butcher' Duke of Cumberland against the clans after the battle, and by the daring adventure of the prince's five months as a fugitive from the Hanoverian forces. This 'secret portrait' of him, a smudge which only takes shape when reflected on a curved cylinder, is an example of how his legend was kept alive through his years of exile from his 'lost kingdom'.

THE FRIENDSHIP WHICH GAVE DR JOHNSON IMMORTAL FAME

MAN OF LETTERS *Samuel Johnson, clumsy and uncouth, but one of the great minds of his age, was already a legend when he met Boswell.*

On Monday, May 16, 1763, one of the most momentous meetings in the history of English literature took place in a Covent Garden bookseller's back-parlour. James Boswell, an aspiring young author, was drinking tea with the bookseller, Tom Davies, and his wife, when Davies suddenly caught sight of Samuel Johnson through the glass door.

He 'announced his awful approach to me', wrote Boswell of the meeting, 'somewhat in the manner of an actor in the part of Horatio, when he addresses Hamlet on the appearance of the ghost'.

Johnson was 53, and already a legend. Author of the famous *Dictionary*, he was celebrated for his caustic wit and eccentric personal appearance. Boswell, a diminutive Scotsman, was only 22, brash and ambitious, and determined while in London to cultivate the English literary scene.

Boswell's opening gambit was inauspicious:

'Mr Davies mentioned my name ... I was much agitated; and recollecting his prejudice against the Scotch ... I said to Davies, "Don't tell him where I come from" – "From Scotland," cried Davies roguishly. "Mr Johnson," (said I) "I do indeed come from Scotland, but I cannot help it." I am willing to flatter myself that I meant this as a light pleasantry. But however that might be, this speech was somewhat unlucky; for with that quickness of wit for which he was so remarkable, he retorted, "That Sir, I find, is what a very great many of your countrymen cannot help." This stroke stunned me a good deal ...'

When Johnson followed this snub with a second scathing remark, Boswell felt 'much mortified', but he 'remained upon the field ... not wholly discomfited'.

It was difficult to deter Boswell and after this first meeting he soon summed up courage to call on Johnson in his 'uncouth' London rooms behind Fleet Street.

This time he was given an extremely amiable reception. 'Give me your hand,' Johnson requested as he bade the young man goodbye, 'I have a liking to you.'

No less likely friendship has existed in the history of English literature. Samuel Johnson came from the provincial middle-classes. His father, Michael, was a struggling bookseller in Lichfield, Staffordshire, who married late, and their first child, Samuel, at birth was a sickly, weak child. His wife was to describe him later as 'lean and lanky ... with the scars of the scrofula deeply visible', and suffering from 'convulsive starts and gesticulations'.

Hampered by illness and lack of money, he was forced to leave Pembroke College, Oxford, after four terms to earn his living. In 1735 he married Elizabeth Porter, a widow 20 years older than himself, who brought him a small dowry, and he subsisted, until the publication of his great *Dictionary* in 1755, by teaching and journalism. He claimed that 'no man but a blockhead ever wrote, except for money'.

The *Dictionary* brought Johnson fame, and the final satisfaction of an honorary degree at Oxford. In 1762 he was awarded a royal pension of £300.

The Scot and the doctor

James Boswell, on the other hand, came from a long line of Lowland gentry. He was son and heir to Lord Auchinleck, a stern and unsympathetic Scottish law-lord, who thought his eldest son feckless, foolish and extravagant.

Boswell was indeed much given to dissipation and debauchery. He was a volatile character, whose moods quickly swung from riotous gaiety to black gloom.

In Johnson he found the second father, guide, protector and spiritual counsellor he had been seeking since childhood. He also found the subject which was to give purpose to his life. The book, the *Life of Samuel Johnson*, with which he crowned their friendship, has been acknowledged as one of the finest biographies in the English language.

Johnson was deeply affectionate and loyal to his friends. 'A man, Sir, should keep his friendship in constant repair,' he wrote, and he loved his fellow human beings, though he frequently derided and often abused them. He was an endless, indefatigable talker, often staying up until the small hours of the morning. 'There is in the world,' he declared, 'no

---

JOHNSON'S MEMORIAL

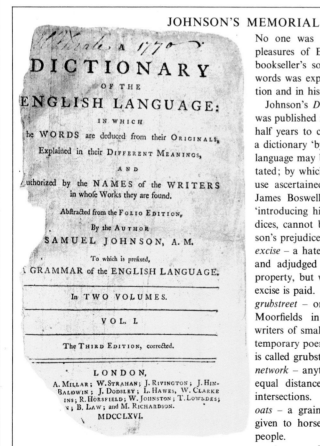

GREATEST ACHIEVEMENT *Title page of Johnson's* Dictionary. *The work took nearly nine years to compile. It revealed many of his prejudices, but brought him fame and a modest fortune.*

No one was ever more intoxicated with the pleasures of English than Samuel Johnson, a bookseller's son from Lichfield. His delight in words was expressed in a life-time of conversation and in his great *Dictionary*.

Johnson's *Dictionary of the English Language* was published in 1755, and took him eight and a half years to compile. His aim was to produce a dictionary 'by which the pronunciation of our language may be fixed, and its attainment facilitated; by which its purity may be preserved, its use ascertained, and its duration lengthened'. James Boswell wrote that Johnson's habit of 'introducing his own opinions, and even prejudices, cannot be fully defended'. Among Johnson's prejudices were:

excise – a hateful tax levied upon commodities, and adjudged not by the common judges of property, but wretches hired by those to whom excise is paid.

grubstreet – originally the name of a street in Moorfields in London; much inhabited by writers of small histories, dictionaries, and contemporary poems: whence any mean production is called grubstreet.

network – anything reticulated or decussated at equal distances, with interstices between the intersections.

oats – a grain, which in England is generally given to horses, but in Scotland supports the people.

pension – an allowance made to anyone without an equivalent – in England generally understood to mean pay given to a state hireling for treason to his country.

BIOGRAPHER *James Boswell produced the great* Life of Samuel Johnson, *but died four years later, haunted by a sense of personal failure.*

real delight (excepting those of sensuality), but the exchange of ideas in conversation.'

During the 21 years of their friendship, these conversations were meticulously recorded by Boswell in the frank journals which he used later as the source books of his great biography.

In 1773 Boswell persuaded Johnson to accompany him on a walking tour of the Hebrides, despite the fact that Johnson loved London and detested Scotland, which he saw as '... a most dolorous country'.

His worst fears were realised: there was dried haddock for breakfast, the windows would not open, and the country 'grew more stoney, and continued naked of all vegetable decoration ... an eye accustomed to flowery pastures and waving harvests is astonished and repelled by this wide extent of hopeless sterility'.

Through storm and discomfort Johnson was mainly philosophical, but he became moody when he lost his large oak walking-stick: 'It is not to be expected that any man in Mull, who has got it, will part with it. Consider, Sir, the value of such a *piece of timber* here !'

The victim of asthma and dropsy, Johnson's last illness was long and painful, but he refused to take opiates because he had prayed he might render his soul to God unclouded. He died in 1784 and was buried in Westminster Abbey.

Memorial of a friendship
Boswell never recovered from his friend's death. His drinking and debauchery became increasingly uncontrollable. However, by an extraordinary act of self-will, he forced himself to complete his *Life of Samuel Johnson,* which came out in 1791, and was immediately acclaimed a masterpiece.

Johnson had put the best part of his genius into his conversation. Boswell's great book rescued these brilliant conversations for posterity and provided the world with a record of a strange and fruitful friendship.

LONDON RISES TO HONOUR THE 'HALLELUJAH CHORUS'

In the 18th century, London's artistic life achieved a sophistication it had not reached before. Painters like William Hogarth and writers such as Dr Samuel Johnson and the satirist Dean Swift were the leaders of a brilliant society. And to their number was added one of the greatest composers of the day – George Frederick Handel.

Handel was born in 1685 in the town of Halle in Saxony, where his father was the local barber and surgeon. Handel did not come from a musical family. His father intended him to become a lawyer, and the infant composer used to practise secretly on a clavichord in the attic while his parents slept. But he eventually won the right to follow a musical career.

From opera to oratorio
Handel settled in London in 1712, but two years after his arrival, the accession of George of Hanover to the English throne placed Handel in an awkward predicament. He had neglected his duties as court composer at Hanover, and the king was displeased. But he won his way back to favour by composing a suite of instrumental pieces, 'The Water Music', to accompany the royal family's progress by barge down the Thames from Whitehall to Limehouse. George was delighted; he welcomed Handel at the new court, and increased his royal pension by £200 a year. In England, Handel's early reputation was largely based on the Italian-style operas he wrote for the London stage. For a while this form of opera was all the rage, and the composer made a fortune. But even at the height of his operatic success, he was not without rivals – the chief of whom was the Italian Bononcini. The poet John Byrom wrote an epigram which was typical of the reaction of the time:

> *Some say, compared to Bononcini*
> *That Mynheer Handel's but a ninny*
> *Others aver, that he to Handel*
> *Is scarcely fit to hold a candle.*
> *Strange all this difference should be*
> *'Twixt Tweedle-dum and Tweedle-dee!*

In the end, it was a change in fashion rather than anything else which ended Handel's operatic enterprise. And though its collapse brought him ill-health and financial difficulties, it led him to devote his talents to a new field, the composing of the great religious works which were to win him immortality.

The series of biblical oratorios, from 'Esther' (1732) to 'Saul' (1739) and 'Israel in Egypt' (1739), culminated in his magnificent 'Messiah' which he composed in the amazingly short time of 23 days. At the first London performance in 1743, the king himself set the precedent of rising to his feet for the 'Hallelujah Chorus'.

On April 6, 1759, Handel attended a triumphal performance of 'Messiah' at Covent Garden. As the oratorio ended, he collapsed. Eight days later he died.

He had earned an honoured place in the nation he had made his own and had himself said, of the future George III, 'While that boy lives, my music will never want for a protector'. It has not wanted for a British protector since. And audiences listening to 'Messiah' today must often echo Handel's own feelings as he wrote it: 'I did think I did see all heaven before me, and the great God himself.'

HALLELUJAH! *Handel (above) directed performances of his most famous oratorio, 'Messiah', from this organ keyboard.*

Victory at Quebec wins Britain a new empire

A HERO'S RELIC
James Wolfe died from three bullet wounds as his men went on to capture Quebec. His body was brought home wrapped in his dressing-gown, now at Quebec House, Westerham, Kent.

In the middle of the 18th century, England and France were locked in a struggle that brought bloodshed and heroism to four continents. The prize at stake was not glory or prestige, nor even colonial conquest for its own sake: it was trade.

Scattered across the face of the globe were lands rich in the resources eagerly demanded by an economically expanding Europe – cotton and tea in India, slaves in Africa, sugar, tobacco and coffee in the Caribbean, fish and furs in North America. Few men were more aware of the value of trade than the British war minister, William Pitt. He was willing to subordinate all foreign policy to its demands. And few places were more crucial in Pitt's eyes than Canada – for Canada seemed the key to the commercial exploitation of the entire North American continent.

French and English interests had competed in Canada since the first settlers arrived in the 16th century. But England had carelessly thrown away her early military success there – much to the disgust of her American colonists. So, when in 1757 Pitt took over the conduct of the latest round of hostilities, the Seven Years'

War, he was determined not to let the prize slip from England's grasp again.

Whether Pitt could achieve his ambition hinged in the end on the fortunes of a remarkable expedition which crept, with infinite care, up the St Lawrence River in June 1759. Its target was the town of Quebec, 700 miles from the Atlantic Ocean, and the strategic gateway to a successful attack on Canada.

Quebec was a natural fortress which had defied a major English attack in Queen Anne's time. Many – including the French themselves – believed it to be impregnable.

The expedition's commanders were men of Pitt's own choice – young talents new to high command, and ready to rise to their leader's confidence. In charge of the 35 warships and 119 troop transports was Sir Charles Saunders, a brilliant sailor still in his mid-forties, who had once sailed round the world with the explorer Commodore Anson. The 8600 troops aboard Saunders' ships were the responsibility of an even younger leader, James Wolfe.

The great commander
Wolfe was a man born for a hero's life. In an age when advancement was so often won not by merit but by money, Wolfe had risen by his talents alone. He had been an officer at the age of 16, a captain at 17, lieutenant-colonel at 23, and now, at 32, he was a major-general. This dizzy climb to fame had brought him the enmity of less-favoured colleagues; but his own soldiers idolised him. Like many great commanders, Wolfe spared no pains to ensure the comfort of the ordinary fighting man, sharing his hardships and dangers. Although he was a man of frail constitution and gangling physique, he was full of reckless courage, tremendously energetic, agile and brimming with ideas. His temper was explosive, his aspirations boundless, his standards exacting. 'He looked upon danger,' said Horace Walpole, 'as the favourable moment that would call forth all his talents.'

Wolfe's whole attitude to soldiering was summed up in his memorable retort to a military engineer who boasted that he was 'slow and sure': 'Quick and sure, Sir – a much better maxim.' And yet this dashing soldier was also the man who admitted, on the eve of his last battle, that he would rather have penned Gray's famous *Elegy* than win a victor's crown in war.

Assisting the two leaders of the Quebec expedition was a notable array of other talents, including the young James Cook, soon to become England's most successful explorer. Cook had the task of reconnoitring the shoals

FALL OF QUEBEC *Under cover of darkness, Wolfe's troops sailed down the St Lawrence to storm the Heights of Abraham from a track up the hill-side. Within minutes the town (in the background) had fallen to Britain's Redcoats, and France's hold on Canada was broken.*

and shallows of the great river, right under the eyes of the French. The work took many months, but thanks to Cook's charts, the armada reached its destination unscathed – in itself an amazing feat of nerves and planning.

But this success was not matched elsewhere in Canada, where British armies were battling vainly against French forts and Indian war-bands. Wolfe's expedition lacked the support it had relied on. The first assault on Quebec in July 1759 was a disastrous failure. Precious lives were lost; Wolfe himself fell sick with a fever; the great French general Montcalm was able to muster reinforcements and hasten to the defence of the city. On September 2, Wolfe, outnumbered and frustrated, wrote his despairing last dispatch to Pitt. He felt that his health was ruined, his expedition a failure, his career at a shameful end.

The crucial discovery
Suddenly the English had a stroke of luck which was to change their fortunes overnight. A scouting party, combing the riverbanks for a route into the citadel, made the crucial discovery: a small track led up to the Heights of Abraham overlooking the town. It was a track so sheer and narrow that the French had barely given its defence a thought. This was a vital weakness, and Wolfe used it brilliantly.

GENERAL'S DEATH *Mortally wounded as he led the attack on Quebec, James Wolfe learnt as he lay dying that victory was certain. On hearing the news he smiled and said: 'God be praised, now I can die in peace.' An eye-witness wrote: 'The smile never left his face until he died.'*

William Pitt: A genius plagued by ill-health

William Pitt, known to his contemporaries as 'the Great Commoner', was a man of deep and fertile contrasts. A grandson of a self-made magnate, 'Diamond Pitt', he was born outside the Whig aristocracy that ruled England in the 18th century. His personality was flamboyant, yet flawed by a manic instability which sometimes goes with genius.

Pitt was lonely and egotistical, and haunted by physical and mental ill-health, but he brought to politics an efficiency and honesty that set new standards in a lax and corrupt age. He was an inspired orator and England's first popular politician. He found firm support from the hard-headed businessmen whose pockets his fervent imperialism promised to line. Destructive in Opposition, he later led his country from crisis to victory.

Though Pitt entered the Commons in 1735, his rebel temperament deprived him of the highest office for 20 years. When at last he came to power, his recipe for national greatness was simple. Power came from wealth, and wealth from trade. France was England's great rival, to be driven from her trading posts abroad and swept from the seas.

In four years as war leader, Pitt smashed France's naval power and hit unerringly at her bases in India and the Americas. Horace Walpole said: 'We are forced to ask every morning what victory there has been for fear of missing one.' But in 1762 a new king, George III, decided to make peace. Pitt resigned in bitterness, his self-imposed task of saving the nation incomplete. And though he was later to recapture power, he was never again to achieve the greatness that had led his country to victory in the Seven Years' War.

ECCENTRIC GENIUS *William Pitt led Britain to victory in the Seven Years' War. But his later career was marred by outbreaks of physical ill-health, deep depression and insanity.*

Towards 2 a.m. on the morning of September 13, Wolfe's flagship, the *Sutherland*, raised the signal for the assault to begin. His 4000 troops had spent the night waiting in readiness on board the other ships; now the squadron floated noiselessly downstream with the tide, protected by a moonless sky. Challenged by a French sentry, the identity of the English force was disguised by a Highland officer who responded in fluent French.

The surprise was complete. The English swarmed up the path, and re-formed above in perfect order. When the French at last launched their counter-attack, they advanced carelessly, losing formation. Wolfe met them at the head of his men, reckless as ever.

Within minutes he had fallen, mortally wounded. An officer sought to encourage him, crying 'They run, see how they run!' 'Who runs?' demanded Wolfe, and was told: 'The enemy, Sir; Egad, they give way everywhere.' As he lay dying with victory assured, Wolfe issued a final order to cut off the French retreat. 'God be praised,' were his last words, 'now I can die in peace.'

It was a hero's death indeed, and a hero's burial at Greenwich followed. Wolfe had risen nobly to the challenge of leadership on the Heights of Abraham. His men went on to capture Quebec, and in 1760 all Canada fell to the English. Though Wolfe did not live to see it, his was the bravery that won an empire.

239

A NEW ART TRANSFORMS THE ENGLISH LANDSCAPE

The landed aristocracy of Georgian Britain regarded themselves as the most cultivated and educated class in the island's history. They were also perhaps the richest and most leisured. Many of them devoted their resources of time, money and educated taste to a single objective: the building of superb country houses which were to be the envy of their neighbours and the wonder of posterity.

They were not the first generation of British aristocrats to be preoccupied with the building of beautiful houses. But their aspirations went much further than even the most ambitious building schemes of their Stuart or Tudor ancestors. For the 18th-century landowner felt impelled to create not just another enormous mansion in the latest style, but a whole new landscape in which to enclose it. To fulfil the needs of these rich patrons a new kind of designer was born – the landscape gardener.

These gardeners and their patrons knew that they would seldom live to see the fulfilment of their dreams; their avenues of chestnuts and hilltop clumps of beeches took as much as a century to reach maturity. But the men of the 18th century were supremely confident that posterity would approve of all their works. Such confidence was justified; their mature gardens have won a place among Europe's supreme works of art – and no later generation has possessed the resources of patience or taste to rival their achievements.

Transforming the landscape

Of all the 18th century's many men of taste, few were more wealthy than Richard, the 1st Earl Temple, who inherited three fortunes, married into a fourth and made a fifth in politics. And of all the great estates created or improved in that century, none was more remarkable than the garden Temple brought to perfection at Stowe in Buckinghamshire. These gardens were the marvel of their age, and the men who helped in their design – William Kent, James Gibbs and Capability Brown – carried the inspiration of Stowe into countless estates in every part of England.

The work of transforming Stowe lasted for more than 50 years. It was begun by Temple's uncle, Lord Cobham, soon after he returned to England in 1715, enriched by his years as a general in Marlborough's wars and his marriage to an heiress. He employed, among others, the architect William Kent, and encouraged him to create an inspired succession of 'fantasy buildings'. To reach these carefully sited ornaments Kent laid out winding paths, and to show them to their best advantage he cleared informal vistas. In tune with the prevailing Classical mood he was trying to create,

Kent gave them such names as the Elysian Fields and the Grecian Valley.

By 1749, when Lord Temple inherited the property from his uncle, Stowe was already one of the finest country estates in the kingdom, due in the main to the labours of its head gardener, Lancelot 'Capability' Brown. Later one of the greatest landscape gardeners of his age, Brown left in 1751 to form his own business. Over the next 30 years Temple saw the fruits of Brown's years of planning and planting, the design which was to give Stowe its 'natural' grace.

Mountains of earth were moved, water courses were re-channelled, thousands of trees and shrubs were planted. An old watermill and other relics of an ancient village were demolished; the church was spared, but carefully screened from view by a dense grove of trees. Nothing was to clash with the ideal world which Temple determined to create.

An aristocrat's dream

By the time the work at Stowe had been completed, over 30 follies, temples, obelisks, ornaments and pavilions had been built and, perhaps most perfect of all, the Palladian bridge. Its proportions were designed to be seen mirrored among water-lilies, as an expression of perfect tranquillity.

But among all the attractions of Stowe, the most important was the great house itself. It had two roles to play in Temple's grand design: firstly, as the centre of the whole creation, the crowning glory of all the many views; secondly, as the main vantage point, from which the most breathtaking vistas opened out in each direction. Lord Temple was determined to give Stowe a house worthy of its surroundings. He asked Robert Adam, the greatest architect of the day, to design the South Front. The final building is an adaptation of Adam's plans.

It is this front that the visitor to Stowe sees first, framed in the Corinthian Arch, from a mile away across the lake. Its three linked pavilions in honey-coloured stone are simple enough, but the proportions are flawless. Dominating the wide landscape, they are the ultimate expression of the aristocratic ideal.

The view that unfolds from the South Front of the house, looking back towards the arch, is equally impressive. Stowe's dreaming world stretches out again, with all its individual works of art coming together as a perfectly balanced landscape. In it, even the movement of the wind in the trees, the shimmering light on the lake and the clouds in the sky seem to contribute to the ideal composition. Through this inspired union of art and nature, Stowe tells more about the tastes of the 18th century than any other house in England.

CROWNING GLORY *Determined to give Stowe a fitting house, Lord Temple himself adapted Robert Adam's designs for the South Front.*

CLASSICAL HEROES *Designed by William Kent in 1734, this temple honoured classical poets, philosophers, scholars and law-makers.*

TRIBUTE TO A QUEEN *This temple was named the Queen's Temple in gratitude to Queen Charlotte for her devoted nursing of George III in 1789.*

GARDEN ARCHITECTURE *John Vanbrugh's original Rotondo was adapted in 1721 to fit in with the fluid sweep of the newly landscaped gardens.*

THE PERFECTION OF STOWE *The superb 18th-century Palladian bridge dominates the lake in the grounds of Stowe. It is one of more than 30 works of architecture – temples, arches, follies, monuments and pavilions – all carefully positioned by the many designers who worked there.*

FAMOUS BRITONS *The Temple of British Worthies was built in 1735 to complement the Temple of Ancient Virtue across the river. Among the 16 busts of British celebrities are Bacon, Shakespeare and Milton.*

MEMORIAL *A monument in the grounds to the explorer Captain Cook.*

A SELF-MADE GENIUS

Of all the men who laboured to make Stowe the most perfect country house in England, Capability Brown (right) is the most renowned. He earned his nickname – 'Capability' – from the phrase he invariably used when looking at a garden: 'I see great capability of improvement here.'

Brown learnt his craft at Stowe, where he was made head gardener in March 1741 by Lord Cobham. He stayed on at Stowe for ten years before branching out into business on his own. He went on to transform more than 100 important gardens. Among his clients he numbered George III, for whom he worked at Kew.

Forsaking the old formal style of garden, Brown's two occupations were the provision of 'vistas' (views), and the creation of natural settings for his patrons' houses. William Cowper, the 18th-century poet, wrote of him:

The omnipotent Magician Brown appears.
He speaks; the lawn in front becomes a lake;
Woods vanish, hills subside and valleys rise
And streams – as if created for his use –
Pursue the track of his directing wand.

The concept of gardening he evolved at Stowe dominated much of the English countryside.

A SCULPTURED LANDSCAPE *Almost lost in mist, the Corinthian Arch, designed in 1765, crowns the horizon in this view looking from the house across the lake. The landscape gardeners of the time strove after a 'grand design' – a harmony between architecture and nature.*

The 50 years of power and plenty

Victory in the Seven Years' War gives Britain mastery of the oceans and provides the impetus for Industrial Revolution

Stubborn, simple and well-meaning, the 22-year-old George III ascended the British throne in 1760, determined to follow his mother's advice to 'be a king'. He was the first British-born monarch to rule his country since 1714, and he believed that he possessed something that his two predecessors had lacked – the ability to understand the turbulent nation he had been called upon by God to lead.

In his own mind, George was convinced that his two Hanoverian predecessors, George II and George I, had been tricked by unscrupulous politicians into giving up many of the customary rights of a king. He, unlike them, had been born in England. He was determined to assert himself. And it was the Whig politicians, who had monopolised power since the Hanoverians had come to Britain in 1715, who were the targets of his hatred.

But great events far outside George's ken were now beginning to change the face of Britain. The Industrial Revolution was forcing millions into new occupations and new attitudes to their lives. Many Britons were beginning to question the established order of things and make demands for change. George, however, steadfastly set his face against reform – and in this much of the nobility followed him.

Nothing displayed the way the privileged lived more eloquently than Syon House (pp. 246–7). This was the home of the Duke of Northumberland, 'a person of extensive knowledge and correct taste', as his architect Robert Adam called him. But while Adam was creating the splendidly extravagant rooms of this mansion in Middlesex, the other England was revealing itself only a few miles away. A radical politician, John Wilkes (pp. 248–9), became the hero of the people when he defied king and court by standing up for the right of the Press to publish what it chose. Wilkes's long fight with George III and his ministers ended in an honourable draw, but not before a mob several thousand strong had rioted outside the prison where Wilkes was held

WEALTH FROM THE WORLD

East Indiamen, symbols of Britain's wealth under George III, lie at anchor at their dock in London. Their cargoes – sugar, cotton, rum, spices and tobacco – were all in great demand in mid-18th century Britain.

Britain's new wealth had largely been created by success in war. The nation's leader, Lord Chatham, taught his countrymen that trade followed the flag. The genius of military commanders such as James Wolfe and Robert Clive had won Canada and India for the British.

Not only did these riches display themselves in houses and estates all over the country. They were also invested in the factories of the Industrial Revolution. The mastery of the seas helped make Britain the workshop of the world.

243

A NEW AGE *The new age of industry even utilised children in the mills and factories. But the miracles of the Industrial Revolution were enthusiastically welcomed by the British, who saw the development first of water-power and then of steam as the bringers of a new prosperity. The mill-owner Joseph Arkwright expressed this confidence when he boasted that the machine he had invented – the spinning-frame – would enable him to 'pay the National Debt'.*

TOWNS AND ROADS *The bustle of the Tottenham Court Road turnpike depicted by Rowlandson. Britain's primitive roads were ill-equipped to meet the demands of the industrial age. The late 18th century saw the beginnings of a great road-building programme to link the new cities of the Midlands and North with the capital.*

A WORLD OF ELEGANCE *For the rich, the late 18th century was an age of pleasure and elegance. The fashionable paid for their pleasures with the rents from vast acres of prosperous farmland and by shrewd investment in the new industries. However, this flamboyant display of wealth increasingly aroused the envy and the resentment of the poor, who were becoming attracted by radical ideas.*

captive. The outburst claimed 16 victims who were shot down by the government troops. This was the first stirring of discontent.

However, the real pressure for change was centred not in the capital but in the new towns springing up in the North and the Midlands. It was in George's reign that the foundations of Britain's industrial prosperity were laid. Roads that had been left unrepaired since the days of the Romans were now resurfaced. Canals, in which France had previously led the world, were built at an unprecedented speed. The first major canal (pp. 250–1) was commissioned by the Duke of Bridgewater, from the engineer James Brindley. The cost of transporting goods by canal was about one-third that of road transport. A network soon linked the new centres of industry.

With the coming of canals, new markets were open to enterprising businessmen who knew how to exploit their opportunities. Adam Smith, the first intellectual of capitalism, proclaimed the merits of the 'division of labour'. Shrewd merchants, such as Josiah Wedgwood, put Smith's theories into practice, establishing so-called 'manufactories' where primitive production lines were set up.

A slow progress towards democracy

Others found an outlet for their energies in the expanding British Empire. Victory in the Seven Years' War (1756–63) won Britain vast new territories in Canada and India. The empire now became a place where men wished to settle. Captain James Cook's great voyages of exploration in the Pacific (pp. 252–3) led the government to encourage settlement there.

Just as George III's government was starting to encourage these new settlements, it lost the oldest settlement of all. The North American colonies broke away to declare their independence in 1776. Bitter years of fighting followed. But these made little difference to the way of life in Britain itself. As the war reached its height, English painters were producing their finest work for their aristocratic patrons (pp. 254–5). In George Stubbs, Britain had a painter of horses of unequalled technical brilliance. Thomas Gainsborough applied the same acute powers of observation to his sensitive portraits of the rich and noble.

In 1781 the British surrendered at Yorktown (pp. 256–7). After this defeat, even George III recognised that victory was impossible. For George himself the blow was a bitter one. Not only was it an affront to his crown, but it was the direct result of the disastrous policies that he had obstinately pursued.

Defeat was to bring change to Britain itself. Discredited by its American policy, Lord North's government fell, and a year of crisis followed. In 1783 George resolved it by a bold stroke – he appointed Lord Chatham's 24-year-old son, William Pitt, as his Prime Minister. The appointment was ridiculed, but Pitt was to be no royal stooge. He embarked on a programme of financial reform and administrative reconstruction that was ultimately to spell the end of royal power as George III understood it.

Even Pitt found it difficult to carry his programme through when faced with determined royal obstruction. But George's patronage of the arts and sciences was more enlightened than his political policies. He commissioned the architect James Wyatt to remodel Windsor Castle in the Gothic style. He was an enthusiastic collector of books and paintings, and wrote articles about agriculture under a pseudonym. He followed his mother in encouraging the development of the botanical gardens at Kew (p. 258), where many significant advances in the scientific study of plants were made.

Such interest in scientific and technical problems was characteristic of educated Englishmen of the time. It was the common bond that united the members of the Lunar Society of Birmingham (p. 259), for example. James

Watt, a prominent member of the society, was typical of those who found a practical application for scientific knowledge. Developing and improving on the work of previous inventors, he built a revolutionary steam engine that was soon used to power the cotton-spinning factories springing up in Lancashire. The accelerating pace of industrial expansion required new fuels and new materials. Coal provided the power that turned Watt's engines. Cast iron to make the new machinery was produced in vast quantities at ironworks such as Coalbrookdale (pp. 260–1), where three generations of the Darby family were the most famous ironmasters in England.

The pace of change increases

Britain's aristocrats, however, still thought that agriculture was the only real source of wealth. Their education was based firmly on a study of Classical literature with a 'Grand Tour' of Europe as its traditional conclusion. The influence of the Classical tradition and of Italy – the centrepiece of any Grand Tour – can be seen in such great houses as Woburn Abbey in Bedfordshire (pp. 262–3), remodelled during the 1780's as a treasure house to display the magnificent collections of the wealthy dukes of Bedford.

The forces of change were given still more impetus when the French Revolution broke out in 1789. Many Britons welcomed it, and revolutionary clubs were founded in London and other cities. The ideas of the revolution struck an answering chord in the work of a new generation of poets (pp. 264–5) – Wordsworth and Coleridge, who deliberately set out to capture the authentic voice of ordinary people in their works, and Blake, whose vision made no concessions to the conventions of the day.

But the events in France – the execution of Louis XVI and his queen in the 'reign of terror', and the military menace posed by the revolutionary armies – made the rulers of Britain determined to stamp out the message of *Liberté, Egalité, Fraternité* (Liberty, Equality, Fraternity) both at home and abroad. In 1793 war broke out with France. The struggle which followed was to last – with one short break – for 23 years.

Fighting alone against revolution

As the French armies swept in their all-conquering path across Europe, Britain was left to fight alone. Invasion was the main danger, but it was overcome by the bravery and superiority of the Royal Navy. On October 21, 1805, a succession of victories was crowned by Nelson's triumph at the Battle of Trafalgar (pp. 266–9). Though Nelson himself was killed, he left his country a priceless legacy in his lasting improvements to the organisation and strategy of the Royal Navy. 'England has saved herself by her exertions,' Pitt declared after the victory, 'and will, as I trust, save Europe by her example.'

Pitt was not to see his prophecy fulfilled, for he died in the following year. Though Britain ruled the seas, France still dominated the entire continent of Europe. In 1808, however, British forces under Sir John Moore landed in Spain. Though Moore was defeated by Napoleon, his selfless bravery on the retreat to Corunna (pp. 270–1) saved his army. It was to return to drive the French from Spain and invade France itself.

The king in whose name victory was to be won was now incurably mad. For 50 years he had tried to dominate events. Though he had another ten years to live, he spent them in isolation at Windsor. Power passed to his hated eldest son who assumed the Regency. But even though George III had lost his battle to 'be a king', in his reign he had seen the foundations laid of the supremacy that was to take his country to world dominance.

THE VOICE OF THE MOB *Despite the spread of wealth, political power remained firmly in the hands of the aristocracy. The common man could only make his voice heard through violence, as in 1780 when the Gordon Riots (above) swept London. Led by Lord George Gordon, these started off as a peaceful protest against a plan to give Catholics some political rights, but they soon turned into an orgy of destruction which was only quelled by armed force.*

CONSTITUTION'S GUARDIAN *Edmund Burke, a prominent Whig, believed that the English constitution was incapable of improvement. He attacked George III for his attempts to increase royal power, and supported the American colonists.*

INTO BATTLE *The Prime Minister, William Pitt, rides George III into battle against revolution in this cartoon of 1793. In that year war broke out with revolutionary France, and a struggle began that was to last, with one short break, for 23 years. Pitt, too, had once been a reformer, but his fear of the revolutionary ideas which had overthrown the French monarchy led him to adopt a policy of repression. Measures such as the 'Gag Acts' restricted freedom of speech.*

A PALACE INSPIRED BY THE GLORY OF GREECE AND ROME

The aristocrats of George III's Britain spent fortunes on indulging their taste for flamboyant display. Riches from a newly won empire poured into their hands – together with the profits from their lands, and from the careful investments they made in the factories of the Industrial Revolution.

Inevitably, they compared themselves with the proud rulers of another empire, ancient Rome. The Romans, too, had thrived on the wealth of foreign territories, and prided themselves on the riches of their estates. The buildings which had provided a background to their lives had been made to last – and their ruined splendour provided the great inspiration of England's 18th-century aristocrats.

On their 'Grand Tours' of the Continent, young English nobles marvelled at the grave palaces and silent temples of Classical Rome. They returned with the resolution to provide their own lives with the grandeur and the beauty of a vanished imperial world.

A freshness of vision

In Britain in the 1760's an architect emerged who had the skill to exploit this demand for Classical palaces. He was Robert Adam, a man who had made his own Grand Tour, armed with a sketch book. But Adam was more than a correct follower of antique models. He was by far the most creative genius ever to work on the interiors of great houses in Britain – in such staggering displays of virtuosity and imagination as the five great reception rooms at Syon House, near London. There he evolved a style which was to revolutionise British architecture.

Robert Adam mastered the basic principles of his craft from his father, a prosperous Edinburgh architect. During his Grand Tour, which lasted for four years, Robert was greatly influenced by the ruins of Emperor Diocletian's palace at Spalato (now Split, in Yugoslavia). He returned home in 1758 bursting with ideas, self-confidence and a determination to make a name for himself.

Adam was now 30 years old. He went into partnership with his brothers, James and William, and together they took the fashionable world by storm. Robert's secret was his conviction that the whole effect of an interior could be marred if its furniture and fittings were unrelated to the architectural design. So he designed furniture of all descriptions – carpets, fireplaces, tapestries, embroidery, plate and mirrors – to go in the houses he built.

Not only did Robert have the freshness of vision which speedily brought him to the head of his profession, but also he was a personable young man. He was quickly accepted into high society, where he made many valuable contacts. One of these was the diarist Fanny Burney,

who met Robert Adam soon after he arrived in London. She wrote that he was 'very sensible, very polite and very agreeable'. After supper on that occasion, the guests sang, but, she recorded, 'none shone more than Mr Adam; though, in truth, he had little or no voice... yet he sung with so much taste and feeling that few very fine voices could give such pleasure'.

Inspired by imperial Rome

Commissions poured in. And one of the first was Syon House, where Adam started work in 1762. There he designed the reception rooms as a unity, varying the form and height of the apartments to avoid monotony.

Syon House was the seat of Sir Hugh Smithson, who in 1750 had succeeded in laying claim to the ancient earldom of Northumberland. In keeping with his new status, the earl employed the most fashionable artists and craftsmen of the day. His portrait was painted by Thomas Gainsborough, his grounds laid out by Capability Brown and for his splendid apartments at Syon he chose Robert Adam, who was commissioned to refashion them 'in the antique style'. For his part, Adam 'endeavoured to render it a noble and elegant habitation, not unworthy of a proprietor who possessed not only wealth to execute a great design, but skill to judge of its merit'.

Adam's original plans were too ambitious, even for the purse of the proud earl, but his scheme for the principal rooms survived unchanged. In them he matched Classical simplicity of line with vibrant colours. Each interconnecting room varied in atmosphere and style, to give the visitor a succession of pleasing experiences.

The deliberate coolness of the neo-Classical Entrance Hall, dominated by a statue of the god Apollo, was designed to make a striking visual contrast with the following room, the Ante-Room, which is one of the most brilliantly glowing chambers that Adam ever designed.

The Ante-Room was enhanced still further by relics from imperial Rome itself. Adam had learnt that some ancient Roman columns made of green marble had been discovered on the bed of the River Tiber. He persuaded his patron to buy them, and ranged them around the walls of the ante-chamber. Each of the 12 columns was crowned by a gilded statue, and the atmosphere of glittering imperial luxury was enhanced by a highly polished floor.

The mood changed again with the restrained gracefulness of the State Dining Room. Adam gave this long, wide room a cool, detached atmosphere, where the earl and his male guests could engage in serious political debate over the after-dinner port. No wall-hangings or curtains which might retain the smell of

ARTISTIC GENIUS *The young Robert Adam took London by storm, and soon established himself as the most fashionable architect of the day.*

food were permitted. Copies of antique statues, painted in restrained shades of ivory, gazed at the diners from niches in the walls.

Beyond the dining room there followed the Red Drawing Room. Its walls were covered with Spitalsfield silk, in an explosion of rich colour. Adam himself designed the carpet, which was woven by Thomas More, a leading craftsman of the day. The blaze of painted medallions on the ceiling was executed by the fashionable artist Angelica Kauffman.

Palaces for the aristocracy

But it was the last of this great series of rooms which had the greatest impact. The Long Gallery – 136 ft in length and 14 ft wide – was designed, as Adam wrote, 'in a style to accord great variety and amusement'. The room also set him the greatest challenge, for its length and width meant that it was impossible to achieve the perfect balance of Classical proportions. So Adam filled it with columns, carved doorways and book-cases, installed clusters of furniture of his own design and crowned it with an exquisite moulded ceiling, designed to exaggerate the width.

At Syon, Adam showed his mastery of all forms of design. And, after his triumph there, British architecture was never the same again. Adam went on to greater and greater triumphs, such as Kenwood, near Hampstead, Osterley, near Brentford, and Keddlestone in Derbyshire. In the last year of his life alone, when he was 63, he designed 25 private houses and eight public buildings. And when he died he was buried in Westminster Abbey, with five great noblemen among his pall-bearers. They had reason to pay him tribute. For he had created a world in which they could display their dreams of classical grace and grandeur.

GRANDEUR OF ROME *Twelve columns of green marble dredged up from the muddy floor of the River Tiber in Rome, were brought to Syon House, London, by Robert Adam, for his classic Ante-Room.*

SYMPHONY IN RED *The Red Drawing Room, with its crimson Spitalsfield silk walls and carpet designed by Adam, is famous for its doorways which are decorated with ormolu on panels of ivory.*

INTRICATE DETAIL *The patterns in gold-leaf above the columns in the Ante-Room reveal Adam's love of elaborate ornament.*

TOTAL CONCEPT *Adam believed that décor and architecture should blend together. In the Long Gallery, the elaborate ceiling, the carpet, the 11 windows, the two fireplaces, the three doorways and all the furniture and materials were designed by Adam as matching parts of his overall concept.*

The struggle to win Reform

Triumph at Waterloo brings no peace to a nation divided into rich and poor, but the threat of revolution forces Britain along the road of reform

In 1810 the threat of French domination still hung over Europe. England, alone among the nations that had taken up arms against France, had managed to avoid defeat at the hands of Napoleon. But under the impetus of war, its two nations – rich and poor – had moved further apart. The poor suffered under the combined weight of low wages and high wartime prices, while the aristocracy flung itself into exuberant extravagance.

The spendthrifts of the aristocracy found their natural leader in George, Prince of Wales, who became Prince Regent when his father finally went mad in 1810. Gamblers and dicers lounged in the royal staterooms. Fashions came and went with the seasons. Low necklines and German waltzes gave the impression that the British upper classes had surrendered to frivolity and vice. At the Royal Pavilion in Brighton (pp. 278–9), the stately pleasure dome of Regency England, the Prince Regent escaped from the tedious business of government by indulging himself in gambling, drinking and 18-course banquets. And men of all classes followed his example (pp. 276–7).

While the Prince Regent dallied, the Duke of Wellington was winning the war for Britain. In the Peninsular War in Spain, his armies took the offensive against the French, forcing them back across the Pyrenees and into their own territory. For its part, the British government poured out subsidies to every nation in Europe willing to fight Napoleon. In 1812, Britain's expenditure rose to the unprecedented figure of £118 million; by the end of the war in 1814, when Napoleon abdicated, the National Debt had risen

A DIVIDED NATION

The rich of the West End rub shoulders with the poor from the slums of the East End during a parliamentary election held in Covent Garden in 1818. The popular mood was demonstrated in banners calling for 'Universal Suffrage' and 'Magna Charta'. But they went unheeded.

Covent Garden, little changed today (inset), was one of the few places where the great debate could be carried on, as elections in the City of Westminster were relatively free.

The two nations of Regency England were in constant conflict. The poor demanded greater freedom; the rich replied with repression.

But by 1832 the reformers' demands could only be resisted at the cost of revolution. In that year Parliament was finally reformed.

273

DEATH IN THE COMMONS *Spencer Perceval (left), Prime Minister of England, meets his death at the hands of the insane Francis Bellingham in the lobby of the House of Commons on May 12, 1812. Bellingham killed Perceval for personal reasons, but his crime was seen as part of the unrest that was sweeping England at the height of the Napoleonic Wars. The unrest stemmed from Napoleon's 'Continental System', which had closed Europe to British trade and thrown thousands out of work at home.*

REFORM AND REPRESSION *The coming of peace in 1815 did not diminish the suffering which led to demand for reform. A trade slump in 1819 gave rise to widespread agitation and, on August 16, some 50,000 people assembled at St Peter's Field, Manchester, to press for reform. The local magistrates panicked and sent in the yeomanry; in the 'Peterloo massacre' 11 were killed.*

POPULAR VOICE *The cartoonist George Cruikshank summed up the mood of popular discontent with England's system of government under the Regency. A Briton is shown in rags, with his mouth padlocked to stop him spreading sedition against king and constitution. The government's response to popular discontent was not reform but repression.*

274

from £252 million to £861 million. And when the 'Corsican tyrant' returned to France a year later, it was Wellington who again defeated him. By crushing Napoleon at the Battle of Waterloo in 1815 (pp. 280–3) he laid the foundations for a lasting peace. The duke arrived back in England as a conquering hero. By 1818 he had been made a cabinet minister and the leader of the Tory Party in the House of Lords. For the following 20 years, his prestige and influence were decisive factors in British politics. 'The duke is against it!' was often enough to damn any proposal.

The effect of peace was to turn men's minds either in hope or in fear away from the French peril, and towards those currents of change that had for so long been dammed up by the national effort against Napoleon. The country to which the duke returned seemed both to him and his colleagues in the government to be almost as dangerous a place as the Continent. Wellington had not fought revolutionary France to see its insidious principles established in his own country.

In the early 19th century, the House of Commons was an exclusive club rather than a body representing the people of Britain. Nearly all its members came from the land-owning aristocracy – most of them men who had little knowledge of or sympathy with the lives of men less fortunate than themselves. Peace brought great hardship and unemployment, as the soldiers returned and the demand for British manufactured goods, which had been stimulated by the war, fell off sharply.

The House of Commons, however, was only concerned to protect the wealth and privileges of the aristocracy. It repealed the income tax William Pitt had imposed in 1793 to help pay for the war; and it passed the Corn Laws, which forbade the import of foreign wheat at low prices. This kept up the high wartime price of food.

The result was deep unrest throughout the country. Mobs surrounded Parliament, holding up rope halters and crying 'No starvation! No landlords!' The home of the minister who had introduced the legislation was sacked. Riots by farm labourers in the south and strikes by coal miners in the north culminated in a great reform meeting in London in December 1816. Demands for the abolition of the Corn Laws and for the reform of Parliament swept the country, but the Tory government's frightened response was to suspend *Habeas Corpus*, so that agitators could be imprisoned without trial, and to outlaw 'seditious meetings'.

Two nations – bitterly divided

In 1819 trouble flared up again. This time the centre was not London but the north, the heart of the industrial challenge to the traditional power of the landed aristocracy. At Manchester, the home of the cotton industry and the most important of the growing towns which were still unrepresented in Parliament, a great meeting was held to petition the government for parliamentary reform. It attracted an enormous crowd of 50,000. The local magistrates ordered in the troops of the county yeomanry to disperse the crowd. In the resulting chaos 11 people were killed and 400 injured. The tragedy quickly became known as the 'Peterloo massacre', and a legend was born of popular resistance to repression and tyranny.

Peterloo did not stop the demand for reform and, in the following year, the monarchy itself became the subject of open attack. When George III at last died, his son, George IV, was determined that the wife he so hated, Caroline of Brunswick, should not be crowned queen, and demanded that the government bring in a Bill for her divorce (pp. 284–5). Caroline was a vulgar, brassy woman, but the mob thronged the streets of London in her support and, when the divorce was abandoned, howled with delight. Never had the prestige of the crown sunk so low in the eyes of the British people.

Contempt for George IV was reflected in the verses of Shelley, Keats and Byron, the greatest poets of the day (pp. 286–7). Shelley and Keats had both been inspired by the ideals of the French Revolution, while Byron, who was to die for the liberty of a foreign land, railed against 'the fourth of the fools and oppressors called George'.

But it was technological, not intellectual, ferment that was to speed reform. The Royal Institution spread the knowledge of modern science. Under its auspices, the most brilliant scientists of the day, among them Davy and Faraday (p. 287), lectured to vast audiences of both high and low. And their work in their laboratories – particularly in the field of electricity – was soon put to practical use in transforming Britain still further.

FIRST POLICE *In the 1820's the government realised that only reform would stave off revolution. One of the reforms introduced by Sir Robert Peel, the Home Secretary, was an efficient civilian police force. Its members were nicknamed 'Peelers' or 'Bobbies' after him. Previously, the only force that the government could call on to preserve law and order in times of unrest had been the army.*

Reform changes the face of Britain

Another revolution was the coming of railways. In 1829 Stephenson's *Rocket* (pp. 288–9) finally convinced sceptics that self-propelled locomotives were safe and efficient. So began the great railway boom that was to affect every aspect of life in Britain. The railways gave Englishmen the feeling that industrial success was a noble and glorious objective for any civilised nation. The liberal headmaster of Rugby School, Dr Thomas Arnold, looked down from a bridge on a passing train and exclaimed: 'I rejoice to see it and to think that feudality is gone for ever.' Any remaining 18th-century prejudice against trade was banished; 19th-century England saw the railways as portents of an ever-increasing prosperity. Their importance was reflected in the painting 'Rain, Steam and Speed' by William Turner, who gave artistic expression to the new age just as John Constable had to the old (pp. 292–3).

The pace of change was reflected in the politics of the 1820's. At the Foreign Office, George Canning turned his back on the despotic powers of Europe and recognised the new democratic republics of South America. At the Board of Trade, William Huskisson eased the lot of the poor and gave a spur to industrial advance by reducing the customs duties on imports, including food. In 1825 a major step was taken to secure the rights of workers. The Combination Acts, which prevented workers from forming Trades Unions to press for higher wages or better working conditions, were repealed. And at the end of the decade, even the Duke of Wellington, who had now become Prime Minister, was forced to yield. In 1829 Roman Catholics were allowed to become Members of Parliament.

But there was one demand the Tories would not concede – reform of Parliament. By 1830 this had become irresistible. Severe famine had provoked outbreaks of mob violence and arson, while the large industrial towns of the north and Midlands chafed under their exclusion from Parliament.

Two years of bitter agitation followed. At a General Election the Tories were thrown out of power and the Whigs took office after 50 years in Opposition. To save the constitution, Lord Grey's government introduced a sweeping Reform Bill (pp. 290–1), abolishing the corrupt 'rotten boroughs' and giving the middle classes the vote. But the House of Lords threw out the Bill, and for several weeks Britain stood on the brink of revolution.

Now a new figure had the decisive voice. For George IV had died in 1830 and his moderate brother, William IV, was on the throne. He promised to create new peers to ensure the Bill's passage. Opposition collapsed and the Reform Bill became law.

In spite of its name, the Reform Act achieved only a small measure of reform. But it was a symbol. It showed that the landed aristocracy could be forced to share its power. And its passage was a sign that new forces were arising to change the face of British society.

PLOT AND CONSPIRACY *Radical fervour reached its height in the Cato Street Conspiracy of 1820. A group of conspirators, led by Arthur Thistlewood, planned to blow up the entire British cabinet over their dinner. Their heads were to be exhibited to the mob at the Mansion House, where Thistlewood was to be proclaimed president of a provisional government. But the plot was betrayed and the conspirators were arrested at their Cato Street headquarters (above).*

REFORM AT LAST *The Duke of Wellington – once the hero of Waterloo but now a hated reactionary – is surrounded by an angry mob outside his London home, Apsley House, in 1832. In that year, the demand for parliamentary reform grew so great that a Whig government passed the Great Reform Bill. This was only achieved after a year-long resistance by the House of Lords had brought Britain to the brink of revolution.*

WHEN PLEASURE RULED

No era in Britain's history has ever been as devoted to pleasure as the Regency. Even though the country was involved in a war with France, this only gave an added zest to its citizens' pursuit of amusement. With the extravagant figure of the Prince Regent as their example, high and low-born alike flung themselves into every kind of enjoyment. The robust amusements of the age, such as bull-baiting, prize-fighting and cock-fighting, attracted an enthusiastic following from every class of society. One of the nation's greatest figures, the Duke of Wellington, observed that there was 'nothing the people of this country like so much as to see their great men take part in their amusements'. And the popular ideal of the gentleman was of a fighting sportsman, ready at the slightest excuse to defend his honour with his fists or his pistols. Even after duelling was made illegal in 1828, duels continued to be fought.

Excess was the keynote of the age. Lord Petersham, a prominent dandy, took extravagance to the point of eccentricity. He indulged his fondness for snuff by keeping 3000 lb. of it permanently in stock, using a different snuff-box every day of the year, and painting his carriage snuff brown. Gambling to extremes was a universal passion. The rich squandered fortunes at the card tables of clubs such as Crockford's – whose owner made £1 million from it – while the poor patronised fairground gaming booths. In their pleasures, if in nothing else, the British were united as never before.

NEW DANCE *Introduced from Austria, the waltz created a sensation in England. It was thought immodest, and it took years before the waltz was accepted in fashionable circles.*

IN THE COUNTRY *Shooting duck in winter was a favourite country sport – but confined to the upper classes. It was illegal for anyone but a squire or his eldest son to shoot game.*

RARE RELAXATION *An engraving by Rowlandson of a country fair. Seasonal fairs were the high points of the rural year, giving country folk a rare chance to enjoy themselves and buy small luxuries from travelling pedlars.*

NATIONAL SPORT *Boxing had the greatest claim to be considered the national sport of Regency England. Prize-fighters such as Tom Cribb, who fought 76 rounds to become British champion, had a special status in high society and could win huge rewards from their noble patrons. But the price of fame was high; there were few rules and boxers fought bare-fisted until they fell.*

STAGE-STRUCK *Edmund Kean, the great Shakespearian actor, falls to the ground in one of his most famous scenes – the death of Richard III. His other famous roles included King Lear and Othello. Well-known actors were idolised by working people as well as by aristocrats. Attempts to raise London gallery prices caused riots in the theatres during this period.*

DANDY *Though neither rich nor high-born, George 'Beau' Brummel was the arbiter of Regency taste. He dressed with exquisite care, preferring sober perfection to showy display.*

COURAGE *Fencing was an upper-class sport, esteemed as a school for duelling. The Regency saw the heyday of duelling.*

SCANDAL AND ROMANCE *London's courtesans were patronised by the famous. A cartoon shows Harriette Wilson, once mistress of the Duke of York, receiving compliments from her admirers.*

THE GAMBLERS *Card-playing was a favourite pastime. While rich rakes lost fortunes overnight in their clubs, families enjoyed whist (above).*

BLOOD SPORTS *Cruelty was no barrier to pleasure in Regency England. Standards were less squeamish than now, and men of all classes found amusement in any kind of blood sport – especially if it also provided an opportunity to indulge their passion for gambling. At the Westminster rat pit (above), bets were placed on the terrier most likely to kill the greatest number of rats in a given time.*

FANTASY PALACE BUILT FOR A PRINCE OF PLEASURE

A contemporary said of the Prince Regent that he was 'a bad son, a bad husband, a bad monarch and a bad friend'. But posterity has taken a kinder view because of the prince's one redeeming feature: bad in so much else, he had good taste and he was one of the greatest patrons of the arts ever to occupy the throne of England.

He created the royal collection of paintings;

he was responsible for the foundation of the National Gallery in London; he encouraged the great plan for rebuilding the West End of London, including the creation of Trafalgar Square, Regent Street and the terraces of Regent's Park. Above all, he created at Brighton a seaside palace which ranks as one of the most inventive and enjoyable works of architecture in Britain.

In his role as art collector and builder of palaces, George's worst failings – his extraordinary vanity and egoism, his limitless extravagance and wild irresponsibility in money matters – were turned to virtues. His vanity prompted him to dream of palaces of unparalleled splendour. His extravagance permitted him to fulfil even his wildest dreams. The marine pavilion at Brighton evolved from 40 years of this royal folly.

George, Prince of Wales, was just 19 when he began a lifelong association with Brighton. In 1783 he was persuaded that sea water would help cure some uncomfortable glandular swel-

EGYPTIAN INFLUENCES

As the French armies swept through Egypt in 1798, their commander, General Bonaparte, became obsessed with the ancient world of the pharaohs. He sent antiquities back to Paris, where Egyptian design soon became the rage. Despite the barriers of war, the fashion spread to England, where the Prince Regent introduced it into Brighton Pavilion.

NILE-INSPIRED *A couch shaped like an Egyptian river boat.*

BACK IN TIME *A clock in an ancient setting.*

SPHINX *Armchair for state occasions.*

CHINESE EXTRAVAGANZA *The Prince Regent's taste for Chinese art was given full flight in the Banqueting Room. Its centrepiece, a 1 ton chandelier with a lotus flower motif, hung from a gilded dragon in the dome. A typical menu for a banquet there listed 116 dishes.*

ORIENTAL FANTASY *It fell to John Nash to try to unify the Prince Regent's fashionable fantasies with a plan for the pavilion, shown here in a cross-section. He was inspired in 1815 by a book of Indian scenes painted by Thomas Daniell, which he had borrowed from the prince's library. But the prince's finances were in a precarious state and the* Prime Minister, Lord Liverpool, the Foreign Secretary and the Chancellor of the Exchequer warned him that Parliament would never vote further expenditure on the house. At last work began with a gift of £50,000 from the prince's mother, Queen Caroline. By 1820, when work finished, the pavilion had cost the enormous sum of £155,000.

lings in his neck, and he travelled to the quiet fishing village of Brighton for the first time.

Two years later, the young prince secretly married Mrs Fitzherbert, a beautiful widow of 25 who, as a Roman Catholic, was ineligible as a wife for the heir to a Protestant throne. He brought her to Brighton where he leased a house overlooking the Steine, a wide stretch of grass where fishermen spread their nets to dry.

But no modest seaside house was good enough for 'Prinny', as his friends affectionately called him. In 1787 he commissioned the architect Henry Holland, who had re-built Carlton House in London for him, to design a 'marine pavilion' on the site. The first pavilion – a bow-fronted house of pure Classical design – was completed in the same year.

The prince's taste, however, was constantly changing. In 1802 he was given a roll of Chinese wallpaper, and he immediately made plans to add a Chinese gallery. This was the beginning of the oriental decorations which soon spread to other parts of the house.

Even as the designers and craftsmen were at work on these elaborate Chinese decorations, the fickle prince had fallen in love with a new fashion – the romantic and glittering style of India's Mughal emperors. His imagination had been fired by Thomas and William Daniell's *Views of Oriental Scenery*. He ordered the most elaborate stable block ever built in Britain, including an iron and glass cupola 80 ft wide and 65 ft high, all in Indian style.

This building took six years to complete, and cost £70,000 – well over £1000 for each of the royal horses. The prince liked to remark that even his horses were now housed in a palace. William Hazlitt, the contemporary writer, took a more critical view: 'The King's horses (if they were horses of taste) would petition against such irrational lodging.'

The Prince Regent now had two exotic styles – Chinese and Indian – warring with each other inside the shell of a conventional Classical house. He was in need of an architect with the inventive power to unite the styles into the 'stately pleasure dome' of his dreams. The one man in Britain with the type of skill that was needed was John Nash, a self-taught speculative builder, who was already at work on his superbly dramatic transformation of the West End of London.

A prince and his architect

Nash was appointed Surveyor-General of royal buildings, and in 1815 began work on the pavilion. It took five years to complete. The exterior was transformed into an exotic version of Indian architecture, with a large bulbous dome built over the central salon and flanked by smaller domes on either side.

But it was inside that the extravagant fantasy was at its most imaginative. Writhing dragons rioted across the walls of the Music and Banqueting rooms whose roofs were shaped like Saracen tents. In the Banqueting Room hung a magnificent chandelier, which cost over £5000.

Even in the Great Kitchen, the supporting pillars of the high roof were made to look like palm trees. Here, the most celebrated chef of the day, Carème, presided over the ovens, with 15 chefs under him.

A prince's legacy

The Prince Regent's guests found the enormous meals, the stuffy heat, the dazzling architecture and their host's endless mealtime monologues somewhat overpowering, but nevertheless impressive. The prince's subjects, suffering from unemployment and poverty, were less easily pleased. In Parliament, one member of the Whig opposition summed up the feelings of the people when he described the pavilion as 'that squanderous and lavish profusion which resembled more the pomp and magnificence of a Persian satrap than the sober dignity of a British prince seated in the bosom of his subjects'.

Throughout the rest of his reign the pavilion continued to arouse the wrath of George's subjects. It was not until 100 years later that his extravagant folly was to be fully appreciated and enjoyed by the British people.

ROYAL WHIM *The wit Sidney Smith said of the Prince Regent's masterpiece, it was as if 'St Paul's had gone down to the sea and pupped'. But no sooner was the glittering oriental pavilion at Brighton completed in 1820, than the fickle prince lost interest and seldom visited it again.*

Victory at Waterloo–and Europe's fate is decided

WELLINGTON'S TRAVELLING CASE

The Duke of Wellington's travelling case, which accompanied him from his first campaigns in India to his last battle, Waterloo in 1815. It contains razors, nail scissors and medicine, and it now can be seen at Apsley House, London. But, unlike many of his junior officers, Wellington was a soldier, not a fashionable dandy.

As the long afternoon of Sunday, June 18, 1815, wore on, the city of Brussels was in a state of panic. Since 3 p.m. refugees had been pouring in from south of the capital. Twelve miles away, on the field of Waterloo, the Duke of Wellington, with his Allied army, was barring the way of 70,000 French veterans under the command of Napoleon. The grumbling thunder of the guns grew louder, and rumours of Wellington's defeat swept through the city. 'I never saw such consternation,' wrote the diarist Fanny Burney. 'We could only gaze and tremble, listen and shudder.'

Only a few days previously, everyone in the Allied camp at Brussels had been supremely confident of victory. Leisurely preparations were being made for the invasion of France. Napoleon, whose untimely return from exile on the Mediterranean island of Elba had plunged Europe into renewed war, would finally be overthrown.

The Prussian army, under Marshal Blücher, numbered 113,000 men – almost as many as the largest striking force the French could possibly raise. Wellington's own army was 70,000 strong. And further east, 500,000 Austrians and Russians were massing.

But Napoleon struck first. He had made his reputation by daring – and now he risked everything on a lightning last throw, hoping to meet and defeat his enemies one by one. On June 15 his forces smashed through the feeble

NAPOLEON *In this contemporary picture, the French emperor is shown formed out of corpses and symbols of death – a reminder that his career as self-made master of Europe was built on pitiless conquest. Only the British, the 'nation of shopkeepers' he despised, held out; and at Waterloo in 1815 they brought him down.*

frontier posts at the Belgian border. Wellington's main object was to keep in touch with the Prussians, so he ordered an immediate concentration of his forces. But the British were slow to obey their commander's orders, and by the end of the following day Napoleon had defeated the Prussians at Ligny.

Despite their defeat, the Prussians had managed to retire in good order. They kept in touch with the British, who now took up a defensive position at Waterloo and waited in a downpour for their allies to join them. Wellington was quietly confident as he went off to a glittering ball given by the Duchess of

THE IRON DUKE *Wellington's great victories against the French made him a popular hero.*

A GAMBLE THAT FAILED *Seeking the chance of a quick victory, Marshal Ney sent 5000 French horsemen against the British infantry squares at Waterloo. The French charged five times, but each time they were beaten back, suffering huge losses. The dead and wounded riders reminded Wellington of overturned turtles as they sprawled in the mud. Ney's gamble failed and the battle was lost when Blücher and his Prussians arrived to complete the French rout. A few days later Napoleon abdicated and went into exile. He had finally lost his throne.*

Richmond in Brussels. At 2 a.m. on June 18, Wellington retired to bed, slept for six hours and then rode out to see his troops. The French were there and about to attack – but the Prussians had not yet arrived. Wellington's plans had miscarried. He now had to face Napoleon's veterans alone; defeat seemed to many to be very near.

Two men of action

All would now depend on the quality of the two commanders and the bravery of the men they commanded. Wellington and Napoleon had both been born in the same year – 1769. Both men were outsiders. Wellington's family was poor, and its Irish peerage laughed at by English nobles. Napoleon's home, Corsica, only became a French possession in the year of his birth, and the emperor always spoke French with a strong Italian accent.

Both men had tremendous energy and were capable of going without sleep for days on end. Officially they denigrated each other's abilities, but there was a grudging respect between them. When he heard the details of one of the duke's campaigns, Napoleon remarked: 'Only Wellington and I are capable of carrying out such measures.'

In public, however, Napoleon scorned the duke. He told his chief-of-staff, Marshal Soult: 'You think he is a great general? I tell you that Wellington is a bad general, that the English are bad troops and that this will be a picnic.' The emperor also believed that there did not seem to be much greatness about a man who had made his reputation by always fighting on the defensive. Napoleon exclaimed contemptuously: 'There's a man for you! He is forced to flee from an army he dares not fight.' Now the two men were to meet on the battlefield for the first time – with Europe as the prize.

Man for man, Wellington's troops were probably inferior to the veterans of the *Grand Armée*. Out of every 100 men only 18 were actually British. The rest were Hanoverians, Brunswickers, Belgian and Dutch. The duke tersely described them as: 'The scum of the earth; they have all enlisted for drink.' But he valued their loyalty, and to this end he wore the national cockades of all the allies in his hat; he also forbade the playing of 'Rule Britannia' by his regimental bands.

Wellington's men wore more or less what they liked. One officer wrote: 'Provided we brought our men into the field well appointed, with the 60 lb. of ammunition each, Wellington never looked to see whether their trousers were black, blue or grey.' The smartest soldiers were probably the light dragoons, who wore blue coats with very tight breeches.

Most of the cavalry discarded their standard-issue swords, preferring to fight with captured French weapons. To even the score, Napoleon's men marched in boots made in Northampton. The British muskets were better than those of the French, but they were difficult to fire in wet weather.

On both sides, the men would do their duty – either from enthusiasm or from threat of punishment. Wellington stated: 'I have no idea of any great effect being produced on British soldiers but by the fear of immediate corporal punishment.' Napoleon, on the other hand, inspired devotion in his men. He always addressed his soldiers as *mes amis*, and did his best to provide for wounded veterans.

Now, both commanders were making their final preparations. By 11 a.m. Wellington was riding along the ridge at Mont St Jean. He was wearing a strange mixture of military and civilian dress – a low cocked hat, a plain blue coat, white buckskin breeches and highly polished top boots.

From his horse, Copenhagen, Wellington could see the French columns as they formed up ready for battle. He did his best to hide his concern, but he wrote later: 'It was already quite clear that we should have a terrible day.'

Soon afterwards, a fierce skirmish broke out between troops commanded by Jerome Bonaparte, Napoleon's youngest brother, and eight companies of guards around the Château Hougoumont, a manor house at the southern end of the British line. This was the weakest point in Wellington's defence, but Napoleon only meant this as a diversionary attack. He put his faith in one swift decisive blow on the British centre, which he believed would be enough to hurl the stiff-necked Redcoats into retreat. 'I shall hammer them with my artillery,' he declared to his staff, 'charge them with my cavalry to make them show themselves, and, when I am quite sure where the actual English are, I shall go straight at them with my Old Guard.'

'The French came on in the old style'

The first part of Napoleon's plan went into operation at 1 p.m., when 80 French guns began a ferocious bombardment of the centre. This lasted for 30 minutes and then 16,000 French grenadiers and *tirailleurs* (sharp-shooters) moved forward, sending several Belgian units into panic-stricken flight.

But veterans of the war in Spain, such as the 79th Highlanders and the 95th Rifles, held their fire until the enemy were only 20 yds away. Then, from their extended line, they poured in a tremendous disciplined volley, and, as the startled French tried to deploy, the British charged with fixed bayonets. The French attackers broke and ran. Wellington later recalled: 'The French came on in the old style – and we drove them off in the old style.'

Then things started to go wrong for the British. The fleeing Frenchmen were pursued by the Household Cavalry and the Scots Greys. The Scots Greys had been given rum before the battle and their blood was up. They charged headlong into the centre of Napoleon's army, where they were cut to ribbons by a French counter-attack. With the loss of some of his

THE EMPEROR FLEES *With defeat inevitable, Napoleon's hand-picked Old Guard clears the way for his flight, which was so hasty that he left behind hat and sword. Two days later he abdicated.*

best cavalry, Wellington's position was critical.

A lull followed, during which Wellington decided to reposition some of his troops. It was at this moment that Napoleon's brilliant subordinate, Marshal Ney, made a disastrous error that was to cost his master the battle.

Determined to seize the chance of quick victory, Ney launched 5000 heavy cavalry, perhaps the finest in the world, against the British position. This move – sending cavalry against intact squares of infantry supported by artillery – was against all the textbook rules of

LAST STAND *As twilight fell, the survivors of the Old Guard were surrounded by the British. Even in defeat they refused to capitulate and managed to retreat to safety. Their commander, General Cambronne, is said to have shouted: 'The Old Guard dies, but does not surrender.'*

war. But by such unorthodoxy Napoleon's marshal had made his reputation.

Five times the French charged – and five times they were repulsed. The slaughter on both sides was prodigious. Inside each tightly packed British square was a small area for dying infantrymen and crude battlefield surgery. Between the squares lay the fallen French cavalrymen.

Ney did capture the farmhouse outpost of La Haye Sainte, giving the French a chance of overrunning Wellington's Hanoverian auxiliaries and breaking the British line. Had Napoleon given Ney infantry support, the French might still have won the day. But Napoleon refused to commit his reserves and Wellington had time to plug the gap.

As Wellington sent in British regiments to stiffen the Hanoverians, he replied to a mes-

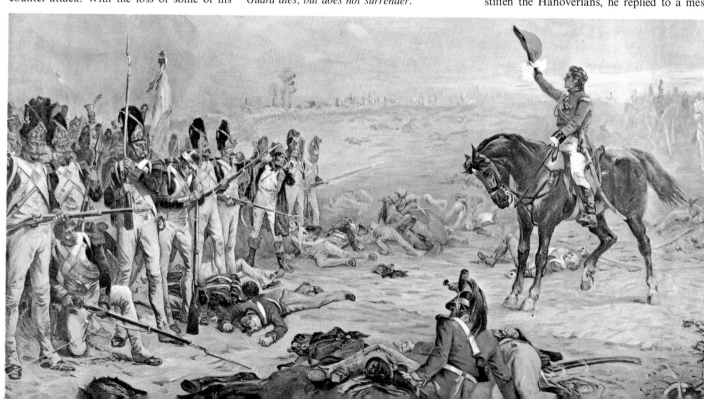

Wellington described his men as 'the scum of the earth; they have all enlisted for drink'. And drunkenness, looting and rape were their chief preoccupations off the battlefield. But on duty, discipline was rigid. They obeyed orders without question and, at Waterloo, one-third of the British regulars were killed or wounded. A quick death was a blessing because wounds were usually fatal. A shattered limb meant amputation – without anaesthetics. Gangrene and tetanus killed thousands. Even for fit men conditions were appalling. They were ill-fed and badly paid (each private's prize for winning at Waterloo was £2 11s 4d). Disease was rife.

Nor could a soldier expect promotion. The purchase system, by which the wealthy could buy commissions, made it almost impossible to rise from the ranks.

The British Hussar took his name and his distinctive shoulder cape, worn by all such regiments, from Hungary.

In contrast to the red coats of the other regulars, the Rifle Brigade's green-and-black uniform was fine camouflage.

These infantrymen, the mainstay of the line, wore the red coats which distinguished the British army from all others.

sage from Sir Colin Halkett, commanding a brigade of the 3rd Division. Halkett asked if he could retreat a little. Wellington replied: 'Tell him what he asks is impossible. He and I and every Englishman on the field must die on the spot which we occupy.'

'À Bruxelles, mes enfants'

It was at this moment, when all seemed uncertain, that Wellington observed to his anxious staff: 'Hard pounding this, gentlemen, but we will see who can pound the longest.' Throughout, he had been glancing at his watch. Now, at long last, a staff-officer brought the message he had awaited: the Prussians were arriving. With their gun-carriages axle-deep in mud, Blücher and his men had taken a day to come 9 miles.

Napoleon, too, knew that his gamble was on the brink of failure. At 6.30 p.m. he ordered his last throw – an all-out attack by his finest troops, the hand-picked Imperial Guard. The emperor stood before his soldiers, shouting *'A Bruxelles, mes enfants, à Bruxelles'*.

The Guard advanced in two massive columns to make a frontal assault on the British lines on the crest of the ridge. In front of each regiment rode a general – the hardened men who had marched in triumph into every European capital but one – London. In the face of this tremendous onslaught, the British held their formation, but the Guard pressed on.

Suddenly the initiative was taken from Wellington by the action of John Colbourne, commander of the 52nd Rifles, the most experienced regiment of the British Army. Without orders, Colbourne ordered his men to wheel out of line and take up position on the French left. It was dangerous to leave this gap, but the gamble succeeded. The astonished Guard halted, and poured a volley into the 52nd which brought down 140 of its men. But the 52nd's reply was decisive. Every British bullet seemed to find its mark. The Guard broke and fled.

Wellington had been appalled by Colbourne's recklessness. But, as he saw the Guard crumble, he muttered: 'Oh damn it! In for a penny, in for a pound!' He ordered a general advance.

'À damn near thing'

The drifting smoke and the low clouds brought on an early dusk. In the twilight, the French army dissolved. The day had been won by Wellington's men, and the arrival of Blücher made the enemy give up all hope. But the remnants of the Old Guard fought on to give their emperor the chance of escape.

The victorious commanders, Wellington and Blücher, met about 10 p.m. The 72-year-old German gasped *'Quelle affaire'* – as the duke observed, about the only French he knew.

Wellington rode on into the darkness. On the field lay 45,000 dead and wounded men, 15,000 of his own – the rest French. The bodies were still there as the sun rose. Many remained for days and all distinction between friend and foe was lost amid the cries of the dying.

Wellington had triumphed. His victory secured the peace of Europe for 33 years. But there had certainly been times when the French had the upper hand. Wellington observed that 'it was a damn near thing – the nearest run thing you ever saw in your life'.

The 'Iron Duke' who dominated a generation

After his triumph at Waterloo, Wellington had over 30 years of active life in front of him. His first decision was to abandon the army for politics. But his military reputation was a liability as well as an asset in his subsequent career. With Napoleon's example before them, many believed that the duke, too, might have dreams of supreme power.

There were alarming straws in the wind. Wellington, a diehard Tory, was on the side of repression at home and abroad. When anything went wrong, whether connected with politics or not, the duke was liable to exclaim: 'Hah! here's liberality again.'

Wellington believed that the British constitution was perfect and incapable of improvement. What others – particularly the less privileged – thought of as anomalies and abuses were to him its finest features. But for all his apparent rigidity, Wellington had his priorities clear. Experience as a soldier had taught him that exposed positions had sometimes to be given up to defend more crucial points. As Prime Minister, in 1828, he conceded Catholic emancipation – the right of Catholics to sit in Parliament – in the teeth of the opposition of his own party, to avoid revolution in Ireland.

Soon after the passage of the Great Reform Bill in 1832, Wellington returned to the army. He became commander-in-chief for life. 'Consult the Duke' was a precept for every statesman, diplomat and soldier. And when he died in 1852 the nation honoured its 83-year-old hero with a state funeral in St Paul's.

THE COACHMAN *Wellington became Prime Minister in 1828. 'The man wot drives the sovereign' was a jibe at the power he held.*

A scorned queen puts the monarchy on trial

WHERE A QUEEN SPENT HER EXILE

The Ranger's House in Greenwich Park, London, where Queen Caroline, wife of the Prince Regent, set up home after being forced to leave the court in 1798. She lived there for 16 years, learning to play the harp, paint, and even tending her own vegetable garden.

A QUEEN ON TRIAL *Caroline (seated centre right) at the House of Lords in 1820. Her trial was held in the annexe of the House, which was specially built for the occasion. Although she was allowed to attend the hearings, she was refused the right to give evidence.*

In the mid-summer of 1821 England crowned its new king, George IV, in Westminster Abbey. No expense was spared to make the occasion unforgettable. In total, the coronation cost £250,000. Every resource of an age devoted to flamboyant display and luxury was brought into play by the king.

As the royal procession neared the sacred precincts of the abbey, George's efforts were rewarded. The spectators were reduced to stunned silence. Then the cheers rang out. At the head of the procession walked the King's Herb Woman and six handmaidens, scattering herbs along the way. They were followed by the officers of state, carrying the crown, orb, sceptre and the sword of state, and three bishops, bearing the paten, chalice and Bible. The peers and Privy Councillors, majestic in their state robes, came next. Finally, George himself appeared. He walked slowly beneath a cloth-of-gold canopy. Behind him, pages supported a 27 ft long train of crimson velvet decorated with gold stars.

One person, however, was missing from her place in the abbey – George's wife, Caroline of Brunswick. No invitation had been sent to the rightful Queen of England. Early on Corona-tion Day she went to each of the abbey doors in turn and demanded admittance. But she was turned away by the ushers as the mob shouted 'Shame!' and 'Off! Off!'

Such was the end of a tragedy which had come close to shaking the throne of England to its foundations. George and Caroline had been estranged for years – almost since their first meeting in 1795.

On that occasion, George, then Prince of Wales, turned to his companion, Lord Malmesbury, and audibly whispered: 'I am not well, pray get me a glass of brandy.' He had been persuaded to marry her only as part of a bargain for Parliament to pay off his debts.

Scandal in Italy

Since 1814 Caroline had been living in Italy. While his father had lived, George was content with such a separation. But when he became king he determined to prevent Caroline from returning to England as queen. In February 1820 he laid papers before his cabinet relating to the adulterous conduct of his wife, and demanded a divorce. According to his charges, Caroline had been living in Milan 'in a most unbecoming and disgusting intimacy' with Bartolemo Bergami, an Italian of low birth whom she had made her Chamberlain.

George's own reputation, however, did not bear close examination. His mistresses had been many – and his people knew it. And so the cabinet, while agreeing to omit Caroline's name from the royal prayers in the prayer book, refused to agree to the king's demand for a divorce. For four months, George fumed against his ministers.

It was Caroline herself who forced the issue. Beside herself with anger at George's attempts to deny her legal rights, she landed at Dover on June 5, 1820. She meant, she said, to secure those rights or blow her husband off his throne.

Caroline swiftly proceeded to London, where the mob gave her a tumultuous welcome. They believed her to be a wronged woman – and it was their duty as Englishmen to protect her.

The government made a last offer to Caroline – a life annuity, on condition that she stayed out of England. This she rejected, and on July 5 the cabinet reluctantly introduced a Bill of Pains and Penalties in the House of Lords, depriving Caroline of her crown and dissolving her marriage.

In the House of Lords the debates were long, the details fascinating. An Italian fisherman testified that Caroline and Bergami had kissed in his boat. There were tales of meetings in secret grottoes, noises behind locked doors and hints of an illegitimate child.

But the defence proved that Hanoverian

284

George IV: A prince who lost his charm

George IV was one of the most controversial kings in British history. When he died in 1830, *The Times* wrote that 'there was never an individual less regretted by his fellow creatures than this deceased king'.

Yet, in his early years, George had been a handsome and witty prince, who had been idolised by society. He knew more about the arts than any prince in Europe. He was such an excellent mimic that his friend George 'Beau' Brummell declared that he could have been the finest comic actor in Europe.

Above all, George was a connoisseur of paintings and a generous patron of architecture. He did much to give his country objects and buildings of great beauty. The splendid pavilion at Brighton, with its domes, minarets and 'Chinese' furniture, was a permanent contribution to English life. And George persuaded the government to pay £300,000 for the Angerstein Collection of Dutch paintings, which was to become the nucleus of the National Gallery.

Corrupt and extravagant

But George was also the victim of a taste for self-indulgence. At the early age of 52 the once-slim Prince Charming had turned into a 'voluptuary' whose backside was one of the sights of society.

By the time George came to exercise political power, his character had been warped by the company of rakes. Moreover, George's extravagance did much to turn his people against him. At one time his debts amounted to as much as £600,000 – squandered, so his subjects believed, on drink, gambling and women. Leigh Hunt, a radical poet, described him as 'a man who has just closed half a century without one single claim on the gratitude of his country'.

George disliked ridicule more than anything else, and Hunt was imprisoned for two years for seditious libel. But such attacks swelled, and soon after he became king in 1820 George withdrew into isolation. He was now a sick man, troubled by insomnia and sapped of energy by the large doses of laudanum he took with cherry brandy for his gout.

Refuge in fantasy

George's last years were spent almost totally at Windsor. The rapidly ageing king was now filled with tortured longings for what he might have been, and what he might have done. He convinced himself that he had commanded a division at Waterloo and won the Goodwood Cup on his own horse. But at least he could meet his death with bravery. In the early hours of June 26, 1830, he awoke his page, Thomas Bachelor, with the cry: 'Good God, what is this?' Clutching Bachelor's hand, George continued: 'My boy, this is death.'

---

diplomats had bribed some of the Italian witnesses. Moreover, Caroline's English servants told a different story. Lady Charlotte Lindsay had observed no improprieties in the queen's conduct.

From triumph to humiliation

In November the bill was passed by nine votes. But this was too small a majority to take it to the House of Commons and the government abandoned it. They also played their trump card – they dissolved Parliament. By January, when it met again, support for the queen had died down, especially when it became known that she had accepted an annuity of £50,000 from the government. Her appearance at the coronation was her last throw. In August she died, according to her supporters, of a broken heart, but according to her doctors, of an overdose of magnesia.

Caroline was the most unlikely symbol for a popular revolution. She was fat, unwashed and given to barrack-room language. In Italy she had gone about in a mother-of-pearl carriage supposed to look like a sea-shell, wearing large pink feathers in her hat, a low-cut pink bodice and a short white skirt, revealing her short fat legs. But for a few months her cause became the outlet for all the ills of an England ruled by a reactionary king.

VICTIM OF THE SATIRISTS

Contemporary satirists had a field day with the luckless George IV. His size, his extravagance and his infidelity made him a constant butt for cartoonists such as George Cruikshank and James Gillray. The king hated their caricatures, which he referred to as 'licentious abominations'. And from 1819 to 1822 more than £2600 of taxpayers' money was paid out to cartoonists in a vain attempt to stop them ridiculing their king.

A reflection published during the divorce crisis argues that the royal couple were as bad as each other – 'Kettle abusing the pot'.

James Gillray's view of the king – 'A voluptuary under the horrors of digestion' – was one of many cartoons mocking George for his excesses.

A WORLD OF BEAUTY – THE VISION OF THREE POETS

Keats, Byron and Shelley, three of England's greatest Romantic poets, all died young. And all three lived and wrote as if they had some premonition of the tragic shortness of their lives. They were desperately aware of the need to cram a lifetime's experience into the years of youth.

Keats died in Rome, from tuberculosis, at the age of 25. Shelley drowned the next year, aged 30, while sailing off the Italian coast; and Byron was 36 when he died of fever, playing a leading role in the Greek struggle against the Turks.

'Mad, bad and dangerous to know,' Lady Caroline Lamb wrote in her diary, after her first meeting with George Gordon Noel, the 6th Lord Byron.

When the first two instalments of 'Childe Harold's Pilgrimage' appeared in 1812, Byron became the most notorious, most desirable guest in any fashionable drawing-room. His dark good looks coupled with the hints he let drop of strange doings in his past, made him irresistible to society women.

In 1815, partly to extricate himself from a tedious affair with Lady Caroline Lamb, and partly to solve his financial problems, he married Anna Isabella Milbanke, the spoilt and priggish daughter of a coal-owning squire. The marriage was a disaster. Byron awoke on his wedding night exclaiming: 'Good God, I am surely in hell.' Anna Isabella left him the next year after the birth of their daughter.

There was only one woman throughout his life whom Byron really loved: his half-sister Augusta Leigh. She laughed at him, coaxed him out of his black humours – and returned his love. In 1816, when the scandal of their affair broke in London, Byron was forced to leave the country. He lived the rest of his life trailing what he called his 'Pageant of a bleeding heart' through Europe.

Byron in exile became England's best-known poet, but towards the end of his life a note of world-weariness crept into his writing.

To his fellow poet Tom Moore, his former drinking companion, he bade farewell:

> So we'll go no more a roving
> So late into the night,
> Though the heart be still as loving,
> And the moon be still as bright.
>
> For the sword outwears its sheath,
> And the soul wears out the breast,
> And the heart must pause to breathe,
> And love itself have rest.

The end came suddenly. Byron was almost shipwrecked as he sailed to Greece to help in the struggle for independence against Turkey. He caught fever in the small swamp village of Missolonghi, and died four months later.

Two years before, Byron had been present at the scene of Shelley's death. When Percy Bysshe Shelley's body was washed ashore in the Bay of Lerici, in Italy, it was Byron who arranged the pagan funeral cremation.

POET'S PYRE *After he was drowned, Shelley was cremated on the beach watched by his friends, including Lord Byron (in white scarf). One of them snatched the poet's heart from the pyre.*

ROMANTIC EXILES *Shelley, Keats and Byron.*

The two poets had been close friends. Shelley had been forced to leave England in the same year as Byron, after the uproar caused when he declared himself an atheist and believer in free love. He eloped with Mary Godwin, author of *Frankenstein*, the world-famous horror story. His first wife, Harriet, drowned herself shortly afterwards.

From his earliest attempts at writing, Shelley had dreamt of reforming the world. But his real gift was for lyric poetry. In his years of exile, he wrote some of the most haunting songs in the English language, capturing with heart-rending poignancy what he saw as the fundamental human dilemma:

> We look before and after,
> And pine for what is not:
> Our sincerest laughter
> With some pain is fraught;
> Our sweetest songs are those that
>   tell of saddest thought.

Shelley drowned with a copy of the poems Keats published in 1820 in his jacket pocket – the poems that were to bring Keats the recognition he had craved all his life. But fame came too late. He was already dying when the poems were published.

John Keats's father was a Finsbury innkeeper. Both his parents died while he was still young, and he was apprenticed to a surgeon. But he confessed: 'I find I cannot exist without Poetry – half the day will not do.'

Keats gave up medicine, and moved to Hampstead, where he fell in love with his 17-year-old neighbour, Fanny Brawne. Their relationship was at once a torment and a delight. Fanny loved parties and company; Keats was poor, jealous and possessive. Nevertheless, during 1818 and 1819, the years of his infatuation with Fanny, he wrote almost all his greatest poetry.

In 1818 Keats nursed his younger brother until his death from tuberculosis, and contracted the disease himself. Racked by coughing, desperately poor, and with his poetry as yet largely ignored, Keats knew there was no hope of his surviving the English winter of 1820. With grim foreboding he wrote:

> When I have fears that I may cease to be
> Before my pen has glean'd my teeming
>   brain,
> Before high-piled books in charactery
> Hold like rich garners the full ripen'd grain.

But already he had written enough to assure him the place he craved 'among the English poets after my death'.

Keats's friends and publisher clubbed together to send him to spend the winter in Italy with the painter Joseph Severn. After a storm-racked and painful sea journey they reached Rome, and took lodgings in the Piazza di Spagna. There, far from home and all he loved, full of self-doubt, jealousy and bitterness, Keats passed his last few months.

MEN OF SCIENCE PURSUE THE MYSTERY OF ELECTRICITY

EXPERIMENTAL GENIUS *Michael Faraday, son of a blacksmith, pictured in his laboratory in the Royal Institution where he experimented with electromagnetism, giving the world the electric motor and the dynamo. His start in science was as laboratory assistant to Sir Humphry Davy.*

Few men made a greater impact on 19th-century science than Humphry Davy and Michael Faraday. As well as being prolific inventors, both were gifted lecturers and were able to kindle an enthusiasm for science in the minds of ordinary people.

Davy was the eldest of a large Cornish family and became fascinated by science when apprenticed to a Penzance surgeon. He became his own guinea pig. On one occasion he had to be revived by friends after inhaling nitrous oxide (laughing gas).

In 1801, at the age of 23, he was appointed assistant lecturer in chemistry at the newly founded Royal Institution in London, which provided working and lecturing facilities for scientists. He used voltaic cells (the first batteries) to discover and isolate the elements sodium, potassium, boron, calcium, magnesium, barium and strontium. Davy's studies of the explosive qualities of fire damp mixed with air led to his invention of the safety lamp. This was to save the lives of thousands of miners.

One of those who listened to his lectures at the Royal Institution was a bookseller's apprentice, Michael Faraday. In 1812 the 21-year-old Faraday applied to the great scientist for a post in the institution, and Davy made him his personal assistant. Around 1820 he turned to physics, concentrating on the newly discovered phenomenon of electromagnetism.

European scientists had discovered that an electric current would cause a pivoted magnetic needle to move. Faraday and Davy attempted to reverse the process. They failed. But Faraday continued with his tests.

On Christmas Day, 1821, the breakthrough came. Mrs Faraday, busy with the dinner, heard her name called. Rushing to the laboratory, she found her husband staring at a bar magnet standing in a bowl of mercury. A wire suspended above it was rotating around the magnet in response to an electric current. It was the prototype of all electric motors.

The principles of electricity

In a dazzling succession of linked discoveries, Faraday now proceeded to evolve the principles of the form of energy which in a few generations was to transform life on earth, providing heat, light and power for a multitude of purposes.

In the openness of his nature, the great scientist shared these findings with a wide audience. His Friday evening lectures inspired a whole generation.

Faraday achieved these later triumphs without the aid of his master and friend, Davy. The two men had quarrelled in the 1820's after Faraday published the results of his electromagnetic experiments without acknowledging Davy's efforts. But their joint achievements had laid the foundations for the partnership between science and industry; and it was this partnership which made Britain the leading industrial power of the 19th century.

Stephenson triumphs–and the railway age begins

HERALD OF THE RAILWAY AGE
George Stephenson's Rocket *launched a transport revolution when it made its first journey in 1829. Yet so quick was the pace of technical change it sparked off that it ran for less than ten years. In 1862 it was given to London's Science Museum. The steam breakthrough was said to have raised train speeds from 'those of a carthorse to more than those of the fastest racehorse'.*

LINE TO SUCCESS *The* Fury *on the Liverpool and Manchester Railway, the world's first successful commercial line. But its opening in 1830 was marred by tragedy. The politician William Huskisson was run down by a train and killed – the world's first railway casualty.*

A revolution that was to change the face of the world began in a field at Rainhill, just outside Liverpool, on an October day in 1829. Several thousand people had gathered to watch the trials the directors of the Liverpool and Manchester Railway were holding for a locomotive to be used on their new line. They had offered a prize of £500 for an engine that could meet the testing standards they had laid down – to pull 20 tons at a speed of not less than 10 mph.

The scene at Rainhill was like a race meeting. Bets were being laid and there was a special stand for the 'beauty and fashion' of the area. All the spectators were impatiently waiting for the contest to begin.

Resistance to the competition had lasted almost up to the last minute. Old-fashioned pessimists still advocated horsedrawn trains. Inventors were toying with madcap schemes for driving trains by hydrogen gas or carbonic acid. The engineering establishment argued that stationary steam engines hauling trains by ropes were both cheaper and safer. One engineer, Nicholas Wood, stated categorically that 'no locomotive can travel more than eight miles an hour'.

But the designer of the line, George Stephenson, argued that improvements in locomotive design had met these objections. He persuaded his reluctant directors to hold the competition. But Stephenson was not a disinterested party. He had already decided to try to win the prize for himself.

Building the 'Rocket'
At his Newcastle works, Stephenson built a revolutionary new steam engine and named it the *Rocket*. After tests on the Killingworth Colliery Railway, near Newcastle, the engine was dismantled and sent to Liverpool by sea.

Compared to the cumbersome machines in use on the Stockton and Darlington Railway, the *Rocket* was a streamlined masterpiece. Its most revolutionary feature, invisible to the casual spectator, was its boiler.

Earlier boilers had simply been large tanks of water. But the *Rocket's* consisted of 25 narrow copper tubes around which flames from the fire-box passed freely. The effect was a dramatic increase in the quantity of steam produced and thus in the power of the engine. At first, difficulties were experienced in preventing leaks in the boiler tubes. But in September, only a month before the all-important trials, George Stephenson's son and partner, Robert, announced that 'the engine is capable of doing as much, if not more, than set forth in the stipulations'.

The trials began on October 6, 1829. There were five entries, each of which had to make 20 trips up and down a flat stretch of line about 2 miles long. One entry, the *Cycloped*, was disqualified at the start, when it was discovered to consist of a horse in a frame. Of the others, the *Sans Pareil* was a copy of one of Stephenson's earlier designs and the *Perseverance* could manage only 5 mph. The only serious challenge came from the strange-looking *Novelty*, with its vertical boiler. It reached 28 mph, but it could not pull heavy trucks and frequently broke down.

GEORGE STEPHENSON *A fireman's son with little formal education, he created the railway age.*

The *Rocket* was tested at 8 a.m. on October 8. Tension increased in the crowd, for it took 57 minutes after the boiler fire was lit to raise a head of steam. But then the engine ran for 35 miles at an average speed of 15 mph.

The crowd was stunned by a performance beyond their wildest expectations. They were even more amazed when, running on its own, without carriages or trucks, the *Rocket* reached the undreamt of speed of 35 mph.

A new iron age
The Stephensons had triumphed; the argument of fixed engines versus locomotives had finally been settled. James Cropper, formerly a fervent advocate of the fixed-engine principle, threw up his hands and exclaimed: 'Now has George Stephenson at last delivered himself.'

At the end of the day, the crowds who had gathered that morning at Rainhill made their way home. They were smoke-grimed, excited and slightly incredulous. They had witnessed the first day in a new age of transportation. As one commentator wrote: 'The experiments have established principles which will give a greater impulse to civilisation than it has ever received from any single cause.'

For the next 16 years, until his retirement, Stephenson devoted himself to developing the railway age. There was hardly a scheme in which he was not consulted or an important line built without his help and advice. When he died in 1848, he had seen his country transformed by the locomotive that he had helped to create. Stephenson had won himself a high place in the great line of English inventors.

PIONEERS OF STEAM
The success of George Stephenson's *Rocket* on the Liverpool and Manchester Railway was the climax to over 20 years of hard work on the challenge of steam locomotion. Railways had been pioneered by the mining industry, which needed to transport coal and iron ore in bulk. In 1804, Richard Trevithick, a Cornish mining engineer, produced the first steam engine designed to run on rails. It hauled 10 tons of iron ore and 70 men along a colliery track in Wales at a speed of almost 5 mph. Trevithick and other pioneers improved this early invention, but it was George Stephenson who made the decisive breakthrough. In 1825 his experiments at Northumbrian mines were crowned by the opening of the 27 mile Stockton and Darlington Railway, where coal was carried partly by horse and partly by steam power. He went on to become the official engineer of the Liverpool and Manchester line. From these achievements sprang the railway age.

Richard Trevithick's engine Catch-me-who-can *running on its circular track at Euston in 1809. Crowds came to see it from all over London. He charged passengers 1s a ride.*

Iron rails transform the face of Britain

With the opening of the line linking Liverpool and Manchester on September 15, 1830, the railway age began in earnest. This was the first line to rely entirely on steam locomotives and to carry a high proportion of passenger traffic. Success was instantaneous. After this, there was no stopping the advance of the iron road.

Soon, armies of navvies were employed building railways. At the peak, in 1847, there were 250,000 of them at work all across the country. Their equipment was primitive. 'Spoil' (soil) was moved in small barrows; the great cuttings and embankments were literally created with pick and shovel. The navvies themselves were frequently undisciplined. They lived in squalid hutment townships and spread terror to the surrounding villages on pay nights.

But despite these handicaps, the results were astonishing. In the 15 years after the Liverpool and Manchester line was completed, there followed the London and Birmingham, the London and Southampton, the Grand Junction, the Great Western and many smaller lines. Railways brought travel to the lives of millions – particularly after third-class fares were fixed at 1d a mile in 1844. In stagecoach days, the return fare from Manchester to London was £3 10s. In 1851 the railways offered a special cheap ticket at 5s.

The impact of the railways changed the face of Britain. But their impact on ordinary people was even greater. Towns and villages, which had remained little changed since the days of the Middle Ages, were awakened into a new age by the coming of steam.

THE RAILWAY AGE
Railway companies mushroomed after the success of the Liverpool and Manchester Railway. But much railway development was haphazard. Even the Great Western (insignia below right), which was formed in 1835 to build a line from London to Bristol, went its own way by refusing to adopt Stephenson's standard gauge for its tracks. And many smaller companies ran uncoordinated lines.

It was not until 1921 that Parliament resolved the situation by authorising 120 companies to be merged into four. The London Midland and Scottish (insignia below left) was the largest of the merged companies.

TO ENGINEERS AND IRON FOUNDERS.
THE DIRECTORS of the LIVERPOOL and MAN-CHESTER RAILWAY hereby offer a Premium of £500 (over and above the cost price) for a **LOCOMOTIVE ENGINE**, which shall be a decided improvement on any hitherto constructed, subject to certain stipulations and conditions, a copy of which may be had at the Railway Office, or will be forwarded, as may be directed, on application for the same, if by letter, post paid.
HENRY BOOTH, Treasurer.
Railway Office, Liverpool, April 25, 1829.

BIRTH OF THE 'ROCKET' *This advertisement by the Liverpool and Manchester Railway was the chance George Stephenson had been waiting for to prove his theories. His* Rocket, *with its revolutionary boiler design, proved far superior to its four rivals during trials at Rainhill in 1829. The engine was the basis from which all future locomotive designs followed.*

Reform or revolution? Britain makes its choice

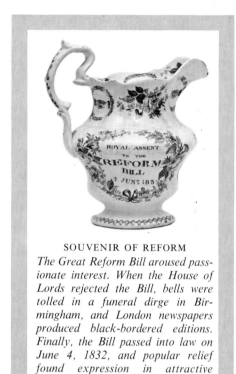

SOUVENIR OF REFORM
The Great Reform Bill aroused passionate interest. When the House of Lords rejected the Bill, bells were tolled in a funeral dirge in Birmingham, and London newspapers produced black-bordered editions. Finally, the Bill passed into law on June 4, 1832, and popular relief found expression in attractive souvenirs, such as this Swansea-ware jug. Similar pieces are on view at the Glynn Vivian Art Gallery, Swansea.

In 1832 it seemed to many Englishmen that their country stood on the brink of revolution. Only two years before, the King of France had been overthrown. Could the same thing now happen in England?

Since the end of the Napoleonic wars against France 17 years earlier, England had been ruled by diehard Tories, who feared all change and were determined to keep things as they had been in the peaceful days of the 18th century. The power of these men – aristocrat, squire and parson – was based firmly on wealth from land. But the Industrial Revolution was rapidly sweeping this England away. And the pressures that resulted meant that political change could be resisted only at the government's peril.

The question of reforming Parliament had been debated for the previous 60 years. In the General Election of 1830 it became the key issue. Though the Tories managed to hold on to office for a few weeks, they were soon voted out. The Whigs came in, determined to carry through reform. Their Bill, which was to transform parliamentary government in Britain, was introduced into the House of Commons by the Paymaster-General, Lord John Russell, on the evening of March 1, 1831.

Russell declared that 56 'rotten' boroughs – seats such as Bossinney in Cornwall where the two members were elected by one voter – would be disfranchised. A further 30 would lose one of their two members. The seats gained would be given to the new towns.

As the names rolled from Russell's lips, most members looked stunned. Some grew purple with rage and a few just laughed at the absurdity of it all. To them, it seemed that Russell and the government had gone mad. But ardent reformers were delighted.

On the verge of revolution

At first, it seemed that the Bill would soon be passed. On March 23 its second reading was carried by one vote. But a ferocious struggle was to follow as the Tories fought to defeat the measure. In vain, the Whig politician Macaulay appealed to them to: 'Save property, divided against itself. Save the multitude, endangered by their ungovernable passions. Save the aristocracy, endangered by its own unpopular power. The danger is terrible. The time is short.' In April the government was defeated in committee. William IV dissolved Parliament and a General Election was called. The Whigs were returned with a majority of 130. They introduced a second Bill which passed the Commons in September 1831. But after five days of debate the Lords rejected it.

The details of the Bill were now the obsession of millions. At once, rioting broke out. The Tory leaders were soon in danger. Mobs attacked the Duke of Wellington's London home, Apsley House. In Bristol the Mansion House, the gaol, the customs house and the Bishop's Palace were destroyed by rioters and their contents looted. The bishop's champagne, claret and port were taken from his cellars and sold on College Green for 1d a bottle.

In this hour of peril, the government persevered and introduced yet another Bill in December. Again it passed through the House of Commons – but on May 7, 1832, in a last-ditch stand, the Lords wrecked it with a series of drastic amendments.

Now the decision between reform and revolution lay with one man – William IV. The Prime Minister, Lord Grey, asked the king to create enough peers to ensure the passage of the Bill. William IV refused, Grey resigned and the king begged the Duke of Wellington to form a government.

Armed resistance was planned if a Tory government looked like succeeding. And there were other ways of making things impossible for them. A leading agitator, Francis Place,

REFORMED PARLIAMENT *A painting of the first meeting of the reformed House of Commons in 1833. The Whig government benches are on the left. The Prime Minister, Lord Grey, stands third from the left. His adversary, Wellington, stands third from the right.*

launched the slogan – 'To stop the Duke, Go for Gold' – and people rushed to change their banknotes into sovereigns, threatening the national economy.

The triumph of reform

Wellington believed that his duty was, above all, to the king. He was prepared to pass a Reform Bill of his own to stave off revolution. But his supporters refused to follow him, and within a week Grey was back in office.

Grey called upon the king to give him a pledge that the Bill would be passed 'unimpaired in its principles and its essential provisions'. The king finally agreed to create Whig peers and the threat brought the House of Lords to heel. On June 4, the Great Reform Bill passed into law.

Few of those who had cried for 'the Bill, the whole Bill and nothing but the Bill' became voters when the measure was passed. In the new manufacturing towns, most of the seats were filled by the new industrialists – men who were, in fact, less sympathetic to the workers than the landed squires they replaced in Parliament. In 1831 there were about 300,000 voters. Russell's proposals increased the number to 500,000 – about 4 per cent of the population. Yet the flood-gates of change had been opened. Britain had taken a decisive step along the road to democracy.

William IV: A sailor sets a safe course

William IV, the third son of George III, was not expected to become king and so was not educated for monarchy. At the age of 13 he was sent to sea and there he acquired a nautical directness and a taste for strong language that he never lost. His chief characteristic was a blunt tactlessness which earned him the nickname 'Silly Billy'.

It was not until the Duke of York died in 1827 that William became heir to his eldest brother's throne. Yet he turned out to be a conscientious sovereign. Despite his age – he was 64 in 1830 – he was in robust fettle, and could scarcely contain his glee at becoming king. For months he had been practising his royal signature – 'William R'. There were 48,000 papers to deal with and he would work far into the night, with a basin of warm water to bathe his fingers. His delight was summed up in his stage whisper – 'Who is Silly Billy now?' – as the Privy Council gravely lined up to kneel before their new monarch.

William ruled England at the beginning of a hectic period in English history – and one which might have seen revolution. But, by consenting to a dissolution of Parliament in 1831 and agreeing to create Whig peers if necessary to pass the Reform Bill in 1832, William behaved, as his Prime Minister, Lord Grey, said, 'like an angel'. And his common sense helped to raise the public prestige of the monarchy from the depths of scandal to which his brother, George IV, had brought it.

NEW BROOM *William IV was popularly welcomed as a sober contrast to the indulgent George IV. He is shown here as an exciseman, eager to clear the decks for a fresh start.*

FROM HUSTINGS TO POLLING BOX

The Great Reform Bill of 1832 was only a first step in Britain's long road to full democracy. Though Parliament itself had been reformed, the conditions under which its members were elected remained the same as in the 18th century. Votes were still cast in public on the hustings, and this inevitably encouraged open bribery and corruption. Candidates spent vast sums of money purchasing votes, particularly in small constituencies. Voters could sell their votes for a fixed price, or to the highest bidder. The novelist Charles Dickens captured such a scene in the 'Eatanswill' election in *The Pickwick Papers*.

At Ilchester in 1802 the price for each of the 60 voters was £30. Alternatively, the candidates 'treated' the electors, plying them with food, drink and entertainment in an attempt to win promises of support. The cost of such an election could be astronomical. In 1807 the three candidates fighting the Yorkshire seat spent almost £500,000 between them on their campaigns.

The other evil of public voting was that it opened the way for intimidation of the voters. A powerful landlord could easily browbeat his tenants into voting for the candidate of his choice. Any tenant who refused to do so risked eviction. This fate befell 100 voters in Cardiganshire after one election.

Some British politicians felt that there was nothing wrong with this state of affairs. The Whig politician, Lord Palmerston, remarked that 'to go sneaking to the ballot box is unworthy of the character of a straightforward and honest Englishman'. But most Parliamentary reformers knew that while voting was not secret, real democracy was impossible. They pressed for the introduction of the secret ballot. Two Bills to introduce it were defeated in 1870 and 1871, but the following year it became law. Britain had taken another step towards democracy.

One of the earliest by-elections to be held under the terms of the Ballot Act, which passed into law in 1872, was at Taunton in October 1873. These contemporary prints show a working man casting his vote by secret ballot, and policemen carrying off the sealed ballot boxes to the final count (right).

A NEW ART DEDICATED TO THE WORSHIP OF NATURE

In the years that followed the French Revolution, another revolutionary force swept through Europe, profoundly affecting the works of man in poetry and art. This great new inspiration, known as Romanticism, drew its strength in Britain from the beauty of the countryside. In literature its prophets were the poets Wordsworth and Coleridge. In art, the Romantic movement found expression in the paintings of two of the world's finest landscape artists, John Constable and Joseph Turner.

Turner was born in 1775 and Constable a year later, and both devoted their lives to the task of capturing nature in paint. Yet the two men saw nature quite differently. Turner yearned for drama, emotion and passion in nature. He loved craggy mountains, thundering waterfalls, raging seas and storms. Constable, on the other hand, experienced nature simply and submissively. He loved tranquil summer scenes with a breeze fluttering the leaves and sending ripples across sparkling water. He wrote: 'The landscape painter must walk the fields with a humble mind.'

A struggle for recognition

Constable was a countryman, the son of a prosperous Suffolk miller, who sent him to London to the Royal Academy School. By the time he was aged 27 he realised that his talents lay exclusively in landscape painting. Although this form of art was then unfashionable, he spent most of his time in the countryside, his pockets filled with sketchbooks. He wrote: 'The sound of water escaping from mill dams, willows, old rotten planks, slimy posts and brickwork, I love such things ... these scenes made me a painter and I am grateful.'

For years he could sell little of his work in Britain. His first recognition came from France. In 1824 his eldest son was dying and his wife was suffering from tuberculosis. Constable himself was 48 and ill from worry over expenses. To raise money, he decided to sacrifice his masterpiece, 'The Hay Wain', to a French dealer who had offered him £125 for it.

PRELIMINARY WORK *This was Constable's sketch for his 'Leaping Horse'.*

CLOUD EFFECTS *'Seascape Study with Rainclouds' was one of Constable's many studies of the drama of the skies.*

SUMMER IDYLL *Constable's masterpiece 'The Hay Wain', dated 1821, was sold to a French dealer for £125.*

VISION OF LIGHT *Turner painted this view of Petworth Park, Sussex, in his last years when he had become obsessed by the desire to depict the beauty of light in his work.*

VIOLENT SEAS *Turner was fascinated by the drama of nature. He found beauty in violence in his 'Shipwreck'.*

Later that year, the dealer exhibited the picture at the Paris Salon and it became famous overnight. The French king, Charles X, awarded Constable a gold medal and tried to buy the picture for the nation. But the dealer had already sold it to a private collector for £834.

But even this success did nothing for Constable's reputation in England. In France, the great painter Delacroix said that Constable was 'pursuing nature, while we are merely occupied in imitating pictures'. Constable, too, was conscious that he was breaking new ground. He wrote: 'When I sit down to make a sketch from nature, the first thing I try to do is to forget that I have ever seen a picture.'

It was precisely this break with convention that made it so difficult for Constable to win recognition. Year after year, his pictures were ridiculed at the Royal Academy's annual exhibition, and it took him ten years to win admission to its ranks.

But Constable was not a man to become embittered. He drew consolation from his love for his wife, his unswerving passion for the countryside and his simple fidelity to the things he thought important. He wrote: 'I never saw anything ugly in my life.'

Inspired by light and drama

Unlike Constable, Joseph Mallord William Turner, the son of a London barber, was quick to win both fame and fortune. As a child he had been starved of air, space, light and sun, and his life became a constant quest for all these things. For more than 60 years he lived almost all the daylight hours with either a pencil or a brush in his hand. He produced 25,000 oil paintings, watercolours, etchings and drawings in his lifetime. He never married.

At the age of 11, Turner left his father's cramped shop to go to the Soho Academy, where he received drawing lessons. It was not easy for a poor boy to gain the necessary training. One of his teachers gave him up as hopeless. 'Better make him a tinker or a cobbler,' his father was told. 'He will never make an artist.' But Turner possessed a single-minded ambition. It was this, and his father's sacrifices, that took him to the Royal Academy School and then to the studio of Sir Joshua

NEW IMAGES IN ART *In his 'Rain, Steam and Speed', Turner pictured the new age of transport that was transforming the English landscape. Ignoring his critics he developed a revolutionary impressionistic technique that was to inspire later generations of 19th-century artists.*

Reynolds. In 1802, at the age of 27, Turner was already exhibiting at the Royal Academy.

Contemporaries described Turner as blunt to the point of rudeness, careless in dress and, with his pronounced nose, far from good looking. But his intensity carried all before him. A friend wrote of him: 'His temperament was full of audacity, self-centred, self-reliant, eager for success . . . no man ever loved fame and money more than he did, and no man condescended less to opinion.'

Both artists were fascinated by the effects of the sky. For Constable, landscaping clouds was the ultimate expression of sentiment. For Turner, they had a symbolic meaning. Constable wrote of him: 'He seems to paint with tinted steam, so evanescent, so airy.' After his first visit to Italy his paintings achieved even greater lightness and brilliance.

Up to the age of 40, Turner enjoyed continuous success and recognition. But then he decided to paint only what suited him. He was

determined to push beyond the accepted frontiers in search of the mystery of light. In his dedicated pursuit he moved beyond the understanding of his contemporaries.

Paintings such as the masterpiece 'Rain, Steam and Speed' were dismissed as 'Mr Turner's little jokes'. A critic commented on another picture: 'It looks as if he has been throwing eggs at the canvas.' But by now Turner was painting for himself alone – and for the future. The radiant canvases found in his studio when he died aged 76 became the inspiration for later generations.

Rooted as they were in their absolute fidelity to the countryside, the two great landscape artists had moved into another world. In their struggle to reproduce such things as the glimmer of light through mist, the hint of rain in a spring sky, the dance of leaves stirred by a breeze or the reflections in a rippling stream, they anticipated the school of Impressionists who were to transform the art of the world.

The decades of triumphant change

Victoria's long reign sees Britain transformed – from a land of farmers and small shopkeepers to an industrial giant dominating the world and ruling over a vast empire

Queen Victoria's reign lasted 64 years, the longest in British history. When she came to the throne in 1837, she was an 18-year-old girl. By the time she died in 1901 she had made her impact felt on every part of British life. Between her coronation (pp. 298–9) and her death, she saw Britain change beyond recognition. She saw the country linked by railways; she saw electric trams and even the first motor-cars. She saw sail give way to steam at sea. She was, said her last Prime Minister, Lord Salisbury, 'the bridge over that great interval which separates old England from new England'.

Her reign saw the British Empire extended to the far corners of the globe. Industry sprawled its smoky cities over Britain and the population trebled. Modern politics were born. Religion came under attack. And the worship of progress became almost a new creed.

Queen Victoria reigned; she did not rule. But she made her preferences for one Prime Minister over another very clear. She deeply admired Lord Melbourne and Benjamin Disraeli, but could barely tolerate William Gladstone. She made no secret of her feelings in her voluminous private diaries. Power, however, had passed firmly from the crown into the hands of the politicians – and the people.

Victoria's influence on her people was direct. In her simplicity and honesty of manner and in her devotion to her husband, Prince Albert, and their nine children, she set the tone for the nation. Her concept of her 'duty'

THE GRANDMOTHER OF EUROPE

By the time of her Golden Jubilee in 1887, Queen Victoria had mellowed from the naïve young girl who had come to the throne in 1837 into the dominant figure among Europe's monarchs. Amongst the family group in this

painting with the 68-year-old Victoria (1) are her eldest son, the Prince of Wales later Edward VII (2), his wife, Princess Alexandra of Denmark (3) and the queen's eldest daughter, Victoria (4), who had married Crown Prince Frederick of Prussia in 1858 and was Empress of Germany for 99 days in 1888. Two granddaughters who became queens are also shown. Princess Maud (5), youngest daughter of Edward VII, married King Haakon of Norway in 1896. Alix (6), daughter of Princess Alice, married Nicholas II, the last Tsar of Russia, in 1894. Also Sophie, one of Princess Victoria's daughters, married King Constantine of Greece in 1889. Queen Victoria's direct descendants also ruled Sweden, Spain and Romania.

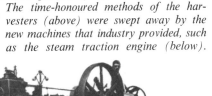

REVOLUTION IN THE FIELDS *In the 64 years of Victoria's reign, a revolution transformed the traditional pattern of agriculture in Britain. The time-honoured methods of the harvesters (above) were swept away by the new machines that industry provided, such as the steam traction engine (below).*

IN THE CITIES *The bustling prosperity of Victorian life was reflected in the great cities of Britain. The demands of a growing population meant that old-fashioned traders (above) soon found themselves outclassed by modern shops (below). These provided cheap food from all over the world for the teeming millions of Victorian Britain. But agriculture at home declined in the face of this competition.*

never faltered. It was a concept that many Victorians extended to their own lives in an age when moral improvement and social reform were dominant topics. When she died, Archbishop Temple paid her a simple tribute: 'She was a good woman.'

Next to the queen, the chief figures of the Victorian age were the architects of change. These included engineers such as Isambard Kingdom Brunel (pp. 300–1), who built railways and the first great ocean liners. The average family travelled more and were better educated and better read than their ancestors. They were proud of the progress their society was making. The 'penny post' of 1840, the introduction of piped water and gas, the building of the London Underground were all objects of Victorian pride, and helped build confidence in the future. And the Great Exhibition of 1851 (pp. 302–3) was a fitting monument for this certainty. Held in Hyde Park beneath Joseph Paxton's glittering glass frame, it was a British workshop for the world to admire and a temple for the worship of progress.

But there were some who revolted against the material world. The Pre-Raphaelite movement (pp. 304–5), which began in 1848, produced works of art far removed from average Victorian taste. The paintings of Dante Gabriel Rossetti, John Everett Millais and William Holman Hunt evoked the romance of the long-past medieval age. Edward Burne-Jones and William Morris extended the influence into glass and furniture. But the freedom expressed in both the art and the lives of the Pre-Raphaelites scandalised many of Victoria's sober-minded subjects.

Spreading the benefits of civilisation

Such people preferred to admire the heroism of the rank-and-file soldiers of the Crimean War, fought against Russia from 1854 to 1856. Stories of their sufferings, and of the dedication of the war's great heroine, Florence Nightingale – 'the lady with the lamp' – touched and inspired ordinary people. And the Charge of the Light Brigade at the Battle of Balaclava (pp. 306–7) became one of the great stories of British heroism on foreign soil.

The Crimean War was the first to be fully reported in the daily Press by a group of war correspondents led by William Russell of *The Times*. Their reports gave a great boost to the new mass-circulation newspapers which were helping both to inform and to create public opinion.

Most novels, such as Charles Dickens's *Bleak House* and *David Copperfield*, first appeared in serialised form in newspapers or magazines. Dickens (p. 308) intended that his novels should not only entertain but also expose the evils of Victorian society. His vivid pictures of the life of the poor, huddled into airless factories and living in slums, were a direct appeal to the social conscience of the middle classes. At the other end of the literary scale, the romantic and passionate novels of the Brontë sisters (p. 309) were a reaction against the restrictions of middle-class society.

But whatever cruelties and injustices existed at home, Victorians believed that it was their mission to carry British civilisation to the far corners of the world. In India, it was believed that the slow introduction of British culture and standards would lead to the moral improvement of the people. So the outbreak of the Indian Mutiny (pp. 310–11) was a considerable shock to public opinion. But the crushing of the mutiny with the recapture of Cawnpore and the relief of Lucknow re-established confidence. The mutiny, too, ended the rule of the East India Company and substituted that of the crown. But it did more than that. It widened a gulf between rulers and ruled that could never be bridged.

At home, the functions of government grew more complex and there was an outcrop of both civic and national buildings to house them. Massive new town halls graced cities such as Manchester and Leeds. In London a disastrous fire at

Westminster gave the government a chance to create a new building to house Parliament (pp. 312–13). Charles Barry won the competition to build it, but it was not finally completed until after his death. Built in the Gothic style, it was the first palace for modern democracy.

'Wider still and wider'

But the House of Commons, echoing the sentiments of most of its members, still barred atheists, as the radical Charles Bradlaugh found when he tried to take his seat in the 1880's. Many regarded Charles Darwin's *Origin of the Species* (pp. 314–15), published in 1859 and the sensation of the age, as a blasphemy. By suggesting the revolutionary theory that man had developed from lower forms of life, Darwin was flying in the face of established religion and casting doubt on the biblical story of the Creation.

Religion, too, lay behind much of the ardent imperialism of the last decades of Victoria's reign. Christian conscience urged the campaign against slavery and encouraged the exploration of Africa – the 'Dark Continent'. For all his fame as an explorer, David Livingstone (pp. 316–17) considered himself first and foremost a missionary. H. M. Stanley, with whom Livingstone's name is forever linked, was a journalist turned explorer. But he, too, regarded it as his duty to spread the knowledge of civilisation to Africa.

Paradoxically, the age of imperialism coincided with a noticeable change in the Victorian mood. The boom years of prosperity which had produced the Great Exhibition had extended through the 1860's, but by the 1870's there was a feeling of economic uncertainty. Foreign competition seriously threatened Britain's exports for the first time.

But progress at home continued. The Reform Acts of 1867 and 1884 gave most men the right to vote. Trade unions were beginning to gather strength. Primary education became compulsory. All these factors combined to make politicians aware, almost for the first time, of the need to woo the electorate. William Gladstone's exhausting political speaking tour of 1879 was the first modern political campaign. His great rival, the Tory leader Benjamin Disraeli, denounced it as demagogy. But within a decade all politicians were following Gladstone's example.

The symbol of the age

Victorians turned to their queen as the true symbol of the age. Her two jubilees, the Golden Jubilee of 1887 and the Diamond Jubilee of 1897 (pp. 318–19), were displays of unashamed patriotism. They gave a chance to show the world, through the naval reviews at Spithead, that it was Britain's might at sea which had won her an empire.

But this confidence was shattered by the disastrous beginning of the Boer War in South Africa, when a handful of farmers inflicted three heavy defeats on Britain's highly trained regulars in the disastrous 'Black Week' of December 1899. Once again the queen spoke for the nation with the terse statement: 'We are not interested in the possibilities of defeat; they do not exist.' Soon the tide turned in Britain's favour. But the event of the war that brought the greatest enthusiasm was the relief of Mafeking (pp. 320–1).

Late Victorian confidence concealed the symptoms of an unhealthy society. With Germany in the ascendant in Europe, a policy of 'splendid isolation' was becoming unwise and outdated. And, at home, the worst results of over-hasty industrialisation were becoming clear. The Victorians bequeathed to the 20th century an unparalleled heritage of prosperity. But they also left a legacy of social problems which were to hamper their descendants in the changed circumstances of a new world.

NEW LEARNING *Under Victoria, many social reforms were introduced, especially in the field of education. A dame's school (above) was the only form of learning that most people received until the 1871 Education Act set up a state system of education and state schools (below).*

A REVOLUTION IN TRANSPORT *No innovation transformed Victorian Britain more than the rapid development of the railways. The stage-coach (above) was soon made obsolete by the train (below). And legislation to fix cheap fares meant that ordinary people were able to travel widely for the first time in history.*

The day Victoria remembered as the 'proudest of my life'

CROWN FOR A QUEEN

This new Crown of State was made for Victoria to wear towards the end of the Coronation Service – because the traditional St Edward's Crown was too heavy for the slender girl queen. The crown, which can be seen at the Tower of London, has 3000 precious stones, including the great ruby given to the Black Prince and worn by Henry V at the Battle of Agincourt.

One of the first things Victoria did after she became queen in 1837 was to deliver a colossal snub – to her mother. It was an extraordinary thing for an 18-year-old to do, particularly as she had just attended her first Privy Council meeting, and delighted her ministers with her self-assurance and dignity.

'And now, Mamma, am I really and truly queen?' she asked her mother.

'You see, my dear, that it is so.'

'Then, dear Mamma, I hope you will grant me the first request I make to you as queen. Let me be by myself for an hour.'

The snub had its justification.

Victoria's father had died when she was eight months old, and she was brought up by her mother, the Duchess of Kent, an ambitious and prudish woman who made Victoria wear a sprig of holly on her collar to make her sit erect at the table. The duchess disapproved of Victoria's uncle, the bluff William IV, and kept her daughter as much as possible away from his court, occupying frugal rooms in Kensington Palace. The princess was never allowed to be alone. She had to sleep in her mother's room, and her days were carefully arranged so she would always have the company of her governess, Baroness Lehzen, the daughter of a Hanoverian clergyman.

Nevertheless, Victoria loved and trusted this forbidding governess, as she admitted frequently in her diary. But she detested the Comptroller of her mother's household, Sir John Conroy, who had ambitions of carving for himself a career as the power behind the future throne. He had a dominating influence on the duchess – it was said the princess had once surprised him in her mother's arms. Certainly, Victoria disliked him, because, shortly after she became queen, she dismissed him with an annuity and made certain that his relationship with her mother was absolutely broken.

A new queen launches a new age

It was never completely certain that Victoria would inherit the throne. When George IV became king, she was only third in line to the throne, after the Duke of York, who died in 1827, and the Duke of Clarence, who became king as William IV in 1830. But the likelihood was always there.

Her mother and Sir John arranged a series of semi-royal progresses for the princess around the country, meeting county families and civic dignitaries. These tours aroused the fury of the king, particularly the salutes, and at a formal palace dinner he publicly expressed his fear that he might die before his niece came of age, and that a regency would fall into the hands of 'evil advisers'. Victoria was reduced to tears by this declaration, and the duchess made as dignified an exit as she could muster.

The king's fears were justified. When only 16 years old, Victoria caught typhoid fever in Ramsgate. Sir John, abetted by the duchess, tried to persuade her into signing a document which promised him the key position of her secretary when she became queen. Even though she was desperately ill, she found the strength and courage to refuse.

The hard lessons of her early years gave Victoria a mature self-confidence which, added to her youthful freshness and vivacity, made her a natural popular heroine, a perfect focus of the coronation festivities. It seemed to her subjects that she symbolised the dawning of a new era of peace and prosperity, a new spirit after a period of political discord and a succession of uninspiring monarchs.

The manner in which she was first hailed queen became a romantic legend even before she was crowned. William died in the small hours of June 20, 1837, and immediately the Archbishop of Canterbury drove to Kensington Palace.

Victoria donned her dressing-gown when she heard the archbishop had arrived – at 5 a.m. She stood in her night clothes while the elderly cleric knelt before her and broke the news of her uncle's death. 'Since it has pleased Providence,' she wrote in her diary that day, 'to place me in this station, I shall do my utmost to fulfil my duty towards my country.'

Immediately after she became queen, she gave orders that her bed should be removed from the duchess's room, and that her meals should be served with nobody else present. She recorded with pride that she had given audiences to the Archbishop of Canterbury, the Lord Chamberlain and the Prime Minister – 'of course, quite alone'.

At 4 a.m. on the day of her coronation on June 28, 1838, Victoria was woken by the guns of the Royal Horse Artillery thundering a royal salute. She ate only a little breakfast

before she drove to Westminster Abbey, through rapturously cheering crowds. Her reception overwhelmed her.

The procession reached the abbey just after 11.30, but the ceremony was marred by hitches. The Archbishop of Canterbury got muddled, and gave the heavy orb to the new queen at the wrong moment. Then he put the coronation ring on the wrong finger, so that it proved painful and difficult to take off afterwards. And another incident came close to ruining the ceremony. The 82-year-old Lord Rolle overbalanced as he tottered up the stairs to the throne to kiss the royal hand. He fell backwards to the bottom of the steps, but Victoria rose from the throne and went to help the old man back again. It was a gesture that was taken as an indication of the new monarch's sympathy and generosity.

Pomp and pride
At the palace that evening, her Prime Minister, Lord Melbourne, had tears in his eyes when he told her she had carried off the whole occasion quite beautifully.

In public she had acquitted herself as a woman; now, in private, she could be a girl again. She rushed straight up to her private rooms, took off her ceremonial robes and gave her dog, Dash, his evening bath. With evident happiness in her heart, she noted in her diary – underlining her emotions – 'I cannot say how proud I feel to be the Queen of such a Nation. I shall remember this day as the proudest of my life.'

DAY OF SPLENDOUR *One month after her 19th birthday, Victoria was crowned at Westminster Abbey on June 28, 1838 in a service starting just after 11.30 a.m. She receives the Sacrament from the Archbishop of Canterbury (left) and is shown in her coronation robes (above). That evening she said that she had 'the gratifying feeling that her duty had been done' – but that her feet were tired after the long service.*

Victoria: The monarch who vowed 'to be good'

FAMILY GROUP *Victoria and her husband, Albert, the Prince Consort, with (left to right) some of their children – Alfred, Edward, Prince of Wales, Alice, Helena and Victoria.*

The image of Queen Victoria which emerges from history is of a severe old lady dressed in black and with a white-ribboned bonnet – the symbol of an age of austere morality.

But this was far from being the whole story. When she died, she had been in mourning for 40 years for her adored husband, Prince Albert; and, with children and relatives occupying nearly every throne in Europe, her influence was immense. But these facts obscure the real woman.

In her youth she had been a pretty and fun-loving girl who loved to dance, and often lapsed into fits of giggles. Later, she became a devoted mother and doting wife. But she seemed unable throughout her life to manage without the support of a series of strong-willed masculine men. At various times she was popularly called 'Mrs Melbourne', after her elderly Prime Minister at the beginning of her reign, 'Queen Albertine', after her husband, and even Mrs Brown, after John Brown, her Highland servant. Another man whom she came to trust and rely on was the Conservative Prime Minister, Benjamin Disraeli.

But her passionate love for her husband eclipsed all others. She idolised him with an intensity almost cloying: 'I should like to fall at his feet . . . for I feel how unworthy I must be of one so great and perfect as he.'

The 'widow of Windsor'
Albert's death, after 21 years of marriage, devastated Victoria. For the rest of her life she wore widow's weeds, and refused to have his room changed in the smallest detail, except for the fresh flowers she strewed on his bed. Even five years after his death, she excused herself from opening Parliament, because she did not wish to be a 'spectacle of a poor, broken-hearted widow, nervous and shrinking, dragged in deep mourning'.

The strange consolation of her widowhood was John Brown. He was brusque with everyone, and even called the queen 'wumman'. But nobody could communicate with her except through him, and she did not seem to mind when he drank too much whisky.

But she never forgot Albert – the one man who had shared her own naïve resolution 'to be good'. By her wish, she was buried beside him in the mausoleum at Frogmore, in the grounds of Windsor Castle.

FAVOURITE HOME *In the early years of her marriage, Victoria's favourite home was Osborne House on the Isle of Wight. She shared her desk with Albert, who sat on her left and helped her with state business. Bell pushes (near the right-hand table leg) summoned equerries or staff.*

A man of genius builds steamships of iron

REVOLUTIONARY STEAMSHIP
Brunel's Great Britain, *constructed of iron and driven by propeller, revolutionised ocean travel. Abandoned in the Falkland Islands after being caught in a storm off Cape Horn in 1886, she was towed back to Bristol in 1969, exactly 126 years to the day after her launching there.*

Confidence was one of the hallmarks of the Victorian era. Confidence in progress and the ability of Britons to overcome any obstacle. Confidence in Britannia's mastery of the waves.

It took confidence on a massive scale, in the days of wooden-hulled ships, to build an ocean liner of metal and powered by steam. But Isambard Kingdom Brunel, designer of the *Great Britain*, and an outstanding engineer, had a faith in himself that was remarkable even by Victorian standards.

Revolution at sea
The *Great Britain* was the world's first all-metal liner. She had technical innovations which, though they had been experimented with before, were now combined for the first time. Iron hulls were now 20 years old, and screw propellers had been invented by Leonardo da Vinci in the 15th century, but nobody had brought them together before, and, above all, never on such a scale. The *Great Britain*, at 320 ft, was by far the biggest ship ever built, half as big again as the largest warship in the Royal Navy.

When she was launched, Brunel was just 37 years old and at the very height of his powers. He had already established his reputation by building the 110 mile London to Bristol railway for Great Western Railways.

When a critic questioned the wisdom of so long a rail link, he retorted: 'Why not have it longer and have a steamboat to go from Bristol to New York?' It was following up this idea which led Brunel into ship-building, and he started to design his first ship, the *Great Western*. Launched in 1836 with a length of 236 ft, she was already larger than any steam vessel afloat.

Quest for perfection
Brunel was determined to show that it was possible to make the transatlantic crossing by steam alone, which many thought impossible. The *Great Western*, however, made the crossing from Bristol to New York in a record 15 days, and with 200 tons of coal to spare. Before long, the ship was running the first regular steamship service across the Atlantic.

Immediately, Brunel set to work on the design of an even more ambitious ship, the *Great Britain*. In his constant search for perfection, he completely redesigned his original plans after deciding to have a propeller rather than paddles. Then he decided to build·in iron, rather than wood, even though the timber for the ship had already been bought. Once again, he redesigned the ship.

The following year, Queen Victoria visited the *Great Britain* when the ship was anchored in the Thames to be finally fitted out. She marvelled at the luxury of the 64 staterooms, the music rooms, the rich panelling and the 1200 yds of Brussels carpet.

Six months later the *Great Britain* made her maiden voyage to New York, but a year later disaster struck. She was outward bound when a navigational error ran her aground on rocks in Dundrum Bay, Ireland. All the passengers were safely landed, but the ship lay stranded with 10 ft of water in her holds; and there she stayed throughout the winter until she was refloated and repaired. The grounding was a financial disaster for her owners for the esti-

ROYAL LAUNCHING *An engraving of the launching of the* Great Britain, *Brunel's revolutionary iron-hulled, screw-driven liner, by Prince Albert on July 19, 1843. She plied a successful transatlantic steamship service for a year before she ran aground on the Irish coast. She was eventually towed off by the* Birkenhead.

STEAM AND SAIL *A contemporary lithograph of the* Great Western *crossing the Atlantic. The journey took her 15 days and five hours.*

mated cost of repairs was more than £21,000. But it vindicated Brunel's use of iron in ship-building, for any timber ship would have broken up in the winter storms.

Far from being dismayed, Brunel was soon busy with an even bigger ship-building scheme. His *Great Eastern*, 692 ft long, was the most ambitious construction project of her day, but was dogged with problems, few of Brunel's making. It took three and a half years to get her into the water, and broke Brunel's health.

An iron memorial
But the *Great Britain* sailed the seas for 41 years. After her grounding, she was sold, refitted and put on the Australia run as a passenger liner, where she worked for 23 years. She was a troop carrier in the Crimean War, carrying complements of 1650 troops and 30 horses. In 1882, an ageing ship, she was sold again, converted to carrying a cargo of coal, and put on the route to San Francisco. In 1886 she was caught in a storm while rounding the Horn and grounded, this time deliberately for safety, in the Falkland Islands. There she lay, rusting but indestructible, for 83 years, used only as a nesting place for sea birds.

But the *Great Britain* was to make one last voyage. In 1969, financed by public subscription, she came home on a specially designed raft, and sailed under Brunel's own Clifton suspension bridge and up to Bristol Docks – a permanent memorial of the revolution from sail to steam.

RAILWAY BUILDER

There was hardly any aspect of engineering in which Brunel's versatile genius did not make an impact. He was only 27 when in 1833 he was appointed engineer for the proposed London to Bristol Great Western Railway. He took to a horse to survey the route himself, rarely working less than 20 hours a day. He supervised every detail of the construction and design of the railway – bridges, tunnels, the architecture of the stations, even the quality of the coffee at a station hotel. He would throw off his coat and work alongside the navvies, who affectionately called him the 'Little Giant'.

The railway was built in stages and completed in 1841. Brunel left his mark everywhere – his bridge at Maidenhead, the 3000 yd long Box Tunnel near Bath, the 2 mile long Sonning cutting, and a new town for railway workers at Swindon. On the broad-gauge line he laid down, the London to Bristol express took four hours on its inaugural run. Brunel supervised the first journey from the footplate.

The Great Western's broad-gauge track took huge engines with 9 ft high driving wheels.

An engineer to whom nothing was impossible

On the flood tide of the Industrial Revolution a new breed of men began to emerge. Their confidence and dynamism were unbounded. They felt they were in possession of the materials and techniques for building a new world – and in many ways they succeeded.

In this vital age, which brought Britain to a peak of economic power, the outstanding man was Isambard Kingdom Brunel, son of a refugee from the French Revolution. His father, himself a brilliant mathematician and a successful engineer, sent the young Isambard to France to complete his education in mathematics, and afterwards took him into the family firm. It was typical of Brunel's ambition that, before he was 19, he was complaining in his diary of his father 'stifling' him. 'I will not suffer it,' he wrote. But by the age of 21, he was in charge of the Thames Tunnel, the world's first tunnel under a navigable river.

His energy was immense. No detail of any project in which he was involved escaped him. He worked 20 hours a day, chain-smoking cigars to keep himself going. Civil engineer, engine designer, bridge-builder – no branch of his profession seemed beyond his capacity. His bridges at Maidenhead, Saltash and Clifton stand today as monuments, not only to his engineering skill, but also to his artistic creativity; for nothing would satisfy him but perfection.

Looking to the future
Innovation was what he lived by, and luckily he had the knack of persuading committees and boards of directors of the practicability of his plans. Nothing was 'impossible' to him.

Brunel's unremitting search for new techniques, and his willingness to experiment, always made him a controversial figure. Although many of the projects he attempted were triumphantly successful, many others were judged disasters at the time.

His Thames Tunnel from Wapping to Rotherhithe was dubbed the 'Great Bore' by *The Times*, but it is still part of the London Underground rail system. His steamship *Great Britain* bankrupted the company which built it, but is now regarded as a milestone in the evolution of ship design. His *Great Eastern*, for over 40 years the largest ship ever built, was furiously attacked by the Press, who accused Brunel of 'megalomania' because of it. It was dogged by minor setbacks which seemed insoluble at the time, and was a financial disaster. Yet today it is regarded as the prototype of modern luxury liners.

The problems of the *Great Eastern* killed Brunel. The day before her trials, Brunel collapsed on her deck. And the news of a boiler explosion on board was the final blow. He died on September 15, 1859, aged 53.

FINAL PROJECT *An enormous shadow loomed over the last years of Brunel's life – that of the* Great Eastern. *Nearly 700 ft long, and popularly known as the 'Leviathan', it was more than 40 years before a bigger ship was built anywhere. She was intended for the Australia route, but changing circumstances, such as the opening of the Suez Canal, made her uneconomic even before she was launched – she ended up laying Atlantic telegraph cables. The difficulties of her construction (above) exhausted even the prodigious energies of Brunel (right), and led to his death shortly after she was completed in 1859.*

Prince Albert creates a showcase of British power

Throughout the gloriously hot summer of 1851, Englishmen from the provinces and visitors from abroad descended upon London to attend the Great Exhibition in Hyde Park. The world's first industrial giant, confident in its overpowering strength, had invited the nations to join it in the first international exhibition in history.

The exhibition was the brain-child of the queen's husband, Prince Albert. Albert was a true representative of his age, a passionate believer in the moral and material rewards to be reaped from the progress of science and industry. The world, he believed, stood at the threshold of a new age of international co-operation and prosperity. It was 'England's mission, duty, and interest', he said, 'to put herself at the head of the diffusion of civilisation and the attainment of liberty'.

The Great Exhibition, the most ambitious scheme of Albert's fertile imagination, was to proclaim both the dawning of that new world and Britain's leadership of it.

Albert first put the scheme forward in 1849. For two years he had to fight the opposition of rural squires and powerful organs like *The Times*, who feared the relentless march of industry. In the proposed felling of Hyde Park's trees to make room for the exhibition, they found a symbol of industry's indifference to the traditional world of agricultural England. Albert would not be beaten. He cajoled, argued and persuaded. He launched a public subscription. And by January 1851 he had won parliamentary approval for the exhibition.

Made of iron and glass

The first stage of Albert's great work was over. Ahead lay the more daunting task of getting everything ready for the opening in May, a mere 22 weeks away. The building itself, designed by Joseph Paxton, was 1500 ft long and covered 26 acres – three times the size of St Paul's Cathedral. To build it workmen laboured through the winter nights, aided by huge bonfires of scrapwood. Miraculously the building was finished, outfitted and filled with exhibits exactly on time, ready for the royal opening.

The completed exhibition hall was a splendid sight. Paxton's revolutionary building caught perfectly the note of confidence in Britain's industrial future. It was the first building made only of iron and glass. It was also the world's first prefabricated structure (which accounted for the speed with which it was put up). It silenced the critics who had stormed against the invasion of Hyde Park by bricks and mortar. Its glittering dome soared above the elm trees, and when the exhibition was over it was easily dismantled and moved to Sydenham, south of London.

A 'fairy-tale palace'

With the sun shining into it, Paxton's monumental building seemed to Queen Victoria like a 'fairy-tale palace'. The magazine *Punch* called it the Crystal Palace, and the name stuck. William Thackeray, the novelist, was moved to poetry:

> As though 'twere by a wizard's rod
> A blazing arch of lucid glass
> Leaps like a fountain from the grass
> To meet the sun!

Reporting the opening of the exhibition on May 1, *The Times* forgot its early hostility and spoke out in fulsome praise: 'There was yesterday witnessed a sight the like of which has never happened before, and which, in the nature of things, can never be repeated. They who were so fortunate as to see it hardly knew what most to admire, or in what form to clothe the sense of wonder, and even of mystery, which struggled within them.'

No one was more impressed than Queen Victoria herself. She left her own description of the opening day in her journal: 'The glimpse of the transept through the iron gates, the waving palms, flowers, statues, myriads of people filling the galleries and seats around, with the flourish of trumpets as we entered, gave us a sensation which I can never forget, and I felt much moved... The tremendous cheers, the joy expressed in every face, the immensity of the building – all this was moving indeed, and it was and is a day to live forever.'

On display were more than 100,000 objects from 14,000 exhibitors from all over the world. Though half the space was allocated to foreign products, the exhibition was no less a British showplace, and Britain provided the most impressive examples of engineering and invention. There were models of suspension bridges,

THE CRYSTAL PALACE *The Great Exhibition of 1851 is formally opened by Queen Victoria and Prince Albert. The queen wrote that she was 'filled with devotion' by the ceremony.*

EXHIBITION BUILDERS *Navvies, engaged on the construction of the Crystal Palace, breakfast beside the almost-completed glass building.*

a lighthouse and even a scale model of the entire Liverpool docks. Working machinery included a boiler house and steam pumps.

Among the mechanical marvels of the age were many weird inventions. There was a machine for folding envelopes; a sportsman's knife with 80 blades; a model of the floating Church for Seamen in Philadelphia; a stove designed in medieval Gothic style. In the clothing section could be seen Australian hats made of cabbage-tree leaves; cuffs spun and knitted from the wool of French poodles; and a shirt cut on mathematical principles.

Marvels of an age
The exhibition was a global supermarket, a gigantic jumble of hardware, textiles, precious metals, works of art and ornamental bric-à-brac.

Apart from its curiosities, the exhibition was an important event in the formation of Victorian life and manners. Its message was that Britain led the world in the manufacture of useful articles which were made to last, and which were available at reasonable prices.

After 1851 the label 'Made in Britain' was a guarantee respected throughout the world.

Just as important, the exhibition marked the entrance of the skilled working man into the ranks of the 'respectable' in Victorian society. It was from such men that the wonders of the festival had come. The 'swinish multitude' and the 'great unwashed' became phrases of memory only. The future lay with the 'respectable artisan'.

Great care had been taken to ensure that the exhibition would be open to all. Although admission on the first two days was restricted to those wealthy enough to pay £1, the cost was then lowered to 5s and after the first month there were 1s entrance tickets for four days each week.

All over Britain, special excursions to the exhibition were organised. Working men saved up a few pence every week, and many employers gave their workers extra holidays so that they could visit the exhibition. The Admiralty even offered to provide transport for the Portsmouth dockyard workers in case they could not afford the train fare. For the first time in Britain, people from all walks of life mingled together in a common celebration of their country's achievements.

Memorial to a prince
Financially, the exhibition was a greater success than anyone had dared to hope. In the six months that it was open, more than 6 million people attended it. It cost £335,742 to mount, but when the accounts were tallied – including the proceeds from the sale of 1,092,337 bottles of mineral waters, 934,691 Bath buns and 870,027 plain buns – the profit was discovered to be £186,437.

Paxton was rewarded with £5000. The rest went, as Albert desired, to help to pay for that ambitious project with which Queen Victoria permanently fixed the memory of Albert in the English mind. This was the great cluster of museums, including the Science Museum and the Natural History Museum, which now grace South Kensington. They stand just down the road from the site where the Crystal Palace had, for a season, held the attention of the world.

Victorian Britain – the 'workshop of the world'

The Great Exhibition was not simply a celebration of manufacturing invention. It was also a temple in praise of work. For the Victorians, work was more than an economic necessity; it was a moral virtue. The best-selling book of the mid-Victorian era was Samuel Smiles's *Self Help*, a long treatise on the rewards of industry, self-reliance and thrift, published in 1859.

Everywhere in Victorian England there was ceaseless activity. England had become the 'workshop of the world'. At the 1851 census it was discovered that, for the first time, more than half the population lived in towns. Manchester was the centre of the cotton industry. Knives, scissors, buckles, corkscrews and guns were made at Birmingham. Woollen stockings were made at Leicester and cotton ones at Nottingham.

'Dark satanic mills'
Much manufacture was still on a small scale – women and children in the textile industry often worked at home – so that men could still take personal pride in work which retained something of the craft about it.

But where factories sprang up – as at Northampton, centre of the 'sweated' shoe-making trade – hardship and cruelty followed. Children and women worked long hours for low wages. They went home in the evening to overcrowded tenements and unsanitary basements. And the air that they breathed was, for the first time, becoming polluted.

Two decades of prosperity were ushered in by the Great Exhibition. The number of men employed in ironworks rose from 80,000 to 200,000, exports nearly trebled, and savings deposits increased from £30 million to £53 million. The high expectations of 1851 were met. But they were only accomplished through the sufferings of thousands in Victorian England's 'dark satanic mills'.

INGENIOUS DESIGNS
Though the Great Exhibition was a showplace for great inventions and massive machines, small-scale products were not neglected. The beginnings of mass production had not entirely destroyed the tradition of individual workmanship, and objects such as cutlery, chinaware and ornaments were examples of skilled craftwork. The style of the period was florid and elaborate, and characterised by dense decoration.

A cut-throat razor by Hawcroft & Sons of Sheffield, its blade engraved with a view of the Crystal Palace.

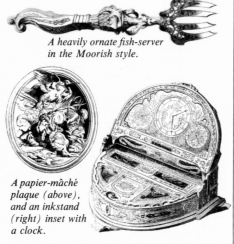

A heavily ornate fish-server in the Moorish style.

A papier-mâché plaque (above), and an inkstand (right) inset with a clock.

HALL OF INVENTION *The machinery section of the exhibition housed much of the best of Britain's achievements in engineering.*

TURBULENT PASSIONS OF A BROTHERHOOD OF ARTISTS

The Pre-Raphaelites, the most striking, original group of English painters, first came together in 1848 – a significant date, for 1848 was a year of political revolutions throughout Europe. John Everett Millais, Dante Gabriel Rossetti, William Holman Hunt and their colleagues were idealistic young painters totally caught up in the revolutionary spirit of the age.

They were given the name Pre-Raphaelites because of their shared belief that art had pursued false objectives following the death of the 16th-century Italian master Raphael. They were determined to recapture the mystical interpretation of nature by earlier artists, and

they revolted against classical themes. Above all, they despised the artistic 'establishment' – in particular, the Royal Academy.

These precocious young men saw themselves not merely as the founders of a new movement, but as a closely knit band of devotees dedicated to the ideals of truth and beauty. For a while the studios in which they worked together, sharing models and inspiration, had the atmosphere of a monastic cloister.

They called their association the Brotherhood, savouring its suggestion of democracy and its overtones of the past. And their determination and solidarity were strengthened by the hostility of the Victorian art world to their

ideas. Few of their paintings were sympathetically received, and some Royal Academicians began a deliberate campaign to denigrate their work in the Press. Charles Dickens, in *The Atheneum*, launched a vitriolic attack on Millais's 'Christ in the House of His Parents' as 'revolting and loathsome'. He went on: 'In the foreground of that carpenter's shop is a hideous, wry-necked, blubbering red-haired boy in a night-gown who appears to have received a poke from the stick of another boy . . . and to be holding it up for the contemplation of a woman so horrible in her ugliness that . . . she would stand out from the rest of the company as a monster in the vilest cabaret in France or the lowest gin-shop in England.'

The Pre-Raphaelites, however, were not entirely without friends. John Ruskin, the respected author, critic and social reformer, was an ardent patron, and supported Millais and Rossetti with gifts and commissions, while also introducing them to prospective clients.

The Brotherhood broken

The collaboration was short-lived. The Brotherhood broke up, its members driven apart by their own differences. The wild and depressive Rossetti took a dislike to Ruskin and found co-operation with his former colleagues difficult. Holman Hunt left the group to travel in the Middle East. Millais fell in love with Mrs Ruskin, whom he later married; his financial success and his membership of the Royal Academy made him a member of the 'establishment', and earned him the contempt of the Brotherhood.

By 1854 the original Pre-Raphaelites had gone their separate ways, and the movement was dead. But its influence lived on. It was the inspiration for William Morris and his Arts and Crafts Movement, and it also inspired Aubrey Beardsley and the Art Nouveau of the early 20th century.

DROWNED BEAUTY *For full realism of effect Millais posed his model for 'Ophelia' in a bath.*

METICULOUS DETAIL *John Everett Millais (below), the son of an Anglo-French family from Jersey, paid little attention to his schooling, and was expelled for biting a master's hand. But his doting parents encouraged his gifts and helped him to establish a reputation as a painter of religious and historical subjects. He exhibited his first picture at the Royal Academy at the age of 17. Millais painted with meticulous attention to detail, recording every leaf and flower in the lush background of his painting of 'Ophelia' (above), and every woodshaving in 'Christ in the House of His Parents' (right). But Millais's allegiance to the Pre-Raphaelite Brotherhood was only an early phase in a brilliant career.*

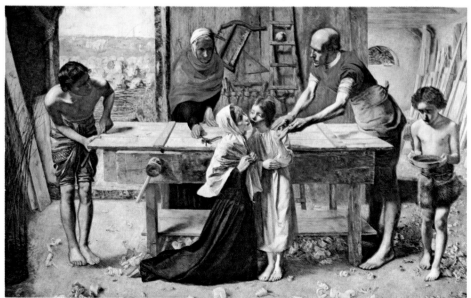

RELIGIOUS OUTRAGE *Millais's 'Christ in the House of His Parents' was reviled by Charles Dickens.*

LEAVING THEIR HOMELAND *Ford Madox Brown's 'Last of England'*.

ARTIST'S INSPIRATION *Elizabeth Siddal (left) and Jane Morris (right)*.

SEEKER FOR TRUTH *Ford Madox Brown (left), though never a member of the Brotherhood, was its most important single influence. Setting 'truth above originality . . . to be true no matter whence the truth comes', he was already an established artist when Rossetti became his pupil in 1848. That same year Brown eloped with a Herefordshire girl of 15. Both of them are shown in his 'Last of England' (above)*.

IDEALISED LOVE *Rossetti's 'Dante's Dream' was painted in 1871*.

SPIRIT OF ROMANCE *Dante Gabriel Rossetti (left), central figure of the Pre-Raphaelites, worshipped women with a passionate, mystical devotion. But it was a platonic love, inspired by the pure emotion that his namesake, the Italian poet Dante, felt for his ideal, Beatrice.*

As a poor, unrecognised artist, Rossetti fell in love with Elizabeth Siddal, a milliner's daughter, whom the Pre-Raphaelites used as a model. They became engaged in 1850, but were not to marry for another ten strange and often tormented years. Rossetti adored her as a goddess of virginity and beauty, but at the same time took as his mistress another model, Sarah Cox, an exotic sensuous young woman, quite in contrast to the ethereal Elizabeth. Rossetti found another aspect of woman's 'ideal' beauty in Jane Burden, later the wife of the designer William Morris – and Rossetti's innocent attachment to her cost him Morris's friendship. He eventually married Elizabeth in 1860, but the marriage was short-lived. She gave birth to a dead child the following year, and never recovered from the experience. Suffering from consumption and depression, she committed suicide in 1862.

Rossetti's grief was so profound that he laid the manuscripts of his poems beside her in her coffin. But seven years later his friends persuaded him to have them exhumed, and they were published with enormous success in 1870. His last literary effort, Ballads and Sonnets, *appeared in 1881. The rest of his life was riddled by ill-health, depression and drug addiction. Outbursts of anger and ingratitude lost him most of his friends, and towards the end he found comfort only in his work.*

PLEASURES OF LOVE *Holman Hunt's 'The Hireling Shepherd'*.

MORAL STRENGTH *None of the Pre-Raphaelites fought harder for his ideas than Holman Hunt (left). His parents were poor, and strongly opposed to his becoming a painter but he achieved his aim. He saw his task as 'to serve as high priest and expounder of the excellence of the works of the Creator', and many of his subjects were biblical in origin. 'The Hireling Shepherd' (above) describes the story of a young shepherd who neglected his sheep for love.*

The Light Brigade charges into the 'valley of death'

BUGLE OF BALACLAVA
Among the first to die as the Light Brigade thundered towards the Russian guns at Balaclava was the bugler of the 17th Lancers. His bugle was found on his body afterwards. It can be seen today in the 17th/21st Lancers Museum, Belvoir Castle, Lincolnshire.

The dashing, pointless sacrifice of the Light Brigade at the Battle of Balaclava in October 1854 came as the muddled climax to a foolish war – a war which had been muddled even in its origin.

Exactly a year before, Russia had gone to war with Turkey on the pretext of defending the Christian subjects of the Turkish empire. Britain saw this as evidence of Russian ambitions to threaten the Indian empire. Driven on by popular fervour, the British government, together with France, concluded an alliance with Turkey – the 'Sick Man of Europe'. An expedition was dispatched to the Black Sea in February 1854; war was declared in March. The Crimea was to remain the focus of the British war effort.

Britain had fought no major campaign since the Napoleonic wars 40 years earlier, and both government and people basked in the reflected glory of Waterloo. They believed that the same methods would bring them victory.

They were to be proved abysmally wrong. Britain's armies were untried; their organisation and administration were hopelessly defective. Worst of all, the standard of command was appalling. There was no general of outstanding ability, no one remotely approaching the stature of Wellington. The evils of the purchase system had eaten away at the standards of the entire officer corps. Promotions were bought and sold, and the effect was that high rank and command went not to the most able, but to the wealthiest. Such men were totally unequipped to face the taxing conditions of modern war. The fatal weaknesses of the structure were clearly demonstrated in the men who presided over the destruction of the Light Brigade.

Lord Raglan, the commander-in-chief, had not seen active service since Waterloo, and had never commanded an army in the field. Though a conscientious man, he completely lacked the power of decision. Lord Lucan, the commander of the cavalry division, was a

INTO THE VALLEY OF DEATH *With Lord Cardigan galloping ahead, this Victorian lithograph shows the 17th Lancers leading the Charge of the Light Brigade. Confused orders led to this fatal attempt at a frontal assault on the massed Russian guns at Balaclava. The heroism of the charge was immortalised in Tennyson's famous poem 'Charge of the Light Brigade'.*

WAR COUNCIL *Lord Raglan, Omar Pasha and General Pélissier meet to discuss Allied strategy.*

WAR AGAINST WINTER *An inadequate and disorganised supply system left most British troops ill-equipped to survive the rigours of a Russian winter. The lucky ones, like these sheepskin-coated soldiers, found their own supplies. But many more died, victims of official negligence.*

man of undeniable courage, but was quick-tempered, imperious and quarrelsome. And the man who led the Light Brigade itself, Lord Cardigan, was one of the most incompetent officers in the army.

Arrogant and self-satisfied, Cardigan had purchased the command of a regiment of the Light Brigade just two years after having been removed from a previous command in disgrace. His new regiment had been famous in peacetime London as the 'Cherry-Pickers' – in reference to the bright red trousers Cardigan had had designed for them. But, smart and disciplined though they were on the parade-ground, Cardigan and his resplendent troops had never been tested in the iron school of war.

Forewarned but not forearmed

Their test came on the afternoon of October 25, 1854, at Balaclava. It was to be one of the most gruelling in the history of British arms.

Balaclava was a small harbour on the south-western coast of the Crimea. It had been chosen by the French and British allies as their base for their assault on Sebastopol, the key to the Russian defensive system in the Crimea. The bombardment of Sebastopol had begun on October 17. Pounded by unceasing artillery fire, the Russians decided that their best hope of saving the fort lay in attacking Balaclava.

Early in the morning of October 25 the attack was launched. It took the British by surprise, for although Raglan had been forewarned, he had already been deceived by several false alarms and decided to ignore this fresh information. The battle was dominated by complete confusion from the very start.

Raglan chose to direct his army from a vantage point on the hills above the main field of battle, and it was from this remote command post that the fatal course of events was set in train. The Russians had captured a number of British guns and, anxious to recover them, Raglan dictated his famous order to his Quartermaster-General, General Airey: 'Lord Raglan wishes the cavalry to advance rapidly to the front – follow the enemy and try to prevent the enemy from carrying away the guns. Troop Horse Artillery may accompany. French cavalry is on your left. Immediate.' The order was signed by Airey.

Into the jaws of death

Raglan's brief order was disastrously ambiguous. It was carried down to Lucan's cavalry on the plain below by an enthusiastic young aide-de-camp, Captain Nolan. Nolan had watched with mounting frustration all day as his beloved light cavalry stood idle and inactive. Now, beside himself with irritation and anger, he swooped like an avenging angel from the heights, bearing the message that was to spell the doom of the Light Brigade.

Lucan, not having Raglan's bird's-eye view of the battlefield, could not understand which guns Raglan meant. Perplexed, he asked Nolan for clarification. Impatient of the delay, Nolan flung out his arm in front of him. 'There, my Lord! There is your enemy! There are your guns!' he shouted.

But to Lucan, Nolan seemed to be pointing at the only guns he himself could see. These were not the captured guns, but a bristling Russian battery lying at the end of a valley protected on both sides by even more artillery. A frontal assault on these would be doomed to disaster. But standing orders laid down that the Commander-in-Chief's orders had to be obeyed without question. Despite his doubts, Lucan gave Cardigan the order to advance and the Light Brigade, immaculate and sparkling, trotted forward.

At first, nobody realised that a catastrophic error had been made. Then Nolan, suddenly seeing that the orders had been misinterpreted, galloped furiously across the front of the advancing cavalry, shouting and waving in an effort to halt the charge. But, before he could give warning, a Russian shell blew a hole in his chest.

The brigade continued its advance, moving towards the blazing guns at a steady pace. Its formation was perfect; not one man faltered, and as each trooper fell, so the ranks closed up.

On the heights above, the Allied General Staffs watched, appalled but powerless. The French general, Bosquet, was deeply impressed by the brigade's unwavering discipline under such shattering fire. But he commented: '*C'est magnifique, mais ce n'est pas la guerre* (It is magnificent, but it is not war).'

'A mad-brained trick'

Six hundred and seventy-three British cavalrymen dashed into an inferno of Russian fire. They reached the battery and began their hopeless hand-to-hand engagement with the 20,000 waiting Russian troops. But so shaken were the Russians by the disciplined courage of this charge that for a moment they lost their nerve. Had the Light Brigade received immediate support, they might have forced the enemy into retreat. But the brigade was alone. Faced with such desperate odds, it wheeled and retired, running the gauntlet of the Russian guns a second time. In 20 minutes, 247 men had been wounded or killed; over 500 horses also died; and the Light Brigade ceased to exist as a fighting unit.

Cardigan, turning to the remnants of his men, said tersely: 'Men, it is a mad-brained trick, but it is no fault of mine.' A voice replied: 'It was nothing, my lord, and we are ready to go again.' And late on the same evening, the shocked Raglan summoned Lucan to give his own bitter judgment: 'You have lost the Light Brigade.' But the loss of the Light Brigade was to develop into more than mere recriminations amongst generals. The disasters of the Crimea spelt the end of the old British army. In the future wealth would not be the sole key to advancement.

Heroine and hero of an inglorious war

The wild enthusiasm with which Britons greeted the outbreak of the Crimean War in 1854 had turned to disillusionment and anger by the time peace was made two years later. This remarkable turn-about was the work of two extraordinary people, Florence Nightingale (right) and William Russell, who made people aware for the first time of the sufferings which common soldiers had to endure in war.

Russell was the first great war correspondent. He sent back to *The Times* graphic descriptions of the lack of clothing, ammunition, proper quarters, food and medical supplies and treatment. The British were used to hearing that their soldiers were brave. Now they heard in addition that they were filthy, frozen, starved and badly led.

It was Russell's reports which fired the imagination of Florence Nightingale. With 38 volunteer nurses, she arrived at Scutari, the main British base, in November 1854.

The army hospital there was filthy – the wounded lay virtually unattended in beds infested with lice and fleas. More than half of the men who died in the war had contracted a fatal disease in the hospital.

With determination and patience, Florence Nightingale overcame the doctors' suspicions. Then she set to work, cleaning, repairing and providing new medical equipment.

Above all, she brought comfort and care to the virtually abandoned men, and was said never to leave the side of a dying man. The official medical staff were jealous to the last. But to the men she was a ministering angel – the 'lady with the lamp'. And to the British public she was the great heroine of the war.

WILLIAM RUSSELL *As* The Times *correspondent, he set a new style of realistic war reporting.*

LESSONS FROM LIFE INSPIRE A GREAT STORY-TELLER

On a December evening in 1833 Charles Dickens, an unknown political reporter of 21, was on his way to the House of Commons when he saw a new number of the *Monthly Magazine* in a Strand bookshop. Weeks before he had sent a story to its editor, but had heard nothing from him. He was supporting his entire family on his earnings and could ill afford the half-crown it cost, but he bought the magazine.

Turning the pages he saw his own name in print for the first time. His hands and knees shook, tears blinded his eyes; he was forced to step into Westminster Hall to recover his composure, and there he read the story before going on to his evening's work.

Nine years later, after the publication of his *Sketches by Boz*, and five other novels – among them *The Pickwick Papers*, *Oliver Twist* and *The Old Curiosity Shop* – Charles Dickens, now married and father of four children, was the most widely read author in the world.

A large part of Dickens' especial appeal for the sentimental Victorian reading public lay in his talent for presenting the grotesqueries of his world through the startled, bemused and innocent eyes of childhood. He never forgot the hardships of his own boyhood.

Stories drawn from life

Charles was only 12 when his father was gaoled for debt, and he was sent out to earn his living in a rat-infested factory. He lived alone in cheap London lodgings, and wandered the streets and wharves by night. The raggle-taggle low-life of London he knew so well during these years furnished much of the atmosphere and vast range of comic characters in his books; and his most touching descriptions of oppressed children, like David Copperfield, Nicholas Nickleby or Oliver Twist, are based on his own experiences.

Crusader and entertainer

Wilkie Collins, Dickens' close friend and fellow novelist, advised him that the best formula for the novel was to 'make 'em laugh, make 'em cry – but make 'em wait'. Dickens' books admirably bore out his advice. His range of comic characters is unequalled, and his readers were made to 'wait' by the serial form in which his books appeared, which called for a constant series of climaxes to sustain interest. So skilled was he in maintaining the excitement, that the ship taking the latest episode of *The Old Curiosity Shop* to America was met in New York by a crowd on the harbour which surged forward, shouting 'is Little Nell dead?'

But Dickens was more than just a great entertainer. Dedicated to social reform, he relentlessly attacked the abuses of Victorian

ASKING FOR MORE *Oliver Twist asks for more gruel in Cruikshank's illustration.*

CONVIVIALITY *Dickens' account of Mr Pickwick and his club brought him fame.*

FROM LIFE *The hapless Mr Micawber in* David Copperfield *is modelled on Dickens' father.*

NOVELIST
Dickens in middle life.

society. The wicked cruelty of schools and orphanages, the corruption and incompetence of the Poor Laws and the law courts were all mercilessly attacked in his books.

Throughout his life Dickens drove himself with an almost unbelievable energy, sometimes to the very limits of exhaustion – writing, editing, travelling, entertaining, dining out, acting and producing his own plays.

Year by year he drove himself on, digging deep into his childhood memories to create the countless fascinating characters that fill the pages of his books. And when he was more than 50 years of age he took up the even more arduous profession of public lecturer.

Dickens revelled in the chance to display his theatrical talent, and as fruit of this tireless energy he left £93,000 in his will. But he had worn himself out. He knew the end was at hand, and he wrote desperately, trying to finish his last great novel, *Edwin Drood*, before death came. For once he was defeated. On June 8, 1870, he collapsed after dinner with his daughter, and died the next day.

RESTING PLACE *In* Great Expectations, *Pip, the novel's hero, said that these graves – at Cooling, Kent – belonged to his family.*

HUMBLE BEGINNINGS *This forge and cottage in Chalk, Kent, were the model for Pip's home before he heard of his 'great expectations'.*

TRAGIC GENIUS FLOWERS IN A YORKSHIRE PARSONAGE

THREE SISTERS *Anne, Emily and Charlotte Brontë, painted by their brother, Branwell, who placed his self-portrait in the middle of the picture. He later painted it out. After an unrequited love affair, Branwell took to drink and drugs. He died of consumption at the age of 31 in 1848. Within seven years his three sisters had followed him to the grave.*

In July 1848 the publisher George Smith was working in his London offices in Cornhill when two small, shy, old-fashioned ladies were shown in. One handed him a letter written to Currer Bell, author of *Jane Eyre*, which he had published with resounding success the previous year. 'You see,' she explained 'we are three sisters.'

Her real name was Charlotte Brontë and her companion was her sister, Anne. A third sister, Emily, was at home in Yorkshire. All three had published books under pseudonyms, as Currer, Acton and Ellis Bell – for fear that prejudice against women would hinder their chances of success.

From success to tragedy

Charlotte, Emily and Anne, together with their brother, Branwell, were brought up in the bleak Yorkshire village of Haworth. Their father, a temperamental isolated Irishman, was rector; their mother died while they were very young. Few people visited the rectory, and the children, forced in on the world of their own imagination, inhabited a secret, self-centred literary realm, producing poems and romantic stories by the thousand. Charlotte and Branwell recorded the chronicles of Angria, a land entirely populated by handsome heroes and passionate women; Emily and Anne wrote of Gondal, an altogether sterner country of windswept moors and hills.

Charlotte and Emily, anxious to earn a living, attempted to teach as a career. Leaving Anne at home, they took up positions as student-teachers in a school in Brussels. Desperately homesick, they returned home, and turned to professional writing. In 1848 their first novels came out.

Anne's *Agnes Grey*, and her only other work, *The Tenant of Wildfell Hall*, were solid but uninspired books. Success eluded Emily's *Wuthering Heights* for many years, but Charlotte's *Jane Eyre* was an instant success.

Jane Eyre became one of the great heroines of English literature. Plain, passionate, intelligent, independent and, finally, triumphant, she was a projection of Charlotte's own nature, isolated at Haworth.

The inspiration for Emily's *Wuthering Heights*, on the other hand, was almost mystic. Emily rarely moved outside Haworth, her world was totally circumscribed by the Yorkshire moors and the vividness of her imagination. *Wuthering Heights*, one of the most remarkable novels in the English language, set the eternal drama of love and passion against the wild moors.

But just as success seemed within reach, the family was devastated by tragedy. In 1848 Branwell died of consumption, aged 31. Emily, a year younger, caught cold at his funeral, and died three months later, and Anne soon followed them to the grave.

Alone now, Charlotte stayed on at the rectory and wrote her last novel *Vilette*. In 1855, after years of spinsterhood, she married her father's curate. Her happiness was short-lived. Within a year she was struck down by fever, and died before she could give birth to the child she was carrying.

A handful of Britons – the heroes of the Indian Mutiny

SPARK OF REVOLT

A cartridge from the Royal Small Arms Factory, Enfield, of the same type as those which provoked the Indian Mutiny. Hindus and Muslims were outraged because some of the cartridges were greased with fat from cows and pigs – both of which had a religious significance.

DEFENDER *Sir Henry Havelock reinforced the besieged Lucknow garrison but could not fight his way out.*

RELIEVER *Sir Colin Campbell and his seasoned troops raised the siege of Lucknow in November 1857.*

On July 2 a shell hit his bedroom as he lay exhausted on his bed. Two days later he died, and was buried in a mass grave.

Now, without their leader, the British forces faced the ordeal of the long Indian summer. There were 1800 men, women and children, together with 1200 loyal native troops. The mutineers were not the only enemy, for the beleaguered garrison had to fight a second battle against heat and starvation. The garrison lived in daily hope of relief, but, as the weeks went by in silence, morale fell.

No source of food was neglected. On one occasion, 150 sparrows were shot and made into a curry. On another occasion, when a shell splinter shattered a cooking pot and plastered a group of officers with what was to be their meal, the ravenous men licked the food from their clothes and bodies. There was no room for pride.

Meanwhile, the guns of the besiegers took a daily toll. Those who were not killed out-

RELIEF ARRIVES *The Queen's Bays, part of Sir Colin Campbell's 5000-strong relief force, charge the rebel Indians outside Lucknow in November 1857. The cavalry charge was the final stage of Campbell's carefully organised relief expedition. His troops led the besieged British out of Lucknow to safety, but the city itself was abandoned to the Indians, and was not recaptured until March 1858.*

In 1857 British rule in India hung in the balance as thousands of rebels rose against the handful of Britons who held their country in thrall. The mutineers' aim was simple – to drive the British out. And to achieve this it was essential to capture the garrison cities which were the centres of imperial power.

Such a city was Lucknow, the capital of the northern province of Oudh. It was there that a siege took place which passed into Victorian history as an epic of courage against overwhelming odds.

The Indian Mutiny broke out in the middle of May 1857. Within a few days, Sir Henry

Lawrence, the Commissioner of Oudh, was facing the responsibility of protecting the lives of the terrified European community in Lucknow, now isolated in a sea of rebellion.

Cut off and alone

Hastily, Lawrence completed makeshift arrangements to withstand a siege. His own Residency building was chosen as the centre of refuge. Stores were hurriedly assembled. Earthworks were thrown up in a rough-and-ready system of fortifications. And outside them gathered the Indian rebels, whose numbers reached 20,000 at the height of the siege.

Lawrence was one of the first casualties.

right had to suffer the agonies of the primitive hospital. Without antiseptics or anaesthetics, operations were performed in a chaos of flies, dirt and filthy linen. Gangrene and death were the inevitable result. Outside the hospital, dysentery, diarrhoea, scurvy and lice made everyone's life a daily torment.

But on September 23 a loyal native reached Lucknow with the news that relief was at last on the way. And two days later, Sir Henry Havelock fought his way into the city. At a heavy cost, his troops joined the garrison and were met with frantic joy.

But this joy was short-lived. The force that Havelock had brought into the city was, even when joined with the surviving members of the garrison, too weak to fight its way out. The siege continued to take its toll.

However, Havelock's brave attempt had not been in vain. For Sir Colin Campbell, who had now arrived from Britain with reinforcements, determined to make the relief of Lucknow his first priority.

End of the ordeal

On November 9 Campbell began his advance from Calcutta. News of it soon reached Lucknow's garrison and a clerk, Henry Kavanagh, volunteered to disguise himself as a rebel and make his way through the enemy lines to guide Campbell and his forces. It was a hazardous venture, for Kavanagh was 6 ft tall, with red-gold hair and brilliant blue eyes. But he succeeded in his desperate mission and, even though he was a civilian, he was later given the supreme award for courage on the field of action – the Victoria Cross.

ROLL OF HONOUR *An unknown drummer boy painted this memorial to the men of the 32nd Light Infantry Regiment who died defending Lucknow. Rebel gunners took a heavy toll of the British during the long siege.*

By November 13 Campbell's army of 5000 men had reached the outskirts of the city. On the following day he began a carefully planned assault, capturing one by one the large buildings which lay as strongpoints along the route to the Residency. Meanwhile, Havelock led his troops out from the Residency to harass the enemy from the rear.

Finally, only a few hundred yards separated the two British armies. Heedless of the flying bullets, Havelock rushed forward to meet Sir Colin and congratulate him. The relief of Lucknow had finally been achieved.

Campbell had fulfilled his mission. The siege of the Residency had been raised. Those who survived it were evacuated to safety. For them, the four-month ordeal was at an end.

Ruling the 'brightest jewel' in the empire

The ferocity of the mutiny which swept India in 1857 came as a profound shock to the British. But only a blow of this magnitude could have forced home to them the inadequacies of their rule in India.

Starting in the 18th century, a commercial enterprise, the East India Company, had gradually taken over the administration of the ramshackle native states with which it came into conflict. By the 1850's, it controlled vast areas of India.

But no commercial concern could hope to rule so great an empire effectively. The British government had been forced to intervene, but all that it achieved was an uneasy system of dual control, which made efficient administration almost impossible.

And the physical problem of ruling an empire which lay so far from the centre of imperial power in Britain seemed almost insuperable. Britain's regular army was far too small to garrison India. So the East India Company was charged with raising locally recruited native troops. The largest was the Bengal Army. It was made up of Hindus from the provinces on the River Ganges, which had a long-established military tradition.

These soldiers were the famous Sepoys. But though they subdued their own country on behalf of their British masters, they were given little reward for their services. Though frequently men of high caste, they were treated with contempt by their British officers. Yet the British always took their loyalty for granted.

But in May 1857, the Sepoys of Meerut, near Delhi, rose against their officers. They had recently been issued with a new type of cartridge, which had to be bitten before being loaded into a rifle. And, ignoring official instructions, the manufacturers had greased some cartridges with the fat of cows and pigs – even though the cow was sacred to Hindus and the pig unclean to Muslims.

The Sepoy mutiny was welcomed by many Indian princes, who saw their chance to expel the British intruders. The revolt spread quickly over northern and central India. Delhi fell to the rebels, and Lucknow was besieged.

The tide turns

The British, surprised and outnumbered, fought back with desperate determination. Reinforcements were rushed out from Britain and, with the recapture of Delhi and the relief of Lucknow in the autumn, the tide turned against the rebels. After that came a long mopping-up operation, in which the British took savage reprisals.

But the mutiny at last inspired the British government to decisive action. In 1858 India was removed from the control of the East India Company and placed under the direct rule of the British government. And for the next 79 years, India remained Britain's proudest possession – the brightest jewel in her worldwide empire.

MILITARY LIFE *After the mutiny, the British Army played an increasingly important role in India. It was the rock on which the Indian Empire stood, and more than any other group it stamped the style of British India. Though native troops remained the backbone of the Indian army, many more British officers were appointed, including medical staff (above). Artillery was kept in British hands – even the Maxim gun detachment (left) is composed entirely of British soldiers. And every British regular regiment took its turn to serve in India.*

MASTER AND PUPIL BUILD A PALACE FOR DEMOCRACY

THE DESIGNERS *The talents of Augustus Pugin (left) and Charles Barry combined to create the new Palace of Westminster.*

FAMOUS SKYLINE *The Palace of Westminster, seen here from the Thames, was rebuilt after a fire in 1834. Completed in 1867, it has 1000 rooms, 100 staircases and 2 miles of corridors.*

Throughout centuries of monarchical rule, Britain's finest architects, artists and craftsmen devoted their talents to building and decorating magnificent palaces for royalty. In the 19th century the balance of power shifted irreversibly from the monarchy to the people. And, suitably, a new palace was built which was to become a unique monument – a palace for democracy.

It was a monument which came into being by accident. On the night of October 16, 1834, workmen burning a large pile of old wooden Exchequer tallies over-stoked the furnace in the old Westminster building which had been the home of Parliament. The flues became too hot and fire spread rapidly through the timber-framed building.

Firemen managed to save Westminster Hall, dating back to 1097, and St Stephen's Chapel. But the rest of the building was gutted.

Building from the ruins

Not everyone saw the fire as a disaster. *The Times* pointed to the deficiencies of the old building and urged that the new Houses of Parliament should be 'well considered of space, form, facility of hearing, facility of ventilation, facility of access and amplitude of accommodation for the public as well as for the members themselves'.

A national competition was held for the design of the new building with the stipulation that the prevailing style should be 'Gothic or Elizabethan', both of which were then fashionable. Charles, later Sir Charles, Barry won the competition. But his entry was based on a set of 'exquisite and minute drawings' which were

largely the work of his brilliant 23-year-old assistant, Augustus Pugin.

Barry's own special interest was Classical architecture, evident in his earlier buildings such as the Travellers Club and the Reform Club in Pall Mall. In 1844, four years after construction of his new Westminster Palace began, he realised he would need considerable help with the ornate and complex Gothic detail. He turned again to Pugin, who was by now widely acclaimed as the master of the 19th-century Gothic style.

A partnership between equals

'I am in a regular fix,' Barry wrote to his former employee, begging him to help with the decoration of the House of Lords. Pugin at once accepted, and for the next seven years the two men – different in taste and character – worked together to produce one of the greatest British buildings of the 19th century.

While Barry was a staid, methodical architect, Pugin was an erratic genius. He dressed unconventionally in a wide-brimmed hat with a huge cloak to hide his shabby clothes. He often made his beautifully detailed sketches while sailing in the open sea, and he once said that the only two things worth living for were 'Christian architecture and boats'.

Pugin thought little of his fellow architects, calling them 'villains' and their work 'deplorable' and 'execrable'. Although he did not share Barry's love of Classical design, he later paid tribute to his skill, admitting that he could never have planned a building as large and logical as the Houses of Parliament. Barry, in turn, said that he himself did not have the

inventiveness to produce the infinite variety and beauty of Pugin's details.

To Barry, the palace owes the surprising simplicity of its basic design: a single spine beginning with the House of Commons at the north and running southwards through the three major lobbies, the House of Lords, the Princes' Chamber and the Royal Gallery. Barry's great plan was completed by the two towers which balance one another at either end of the enormous building – the impressive Victoria Tower and the 320 ft high Westminster Clock Tower which houses Big Ben.

Wealth of detail

Inside, it is Pugin's brilliance that is supreme. He wrote: 'I strive to revive, not invent.' But when invention was called for, he produced a seemingly inexhaustible wealth of ideas, crowding thousands of tiny details into such rooms as the octagonal Central Lobby, the intricately patterned Queen's Robing Room and the moodily romantic corridors.

Into these spectacular chambers – lit by narrow shafts of light from hidden Gothic windows – Pugin put exquisite mosaic patterns, carved reliefs and tracery, intricate ceilings, carved panelling, gilt and bronze statuettes.

'Gravely gorgeous'

Nothing was too small for his inventiveness. Umbrella stands, coat-hooks, lamp-brackets and even inkstands were made in Gothic style to Pugin's design.

The culmination of the partnership between Barry and Pugin came in one magnificent chamber – the House of Lords. The great throne, with its huge canopy and metal candelabra, dominates the brown-and-gold chamber, vividly warmed by its scarlet morocco seats, its azure carpets and its rich gilding. Repeated intricate details, the panelled ceilings, the frescoes and hidden niches all contribute to the impression of breathtaking splendour. An early American visitor, the author Nathaniel Hawthorne, commented: 'Nothing could be more magnificent and gravely gorgeous.'

Yet the Palace of Westminster brought little but trouble to Barry, who was under constant attack from critics and various committees. He had many problems with the Royal Com-

ARCHITECT'S TRIUMPH *The House of Lords, with its brilliant colour and Gothic tracery, is dominated by Pugin's gilded throne, used by the monarch on State occasions.*

mission of Fine Arts which had been set up to help with the decoration of the palace. Eventually the commission took complete charge of the gigantic and melodramatic murals.

Barry also had a long-standing argument with Edmund Beckett Denison, the designer of the clock and Big Ben itself, the 14 ton bell which was named after Sir Benjamin Hall, the Commissioner of Works. Despite the varying problems – the initial failure of the clock to work, the cracking of Big Ben I and II – the bell, still cracked, has loudly chimed the time for over 100 years. And the 14 ft minute hand of the huge clock, 22.5 ft in diameter, has continued to travel over 100 miles a year ever since it was erected.

Both Barry and Pugin died before Westminster Palace was completed in 1867 – Pugin, only 40 years old and insane, died in 1852, and Barry in 1860. In the years that followed their deaths the building fulfilled its lofty purpose. Its magnificent debating chambers became the sounding board for great orators and the scene of dramatic events, a fitting stage for the triumph of the democratic ideal.

CLASH OF TWO GIANTS

The newly built Palace of Westminster was dominated during its first decades by two of the greatest Parliamentarians in Britain's history – William Ewart Gladstone and Benjamin Disraeli.

Disraeli, the unlikely leader of the Conservatives, was of Jewish origin, a dandy who wore his dyed hair in ringlets and looked on politics as an exciting game. When he became Prime Minister in 1868 he commented flippantly that he had reached the 'top of the greasy pole'.

Gladstone, the austere and high-minded leader of the Liberals, had no time for frivolities, and saw politics as a Christian mission. Disraeli said

he did not mind Gladstone always having an ace up his sleeve, but objected to his presumption that God had put it there.

Disraeli's flamboyance found an outlet in the empire-building adventures which Gladstone thought were reckless, expensive and immoral. Gladstone preferred reforms at home. His policy was 'peace, retrenchment and reform'.

The two great rivals disliked each other intensely. Facing one another across the floor of the House, they provided a long-running drama which perfectly matched the richly theatrical architecture that Barry and Pugin had created.

Souvenir plates of Gladstone (left) and Disraeli.

THE QUIET SCIENTIST WHO OUTRAGED VICTORIAN SOCIETY

THE VOYAGE OF THE 'BEAGLE' *Charles Darwin (above) was just 23 when he set sail as ship's naturalist in the* Beagle *(left). The voyage led to Darwin's theory on the evolution of species which shook religious beliefs.*

To the average Christian in the 19th century every word in the Bible was still literally true. The world had been created by God in six days and man had been created in his image. All the creatures of the world had survived the Flood only because Noah had taken two of each species on board the Ark. Charles Darwin's theory of evolution by natural selection shattered these beliefs. It struck at the very roots of society, undermining man's belief in his natural superiority, the inheritor of the universe.

Darwin developed this revolutionary theory during the five years he spent as naturalist on the survey ship HMS *Beagle*. On his return to London in 1837 he was already famous, simply because of the sheer volume of scientific material he had collected.

Voyage of discovery

Like so many men of genius, Darwin developed late. His interest in natural history was encouraged at Cambridge, where he became friends with the Cambridge botanist Professor John Henslow, to whom he confided his mania for collecting beetles: 'I will give a proof of my zeal: one day, on tearing off some old bark, I saw two rare beetles, and seized one in each hand; then I saw a third and new kind, which I could not bear to lose, so that I popped the one which I held in my right hand into my mouth.'

Professor Henslow recommended Darwin for the unpaid post of naturalist aboard the Admiralty's survey ship, HMS *Beagle*.

The *Beagle* sailed from Plymouth on December 27, 1831. By the time she returned five years later, Darwin was halfway to re-

shaping the landscape of 19th-century thought. At sea he was possessed by an almost super-human energy, a magical vitality that he was never again to recover.

Whenever the ship touched land, he threw himself into energetic exploration and inquiry. He roamed the rain forests of South America; he climbed the Andes mountains; he undertook long and hazardous treks that would have exhausted the most seasoned explorers. And throughout it all he was collecting specimens of rare plants and animals.

Darwin recorded his observations, with painstaking detail, in *Zoology of the Voyage of HMS Beagle*. The birds, the animals and the flowers he saw only sharpened the conflict he now began to feel between his observations and his acceptance of the biblical account of the Creation of the natural world.

This conflict finally came to a head in the Galapagos Islands in the eastern Pacific. Darwin noticed that the islands had few varieties of land birds but that there were many different finches, all extremely similar except in the size of their beaks. He was struck by the thought that each species appeared to have been 'modified for different ends'. It was as if finches had developed on these isolated islands to fill roles normally filled by other birds.

Here at last was the clue to Darwin's dilemma. Either every one of these species had been separately created, or an ancestral pair of finches had arrived and their offspring, colonising new islands, had evolved into separate species.

With mounting excitement Darwin wrote at the time: 'Here we seem to be brought

somewhat near to that great fact, that mystery of mysteries, the first appearance of new beings on earth.'

He was 28 when he returned to London. Within weeks he was jotting down the beginnings of the theory that was to make him world famous and change the history of science: 'If we let conjecture run wild, then animals – our fellow brethren in pain, disease, death, suffering, and famine, our slaves in the most laborious works, our companions in our amusements – they may partake from our common origin in one ancestor, we may all be netted together.'

The final inspiration

In the following months this conjecture slowly became conviction. Darwin realised that species develop in different directions when isolated from one another – and that they are not immutable.

He was halfway to making his momentous discovery. But he still could not solve 'that mystery of mysteries' – the force which drives species to change, over many thousands of years, to suit varying environments.

The explanation came to him suddenly two years later. He was reading the *Essay on Population* by the Rev. Thomas Malthus. Malthus argued that human populations multiplied faster than the available food supply. If this were also true of animals, then they had to compete to survive. Darwin rightly concluded that in this deadly competition only those animals endowed with favourable characteristics – with slightly longer legs, thicker fur or stouter beaks – would survive. This was the basis for Darwin's theory of the

DARWIN'S FINCHES

Of all the thousands of species of animal life that Charles Darwin described during his five-year voyage on board the *Beagle*, the finches of the Galapagos were among the most important, for they eventually provided the most telling evidence for his epoch-making theory. Darwin noticed that there were about a dozen different species of finch and that they filled many different roles. One species feeds from the flowers of cacti and has a beak well suited for this purpose. Another species, with a tit-like beak, probes bark and leaves for insects; and others have parrot-like beaks, well adapted for cracking large seeds.

Darwin knew at once that the natural oddities of the Galapagos Islands had brought him near to 'that mystery of mysteries', the origin of species. But it was to be many years before he appreciated the full significance of the finches. Ten years after his voyage, he wrote hesitantly: 'One might almost fancy that, from an original paucity of birds on this archipelago, one species had been taken and modified for different ends.' And another 14 years were to pass before he set out to show that this 'fancy' was scientific fact. In Darwin's book, *The Origin of Species*, the finches finally emerged as perhaps his most convincing evidence that new species arise through the process he described as 'natural selection'.

This tree finch feeds like a European tit by probing bark and gleaning leaves for insects.

Ground finches have powerful beaks to crack large seeds.

Cactus-eaters have long pointed beaks to probe the flowers of cacti for their food.

Warbler finches glean insects with thin bills.

Another tree finch has a hooked beak for reaching insects.

THE PROTAGONISTS

When Darwin published his theory of evolution in *The Origin of Species* in 1859, Victorian society was incensed. The challenge to the biblical account of Creation threatened man's view of his God-given superiority, and the clergy took it up at a famous meeting of the British Association at Oxford in June 1860. Samuel Wilberforce, Bishop of Oxford, led the concerted attack and declared beforehand that he was out to 'smash Darwin'. He told a packed and hushed hall that the theory was 'casual', 'sensational' and contrary to the divine revelations of the Bible. He then turned on the biologist, T. H. Huxley, a champion of Darwin's theory, and demanded to know whether it was through his grandmother or grandfather that he claimed to be descended from the apes. Huxley was infuriated by the insolence of the question, and heatedly replied that he would prefer to be descended from an ape than from a cultivated man who prostituted his culture and eloquence to prejudice and falsehood. During the uproar that followed one woman fainted, and Wilberforce's supporters angrily demanded an apology. *The Descent of Man*, published in 1871, excited renewed public furore. But by Darwin's death in 1882, at the age of 73, his controversial theories were widely accepted. They form the basis for all modern biology today.

Thomas Huxley.

Bishop Samuel Wilberforce.

survival of the fittest, which he called the 'principle of natural selection'. This theory was to have far-reaching implications, not only in the scientific world, but on man's whole view of himself in the universe.

Darwin put up a tremendous fight against the conclusions he had been forced to draw. He wrote 'disbelief crept over me at a very slow rate but was at last complete'. He himself knew how reluctantly he had reached his conclusions, and he realised how outrageous they would appear to the public.

He made a rough outline of his theory, and locked it in a drawer with a letter to his wife, asking her to publish it in the event of his death. Then for 20 years he kept his heretical ideas from the public.

He had married his cousin Emma Wedgwood, and lived at Down in Kent. He adored his family, and when any of his ten children were ill, he would keep them beside him in his study while he worked. During these years his studies were hampered by daily headaches, and even these may have had their origin in the overwhelming guilt he felt at the ruthless implications of the theory he had developed.

Pilloried by the public

In the event his hand was forced by Alfred Wallace, another naturalist, who had independently arrived at a similar theory, and had written in June 1858 to tell Darwin of his findings. Papers from both men were read at the Linnean Society in London the following month; they caused little stir, but the following year Darwin published his theory as a book, *The Origin of Species*.

Public reaction was intense. Darwin was mercilessly criticised and abused. But he persevered with his work, and in 1871 he compounded the outrage he had already caused by publishing *The Descent of Man*, which advanced the belief that men and apes were descended from a common ancestry.

Darwin had expected the public execration. He knew that the acceptance of his theory would need time. He was prepared to sacrifice his private happiness to the cause of science.

When the outcry finally died down, the living world was seen to be a different place, and Charles Darwin was responsible for this change. The quiet, unassuming family man, working slowly but doggedly in his isolated country house, pursuing the solutions to the most basic questions about the natural world, became the father of modern biology. He wrote that his success was due to 'love of science, unbounded patience in long reflecting over any subject, industry in observing and collecting facts, and a fair share of invention as well as of common sense'.

He never stopped working: 'When I am obliged to give up observations,' he wrote, 'I shall die.' He collapsed at work on April 17, 1882. Two days later, he died of a heart attack at the age of 73.

Livingstone fulfils his destiny in darkest Africa

FIXING THE UNKNOWN
Livingstone kept accurate daily records on his journeys, no matter how terrible the conditions, with observations of his position, data on flora and geology. These went to the Royal Geographical Society, who still keep the sextant he used.

On April 18, 1874, Dr David Livingstone was buried in Westminster Abbey. Benjamin Disraeli, the Prime Minister, and the Prince of Wales attended. Dense crowds, many openly weeping, lined the funeral route. Florence Nightingale called him 'the greatest man of his generation'.

Livingstone was a national hero because he combined the virtues Victorians admired most – indomitable courage, stern morality and boundless faith. Yet by his own exacting standards, he had failed.

Tragically for him, it was only after his death that the ideas which drove him on were realised. Two months after his death the British brought to an end the slave trade in East Africa. And within 20 years, Nyasaland (now Malawi), Uganda and Kenya were incorporated into the empire.

Nothing exemplified the extraordinary tenacity of Livingstone more than his struggle to educate himself. From the age of ten, he had worked a $12\frac{1}{2}$-hour day in the Blantyre cotton mills for six days a week – but somehow he found time to learn to read and write. Through sheer hard work he went on to graduate in medicine in Glasgow, and later to be ordained a priest.

Hardship and privation

He sailed for South Africa in 1841, aged 28, to a life of incredible hardship. But he was 40 when he made his first real expedition across Africa from west to east between 1853 and 1856. It was the first crossing of the continent by a white man, and followed for the most part the Zambesi River. On his way he discovered the Victoria Falls, one of the world's great scenic wonders, which he named after the queen.

His accomplishment made him an overnight hero in England, but it had fired him with a burning ambition which was to dominate the rest of his life. On his way he had encountered the horrors of the slave trade, and he determined that the only counter to it, and the inter-tribal wars in its wake, was the introduction of trade and settlement by British colonisers.

With government backing he returned to the Zambesi in 1858 to prove his conviction that the river was navigable. The Kebrabassa Rapids proved him disastrously wrong, and he turned his attention to the area around Lake Nyasa. Once again he failed, and he returned to England in 1864, now 51, with his reputation in ruins.

But nothing could keep him from his heroic quest to stamp out slavery. In 1866 he returned to Africa, hopelessly ill-equipped, short of money and without European companions. As well as the problem of slavery, he had also become obsessed with finding the source of the Nile, the great geographic question of the time. His previous guesses and conclusions had been wrong. He went south instead of north from Lake Tanganyika. His hardships were incredible, his money ran out, his bearers abandoned him. There were rumours of his death. To the outside world he was 'lost'.

The man sent to find him was the 28-year-old Henry Stanley, a journalist from the *New York Herald*. His editor's briefing was blunt: 'Find Livingstone if he's alive, or his boots

HISTORIC FRIENDS *Though Livingstone (above) and Stanley (left, in a studio pose) were only together five months after their historic meeting (right), Stanley was inspired to devote his life to African exploration. When Livingstone died, his loyal servants embalmed his body and carried it 1000 miles to the coast for burial in his homeland.*

if he's dead.' In accordance with these instructions, Stanley followed every clue and rumour he could find in the huge continent. His journey took him 236 days and 1000 miles to the village of Ujiji on the shore of Lake Tanganyika. On November 10, 1871, dressed in a freshly pressed flannel suit and with glistening boots, Stanley arrived at the village and pushed through the crowd of Africans who thronged around the sick, old man he had come to find. Raising his hat he uttered the words which have passed into history – 'Dr Livingstone, I presume?'

A national hero

Though the two men were only together five months, Livingstone made a deep impression on Stanley. The stories he published in England re-established Livingstone as a national hero, then he himself returned to Africa to follow in Livingstone's footsteps. He discovered the source of the Congo River, and finally discovered the source of the Nile.

Livingstone had died two years after their historic meeting. His servants had found him dead, kneeling as if in prayer next to his camp bed. Constant dysentery had killed him. One of the last things he wrote had been: 'Nothing earthly will make me give up my work in despair. I encourage myself to the Lord my God and go forward.'

Crusade to end the curse of slavery

The campaign against slavery was started by a small band of dedicated campaigners in Britain during the 18th century. But it took many years before the world accepted their views.

While William Wilberforce and the abolitionists were fighting against slavery, the trade had never before reached such a peak of intensity. Liverpool and Bristol founded their wealth on shipping cloth to West Africa on the so-called 'Middle Passage'. The cloth was bartered for slaves in the malaria-ridden swamps of the African coast. The slaves were in turn exchanged for tobacco, sugar and cotton in the West Indies and America.

Estimates from the logs of British ships alone are that the trade involved 85,000 slaves annually during the 18th century. Records for 1771 show that 58 slave ships sailed from London, 25 from Bristol and 107 from Liverpool. In these ships the slaves were packed literally like sardines, head to toe, with 18 in. width in which to lie and not enough headroom in which to sit up. Sometimes only half a slave cargo survived the crossing across the Atlantic to the plantations of the Americas.

Britain leads the way

The abolitionists, inspired by a vigorous evangelical Christianity, had their first success when a British judge, Lord Mansfield, ruled in 1772 that no one could be a slave in Britain itself. And from this time on, the British abolitionists built up an intense and relentless pressure on the government. In 1807 they succeeded at last in persuading Parliament to ban the carrying of slaves by British subjects in British ships.

But this was only a beginning. Britain's pioneering stand led her into a series of campaigns to ensure that first the slave trade, and eventually slavery itself, was outlawed throughout Africa, America and the European colonies of the Caribbean. By the 1820's, most European nations had followed Britain's example and forbidden their subjects to participate in the trade.

Fighting the slavers

Nevertheless, a vast illicit traffic in slaves flourished to supply the continuing demand for African manpower – for, though trading was illegal, slavery was still allowed.

Britain used her naval power to police the West African coast and arrest any ship engaged in the trade. The centre of this blockade was Sierra Leone, which was formerly called the Slave Coast. Its port, called Freetown, became a settlement for freed slaves, who prospered from re-victualling Royal Navy warships which often spent up to three years on patrol without the crew or its officers leaving the ship. Further north on the coast another settlement for freed American slaves

was established and called Liberia. But the slave smugglers, in order to maximise the profit of the risky voyage, now crammed slaves even more densely into their holds. If detection and arrest by a British patrol seemed likely, the entire human cargo was usually thrown overboard.

Nor were these cruelties confined to the slavers from Europe. The traders seldom left their ships to venture into the tractless and malaria-ridden interior of the continent. It was Africans themselves who initially caught the slaves, the strong preying on the weak, in constant, bloody slave wars.

In Britain the abolitionist campaign achieved its greatest success in 1833, when Parliament abolished slavery throughout the empire, and slaves already there were given their freedom. The British public cheerfully paid £20 million compensation to slave owners in the colonies. And in the course of the next 50 years the nations of Europe and the Americas followed Britain's example.

New horizons open

The ending of the slave trade was more than a mere philanthropic gesture. Until abolition, Europe's interest in Africa had been dominated by slavery. The Africans themselves were regarded more as animal resources than human beings. Abolition opened new horizons – Africa became a source of human and scientific interest, and attracted missionaries, explorers and settlers. The ending of the slave trade put a huge new continent on the map.

HUMAN GOODS
Manacles or logs to prevent escape were used by the Arab slave-trader Tippu Tip (above).

ing Leeds and Bradford war-profiteers now reading *John Bull* on Scarborough Sands'.

He was killed on November 4, 1918, during the crossing of the Sambre Canal, one week before the Armistice was signed. He was 25.

Among the papers found after Owen's death in 1918 was a draft preface to his planned volume of poems. It sums up his aims as a poet of pity, who saw his duty as to 'warn':

'This book is not about heroes. English poetry is not yet fit to speak of them.

Nor is it about deeds, or lands, nor anything about glory, honour, might, majesty, dominion, or power, except War.

Above all I am not concerned with Poetry. My subject is War, and the pity of War. The poetry is in the pity.'

In drawing attention to the pity of war,

Sassoon and Owen, and the artists who also went to the Front, had lived up to their great ideal – to warn future generations. Determined to find new ways of communicating their indignation, these young poets and artists were the forerunners of the modern movements which were to transform literature and art in the next decades. Their influence survives in the arts of today.

NIGHTMARE LAND *Paul Nash served with the Artists' Rifles in France and was appalled by the landscape blasted by mortars and shells. 'I am no longer an artist interested and curious,' he wrote. 'I am a messenger who will bring back word from the men who are fighting to those who want the war to go on for ever...it will have a bitter truth and may it burn their lousy souls.' His picture of the 'Menin Road', painted in 1917, was intended to rob war of the 'last shred of glory'. For the rest of his life he suffered from the effects of poison gas.*

IMAGE OF VIOLENCE *Christopher Nevinson was unfit for active military service, but served in France in 1914 with the Friends' Ambulance Unit. His abstract pictures express his horror at the sufferings of the wounded and the ruthlessness of war. 'La Mitrailleuse' (The Machine Gun) is a terrifying view of mechanical efficiency.*

'MASS-MURDER' *Percy Wyndham Lewis was the founder-member of the most modern movement among artists – the Vorticists. Their aim was 'to build up a visual language as abstract as music'. In his painting of 'A Battery Shelled', Wyndham Lewis used the bleak war landscape of cogs and wheels and abandoned, inhuman machinery to build up an impression of mechanical violence. He himself went to the Front in 1914 as a Bombardier, and he wrote later: 'I have never been able to regard modern war as good or bad. Only supremely stupid. The greatest wickedness is the perpetuation of foolishness these carnivals of mass-murder involve.'*

Victory hangs in the balance off the coast of Jutland

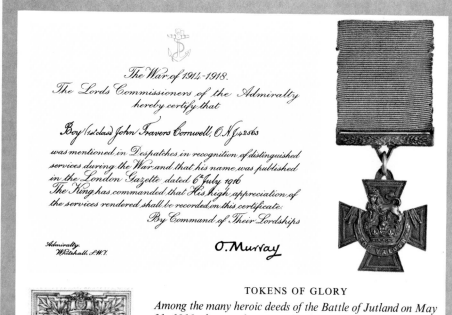

TOKENS OF GLORY

Among the many heroic deeds of the Battle of Jutland on May 31, 1916, the one that most deeply moved the British public was the story of the 'Boy VC', John Cornwell. Aged only 16, Cornwell was one of the gun-crew on board the light cruiser Chester *when she was attacked by four German ships. Within minutes, one-fifth of the* Chester's *crew were killed or wounded, including all of Cornwell's comrades. But he stuck to his post until he, too, was killed. He was awarded a post-humous VC. His medal (above right), the certificate of his mention in dispatches (above left) and a commemorative stamp (left) are all in the Imperial War Museum, London.*

A thickening North Sea mist enveloped the British Grand Fleet, steaming towards the Danish coast from its base at Scapa Flow. The 24 battleships advanced in six parallel columns, with cruiser squadrons scouting ahead. On the forebridge of the flagship, HMS *Iron Duke*, Admiral Sir John Jellicoe peered at the blurry line where sea and sky met. Listening to the thunder of gunfire from the south, the admiral's calm vanished for a moment. 'I wish,' he suddenly remarked to his staff, 'someone would tell me who is firing and what they're firing at.'

A battle with no room for error

It was about 6 p.m. on May 31, 1916. The Battle of Jutland, the only great sea battle of the First World War, was just beginning. During the afternoon, scant and contradictory reports had reached Jellicoe from the Commander-in-Chief of the Battle-Cruiser Fleet, Vice-Admiral Sir David Beatty. They indicated that Beatty's ships were in action with enemy battle-cruisers, and the whole German High Seas Fleet was steaming northwards. Now the two battle fleets were just concealed from Jellicoe's own ships by the misty horizon. At any moment he would have to decide how to deploy his great fleet for battle – and decide quickly.

Yet he lacked essential information – where exactly Beatty was, and how his ships had fared. Above all, Jellicoe did not know the precise location and course of the German fleet.

Shortly after 6 p.m., Jellicoe saw Beatty's flagship *Lion* emerge from the murk at full speed, smoke pouring from her fo'c'sle. A signal lamp blinked in *Lion*: 'Have sighted enemy Battle Fleet, bearing SSW.' Now, with the two main fleets still invisible to each other,

INTO BATTLE *Admiral Sir John Jellicoe (above left), the Commander-in-Chief of the Grand Fleet, refused to risk Britain's naval supremacy by over-hasty action against the German High Seas Fleet in the North Sea. But when the British broke the German radio code and thus secured advance knowledge of Admiral Scheer's plans, Jellicoe felt confident to go into action at Jutland. Vice-Admiral Sir David Beatty (above right) used his battle-cruisers to lure the German fleet into action against the British Grand Fleet of 24 battleships under Jellicoe. One of the worst-damaged German ships at Jutland was the battle-cruiser* Seydlitz *(right). She was hit by 21 heavy shells, and a torpedo which blew a 39 ft hole in her bows. Half-waterlogged, and with one in ten of her crew killed or wounded, the* Seydlitz *still managed to limp back to port at Wilhelmshaven.*

but converging at a combined speed of over 50 knots, Jellicoe had at last to decide his battle dispositions. An error of judgment on his part could, as Winston Churchill wrote, 'lose the war in an afternoon'.

At 6.15 p.m., Jellicoe ordered the deployment to begin, and his fleet formed into line of battle behind the port wing column. The moment Jellicoe had been waiting and hoping for since the war had begun in 1914 had arrived.

Except for occasional sorties, the German High Seas Fleet had so far remained in its heavily protected coastal waters. But in 1916 its new Commander-in-Chief, Vice-Admiral Reinhard Scheer, decided that, with the German army hard-pressed on every front, the German navy could no longer remain aloof. His plan was to bait a portion of the British fleet into a trap, and destroy it. His battle-cruisers, under Vice-Admiral Hipper, were to supply the bait, sailing northwards past the Danish province of Jutland.

Now, chasing Beatty's Battle-Cruiser Fleet northwards at top speed, Scheer believed that his plan had succeeded brilliantly. For he had no idea that Jellicoe's Grand Fleet was just out of sight ahead of him.

Suddenly, Scheer saw in the gloom ahead of him an interminable line of British battleships. At once he ordered his fleet to reverse course. Within minutes Jellicoe lost sight of his prey. Yet he hesitated to start an immediate pursuit, fearing that Scheer meant to entice him into a submarine ambush. Instead, he held to his course towards the south-east, so getting between Scheer and his base.

During this encounter, the British battle-cruiser, HMS *Invincible*, was hit in a magazine, blew up and sank. Soon after 7 p.m., Scheer started eastwards again – only to find Jellicoe across his course once more. The German fleet wallowed in confusion, pounded by ferocious British gunfire. In desperation, Scheer ordered his battle-cruisers on a 'death-ride' against the British line, in order to cover his fleet's escape.

Once more Hipper's ships steamed into action against the Grand Fleet. Then, having covered Scheer's retreat, they turned and steamed away. They had been in action all day and their crews were exhausted. Yet though appalling damage was inflicted on them, not a single German ship in the squadron was sunk.

Command of the seas assured

Between 8 and 9 p.m., the German fleet was sighted a third time, lying to the westward in the fading light. But neither Jellicoe nor Beatty steered to close with the enemy. The Grand Fleet held on a south-westerly course, still running between Scheer and his base at Wilhelmshaven.

That night, in a desperate dash for home, Scheer smashed through British cruisers and destroyers in the rear of the Grand Fleet. And so the greatest sea battle since Trafalgar sputtered out. By morning, the German High Seas Fleet, though badly mauled, had reached its base. The Germans claimed the victory, for they had sunk 111,980 tons of British ships against their own losses of 62,233 tons; and they had inflicted 6945 casualties while receiving only 2921.

But, strategically, success at Jutland lay with the British. The war saw no other naval battles. The German fleet only ventured to sea on three occasions during the rest of the war. An American journalist wrote: 'The German High Seas Fleet had assaulted its jailer; but it is still in jail.'

The unseen menace of Germany's U-boats

'THE U-BOATS ARE OUT!' *A German war poster glories in the work of the U-boats, which brought Britain to the verge of defeat in 1917.*

Throughout the First World War, the sea was Britain's jugular vein, for her national life depended on imports of food and raw materials. From the beginning of 1915, even though they were shackled by international law, which forbade sinking at sight without warning, the U-boats quadrupled the monthly British tonnage sunk. Then, in February 1917, Germany began to use her submarines in an even more deadly fashion, by freeing them of all restrictions under international law. The Germans knew that to sink ships on sight would probably bring America into the war. But they believed that this move would defeat Britain before America could mobilise her strength.

The effects were dramatic. In April, one out of every four ships that left Britain never returned. The First Sea Lord, Sir John Jellicoe, confessed that 'there is absolutely no solution that we can see'. With only six weeks' food left, Britain faced starvation.

But then, just as dramatically, the answer was found – the convoy system. Convoys could be protected by naval escorts and, by concentrating merchant ships in large groups, the number of targets for the U-boats to attack was drastically reduced.

By the autumn of 1917 all British vessels moved in convoys, and losses fell by nearly two-thirds. By the end of the war the U-boat had dwindled into a mere nuisance. But the margin between victory and defeat had been frighteningly narrow.

A summer of victories – and the First World War ends

THE FINAL BLOW
As the German armies crumbled in the summer of 1918, victory was at last in sight. This poster, now in the Imperial War Museum, called for one last national effort to beat the foe.

In the high summer of 1918, only months before the armistice, the British army won its most brilliant victory of the war. This time there was no long preliminary bombardment; none of the elaborate and obvious preparations which on previous occasions had warned the enemy long in advance that an offensive was imminent.

At 4.20 a.m. on August 8 the guns opened fire, creating a slowly advancing curtain of annihilation. Close behind came nearly 500 tanks, including the new 8 mph 'Whippets', grinding forward through the ground-mist. They were a shield of steel for the advancing British, French, Australian and Canadian infantry divisions.

The second Battle of the Somme was opening, and it was an astounding contrast to the first battle two years before. Yet it was planned and directed by the same Commander-in-Chief, Sir Douglas Haig, and the same army commander, Sir Henry Rawlinson.

Taken completely by surprise, the Germans collapsed. By nightfall, Canadian troops had advanced over 8 miles, and what General Ludendorff called 'the blackest day of the German army in the history of the war' had come to an end. German losses totalled 27,000 men killed, wounded and missing. But even

more alarming to Ludendorff than the collapse of the German front on the Somme was the disintegration of his soldiers' morale. Only three days later he warned the Kaiser that the war must be ended. This was the measure of Haig's success.

Yet barely six months earlier, on March 21, Ludendorff had launched the enormous spring offensive – the *Kaiserschlacht* (Emperor battle) – with which he intended to win the war for Germany. At first the Germans had achieved striking gains, breaking through the British Fifth Army front, and starting to drive a wedge between the British and French armies. But after the French Marshal Ferdinand Foch was appointed Allied Supreme Commander, dogged resistance brought the Germans to a halt just short of the key railway centre for the British front – Amiens.

From victory to victory

Later, but smaller, German offensives, first against the British in Flanders, then against the French along the Aisne and round Rheims, were also blocked after early successes. On July 18 the French opened the Allied counter-offensive with an attack led by tanks, at Villers-Cotterêts. Now, on August 8, it was the turn of the British.

The second Battle of the Somme was only the first of a series of crushing blows struck by Haig as part of the general Allied offensive of 1918. Nine more attacks were to follow before the armistice.

By the last week of September, Haig had

THE END IN SIGHT *German infantry surrender to Australian troops near the Hindenburg Line in September 1918. A few days later, the German commanders, Hindenburg and Ludendorff, told Kaiser Wilhelm II that Germany was defeated and warned him that the war must be ended.*

reached the Hindenburg Line, the most formidable of the German positions on the Western Front. It was a maze of strongpoints, trenches, pill-boxes and barbed wire. From England, the Chief of the Imperial General Staff, Sir Henry Wilson, warned Haig that the War Cabinet 'would become anxious if we receive heavy punishment in attacking the Hindenburg Line without success'.

The cabinet was still thinking in terms of the stalemate battles of 1916 and 1917. Its members were planning to achieve victory only in 1919. But Haig realised that the German army was tottering at last. The time had come to garner the fruits of the earlier terrible battles of attrition.

Between September 27 and 30 the armies of the British Empire smashed their way through the Hindenburg Line, and the French and Americans drove back the enemy on their sections of the front. On October 4 Germany

A NEW HORROR

By 1918 the new technology of war had reached its peak. Massed artillery bombardments, machine-guns, barbed wire, flame throwers – these and many other innovations had combined to make life in the trenches a living hell for soldiers of both sides.

Of all these new inventions it was poison gas that was most feared. The Germans first used gas at Ypres in 1915. It took the Allies by surprise, and French troops were seen clutching at their throats and choking as they ran. Though the Allies condemned this as an example of 'German barbarism', they were soon using gas in their turn. By 1918 millions of gas shells were being fired by both sides.

British gas victims line up for medical treatment at a dressing station. It took a year for an effective form of gas mask to be developed.

A menace from the air ends Britain's isolation

Britain suffered 52 air raids during the First World War, and 5806 tons of bombs were dropped, killing 557 people and injuring 1358. These casualties were slight by the standards of the Second World War, but even this limited toll had a profound effect on the morale of a people who had never experienced war at first hand.

At first, the German air threat to Britain was based on the Zeppelin, a hydrogen-filled airship. But the Zeppelin was only the first of a new race of war machines. In 1917 a new and more dangerous threat appeared in British skies – the Gotha bomber.

Terror in the skies
When an area was raided, industrial production would drop by 25 per cent because of absenteeism. And there was a public outcry at the lack of effective protection from air attack. Slowly an air-defence system was built up. By the end of the war, London and other important cities were protected by guns, searchlights, sound locators and fighters.

By 1918 the newly founded Royal Air Force numbered 22,000 planes. It was the largest air force in the world.

Yet the British were slow to learn the full lessons of air power. At the end of the war, the RAF was drastically run down. And 20 years later, on the eve of another war, British air power had once again to be built up almost from scratch.

The Daily Chronicle

LONDON, TUESDAY, NOVEMBER 12, 1918.   ONE PENNY

+ No. 17.702.

END OF THE GREAT WORLD WAR.

Extra Late Edition.

SURRENDER OF GERMANY.

ARMISTICE SIGNED.

ALL FIGHTING SUBMARINES TO BE HANDED OVER.

The end of the world-wide war was announced yesterday in the House of Commons by the Prime Minister in the following historic declaration:—

The Armistice was signed at five o'clock this morning. Hostilities ceased on all fronts at 11 a.m. to-day. . . . Thus came to an end the cruellest and most terrible war that has ever scourged mankind. I hope we may say that thus, on this fateful morning, came to an end all wars.

CHIEF POINTS IN CONDITIONS OF ARMISTICE.

End of fighting by air, land and sea.

Evacuation of invaded lands—Belgium, France, Alsace-Lorraine, Luxemburg—and repatriation of all inhabitants of those lands, within 14 days.

Evacuation of countries on left bank of Rhine within 31 days.

and all stocks, shares and money removed.

Restoration (to Allies in trust) of Russian or Rumanian gold yielded to, or taken by, Germany.

What Germany Surrenders.

Germany to surrender, in good condition:—

[J. Russell & Sons.

With you I rejoice and thank . . . d for the victories which the Allied arms have won, bringing hostil . . . ys to an end and peace within sight.

[King, . . . er, from the balcony of Buckingham Palace.

EX-KAISER A FUGITIVE.

UNCONFIRMED REPORT OF THE SHOOTING OF CROWN PRINCE.

PROBABLE INTERNMENT OF WILLIAM II.

HINDENBURG REMAINS AT GERMAN MAIN HEADQUARTERS.

William II. has fled to Holland, and as he crossed the frontier wearing a military uniform and sword, it is believed he will be interned.

Hindenburg, contrary to report, has not fled with his fallen master, but accompanying the party were the Kaiserin and at least one of her sons.

The following message was received at a late hour last night:—

AMSTERDAM, Monday.

It is reported that the Crown Prince has been shot. Details are lacking.—Central News.

HOW THE KAISER CAME.

CHANGES INTO CIVILIAN ATTIRE REACHING HOLLAND.

From "The Daily Chronicle" Special Correspondent, George Renwick.

AMSTERDAM, Monday.

It was on Sunday morning, almost precisely at 7.30, that the ex-Kaiser William II. saw the last of Germany and crossed the Belgian-Dutch frontier into exile.

On Saturday evening a German general arrived at Maastricht, and put himself into communication with the Dutch authorities, informing them that the ex-Kaiser would arrive on Dutch territory on the following day. At the hour I have mentioned a train of ten automobiles approached the little half Belgian half Dutch village of Mousend, and drew up in the neighbourhood of the Custom Office. . . .

upon another train. The two trains were under Dutch escort to Eysden, and kept there pending instructions from The Hague.

Here again the Kaiser appeared on the platform, this time in civilian clothes, and walked about for a little while. The larger number of the suite, however, kept out of sight.

It was in the train at the little station of Eysden that the ex-monarch spent the first night of exile. The station was held by soldiers and mounted police, and the public were kept at a good distance.

GEORGE RENWICK.

HINDENBURG REMAINS.

TO RECEIVE SOLDIERS' COUNCIL AT HEADQUARTERS.

AMSTERDAM, Monday.

A Berlin . . . .

VICTORY AT LAST *The* Daily Chronicle *front page for November 12, 1918, proclaims the end of the war and the Kaiser's flight from Germany to exile in Holland. After four years of bloodshed, in which over 8 million soldiers on both sides perished, Germany had finally surrendered.*

---

asked President Woodrow Wilson of the United States to settle the terms of an armistice.

But throughout the month of October, while peace negotiations went on, the Allied armies kept up their remorseless offensives, first on one sector of the front and then another. They cleared the Belgian coast and drove the Germans steadily off French soil.

'The end of a frightful four years'
This pressure was not confined to the Western Front. Far off in Syria, the British pursued a routed Turkish army back to Damascus, and then beyond Aleppo. On October 30 Turkey signed an armistice. The day before, Bulgaria, defeated by an Allied army based on Salonika, had asked for terms. On November 3, Germany's sole remaining ally, Austria, signed an armistice.

In Germany itself, revolution broke out. Yet the German army fought on. Then, at last, on November 11, an armistice was signed by the new republican German government,

which had come into power two weeks earlier when the Kaiser abdicated.

It was the soldiers of the British Empire who played the greatest part in the final triumphant campaign on the Western Front. They took 188,700 prisoners, as against 196,070 by the French, Belgian and American forces. They captured 2840 guns, compared to the 3775 taken by their three allies.

In November 1918, the greatest war Britain had yet fought was over. On Armistice Day a British regular officer, Brigadier-General Jack, summed up the war in his diary: 'Incidents flash through the memory: the battle of the first four months: the awful winters in water-logged trenches, cold and miserable: the terrible trench assaults and shell fire of the next three years: loss of friends, exhaustion and wounds: the stupendous victories of the last few months: our enemies all beaten to their knees.

Thank God! The end of a frightful four years . . .'

A NATION ON RATIONS

Air raids were only one of the dangers that the British had to face at home in the last two years of the war. By the middle of 1917, the success of the German U-boat campaign had brought Britain close to starvation. Thousands waited patiently in line outside the shops for food. A new word was borrowed from France to describe this phenomenon – the queue.

In February 1918, for the first time in Britain's history, rationing was introduced in response to popular demand. But, paradoxically, this revolutionary step was no longer necessary. The U-boat's moment of supremacy had been ended by the convoy system, and the consumption of food was not heavily restricted. It was in Germany – victim of the Royal Navy's blockade – that there was starvation.

A 1918 ration book. Rationing was not fully abolished until three years after the war.

Nine days that shook Britain to its foundation

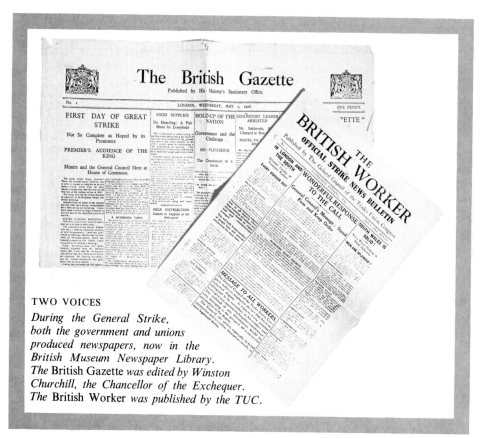

TWO VOICES

During the General Strike, both the government and unions produced newspapers, now in the British Museum Newspaper Library.
The British Gazette *was edited by Winston Churchill, the Chancellor of the Exchequer.*
The British Worker *was published by the TUC.*

For nine days in May 1926, Britain's industrial life was brought to a standstill. On the orders of the Trades Union Congress, over 2 million workers in vital sectors of British industry – including miners, dockers, printworkers, shipbuilders and workers in transport, power and construction – downed tools from midnight on Monday, May 3. The stoppage was total.

A nation at a standstill

The threat of a General Strike had been looming over Britain for a year, provoked by the crisis in the mining industry. In April 1925 Britain had returned to the gold standard, restoring the old pre-war exchange rate between sterling and the dollar. But this step was inspired more by illusions about Britain's financial strength than by sound economic principles. It forced exporters to raise their prices abroad.

The coal industry was among the worst hit. In June 1925 its owners announced that the only way out of their crisis was to reduce wages and lengthen working hours.

The miners rallied under the slogan 'Not a penny off the pay, not a minute on the day', and prepared to resist the demands of the owners. A strike in the pits was averted at the last moment, when the government decided to grant a temporary subsidy to the mining industry, and to appoint a Royal Commission under Sir Herbert Samuel to investigate its problems. But the government had only bought time. In March 1926 both sides rejected the Samuel Commission's recommendations. On May 1 the miners were locked out by their employers.

Immediately, the TUC called for a nationwide stoppage in chosen sectors of British industry. Their object was to force the government to find a satisfactory solution to the mining dispute. And the government, the nation – even the TUC – was astounded by the response as Britain's workers rallied to support the miners. In most of the affected areas, the strike was almost 90 per cent solid. Britain had never seen anything like it.

Fear of revolution

In this situation, unprecedented countermeasures were adopted. The trade unions had taken on the government, and their challenge could not be allowed to succeed. The Prime Minister, Stanley Baldwin, was already prepared. His plans to meet the strike had been laid in the autumn of 1925, and now they swung smoothly into action.

The major tasks facing the government were the preservation of order, and the distribution of food and other essential supplies. Warships moved into position off major ports and rivers. The navy went into the docks to unload waiting ships. The army was given responsibility for food distribution. Civil commissioners were appointed to supervise operations in each of ten areas into which the country was divided. Hundreds of special constables were sworn in. Most heartening of all for Baldwin and his colleagues was the response to their appeal for volunteers. Thousands of them were soon at work.

But, though many feared that the strike was the first step on the road to a violent revolution, there was far less violence than had been expected. The peaceful nature of the strike had been foreseen by the socialist writer Beatrice Webb, who suggested that it would 'turn out to be a batch of compulsory Bank Holidays without any recreation and a lot of dreary walking to and fro'.

And for many, it was a nine-day Bank Holiday – including a good deal more entertainment than Beatrice Webb thought.

Volunteering to beat the strike

London was the centre of the tremendous volunteer operation to counter the strike's effects on the nation's political and commercial life. Thousands of people left their desks, their homes or their colleges to register for work.

Among them were hundreds of undergraduates who ran London's bus services with style and wit. To travel on their vehicles was more a jaunt than a journey, for their progress was unreliable. Many drivers were ignorant of the routes. Some made wide detours to deliver passengers to special destinations. Others were obstructed by angry pickets. The volunteers had their own answer to this last threat: 'The driver of this bus is a student of Guy's Hospital', was the notice chalked on one vehicle; 'The conductor of this bus is a student of Guy's. Anybody who interferes with either is liable to be a patient of Guy's.'

Victory for the government

Other volunteers had the chance to fulfil schoolboy ambitions to become enginedrivers. Westminster Underground station was manned by two lords, a knight, and an army major – all MPs. Volunteers kept some daily papers going. Lady Edwina Mountbatten became a telephonist for the *Daily Express*, and eminent readers of *The Times* – including two duchesses, a viscountess and the daughter of a marchioness – drove lorries to distribute the paper. And the government, too, produced its own newspaper – the *British Gazette*.

Only a handful of clashes disturbed the prevailing calm. Army escorts for food convoys were a common sight in London. But in general the strikers were orderly. In Plymouth there was even a football match between

Police and Strikers (the Strikers won 2–0).

On May 12 the TUC called off the strike. Never wholeheartedly in favour of such massive industrial action, the TUC had conducted negotiations with the government throughout the nine days. They reached a compromise settlement of the miners' issue: only when the mine-owners had adopted the Samuel Commission's reorganisation proposals would a wage reduction be permitted.

But the miners themselves rejected this plan. They stayed out for another six months, until starvation forced them back to the pits.

Lessons from failure

The miners felt betrayed by the failure of the General Strike. But for many trade unionists, the lessons of the strike were of lasting importance. They realised that they could not lead Britain's workers towards revolution. The threat of class war receded, and Britain's trade union and Labour leaders prepared for the time when the processes of democracy would give them a real chance to wield power.

VOLUNTEERS *Undergraduates unloading milk churns at King's Cross Station. Students from Oxford and Cambridge responded in their hundreds to the government's call for volunteers at the start of the strike. In London they ran buses and trains.*

SHOW OF FORCE *As the strike went on, the government resolved on an open show of strength. On Sunday, May 9, six days after the strike had begun, troops and armoured cars escorted a food convoy through the East End of London. Three days later, the strike was called off.*

MEN OF ACTION *Guarded by soldiers, sailors unload rations for their comrades sent into Neasden power station to supply electricity. Troops were also used in the docks, where pickets were deterred by the threat of machine-guns.*

In 25 years a new party rises to power

TO-MORROW – WHEN LABOUR RULES

NEW AGE *The men, women and children of Britain look forward to a better future 'when Labour rules' in this 1922 election poster.*

In January 1924 a new era dawned in British politics. Ramsay MacDonald became the country's first Labour Prime Minister. In the general election of December 1923 the Conservatives had lost over 90 seats, and their government was defeated when the new Parliament met. Since its foundation in 1900, the Labour Party had made dramatic progress. In less than 25 years, the number of Labour MPs had risen from two to 191. Now Labour, as the next largest party in Parliament, was called on to form a minority government.

Observing the conventions

Many traditionalists viewed the prospect of a Labour government with horror. But their fears that Britain was heading for revolution, proved groundless. For thoughts of revolution were far from Ramsay MacDonald's mind.

When George V invited him to form the new government, MacDonald assured the king that there would be no concessions to Labour's fiery left-wingers. He promised to prevent his followers from celebrating victory by singing the 'Red Flag' in the House of Commons. And MacDonald also insisted that his ministers must observe the customary etiquette by wearing court dress at Buckingham Palace.

Many Labour voters saw this as treachery to the ideals of the movement, and reacted with bitterness. But MacDonald's government needed the votes of the 158 Liberal MPs in order to survive. In this situation, Labour had no hope of adopting radical measures.

The first Labour government lasted only eight months. Five years later MacDonald formed a second government – again in a minority. And in 1931, in the throes of the economic depression, MacDonald agreed to form a National Government with the Conservatives and Liberals. Shocked by this 'betrayal', the Labour Party split in two. It was to be 14 years before a reunited Labour Party swept to power, with an overwhelming mandate, to fulfil the goals which its founders had cherished.

A king renounces his throne for 'the woman I love'

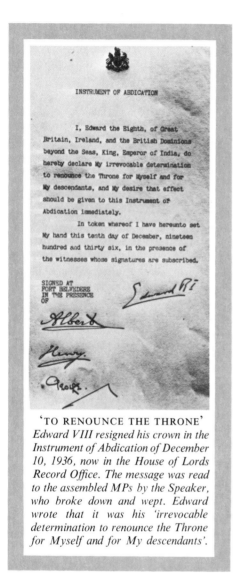

'TO RENOUNCE THE THRONE'
Edward VIII resigned his crown in the Instrument of Abdication of December 10, 1936, now in the House of Lords Record Office. The message was read to the assembled MPs by the Speaker, who broke down and wept. Edward wrote that it was his 'irrevocable determination to renounce the Throne for Myself and for My descendants'.

Edward Albert Christian George Andrew Patrick David Windsor reigned as Edward VIII for just 325 days. At 10 a.m. on Thursday, December 10, 1936, the still-uncrowned king-emperor abdicated. On the following evening, he broadcast to the people of Britain and the empire: 'A few hours ago I discharged my last duty as King and Emperor. I now quit altogether public affairs, and I lay down my burden.' Within hours of this statement, the ex-king had boarded the destroyer HMS *Fury* in Portsmouth Harbour, and slipped out of England to join the woman he loved, in a lifetime of exile.

In the quarter of a century since he became Prince of Wales in 1911, Edward had done much to endear himself to his subjects. Dashing and debonair, he had provided a refreshing contrast to the austere and restricted life of his parents, George V and Queen

Mary – to their disapproval. And in adult life, Edward reacted sharply against the atmosphere of hallowed tradition and strict convention that had enveloped his childhood upbringing. During the First World War, he asked to be allowed to fight at the Front, but had to be content with being attached to the General Staff in France. And in the 1920's he relaxed from official duties at parties, nightclubs and country weekends – a foretaste, it seemed, of the more informal style he would adopt as king.

There was another side to Edward's unorthodoxy. Notwithstanding his indulgence in fashionable pleasures, the prince also revealed a strong social conscience. In 1926 he shocked many of his subjects by contributing to the miners' relief fund after the General Strike. Ten years later, as king, he made his own views clear when he saw the misery of the depressed mining valleys of South Wales. His comment was: 'Terrible, terrible, something will be done about this.' It seemed evidence of more than formal sympathy with the plight of the unemployed.

Dislike of convention

Edward's party-going and his social concern were not contradictions, but the two sides of a single coin. The keynote of his character was a deeply felt dislike of the formal conventions that bound his life. Edward's ambition was to give the English monarchy a more modern appearance, to make it more accessible to millions of ordinary people.

It was this genuine commitment to the monarchy as an institution that led Edward to abdicate when he felt that he could not live up to its demands. He had often doubted his ability and, as he said in his abdication broadcast: 'I have found it impossible to carry the heavy burden of responsibility and to discharge my duties as a King as I would wish, without the help and support of the woman I love.'

Keeping the royal secret

That woman was an American, Mrs Wallis Ernest Simpson, whom Edward had met in 1931. The prince soon fell in love with her. Three years later, Henry 'Chips' Channon, a prominent member of high society, noted that Mrs Simpson 'already had the air of a personage who walks into a room as though she almost expected to be curtsied to'.

According to the rigid standards of the age, Mrs Simpson was an unsuitable candidate for the hand of the future King of England. She had divorced her first husband and was now in the process of dissolving her second marriage. Since the Church of England then refused to

SMILE THAT WON AMERICA *Edward conquered the United States during his tour of 1919, when this photograph was taken.*

bless the marriage of divorced people, Edward could neither go through a religious wedding ceremony with Mrs Simpson nor have her crowned as queen. As king, he was 'Supreme Governor of the Church of England', so his dilemma was more than a personal one.

The new king and Mrs Simpson were frequently in each other's company after his accession in January 1936, and in the summer went on a holiday cruise together. But for months after the royal romance was common knowledge throughout the world, the British Press voluntarily kept silent.

It was on December 1 that Bishop Blunt of Bradford made a public comment on the king's 'need for grace', and the long-awaited storm broke. The bishop's remarks were reported in the *Yorkshire Post*, and two days later an editorial in *The Times* spoke openly of a 'marriage incompatible with the Throne'.

Marriage or the throne

The crisis came at the end of a dismal year for Britain. Hitler had occupied the Rhineland in March; Mussolini's troops had conquered Ethiopia in May; and the Spanish Civil War had broken out in July. The world's political future looked grim. 'For the monarchy to lose the affection and respect of the people would be to imperil the continuance of the Empire, and thus to add immensely to the perils of this troubled world,' declared the *Church Times*. 'If the King marries Mrs Simpson, relations between the Church and the State must be fundamentally affected.'

Stanley Baldwin, the Prime Minister, rallied his cabinet firmly behind Church opinion. The king must choose between the crown and Mrs Simpson. Sympathisers with Edward wondered whether Baldwin's firmness had anything to do with the king's indignation at what he had seen in South Wales. His comments could have been taken as a criticism of the government's

THE SPORTING PRINCE *Edward is pictured after a successful partridge shoot on the estate of Sir Walford Selby, the British Ambassador to Austria. On such holiday visits abroad, Edward would combine business with pleasure, using his trips to show the British flag as well as to relax.*

VALLEYS OF GLOOM *Crowds surround Edward during his tour of industrial valleys in Monmouthshire in 1936. The poverty he found among the unemployed miners deeply shocked him, and he said that 'something will be done'. It was this social conscience which helped to establish his popularity.*

policies. 'God save the King from Baldwin!' declared the demonstrators' placards.

But despite such proof of his public popularity, influential opinion was against the king. And in this ultimate test of duty, Edward did not fail. He knew he must marry the woman he loved, and his government had made it clear that he could not remain king if he did so. Less than a week after the crisis broke, on December 5, Edward agreed to abdicate.

'Now we all have a new King'

It took another five days for the legal and constitutional arrangements to be completed. Baldwin's government drew up the formal Instrument of Abdication and rushed it through both Houses of Parliament. On December 11, 1936, Edward spoke to the public as a private citizen, first declaring his allegiance to the new king, his brother Albert, Duke of York. He ended: 'Now we all have a new King. I wish him, and you, his people, happiness and prosperity with all my heart. God bless you all. God save the King.'

IN EXILE *Edward married Mrs Simpson in June 1937 at Château de Cande, near Tours, France.*

George VI: A shy man devoted to his duty

Albert, Duke of York, had not been trained for kingship. Aged 41 when he came to the throne, adopting the title of George VI, he was shy and nervous, and suffered from an acute stammer. On the first night of his reign he admitted his fear to his cousin, Lord Louis Mountbatten: 'I never wanted this to happen. I'm only a naval officer, it's the only thing I know about.'

Yet, due to his courage, his doubts were not borne out and within a few years of his accession, the king was even more popular than his brother had been.

With medical assistance, George mastered his embarrassing stammer. He continued to support projects such as his Duke of York's camps – where, in shorts and shirtsleeves, he mingled with boys drawn from both public schools and slum areas.

But the supreme test of George's life came in 1939. In rising to this challenge, he leant heavily on the extraordinary gifts of his wife, Queen Elizabeth. The daughter of the Earl of

INTO THE LIMELIGHT *George VI said that he had 'never seen a state paper' before coming to the throne after his brother's abdication in 1936.*

Strathmore, she was the first British-born queen since the 17th century, and she was blessed with the rare gift of a popular touch.

In Britain's darkest hour, the king and queen lived and suffered in the midst of their people. They accepted rationing, they refused to leave England and, in September 1940, they even lived through the bombing of Buckingham Palace.

George personally introduced the George Cross and Medal, to recognise civilian heroism and, again on his own initiative, he bestowed the George Cross on the Mediterranean island-fortress of Malta. George's undemonstrative leadership was recognised by his wartime Prime Minister, Winston Churchill. He told the king: 'Your Majesties are more beloved by all classes and conditions than any of the princes of the past.'

Britain stands alone to face its 'finest hour'

MISTRESS OF THE AIR

A Spitfire – the plane that won the Battle of Britain – can now be seen at the RAF Museum, Hendon. Designed by the brilliant R. J. Mitchell, it had a top speed of 361 mph and its manoeuvrability made it more than a match for its German counterpart, the Messerschmitt 109. The Spitfire's success made it a legend, and even the German pilots envied the RAF the plane. When Göring asked a pilot what planes he would like, he answered 'Give me a squadron of Spitfires'.

Only two weeks after Germany launched her long-awaited offensive in the West on May 10, 1940, the British cabinet was discussing the possibility that France would soon be defeated. If this happened, could Britain survive alone?

This was the question that the newly appointed Prime Minister, Winston Churchill, put to the chiefs of staff at the end of May, just as the British army was beginning its evacuation from Dunkirk. They answered: 'The crux of the matter is air superiority.' For the British army, after its losses in France, did not have the strength to drive out an invader.

Battle in the sky

The Germans, too, were aware of the crucial importance of air power when, after the fall of France in June, they began to plan Operation Sealion – the invasion of England. Because of the strength of the Royal Navy, it would only be possible to launch an invasion if the *Luftwaffe* had first won air supremacy.

Reichsmarshal Hermann Göring, commander of the German air force, had no doubts that his invincible *Luftwaffe* would succeed. It had triumphed in the skies over Poland, Norway, France and the Low Countries: now it would crush the outnumbered Fighter Command of the Royal Air Force.

On July 10, Göring opened the first phase of his air offensive – attacks on Channel ports and shipping. But it was not until August 13 – *Adlerstag* – ('Eagle Day'), as the Germans optimistically dubbed it – that the Battle of Britain began in earnest. The pattern set on that day was to be followed throughout the

blue-skied summer of 1940. German planes took off in waves from their bases in northern France, took up formation high over the Channel and headed inland over the English coast. Their targets were the RAF airfields. For the first time, the British watched what was to become a familiar spectacle: vapour trails stretching across their skies; glinting specks twisting in combat, high in the sunshine.

The *Luftwaffe* had about 2500 aircraft available for its offensive; 800 of them were Messerschmitt 109 single-seat fighters. Fighter Command numbered no more than 700 serviceable Spitfires and Hurricanes. England's salvation depended on these aircraft and the 1400 men who were now to win immortality as 'the Few'.

But, though outnumbered in the air, the pilots had a major advantage over the Germans. Britain's southern and eastern shores bristled with a chain of radar stations, the first in the world. Radar provided accurate and early warning of the position and direction of approaching enemy squadrons.

And Fighter Command was the most advanced air-defence organisation in the world. Its centre lay in Command Headquarters at Stanmore, Middlesex, where the

'THEIR FINEST HOUR' *Fighter Command had a strength of just over 1400 pilots at the start of the battle, but in August alone 300 of them were lost. Waiting in their messes (above) until the alert sounded, pilots would 'scramble' for their planes – in this case Hurricanes (below). Fighter Command flew 600 sorties a day during July and August. Its great victory over the* Luftwaffe *on September 15 turned the tide of battle decisively in Britain's favour.*

information from radar stations and observation posts was plotted on maps and charts. These gave the head of Fighter Command, Air Chief Marshal Sir Hugh Dowding, a continuous picture of the fighting, enabling him to supervise and co-ordinate all operations.

Tactical control of the battle lay in the hands of group and sector commanders, who had their own subsidiary operations rooms. These 'ops rooms' gave the pilots in the air up-to-date information and instructions.

'Their finest hour'

From the very start of the battle, the Germans found that they were failing to achieve the decisive successes they had expected. Time and again their formations would find British fighter squadrons waiting for them. German aircraft losses were consistently higher than those of the British.

Then, on August 24, the Germans changed their tactics. Instead of dispersing their efforts over many targets, they began to concentrate on Fighter Command's own airfields and sector stations – and the sector stations, with their vital communications centres, were the key to British control of the battle.

Within a fortnight, the fighting had swung heavily against the defenders. As the airfields and sector stations were knocked out or badly damaged, Fighter Command's efficiency began to suffer. Losses in the air were mounting dangerously. Between August 24 and September 6, the British lost 295 fighters totally destroyed and another 171 badly damaged. But the aircraft factories only managed to produce 269 new machines.

The brave young pilots were as indispensable as their aircraft – and now the original band who had led the fight to defend their country only a few weeks earlier were sadly depleted in number. In August, 300 fighter pilots were lost, and the flying schools could provide only 260 young and inexperienced replacements. By the first week of September, Dowding knew that the tide of the battle was turning against him.

But then a German mistake gave Fighter Command a much-needed respite. On September 8, stung by a British raid on Berlin, Göring switched his offensive from the hard-hit airfields and sector stations to London. For Londoners, it was the start of the Blitz, but the Air Ministry was able to seize the opportunity to rebuild its strength. The pendulum of aircraft losses once again began to swing against the Germans, who now prepared for the climax of the battle. This came on September 15. The Germans launched a huge raid on London, intending it to be the final blow against both Fighter Command and British morale. It was to pave the way for invasion but instead, though much damage was done to London's docklands, the *Luftwaffe* lost 60 aircraft to the RAF's 26.

The events of the day made it plain to Hitler that the RAF was far from defeated, and therefore invasion was impossible. Two days later, he postponed the invasion.

The Battle of Britain, the first decisive battle in history to be fought solely in the air, had been won by the RAF. Hitler had met his first defeat. But when the *Luftwaffe* faced up to the fact that it had lost the Battle of Britain, it at once switched to another strategy – one that had never been known to fail – the terror bombing of cities. For the British people a new and brutal word was about to enter the language – the Blitz.

The first major raid on London came on September 8, 1940. From 5 p.m. onwards, hundreds of Nazi bombers struck at the docks of the East End. The first waves carried incendiaries and, guided by the light of the fires, successive waves of attacks continued into the night, and until 4.30 the following morning.

Striking at the capital

The destruction was immense, and London's civil defence was stretched to its limits. By the time the bombing ceased, there were nine huge fires, and countless smaller blazes. The fire officer trying to deal with the biggest blaze of all, in the Surrey Docks, sent a message to his superiors: 'Send all the bloody pumps you've got. The whole bloody world's on fire!' The casualties were equally tragic; 430 Londoners were killed, 1600 seriously injured and thousands made homeless.

This was the scene that the British and their leaders had dreaded for years. Thanks to the bravery and skill of the RAF, the *Luftwaffe* was soon prevented from bombing London

NERVE CENTRE *At Fighter Command headquarters at Stanmore, Middlesex, a constant watch was kept on the enemy. There, Sir Hugh Dowding commanded the battle which saved Britain.*

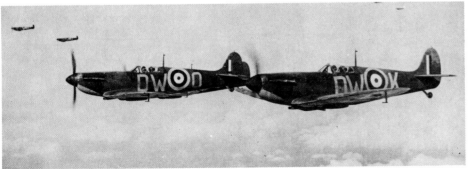

SPITFIRES IN THE SKY *Guided by the top-secret radar system, Spitfire squadrons such as these above, from Biggin Hill, Kent, helped to fight off the* Luftwaffe *during the Battle of Britain. The public collected scrap metal and gave their pots and pans to help build them.*

BACKROOM BOYS *While the 'few' were in the skies, ground teams worked unremittingly to provide new planes and ammunition.*

349

and the other cities of Britain by day. But for the next 76 nights, with the exception of November 2, when bad weather grounded Göring's planes, London was attacked as no city had ever been. Night after night, the anti-aircraft guns deployed in and around London kept up a non-stop barrage.

With these night attacks, the government had to come to terms with a new situation. Before the war, all civil defence plans were based on the belief that the enemy would strike one overwhelming blow by day. No one had foreseen continuous raids lasting from 14 to 16 hours. Nor had anyone expected that people would have to hibernate by night, nor that thousands of homeless would have to be cared for. By November, London had 250,000 of them – men, women and children.

Welfare services for the victims of the Blitz were swiftly organised. The Underground was opened as shelters, and the Aldwych branch was even completely closed and turned into a deep shelter. By the end of September, more than 177,000 people were taking refuge every night in the 'tube'. And some Londoners looked further afield for a shelter from the bombs. Several thousand took refuge in the caves at Chislehurst in Kent. Special trains were run there each evening, and life soon became so organised that the inhabitants of the caves had their own concerts, church services – and even a barber's shop.

All the capital's citizens showed defiant courage. Thousands volunteered to serve as air-raid wardens or firewatchers. Despite the bombing, essential workers stuck to their posts. And, by widening their attacks over the whole capital, Göring's raiders created a unity of spirit never seen before.

'London can take it'

During the day 'Business as usual' was London's slogan. By night the need was for cool courage. When the BBC was bombed as the news was being read, listeners heard a muffled crash and a voice assuring the news reader that it was 'all right'. The news then continued without a break.

Throughout London, signs appeared in shattered shop-fronts. 'Blast !' was the briefest, 'More open than usual' the most common. Soon, bomb stories became so common that some Londoners wore badges bearing the slogan 'I've got a bomb story too!' London was the country's only major sufferer for two months. Despite the black-out, the great U-bend of the Thames glinting in the dimmest moonlight made it impossible to hide the position of the city. The capital was the natural target of the *Luftwaffe* in its attempts to break British morale and force Britain to sue for peace.

Then, in November, the *Luftwaffe* again changed its tactics. London, it was clear, could not be bombed into submission. From November 18 to January 19, London experienced only six full-scale raids – though one of them, on December 29, was more destructive than any that had gone before. For the second time, 270 years after Sir Christopher Wren had rebuilt the city, all London seemed to be ablaze. Only the bad weather, which prevented the *Luftwaffe* returning to the attack, saved the city from complete destruction.

But, by this time, London was not alone. Göring's attack had spread over the entire country. And the luckless city of Coventry was its first victim.

On November 14, the *Luftwaffe* attacked Coventry for ten hours, using a new direction-finding method based on following radio

HITLER'S TARGET *The great U-bend of the River Thames made it easy for the Luftwaffe's bombers to pinpoint central London, even during the blackout. Much of the East End was soon reduced to rubble. Casualties were heavy, with thousands killed and many more made homeless. Many historic monuments were also destroyed – including the House of Commons in May 1941.*

BANK STATION *The damage after the* Luftwaffe *hit the Bank Underground station in London in January 1941. Below – cheers for Winston Churchill as he meets Manchester bomb victims after the* Luftwaffe *struck the city.*

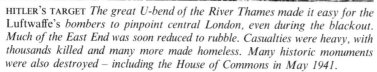

MERCY MISSION *Rescuers freeing the landlord of a public house. Bombing united rich and poor. When Buckingham Palace was hit, the queen said: 'It makes me feel I can look the East End in the face.'*

waves – the *Knickebein*. It was a vital target as a centre of the British armaments industry. But no attempt was made to pinpoint its factories. Incendiary-carrying pathfinders first set fire to the medieval city centre which, with its 500-year-old cathedral, was soon totally destroyed. Then hundreds of tons of bombs were poured down in one concentrated attack. One-third of the city was destroyed, and over 4000 of its citizens were killed.

Climax of the offensive

Delighted with the success of their attack, the Germans coined a word to describe the fate of Coventry. It was the verb *Coventrieren* – 'to coventrise'.

Other cities soon came to understand the meaning of the word. On November 24, Bristol was 'coventrised'. Merseyside, Southampton, Portsmouth, Plymouth, Birmingham – even far-away Belfast – suffered the same blows. In Merseyside's 'May Week', Liverpool and its neighbours were bombed unmercifully for eight successive nights in May 1941. Morale shuddered – but it did not break. Even in Coventry itself, armaments production at the giant Morris Motors factory was back to normal within six weeks of the devastating November raid.

Finally, on May 10, London itself was 'coventrised'. It was the worst air-raid the city experienced in the course of the war; 1436 were killed and 1792 were injured. Fires raged from Hammersmith in the west to Romford in the east. The House of Commons was burnt to the ground, the Tower of London and Westminster Abbey were hit. In the British Museum 250,000 books were burnt. More than 2200 separate fires were burning, and they raged for 11 days.

But the final blow never came. For, despairing of his attempts to break Britain's morale, Hitler had already ordered the abandonment of Operation Sealion – the invasion of Britain – and most of the *Luftwaffe* was now transferred to the east to prepare for action against Russia.

The Blitz was never to be resumed on the same scale. In its eight months, 43,000 had died, 86,000 had been seriously injured, and 151,000 more were slightly hurt. But Britons had shown that, in Churchill's words, they 'could take it'. And the experience had united them as never before.

RAZED CITY *The Germans coined a word for their destruction of Coventry in November 1940 – the verb* Coventrieren, *'to coventrise'. The* Luftwaffe *used a complex system to guide their bombers on to the target. Transmissions from two radio stations were arranged so as to intersect, and the bombers were guided 'blind' to their destination. The British had hitherto been able to distort the beams, but the Germans had now improved their methods. The horror of Coventry was the result. Within hours the city was destroyed.*

ON GUARD *The threat of German troops landing was real, and air-raid wardens were taught to use a gun. The king practised shooting in the palace gardens.*

Churchill's voice speaks for a united nation

UNITED FRONT *This poster symbolised the new mood of defiance against the enemy after Winston Churchill became Prime Minister.*

Winston Churchill presented himself and his new war cabinet to the House of Commons on May 13, 1940, with these stirring words. 'You ask, what is our policy? I will say: It is to wage war, by sea, land and air, with all our might and with all the strength that God can give us; to wage war against a monstrous tyranny, never surpassed in the dark, lamentable catalogue of human crime. That is our policy. You ask, what is our aim? I can answer in one word: Victory – victory at all costs, victory in spite of all terror; victory, however long and hard the road may be; for without victory there is no survival.'

Churchill was 66 years old. Throughout the previous decade of mounting tension in Europe he had been a lone, scorned voice. Now he was Prime Minister when Britain was in the most desperate plight of her history. By the end of June, after the fall of France, it seemed impossible that she could survive against the combined power of Nazi Germany and Fascist Italy.

Yet Churchill knew that this was a time not for reason, but for faith: for a simple, stubborn refusal to give in. And the British people were at one with their Prime Minister.

Churchill gave superb expression to the nation's mood. His towering personality symbolised a Britain embattled and unafraid.

Churchill did not seek to disguise the tremendous challenge facing the British. He offered them, he said, 'nothing but blood, toil, tears and sweat'. By openly admitting the grim reality, and by inviting every citizen to join him in lifting Britain from the depths, Churchill rendered the greatest single service of his career to his fellow countrymen.

Victory in North Africa – and the tide of war turns

DECORATION OF WAR
The Africa Star was awarded to all the troops who fought in the desert campaign in North Africa, which lasted from June 10, 1940, to May 12, 1943. This medal can be seen in the Imperial War Museum, London.

In the summer of 1942, British fortunes in the Second World War had reached their lowest point since the grim days of the fall of France two years before. In the Far East, the Japanese had conquered the 'impregnable' fortress of Singapore. In North Africa, the only front on which the British army faced its German and Italian enemies, the Eighth Army had just suffered a resounding defeat.

Since May 26, Erwin Rommel, the brilliant commander of the German *Panzerarmee Afrika*, had driven the British back 400 miles across the burning North African desert and deep into Egypt. He had captured the key stronghold of Tobruk, taking over 30,000 prisoners and masses of equipment. Now the British prepared to make a last-ditch stand at El Alamein. Defeat would open the way to Cairo and the Suez Canal.

Although the advance had taken its toll by reducing Rommel's strength to less than

9000 German and Italian troops and 60 tanks, he believed that success lay within his grasp. On the morning of June 30, the last of the retreating British took up position at El Alamein. Towards noon a sandstorm swept up, as thick as a London fog but oven-hot. The British peered into the billowing murk, waiting for it to form into the shapes of the German tanks which were pursuing them into the heart of Egypt. Then, out in the west, something moved – tanks, trucks and guns. A salvo crashed out from a battery of British field artillery. These were the first shots in the

FOES IN THE DESERT *Montgomery (above) and Rommel (right) had very different ideas on generalship. Rommel was a gambler, full of dash and daring, while Montgomery was more cautious. He never took unnecessary risks. But both men possessed the ability to get the best out of their troops. Their methods – putting their men 'in the picture' – and their insistence on constant contact with the soldiers in the front line shocked some of their contemporaries.*

two battles of El Alamein which were to decide the campaign in the Western Desert.

On July 1, Rommel attacked, swinging his forces south around the British position in a characteristically bold attempt to encircle his foe. But this time he found himself in trouble from the start. The German attack was hammered by British artillery from three sides.

Waiting to strike
For Rommel now faced a new opponent – General Sir Claude Auchinleck, the Commander-in-Chief Middle East, who had taken over direct command of the Eighth Army. Auchinleck told his troops: 'The enemy is stretching to his limit and thinks we are a beaten army. He hopes to take Egypt by bluff. Show him where he gets off.'

This was the beginning of a three-week duel between Rommel and Auchinleck. By mid-July Rommel was afraid that his own front would collapse under Auchinleck's blows.

In the last week of that month, Auchinleck tried to complete his success by destroying Rommel's army. Though his attacks failed to break through, he had saved Egypt.

But Churchill dismissed Auchinleck

when he refused to promise him an early renewal of the offensive. General Sir Harold Alexander was appointed C-in-C Middle East, and Lieutenant-General Sir Bernard Montgomery commander of the Eighth Army.

Montgomery, aged 55, was a master of the arts of leadership – a dedicated professional. He soon faced his first serious challenge. At the end of August, Rommel made a last attempt to break through to the Nile, but his gamble was defeated.

Despite Churchill's urgings, Montgomery refused to launch his own offensive until he was ready. He paused for nearly two months while the Eighth Army was reinforced with fresh troops and new equipment, including 300 American tanks. Montgomery's instructions to his men were to 'hit the enemy for six' and drive them out of North Africa.

Rommel knew that a British offensive was imminent and made his own preparations to meet it. He built a 4½ mile deep defensive zone between the Qattara Depression and the sea. There he had sown 'Devils' Gardens' of minefields, belts of barbed wire and pillboxes. Montgomery's solution to the problem that Rommel had set was to be equally methodical.

When the second Battle of El Alamein opened on October 23, Montgomery enjoyed complete superiority in the air and odds of two to one in men, tanks and guns over the combined German and Italian forces – despite the reinforcements they had received. At 9.40 p.m. the British artillery opened fire: 1000 guns began their barrage. The infantry advanced, their paths marked by shielded lamps and white tapes. But the attack failed to reach its objective, and co-operation between the armour and infantry broke down. Montgomery had to think again.

Defeat for the 'desert fox'

A 12 day struggle followed. It saw a piecemeal grinding forward by the Eighth Army, as Montgomery used his superior strength to wear the enemy down. On November 2, the British armour at last broke through into the open desert. Two days later, after a final tank battle at odds of 90 against 700, Rommel gave the order to retreat.

Thanks to Montgomery's resolution and his soldiers' dogged courage, Britain at last had a resounding victory to cheer after a grim year of defeat.

Winning the battle of the Atlantic

SINK THE 'BISMARCK'! *It took the Royal Navy seven days to finally corner the battleship* Bismarck *(above). The end of the* Bismarck, *which Hitler had boasted was unsinkable, was master-minded by Admiral Sir John Tovey (right).*

El Alamein was the turning point for Britain on land. The war at sea was to be won, six months later, in the North Atlantic.

Until 1943, the Battle of the Atlantic had run very much in Germany's favour. A vital lifeline for Britain, the North Atlantic was also an essential supply route for the eventual invasion of Hitler's Europe.

'Our worst evil'

The British had one great success – the sinking of Germany's finest battleship, the *Bismarck* in May 1941, at the cost of Britain's most powerful battle-cruiser, HMS *Hood*. After this, the German surface fleet played little part in the Atlantic struggle. But the victory did not stop the U-boat menace. In 1942 the Allies lost 1664 ships, a total of nearly 8 million tons. And 1160 of them were sunk by U-boat attacks, which Winston Churchill described as 'our worst evil'.

In March 1943 500,000 tons of shipping were sunk in just 20 days. The Germans were on the point of finally cutting the North Atlantic lifeline. Yet within two months the U-boats had been defeated. An all-out effort mobilised escort carriers now released from the North African landings; 40 long-range bombers were made available by the USA; and improvements in radar meant that surface ships could now detect U-boats without themselves being detected.

In the first three weeks of May alone, no fewer than 31 U-boats were sunk. On May 24, 1943, Admiral Doenitz acknowledged defeat by withdrawing his submarines from the Atlantic. From now on the sea lanes were open to feed the final offensive in Europe.

AT THE BATTLEFRONT *British troops capture a German tank and its crew at El Alamein. The Germans lost 15,000 men killed, wounded and captured during the battle, and over 200 of their 250 tanks were seized or destroyed.*

SURRENDER *German prisoners are rounded up at El Alamein. The Prime Minister, Winston Churchill, saw the victory as a turning point in the war. He said: 'This is not the end. It is not even the beginning of the end. But it is, perhaps, the end of the beginning.'*

The Allies invade France as the 'longest day' dawns

FLOATING MEMORIAL
The cruiser Belfast *took part in the bombardment which supported the Allied landings on the beaches of Normandy in June 1944. The ship is now a floating museum and is moored in the Thames near Tower Bridge.*

In the spring and summer of 1944, the whole of southern England was one vast military camp. Quiet country lanes rang to the marching feet of Allied troops, while a never-ending stream of traffic – guns, tanks, lorries and jeeps – crammed the main roads. Both the men and their machines were heading in one direction – towards the sea.

The British knew full well that the long-awaited Second Front – the invasion of France – was imminent. Winston Churchill had broadcast that 'the hour of our greatest effort and action is approaching'. And across the Channel, the Germans, too, waited for the Allies to strike. Field-Marshal Rommel, commander of the Nazi defences on the French coast, commented to his aide: 'Believe me, Lang, the first 24 hours of the invasion will be decisive... for the Allies, as well as for Germany, it will be the longest day.'

'The sound of shells bursting'
On June 6, 1944, at 6.35 a.m., the longest day dawned as the first wave of landing craft grounded on the Normandy beaches. 'The wind was bringing them now the sound of shells bursting ashore,' wrote the novelist Alexander Baron, an official government observer of the D-Day landings. 'Each man could feel the thudding detonation somewhere

inside him. The talking stopped. Men took up their rifles and machine carbines; there was a clack of bolts being drawn and rammed home. The slow, wallowing motion of the landing craft eased; they were coming into shallower water. There was smoke across the beach ahead, and the black plumes of explosions, each with a cherry-red flicker at its heart. The landing craft nosed ashore through a mass of floating rubbish.' Operation Overlord was under way.

The Normandy invasion was a combined operation, the fruit of meticulous planning at every level. Since January 1943 plans for the Second Front had been going ahead. It was the British Combined Operations Headquarters which had originally studied the technical problems of seaborne landings and developed the necessary specialist equipment, such as landing-ships and craft with unloading ramps.

The supreme commander of the operation, General Dwight D. Eisenhower, was American. His deputy, Air Chief Marshal Sir Arthur Tedder, was a Briton. So, too, were the naval commander, Admiral Sir Bertram Ramsey, the air commander, Air Chief Marshal Sir Trafford Leigh-Mallory, and the commander of the ground forces, Field-Marshal Sir Bernard Montgomery. Montgomery was also responsible for drawing up the final assault plan for the Allied forces.

Battle of wits
The scale of the expedition and the numbers involved dwarfed all historical precedents. One and a half million American troops had been shipped across the Atlantic to join 2 million Allied soldiers, of a dozen different nationalities, already mustered in England. As Eisenhower joked: 'Only the great number of barrage balloons floating constantly in British skies kept the island from sinking under the seas.'

Over 5000 ships – transport vessels and warships – were assembled for the passage across the Channel. More than 10,000 aircraft took part. On the first two days of the invasion alone, 20,111 vehicles of all kinds and 176,475 men were to be landed.

The landing itself was only the first hurdle. Although the Germans had not completed their 'Atlantic Wall' of fortifications, they had made all French Channel ports impregnable. Hitler was convinced that, without a large port, the Allies would be unable to land enough troops to avoid being swept back into the sea.

It was British inventive genius that solved this crucial problem. As a substitute for a

INVASION FLEET *An armada of 2700 vessels loaded with men and equipment made the first landings. They went unnoticed by the Germans until dawn broke on June 6.*

THE D-DAY COMMANDERS *In the front from the left are Tedder, Eisenhower and Montgomery. At the back from the left: Bradley, Ramsey, Leigh-Mallory and Bedell Smith.*

seaport, two artificial harbours – called 'Mulberries' – were towed across the Channel after D-Day. Thanks to them 326,547 men, 54,186 vehicles and 104,428 tons of supplies were brought ashore during the first six days of Overlord. The Mulberries shattered the basis of German strategic calculations.

Taken by surprise
The Allied landing achieved complete tactical as well as strategic surprise. It was accomplished in poor weather during a period of full moon, and at low tide – a threefold feat that the Germans had thought impossible. And an elaborate deception plan had in any case convinced the German High Command that the invasion would come further north – in the Pas de Calais.

Months of bombing of German defences and communications reached their climax on

HEROES ON THE BEACHES *A commando unit sets out on one of the toughest assignments of the D-Day landings. They had been ordered to link up with the paratroops who had been dropped behind the German defences. They had been warned that they faced casualties of up to 84 per cent, but were told: 'No matter what happens we must get on to the beaches'.*

D-Day itself, when heavy bombers alone dropped over 10,000 tons of bombs. The German defences along the coast were not totally destroyed by this onslaught, but they were badly damaged and disrupted.

There were only two serious hold-ups on D-Day itself; on an American beach – code-named 'Omaha' – where the assault force ran into a German infantry division on exercise, and near Caen in the British sector, where a counter-attack by a German Panzer division almost penetrated to the coast. But by night-fall on June 6 the Allies were firmly ashore. By the end of the following day, they were in occupation of a beachhead 60 miles long and up to 12 miles deep. Montgomery wrote that 'all anxiety had passed'. The months of preparation had been crowned with complete success: the Germans had lost the battle of the 'longest day'.

HITLER'S LAST THROW

As soon as the Allies landed in France, Britain came under bombardment by a new German weapon – the V1. This unmanned flying bomb was the first of Hitler's 'revenge' weapons developed at the Peenemünde testing grounds. Its range was 150 miles and its warhead was 1870 lb. Another was shortly to follow. In September the first V2 rocket (below) fell on Britain. Hitler had hoped to have these weapons in service earlier. But British Intelligence

had discovered his plans. A massive bombing raid on Peenemünde in 1943 put back the German development programme by a year – and probably saved the D-Day invasion itself from disaster.

Welfare for all in the midst of war

CELEBRATION *The leading British field commander of the war, General Montgomery, is given due credit in this flag made for V-E Day.*

While Britain was still in the grip of war, the post-war future was already being shaped. Popular feeling ran strong. People were determined that this time they would create 'a land fit for heroes to live in'. The privations of war had united rich and poor in a common purpose. The end of the war, when it came, should signal a new dawn for a united Britain.

One wartime document best summed up the mood and aspirations of the average Briton. Published in 1942 under the unpromising title 'Social Insurance and Allied Services', and popularly known as the Beveridge Report, it was a blueprint for the kind of society which the British hoped to see emerge after the war.

The report had been prepared for the government by the economist Sir William Beveridge. It took as its starting point that every working person in the land should be able, with one weekly payment, to ensure his employment, sickness pay and pension.

Security for all

It was a revolutionary concept. Beveridge answered the demand for social justice sparked off by the sufferings of the 1930's, when millions had queued for the dole. His new society was based on equality not charity. Thus the Welfare State was born.

When the Labour government was swept to power in 1945, the Beveridge Report became the basis for its far-reaching social legislation. The new age, it seemed, had really arrived.

Out of the many measures that were passed into law, the most momentous was the founding of the National Health Service in July 1948. The Minister of Health, Aneurin Bevan, faced opposition from many doctors and surgeons when he introduced this ambitious venture. But the establishment of state medical treatment for all, regardless of income, was to remain a part of British life.

By the time the Conservatives returned to power in 1951, the Welfare State was accepted by all. The principles embodied in the Beveridge Report had come to stay.

Team spirit takes the British to the summit of the world

THE VICTORS *Edmund Hillary (left) and Sherpa Tensing (right) prepare for the last assault. Tensing carries the Union Jack they were to plant on the summit. They had only enough oxygen for one attempt, and if the weather had broken they would have been forced to turn back. Their last meal was of sardines, crackers, honey and dates.*

DOUBLE CELEBRATION

News of Everest's conquest reached Britain on Coronation Day. Eager crowds bought newspapers outside the Abbey. A copy of the News Chronicle, *now in the British Museum Newspaper Library, captures the mood of the moment.*

TEAM SPIRIT *The 1953 Everest expedition, under the leadership of Colonel John Hunt, relied on flawless teamwork between Hunt and his carefully selected team and a band of 20 Sherpas recruited in Nepal. In this group photograph, Edmund Hillary, John Hunt and Sherpa Tensing are fifth, sixth and seventh from the left in the back row.*

BASE OF OPERATIONS *Base Camp for the assault was set up at 17,900 ft. From there, the equipment needed for the attempt on the summit was slowly carried up the mountain. It took a month to establish a camp on the South Col, but this slow progress was deliberately planned by Hunt to gradually acclimatise his men to greater and greater heights.*

Mount Everest has magnetised climbers ever since it was discovered to be the world's highest peak in 1852. But the supreme challenge of its 29,028 ft was not finally beaten until May 29, 1953 – after 12 unsuccessful attempts which had cost 12 lives. At 11.30 a.m., a New Zealander, Edmund Hillary, and a Nepalese Sherpa, Tensing Norkay, became the first men to stand on the summit of the world.

'I looked at Tensing,' Hillary wrote later, 'and in spite of the balaclava, goggles and oxygen mask all encrusted with long icicles that concealed his face there was no disguising his infectious grin of pure delight as he looked all round him. We shook hands and then Tensing threw his arms around my shoulders and we thumped each other on the back until we were almost breathless.'

This achievement was more than the work of just two men. Behind the 15 minutes that Hillary and Tensing spent on the summit of Everest lay months of planning and training, and years of hard-won experience.

Colonel John Hunt, a 42-year-old soldier and climber, was chosen to lead the expedition. His party numbered ten climbers – eight Englishmen and two New Zealanders – along with a doctor and a number of reserves. All were tough and experienced mountaineers. When the expedition reached Nepal in March 1953, its members were joined by a band of 20 Sherpas – the hardy hillmen of the Himalayas. Led by Tensing, five of the most experienced were picked out to join the assault team itself.

These men, climbers and Sherpas, were the backbone of the expedition as it set out on the assault from the Base Camp at 17,900 ft in April. Hunt and his men climbed higher and higher until, just over a month after the expedition had set out, the final camp was established at 24,000 ft, 5028 ft below the summit. From there, Hunt had decided to launch two assaults on the summit itself. The first would use light-weight oxygen equipment; if it failed, a second attempt would be made, using a heavier but longer-lasting oxygen system.

The first assault, by Tom Bourdillon and Charles Evans, was made on May 26, but it was beaten back at 28,700 ft by lack of oxygen. Now Hillary and Tensing, assisted by a three-man support party, prepared for their own attempt.

On May 28, the five men established a camp on a ridge at 27,900 ft. At 2.30 that afternoon, the support group left Hillary and Tensing on their own to pitch their tent and rest before launching their attempt on the summit.

The final assault

As soon as it was light the next morning, the two men were ready to go. Their climb first took them through soft snow, then up a steeper slope of hard snow, broken by a formidable 40 ft rock face. After climbing this difficult obstacle, they found themselves on a hard snow ridge once more, fighting for every breath as they made their way up the steep slope. Then, suddenly, the summit itself stared them in the face. A few steps more and the climb was over.

On the summit, Tensing buried some biscuits and sweets, gifts to the mountain's gods. Beside them, Hillary laid his own religious offering – a small crucifix given to him by Hunt. Tensing posed for Hillary's camera, waving his ice-axe with a string of flags attached – the flag of the United Nations, the Union Jack and the flags of Nepal and India. Everest was conquered at last.

SYMBOL OF UNION *The first Commonwealth tour of the queen's reign was in 1954. It was the first of her many personal triumphs.*

Elizabeth II: Symbol of Britain's future

The coronation of Elizabeth II, in June 1953, was the occasion for a display of public pageantry and loyalty unsurpassed in living memory. Winston Churchill spoke for all the new queen's subjects when, on Coronation Day, he hailed 'the gleaming figure whom providence has brought to us – and brought to us in times where the present is hard and the future veiled'.

Young, pretty and above all determined to do her duty, Elizabeth II symbolised, from the moment she came to the throne, values that her people hoped might inspire a new age. She was quick to seize on one invention that was transforming the life of Britain. At her personal insistence, television broadcast the coronation ceremony from within Westminster Abbey itself. And this direct link with millions of British people aptly heralded the new spirit of her reign.

Elizabeth's training for the throne began early. Edward VIII's abdication in 1936 made her the heir presumptive to the throne, and during the Blitz the 14-year-old Elizabeth broadcast to the children of an embattled Britain. As the war continued, she took on more and more public duties.

Duty has dominated the queen's life ever since. Her evident pleasure in the long-established routines of royal life, with its cycle of quiet domestic occasions in long-familiar places – Windsor, Sandringham and Balmoral – have made her a symbol of permanence in a changing world. At the same time, the innovations introduced into the monarchy, many of them by her forceful husband, Prince Philip, have brought the crown into closer touch with its subjects than ever before.

HUMAN CHAIN *A team of Sherpa porters make their way up the mountain with the vital supplies and equipment for the assault.*

ON TOP OF THE WORLD *Sherpa Tensing stands on the summit of Mount Everest at 11.30 a.m. on May 29, 1953. Hillary took the picture.*

THE WAY WE LIVE

The decades from the 1950's to the 1980's saw the British way of life transformed. More than twice as many people owned homes, rather than renting them; car owners increased from just under 2 million in 1939 to nearly 20 million by 1980. Television had reached 97 per cent of households by 1984, spreading a uniform culture. 'Most of our people have never had it so good', claimed Prime Minister Harold Macmillan in 1957.

For many, the prosperity bubble burst in the late 1970's when world oil prices soared. Unemployment rose from 600,000 in 1974 to 3 million in 1982. From 1969 troops had to be stationed in Northern Ireland to curb nationalist extremists; and in mainland Britain social frustrations and industrial strife resurrected barriers separating affluent south from depressed north.

Yet, as 1984 ended, there were signs of hope. With inflation cut, a slow recovery held promise of new stability. The microprocessor, which had brought computers and other electronic devices into many thousands of homes, kept alive the dream of a second Industrial Revolution.

PUBLIC EYE *Recognising the desire of newspaper readers and television viewers to share vicariously in Royalty's more private moments, Britain's Royal Family has co-operated with the probing eye of the camera. Here the Prince and Princess of Wales, with their children Prince William (born 1982) and Prince Henry (born 1984) pose informally for the camera of the Prince of Wales' uncle, professional photographer Lord Snowdon.*

MARATHON *A passion for physically demanding recreation contributed to the growing popularity of marathons, in which daily joggers as well as trained athletes sought to complete a 26 mile course. Here some of the 22,000 runners in the 1984 London Marathon cross Tower Bridge.*

ARMCHAIR SPORT *Television coverage of sponsored sport aroused public interest in most athletic skills. Daley Thompson, here throwing the discus, won Olympic Gold Medals in Moscow (1980) and Los Angeles (1984) for the ten events, spread over two days, that constitute a modern decathlon.*

MINI REVOLUTION *Designed by Sir Alec Issigonis and launched in 1959, the Austin and Morris mini cars represented a complete revolution in car design – and a breakthrough for Britain's export trade. More than 5 million minis have been made since the first came off the assembly line. Early models, such as this one pictured at Silverstone, proved themselves in races and rallies.*

THE SWINGING SIXTIES *Britain's social revolution of the 1950's spilled over into the 'swinging sixties', when the young, questioning accepted conventions, evolved a highly individual and more permissive way of life. In 1964 a young designer, Mary Quant introduced the mini-skirt to a stunned world. It is worn (left) by Twiggy, a favourite model of the period. The 1960's charted the discovery and rise of* the Beatles (above). *This pop group's Liverpudlian accents and irreverent humour, together with the catchy lyrics of their songs, captured the mood of the young. Their records sold millions all over the world. One of the most successful, 'Sergeant Pepper's Lonely Hearts Club Band' (of which a detail from the sleeve is shown), was released in 1967. The group split up in 1971.*

LORD OF THE THEATRE *British actors attained their widest renown after 1945. In 1970 Laurence Olivier – seen (right) as King Lear in the 1983 television production – became the first actor to be honoured with a peerage.*

MAN OF MUSIC *Benjamin Britten, the composer.*

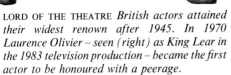

STREET CARNIVAL *The 1960's brought an influx of mainly Caribbean and Asian immigrants, creating a multi-racial society over the following decades. London's Notting Hill Carnival developed into an object lesson in the wise handling of race relations, making this annual event a fine example of integrating Commonwealth cultures.*

REVIVAL *An upsurge of interest in music and dance began in the 1950's. Among composers, Benjamin Britten stood out, especially for his 'War Requiem', first performed in 1962. Ice dancing, uniting the expertise of skating with the grace of ballet, was exemplified by Jayne Torvill and Christopher Dean (above).*

LAND OF HISTORY

An A–Z guide to the places where history was made

The currents of British history have swept like a tide across the land, affecting even the most remote villages and valleys. Every place has its story – meadows where kings and rebels clashed for the crown or mansions where nobles schemed for power. Individual places have also cast their spell over the history-makers – men and women who contributed to our cultural heritage or shaped the nation's destiny in the world of action. *Land of History* recounts the great events which have taken place at more than 300 sites in Scotland, England and Wales, and tells the stories of many famous men and women in their favourite places.

PROUD FORTRESS *Standing on a rocky site, the ruins of Dolwyddelan Castle in Gwynedd are a memorial to the medieval struggles between the English and the Welsh. It was the birthplace of the Welsh hero, Llewelyn the Great.*

Places which are open to the public are marked with an asterisk, but visitors should check opening times before going to see them.

A

Abbotsford, *Borders*

In 1811 Sir Walter Scott bought a farm on the banks of the River Tweed. The property consisted of 110 acres of rough land and a farmhouse, into which Scott, his family and his servants moved in 1812. He decided to call the place Abbotsford* because monks used to ford the river near the farm.

Two years after settling at Abbotsford, Scott began the *Waverley* novels, whose success made him a rich man. But he spent his income on buying more land, and by 1820 his estate had grown to 1400 acres.

Scott's ambitious plans for transforming the farmhouse into a man-

sion were not carried out until 1817. He first enlarged the house, but in 1822 he pulled it down and built the mansion of turrets and battlements that still stands today. It cost Scott £76,000 and untold energy to build Abbotsford. Every detail of its construction was carried out under his supervision.

In order to pay for Abbotsford, Scott became involved in publishing speculation. Disaster struck in 1826, when the publishing firm of Constable, and Ballantyne's the printers, which had become enormously successful through Scott's writings, overreached themselves and went bankrupt. Scott, who was closely connected with the affairs of both firms, found himself liable for debts of £117,000.

While desperately striving to hold on to Abbotsford, Scott set about repaying his debts through his writings. In six years he paid back £70,000, but the effort proved too much and by the beginning of 1832 he was too ill to work. After a visit to the Mediterranean, Scott returned to his beloved Abbotsford, where he died in September 1832.

DREAM CASTLE *Abbotsford was the mansion built by Sir Walter Scott (above right) to fulfil an ambition to live in baronial splendour.*

Aberdeen, *Grampian*

Until the mid-18th century Aberdeen was fought over by one army after another.

In 1296 Edward I garrisoned troops in Aberdeen Castle. Two years later the Scots patriot William Wallace tried to dislodge them, without success. The English set fire to the town to delay him, and Wallace retaliated by burning their fleet in the harbour.

Early in the 1300's, Robert Bruce

raised an army of Aberdonians for one of his campaigns. Returning home, his soldiers captured and destroyed Aberdeen Castle, killing all the English garrison, despite pleas for mercy from the local monks.

Aberdeen resisted the campaign by the Covenanting movement of 1638 against Anglicanism. The Covenanters occupied the city and held four burgesses hostage against payment of a heavy fine. Aberdeen surrendered, agreeing to adhere to

the Covenant. But during the following 12 years there was sporadic fighting in the streets of Aberdeen between the Covenanters and their opponents.

During the first Jacobite rising, in 1715, the Old Pretender, James Stuart, lodged in Castlegate*. Thirty years later the British commander-in-chief, Sir John Cope, camped at Aberdeen before going on to his defeat by Prince Charles Edward Stuart at the Battle of Prestonpans. (See p. 413.)

But disaster was in store for the prince. In February 1746 part of the rebel army reached the town after their long retreat from Derby, and left it again only two days before the arrival of British troops under the Duke of Cumberland. The duke stayed six weeks and gave a ball at Marischal College* before marching on to Culloden, where his troops routed the prince and his followers. (See map, p. 380.)

Abergavenny Castle, *Gwent*

The foulest deed in the history of Abergavenny was the massacre of the Welsh chiefs of Gwent by the Anglo-Norman Lord William de Braose. In 1176 he invited them to the castle* to celebrate Christmas, but at a signal from de Braose his men-at-arms slew them all. This was supposedly in revenge for the death of his uncle.

Fifty years later the Welsh avenged themselves on the de Braoses by killing William's grandson. In the reign of Henry VI, the castle was taken over by Richard Neville, Earl of Warwick, known as the Kingmaker, and its remains still belong to the Neville family.

Abingdon, *Oxon*

The final parting between Charles I and his queen, Henrietta Maria, took place at Abingdon on April 17, 1644. Early in the Civil War the queen went to live at the king's headquarters in Oxford. But when the position of the city became insecure in the spring of 1644, the king decided to move Henrietta Maria, then seven months pregnant, to Exeter.

The queen left Oxford, accompanied by the king, Prince Rupert and the Duke of York. At Abingdon the queen fell on her knees before her husband, pleading with him not to permit their separation. But Charles, raising and embracing

his wife, begged her not to distress him with further pleading. Overcome by grief, the queen fainted. When she recovered in the carriage taking her to Exeter, she was 30 miles away from Abingdon. Her daughter, Princess Henrietta, was born at Exeter in June, and in the following month the queen sailed from Falmouth for France.

Aldeburgh, *Suffolk*

This small seaside and fishing town among the marshes has been an important musical centre since Benjamin Britten founded a festival of music and the arts there in 1947. Britten's opera 'Peter Grimes' is set in Aldeburgh and is based on 'The Borough', a long poem by the local poet, George Crabbe (1754–1832).

The Victorian novelists George Meredith and Wilkie Collins lived there. Alde House was for long the home of Elizabeth Garrett Anderson (1836–1917), one of the first women doctors, who was elected mayor of Aldeburgh in 1908—the first woman mayor in England.

Alloway, *Strathclyde*

Robert Burns, Scotland's national poet, was born in 1759 at Alloway, in the kitchen of a two-roomed, clay-and-thatch cottage* built by his father. He went to school for a time at nearby Alloway Mill, and was later taught at a small private school set up by his father and some neighbours.

When Burns was eight, his father took an unprofitable farm at Mount Oliphant, 2 miles away. By his early

POET *Born at Alloway, Robert Burns lived his last years at Dumfries, where this silhouette was cut.*

teens Burns was his father's chief labourer. He took refuge from his hard life in poetry and love affairs. As he went about his work on the farm he composed verses for songs, and invented new ballad forms.

After his father's death, Burns moved to Mossgiel, where he fell in love with Jean Armour. Because Jean's father persistently refused to let her marry him, Burns decided to emigrate to Jamaica. In order to raise money for the journey, he published his *Poems, Chiefly in the Scottish Dialect* in 1786.

The acclaim with which these poems were received persuaded Burns to stay in Scotland. He went to Edinburgh, where he was lionised by fashionable society, and later he visited the Border country and the Highlands.

Burns married Jean Armour in 1788, obtained the post of excise officer at £50 a year, and settled at Ellisland Farm near Dumfries. When the farm failed in 1791, he moved to Dumfries. In his last unhappy years, the poet wrote prolifically. But his radical views offended friends and admirers, and his heavy drinking and womanising led to a breakdown in his health. He died prematurely, aged 37, on July 21, 1796.

Alnwick Castle, *Northld*
Alnwick Castle*, which survived centuries of siege and Scottish invasions, was the principal seat of the Percy family. (See pp. 98–99.)

War was a way of life for the Percys. Henry, 4th Lord Percy and Earl of Northumberland (1342–1408), joined Henry of Lancaster against Richard II. But, after Lancaster had become Henry IV, Northumberland felt he had not been sufficiently rewarded for his help and, with his son, Harry Hotspur, rebelled unsuccessfully. The Percys lost Alnwick as a result, but Henry V restored it to them. During the Wars of the Roses the Percys again managed to survive. But in the religious conflict of the Reformation the Roman Catholic Percys again fell foul of the throne. Sir Thomas Percy, brother of the sixth earl, was executed at Tyburn for his part in the Pilgrimage of Grace of 1536. And the seventh earl, Thomas, nephew of the sixth, was executed by Elizabeth I for conspiring with Mary, Queen of Scots, as was his son, Henry.

Disfavour persisted under James I. The ninth earl spent 15 years in the Tower on the suspicion of being involved in the Gunpowder Plot of 1605.

Alton, *Hants*
Scars on the main door and walls of the parish church of St Lawrence* tell of the final heroic scene in the Civil War Battle of Alton in 1643.

Royalist troops under Lord Crawford who were quartered in the town were surprised by Sir William Waller and his Roundheads. Crawford, who was unprepared, slipped away with the cavalry and fled to Winchester, leaving a Captain Bowles and the infantry to hold off the enemy.

Bowles was forced back into the town and with 80 men made a last stand in front of the church. As they were beaten back into the building the brave captain was killed and the survivors surrendered. Marks of cannonballs and even bullets themselves can be seen in the walls.

Anglesey, *Gwynedd*
When the Romans invaded Britain in AD 43, Anglesey was a stronghold of the Druid religion. Seeing the power of the Druid priests as a threat to their own dominance, the Romans launched an attack on the island in AD 61.

For a year, the Roman leader, Suetonius Paulinus, prepared for the invasion of Anglesey. Special ships were built to ferry his infantry across the Menai Strait. His cavalry swam the shallows on the night of the attack.

When the Romans reached the island, they were confronted by a line of fierce warriors standing on the shore. Behind the warriors ran frenzied black-clad women, bearing flaming torches. In the rear, where huge sacrificial fires blazed, stood the white-robed Druid priests, lifting their hands to heaven and uttering frightening curses.

Undaunted by this chilling sight, the Romans ruthlessly cut down the warriors, the women and the priests. Those who were not slain by the sword were thrown into the fires. When the slaughter ended, the Romans chopped down the thick groves of oak trees that were the sacred places of the Druids.

At the height of their onslaught

the Romans hastily withdrew to deal with Boudicca's uprising at Colchester. But they returned 17 years later, completed their conquest of the island and finally destroyed the Druids' stronghold.

Later, Anglesey became a stronghold of the Welsh princes of Gwynedd. It was not finally conquered by the English until 1282–4.

Antonine Wall, *Strathclyde-Central*
Three legions constructed Britain's second Roman wall* during the year AD 143. The wall, named after Emperor Antonius Pius, stretched for about 37 miles from Bridgeness on the Firth of Forth to Old Kilpatrick on the River Clyde. Built of turf on a stone foundation, the wall had a series of 12 forts, placed at intervals of 2 miles, on its southern side. The Romans hoped it would relieve the main frontier, Hadrian's Wall, from the attacks by Scottish tribes. (See pp. 38–39.)

The wall was breached in 155–8, and again in 184, when marauders overwhelmed the Roman garrisons and ravaged the Lowlands. Following this attack the Romans rebuilt the wall, but soon afterwards the legions were withdrawn from the fortifications and by 200 the Antonine Wall stood abandoned.

STONE OF SCONE *The custodian at Arbroath Abbey (right) uncovers the missing stone, left there by Scots Nationalists (below) in 1951.*

Arbroath, *Tayside*
Early on Christmas morning in 1950, three young Scotsmen and a girl raided Westminster Abbey. Their target was the ancient Stone of Scone, symbol of their nation's independence, which had been taken from Scotland 654 years before by Edward I.

With police looking for them throughout Britain, they lay low until the following April, when they conveyed the stone secretly to Arbroath and left it in the ruined abbey* there.

They did so remembering the Scottish Declaration of Independence, drawn up by the nobles and commons of the kingdom at Arbroath Abbey in 1320: 'For so long as a hundred of us are left alive, we will yield in no least way to English dominion. We fight not for glory nor for wealth nor honours; but only and alone we fight for freedom, which no good man surrenders but with his life.'

This ringing declaration was the culmination of a struggle between Scotland and England which had raged since 1290, when Margaret, the Maid of Norway and child-queen of Scots, died in the Orkneys at the age of seven. She was the last of the House of Canmore.

Edward I of England had betrothed his son to Margaret, and after her death considered himself master of Scotland. Since there were at least 13 claimants to the vacant throne, Edward faced a confused and disunited opposition. It was only after his death that Robert Bruce, who had rallied the Scots behind him, was able to expel the English at Bannockburn in 1314. (See pp. 88–89.)

Although the pope did not recognise the Arbroath Declaration until 1326, the document established Scottish sovereignty and acknowledged Bruce as king.

Arbury Hall, *Warks*
George Eliot, the 19th-century novelist, whose real name was Mary Ann Evans, was born in 1819 at South Farm on the Arbury estate, where her father was agent. She was christened in the 13th-century church at Chilvers Coton.

In 1820 the Evans family moved to nearby Griff House and lived there until 1841. From an early age Mary drove round the estate with her father. Her childhood memories of village life in the Warwickshire countryside are reflected in her early successful novels, such as *Adam Bede* (1859), *The Mill on the Floss* (1860) and *Silas Marner* (1861).

NOVELIST *Mary Ann Evans, born at South Farm, won fame as George Eliot, author of* Adam Bede.

Arbury Hall* is the 'Cheverel Manor' described in *Mr Gilfil's Love Story*; and Chilvers Coton, now a suburb of Nuneaton, is the 'Shepperton' of the same story, which appears in *Scenes of Clerical Life*.

Ardvreck Castle, *Highland*
In 1650, a year after Charles I was executed, James Graham, the Marquess of Montrose, led an invasion force into Scotland on behalf of the exiled Charles II. After the rout of the Royalist forces at Carbisdale, Montrose sought refuge at Ardvreck Castle*, the clan centre for the Macleods of Assynt.

The Roundheads' offer of £25,000 for Montrose's capture was too tempting for Macleod, who betrayed his guest to General Leslie at Tain. Montrose was taken to Edinburgh where, on May 21, 1650, he was hanged. (See Montrose, p. 408.)

Arundel Castle, *W Sussex*
For more than 700 years the Dukes of Norfolk and their ancestors have lived at Arundel Castle*. The 11th-century keep is the work of Robert

Montgomery, who came over with the Conqueror; he also built a great gatehouse. The castle was destroyed by the Roundheads during a 17 day bombardment in the winter of 1643–4. It was rebuilt in the 18th century and extensively restored between 1890 and 1903.

The earldom of Arundel dates from 1139, when William de Albini acquired the castle and other estates by marrying Adeliza of Louvain, widow of Henry I.

During the 13th century the title and lands passed to John Fitzalan who, with Henry III, was captured at the Battle of Lewes in 1264 by Simon de Montfort.

Arundel Castle remained the home of the Fitzalans for 300 years until it passed by marriage to the Howard family, the Dukes of Norfolk, in 1580.

Spies and messengers connected with Catholic conspiracies against Elizabeth I passed through Arundel on their way to and from Flanders, but Elizabeth's spies were alert; the 4th Duke of Norfolk was arrested and executed. His son, Philip Howard, Earl of Arundel, was sent to the Tower in 1589, where he died six years later. Elizabeth confiscated Arundel town and castle, but the family earldom was restored by James I in 1604.

Ashby de la Zouch Castle, *Leics*
In the 12th century the Norman manor house of Ashby was held by a Breton nobleman, Alan la Zouch. By the time of the Wars of the Roses, Ashby had a Lancastrian owner, the Earl of Ormonde. When he was beheaded after the Battle of Towton in 1461, Ashby became the property of the crown. In 1464 the manor was granted to the first Lord Hastings, who was Lord Chamberlain to Edward IV.

Hastings rose swiftly to a prominent position in Edward's court, and in 1467 obtained permission to transform Ashby manor house into a castle*. But in 1483 he was found guilty of treason and executed by Richard III.

During the Civil War, one of Hastings' descendants, Colonel Henry Hastings, garrisoned Ashby for the king. The town was captured by Parliament in 1644, but the castle held out until forced by an outbreak of plague and lack of food to surrender on February 28, 1646. Three years later, following

Parliament's order that the castle be 'slighted', the south wall and all the outer part of the building were destroyed by gunpowder.

Ashingdon, *Essex*
The Battle of Ashingdon in 1016 ended a campaign by Edmund Ironside, to keep Canute's Danes from capturing London.

Although far fewer in numbers, the Danes inflicted a heavy defeat on the Saxons. But Canute decided to come to terms with Edmund. They agreed that Edmund should rule Wessex and Canute be made ruler of London and the land north of the Thames. But Edmund died before the year was out and Canute became king of all England.

Ashridge, *Herts*
Ashridge House was one of the homes of the children of Henry VIII. In 1553 Princess Elizabeth, later queen, fled there from the court of her Catholic sister, Queen Mary.

In January 1554 Elizabeth was suspected of being involved in Sir Thomas Wyatt's rebellion in Kent. Mary sent three councillors to Ashridge to arrest her sister and bring her to London to be interrogated. When she came to court at the end of February, Mary refused to see her; Elizabeth stayed in apartments at Whitehall.

The evidence against Elizabeth was flimsy. Letters were found from Wyatt to her, but no written reply from her was found. She was imprisoned in the Tower and expected execution, but the government had no evidence to convict her of treason.

At his execution, Wyatt declared Elizabeth innocent of involvement in his conspiracy, and after two months in the Tower she was allowed to go to Woodstock, where she was closely watched by the government for another year.

At Ashridge only the barn remains of the Tudor building.

Aslockton, *Notts*
This tiny village was the birthplace of Thomas Cranmer, the first Protestant Archbishop of Canterbury, who bequeathed to Englishmen the 1549 Book of Common Prayer, most of which he compiled himself.

Henry VIII promoted Cranmer from divinity lecturer to archbishop in three years, because he

had devised a means of annulling the king's marriage to Catharine of Aragon. Cranmer pronounced Henry legally married to Anne Boleyn, but only three years later he had to find grounds to undo that marriage.

Cranmer shifted his religious principles to suit Henry's changing views. But his career came to an end at the stake when he refused to abandon his beliefs under the Catholic Mary. (See pp. 136–7.)

Aston, *W Midlands*
Association football was transformed from an amateur pastime into a professional game during the late 19th century. One of the most successful clubs of the time was Aston Villa. Like many other clubs, it began as a church organisation. The first meeting was held in 1874 under a lamp post near Villa Cross Wesleyan Chapel, Aston.

During the 1880's most of the players became professionals. In the 1887 Cup Final at Kennington Oval, London, the club beat their neighbours, West Bromwich Albion, 2–0 to win the FA Challenge Cup.

By the end of the 19th century, Aston Villa had taken the FA Cup twice more and had been Football League champions five times; in 1897 it won both competitions, a feat not repeated for 64 years. The glory the club won did much to spread the professional game.

AMATEURS *England play Scotland in 1878. Many clubs, including Aston Villa, turned professional in 1885.*

Auchinleck, *Strathclyde*
The family of James Boswell (1740–95), diarist and biographer of Dr Johnson, became lairds of Auchinleck when Thomas Boswell obtained

the estate from James IV. Thomas died with the Scottish king, fighting the English on the field of Flodden in 1513.

The present house was built by James's father, Lord Auchinleck, a judge who disapproved of his son's conduct and threatened to disinherit him. Upon his father's death in 1782, James became laird, and is buried in the church. After his death it was believed that his heirs had burnt his papers, but later his revealing and bawdy *London Journal* was found at Auchinleck.

Audley End, *Essex*
The lands of the Benedictine priory of Saffron Walden were granted at the Dissolution of the Monasteries to a firm supporter of Henry VIII. He was Thomas Audley who had succeeded Sir Thomas More as Lord Chancellor.

As Lord Audley of Walden, he transformed the Prior's house into a comfortable home. On his death in 1544 the house passed to his daughter, Margaret, who was the second wife of Thomas Howard, 4th Duke of Norfolk. Howard was executed for treason by Elizabeth I and Walden passed to his elder son, Lord Thomas Howard.

Lord Thomas played a notable part in the defeat of the Armada. He was created Baron Howard de Walden in 1597, and became a favourite of James I.

In 1603 Howard, now Earl of Suffolk, had begun to build a new house at Audley End*. It took 13 years to build and is reputed to have cost £200,000—a gigantic sum for those days. Meanwhile, he was appointed Lord High Treasurer of England, and King James is said to have observed that Audley End was 'too big for a king, but might do for the Lord Treasurer!' But Howard's downfall came in 1618 when he was committed to the Tower of London and fined £30,000 for embezzlement.

Audley End became a royal palace after the restoration of Charles II in 1660. It reverted to the Suffolks in 1701 and later, on the advice of architect Sir John Vanbrugh, was greatly restored and much reduced in size. In 1745 the Suffolk line failed.

Lady Portsmouth bought the house and park and made further alterations. The property was bequeathed to her nephew, who became a field-marshal, and in 1784 succeeded to the barony of Howard de Walden. Four years later he was created Baron Braybrooke. He employed Capability Brown to landscape the gardens and Robert Adam to build bridges and temples.

Title and property passed in 1797 to Braybrooke's kinsman, Richard Aldworth Neville. He and his son, the 3rd Lord Braybrooke, were responsible for the final embellishments to the house, now the property of the nation. Although little remains of Thomas Howard's Audley End, the successive restorations were carried out with such feeling for the original design that it still has the look of an early-17th-century mansion.

Avebury, *Wilts*
The village of Avebury lies inside a circle of earth-works and standing stones*—the largest stone circle in Europe. Its exact function is still a mystery. The structure dates from about 2000 BC—the close of the Stone Age and dawn of the Bronze Age. The site seems to have been some kind of ritual centre for the local herdsmen and farmers. But in the Middle Ages many of the stones were overthrown and buried because the inhabitants of Avebury feared their pagan associations. The vandalism claimed a victim: under a tumbled sarsen was found a crushed skeleton.

Aylesbury, *Bucks*
In the bitter divisions of the Civil War, the town of Aylesbury and the Pakington family, the lords of the manor, were on different sides. In these years of struggle the Pakingtons supported the king—and the town, Parliament.

On November 1, 1642, the Royalist general, Prince Rupert, entered the town by surprise. But the tables were turned when Roundhead reinforcements united with the garrison and forced Rupert to retreat.

The radical reformer John Wilkes, who was Aylesbury's MP from 1757 to 1764, kept up the tradition of struggle against arbitrary rule. Wilkes founded the journal, *The North Briton,* in which he attacked George III and the government of the day. He lived in the 18th-century Prebendal House, now a school. (See pp. 248–9.)

SHAW'S CORNER *The playwright George Bernard Shaw (left) settled in Ayot St Lawrence in 1906. He wrote some of his most famous plays in the study (above), preserved today as he left it.*

Ayot St Lawrence, *Herts*
When George Bernard Shaw and his wife were looking for a house near London in 1906, they came upon a tombstone in the graveyard of Ayot St Lawrence. 'Jane Eversley. Born 1825. Died 1895. Her time was short,' ran the inscription. Shaw instantly remarked: 'Then this is the place for me.'

Shaw bought the old rectory and retreated to its seclusion at weekends. He wrote there large portions of some of his most famous plays, including *Pygmalion, Heartbreak House, Back to Methuselah,* and *Saint Joan.* The villagers christened the house 'Shaw's Corner'*.

Even at the age of 94, in 1950, Shaw liked to prune and top the trees in his garden rather than leave it to his gardeners. It was in September of that year, while working on the trees, that he fell and broke his thigh. The injury was a major cause of his death three months later. His ashes were scattered in the garden he so loved.

Ayr, *Strathclyde*
Ayr was the scene of one of the most appalling massacres in Scottish history. In 1297 the English captured the town and used the barns in Ayr as a barracks. Wallace set fire to them—with 500 soldiers inside—as a reprisal for the hanging of leading Scotsmen. He went on to sack the castle and, it is claimed, to slaughter 5000 more English soldiers.

In 1315, a year after the Scots victory at the Battle of Bannockburn, Robert Bruce called a Scots parliament at the old parish church of St John's to decide the Scottish succession. Eventually the crown passed to Robert II, Bruce's grandson, and from him descended the Stuarts. The church was incorporated into a fort built by Oliver Cromwell in 1652. Cromwell also gave money for the building of a new church*, which still stands.

John Loudon McAdam, the inventor of the 'macadamising' system of road-building, was born at Ayr in 1756. While he was still at school he built a model section of a local road, and began experimenting with different kinds of road-building materials in the 1780's. The first macadam road of crushed stone and tar was constructed at Maybole in 1797. McAdam became surveyor of roads for Britain in 1827, and by the time of his death in 1836, his name was synonymous with his invention.

B

Bala, *Gwynedd*
In 1324 Edward II founded Bala as a royal borough. The town is situated at the northern end of Lake Bala, the largest natural lake in Wales. According to legend, the old town was swallowed up by the lake.

Bala was a stronghold of Welsh Methodism in the 18th century. In 1865 a group of Methodists left Bala to found a colony in Patagonia, a province of Argentina. Even today some of their South American descendants still speak the Welsh language as well as Spanish.

Balmoral Castle, *Grampian*

The manor house of Balmoral, set in the Scottish Highlands, was Queen Victoria's favourite retreat. As she wrote in her diary: 'Every year my heart becomes more fixed in this dear Paradise and so much more so now that all has become my dearest Albert's own creation, own work, own building, own laying out . . . and his great taste and the impress of his dear hand have been stamped everywhere.'

Victoria and Albert fell in love with Balmoral in 1848 and they spent many happy holidays there, although the house was too small for the needs of a growing royal family. Between 1852 and 1855 the old dwelling was demolished and the present building erected under Prince Albert's direction.

After Albert's death in 1861 the queen looked on Balmoral as a permanent memorial to her husband. She rarely spent less than five months of each year there, and enjoyed being the laird of this private estate, visiting the cottages of the labourers and interesting herself in their lives.

None of Victoria's children and few of her visitors shared her affection for the Scottish home. But later generations of the royal family have rediscovered the walks, picnic sites and views so beloved by Victoria and Albert.

HIGHLAND VISITORS *Tsar Nicholas II (fourth left) and Empress Alexandra (third right) with Queen Victoria (centre) at Balmoral in 1896.*

Balquhidder, *Central*

The real Rob Roy—the model for Sir Walter Scott's novel—was a MacGregor, who spent much of his life in and around Balquhidder and is buried there.

Rob Roy started out as a cattle dealer with a good education and a mastery of swordsmanship. Taking advantage of the feuds and raids between the cattlemen of the area, Rob built up a flourishing protection racket.

Legend says that he once advanced the rent money owed by a tenant of the Duke of Montrose. Rob told the tenant to get a receipt from the agent when he came, then laid in wait for the man and stole the money back.

Once, hearing that soldiers were looking for him, he disguised himself as a beggar, lured the soldiers into a house in pairs, then bound and disarmed them.

When Rob lay dying at Inverlocharaig in 1734, he insisted on being dressed, sword and all, to receive a former enemy who came to call. Collapsing after his visitor had left, Rob bade his piper play 'Cha till mi tuille' (I shall never return) until he died.

Bamburgh Castle, *Northld*

Founded in the 6th century, Bamburgh Castle* was the seat of the Northumbrian kings. It was rebuilt by both Henry II and Henry III as a bastion against the Scots. David II of Scotland was imprisoned there after his defeat by Edward III at Neville's Cross in 1346.

In the churchyard of Bamburgh parish church is a monument to Grace Darling. On the stormy night of September 7, 1838, she rowed with her father—the Langstone Lighthouse keeper—to rescue the nine survivors of the *Forfarshire*, wrecked on the Farne Island rocks a mile away.

Banbury, *Oxon*

In AD 624 Banbury was given to St Birinus, a missionary to the West Saxons, who became Bishop of Dorchester on Thames, and for

FAMED CROSS *The medieval Banbury cross, celebrated in the nursery rhyme, was replaced in 1860.*

1000 years the town enjoyed peace under Church rule.

Tranquillity came to an end with the Civil War, when the town held out for Charles I. The 12th-century castle was twice besieged by Parliamentary forces. In 1644 it was relieved by the Royalists, but in 1646 it surrendered. The townsfolk then petitioned Parliament to destroy the castle which had caused them so much hardship, and in 1648 it was demolished.

Banbury's famous cross*, mentioned in the nursery rhyme 'Ride a cock-horse', was torn down by Puritans, who regarded it as popish. The 'fine lady' of the rhyme is thought to be Celia Fiennes, who became celebrated for her horseback journeys throughout England and published her *Journeys* in 1702. She was a member of the Fiennes family, who still live in nearby Broughton Castle.

Bannockburn, *Central* See p. 88

Bardsey Island, *Gwynedd*

The oldest monastery in Wales is said to have been founded on Bardsey in 516 by St Cadfan. The monks at Bangor-is-Coed are thought to have taken refuge on Bardsey after their monastery was destroyed in the 7th century.

Traditionally the burial ground of 20,000 monks, the island became famous as a place of pilgrimage in the Middle Ages.

In 1550 the monastery became a pirates' storehouse, and for the next century Bardsey was a centre of a flourishing smuggling industry.

Barnard Castle, *Durham*

Built in the early 12th century Barnard Castle, now in ruins*, was the stronghold of John Balliol, whom Edward I made King of Scotland in 1292, and also of his son, Edward, King of Scotland under Edward III's protection.

In the mid-15th century the castle passed to Richard, Duke of Gloucester, later Richard III, who had married Anne Neville, daughter of Warwick the Kingmaker.

It is said that Richard's brother, the Duke of Clarence, tried to stop the marriage, to prevent his brother from sharing in the vast Neville inheritance. He persuaded Anne to escape Richard's attentions by disguising herself as a kitchenmaid in his household. But Richard recognised Anne despite the disguise and abducted her from his brother.

Barnet, *Gtr London*

An obelisk* on Hadley Green, just north of Barnet, marks the spot where Edward IV defeated and killed Warwick the Kingmaker at the Battle of Barnet on Easter Day, April 14, 1471. Edward had originally been set up as a puppet king by the Earl of Warwick. When Edward showed signs of becoming his own master, Warwick plotted against him, and allied himself with the Lancastrians. He drove Edward into exile in the Low Countries, and restored the deposed Henry VI.

After six months, Edward came back to England with 2000 men. In a month he had captured Henry VI and gathered an army 10,000 strong. In a three hour battle in the morning mist near Barnet, the 15,000-strong Lancastrian army led by Warwick was routed by the Yorkists.

Bass Rock, *Lothian*

According to an old Scottish saying, an impossible task is 'like building a bridge to the Bass'. Bass Rock, a mile out in the Firth of Forth, its walls rising 350 ft from the sea, has been a refuge, prison and fortress.

St Baldred, the early Christian missionary, made his recluse's cell* there in the 7th century. A thousand years later the rock was a prison* for the extremist Scottish Protestants, known as the Covenanters.

After James II's flight from England in 1688, some of his followers were imprisoned on the rock. But they overpowered their gaolers and seized the rock. They held out against the government until 1694.

Bateman's, *E Sussex*
Although Rudyard Kipling was fervently patriotic, he had never put down roots in England until he bought Bateman's*, a 17th-century ironmaster's house, in 1902. He came across it down a 'rabbit-warren of a lane' on a motoring excursion. When he saw Bateman's, he exclaimed: 'That's her! Make an honest woman of her—quick!'

Kipling was born in India where he worked as a journalist. By the time he settled in England he had become a highly successful author. In the first years at Bateman's, he wrote some of his most famous works, including *Puck of Pook's Hill*, *Rewards and Fairies*, and *If*. He was awarded the Nobel Prize for Literature in 1907.

Kipling's later years at Bateman's were overshadowed by misfortune. His only son was killed early in the First World War. From about the same time Kipling was tormented by ceaseless pain, which was caused by an ulcer. He died in 1936.

PATRIOTIC POET *Born in India, Kipling roamed the world before settling at Bateman's near Burwash.*

Bath, *Avon*
Legend says that Bath was founded on the site of the only hot mineral springs in Britain by Bladud, father of King Lear, after his leprosy had been cured by the healing waters.

The Romans built a fine bathing establishment there about AD 54, with a temple dedicated to Sulis Minerva, the goddess of healing. The Saxons founded religious buildings there including an abbey where Edgar, first king of all England, was crowned in 973.

Bath was largely destroyed in the strife which followed the death of William the Conqueror, and in 1088 it was bought for £60 by John

ENGLISH DANDY *An arbiter of elegance, 'Beau' Nash made Bath into a fashionable centre.*

de Villula, a bishop and physician. He founded several hospitals, and the sick and poor went to bathe in the waters. Bath soon became a refuge for beggars from all over the kingdom.

Anne of Denmark, wife of James I, was the first royal visitor to the baths. She went there early in the 17th century, trying to find a cure for dropsy. Samuel Pepys arrived in 1668 and wrote in his diary: 'It cannot be clean to go so many bodies together in the same water.' The town prospered, though it was dirty and rowdy and the accommodation for the increasing numbers of visitors was inadequate.

In 1703 there arrived in Bath a man who was to transform it into a glittering centre of fashion. Richard 'Beau' Nash was a 29-year-old professional gambler, whose sense of taste and elegance re-created Bath in his own image. Nash became master of ceremonies and 'King of Bath'. (See pp. 228–9.)

Battle, *E Sussex*
Fulfilling a vow he made before his victory, William the Conqueror built a Benedictine abbey* on the site of the Battle of Hastings. Work began immediately after the Conquest and the building was conse-crated in 1094. The altar of the now-ruined abbey stood on the spot where King Harold died. A memorial set up in 1903 now marks the place of his death.

Beachy Head, *E Sussex*
The French inflicted a humiliating defeat on the Anglo-Dutch fleet off the chalk cliffs of Beachy Head on June 30, 1690. It was one of the engagements of the lengthy War of the League of Augsburg (1689–97), which was waged by Louis XIV against the Protestant powers.

A strong French fleet, consisting of 80 ships under Admiral Tourville, sailed up the Channel from Brest, and was sighted off the Isle of Wight on June 22. The Anglo-Dutch fleet, commanded by Arthur Herbert, Earl of Torrington, under strength and consisting of only 56 ships, withdrew.

On the evening of June 29, Torrington was ordered by William III to engage, no matter what the odds. The following morning he went into action against the French off Beachy Head.

Torrington's Dutch contingent, with whom he was on bad terms, rashly attacked and was mauled by the French. When Torrington retreated, Tourville and his fleet pursued him as far as Dover but then gave up the chase.

Torrington was arrested and tried by court-martial at Sheerness for not engaging the enemy. He was acquitted on all charges, but was never given another command.

Beaconsfield, *Bucks*
Best known for its association with Benjamin Disraeli, who became Earl of Beaconsfield in 1876, the town was also the home of poet Edmund Waller, and of the influential statesman and political philosopher Edmund Burke.

Burke lived at Gregories, now destroyed, from 1768 until his death in 1797. It was here that he entertained his many artistic and political friends, including Dr Johnson on his return from his Welsh tour in 1774. Burke is chiefly remembered for his belief that social and political change must be based on tradition and custom. In his *Reflections on the French Revolution,* he denounced the excesses of political upheaval. He is buried in the parish church.

Edmund Waller, who praised Cromwell, and later Charles II, in his poetry, lived at Hall Barn for most of his life (1606–87) and is buried in the churchyard. He was sent by Parliament to discuss peace terms with Charles in 1643, but was later banished for conspiring to reinstate the king.

Beaulieu Abbey, *Hants*
King John founded this abbey in 1204 to atone, it is said, for his violent anger against some Cistercian abbots who had refused his demands for money.

The abbey, consecrated in 1246 in the presence of John's son, Henry III, became a place of sanctuary for fugitives from justice. During the Wars of the Roses, Margaret of Anjou, wife of Henry VI, fled there with her son after being defeated by the Yorkists at the Battle of Barnet in 1471.

Another fugitive, the Yorkist pretender to the throne, Perkin Warbeck, fled to the abbey after vainly attacking Henry VII's forces at Exeter in 1497. In 1538, at the time of the Dissolution of the Monasteries, the abbey church was demolished and only the ruins* remain.

The abbey gatehouse became Palace House*, now the home of the Montagu family.

Beaumaris Castle, *Gwynedd*
Beaumaris Castle* was the eighth and last castle to be founded by Edward I in Wales. It was built between 1295 and 1298 by James of St George—the Savoyard engineer who built castles at Flint, Rhuddlan and Conway. (See pp. 86–87.)

In 1400 Henry IV gave the castle to Henry Percy, Earl of Northumberland—father of the famous Hotspur—in gratitude for his help in placing him on the throne.

During the Civil War, the castle, held for the king by the Constable, Colonel Richard Bulkeley, was attacked by the Parliamentarians under Colonel Mytton. He approached the castle from the landward side, and there were heavy casualties on both sides. To save further bloodshed, the fortress surrendered on June 25, 1646, and remained in Parliamentary hands until the Restoration in 1660. After 1705 the castle was abandoned and fell into ruin.

In the porch of the parish church at Beaumaris stands the carved stone sarcophagus of King John's

367

Dunnottar Castle during the siege.

Anne Lindsay, a kinswoman of the governor's wife, left the castle with the papers stitched into a belt. The regalia were lowered over the wall to a serving woman, pretending to gather seaweed, who hid them in her basket. They remained concealed under the floor of the parish church at Kinneff, a few miles away, until the Restoration of 1660, and are now in Edinburgh Castle.

A terrible moment in the history of Dunnottar Castle came in 1685, during the rebellion of Monmouth and Argyll. A group of 122 men and 45 women—all zealous Covenanters—were herded into the dungeon, now known as the Whig's Vault.

Packed tight, the captives could not sit, lean or lie down, and many of them died. Some took the oaths of allegiance required of them to gain their freedom, but the others were sent into exile.

Dunstable, *Beds*
In 1533 Archbishop Cranmer held a court in the Lady Chapel of Dunstable Priory, for the divorce of Catharine of Aragon. The proceedings lasted two weeks.

On May 23 Cranmer pronounced the dissolution of the marriage between Henry VIII and Catharine, and confirmed the legality of the king's marriage to Anne Boleyn. Catharine stubbornly refused to take any part in the divorce proceedings. (See Buckden, p. 372.)

Dunstable was founded by the Romans who set up a small posting station at the point where Watling Street crossed the prehistoric Icknield Way. In 1132 Henry I founded an Augustinian priory, around which the town developed, and built a palace at nearby Kingsbury.

Dunwich, *Suffolk*
During a great storm of 1740, the town of Dunwich, the former capital of East Anglia, was almost completely destroyed by the sea.

In the early 7th century the Saxon king, Sigeberht, made Dunwich the centre of his kingdom. By 1086, the town had a bishop's palace, a mint and many richly appointed mansions belonging to local merchants.

Dunwich was one of the leading ports on the English east coast when the sea began slowly eroding the shore in the 11th century. The first storm, in 1287, caused havoc, and

the harbour was wrecked in 1347. Twenty years later 400 houses were overwhelmed by the waves, and by the end of the 14th century half of the town had disappeared.

These disasters reduced Dunwich from a prosperous town to a decaying village. Its fishing industry was ruined. In 1600 the town lost its economic importance when the market place vanished beneath the sea. The last church disappeared early this century. Only a few houses and a graveyard now remain.

Durham, *Durham*
In an age when bishops were powerful, none was greater than the prince-bishops of Durham. They defended by force of arms much of the border with Scotland. They conducted their own courts and minted their own money. The king's writ had no force in the Palatinate of Durham.

The bishops were well suited to their high office. William of St Carileph, who began to build the present cathedral in the 11th century, thought nothing of challenging William the Conqueror, and proudly boasted that he was exempt from the king's justice. Ranulf Flambard, the close confidant and minister of William Rufus and scourge of his fellow churchmen, was Bishop of Durham.

Two centuries later, Bishop Anthony Bek led his troops into battle against the Scots and twice defied the might of Edward I. 'The bishop,' proclaimed Bek's steward, 'is king in his own diocese.'

The present cathedral* was begun in the closing years of the 11th century. It was the first church in Europe to be built with pointed arches and ribbed vaulting. This was the first hint of the Gothic style which was to conquer the Christian world in the years to come. It was a seat fit for England's mightiest prelates. (See pp. 70–71.)

Dynevor Castle, *Dyfed*
Rhodri Mawr—Roderick the Great—who united Wales in the 9th century, built Dynevor Castle in 876 for his son, Cadell, whom he made ruler of Deheubarth (South Wales). From that time the castle became the residence of the Princes of Deheubarth. The old castle now lies in ruins and the present castle was built in 1856.

Late in the 12th century, the Welsh

hero Lord Rhys lived at Dynevor. Because he had become a menace to the English, Henry II determined to force him into obedience.

Rhys's men were afraid of the freckled-faced English king, because an ancient prophecy foretold that a freckled-faced man who crossed the ford of Pencarn would bring disaster to the Welsh.

Rhys was encouraged when Henry's army crossed the river at another point. But his relief was short-lived. A trumpet blast frightened the king's horse. Bolting along the river bank, the horse plunged into the water at Pencarn ford. After this incident, Lord Rhys paid homage to the king, who made him Justice of Deheubarth. South Wales prospered, and Lord Rhys encouraged a revival of the arts.

Towards the end of his reign, two of Rhys's sons rebelled, imprisoning their father and their brother, Howell, at Dynevor Castle. The brothers blinded Howell, but he knew the castle so well that he was able to find his father and release him. After escaping, Lord Rhys and his son recaptured the castle.

Eastchurch, *Kent*
The early pioneer air pilots, such as Moore-Brabazon, Rolls and Sopwith, made many flights from Eastchurch. They flew over the Swale, between the Isle of Sheppey and the Kentish mainland, and off Leysdown at the eastern end of Sheppey.

In 1909, at Shell Beach, near Leysdown, J. T. C. Moore-Brabazon, later Lord Brabazon, became the first pilot to fly a British-built aeroplane for a circular flight of 1 mile. He went on to fly 2 miles in $2\frac{1}{2}$ minutes at varying heights up to 30ft.

Winston Churchill learnt to fly at Eastchurch. In 1910 Short Brothers set up their workshops at the aerodrome. They built many flying-boats which they tested on the Swale. During the Second World War the

aerodrome was taken over by the Royal Air Force, and suffered heavy raids by German aircraft during the Battle of Britain.

Ecclefechan, *Dumf & Gall*
The historian Thomas Carlyle (1795–1881) was born here in a house* built by his father and uncle, who were master masons. The village is the 'Entepfuhl' of his satirical essay, *Sartor Resartus*.

Carlyle, who was a schoolmaster in his early years, wrote his first book, a life of the German poet Schiller, in 1825. His chief works were a work on the French Revolution and a life of Frederick the Great.

His wife, Jane Welsh, a doctor's daughter, suffered much from his gloom and ill-temper during the 40 years of their marriage. They were devoted to each other, but Carlyle often masked his affection for her by his gruff behaviour

She was a woman of wit and beauty, who enjoyed the social life of London. He preferred to shut himself away from the world for hours in a soundproof room at the top of their house in Chelsea, London.

Research was often a dreary burden; Carlyle complained of his thoughts 'all inarticulate, sour, fermenting, bottomless'. He was afflicted by dyspepsia, 'a rat gnawing at the pit of my stomach'. Bouts of sleeplessness and the crowing of 'demon fowls' from his neighbours' gardens drove him to distraction.

The sudden loss of his wife in 1866 was a bitter blow. She was found sitting dead in her carriage one day, just after her dog had been knocked down by another vehicle. Carlyle realised too late how much distress he had caused her, and made a yearly pilgrimage to her tomb.

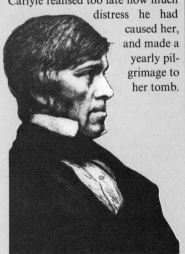

LITERARY GIANT *Born in Ecclefechan, Thomas Carlyle was a major figure of 19th-century letters.*

Edinburgh, *Lothian*
Built on seven hills, Edinburgh has been Scotland's capital for 500 years. Its boundaries extend from the Firth of Forth to the Pentland Hills. Much of the city's grace and dignity derives from the 18th-century streets, squares and crescents of New Town, but its heart is the Royal Mile, linking Holyrood Palace with Castle Rock, the nucleus around which the city grew.

Edinburgh Castle

From its foundation on Castle Rock in the 12th century, Edinburgh Castle* has been the focus of many events in Scottish history.

In 1440 Chancellor Crichton lured his chief rivals, the young Earl of Douglas and his brother, to a banquet there and then treacherously had them beheaded. Half a century later the Duke of Albany, who had been imprisoned by his brother, James III, escaped over the battlements on a knotted rope.

In a small room looking south from the castle, on June 19, 1566, Mary, Queen of Scots, gave birth to a boy. She said: 'This is the son who, I hope, shall first unite the two kingdoms of Scotland and England.' Her wish came true, for the boy was to be crowned James VI of Scotland and James I of England.

Seven years after James was born, William Kirkcaldy of Grange fought desperately to save Edinburgh Castle for Queen Mary against rebel lords. After four months the castle fell, and Kirkcaldy was hanged. During the siege the Earl of Morton bombarded the castle. Later he rebuilt it and added the massive Half Moon Battery.

When Jacobite rebels seized Edinburgh in 1745, the British troops held the castle against them. If the Highlanders had gained access, they might have found the Scottish crown jewels, locked in a cellar. The treasures were discovered by Sir Walter Scott in 1818, and are on display.

Royal Mile

Until the 18th century the Royal Mile was the scene of turbulent upheavals in Edinburgh's life.

In 1520 the Hamiltons, followers of the Earl of Arran, and the Douglases, supporters of the Earl of Angus, met in the narrow street known as Blackfriars Wynd. Neither of the rival families would yield the crown of the road to the other. The resulting skirmish, known as the 'Cleanse the Causeway' riot, led to the Douglases gaining control of Scottish affairs.

Through these same wynds and closes Deacon William Brodie pursued the life of crime which brought him to the gallows in 1788. A respected town councillor and cabinetmaker by day, at night Brodie used impressions that he had taken of his customers' keys to burgle their houses. His career gave Robert Louis Stevenson the idea for *Dr Jekyll and Mr Hyde*.

In 1637 an Edinburgh woman, Jennie Geddes, struck a blow for religious liberty. At St Giles Kirk*, the Anglican order of service was being used when, seizing her stool, Jennie hurled it at the minister's head with the shout, 'Ye'll naesay your mass in my lug!'

A more vigorous protest by the citizens of the Old Town occurred outside St Giles in 1736—the Porteous Riot. A smuggler had earned popular sympathy by robbing the customs house, and when he was being hanged the mob began to throw stones. Captain Porteous, commander of the City Guard, opened fire and killed several townsfolk. He was tried and sentenced to death, but reprieved. The incensed crowd stormed the prison, dragged out Porteous and hanged him.

Princes Street and the New Town

Between 1767 and 1800 the New Town was built as a suburb of the city, with Princes Street as its main thoroughfare. James Craig, a young local architect, prepared the design, which was given its finishing touch by the Adam brothers.

People were reluctant to move beyond the protecting wall of the medieval city until £20 was offered to the first person to build a house in the New Town. Only then did fashionable society make the move.

As the New Town was being built, Edinburgh's importance as an 18th-century cultural centre grew. It produced a brilliant galaxy of men, including Adam Smith, the founder of political economy, the philosopher David Hume, and the engineer Thomas Telford.

Holyrood Palace

According to legend, the Abbey of Holyrood was founded by David I. Thrown from his horse in the marshy land where the abbey now

A KING IN PLAID *Dressed in a kilt, George IV delighted the people of Edinburgh during his 1822 visit.*

stands, the king was about to be gored by a stag when a miraculous vision of a cross appeared between its antlers, at which the animal bounded away. In gratitude the king founded the great church and monastery of the 'holy rood', or cross.

Mary, Queen of Scots, spent the greater part of her troubled reign at the royal palace*, which James IV began developing from the abbey guesthouse in 1501.

In 1745 royal ceremonial was briefly revived at Holyrood for the Jacobite court of Bonnie Prince Charlie. 'He came to the royal palace,' wrote an eyewitness, 'amidst a vast crowd of spectators who, from town and country, flocked to see this uncommon sight, expressing their joy and surprise by long and loud huzzas.'

From Holyrood, on September 20, 1745, Prince Charles marched out to meet the Hanoverian army at Prestonpans; and to the palace he returned victorious next day.

A similar reception greeted George IV on his arrival at Holyrood in 1822, the first official royal visit for two centuries. The king wore pink silk tights and an extremely short kilt. 'As he is to be with us so short a time,' said one Scots lady, 'the more we see of him the better!' It was Queen Victoria who established the present pattern of annual royal visits to Scotland.

Duddingston Village

The churchyard of Duddingston Village was a favourite hunting ground for body-snatchers in the early 19th century. They stole freshly buried corpses to sell to the anatomists, such as the surgeon Dr Robert Knox, at the University of Edinburgh. The array of iron grilles guarding the graves bears witness to this gruesome business.

Doctors did not inquire into the source of bodies which were used for dissection. In particular, an Irish labourer, William Burke, and his accomplice, William Hare, made a handsome profit from body-snatching and selling corpses.

At first Burke and Hare robbed fresh graves. But as the authorities took more precautions to prevent grave-robbing, these so-called 'Resurrection men' turned to murder. Helped by their wives, they lured 15 people to their deaths before discovery. In 1829 Hare, the more villainous of the two, turned king's evidence and Burke's career ended on the scaffold.

On one occasion a life was saved. When John Samuel and Martin Eccles broke into a coffin late one night, the corpse sat up and sneezed. The robbers fled, and the supposedly dead woman lived for several years.

VILLAINY *The gruesome trade of body-snatchers in 19th-century Edinburgh, shown in this contemporary engraving, was stopped in the 1830's.*

Colinton and Swanston

In the hills on the southern outskirts of Edinburgh is Colinton village, where the 19th-century poet and novelist Robert Louis Stevenson spent each summer of his boyhood at his grandfather's house. When he was older he lived at

Swanston, 2 miles towards the hills. 'The road goes down through a valley and then finally begins to scale the main slope of the Pentlands,' he wrote. 'A banquet of old trees stands round a white farmhouse, and from a neighbouring dell you can see smoke rising and leaves ruffling in the breeze. This, with the hamlet lying behind, unseen, is Swanston.'

Throughout his later life, Stevenson looked back nostalgically to the peace of Swanston Cottage.

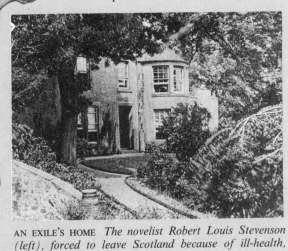

AN EXILE'S HOME *The novelist Robert Louis Stevenson (left), forced to leave Scotland because of ill-health, looked back nostalgically to his home at Swanston (above).*

Elstow, *Beds*

Born in 1628, John Bunyan, the author of *The Pilgrim's Progress,* grew up in Elstow, 2 miles south of Bedford. He was educated at a village school. After being drafted into the Parliamentary army in 1644, Bunyan returned to Elstow in June 1647 to become a tinker. Two years later he married a girl from the village.

During this time, Bunyan underwent a spiritual conflict, described in his autobiography, *Grace Abounding,* and changed from a lively and roisterous young man to a sober Puritan. (See p. 191.)

Ely, *Cambs.*

Saxon resistance to the Normans was centred on Ely, then an island amid the fens. The Saxon leader was Hereward the Wake, who cut his way through William the Conqueror's besieging troops, and vanished from history after 1072.

The cathedral*, on the site of a monastery founded in the 7th century by St Ethelreda, or Aethelthryth, daughter of a king of East Anglia, was begun in 1083, and work went on until the 16th century. An annual fair was held on the feast day of St Ethelreda, or St Awdrey as she became known, at which cheap trinkets were sold. From these trinkets is derived the word 'tawdry', an abbreviation of St Awdrey.

Epworth, *Humberside*

John Wesley, the leader of Methodism, was born on June 17, 1703, the 15th of 19 children. His father, Samuel Wesley, rector of Epworth, was a stern man, whose religious and political convictions brought him into conflict with parishioners. In 1709 a furious mob burnt down the Wesley home. It is said that John was rescued by his nurse only moments before the roof collapsed. Despite this incident, the Old Rectory* was rebuilt, and Samuel remained at Epworth until his death.

At Oxford in 1720, John joined a religious group formed there by his brother Charles. The members were derisively called 'Methodists', because of their strict religious observance.

Evesham, *Herefs & Worcs*

On August 4, 1265, Simon de Montfort and his supporters were defeated at Evesham by Henry III's son, Prince Edward, later Edward I.

Two years before, the barons under Simon de Montfort had revolted against Henry III, and had captured the king and the prince at the Battle of Lewes. But after the revolt, the barons in the west refused to accept de Montfort's lead.

In April 1265 de Montfort marched towards the Welsh borders. At Hereford, Prince Edward escaped from imprisonment and joined his allies.

Prince Edward marched 40 miles overnight from Worcester to Kenilworth, where de Montfort's son was staying. He attacked at dawn, routing the unprepared force and taking the de Montfort banners. Carrying these banners at the head of his forces, Edward intercepted de Montfort at Evesham.

At first de Montfort believed that it was his son advancing towards him. When he realised that the prince had tricked him, he was trapped by the River Avon. His allies deserted him, and he died fighting as Edward's larger force surrounded and crushed his army.

Exeter, *Devon*

An ill-equipped force of 6000 stood before the gates of Exeter in September 1497. Their leader was Perkin Warbeck, a 23-year-old from Flanders, who claimed to be Richard of York, son of Edward IV, and the younger of the two princes in the Tower. The pretender to the English throne received support from the courts of Europe, who wished to embarrass Henry VII.

After landing at Whitesand Bay, near Land's End in Cornwall, the pretender raised an army and marched towards Exeter. But, on learning of the approach of the Earl of Devonshire, Perkin withdrew to Taunton, where he abandoned his followers to their fate.

Perkin finally surrendered to Henry VII who at first treated him with clemency, and he was lodged in the Tower. But, after a foolish attempt at seizing the Tower, he was hanged at Tyburn in 1499.

Perkin Warbeck's assault on Exeter was only one of many which the city has suffered. It was stormed by the Danes in AD 876, and two centuries later it yielded to William the Conqueror.

The Roundheads occupied Exeter at the outbreak of the Civil War, but it was later taken by the Royalists, led by Prince Maurice, in 1643.

Charles I's daughter Henrietta was born there in 1644. Many of its historic buildings were destroyed by German bombing in 1942.

F

Falkirk, *Central*

Edward I marched north in 1298 with 2500 cavalry and 16,000 foot, mostly from Ireland and Wales, to crush William Wallace, the leader of Scots resistance to English rule.

At dawn on July 22 Edward engaged the Scots on the south side of Callendar Wood, near Falkirk. As the king was mounting his horse it was frightened by a trumpet blast and kicked him. With two broken ribs, Edward continued to direct his forces throughout the day.

The Scots infantry stood firm against the onslaught of Edward's cavalry. They eventually gave way before a hail of arrows from the Welsh archers and broke up. Wallace's cavalry fled and about 5000 Scots are said to have perished.

Despite this defeat, Wallace's rising had put steel into Scottish resistance and Edward was able to reoccupy only the southern part of the country.

The second battle of Falkirk took place in January 1746, when Bonnie Prince Charlie surprised and defeated government forces under General Henry Hawley at Bantaskyne, south-west of Falkirk, during the Scots' long retreat north.

Falkland Palace, *Fife*

The palace* was a favourite residence of the Stuart kings. Building began in the late 15th century, but the palace owes its present shape to the efforts of James V, who died there after Scotland's defeat at Solway Moss in 1542.

He had just become the father of a baby girl, the future Mary, Queen of Scots. Recalling that his dynasty had begun with Walter the Steward's marriage to Robert Bruce's daughter, Marjorie, the Scottish king said prophetically: 'It cam wi' a lass and it will gang wi' a lass.' The last Stuart monarch was not to be Mary but Queen Anne, who came to the throne 160 years later.

Falmouth, *Cornwall*

Until the 17th century Falmouth consisted of a hamlet, known as Pennycomequick, and a manor house, Arwennack. The owners of the manor, the Killigrew family, developed Falmouth against opposition from the ancient Cornish ports of Truro, Penryn and Tregony.

Given its royal charter in 1661, Falmouth became a thriving port. In 1688 it became the headquarters of the mail boats or 'packets' to New York. After 1852, when it was replaced by Southampton as the mail port, Falmouth developed a docks industry and, later, it became a popular seaside resort.

AIR SHOW *George V and Queen Mary inspecting new aeroplanes at the Royal Army Aircraft Factory, Farnborough, in 1914.*

Farnborough, *Hants*

The systematic development of the British aircraft industry began at Farnborough in 1910 with the establishment of His Majesty's Balloon Factory. Two years earlier the town had been the scene of the first successful heavier-than-air flight in Britain. On October 16, 1908, the American-born pilot Sam Cody ascended 1390 ft in a demonstration flight in an army aeroplane.

In 1910 Cody won the British Empire Michelin Cup for flying 185½ miles in 4 hours and 47 minutes at Farnborough. His achievement aroused the government's interest in aviation. Within a year the Balloon Factory had been expanded into the Royal Army Aircraft Factory, the beginnings of the present-day Royal Aircraft Establishment.

Farringford, *IOW*

Alfred, Lord Tennyson settled at a farmhouse near Farringford in 1853. He went there after being made Poet Laureate, with a pension of £200 a year granted him by Sir Robert Peel. With Tennyson came his wife, Emily, and their infant son.

Tennyson was a prudent, methodical man, who was prone to depressions. He was unusually tall and of almost Indian appearance with his black hair and beard, aquiline features and dark eyes and skin.

In his first secluded years at Farringford he wrote 'The Charge of the Light Brigade', and finished the first series of *Idylls of the King,* his romantic epic poems about King Arthur and his knights. This was an instant success, and 10,000 copies were sold within a month of publication. Tennyson's other works achieved a popularity unequalled by any other English poet. Among

BEST SELLER *In 1861, at the peak of his popularity, Tennyson, aged 52, posed for this photograph.*

his most ardent admirers was Queen Victoria.

Sightseers flocked to his home. He found them such a nuisance that in 1868 he set in hand the building of a summer residence, Aldworth, in a then remote spot near Haslemere, Surrey. For the rest of his life he divided his time between Aldworth and Farringford.

Tennyson continued to write poetry prolifically until he was over 80. At the age of 74 he went with the Liberal Prime Minister, William Gladstone, on a voyage round Scotland to Scandinavia. On this voyage Gladstone at last persuaded him to accept a peerage, and he became Baron Tennyson of Aldworth and Farringford.

Faversham, *Kent*

In 1551 this estuary town was the scene of a notorious murder that provided the plot for the first domestic melodrama in the British theatre.

The murder victim, Thomas Arden, was a prosperous businessman, collector of the Customs at Faversham and a former mayor. His wife, Alice, fell in love with a tailor called Thomas Mosby. Alice and Mosby decided to murder Arden. They hired two assassins, Loosebagg and Black Will, and all four finally did away with Arden on the night of February 15, 1551, while he was playing draughts in his parlour.

Three of the murderers were caught almost immediately. Alice was burnt at Canterbury; Mosby was hanged at Smithfield; Black Will was burnt at Flushing; Loosebagg appears to have escaped. Arden's half-timbered house, the scene of the crime, still stands in the town.

The story found its way into Holinshed's *Chronicles,* published in 1577, which was the source of much of Shakespeare's historical material. In 1592 an unknown playwright wrote *The Lamentable and True Tragedie of M. Arden of Feversham in Kent*. At one time it was thought that the play was written, or at least retouched, by Shakespeare, but this theory is no longer taken seriously.

Fishbourne Palace, *W Sussex*
See pp. 34–35

Fishguard, *Dyfed*

The last invasion of Britain took place in 1797. On February 22, a small French force landed at a cove near Fishguard. They hoped to rouse the Welsh in an attempt to dethrone George III.

During the voyage to Wales, the leader of the force, General Tate, an Irish-American, had kept his men on short rations. As a result the French satisfied their hunger and thirst by looting the inns and farms of their supposed allies.

The local people, instead of joining the French, fled in terror. However, a woman cobbler, Jemima Nicholas, seized her pitchfork and rounded up 12 French prisoners.

The Fishguard Fencibles, the local militia, were alerted, and the 700-strong South Pembrokeshire Yeomanry marched into the area. As the French were preparing for battle, they saw some figures in red cloaks and tall black hats approaching their assembled ranks.

Imagining that these were troop reinforcements, the terrified French surrendered. These reinforcements were in fact a group of Welsh women, dressed in the traditional costume of their country, who had come to watch the battle.

Flint Castle, *Clwyd*

Flint Castle* was the first of the great fortresses built by Edward I to control the Welsh countryside. Construction began in July 1277.

In 1399 Richard II, tricked by the treacherous Earl of Northumberland into leaving Wales for London, was ambushed on the way to the capital and escorted to Flint Castle. There, he was persuaded to abdicate in favour of his victorious rival, Henry Bolingbroke, Duke of Lancaster, later Henry IV.

A French noble who was with Richard II described the arrival of Henry's army at Flint Castle: 'The host approached the castle and entirely surrounded it, even to the sea, in very fair array. Then the Earl of Northumberland went to Duke Henry and they talked together rather a long while and concluded that he should not enter the castle till such a time as the King had dined, because he was fasting. The table being laid, the King sat down to dinner. The King was a very long time at table; not for anything he ate; but because he well knew, that as soon as he had dined, the Duke would come for him, to carry him off or put him to death.'

Flodden Field, *Northld*

The most crushing defeat in Scotland's history was inflicted by an English army at Flodden, near Branxton, on September 9, 1513.

Taking advantage of Henry VIII's absence in France with the main English army, James IV of Scotland (1488–1513) had crossed the border on August 22, 1513, with a force of about 30,000 men. James captured the castles of Norham and Ford from the English.

Henry's lieutenant in the north, Thomas Howard, Earl of Surrey, hurriedly mustered an army of about 25,000 men at Newcastle and formally challenged James to meet him in battle.

James waited in a strong position on Flodden ridge. Surrey reached Woller Hough, 6 miles from Flodden, on September 6. Failing to tempt the Scots to fight in the plain, he marched north and turned to attack them from the rear.

The battle began late in the afternoon. When the English artillery opened fire the undisciplined Scottish infantry charged forward.

James, believing that the English were in disarray, advanced swiftly downhill with two columns. But his pikemen lost their formation. The English cavalry routed the Scottish left wing, and the English archers, taking the Scottish extreme right wing by surprise, drove it back.

In the centre the Scottish king fought on foot with his nobles. The long and bloody battle continued until nightfall. But at last the shattered remnants of the Scottish army finally admitted defeat. James himself, many of his nobles and 10,000 of his subjects fell in the battle, as well as 4000 English.

Fonthill Abbey, *Wilts*
The wealthy and talented William Beckford (1759–1844) always hated the Classical mansion where he was born. Late in the 1790's he decided to replace it with one of the most exotic and extravagant edifices ever built in Britain.

A product of Beckford's romantic imagination, his new Gothic abbey had a 300 ft high octagonal tower, 120 ft high hall, and 8 miles of surrounding walls. Built at great speed by 600 men, sometimes working all night by the light of bonfires, Fonthill was structurally unsound. The tower collapsed twice during the building operations. In 1825, three years after Beckford had been forced by lack of money to sell Fonthill, the great tower crumbled. Hardly a stone of Beckford's abbey now remains.

Fotheringhay Castle, *Northants*
After the execution of Mary, Queen of Scots, in 1587, Fotheringhay crumbled into decay. The great hall in which the execution took place was built into Connington Manor, Huntingdonshire, now destroyed.

All that remains of Fotheringhay today is a mound, and some stone-work surrounded by railings.

MARY'S CAPTIVE YEARS

After Mary, Queen of Scots, lost her crown and country at the Battle of Langside in May 1568, she was forced to flee to England. Mary was to spend 19 years in exile there, officially as Queen Elizabeth's guest, but in effect her prisoner. During these years she and her entourage were sent from place to place at Elizabeth's orders.

Mary was moved in 1568 from her first 'prison', at Carlisle, because it was near the Scottish border and possible rescue, and taken to the more isolated Bolton Castle.

In 1570 the Earl of Shrewsbury and his wife, 'Bess of Hardwick', were appointed gaolers to Mary. For 14 years the trio moved from one country house to another, and at first they got on well together. But the Scottish queen tricked the earl by sending secret messages to the Catholic Duke of Norfolk. And his wife added to his troubles by accusing him of having an affair with Mary.

Suffering from ill-health and depression, Mary also lived at Wingfield Manor. She stayed occasionally at Chatsworth while the manor was cleaned—as was the custom with large houses in that insanitary age. Buxton spa was not far from Chatsworth, and Mary took the waters there.

After a plot to free her by the northern earls, Mary was taken to Coventry and then to Sheffield, which had two residences fit for a queen—the castle and the manor.

At Chartley, in the autumn of 1586, there was an unsuccessful rescue attempt by Sir Anthony Babington. Then Mary made her last journey, to Fotheringhay. She was tried for plotting Elizabeth's overthrow and, on February 8, 1587, wearing a blood-red petticoat to signify martyrdom, the Queen of Scots was beheaded. (See pp. 144–5.)

Last of Mary's prisons (map, left) was Fotheringhay, where she was executed. A contemporary sketch (above) shows Mary being tried there.

Framlingham Castle, *Suffolk*
Mary Tudor, the rightful Queen of England, found refuge in this castle* during the nine days in which the Protestant claimant, Lady Jane Grey, was attempting to usurp her throne. (See pp. 134–5.)

At Framlingham Queen Mary was the guest of the Catholic Duke of Norfolk. She had been warned that the Protestants would attempt to keep her from the throne and so had stayed away from the death-bed of her half-brother, Edward VI.

At Framlingham, Mary's supporters rallied around her, and soon she was acknowledged as queen.

Gad's Hill Place, *Kent*
Charles Dickens bought Gad's Hill Place (now a school) in 1856, just before he and his wife agreed to separate. He lived there with nine of his ten children (the eldest having left with his wife) until the end of his life, and spent lavishly on improving the property.

He worked in a chalet in the garden editing the periodicals *Household Words* and, from 1859, *All the Year Round,* in which *The Tale of Two Cities* and *Great Expectations* first appeared. At Gad's Hill he also wrote *Our Mutual Friend* and the uncompleted mystery story, *Edwin Drood.* Dickens died suddenly at the dinner table in Gad's Hill Place on June 9, 1870. (See p. 308.)

Glamis Castle, *Tayside*
Sir Walter Scott declared Glamis Castle* to be the noblest specimen of a medieval castle he had ever seen.

The murder of Duncan I by Macbeth, Thane of Glamis, as told in Shakespeare's *Macbeth,* is reputed to have taken place here. In reality Duncan was slain by Macbeth in a battle at Bothouganan, near Elgin, in 1040.

The nucleus of the present castle, rebuilt in the late 17th century, is a 15th-century tower said to contain a secret chamber known only to the Earl of Strathmore and his heir. Reputedly, knowledge of a terrible family secret is similarly confined to the earl, who divulges it to his heir when he comes of age.

Glasgow, *Strathclyde*
The city of Glasgow—the Celtic name, *Gelschu,* means 'beloved green place'—grew up round a 6th-century church founded by St Mungo. Traditionally this was the site of the present cathedral*, which dates from the 12th century. Glasgow University, the second oldest university in Scotland after St Andrews, was founded in 1451.

In early times, this small university town was under the domination of the church. Situated on the River Clyde, it faced away from the profitable trade of the European ports and its river fisheries were its only source of wealth. But although Glasgow was a backwater, its citizens were caught up in the tumult of Scottish history. In 1568 the town joined forces with the Regent Moray to defeat Mary, Queen of Scots, at the Battle of Langside. The site of this conflict is now Queen's Park—named after her.

The city began to prosper after the Act of Union in 1707 opened up the English colonies in the Americas to Scottish traders; its merchants made fortunes out of the trade in sugar, rum and tobacco.

Shoals in the River Clyde prevented large vessels from reaching the city. In the mid-17th century the civic authorities bought 13 acres downstream near Greenock, and Port Glasgow came into being. A century later, engineers managed to clear a channel and large ships were able to reach Glasgow.

Although, in the 1770's, the War of American Independence wiped out the tobacco fortunes, the city had become a centre of trade and

ART NOUVEAU PIONEER
This high-backed chair is typical of the work of Charles Rennie Mackintosh, a Glasgow architect and pioneer of art nouveau. In 1895 he won a competition to produce designs for a new and enlarged art school in Glasgow.

commerce. And, with the coming of the Industrial Revolution, it began to surge forward again. The basis for Glasgow's industrial growth was the huge coal and iron deposits in the surrounding countryside.

By 1834 Scotland had 134 cotton factories, most of them within 25 miles of the centre of Glasgow. Between 1765 and 1861, Glasgow's population soared from 28,000 to almost half a million.

Glasgow and the Clyde achieved world leadership in shipbuilding. In 1811 a Port Glasgow firm built Henry Bell's 30 ton *Comet,* the first steam ship to run commercially in Europe.

Experiments with iron ships began. The *Fairy Queen* was built in a city foundry in 1831. But the peak of Clyde shipbuilding came with the famous liners, the *Queen Mary* (launched in 1936) and the *Queen Elizabeth* (1940).

Glasgow and its university have produced many great men. James Watt (1736–1819), Greenock-born designer of the first economical steam engine. Adam Smith (1723–90) held the chairs of logic and

philosophy at Glasgow, and wrote *Wealth of Nations,* one of the most influential of all books on political economy. David Livingstone (1813–73) studied medicine, applied science and divinity at the university, before he went to Africa as a missionary.

William Thomson, Lord Kelvin (1824–1907), professor of natural philosophy for 53 years, applied his theoretical knowledge of heat, light, sound and electricity to practical problems.

Sir Thomas Lipton (1850–1931), a native of Glasgow, built a butter-and-ham empire of grocery shops over Britain. He was an errand boy at the age of nine and, after working in America, opened his first grocer's shop in Glasgow in 1871. It was soon followed by other shops, and Lipton was a millionaire by the age of 30.

He succeeded in the tea trade because he prepared special blends for different towns after analysing their water supplies. He was a keen yachtsman and made repeated but unsuccessful attempts to win the America's Cup.

Sir William Burrell, a wealthy shipowner and art connoisseur, presented his collection of more than 8000 priceless antiquities and works of art to the City of Glasgow in 1944. It is now housed in a museum* in Pollok Park.

Glastonbury, *Somerset*
The ancient abbey* of Glastonbury was already old when St Dunstan restored it in the 10th century. The monks claimed to be able to trace its foundation back to King Arthur and St Patrick.

When, in 1184, the old wooden church was burnt down, the monks decided to rebuild it with the offerings of pilgrims. In 1191 they pretended that they had found the bodies of Arthur and Guinevere in their cemetery.

Later, the monks claimed to have the Holy Grail—a cup which Christ had used at the Last Supper. The pope granted an indulgence reducing the number of days spent by sinners in purgatory if they made a pilgrimage to Glastonbury.

The monks' myth-making may have been founded on fact. Glastonbury Tor is close to Cadbury Castle, and if the historical Arthur made his base at Cadbury, it is likely enough that Glastonbury was his burial place.

Glencoe, *Highland*
The massacre of 38 MacDonalds of Glencoe in 1692 is one of the most infamous acts in Scottish history. (See pp. 216–17.)

The man whom many Scots held responsible for this outrage was Sir John Dalrymple, later Earl of Stair (1648–1707). William III's chief adviser in Scotland. He said: 'It is a great work of charity to be exact in rooting out that damnable sect, the worst in all the Highlands.'

The legend persists that Stair, using William III's authority, wrote the 'extirpation' order on a nine of diamonds playing card which henceforth was known as 'the curse of Scotland'. This belief may have arisen because the pips on the card resemble the arms of Stair.

Glen Fruin, *Strathclyde*
West of Loch Lomond lies Glen Fruin ('Glen of Sorrow'), the scene of a bloody clan battle in 1603. Horsemen of the Colquhoun clan found themselves in boggy ground, and were helpless against the onslaught of the MacGregors. Two hundred Colquhouns fell to their enemies on the battlefield or in the merciless pursuit.

A hundred Colquhoun widows paraded before James VI (James I of England) at Stirling. Each rode a white horse and carried her husband's bloody shirt on a spear. James was so moved that he outlawed the MacGregors and forbade the use of their name.

Charles II reversed the decision in 1663 in gratitude for their help to the Royalist cause, but William III renewed the ban 30 years later. The MacGregors remained proscribed until 1755.

Gloucester, *Glos*
In the Civil War, Gloucester held out against a Royalist siege for four weeks in 1643. The city's governor, Colonel Edward Massey, was only 23.

This resistance, at a time when the king's cause seemed triumphant, heartened all supporters of Parliament. The trained bands, or militia, of London volunteered to help and marched westwards.

Meanwhile the Royalists had mined the city walls and, on September 5, Charles warned Massey to yield before they were blown up. But that night, with food running

out, the defenders saw a beacon fire signalling that relief was coming. Before morning heavy rain had flooded the Royalist mines and rendered them useless.

By September 8, when the trained bands sighted Gloucester Cathedral*, the besiegers had withdrawn. After the Restoration, as a final act of revenge, the walls which had defied Charles I were destroyed by order of his son, Charles II.

Gotham, *Notts*
During the Middle Ages, Gotham, near Nottingham, was known as 'a village of fools'. This reputation is said to date from the reign of King John in the 13th century.

According to tradition, the villagers purposely acted like fools in order to discourage the king from building a hunting lodge at Gotham. They were afraid that the presence of the court would involve them in great expense and disrupt the life of the village.

The king's servants, flabbergasted by the behaviour of the villagers, are said to have returned to the king and advised him to abandon his plan to live there.

After the success of their ruse, the inhabitants of Gotham are reputed to have said: 'We ween there are more fools pass through Gotham than remain in it.'

Grasmere, *Cumbria* See p. 281.

Gravesend, *Kent*
In the parish churchyard of Gravesend is a bronze statue* commemorating Pocahontas. In 1608, this 13-year-old Red Indian princess, daughter of the powerful chieftain,

INDIAN PRINCESS *Pocahontas, daughter of a chief, saved the life of an Englishman about to be killed.*

Powhattan, rescued Captain John Smith, who was the leader of the colonists in Virginia.

Smith was captured by the Indians, who condemned him to death. Pocahontas placed her head over his as a tomahawk was raised to strike the fatal blow. This act of bravery saved Smith's life and he was freed by Powhattan.

Pocahontas later became a Christian and married a settler named John Rolfe.

When Rolfe brought Pocahontas to England in 1616, together with their infant son, Thomas, she was fêted at the court of James I. In the following year while sailing down the Thames at the start of her return voyage to Virginia, Pocahontas caught a fever and died, aged 22, off Gravesend. The young Indian princess was buried in the chancel of St George's Church.

Greenock, *Strathclyde*
This town, at the 'Tail of the Bank' on the Firth of Clyde, was the deep-water port for Glasgow until the river was opened up for large

SEAFARER *Captain Kidd, shown in this print, was a notorious pirate whose birthplace was Greenock.*

ships in the late 18th and early 19th centuries.

Greenock's most notorious seafarer was Captain William Kidd, born there in about 1645. His father is thought to have been a Covenanting minister.

Kidd served in the West Indies against the French, and was voted £150 by the American colonial authorities for help during riots after the Glorious Revolution of 1688. By the time he was 50 he was prosperous, married and with a home in New York. Then he

went to London, where he received the King's Commission to hunt pirates and share the profits with peers of the realm, including the First Lord of the Admiralty and the Lord Chancellor.

Kidd went to Madagascar, but found few pirates, and began to plunder shipping in the Indian Ocean. He claimed afterwards that he was forced to do so for fear of revolt by the crew, and during a mutinous incident he killed a gunner with a wooden bucket.

Complaints of Kidd's activities began to reach England. The Great Mogul threatened to expel the East India Company from India if the piracy was not checked. Kidd was arrested on his return to America and sent back to England where he was tried and executed in 1701.

Gretna Green, *Dumf & Gall*
For a century runaway lovers made for Gretna Green just over the border where, under Scots law, they could be quickly married without the consent of their parents.

The smithy at Gretna Green still has the anvil over which they were married, but since 1940 the smith has no longer had the right to conduct the ceremony.

Grime's Graves, *Nflk* See pp. 16–17.

Guildford, *Surrey*
In Saxon times, Guildford was a fording place over the River Way. The town was first mentioned in the will of King Alfred of Wessex: 'To Ethelwald, my brother's son, I bequeath the manor at Godalming and at Gyldeford.'

The Norman castle, built in the 12th century, was visited on many occasions by King John, and became a favourite residence of his son, Henry III. Only the castle keep* remains today.

Flemish weavers, invited by Edward III to settle in Guildford during the 14th century, made the town a prosperous centre of the wool trade, which continued to flourish until the 18th century.

Gwennap Pit, *Cornwall*
In 1762 John Wesley, the founder of Methodism, preached at Gwennap Pit* to a crowd of 20,000. The natural amphitheatre is a circular depression, created possibly by the subsidence of a mine. Wesley continued to hold evangelical meetings

at Gwennap Pit until 1788, when he was 85. In 1803, the sides of the pit were terraced; it is still used for Methodist gatherings.

H

Haddington, *Lothian*
A servant girl putting a clothes-horse too near an open fire is said to have caused a blaze which destroyed the town in 1598.

Haddington had been burnt several times before by English invaders. They held it for more than a year in 1548–9 in the face of a Scottish siege, until relieved by the Earl of Rutland.

The county offices, dating from 1833, stand on the site of a palace where Alexander II, son of William the Lion, was born in 1198. The poet William Dunbar (1460–1520) and the religious reformer John Knox (1505–72) are believed to have been born in the town. Knox was educated at Haddington and spent several years as a notary there.

Another native of Haddington was Samuel Smiles (1812–1904), whose book *Self-help* (1857) encouraged many Victorians to better themselves by following the example of great men.

Haddon Hall, *Derby*
One of the finest medieval manor houses in existence, Haddon Hall was the scene in 1558 of the elopement of Sir John Manners and the heiress Dorothy Vernon during her sister's wedding celebrations.

Hadrian's Wall See pp. 38–39.

Hagley Hall *Herefs & Worcs*
After the failure of the Gunpowder Plot, Humphrey Lyttleton, whose family seat was Hagley Hall, hid two of the conspirators, his brother Stephen Lyttleton and Robert Winter, in the hall.

On January 9, 1606, one of the servants found the hiding place

and fetched the local constable, who arrested them. Humphrey was found guilty of harbouring the fugitives and sentenced to death.

Attempting to save his life, Humphrey betrayed the whereabouts of Jesuits thought to be implicated in the plot. But he was executed just the same.

In 1760 Hagley Hall was torn down by Lord Lyttleton and replaced by the present structure.

Halidon Hill, *Northld*
In 1333 Edward III decided to besiege Berwick to try to maintain his shaky control over Scotland. The English army was placed on Halidon Hill, which overlooked Berwick and the road to Duns. Around the hill lay a deep bog. Twice Berwick refused to yield, in the belief that aid was on the way. When help did arrive from Duns, the relief troops sank in the mire and were picked off by archers. The survivors fled before the English knights.

Hambledon, *Hants*
Cricket, originally a medieval game, was polished and organised by the men of Hambledon, whose matches were played in the mid-18th century on Broad Half Penny Down, a mile from the village. Afterwards, the players would gather at the Bat and Ball Inn which was owned by Richard Nyren, who founded the club in 1760 and became its captain and groundsman.

During a memorable match in June 1777, the Hambledon players beat the all-England side by an innings and 168 runs. And the club introduced a third stump to the wicket late in the 1770's. Hambledon lost its dominance when the Marylebone Cricket Club (MCC) was formed at Lord's in 1788. The Hambledon Club was finally disbanded in 1825.

EARLY CRICKETER *A player wields the curved bat popular at Hambledon in the 1700's.*

Harby, *Lincs*
Queen Eleanor, wife of Edward I, died in 1290 at Harby, where she and her husband were spending some weeks hunting. Her body was taken for burial at Westminster.

Each stopping place of the cortège was marked with a cross. Three survive—at Northampton, Geddington and Waltham Cross. The last stopping place was at Charing Cross, London, where a replica of the original stands.

Hardwick Hall, *Derby*

Elizabeth of Hardwick—'Bess of Hardwick'—was known for two great talents: marrying rich men and building great houses. Born in 1518, the daughter of a country squire, she spent the years of her childhood in a one-storey half-timbered house at Hardwick.

Bess was married at the age of 14 to a neighbour named Robert Barlow. He died when she was 15, leaving her a large estate.

Sixteen years later she married Sir William Cavendish, Treasurer of the Chamber. Bess persuaded her husband to buy an estate for them at Chatsworth, on which she built a magnificent mansion.

When Cavendish died, Bess was only 39. Her next husband, William St Loe, died in 1564 or 1565, leaving his entire estate to Bess. Still beautiful, witty and ambitious, and by now very rich, Bess now married her third husband, one of the most powerful men in England—George Talbot, 6th Earl of Shrewsbury.

In 1591 Shrewsbury died. Bess, now 63, promptly began building her final masterpiece—Hardwick Hall. This house is one of the most spectacular triumphs of Tudor architecture, remarkable for having more glass than stone in its walls. It is also an expression of its owner's pride and self-confidence. The old woman had her own initials carved in vast stone letters in the parapet— E. S. for Elizabeth Shrewsbury.

From her bedroom window, Elizabeth had a convenient view of her childhood home, from which she had travelled so far in status and wealth. She died at Hardwick Hall in her 90th year, a remarkable age for Tudor times.

Harlech Castle, *Gwynedd*

Edward I built Harlech Castle* between 1283 and 1290. Because the castle could be defended by fewer than 20 men, it became the stronghold for the desperate few in major wars in Wales.

In 1400, at the beginning of the revolt of the Welsh against the English, Harlech was held by five Englishmen and 16 Welshmen. After a four-year siege, the castle fell to the Welsh leader, Owain Glyndwr. He made it his capital and held one parliament within its walls before his eventual fall.

In 1460, during the Wars of the Roses, Henry VI's wife, Margaret of Anjou, fled to Harlech before going to Scotland to raise recruits against the Yorkists.

The constable of Harlech Castle, Dafydd ap Ieuan, was a staunch Lancastrian supporter. For eight years, he held out against the Yorkists. He boasted that once he had kept a castle so long in France that all the old women in Wales talked of it; and now he would keep Harlech until all the women of France talked about it.

But Dafydd was forced to surrender the castle in 1468 when, according to a contemporary account, the Earl of Pembroke, a Yorkist supporter, 'assaulted the castle in such a furious thundering manner that it yielded to his hands'. The song, 'Men of Harlech', commemorates this siege.

Hatfield House, *Herts*

Hatfield House has been the home of one of England's most illustrious families—the Cecils—for more than 350 years. The mansion was completed in 1612, only months after the death of its conceiver, Robert Cecil, Earl of Salisbury. Before then the old palace had belonged to the bishops of Ely and then to the crown. But in 1607, James I exchanged Hatfield House for Robert Cecil's nearby home at Theobalds.

In 1835 Hatfield House nearly came to an untimely end. The eccentric dowager marchioness lived then in the west wing. Though over 80 she still rode to hounds, entertained lavishly and used language outrageous for a lady. One November night in 1835 she caught her elaborate coiffure in a candle flame. Before aid could be summoned her apartments were ablaze. The marchioness died. The entire west wing was burnt down and only a change in wind direction saved the rest of the house.

The 3rd Marquess of Salisbury (1830–1903) was born at Hatfield. Described by Disraeli as 'the only man of real courage that it has been my lot to work with', Salisbury was Conservative Prime Minister three times from 1885 onwards.

Hawarden Castle, *Clwyd*

In 1839 William Ewart Gladstone, then a 30-year-old MP and 29 years away from his first term of office as Prime Minister, married Catherine Glynne, the heiress of Hawarden Castle.

For 60 years Gladstone and his wife lived at the castle. In 1847 the Glynne estates were badly hit by a financial panic. Gladstone had to work diligently to make the estates economically sound. As a result, he became the largest landowner in the county. His experience gave him training in economics. When he became Chancellor of the Exchequer in 1852, he said: 'It was always a matter of sailing close to the wind in running the estate, and from that I have learned much of benefit to my present administration.'

At Hawarden, Gladstone exercised by cutting down trees. When he became famous, tourists arrived to watch him, with his braces thrown off and his shirt collar unfastened, at work. After this exhibition, he would distribute wood-chippings as souvenirs.

Gladstone died at Hawarden in 1898 and was buried at Westminster Abbey. He had written, 'I desire to be buried where my wife may also be'. After her death in 1900, she was buried privately by his tomb.

TOURIST ATTRACTION *Gladstone (extreme right) loved to chop down trees on his estate at Hawarden. Tourists used to turn up to watch him at work.*

Hayes Place, *Gtr London*

William Pitt the Elder (1708–78), first Earl of Chatham, whose policies brought Britain victory in the Seven Years' War, bought Hayes Place as his country house in 1753. His second son and future Prime Minister, William, and the younger children were born at Hayes. Pitt rebuilt the house, giving it 24 bedrooms, and stabling for 16 horses.

In 1766 Pitt became Prime Minister. He sold Hayes Place to pay for enlarging a house that had been left to him at Burton Pynsent, in Somerset. Within a year Pitt suffered from a nervous breakdown. Believing that only at Hayes Place would he recover, he paid £17,400 to repurchase the house he had sold for £11,780. He died there in 1778.

Helpston, *Cambs*

John Clare, one of the greatest poets of the English countryside, was born in 1793 at Helpston, which he described as his 'old home of homes'. The son of a Northamptonshire labourer, Clare, although he had almost no schooling, began writing poetry at the early age of 12.

In 1820 Clare's first book, *Poems Descriptive of Rural Life*, was well received, but his other volumes failed to sell. Through patrons, Clare secured a small annuity, but it was not enough to keep his large family from sinking into poverty.

In 1841, after years of hardship, Clare went insane, and had to be confined to an asylum at Northampton, where he spent his last 23 years. In a lucid moment, he wrote to a friend: 'If life had a second edition, how I would correct the proofs.'

Holkham Hall, *Norfolk*

Thomas Coke (1752–1842) led the way in the 18th-century revolution in agricultural production. Coke developed the Norfolk system of crop rotation, modified versions of which are practised today. Four crops are grown in turn on the same soil. The first is turnips, introduced as a field crop in 1731 by 'Turnip Townshend'—Viscount Townshend of Rainham Hall, Norfolk.

Barley, oats or peas follow, and then the land is put under clover or grass. In the fourth year wheat is grown. This rotation saves the soil from exhaustion and checks the spread of pests and disease.

Coke also planted winter fodder, for feeding livestock in the cold months. He called farmers' meetings to explain the new methods which had greatly increased the value of his own estate.

Coke encouraged his tenants by granting them long leases. His contemporary, Robert Bakewell, founded modern stockbreeding by his clever crossing of animals.

Honiton, *Devon*
Late in the 16th century, Flemish refugees, whose skill was making fine Brussels lace, settled at Honiton, where they developed a new style. The town became the centre of lace-making in Britain during early Stuart times.

By the beginning of the 19th century, Honiton lace had gone out of fashion. But in Victorian times it enjoyed a revival in popularity. The lace for Queen Victoria's wedding dress was made near Honiton.

COTTAGE INDUSTRY
The typical Honiton style of richly worked flowers and fronds is shown on this lace sampler. Small amounts of this delicate, hand-made fabric are still produced at Honiton. The local industry—founded by Flemish refugees in the late 16th century—was badly hit by the introduction of machine-made lace a century ago.

Horsham, *W. Sussex*
Catharine Howard, one of the ten children of Lord Edmund Howard, was brought up by her grandmother, Duchess of Norfolk, at Horsham and later in London. Living in this free-and-easy household, Catharine, young and attractive, had several lovers—including Francis Dereham, a kinsman, and

her cousin Thomas Culpepper.

Catharine was introduced to the king in 1540 by Stephen Gardiner, Bishop of Winchester. Henry VIII, then 49 and already tiring of his new bride, Anne of Cleves, was captivated by the lively Catharine.

After his divorce from Anne on July 9, he married Catharine privately and publicly recognised her as his wife on August 8.

On November 2 Archbishop Cranmer informed Henry of Catharine's misconduct before their marriage. Henry began inquiries, which revealed meetings between Catharine and her former lovers. Dereham and Culpepper were executed in December 1541.

Catharine steadfastly denied any misconduct since marrying Henry. But on February 11, 1542, Parliament passed a bill of attainder against her, and two days later she was beheaded in the Tower.

Houghton Hall, *Norfolk*
Robert Walpole, Britain's first Prime Minister and the longest holder of that office (1721–42), was born at Houghton Hall, and inherited the estate when he was 24.

Houghton Hall was then shackled with debts. Although, by clever management, Walpole raised its annual income from £2000 to £8000, he remained always in debt because he lived in an extravagant and showy style.

It was on Houghton that Walpole spent the 1000 per cent profit he made on his stock in the South Sea Bubble. He spent 13 years having the hall rebuilt as a Palladian masterpiece. He lavishly refurnished the interior, built up a superb art collection, and had the village of Houghton moved because it was spoiling his view.

Walpole was a good-natured, vivacious, coarsely spoken man with a loud, ill-bred manner, a local accent all his life, and no interest in literature or oratory. But beneath all this he was a shrewd manager of men and money, an indefatigable worker, and a connoisseur of art. His passion was hunting; he kept a pack of harriers at Houghton, held hunts there each November, and was said to open letters from his huntsman before looking at any of his official mail.

When he retired from office, Walpole spent most of his time at Houghton, plagued by gout, and

often heavily drugged by opium administered to relieve his pain. He was buried in the church at Houghton Hall. (See pp. 230–1.)

LAVISH SPENDER *Robert Walpole, the first Prime Minister, lived extravagantly and was always deep in debt.*

Howe of Corrichie, *Grampian*
A great Highland family met its downfall in battle at this spot near Banchory in 1592. George Gordon, 4th Earl of Huntley, who had won the enmity of Mary, Queen of Scots, was making for Aberdeen when her troops defeated him and his followers.

Huntley had taken the advice of his wife. Witches had told her that by nightfall her husband would be lying in the city's tolbooth (town hall) without a wound on his body.

Their prophecy was fulfilled. The earl collapsed and died at his captors' feet. His unmarked corpse was thrown over a pair of fish baskets and taken to the tolbooth, where it lay that night.

Hughenden Manor, *Bucks*
Benjamin Disraeli bought this imposing mansion*, situated in 750 acres of parkland on a wooded spur of the Chilterns, in 1847.

Disraeli, who was Conservative Prime Minister in 1868 and in 1874–80, was devoted to Hughenden and retreated there to recuperate from the pressures of parliamentary life. 'When I come down to Hughenden I pass the first week sauntering about my park . . . and then I saunter in my library and survey my books,' he wrote in his memoirs. He informed a friend that he and his wife, Mary Anne, had 'restored the house to what it was before the Civil Wars, and we have made a garden of terraces in which cavaliers might roam and saunter with their lady loves.'

At his own request, Disraeli was buried next to his wife at Hughen-

den instead of receiving a state funeral. A few days after the burial, Queen Victoria herself visited Hughenden to lay a wreath on the tomb of her favourite minister.

Hull, See Kingston upon Hull, p. 394

Huntingdon, *Cambs*
A small, austere grammar school serves as the only reminder of Huntingdon's most famous citizen, Oliver Cromwell. It was here that he learnt Latin and Greek as a boy and passed his early manhood as a fenland farmer.

Nothing in Cromwell's early life marked him out for greatness. But in 1628 Cromwell began to champion the rights of local farmers and peasants. At the same time he underwent a deep spiritual crisis, from which he emerged as a committed Puritan and a bitter opponent of the High Church policies of Charles I.

Armed with these convictions, Cromwell attended the Parliament of 1628 as MP for Huntingdon. It was the threshold of his great career as a soldier and ruler.

THE PROTECTOR *Oliver Cromwell rose from fenland obscurity to become leader of his country.*

Huntingtower Castle, *Tayside*
The castle*, 2 miles north-west of Perth, was known as Ruthven (pronounced Riven) until 1600, and was the ancient seat of the earls of Gowrie. It was the scene of the 'Raid of Ruthven' in 1582, when a band of nobles, led by the earls of Gowrie and Mar, kidnapped the 16-year-old James VI of Scotland (the future James I of England) by luring him into the castle when he was hunting close by. The boy king wept when the Master of Glamis barred his escape.

The plotters had objected to James's favourite, the Earl of

Lennox. It took James a year to escape. Later he had his revenge. Gowrie was trapped into a confession of treason and executed.

Inveraray, *Strathclyde*

For centuries Inveraray has been the centre of the Campbell clan under their chiefs, the earls and dukes of Argyll. Archibald Campbell, the eighth earl (1598–1661), had 20,000 retainers and was said to be the most powerful subject of the crown in Scotland. A leading Covenanter, he made sure that the Scottish parliament and not Charles I exercised the real power in Scotland.

The king was reconciled with the Covenanters and made Argyll a marquis. Later, Argyll forged an alliance between Cromwell and the Scots against the king, but his plotting led to his execution after the Restoration of Charles II.

Another Archibald Campbell was created first duke in 1701 for his part in the Glorious Revolution of 1688. The second duke was an architect of the Union of Scotland and England in 1707, and helped to put down the 1715 Jacobite Rebellion. The early-15th-century castle* and the town were rebuilt in 1745–80 by the third duke.

Inverlochy Castle, *Highland*

After his early successes against the Covenanters in 1644, the Earl of Montrose, a supporter of Charles I, turned to attack the king's main opponent—the Earl of Argyll, a leader of the Covenanters.

In February 1645 he marched his men from Fort Augustus, through snowbound passes to Inverlochy, where Argyll and his Campbell clan were gathered.

Spearheaded by a force of cavalry, Montrose's wild clansmen, roaring their battlecries, swept down on the unsuspecting Campbells. Before the day ended, 1500 of the defenders lay dead under the walls of Inver-

lochy Castle*. Argyll fled down Loch Linnhe in his galley.

Montrose reported to the king: 'I am in the fairest hopes of reducing this kingdom to your Majesty's obedience.' (See Montrose p. 408.)

Inverness, *Highland*

In the 6th century, St Columba converted the Pictish King Brude to Christianity at his wooden fortress beside the River Ness. The fort is believed to have been where the present town lies. King Duncan's son, Malcolm III, who avenged his father's death at the hands of Macbeth, destroyed the castle.

A stone keep built by David I in the 12th century stood on a summit above the river for 600 years. James I of Scotland (1394–1437) invited 40 Highland chiefs to a parliament in the town in 1427, and then locked them up in the castle. Alexander, Lord of the Isles, celebrated his release a year later by pillaging and burning the town.

When Bonnie Prince Charlie occupied Inverness in 1746 he had the castle blown up, and the present one—used as a courthouse and offices—dates from the 1830's.

Iona, *Strathclyde*

This tiny island off the south-west tip of Mull was the cradle of Christianity in Scotland. St Columba (521–97), a scholar-monk of Irish royal blood, landed there in 563 and persuaded the Pictish king to give him Iona for a monastery.

Columba's conversion of the native Picts led to the gradual spread into their country by the saint's fellow countrymen from Ireland.

St Oran's cemetery* on Iona is the ancient burial place of Scotland's kings. Forty-eight of them lie there, with four kings of Ireland and eight of Norway. The last to be buried was Duncan, slain by Macbeth in 1040.

Thereafter, royal burials took place at Dunfermline.

Ipswich, *Suffolk*

Tudor intrigues may have prevented Ipswich from becoming a great centre of learning. Cardinal Wolsey, born there about 1475, planned to build a great college close to St Peter's Church. It was designed as a 'nursery' for Wolsey's Cardinal College at Oxford, which was later refounded as Christ Church. But the cardinal's enemies were gather-

ing against him and the project, like its creator, was doomed. Henry VIII suppressed the college, and all that remains is the red-brick Tudor gateway.

Charles Dickens stayed at the Great White Horse in Tavern Street, and it was here that one of his characters, Mr Pickwick, entered the wrong bedroom to discover an elderly lady in yellow curl papers.

Isle of Man

In the 9th century the Isle of Man was invaded by the Norwegians who established the island's parliament—the Tynwald. Fought over by the English and Scots in the 13th century, the island was finally taken by Edward III in 1333.

In 1405 Henry IV bestowed it on the Stanleys, who ruled the island for over 300 years.

Jarrow, *Tyne & Wear*

Jarrow is identified with a modern tragedy—the depression of the 1930's and the 'hunger march' of the unemployed to London in 1936.

The inter-war slump closed down the town's shipbuilding and steel industries. Up to 80 per cent of the working people lost their jobs.

The view of Walter Runciman, later Lord Runciman, then President of the Board of Trade, was that 'Jarrow must work out its own salvation'. This phrase kindled a strong reaction which led to the march of 1936, the Jarrow Crusade.

The 200 thin, ill-nourished marchers, led by their militant Labour MP, the red-haired Ellen Wilkinson, took three weeks and

When the seventh earl left to join forces with Charles II in January 1651, he entrusted the island to his wife. Later that year, the local landowners, led by William Christian, forced the countess to surrender the island to the Roundheads. Christian was tried and executed in 1663, after the restoration of Charles II.

In May 1765 the sovereignty of the island, by then a haunt of smugglers, was bought by the crown for £70,000. The crown's representative, the Lieutenant-Governor, presides over the Tynwald, which remains substantially independent of the British Parliament.

Jedburgh, *Borders*

In 1285 Alexander III of Scotland was married to Iolande, the Count of Dreux's daughter, at Jedburgh Abbey*. At the wedding banquet,

five days to cover the 295 miles.

The men slept in schools, drill halls or casualty wards. Local authorities and Labour and Conservative organisations provided baths and hot meals, while relays of medical students cared for blistered feet and minor ailments.

The shabbily dressed hunger marchers reached London in pouring rain. They presented, in the words of one observer, 'the picture of a walking depression'.

There was a huge meeting in Hyde Park and a visit to the House of Commons. Sympathy was widespread, and one or two new factories were set up, but it took the Second World War to give Jarrow's economy the boost it needed.

PROTEST MARCHERS *Widespread unemployment in Jarrow in the inter-war years led to the famous Jarrow 'hunger march' on London in 1936.*

which was held in the now vanished Jedburgh Castle, a ghost is said to have appeared to warn the king of his death. The following year Alexander fell from a cliff on his way to join his queen. His reign had been a period of peace and tranquility, and his death was followed by a struggle for the Scottish crown—a struggle in which Edward I of England intervened.

The abbey, one of David I's four great Border foundations of the 12th century, lay in the path of the English invaders and suffered much damage during the Middle Ages.

K

Kelmscott Manor, Oxon

'A heaven on earth,' was William Morris's first impression of the beautiful 16th-century Cotswold-stone manor which was his country home* from 1871 until his death in 1896. He was a man of extraordinary versatility and genius, who was not only a designer of furniture, wallpapers and textiles, but also an artist, writer and socialist thinker. And in the peace of Kelmscott Manor – 'this many-gabled old house built by the simple country-folk of the long-past times'—he found a refuge from the 19th-century industrialisation of Britain which he loathed.

He never reconciled himself to living in London and, when forced to do so for business reasons, consoled himself with the thought that he could step into a boat outside his home on Hammersmith Mall, Chiswick, and sail up-river 130 miles to Kelmscott.

Kendal, Cumbria

The 12th-century castle*, now in ruins, was the birthplace of Catharine Parr, daughter of Sir Thomas Parr of Kendal, the sixth and last wife of Henry VIII.

George Romney, the 18th-century portrait painter, came from his native Lancashire to Kendal in 1755.

PAINTER *George Romney, who did this self-portrait in 1784 at the height of his fame, learnt his art in Kendal.*

In 1762, having married and set up as a painter, he left for London, leaving part of his savings with his wife and children. He did not return, apart from brief visits, until 1799.

Romney quickly established a reputation as a fashionable portrait painter. His chief inspiration, Nelson's Emma Hamilton, appears in more than 30 of his pictures. At the age of 65, exhausted by his labours, Romney returned to his devoted wife in Kendal, and died there three years later.

Kenilworth Castle, Warks

The Norman castle*, now a ruin, was granted by Elizabeth I to her favourite, Robert Dudley, Earl of Leicester, in 1563.

During her Midlands progress in July 1575, the queen spent three glorious weeks at Kenilworth.

On arrival she was greeted by the porter, in the guise of Hercules, and then by a character from the Arthurian legend—The Lady of the Lake. The clock of Caesar's Tower was deliberately stopped to prolong the fantasy of a midsummer night's dream. Beneath a shower of fireworks—'a blaze of burning darts flying to and fro, gleams of stars coruscant'—devised by an Italian engineer, the queen entered the castle in procession over a bridge built in her honour and guarded by 'gods' and 'goddesses'.

Within the castle Elizabeth attended a series of sumptuous banquets, and was entertained by music, dancing and a performance of the Coventry players. Outdoors there was bear-baiting.

The climax of these lavish entertainments was a water pageant, the Delivery of the Lady of the Lake, with Triton riding on a mermaid

and Proteus upon a dolphin. But when Leicester died in 1588, the queen, still furious at his marriage to Lettice Knollys ten years earlier, insisted that Lettice sell the contents of the castle to meet Leicester's debts to Elizabeth of £34,000.

In 1648 Oliver Cromwell granted the castle to Colonel Hawkesworth and his regiment to meet their unpaid wages. They drained the lake, and pulled down most of the walls to sell the materials.

Kent's Cavern, Devon See pp. 14–15

Keston, Gtr London

William Pitt the Younger (1759–1806) bought Holwood House, a 16th to 17th-century residence at Keston, in 1785. The brilliant son of Lord Chatham, the great war leader, William himself became Prime Minister at the age of 24. For most of the 19 years of his first premiership, Pitt used Holwood, with its 200 acres of land, as his country house. He spent his weekends there to escape from politics, at first wholly occupied by his favourite recreation of landscape gardening.

The sheltered, lonely life of a delicate child had made Pitt shy and ill at ease among society. He would bring one or two friends with him to Holwood, where they breakfasted punctually at 9 o'clock, spent the day walking, riding or reading, and in the evenings, if there were no official papers to be worked on, enjoyed small dinner parties.

For a man whose reputation was made as a finance minister, Pitt's private finances were chaotic. Despite his comparatively simple bachelor life and his salary of about £900 a year over many years, Pitt had debts of £45,000 when his first ministry came to an end. Much to his sorrow, he had to sell Holwood in 1802 and put the proceeds towards paying off his debts.

Killiecrankie, Pass of, Tayside

John Graham of Claverhouse, Viscount Dundee, gathered a Highland army in 1689, and led the first attempt to put James II back on the British throne after the Glorious Revolution the year before.

He won a brilliant victory at the Pass of Killiecrankie in July, but at the cost of his own life. Dundee had been urged to attack the army of William III, led by General Hugh

Mackay, in the pass itself. But his chivalry would not let him put his enemy at such a disadvantage, so the fight took place outside the northern entrance to the pass.

The Highlanders rushed wildly down on the government's inexperienced troops. In the resulting panic-stricken rout, 2000 of Mackay's men died and 500 were made prisoner, though the clansmen were outnumbered two to one.

But in the moment of victory, Dundee was shot beneath the breastplate as he led his troop of cavalry against Mackay's centre. According to Highland legend, he was invulnerable to bullets and was killed by a silver button torn off his own coat. He was taken to Blair Castle*, where he died, loyal to James II to the end. His last words were: 'It matters less for me, seeing that the day goes well for my master.' (See Dundee, p. 382.)

Mackay had left a sentry to guard the pass, and the soldier's first inkling of defeat was the sight of Highlanders rushing towards him. He saved himself with a tremendous 17 ft jump across the River Garry, at a spot which is still known as Soldier's Leap.

Despite this victory, Dundee's death put an end to James's hopes in Scotland—as William III realised. He refused to send troop reinforcements, saying: 'Armies are needless, the war is over with Dundee's life.'

King's Lynn, Norfolk

A small force of Royalists was sent to King's Lynn in August 1643. Under Sir Hamon L'Estrange they fortified the town and beat off the first enemy attacks. One ship crept up the Great Ouse with provisions, but when the enemy cut off the water supply, L'Estrange had to capitulate after a month's siege.

The Royalists, who by then were masters of the North, had missed an opportunity to relieve King's Lynn and overrun East Anglia, the area from which Parliament drew much of its strength.

The town thrived in medieval days on its trade with the Continent. Its importance declined in the 19th century with the development of steam navigation and railways.

Captain George Vancouver, born in New Conduit Street in 1758, discovered Vancouver Island in 1795 and charted the whole of

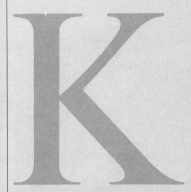

the north coast of North America.

Fanny Burney, the famous 18th-century novelist and diarist, was born at King's Lynn in 1752.

Kingston Hill, *Gtr London*

John Galsworthy, author of *The Forsyte Saga,* was born at Parkfield, a house near Kingston Hill, in 1867. His father later built three houses on a 24-acre site at Combe Warren on Kingston Hill, where the family lived from 1867 until 1886. In the *Saga,* Galsworthy transformed Combe Warren into 'Robin Hill'. He peopled his great sequence of novels with imaginative renderings of his own family. His father, whom he adored, he immortalised as old Jolyon. His irritating mother he turned into silly Aunt Juley. His sister, Mabel, become the sympathetic June Forsyte.

Kingston upon Hull, *Humbside*

Edward I laid out a new town named Kingston (King's Town), on the site of a small trading settlement founded by the monks of Meaux Abbey.

During the Middle Ages, the prosperity of the town was based on trade with northern Germany and the export of wool. Shipbuilding was also important and by the 18th century Hull was famed for its warships.

In 1642 the governor, Sir John Hotham, closed Hull's gates to Charles I on the orders of Parliament. It was the first active defiance against the king at the beginning of the Civil War.

One of Hull's greatest citizens was the reformer William Wilberforce (1759–1833). His efforts in Parliament to abolish the slave trade were rewarded with success in 1807, when a bill prohibiting slave trading by British vessels and the import of slaves into British colonies was passed. He then fought for abolition of slavery abroad. A few weeks after his death in 1833, the government passed an act emancipating slaves throughout the British Empire.

Kirriemuir, *Tayside*

A cottage*, at 9 Brechin Road, Kirriemuir, was the birthplace of the novelist and playwright, Sir James M. Barrie. Barrie, whose passionate love of children sprang from his boyhood experiences, rechristened Kirriemuir 'Thrums', in many of his books.

Barrie's father, a poor weaver

with nine children, sacrificed to send him to school and then to university at Edinburgh. He then went to England where, after struggling as a journalist, he eventually won success with *The Little Minister* in 1897.

His other triumphs included *The Admirable Crichton* and *Dear Brutus.* But the play which won him undying fame was *Peter Pan,* first performed in New York in 1904.

Knaresborough Castle, *N Yorks*

Riding hard from Canterbury, the four murderers of Archbishop Thomas Becket took refuge at Knaresborough Castle* in 1170.

The castle was owned by one of the assassins, Hugh Mauclerk. He and his fellow-conspirators lay low at the castle for a year—riding out the storm of indignation over their action, which had shocked the whole Christian world. None of the neighbouring nobles would eat, drink or talk with them. Finally the pope gave them the penance of serving in the Crusades. The king's displeasure with the murderers soon passed.

By 1399 the castle was owned by Henry Bolingbroke, Duke of Lancaster, who ousted Richard II and supplanted him as king. Richard was briefly held prisoner at Knaresborough before being taken to Pontefract, where he was put to death. (See Pontefract, p. 412.)

The castle was reduced to ruins during the Civil War by the Parliamentary army, which captured it after a six-week siege.

Among Knaresborough's most notorious citizens was the prophetess Mother Shipton, born in 1488. She prophesied metal ships, aircraft and the end of the world in 1991.

L

Lacock Abbey, *Wilts*

Founded in 1229 by a pious widow, Ela Devereux, Countess of Salisbury, Lacock Abbey* was bought and converted into a mansion by Sir William Sharington after its

dissolution by Henry VIII in 1539.

In the 19th century it became 'the first house to have drawn its own picture'. William Henry Fox Talbot (1800–77), whose family had bought the abbey generations earlier, invented the 'calotype' process, forerunner of the modern photographic negative. In 1833 he made the first photographic prints, showing the exteriors and Gothic windows of Lacock Abbey. For this work he was honoured by the Royal Society, who awarded him two medals. These prints are preserved in the Science Museum in London.

INVENTOR *William Henry Fox Talbot, working at Lacock Abbey, made the first photographs in 1833.*

TAKING PICTURES *Talbot's assistants at his photographic studio in Reading, reproduced above from one of his early photographs.*

Lancaster, *Lancs*

Founded by the Norman, Roger of Poitou, Lancaster Castle* became, in the 14th century, the headquarters of the greatest and most powerful of all medieval baronies.

John of Gaunt, who became Duke of Lancaster in 1362, was the son and father of a king, but never became king himself. His frustrated ambition explains his varied and colourful career.

John, the fourth son of Edward III, took his name from the Flemish city of Ghent, where he was born in 1340. While his elder brother, the Black Prince, dissipated his inheritance at his court at Bordeaux, John developed and extended his estates in Lancashire, and made himself the richest and most influential man in England after the king.

In the 1370's John took advantage of his father's senility and the ineffectiveness of the Black Prince to claim a commanding role in English politics. He encouraged Parliament

to attack the clergy, especially the detested William of Wykeham, Bishop of Winchester. But he earned the hatred of the London mob by protecting the heretic John Wyclif at his trial in 1377.

The death of the Black Prince in 1376, and the king's death a year later, left John the most powerful man in England. For four years he ruled in the name of his young nephew, Richard II.

The irony of John's life was that his son, Henry, did win the crown. Within months of his father's death in 1399, he deposed his cousin and made himself king.

Taken by Parliament in 1643, during the Civil War, Lancaster Castle withstood two Royalist sieges successfully.

Bonnie Prince Charlie spent three days in Lancaster Castle in 1745 as he advanced south. It was the castle's last moment of glory. Between 1788 and 1823 the castle was largely rebuilt.

George Hepplewhite, the 18th-century furniture-maker, was apprenticed to a firm in Lancaster before moving to London, where he was to win fame.

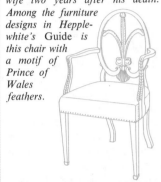

ELEGANT FORM

After leaving Gillow and Son in Lancaster, George Hepplewhite set up a business in London. Hepplewhite was not a prominent craftsman and his reputation is based on the Cabinetmaker's and Upholsterer's Guide, *which was published by his wife two years after his death. Among the furniture designs in Hepplewhite's* Guide *is this chair with a motif of Prince of Wales feathers.*

Largs, *Strathclyde*
In 1263 at the Battle of Largs, the Scottish king, Alexander III, defeated the last attempt of the Norsemen to conquer Scotland. The Norwegian king, Haakon the Old, set out with a fleet of 60 ships, but it was dispersed and largely destroyed by a storm.

Alexander III defeated the remnants of the invading force at Largs. Alexander also regained the Hebrides and the Isle of Man, which had been Norse lands since the late 9th century.

Laugharne, *Dyfed*
In August 1936 the poet Dylan Thomas and his future wife, Caitlin, fell in love while staying at Laugharne Castle House, the home of Richard Hughes, author of *A High Wind in Jamaica*. The couple stayed on there for two years because they had no money to leave. The poet's grave is in the churchyard at Laugharne.

Thomas claimed that the town of Llareggub in *Under Milk Wood*, was not modelled on Laugharne. But every three years a performance is given as a tribute to its most famous literary figure.

Laughton, *E Sussex*
The family seat at Laughton was the home of two Prime Ministers, the brothers Thomas and Henry Pelham. What the writer Horace Walpole said about Thomas would apply to both men: 'His life had been a proof that even in a free country, great abilities are not necessary to govern it.'

Henry Pelham (1695–1754) held office in Sir Robert Walpole's Whig government, and became Prime Minister in 1743. An able parliamentary tactician, he was too readily influenced by others to keep a firm policy of his own.

His brother, Thomas, Duke of Newcastle (1693–1768) succeeded him as Prime Minister when he died. Unable to find or keep a partner to take charge in the Commons, the vacillating Newcastle resigned in 1756, but returned to power in 1757 with Pitt. The partnership survived until George III appointed his favourite, Lord Bute.

Both brothers were buried at Laughton church.

Leeds, *W Yorks*
'The whole town standeth by clothing,' John Leland, the antiquary, wrote of Leeds in the reign of Henry VIII. The first wool merchants of Leeds were the monks of Kirkstall Abbey, whose ruins* still stand on the outskirts of the city. With the coming of the industrial age, the role of the monks was taken over by Leeds businessmen like Benjamin Gotte, the 18th-century entrepreneur whose original factory can still be seen in Wellington Street. In the 19th century Leeds became the largest town in Yorkshire and one of the great manufacturing cities of England.

The town hall* of Leeds is the most imposing of all monuments to the civic pride of the Victorians. The hall, opened in 1858, by Queen Victoria and Prince Albert, amid scenes of great rejoicing, had taken six years to build, and had cost the enormous sum of £122,000.

Leicester, *Leics*
The remains of Leicester's medieval castle* are a reminder that the city, now a thriving industrial centre, was once the possession of proud and rebellious baronial families.

The Grandmesnil family, which received the town from William the Conqueror, rebelled against his son in 1102; and the Beaumont family, who became earls of Leicester in 1107, proved equally fickle friends of the king. Robert Beaumont was one of the first to join the rebellion against King Stephen in 1138. Simon de Montfort, a descendant of Robert's and the ablest antagonist to face a medieval monarch, was Earl of Leicester from 1231 until his death at Evesham in 1265.

In the 15th century, Leicester became a centre of the wool trade and one of the richest towns in England. William Wyggeston was one of the town's leading wool merchants in the early 16th century. His legacy to the city included a chantry, which can still be seen, as well as a hospital and two schools.

Its warlike ways forgotten, Leicester allowed its castle to fall into decay. It was so ruinous that in 1485 Richard III had to sleep at the Blue Boar Inn, now demolished, on his way to fight Henry Tudor in Bosworth Field. After the battle, Richard's body, stripped by looters, was taken to the Grey Friars of Leicester for burial.

In 1530 Cardinal Wolsey, shorn of his power by Henry VIII and carried on a stretcher to be tried in London, reached Leicester and died there. 'I have come to leave my bones among you,' he told the Abbot of St Mary's*.

Eight years later St Mary's itself felt the wrath of Henry VIII and was dissolved. It was the last monument of an age when Leicester stood in the front rank of English towns.

Lemsford, *Herts*
Brocket Hall, near Lemsford, belonged to William Lamb, Viscount Melbourne (1779–1848), Queen Victoria's first Prime Minister. She became very attached to Melbourne and made him her sole adviser. Melbourne served the young queen well, teaching her the principles of constitutional government and the complexities of home and foreign affairs.

Melbourne's early life had little of the prim moral uprightness associated with Victoria. His father had been a dissolute politician, whose career had been advanced by the wit and beauty of his wife—the notorious Elizabeth Milbanke. She lavished attention on William, her favourite son, and according to contemporary gossip his father was Lord Egremont, one of Lady Melbourne's many lovers.

The greatest mistake of Melbourne's life was his marriage in 1805 to the wildly eccentric Lady Caroline Ponsonby. The most celebrated of her affairs was with the poet Byron. Melbourne obtained a separation from her in 1825. Mentally unstable, she died at Brocket Hall three years later.

Lewes, *E Sussex*
One of the major battles of the Middle Ages was fought in 1264, north-east of Lewes. The contestants were Simon de Montfort, leader of the rebellious barons, and Henry III. The aim of de Montfort was to curb the powers of the king, who had won back many of the rights granted to the barons by Magna Carta in 1215.

On May 14, de Montfort drew up his 50,000 men high above Lewes. The king, who commanded nearly twice that number, marched up from the town with his infantry,.

De Montfort's left wing was swiftly routed by the king's cavalry. But the tide of battle turned against Henry when de Montfort's infantry and reserve cavalry launched a fierce attack on the king's infantry.

De Montfort captured both the king and his son, Edward. In the following months, he took the first steps towards founding the parliamentary system by summoning burgesses from the towns and knights from the shires.

Lincoln, *Lincs*
Just outside Lincoln, in February 1141, the greatest battle of King Stephen's turbulent reign was fought.

Ranulf, Earl of Chester, Stephen's most determined opponent, had seized Lincoln Castle* a few months earlier. In London, Stephen waited until he knew that Ranulf had disbanded most of his forces, then hurried north to Lincoln.

The citizens opened their gates to Stephen, who laid siege to the castle. But Ranulf, who had escaped, returned on February 2 with a formidable army.

When the rebels attacked, the king was left to face his enemies with only a few retainers. He fought with savage bravery, but at length was hit by a stone and taken alive.

The citizens paid dearly for their loyalty to Stephen. Many who fled across the river in flimsy boats were drowned. Those who remained were slain and their city was sacked. Stephen himself was imprisoned in Bristol Castle. (See pp. 72–73.)

Lindisfarne, *Northld* See pp. 52–53

Little Sodbury, *Avon*
William Tyndale (1492–1536) was the chaplain and tutor at the manor house at Little Sodbury. During his stay there he began his English translation of the New Testament, parts of which were eventually published in Germany. 'If God spares my life,' he said, 'I will see that a boy who drives the plough shall know more about the Bible than many priests.'

His work aroused intense controversy, both in England and on the Continent. Betrayed to the authorities in Antwerp by a Catholic zealot, Tyndale was tried for heresy, strangled and then burnt.

Liverpool, *Merseyside*
Ireland is the key to Liverpool's early history. King John's two expeditions to Ireland convinced him of the need for a safe harbour from which to embark an army. In 1207 he promised special privileges to all who settled in the small port of Liverpool, and from that time it began to grow.

The boom years of Liverpool began at the end of the 17th century, when it started to rival Bristol as the capital of the American trade. The first American cargo—it was probably tobacco—reached Liverpool in 1648. Cargoes of sugar and cotton followed. The West Indies slave trade was quickly dominated by Liverpool merchants, and contributed handsomely to the town's prosperity until the trade's abolition in 1807.

Victorian Liverpool became the centre of the Lancashire cotton industry, then Britain's largest export industry. The introduction of steamships and refrigerated cargo holds accelerated the town's expansion. Liverpool is still the second port of England.

Built on trade, Liverpool owes its wealth to its good communications. The first docks were completed in 1721, and building was still continuing at Birkenhead at the end of the 19th century. Liverpool's half-mile long landing stage, begun in 1847, is still the largest floating quay in the world.

Liverpool has always valued its links with the industrial Midlands. A network of canals connected it with Manchester and the great textile towns by the end of the 18th century. The first Mersey road tunnel, stretching more than 2 miles

under the river to Birkenhead, was opened in 1934. The second road tunnel, linking Liverpool with Wallasey, was completed in 1971.

Llangollen, *Clwyd*
In the spring of 1778 Lady Eleanor Butler and Sarah Ponsonby, aged 39 and 23 respectively, ran away from their homes in Ireland, determined to lead a life of intellectual retirement together.

Pursued and brought back by their outraged families, the two friends finally set off for Wales later in 1778, having steadfastly refused to be dissuaded from their purpose.

In 1780 they rented a cottage and 4 acres of land at Llangollen, which they named Plas Newydd*. Here they lived for the next 50 years.

The seclusion of their early life together—spent walking, gardening, painting and reading—gradually ceased as stories of their idyllic house and garden and the unconventional way of life attracted an increasing round of visitors. The Duke of Wellington, Sir Walter Scott, Thomas de Quincey and William Wordsworth were among the many celebrated people who came to pay their respects to the 'Ladies of Llangollen'.

Lady Eleanor died in 1829, and two years later Sarah Ponsonby was buried beside her lifelong friend in Llangollen churchyard.

Llantrisant Castle, *Mid Glamorgan*
'The Welsh will never fail you,' Edward II was told when he fled into Wales in 1326, pursued by an army led by his wife, Isabella, and her allies among the barons. The king took refuge at Neath Abbey, but left after a few days, fearing 'lest the Cistercians should suffer from harbouring him'.

Edward's destination was Llantrisant Castle*, which was the home of his companion, Hugh Despenser the Younger. Their guide was a Welsh clergyman, Rhys ap Howel, who betrayed the king's route.

The king and his party, with their baggage, had to struggle towards the castle through a gale. As they came to a bend in the road, they were captured by the Duke of Lancaster.

Edward and his treasure were taken by the duke. But, in the confusion of the skirmish, Hugh Despenser and three of the king's companions escaped to Llantrisant.

Two thousand pounds were offered for Despenser. He was hotly pursued and run to ground in a wood. On the following day, this proud court favourite was executed at Hereford, on the orders of the triumphant Isabella.

Llanystumdwy, *Gwynedd*
David Lloyd George, the Liberal Prime Minister (1916–22) who brought Britain through the First World War, was born in Manchester in 1863 and brought to Llanystumdwy at the age of two. His widowed mother and her three young sons were given a home by her brother, the village cobbler Richard Lloyd. The family was poor. In later years Lloyd George wrote: 'We never ate fresh meat and I remember that our greatest

After his capture, Edward spent the night at Llantrisant Castle and was then escorted to Monmouth, where he surrendered the Great Seal, the symbol of sovereignty. He was murdered ten months later. (See Berkeley Castle, p. 368.)

luxury was half an egg for each child on Sunday mornings.'

Lloyd George became a solicitor at 21 and Liberal MP for Caernarvon at 27, a seat he retained for 55 years. In 1916 he superseded Asquith as Prime Minister, leading Britain to victory and into the postwar period. His downfall came in 1922 when the Conservatives withdrew from his coalition; his attempts during the 1920's at a political comeback failed.

In 1939 Lloyd George bought a farm near Llanystumdwy (which now has a museum* in the grounds). He retired there in 1944 and died in the following year. He is buried on the banks of the River Dwyfor.

WAR LEADER *An eloquent and persuasive orator, David Lloyd George, Prime Minister from 1916 to 1922, led Britain to victory in the First World War.*

Lochindorb, *Highland*
The ruined, 12th-century fortress on an island in the loch was granted in 1371 by Robert II to his fourth son, Alexander, Earl of Buchan, the notorious 'Wolf of Badenoch'. In 1390, when the Church censured the earl for deserting his wife, he took his revenge by burning Elgin Cathedral. He was excommunicated and his half-brother, Robert III, afraid of the consequences of such sacrilege, forced the Wolf to repair it.

Lochranza, *Strathclyde*
Robert Bruce landed at Lochranza ('loch of safe anchorage') on the Isle of Arran in 1306, from Rathlin Island in Ireland, at the beginning

of his campaign for Scottish independence from England.

Although Bruce's army was only 300 strong, the Scottish leader was resolved to defeat the English. According to a legend, Bruce's determination had been inspired by watching a spider trying to weave its web again and again, while he was hiding in a cave on Rathlin. This story was first widely circulated by Sir Walter Scott.

After a year on the Isle of Arran, Bruce crossed to the mainland and began the campaign that was to culminate in the victory at Bannockburn. (See pp. 88–89.)

Longleat, *Wilts* See pp. 160–1.

London (*Inner Boroughs*)

For its first 1000 years London grew from a Roman settlement to a fortress and a port. Just before the Norman Conquest, Edward the Confessor built his palace to the west of the City of London and established the Abbey Church* of Westminster there. After William the Conqueror invaded England in 1066, he was crowned at the Confessor's church.

Outside the eastern walls of the city, the Conqueror erected a great castle, the Tower of London*, to overawe the capital's turbulent citizens. It soon won a grim reputation as the state prison.

A third medieval building of importance, Westminster Hall*, was erected by William Rufus. In 1264 the barons of Henry III gathered in the hall to hold the first Parliament. (See pp. 84–85.)

During the reign of Henry III, it was established that Westminster was the seat of the legislature and the courts, while the walled City of London was the centre of trading. But by the end of the Middle Ages the two cities were linked by the Strand, along which the great built their mansions. These conditions did not change until the Great Fire of 1666 destroyed the timber buildings of the City.

By the late 17th century a new city of brick and stone had arisen on the ground-plan of the old. The disaster gave Sir Christopher Wren the chance of rebuilding the churches of the city, more than 20 of which survive today. His greatest achievement, St Paul's Cathedral*, stood on the site of a 7th-century cathedral.

London's population rapidly grew, and in the 17th century the Earl of Bedford laid out the streets and the square in Covent Garden. Other developers, such as the Grosvenor family, began to build in Mayfair and St James's. In the mid-18th century George III bought Buckingham Palace, and the movement westwards to Belgravia and Kensington gained impetus.

In the 19th century the stucco terraces of John Nash and the termini of the new railways had transformed the city once again. By 1900 London stretched for more than 10 miles in every direction from Charing Cross, and had completely engulfed the surrounding villages and countryside.

NASH FAÇADE *Buckingham Palace was rebuilt in the 1820's by George IV's architect, John Nash, who placed the Marble Arch at the entrance.*

VICTORIAN FRONTAGE *A new wing, hiding Nash's forecourt, was added in 1847, and the Marble Arch was moved to the north-east corner of Hyde Park.*

Buckingham Palace

When George IV succeeded his father, he demanded that his favourite architect, John Nash, undertake the conversion of Buckingham Palace. Originally the home of the Duke of Buckingham, it had been bought by George III for Queen Charlotte in 1762.

Nash's rebuilding, in Bath stone at an estimated cost of £260,000, began in 1826. But his hastily drawn design was criticised—the dome was considered 'a common slop-pail turned upside down'.

Queen Victoria, who moved to Buckingham Palace after her accession in 1837, was appalled by the building's shabbiness. In accordance with her wishes, the deep forecourt was enclosed in 1847 by a frontage which provided more accommodation for her rapidly growing family.

But in the years of her widowhood Victoria rarely came to London. The Prince of Wales, later Edward VII, referred to the palace as the 'sepulchre', but after Victoria's death he moved the court from Marlborough House back to it. Buckingham Palace once again became the centre of the winter and summer seasons.

Bank of England

The City of London has evolved from a crowded, plague-ridden medieval town into one of the world's great financial centres. Within the square mile of the City stand some of Britain's oldest and wealthiest institutions: Lloyd's of London*; the Stock Exchange*;

CITY STRONGHOLD *The builders of the Bank of England deliberately designed it to look like a fortress.*

and the banks, the most awesome being the Bank of England.

With its windowless outer walls, the Bank of England looks like an ancient temple modified to withstand a siege. The bank was founded in 1694, and acquired its present site in Threadneedle Street in 1724. An 18th-century cartoon depicted the Bank as a rich woman sitting on a money box; and so it won the nickname of 'The Old Lady of Threadneedle Street'. Today's building is a modern reconstruction.

Bloomsbury

Originally laid out by the Earl of Southampton during the 1660's, Bloomsbury was developed by successive dukes of Bedford until the mid-19th century. It has several fine squares—Bloomsbury, Bedford, Tavistock, Russell, Gordon, Woburn—around which were built the houses of the rich.

Montague House was bought to house a collection of documents, medals, precious stones and curiosities of natural history, belonging to Sir Hans Sloane (1660–1753). This collection was the nucleus of

Bloomsbury's most famous institution, the British Museum.

In the succeeding 70 years there were many additions to the original collection, and the museum outgrew Montague House. After George IV donated the great library of his father in the 1820's, the building of the present museum* began. It took 24 years to build, and was completed in 1847.

The great domed Reading Room was added in 1857. Since then it has been used by scholars from all over the world, and it was in the Reading Room that Karl Marx wrote *Das Kapital*.

During the first 40 years of this century, a closely knit set of writers, painters and intellectuals lived in Bloomsbury. The leading personalities of the 'Bloomsbury Group' included the biographer Lytton Strachey, the economist John Maynard Keynes and the novelist Virginia Woolf. Their remarkable influence on English letters survived until the Second World War, which dispersed their members and damaged many of the squares where they had lived.

Chelsea

Famous for its writers, poets, painters and eccentrics, Chelsea was a rural hideaway beyond the limits of London until the 19th century. Its peace attracted Sir Thomas More, who built his house there in 1520 to get away from the bustle of Henry VIII's court. There, More was visited by such men as the Dutch theologian Erasmus, and the painter Hans Holbein.

Many others valued the seclusion of Chelsea—'away from the great roads, safe at the bend of the river', as one resident, the 19th-century author Thomas Carlyle, described it. They ranged from the dour Scottish novelist Tobias Smollett to the playwright Oscar Wilde.

Wilde moved to 16 (now 34) Tite Street in 1884. He had already established a brilliant reputation for his outrageousness, his audacious wit and his unconventional dress. His career ended with his arrest at the Cadogan Hotel, Sloane Street, and his trial and imprisonment.

A rival wit and eccentric, the American painter James McNeil Whistler settled in Chelsea in 1866. When his painting 'The Falling Rocket'—an impression of fireworks seen across the Thames from Chelsea—was exhibited in 1877, the art critic John Ruskin accused Whistler of 'flinging a pot of paint in the public's face'. This provoked a lawsuit in which Whistler was awarded a farthing in damages. The cost of the action bankrupted Whistler, who was forced to sell his new house in Tite Street.

Wilde and Whistler were not Chelsea's only eccentrics. The Pre-Raphaelite painter Dante Gabriel Rossetti kept a menagerie in his garden at Cheyne Walk. At various times the garden housed a laughing hyena, chameleons, snakes, wallabies and armadillos.

CHELSEA ECCENTRICS *The cartoonist Max Beerbohm captured the artistic life of Chelsea in this caricature of a gathering in Dante Gabriel Rossetti's garden in Cheyne Walk. Among those included are Whistler and Swinburne, William Morris, John Ruskin and Rossetti himself.*

Covent Garden

The area is famous for both its opera house and for the fruit and vegetable market which stood there for more than 300 years. The name was originally Convent Garden, from a 13th-century monastery garden, which was seized from the church by Henry VIII.

The square was laid out as a residential quarter by Inigo Jones for the 4th Earl of Bedford (1593–1641), whose house (destroyed in 1700) and walled garden formed one side of the quadrangle. The earl asked the architect to put a church on the west side—something inexpensive, 'like a barn'. Jones told him he would get the handsomest barn in Europe, and the result was St Paul's Church*. The portico of the church is the setting for Eliza Doolittle's first encounter with Professor Higgins in Bernard Shaw's play, *Pygmalion*.

In 1661 the principal market for flowers, fruit and vegetables in London was established by royal charter at Covent Garden. The market began as a huddle of shacks and stalls under the Earl of Bedford's garden wall. But in the 19th century it was housed in the market buildings which remained in use until the market was removed to Nine Elms, south of the Thames, in 1974. It was in the market that Charles II is reputed to have found

OPERA HOUSE ON FIRE *The second Covent Garden Theatre was destroyed by flames in 1856, but within two years the present opera house was built.*

STARS OF COVENT GARDEN AND DRURY LANE

When Covent Garden Theatre opened in 1732, there was only one other major playhouse in London—the Drury Lane, which had been established during the Restoration. For a century, the two theatres dominated the London stage.

The great actor-playwright David Garrick (1717–79) took over the management of Drury Lane in 1746, and for 30 years he ran the theatre, which was famed for the brilliance of its performances.

Sarah Siddons (1755–1831) failed in her first performance as Portia at Drury Lane in 1775, but when she returned seven years later in Thomas Southerne's *The Fatal Marriage*, all

London acclaimed her. She and her brother, the tragedian John Philip Kemble (1757–1823), were the theatre's principal attractions, but they left to join Covent Garden after the Drury Lane management failed to pay their wages. Mrs Siddons made her farewell at Covent Garden in 1812, two years before the electrifying début of Edmund Kean (1789–1833) as Shylock. In later years Kean's supremacy was challenged by a new star, Charles Macready (1793–1873). In 1848 Covent Garden went over to opera, and Drury Lane struggled on until the 1880's, when it became the home of melodrama.

Mrs Sarah Siddons, shown here as Lady Macbeth, one of her greatest roles, was without equal in tragic and heroic parts. Off-stage this great beauty could be mercenary and formidable.

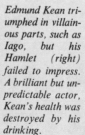

A versatile actor, David Garrick was acclaimed for his tragic roles, such as Richard III (left). As the actor-manager of the Drury Lane Theatre, he dominated the London stage for 30 years.

Edmund Kean triumphed in villainous parts, such as Iago, but his Hamlet (right) failed to impress. A brilliant but unpredictable actor, Kean's health was destroyed by his drinking.

Kean's chief rival, Charles Macready, shown here as Othello, was a fine, rather than a great, actor. Macready disliked his profession, but encouraged the best in the theatre of his time.

an orange-seller named Nell Gwynne, who later became a highly successful actress at the nearby Drury Lane Theatre.

The Royal Opera House*, the third theatre to stand on this spot, dates from 1858. When the second building was opened in 1809, there were serious disturbances because John Philip Kemble, the actor-manager, had put up the admission prices. Performances were marred by the audience shouting 'Old prices!' and Kemble brought in ruffians to keep order. But the nightly uproar grew worse, and the actor George Frederick Cooke had to mime his Richard III because his words could not be heard above the noise. After 68 nights Kemble was forced to yield to the rioters. He apologised and the old prices were restored. The affair was known as the 'O.P. Riots'.

Fleet Street

The short stretch from Temple Bar to Ludgate Hill is a synonym for journalism and the national press. Caxton's assistant, Wynkyn de Worde, set up here in the early 1500's, and printers, stationers and booksellers followed.

In their train came the writers. They lived, as did Dr Samuel Johnson, in the courts and the alleys abutting the street. The doctor's attic den in his Gough Square house* was the birthplace of his great dictionary.

The vitality of Fleet Street has

spawned a host of colourful characters. Greatest of them were the Press barons—men such as Lord Northcliffe and Beaverbrook —who used their publications and purses to champion causes or in attempts to make and unmake governments.

Lord Northcliffe, born Alfred Harmsworth in 1865, started a magazine at his London school when he was 15. He became a journalist, and in 1888 borrowed £1500 to launch a new weekly, *Answers to Correspondents*. After a shaky start, *Answers* achieved an enormous success with a competition which offered the winner £1 a week for life.

In 1896 he founded the *Daily Mail*, the first London paper to sell for ½d. In 1903 the *Daily Mirror* appeared. In 1908 Northcliffe secured control of *The Times*, but his delusions of grandeur grew and his behaviour became irrational. He died in 1922, aged 57.

Lord Beaverbrook, born Max Aitken in Canada in 1879, acquired a paper round at the age of 12 and employed sub-agents in order to make more money. When he grew up he went into finance and was a millionaire by the age of 26. In 1910 he went to London and entered politics as a Conservative. In 1918 he bought the *Daily Express* and founded the *Sunday Express*, using his newspapers as platforms for one of his favourite causes, Empire Free Trade.

Beaverbrook's influence on the political life of Britain was controversial, and his Press campaigns had little success. His finest hour was in the Second World War when, as Minister of Aircraft Production from May 1940, he supplied the aeroplanes which won the Battle of Britain. Lord Beaverbrook died in 1964.

Greenwich

In 1428 Henry V's brother, Humphrey, Duke of Gloucester, built a palace, Bella Court, on the site of Greenwich House, which had been used by English sovereigns since 1300.

On the duke's arrest for high treason in 1447, Queen Margaret of Anjou, wife of his nephew Henry VI, seized Bella Court. She lavished money on extensions and renamed it the Palace of Pleasance or Placentia. After the Wars of the Roses, Henry VII renovated Placentia and renamed it Greenwich Palace.

Elizabeth I's successor, James I, presented Greenwich Palace to his extravagant consort, Anne of Denmark, in 1613. Since the palace had remained unchanged for nearly a century, the architect Inigo Jones was commissioned to build a new residence—the Queen's House or the House of Delight—which was to become one of the finest examples of Renaissance architecture in England.

In 1618 Anne of Denmark died before her residence was completed and all work on it stopped. However, in 1635, after Charles I settled the house on his wife, Henrietta Maria, to mark their reconciliation, Jones returned to his task. The queen was never able to enjoy her House of Delight. Her husband's court left London in 1642—never to return.

After the Restoration, John Webb, son-in-law and pupil of Inigo Jones, enlarged the Queen's House. The house was later used as part of the Greenwich Hospital School, and in 1933 it became the National Maritime Museum*.

During the reign of Charles II, the derelict Greenwich Palace was demolished and Webb was ordered to build another royal residence— the King's House.

In 1688, when William and Mary took over this unfinished house,

they could not afford its completion and instead gave the riverside site to the navy for the construction of a royal hospital for wounded seamen. Sir Christopher Wren supervised the building of the hospital, which was one of his greatest architectural triumphs. After the hospital was closed in 1869, the building became the home of the Royal Naval College*.

It was in the Painted Hall of the Royal Hospital that Nelson's body lay in state for three days in 1805, after his death at the Battle of Trafalgar. According to a contemporary newspaper account, the hall was 'fitted up with peculiar taste and elegance', and many thousands struggled to see the body. 'When the doors finally closed, a multitude that almost extended from Greenwich to London was turned back.'

Hampstead

Since the 18th century, Hampstead has been the haunt of artists, writers and poets. Among the great names who have lived there are Coleridge, Keats, Romney, Constable, Charles Dickens and D. H. Lawrence.

Lawrence is now regarded as one of the most important novelists that Britain produced in this century. But at the time he lived in the Vale of Health in 1915, his pacifism and the fact that he had a German-born wife led to vitriolic attacks on his writings.

His novel *The Rainbow* was prosecuted at Bow Street, where it was described as 'a mass of obscenity of thought, idea and action throughout'. The whole edition of the book was ordered to be destroyed. Lawrence commented bitterly that this persecution marked 'the end of my writing for England'.

Hampstead was kinder to another great figure of the 20th century. In 1938 Sigmund Freud, the founder of psychoanalysis, came to live there after fleeing from the Nazi occupation of his native Austria. He wrote that he found 'the kindliest welcome in beautiful, free, generous England'. And he was delighted with his house in Maresfield Gardens.

Freud's house was inundated with visitors—H. G. Wells, Chaim Weizmann, Salvador Dali among them—and with flowers from well-

MASTER OF FLEET STREET *Taking advantage of a new mass market, Alfred Harmsworth (left) launched the* Daily Mail *(above) in 1896. It was the first newspaper in the world to sell a million copies a day.*

EXILE *Sigmund Freud arrives in London in 1938 after being driven from Austria by the Nazis.*

wishers and with hundreds of letters, some simply addressed to 'Dr Freud, London'.

Only three weeks after his arrival, Freud had to undergo a serious operation for cancer of the jaw, from which he had been suffering for 16 years. But, despite the constant pain, he continued to work on his book *The Outlines of Psychoanalysis* until a few weeks before his death.

On September 3, 1939, he heard the first air-raid siren of the Second World War from his Hampstead garden. Asked whether he thought it would be the last war, he answered that it would definitely be the last for him. He died three weeks later on September 23.

Highgate

In 1386 the Bishop of London agreed, because of the 'deepnesse and dirtie' passage of the highway from London to Barnet, to build a new road through his land on the hills north of London. He set up a gate where a toll could be collected; and from this landmark Highgate acquired its name.

For centuries Highgate, perched on the twin hill to Hampstead, was famed for health-giving qualities of its air. By the 18th century it had become a fashionable village.

In middle age the poet and critic

Samuel Taylor Coleridge retired to Highgate to cure himself of opium addiction. He lived at the home of his doctor, James Gillman, until his death. According to Carlyle, Coleridge spent his last years 'looking down on London and its smoke-tumult like a sage escaped from the inanity of life's battle'.

Within 50 years of Coleridge's death, Highgate had become a

REVOLUTIONARIES IN LONDON

The tomb* of Karl Marx in Highgate Cemetery is a reminder that, for 34 years, the founder of modern Communism lived in obscurity and poverty in London.

From Grafton Street, Kentish Town, the family and a few Socialist friends made regular Sunday excursions to Hampstead Heath during the summer. The group would play games, and return home, singing songs and reciting poetry.

Marx's hours of reading in the British Museum culminated in the publication of the first volume of his major work, *Das Kapital*, a study of capitalism, in 1867. In 1883 Marx

died at his house in Finsbury and was buried in Highgate.

Lenin, the Russian Bolshevik leader, who was profoundly influenced by Marx's thought, first came to London in 1902 to supervise the publication of a left-wing newspaper, *Iskra* (the Spark). He and his wife, Krupskaya, rented two unfurnished rooms in a house (now demolished) in King's Cross.

During the next nine years Lenin returned to London to attend political meetings or to work in the British Museum. In his spare time he explored the city by bicycle or bus. He went to Speaker's Corner, in Hyde Park, to the theatre and the music hall. One landmark Lenin unfailingly went to on his visits was Marx's grave in Highgate Cemetery.

London was a refuge for the two exiled founders of Communism—Karl Marx (top) and Lenin (right). Marx lies buried in Highgate Cemetery (above).

middle-class suburb of Victorian London. Men from the city, on which the poet had gazed with such contempt, were now able to reach the peace of Highgate.

Holland House

Only a wing of Holland House, a Jacobean mansion destroyed by bombs during the Second World War, remains in Holland Park. The

mansion took its name from James I's favourite, the 1st Earl of Holland, whose father-in-law began building it in 1605.

The third earl (who was also the Earl of Warwick) and his wife, Charlotte, were generous hosts to the literary men of the early 18th century. Among those who visited Holland House were the satirist Dean Swift, the poet Alexander Pope and the essayist and politician Joseph Addison. Fifteen years after her husband's death the countess married Addison in 1714. He died three years later.

In 1768 Holland House was bought by Henry Fox, who squandered his own large fortune before acquiring a second by eloping with an heiress. He made a third fortune as a notoriously corrupt minister.

From 1799 until 1840 Holland House was the centre of a brilliant literary and political circle entertained by Henry Richard Fox, the 3rd Lord Holland, and his formidable wife, Elizabeth. Among their guests were the European statesmen Metternich and Talleyrand, the novelists Sir Walter Scott and James Fenimore Cooper, and the celebrated wit Sidney Smith.

Hyde Park

Popularly christened the 'lungs of London' in Victorian times, the five royal parks—Hyde Park, St James's Park, Green Park, Regent's Park and Kensington Gardens— have long been places of recreation for the citizens of London.

Once an estate belonging to the monks of Westminster Abbey, Hyde Park is the oldest of the parks. It passed into royal hands when Henry VIII dissolved the monasteries, and it was transformed by him into a deer park, where his daughter Elizabeth I came to hunt. In 1637 Charles I opened the park to the public.

Charles II made Hyde Park a centre of fashion, but in the reign of William and Mary highway robberies there were common. A roadway leading to Kensington Palace* was hung with 300 lamps to make royal journeys safer. This lighted highway was known as *La Route du Roi*, from which the name 'Rotten Row' is probably derived. In the late 19th century the road was a resort for strollers and riders from Mayfair and Belgravia.

Another social spectacle was ice-skating on the Serpentine, an artificial lake created by George II's wife, Caroline. The queen was responsible for enclosing 300 acres of Hyde Park to make Kensington Gardens. It was her intention to include in the gardens the remainder of Hyde Park (and St James's Park). But when the queen asked the Prime Minister, Sir Robert Walpole, what the cost would be, he replied: 'Three crowns —England, Scotland, and Wales.'

Islington

This area was once a playground for Londoners during the 17th and 18th centuries. Pleasure gardens, teahouses, music and dance rooms, and the more robust attractions of archery, duck-shooting and prize-fights drew Londoners for a day's enjoyment. For the walk back to the city across robber-infested fields, people would gather at the Angel, a coaching inn now demolished, to be escorted in parties by a mounted and armed guard.

In 1683, when Thomas Sadler found an old well in his garden in Islington, he quickly promoted it as a miraculous spa, charging 3d for the waters and the entertainment provided. Out of this grew the first Sadler's Wells Theatre, which was built in 1783. Another popular establishment for entertainment, opened less than a century later, was Sam Collins's Music Hall beside Islington Green.

THE RISE AND FALL OF THE MUSIC HALL

Sam Collins's famous music hall as it was during the 1920's after its heyday.

Collins's Music Hall was one of the 500 halls which were built in late 19th-century London. Whatever their trade or class, Londoners who had a little money to spend and were eager for amusement flocked to these popular places of entertainment for nights of revelry.

The music halls began in alehouses and taverns, where the customers were entertained with songs and comic turns. In 1849 Charles Morton (1819–1904), the enterprising proprietor of the Canterbury Arms, Lambeth, created the first music hall by putting up a special building with a bar, tables and a platform for the performers. Morton's venture was so successful that competitors began building halls throughout London.

Morton, who became known as the 'father of the halls', opened the palatial Oxford Music Hall in the West End in 1861 and was later called upon to manage the London Pavilion (Piccadilly Circus) and the Palace (Cambridge Circus), which he transformed into 'temples of variety'. It was at the Palace that music hall received its highest honour, when George V ordered a command performance in 1912.

This was the heyday of the halls, many of which had become gilt-and-plush theatres and had created stars such as Harry Lauder, Dan Leno, Little Tich, Marie Lloyd, George Robey and Vesta Tilley. But by the 1920's the music halls began to decline in popularity, having lost their audiences to the films, one of whose most famous stars was the English-born music-hall comedian, Charlie Chaplin.

Singer Marie Lloyd (left) and comic Little Tich were idols of the halls.

Kensington

Kensington's royal associations date back over many centuries to the time when it was a tiny village in the centre of a vast hunting preserve stretching west from Westminster. The first king to do more than hunt there was William III, who moved his court into Kensington Palace*.

William chose Kensington as his new abode because of its tranquillity and for reasons of health. The damp fogs rising from the Thames had aggravated his asthma. His taste was shared by his successors— Queen Anne, George I and George II, who all lived there.

Where the monarchy led, fashion followed. According to a foreign visitor of the 1780's, many wealthy Londoners 'who have no country seat of their own, in summer move into Kensington houses for the sake of the good air, the gardens, the fine prospect'. But the area was not safe from thieves. George II himself was accosted by a highwayman who climbed over the wall and 'with a manner of much deference, deprived the king of his purse, his watch and his buckles'.

By the 19th century Kensington was no longer a village, and it received the royal seal of approval when it was made a royal borough by Queen Victoria, who was born in Kensington Palace in 1819.

But it was Victoria's husband, Prince Albert, who gave Kensington its most lasting royal legacy. He inspired the Great Exhibition of 1851 in Hyde Park (see pp. 302–3). With its profits, he and his fellow commissioners embarked on a great programme of museum building which made South Kensington a national monument.

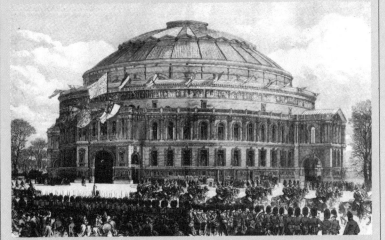

PRINCE'S LEGACY Built to commemorate the life and work of Victoria's Prince Consort, the Royal Albert Hall was opened in 1871.

Lambeth

For seven centuries Lambeth Palace has been the residence of the Archbishops of Canterbury. Stephen Langton, who was archbishop between 1207 and 1228, began making alterations to the original manor house. Over the next three centuries it was transformed into the rambling, turreted red-brick palace* of the present day.

A great part of the palace was built in the early 15th century by Archbishop Chichele, who added the Lollards Tower, reputed to have been a prison for the heretical followers of John Wyclif. Cardinal Morton, Henry VII's Chancellor, who was appointed archbishop in 1493, restored the palace, which had been neglected during the Wars of the Roses, and rebuilt the Gate-house. In Morton's time, Lambeth Palace became a centre of learning.

But in 1381 Wat Tyler's rebels plundered the building and beheaded its resident, Archbishop Sudbury, on Tower Hill. And during the Gordon Riots in 1780 Lambeth Palace was narrowly saved from destruction

Mansion House

Built by George Dance the Elder between 1739 and 1753, Mansion House* is the official residence of the Lord Mayor during his year of office. This dignified building stands on the site of the medieval Stocks Market, whose profits from the sale of fish and meat were used to pay for the upkeep of the old London Bridge.

Apart from private apartments

the Mansion House has a number of chambers for balls, dinners and receptions. The most impressive of these is the grandiose Egyptian dining-hall, where mayoral banquets for up to 350 guests are held. These feasts are prepared in kitchens where, according to one Victorian observer, there were ovens 'large enough to roast an entire ox', and vessels for boiling meat and vegetables which were 'not pots but tanks'.

The tradition of lavish mayoral entertainment, which must be paid for partly by the citizen who holds this high office, dates from the Middle Ages. According to legend, on one splendid occasion, Richard Whittington, thrice Lord Mayor (1397–8, 1406–7, 1419–20), when entertaining Henry V and his queen, burnt not only costly cedar logs but also bonds worth £60,000 to keep his guests warm.

Marylebone

This area of London came into existence in the great building boom of the late 18th and early 19th centuries. It soon became the home of many of the rich and famous—and of a group of men who have added much to the lustre of British science. The area around Harley Street is well known for its medical specialists, and many celebrated doctors have worked there.

But one of the greatest figures of 19th-century medicine deliberately chose to live away from the London medical world which had poured

scorn on his ideas. Joseph Lister (1827–1912) was 50 when he moved from Edinburgh to a house in Park Crescent in 1877, and began his long battle to win acceptance for his theory of antisepsis.

For years he fought against the prejudices of his London colleagues, who refused to accept his conviction that observing rules of hygiene during an operation would prevent wounds from becoming infected. But by his death in 1912, he had seen his theories accepted.

Among the other famous residents of the area were H. G. Wells and George Bernard Shaw, who lived there during his days as music critic of *The Star*. Writing under the pseudonym Corno di Bassetto, Shaw set London laughing by expounding his controversial views not only on music but also on such diverse subjects as women's rights, bicycles and socialism.

The most human story to emerge from Marylebone was the long romantic courtship—immortalised in the play and film, *The Barretts of Wimpole Street*—between the poetess Elizabeth Barrett and her suitor, Robert Browning. For 40 years Elizabeth had been dominated by an intractable father. Then, on the morning of September 12, 1846, she broke the knot that had held her captive by slipping out of the house to marry Browning in the parish church. In later years, Browning returned to kiss the altar stairs at which he and his wife 'had been made happy for life'.

DANCES AND DEBUTANTES *Queen Charlotte's Ball (above) was a high point of the inter-war Mayfair season. Below, a 'deb' advertises a charity ball.*

Mayfair

Speculators and aristocrats together created Mayfair, a name which evokes luxury, fashion and snobbery. The district now bounded by Piccadilly, Park Lane, Oxford Street and Regent Street was open country when Charles II gave his Lord Chancellor, the Earl of Clarendon, a large piece of land in 1664. Clarendon sold portions to his friends Lord Berkeley and Lord Burlington before spending £40,000 on a mansion and garden on his remaining piece. He moved into the house in 1667 but fled into exile the next year to escape trial for high treason. Bankers and speculators led by Sir Thomas Bond bought his estate and on it grew Bond Street, Dover Street, Albemarle Street and Stafford Street. The Great Fire of 1666 had destroyed half the city and noblemen were rushing to buy properties in the new West End.

When Lord Berkeley died, his widow leased his Palladian home to Princess (later Queen) Anne, who became Mayfair's first royal resident. Her presence made Mayfair even more fashionable.

The Earl of Scarborough laid out an estate in north-east Mayfair in 1717. Lord Burlington leased plots behind Burlington House, while the

greatest developer of them all, Sir Richard Grosvenor, created the north-west section.

His mother, Mary Davies, had inherited lands between the Oxford Road and the River Thames. Mary married the wealthy Sir Thomas Grosvenor, and Richard, heir to Mary's land and Thomas's money, laid out Grosvenor Square, Grosvenor Street, Audley Street and the grid of streets around them.

Mary Davies's descendants became dukes of Westminster. The second duke's estate in Mayfair and Belgravia was charged duty of £12 million when he died in 1953.

Shepherd Market, a picturesque huddle of narrow streets, was laid out by Edward Shepherd in the mid-18th century, on the site of the May Fair which gave the district its name. James II had given permission in 1686 for a cattle fair every May. Around it gathered a host of rowdy characters. Finally the neighbours had the fair closed.

Gladstone, Disraeli, Nelson and Wellington lived in Mayfair. Clive of India died at 44 Berkeley Square in 1774 of drugs, either from addiction or to kill pain. Handel wrote the *Messiah* in Brook Street, and the infatuated Lady Caroline Lamb dressed up as a page boy to visit Byron in his chambers at Albany, off Piccadilly.

The rich kept their town houses into the 20th century, but after the First World War office blocks and hotels encroached. And if an era epitomises Mayfair it is the 1920's, when a fashionable Mayfair clique known as the 'Bright Young Things' lived in a whirl of dances, theatre-going, cocktail parties and uncon-

Yours very truly,
Robert Browning.

POET AND POETESS *Robert Browning (right) and Elizabeth Barrett, whose long courtship led to one of the greatest romantic correspondences in history.*

ventional behaviour. Writers such as Aldous Huxley, Evelyn Waugh and Noel Coward so enhanced this little world that it stands for everything that is gay and inconsequential. For the fortunate few, Mayfair in the 1920's was a golden age between the realities of two world wars.

Paddington

Before the 19th century, Paddington was notorious for its dark place in London's history. Within its bounds stood Tyburn, for centuries the capital's chief execution place.

Tyburn's first recorded victims perished in 1196. At first, the executions there were by hanging from the elm trees that grew in the vicinity. Later a gallows was erected. It was a large three-legged gantry, whose triple crossbeams enabled a dozen or more criminals to be hanged at the same time. Its services were much in demand; as late as the early 19th century over 200 petty

offences were punishable by death. (The site where the gallows stood is now marked by a stone on a traffic island near Marble Arch.)

Among the many thousands to die at Tyburn was Jonathan Wild, whose flamboyant career as a professional 'thief taker' had won him great notoriety in the 18th-century London. Operating in the days before there was a police force, Wild brought many criminals to justice. But his own career was more often illegal than legal.

With his intimate knowledge of all types of dishonesty, Wild was able to exploit crime from every angle. He got money from protection rackets, from blackmailing criminals, from the sale of stolen goods (which he might alternatively return to owners for a fat reward), and from rewards given for the criminals he turned over to the law.

Wild's disdain for legal processes was legendary. At his own trial in 1725, for trafficking in stolen goods, he circulated among the jury a list

MORAL EXAMPLE *The fate of Jonathan Wild, executed at Tyburn, is held up as a grim example to criminals.*

of those he had been instrumental in convicting. On the list were the names of 35 robbers, 22 housebreakers, and ten convicts who had returned from transportation—an offence punishable by death.

Many others followed Wild to the scaffold for offences ranging from murder to picking pockets. But Tyburn's day was drawing to a close. The last felon to be hanged there was John Austin in November 1783 for robbery and wounding.

With a new century came a revolution that was to transform the area. The building of Paddington Canal—part of the Grand Union System—in the early 1800's led to a wave of new building. The elegant houses that were erected there were deliberately intended to rival Belgravia—and the area became known as 'Tyburnia'. And the final transformation came about with the coming of the railway. In the 1830's the directors of the Great Western Railway and their engineer, Isambard Kingdom Brunel, decided to build a great terminus there for the line they were building to the west.

Regent Street

Nothing but the line of the street remains of architect John Nash's original plans for Regent Street. He designed it as part of the 'Royal Mile' to link the Prince Regent's proposed new country house in Marylebone (later Regent's) Park with the palace of Carlton House in Pall Mall. Carlton House was pulled down in 1827.

Because of the bankruptcy of the builders and the financial strains of the Napoleonic Wars, the park itself is only a shadow of Nash's grandiose scheme for a fashionable garden suburb. But Regent Street, begun about 1817, benefited from the building boom which began soon after the Battle of Waterloo, and was completed by 1823.

The County Fire Office marked the end of Lower Regent Street, which ran from Waterloo Place to Piccadilly Circus. From there Nash carried the street on a curve—the Quadrant—which led into the final stretch to Oxford Circus.

The original Quadrant consisted of a superb colonnade of 145 columns in front of regular rows of stucco-faced houses. But Regent Street did not long remain as Nash had planned it. The shopkeepers complained that their goods could not be seen in the dim light which filtered through the columns.

In 1848 the colonnade was removed (and part of it was added to one side of Drury Lane Theatre) and the frontages rebuilt. The lower part of the frontage was divided into shops. Above their windows was a long balcony which continued the horizontal curve as the colonnade had done.

Following the rebuilding of the Piccadilly Hotel in Portland stone in 1908, other buildings in Regent Street were gradually heightened and rebuilt in the same stone.

The completion of the rebuilding in 1927 was celebrated by cheering crowds, when George V and Queen Mary drove down a Regent Street decked with flags and flowers.

St James's

Although Britain's sovereigns no longer use St James's Palace as a permanent residence, it has remained the headquarters of court ceremonial, and foreign ambassadors are still accredited to 'the Court of St James's'.

Henry VIII built it on the site of a hospital for leprous women which was dedicated to St James the Less. The only remnants from Henry's time are the Chapel Royal*, and the clocktower gatehouse which faces St James's Street, for a disastrous fire destroyed much of the old palace in 1809.

It was the birthplace of Charles II, James II, Mary II, Anne and George IV. Mary Tudor used it

---

THE GROWTH OF UNDERGROUND LONDON

Digging the first underground.

The world's first passenger-carrying underground railway opened in London in 1863. It was the result of 30 years of struggle. Charles Pearson, an enterprising and far-sighted surveyor of the City of London, saw it as the only solution to the city's road-congestion problems.

The first underground line to be opened was a 3¾ mile stretch from Paddington to Farringdon Road, which was run by the North Metropolitan Railway Company. On the first day, Londoners flocked to the underground railway and in the first six months an average of 26,500 passengers used the line daily.

Pearson, who did not live to see

his scheme fulfilled, had also planned for an underground system linking all the main railway stations in London. In 1868, with the building of the Metropolitan and District line, this project became a reality. There quickly followed a vast network of underground railway tunnels.

Apart from its crucial role as part of London's transport system, the underground railway has served other important functions. During both world wars it was a refuge from bombing raids for thousands of Londoners, and a storehouse for some of London's great treasures, such as the Elgin Marbles from the British Museum.

403

Sheffield

Chesterfield
Haddon
Hall
Hardwick
Hall

Sherwood
Forest

Harby

Lincoln

NOTTINGHAM

LINCOLN

DERBY

Newark

Boston

The
Wash

Holkham Hall
Burnham
Thorpe

Burslem

Newstead
Abbey

Nottingham
Aslockton
Gotham

Castle
Rising

Houghton Hall

Derby

King's
Lynn

Sandringham

Melbourne

LEICESTER

Bourne

NORFOLK

Norwich

Stafford

STAFFORD

Staunton
Harold Hall

Bradgate
Park

Oakham

Helpston

Ashby de la
Zouch Castle

Drayton
Bassett

Leicester

WEST
MIDLANDS

Bosworth
Field

Fotheringhay
Castle

Grime's Graves

Thetford

CAMBRIDGE

Aston

Arbury
Hall

Lutterworth

Ely

Birmingham

Naseby

Huntingdon

Coventry

Rugby

Hagley Hall

NORTHAMPTON

Buckden

Newmarket

Bury St Edmunds

Framlingham
Castle

Dunwich

Bewdley

Kenilworth
Castle

Cambridge

SUFFOLK

Aldeburgh

Warwick
Castle

Worcester

Northampton

Powick
Bridge

WARWICK

Stratford-upon-Avon

BEDFORD

Ipswich

Evesham

Olney

Bedford

Banbury

Elstow

Southill
Park

Audley End

Tewkesbury

Sudeley
Castle

Stowe

Woburn

HERTFORD

Colchester

The Naze

Claydon
House

Dunstable

Stow-on-
the-Wold

Cheltenham

Blenheim
Palace

Woodstock

BUCKINGHAM

Ayot St Lawrence
Lemsford
Rye
House

ucester

GLOUCESTER

OXFORD

Aylesbury

Ashridge

St
Albans

Hatfield
House

Chelmsford

ESSEX

Cumnor
Hall

Oxford

Berkhamsted
Hughenden
Manor

Salisbury
Hall

Cheshunt

berkeley
tle

Kelmscott
Manor

Abingdon

Chalgrove
Field

Chalfont
St Giles

Barnet

Ashingdon

ttle
dbury

Lyford

Sutton
Courtenay

Marlow

Beaconsfield

GREATER

Thames

Medmenham

Cliveden

Hayes
Place

Inner

London

Sheerness

North
Foreland

Windsor
Castle

Syon
House

LONDON

Gravesend

Gad's Hill
Place

Eastchurch

Lacock
Abbey

Calne

Avebury

BERKSHIRE

Kingston
Hill

Richmond

Nonsuch

Bushy
Park

Keston

Rochester

Sandwich

Burbage

Claremont

Biggin
Hill

Down
House

Faversham

Canterbury

Devizes

Farnborough

Sevenoaks

Chartwell

KENT

Walmer
Castle

WILTSHIRE

Guildford

SURREY

Penshurst
Place

Royal
Tunbridge
Wells

Dover

Stonehenge

Alton

Bush Barrow

Old
Sarum

Old
Alresford

Chawton

Horsham

EAST

Brookland

Wilton
House

Selborne

Fonthill
Abbey

Salisbury

Winchester

Tichborne
House

SUSSEX

WEST

Bateman's

Rye

Dungeness

aftesbury

HAMPSHIRE

South
Harting

SUSSEX

Battle
Abbey

Winchelsea

Romsey
Southampton

Hambledon

Arundel
Castle

Laughton

ORSET

Beaulieu
Abbey

Fishbourne
Palace

Shoreham

Lewes

Brighton

Clouds
Hill

Buckler's
Hard

Solent

Chichester
Bosham

Rottingdean

Bournemouth

Portsmouth

Beachy
Head

hester
en

ISLE
OF
WIGHT

Farringford

Osborne
House

Selsey
Bill

Corfe
Castle

mouth

e of
rtland

Scotland & Northern England

Legend

Site or building	▲
Town or village	▪
National boundary	— + — + —
County boundary	— — — —

N

0 — 20
Miles

WESTERN ISLES
Butt of Lewis
Cape Wrath
North Minch
Little Minch
North Minch
Moray Firth

ORKNEY ISLANDS
St Margaret's Hope

Ardvreck Castle
Carbisdale ▲
Tain ▪
Lossiemouth ▪
Turriff ▪
Inverness ▪ ▲ Culloden
Lochindorb
GRAMPIAN
HIGHLAND

▲ Inverlochy Castle
Lumphanan ▲
Aberdeen ▪
Howe of Corrichie
Braemar ▪ ▲ Balmoral Castle
Stonehaven ▪
Dunnottar Castle

Glencoe ▪
Pass of Killiecrankie ▲
TAYSIDE
Kirriemuir ▪
Montrose ▪

Iona
Oban ▪
Dunkeld ▪
Glamis Castle ▲
Dundee ▪
Arbroath ▪

Inveraray ▪
Balquhidder ▪
CENTRAL
Huntingtower Castle ▲ ▪ Scone
Tippermuir ▪ Perth ▪
Tay Railway Bridge
Magnus Muir ▲
St Andrews ▪

▲ Sheriffmuir
FIFE
Falkland Palace ▲

Glen Fruin
▲ Inchmahome Priory
Stirling Castle ▲
Sauchieburn ▪ ▲ Dunfermline
Bannockburn
Burntisland ▪
Bass Rock
Seton Palace ▲ ▲ Tantallon Castle
Dunbar ▪
Old Cramond Bridge
Haddington ▪

Greenock ▪
Antonine Wall
Falkirk ▪
Edinburgh ▪ Prestonpans ▪
Rothesay ▪
Paisley ▪
Glasgow ▪
Carberry Hill
LOTHIAN
Pinkie ▲ Crichton Castle
Halidon Hill ▲

Largs ▪
Blantyre ▪
Cadzow Castle ▲
Borthwick Castle ▲
Berwick-upon-Tweed ▪

Lochranza ▪
Brodick Castle ▲
STRATHCLYDE
Darvel ▪
New Lanark ▪
Coldstream ▪
Abbotsford ▲
Bamburgh Castle ▲

Ayr ▪
Auchinleck ▪
Philiphaugh ▲
Melrose Abbey ▲
Roxburgh Castle ▲
Flodden Field ×

Alloway ▪
Jedburgh ▪
BORDERS
Alnwick Castle ▲

Firth of Clyde
Otterburn ▲

DUMFRIES & GALLOWAY
NORTHUMBERLAND

Dumfries ▪
Ecclefechan ▪
Gretna Green
Hadrian's Wall
TYNE & WEAR

Caerlaveroch Castle ▲
Solway Moss
Jarrow ▪

Stranraer ▪
▲ Buittle
Solway Firth
Sunderland ▪

Whithorn ▪
Neville's Cross ▲
Durham ▪

Cockermouth ▪
DURHAM

St Bees Head
CUMBRIA
Barnard Castle ▲
Stockton-on-Tees ▪
Darlington ▪
CLEVELAND

Grasmere ▪
Richmond Castle ▲
Northallerton ▪
Whitby ▪

Coniston ▪
Scarborough ▪

Kendal ▪
Middleham Castle ▲

Flamboro Head

Peel Castle ▪
Isle of Man

NORTH YORKSHIRE
Lancaster ▪
Boroughbridge ▪
Stamford Bridge ▲

Knaresborough Castle ▲
Marston Moor ▲
York ▪
HUMBERSIDE

Otley ▪
LANCASHIRE
Leeds ▪
Towton ▪
Kingston upon Hull ▪
Welton ▪

Preston ▪
Bradford ▪
Pontefract Castle ▲
WEST YORKSHIRE
Raven

Blackburn ▪
Wakefield ▪
Humber

Bolton ▪
SOUTH YORKSHIRE
Epworth ▪
GREATER MANCHESTER
MERSEYSIDE
Manchester ▪
Sheffield ▪
NOTTS

Liverpool ▪
Mersey

Anglesey
Beaumaris ▪
Conway ▪
Rhuddlan ▪
Flint Castle ▪
CHESHIRE
Haddon Hall ▲
Chesterfield ▪
Sherwood Forest
Harby ▪
LINCOLN

Caernarvon Castle ▲
Denbigh Castle ▲
Hawarden Castle ▲
Hardwick Hall ▲
Lincoln ▪
DERBY

STAFFORD
Newark ▪

426

INDEX

Page numbers in **bold type** refer to a main entry on a subject.
Figures in *italics* refer to illustrations, which are often accompanied by mention in the text
on the same page. The panels provide quick reference to some of the major themes
occurring throughout the book. (*Abbreviations—s.* son of; *w.* wife of)

N

M

MacAlpin, Kenneth, King of
    the Scots 53, 417

Nile, Battle of the 267, 373
Ninian, St 423
Nolan, Captain 307
Nollekens, Joseph 262
Nonesuch *113*, **409**
Nore Mutiny 269, 418
Norfolk, Dukes of 124, 125, *127*, 131, 364, 365, 375, 421
Normanton Down 20
Norris, Henry 127
North, Lord 244, 257, 373, 414
North Briton, The 248, 365
North Midland Railway 377
North Sea oil *323*, 325
Northallerton **409–10**
Northampton 303, 390, **410**
  Assize of 79
  Siege of 81
Northcliffe, Lord 399
Northern Ireland 358
Northumberland, Earls of 95, **98–99**, 108, *141*, 246, *247*, 363, 367, 379, 386, 405
  Percy, Henry ('Hotspur') **98–99**, 363, 367, 405, 411
Northumberland, Duke of (John Dudley) 126, *134*, 135
Northumbria 43, 58
Norwich **410**
Nottingham *175*, 303, **410**
  Castle 66, 175, 410
Notting Hill Carnival *359*
Nuffield, Lord 411

O

Oakham **410**
Oates, Captain Lawrence *331*
Oates, Titus **206–7**
Oban **410**
Odo of Bayeux 64, 69
Offa, King of Mercia 51
Offa's Dyke *51*
Okey, Colonel John 182
Old Cramond Bridge **410**
Old Sarum **410**, 416
Olivier, Sir Laurence (*later* Lord) *359*
Olney **410**
Omar Pasha *306*
Orkney Islands 416
Ormonde, Earl of 364
Orton, Arthur (Tichborne claimant) 421
Osborne, John 359
Osborne House *299*, **411**
Oswald, St 44
Oswy, King of Northumbria 49
Otley **411**
Otterburn **411**

Owen, Robert 409
Owen, Wilfred *338*, 339
Oxford **411**
  martyrs **136–7**
  Provisions of 84
  University **78–79**, *124*, 411

P

Pages, Bastian 143
Paine, Thomas 421
Paisley **411**
Palmer, Barbara 196
Palmer, John 422
Palmer, Samuel 264
Palmerston, Viscount 291, 414
Pankhurst, Christabel (daughter of Emmeline Pankhurst) *332*, *333*
Pankhurst, Emmeline *332*, *333*
Pankhurst, Sylvia (daughter of Emmeline Pankhurst) 332
Paris, Matthew 78
Parke, Colonel 219
Parker, Richard 269, 418
Parliament **84–85**, 397
  Charles I and **172–5**, 184, 187
  Charles II's 194, 207
  'Free' 198
  Long 188–9
  'Merciless' 95
  reform of (1832) **290–1**
  'Rump' 188–9, 198
  taxation and 85, 172–3, 274
Parma, Duke of 150, 151
Parr, Catharine (*w.* Henry VIII) *121*, 393, 420
Parry, Sir Charles Hubert 370
Pascoe, Lieutenant John 266
Paulet, Sir Amyas 140, 145
Paulinus, Suetonius 32–33, 363
Paviland Cave 15
Paxton, Joseph 302–3
Pearson, Charles 403
Peasants' Revolt (1381) 93, **94–95**, 410
Peel, Sir Robert 275, 382, 411
Peel Castle **411**
Pelham, Henry 262, 395
Pélissier, General *306*
Pembroke Castle **411–12**
Pembroke, Earl of 105, 108, 176–7, 390
Penicillin 380–1
Peninsular War **270–1**, 273
Penn, William 375

Penny post 296
Penshurst Place **412**
Pepys, Samuel 200–1, *203*, 208
  quotations from 196, 199, 202, 367
Perceval, Spencer *274*
Percy, Henry *see* Northumberland, Earls of
Percy, Henry ('Hotspur') *see* Northumberland, Earls of
Percy, Thomas 162
Percy, Thomas, Earl of Worcester 98
Perth 227, **412**
Peterborough Abbey 370
Peterhead 227
Peterloo massacre 274, 406
Peter's pence 74
Petersham, Lord 276
Petition of Right 172, 174
Petty, Sir William 209
Petworth Park *293*
Philip, Prince, Duke of Edinburgh 357
Philip II, King of Spain 137, *150*, 153, 419
Philiphaugh 375, 408, **412**
Picts *39*, 47, *53*, 392, 417
Piercebridge 35
Pilgrim Fathers **168–9**, 370, 412
Pilgrimage of Grace 131, 363
Pilgrims 71, 75
Pinkie, Battle of 148, **412**
Pisan, Christine de 99
Pitcairn Island 377
Pitt, William 238, 244–5, 274, 393, 422
Pitt, William (the elder) 231, **239**, 390
Place, Francis 290
Plague (1348–9) **92–93**
  (1665) **200–1**
Plassey, Battle of 223
Plautius, Aulus 31
Plumer, Colonel Herbert 321
Plunket, Oliver 207
Plymouth 351, **412**
Pocahontas, Indian princess *388*, 389
Poincaré, Raymond, President of France *324*
Poitiers, Battle of 91
Pollitzer, Adolf 328
Pomerai, Henry de 416
Ponsonby, Frederick 326
Ponsonby, Lady Caroline 395
Ponsonby, Sarah 396
Pontefract Castle 63, 95, **412**
Poole, Thomas 378
Poor Law 112, 309
Pope, Joseph 371
Popish Plot (1678) **206–7**
Porteous, Captain John 384
Porter, Elizabeth 236
Portland **412**
Portsmouth 351, **412**
Portsmouth, Louise de Kéroualle, Duchess of *198*, 207, 365
Possession Island 253
Potato introduced to Britain *113*

Pottery 17, **251**, *263*, *298*, *381*
Powick Bridge **412**
Prasutagus, King of the Iceni 32
Pre-Raphaelites **304–5**
Prescelly Mountains 18
Press-gang 269
Preston **413**
Prestonpans, Battle of 235, 362, 384, **413**
Pride, Colonel Thomas 188
Priestley, J. B. 370
Priestley, Joseph *259*
Prince Regent *see* George IV
Princetown **413**
Printing 78, **106–7**
Prior Park 228
Pritchard, David 368
Pugin, Augustus *312*, 313, 369
Pulteney, William, (later Earl of Bath) 229
Purcell, Henry *209*
Puritans 160–1, **168–9**, 177, 191, 370

Q

Quant, Mary 359
Quebec, Battle of **238–9**
Quebec House, Westerham 238
Queen Elizabeth, RMS 388
Queen Mary, RMS 388
Queensberry, Duke of *217*

R

Radcot Bridge, Battle of 95
Radio 350, 376
Raedwald, King of East Anglia 51
Raglan, Lord *306*, 307
Raglan Castle **413**
Railways **288–9**, *297*, 300–1, 371, 377, 380, 403, 406
Rainham Hill 391
Rainhill Trials 288
Raleigh, Sir Walter 113, 156, 157, **166–7**, 412, 418
Raleigh, Wat (*s.* of Sir Walter) 167
Ramsay, Admiral Sir Bertram *354*
Ramsay, Isabella 405
Rankin, Duncan 217

Rannulf Flambard 69, 383
Ranulf, Earl of Chester 395
Rathlin 396
Ravenspurn **414**
Rawlinson, Sir Henry 342
Reading 78, 394
Reculver 26
Redman, Henry 122
Redruth **414**
Reform Bill (1832) 275, **290–1**, 369, 410
Regicides *185*
Regni tribe 34
Rennie, John 381
Resolution, HMS 253
Revenge, The 368
Revolution of 1688 193, **214–15**, 371–82, 389, 416
Reynolds, Sir Joshua 233, *263*, 293
Rhodn Mawr (Roderick the Great) of Wales 383
Rhuddlan **414**
Rhys, Lord 383
Rhys ap Tewdr, Prince 86
Rhys ap Howel 396
Rhys ap Thomas 108
Riccio, David *142*, 143, 379, 417
Richard, Prince (*s.* Edward IV) *109*
Richard le Breton 74
Richard le Poore, Bishop 71, 416
Richard of Chichester, St 377
Richard I 62, **76–77**, 380, 412, 419
Richard II 85, 89, **94–95**, 98, 379, 386, 394, 407, 412
Richard III 105, **108–9**, 364, 366, 371, 395, 405, 407, 420
Richborough on Thanet 39
Richmond Castle (N. Yorks) **414**
Richmond-upon-Thames **414**
Ridley, Nicholas *136*, 137, 374
Rivers, Earl 106
Rob Roy 366
Robert (*s.* William I) 375
Robert I of Scotland *see* Bruce, Robert
Robert II of Scotland 365, 396
Robert III of Scotland 396, 414
Roberts, Caroline Alice 328
Roberts, Lord 321
Robin Hood 418
Robsart, Amy 380
Rochester 49, 52, **414**
Rocket, Stephenson's **288–9**
Rocket weapons *355*
Roet, Philippa 96
Roger, Bishop of Salisbury 381
Roger of Poitou 394
Rogers, John 137
Rolfe, John 389
Rolle, Lord 299
Rolls, Hon. C. S. 407
Rolls-Royce 381
Romans
  Antonine Wall **363**
  Art 39, **40–41**

S

U

V

ACKNOWLEDGMENTS

The publishers acknowledge their indebtedness to the following for permission to use their photographs. The details are arranged according to chapter and page number (**bold** figures) and the photographers are given in brackets.

Prehistory 12/13 Stonehenge: (Mike Taylor) **14** Artefacts from Kent's Cavern: Trustees of the British Museum (Natural History) **15** Barnfield Pit, Swanscombe: (Malcolm Aird); Swanscombe skull: Trustees of the British Museum (Natural History); bone fragment: Trustees of the British Museum **16** Grime's Graves: (Penny Tweedie); Grime's Graves Venus: Trustees of the British Museum **17** Clactonian flint: Colchester and Essex Museum (Mike Freeman); hand axe: Trustees of the British Museum (Natural History); flint blade, axe head and arrow head: Devizes Museum (Eileen Tweedy); pots: Devizes Museum (J. Beale) **18** Stonehenge: (Mike Taylor) **19** Silbury Hill: (Malcolm Aird); Avebury: (Penny Tweedie); Dolmen: Susan Griggs (Adam Woolfitt); Castlerigg Circle: Picturepoint **20** Bush Barrow: (Mike Taylor); belt hook and mace: Devizes Museum (Eileen Tweedy) **21** Bell beaker, axe head: Devizes Museum (Eileen Tweedy) **22** Waterloo helmets, Desborough mirror, Battersea shield: Trustees of the British Museum **23** Horse mask, torc: Trustees of the British Museum; limestone head: Gloucester City Museums **23** Mousa broch: Susan Griggs (Michael St Maur Sheil)

Romans 24/25 Hadrian's Wall: Brian Brake, from the John Hillelson Agency **26** Coins (Raymond Gardner) **28** Beach near Walmer: (Malcolm Aird) **29** Coin: (Raymond Gardner); statue of Caesar: Susan Griggs (Adam Woolfitt); the Dying Gaul: Scala **30** Maiden Castle: (Penny Tweedie); coin of Vespasian: (Raymond Gardner) **31** Head of Claudius: Colchester and Essex Museum (Mike Freeman); distance slab: National Museum of Antiquities of Scotland **32** Tombstone: Colchester and Essex Museum (Mike Freeman) **33** Pharos at Dover: Crown copyright by permission of the Controller HMSO; Roman road: (Penny Tweedie); diners and reciter: Colchester and Essex Museum (Mike Freeman) **34** Dolphin mosaic, boy's head: *Sunday Times* **35** Mosaics: Michael Holford; Pierce Bridge plough group: Trustees of the British Museum; hoe and plough share: Guildhall Museum, London (Mike Freeman) **36** Multangular Tower: (Mike Freeman); jet ornaments: Yorkshire Museum (Mike Freeman) **37** Tragic mask: National Museum of Wales; Colchester vase: Colchester and Essex Museum (Mike Freeman); Roman bath: (Michael Holford); strigil and oil-flask: Guildhall Museum, London (Mike Freeman) **38** Hadrian's Wall: Brian Brake, from the John Hillelson Agency; head of Hadrian: Trustees of the British Museum **39** Pictish slab: C. M. Dixon **40** Roman glass: Canterbury Royal Museum (Penny Tweedie); Lullingstone Chi-Rho, Lullingstone wall-painting: Trustees of the British Museum **41** Mildenhall dish and cover: Trustees of the British Museum; Jupiter: Colchester and Essex Museum (Mike Freeman); sphinx: Colchester and Essex Museum (Mike Freeman); dancing lar: Colchester and Essex Museum (Mike Freeman); head of Mithras: Guildhall Museum, London (Mike Freeman)

Saxons 42/43 Sompting church: (Mike Freeman) **44/45** Anglo-Saxon calendar: British Library MS.COT TIB'V (Colour Centre Slides Ltd) **46** Cadbury Castle: Camera Press (Ron Startup) **47** King Arthur: British Library MS.Roy.20 AII f.4; Round Table: Bibliothèque Nationale MS.Fr.343 f.3; Noah's Ark: Bodleian Library roll 172D **48** St Martin's Church: (Malcolm Aird) **49** Bede: British Library ADD MS.39943 f.2; Ixworth cross: Ashmolean Museum (Colour Centre Slides Ltd); Franks casket: British Museum (Michael Holford) **50** Sutton Hoo: (Mike Taylor) **51** Sutton Hoo helmet and buckle: British Museum (Michael Holford); Offa's Dyke: (Keith Morris) **52** Lindisfarne: Tre Tryckare, Cagner and Co. (Brian Seed) **53** Relics of St Cuthbert: Durham Cathedral Library (Colour Centre Slides Ltd); Lindisfarne slab: Crown copyright by permission of the Controller HMSO **54** Coin of Alfred: (Raymond Gardner); the Alfred jewel: Ashmolean Museum, Oxford **55** Skates: (Patrick Thurston); Cnut: British Library MS.Stowe 944 f.6 **56** Shrine of the Confessor: Perfecta Press; Edward the Confessor: Bodleian Library roll 205B **58** Lindisfarne carpet page: British Library Lindisfarne Facsimile f.10v; the Church of St Lawrence: (Mike Freeman) **59** Mouth of Hell: British Library MS.NERO CIV f.39; reliquary cross: Victoria and Albert Museum; Kingston brooch: Merseyside County Museums; Winster Moor brooch: Sheffield City Museum (Colour Centre Slides Ltd); five senses brooch: British Museum (Michael Holford)

Medieval 60/61 Coronation of a king: Master and Fellows of Corpus Christi College, Cambridge; Chair: Woodmansterne **62** Feast, tournament, masons: Trustees of the British Museum **63** Monks cutting planks, dyers at work, reapers and harvestman: Trustees of the British Museum **64** Battlefield at Hastings: John Hillelson Agency (Erich Lessing) **64/65** Death of Harold, Bayeaux Tapestry: (Michael Holford) **65** Halley's Comet: Photo Science Museum, London; comet, Bayeaux Tapestry: (Michael Holford); William I: Dean and Chapter of Wells Cathedral (BPC) **66** White Tower: (Chris Ridley); St John's Chapel: A. F. Kersting **67** Tower of London, MS.illumination: Trustees of the British Museum; *Domesday Book*: Public Record Office; Hereward the Wake: Mansell Collection **68** New Forest: (Keith Morris); death of William Rufus: Mary Evans Picture Library **69** Hunting with bow and arrow: Bodleian Library roll 189A; hunting deer: Bodleian Library roll 189A; William Rufus: Trustees of the British Museum **70** Durham Cathedral, Nave, Durham Cathedral from bridge: (Patrick Thurston) **71** Durham Cathedral, Galilee Chapel: (Patrick Thurston); Durham Cathedral, wall-painting and sanctuary knocker: British Tourist Authority **72** Wreck of the *White Ship*: Trustees of the British Museum **73** Stephen: Bodleian Library roll 205b; illumination from Bury Bible: Master and Fellows of Corpus Christi College, Cambridge MS.2 (Colour Centre Slides Ltd) **74** Canterbury Cathedral: (Malcolm Aird) **75** Manuscript illumination of Becket's death: Trustees of the British Museum; Canterbury pilgrims, MS.illuminations: Trustees of the British Museum **76** Chertsey Abbey tile: Trustees of the British Museum **76/77** Massacre of Saracens: Bibliothèque Nationale Service Photographique **77** Effigy: (G. Croal); Richard I: Trustees of the British Museum **78** Mob Quad, Merton College: (Alain Le Garsmeur); MS.illumination of William of Wykeham: Bodleian Library roll 214.8; Duke Humphrey's Library: Thomas-Photos, Oxford; Merton College Library: BPC (Chris Ridley) **79** Founder's cup: Queen's College, Oxford (Alain Le Garsmeur); giant salt: All Souls College, Oxford (Weidenfeld and Nicolson Ltd) **80** Runnymede: (Keith Morris); King John at Runnymede: Guildhall Library; King John's seal: Trustees of the British Museum; Magna Carta: Trustees of the British Museum **81** King John's tomb: Dean and Chapter of Worcester Cathedral (Derrick Witty) **82** Wells Cathedral, west front: Dean and Chapter of Wells Cathedral (Malcolm Aird); MS.illumination of Wells: Bodleian Library roll 214.8 **83** Wells Cathedral transept: Dean and Chapter of Wells Cathedral (Picturepoint Ltd); Wells Cathedral chapter house: Dean and Chapter of Wells Cathedral (Perfecta Publications Ltd); Wells Cathedral, prior's staircase: Dean and Chapter of Wells Cathedral (Michael Holford); Wells Cathedral, corbels: Dean and Chapter of Wells Cathedral (Malcolm Aird) **84** Westminster Hall: Perfecta Publications Ltd; seal of Simon de Montfort: Trustees of the British Museum **85** MS.illuminations of Parliament (detail): Copyright reserved; Henry III: Dean and Chapter of Westminster Abbey **86** Harlech Castle: (Penny Tweedie) **87** Stonemasons: Pierpont Morgan Library MS.638 f.3; coronation of Edward I: Bodleian Library roll 173G **88** Stirling Castle: (Patrick Thurston); Robert Bruce: Mansell Collection; Battle of Bannockburn: Master and Fellows of Corpus Christi College, Oxford MS.CCC 171 f.265r **89** Edward II: Trustees of the British Museum **90** The Black Prince's shield: Dean and Chapter of Canterbury Cathedral (Penny Tweedie); Battle of Crécy: Bibliothèque Nationale Service Photographique **91** Longbowmen: Trustees of the British Museum; Edward III: Mary Evans Picture Library **92** St Mary's, Ashwell: (Keith Morris); Burial of plague victims: Bibliothèque Royale de Belgique **93** Medical instruments: By permission of the President and Fellows of St John's College, Oxford **94** Groats of Richard II: British Museum (Christopher Barker); Death of Wat Tyler: Trustees of the British Museum **95** John of Gaunt: Mary Evans Picture Library; abdication of Richard II: Trustees of the British Museum **96** Page from *Piers Plowman*: Bodleian Library roll 175A **96/97** Six illuminations from the facsimile of the Ellesmere Chaucer: Trustees of the British Museum **98** Alnwick Castle: (M. Breese); Richard II surrenders: Trustees of the British Museum **99** Coronation of Henry IV: Trustees of the British Museum **100** Stone relief of Henry V: Dean and Chapter of Westminster Abbey (Alain Le Garsmeur); Henry's portrait: National Portrait Gallery (detail); Battle of Agincourt: By courtesy of the Archbishop of Canterbury and the Trustees of Lambeth Palace Library **101** Brasses: Victoria and Albert Museum **102** King's College Chapel – interior: (Michael Holford); King's College Chapel – exterior: Camera Press (Wim Swaan) **103** King's College Chapel – stained glass: (S. Newbury); Eton College – wall-painting: By courtesy of the Provost and Fellows of Eton (S. Newbury); Eton College – Canaletto: By courtesy of the National Gallery, London **104** Helmet: Victoria and Albert Museum (Chris Ridley); the Earl of Warwick: By courtesy of the Marquess of Abergavenny (BPC); Margaret of Anjou: Worshipful Company of Skinners (Percy Hennel); Plucking of the Red and White Roses: By permission of the Right Honourable The Speaker (John Freeman) **105** Battle of Tewkesbury: Bibliotek der Universiteit, Ghent; Henry VI (detail): National Portrait Gallery **106** *Dictes and Syenges*: The British Library (John Freeman); Anthony Woodville and Edward IV: By courtesy of the Archbishop of Canterbury and the Trustees of Lambeth Palace Library **107** Model of Caxton's Press: Crown copyright, Science Museum, London; Edward IV enthroned: Trustees of the British Museum **108** Bosworth: (Michael St Maur Sheil); Battle: Bibliotek der Universiteit, Ghent; Richard III (detail): National Portrait Gallery **109** Princes: by permission of the Trustees of the Wallace Collection

Tudors 110/11 The Ambassadors (Holbein): By courtesy of the National Gallery, London **112** Cellerer: Trustees of the British Museum; emigrants: British Museum (John Freeman); pedlar: British Museum (John Freeman) **113** Hunting at Nonesuch: reproduced by permission of the Syndics of the Fitzwilliam Museum, Cambridge; Campion: Mary Evans Picture Library; Virginia potato: Bodleian Library roll 196c; schoolroom: British Museum (John Freeman) **114** Earl of Dorset: Victoria and Albert Museum; children at table: By kind permission of the Marquess of Bath (John Freeman) **115** Elizabeth Vernon: By kind permission of His Grace the Duke of Buccleuch and Queensberry; Bradford table carpet and cushion cover: Victoria and Albert Museum; Court Musicians and Henry VIII: Trustees of the British Museum **116** Coins: British Museum (Christopher Barker); document: Crown copyright, Public Record Office E101/414/6 f.83V **116** Cabot: Bristol City Art Gallery; **117** Map: Museo Naval, Madrid (Archivo Mas); Henry VII: National Portrait Gallery **118/19** Kitchen and Hall: (John Bethell); others: National Trust **120** Cannon and coins: (Adam Woolfitt); Henry VIII: Walker Art Gallery, Liverpool; Francis I: Cliché Musées Nationaux, Paris **120** Field of the Cloth of Gold (detail): Copyright reserved **121** Catharine of Aragon (detail): National Portrait Gallery; Anne Boleyn (detail): By gracious permission of Her Majesty Queen Elizabeth II; Jane Seymour: Kunsthistorisches Museum, Vienna; Anne of Cleves: The President and Fellows of St John's College, Oxford (Thomas-Photos Oxford); Catharine Howard (detail): Copyright reserved; Catharine Parr (detail): National Portrait Gallery **122** Hampton Court: (Malcolm Aird); Hampton Court, engraving: Crown copyright by permission of the Controller HMSO **124** Missal: By permission of the Governing Body of Christ Church, Oxford (Alain Le Garsmeur); Wolsey: National Portrait Gallery **125** MS.illuminations: Bodleian Library roll 214.5 **126** Hever Castle and lock: By permission of the Hon. Gavin Astor (Malcolm Aird); Anne Boleyn (detail): National Portrait Gallery; Henry VIII and Anne (engraving): Mary Evans Picture Library **127** Thomas Boleyn: Crown Copyright, Victoria and Albert Museum; Thomas, Duke of Norfolk (detail): Copyright reserved **128** Enamel: By kind permission of the Rector of Stonyhurst College (Alain Le Garsmeur); Utopia: British Museum (John Freeman); **128** More and his daughter: Tate Gallery, London (John Webb) **130** Glastonbury Abbey: (Malcolm Aird); Syon Nunnery: Bristol City Art Gallery; *Valor Ecclesiasticus*: Crown copyright, Public Record Office E344/22; Thomas Cromwell (detail): National Portrait Gallery **131** Mells Manor: By kind permission of the Earl of Oxford and Asquith (Gordon Moore); judge: Trustees of the British Museum **132** More and his family: Kunstmuseum, Basel; Fisher (detail): By gracious permission of Her Majesty Queen Elizabeth II; Holbein self-portrait: Weidenfeld and Nicolson Ltd **133** Henry VIII: Baron Thyssen Collection; Prince Edward: National Gallery of Art, Washington D.C. (Andrew Mellon Collection); Anne of Cleves: Cliché Musées Nationaux, Paris **134** Inscription: Crown copyright by permission of the Controller HMSO; Lady Jane Grey (detail): National Portrait Gallery **134** Beheading: Mary Evans Picture Library; document: Trustees of the British Museum **135** Prince Edward: Kunstmuseum, Basel (Hans Hinz, Basel); Prayer Book: Mansell Collection **136** St Mary's, Oxford: (Michael Freeman); Ridley (detail), Latimer (detail), Cranmer (detail), Mary I (detail): National Portrait Gallery; Woodcuts: British Museum (John Freeman) **138** *Liber Regalis*: By courtesy of the Dean and Chapter of Westminster; procession: College of Arms **139** Sir Edward Dymock: College of Arms; Elizabeth I: By kind permission of Lord Brooke, Warwick Castle (John Wright) **140** Hilliard: Victoria and Albert Museum; Leicester: National Portrait Gallery; Hatton: Victoria and Albert Museum; Mary, Queen of Scots: By kind permission of His Grace the Duke of Portland **141** Young Man and a Rose Bush: Victoria and Albert Museum; Elizabeth I: Victoria and Albert Museum; Henry Percy: Ashmolean Museum, Oxford **142** Silver casket: By permission of His Grace the Duke of Hamilton KT, and the National Museum of Antiquities of Scotland (Patrick Thurston); Death of Riccio: National Gallery of Scotland; Rizzio: Mary Evans Picture Library; Mary: Scottish National Portrait Gallery **143** Scene of Darnley's Murder: Crown copyright, Public Record Office SP 52/13* No. 1; Darnley (detail): Copyright reserved **144** Rosary and Prayer Book: By kind permission of His Grace the Duke of Norfolk (Penny Tweedie); Facsimile of warrant: Mary Evans Picture Library; Mary's portrait: National Portrait Gallery **145** Execution of Mary, Queen of Scots: Scottish National Portrait Gallery **146** Goblet: Plymouth City Art Gallery (Michael Freeman); coconut: British Museum (Time Inc. British Empire Series); Drake: National Portrait Gallery; Map: British Museum (John Freeman) **147** Frobisher: Bodleian Library, Oxford; Indians eating maize: British Museum (John Freeman) **148** Longleat – exterior: By kind permission of the Marquess of Bath (Penny Tweedie); Sir John Thynne: By kind permission of the Marquess of Bath (Photo Precision Ltd) **149** Painting of Longleat: By kind permission of the Marquess of Bath; Longleat – interior: By kind permission of the Marquess of Bath (Photo Precision Ltd) **150** Drake's Drum: Plymouth City Art Gallery; Buckland Abbey (Eileen Tweedy); Philip II (detail): National Portrait Gallery; Elizabeth I (detail): from the Woburn Abbey Collection, by kind permission of His Grace the Duke of Bedford (Michael Freeman) **150**/**1** Armada painting: National Maritime Museum, London **151** Howard of Effingham (detail): National Portrait Gallery; Progress: St Faith's Church, King's Lynn (J. R. Freeman) **152** 1st Armada map: National Maritime Museum, London (Time Inc. British Empire Series); 2nd, 3rd and 4th Armada maps, Drake (detail): National Maritime Museum, London **152/3** Armada painting: Tiroler Landesmuseum **153** Armada Treasure: Transworld Feature Syndicate Inc. **154** Shakespeare: National Portrait Gallery; the Globe theatre: Trustees of the British Library **156** Document: By kind permission of His Grace the Duke of Sutherland (British Museum); ring: Dean and Chapter, Westminster Abbey (Woodmansterne); Earl of Essex: from the Woburn Abbey Collection, by kind permission of His Grace the Duke of Bedford (Michael Freeman) **157** Burghley (detail): National Portrait Gallery; Cecil: By permission of the Marquess of Salisbury; Funeral of Elizabeth: Trustees of the British Museum

Early Stuarts 158/9 Execution of Charles I: By permission of Lord Primrose, Scottish National Portrait Gallery; Rubens ceiling: Crown copyright, by permission of the Controller HMSO **160** Arms: Radio Times Hulton Picture Library; St Paul's: Society of Antiquaries of London; James I and Prince Charles: Society of Antiquaries of London **161** Death of Buckingham: By kind permission of the Marquess of Northampton (Henry Cooper); Covenanters: Mary Evans Picture Library; Lord Mayor's procession: Guildhall Library; Hobbes (detail): National Portrait Gallery; Charles II's escape: By permission of the 6th Earl of Arran Will Trust (Christopher Barker) **162** Lantern: Ashmolean Museum, Oxford; gunpowder plotters: Mansell Collection; Fawkes apprehended: British Museum (John Freeman) **163** James I: Crown copyright, Public Record Office (E30/1705); Carr (detail), Buckingham (detail): National Portrait Gallery **164** Tradescant: Ashmolean Museum, Oxford; drawing of plum: Bodleian Library roll 208G **164** Hatfield – south front: By kind permission of the Marquess of Salisbury **165** Marble hall and grand staircase: By kind permission of the Marquess of Salisbury (John Freeman); deed: By kind permission of the Marquess of Salisbury (Basil King) **166** Raleigh's *History*: British Museum (John Freeman); execution: Mary Evans Picture Library; Raleigh: National Portrait Gallery **167** Raleigh in Trinidad: Mansell Collection **168** *Mayflower* model: Crown copyright, Science Museum, London; pilgrims: House of Lords (Phoebus Picture Library) **169** Page from the Bible: British Library (John Freeman) **170** Harvey demonstrating to Charles I: Ronan Picture Library; relics of Harvey: By permission of the Royal College of Physicians of London (Keith Morris); Harvey (detail): National Portrait Gallery **171** Bacon (detail): National Portrait Gallery **172** Account: Crown copyright, Public Record Office SP 116/284 No. 43; Hampden: Mary Evans Picture Library; *Sovereign of the Seas*: National Maritime Museum, London; Speaker of the House of Commons: By permission of the Right Honourable the Speaker (Derrick Witty) **173** Archbishop Laud: National Portrait Gallery **174** Block and axe: Crown copyright by permission of the Controller HMSO; execution: Radio Times Hulton Picture Library; Strafford (detail): National Portrait Gallery **175** Raising of the Standard: Phoebus Picture Library **176** Wilton – south front: By kind permission of the Earl of Pembroke (A. F. Kersting) **177** Double Cube Room: (A. F. Kersting); Inigo Jones (detail): National Portrait Gallery; Inigo Jones watercolour: Devonshire Collection, Chatsworth reproduced by permission of the Trustees of the Chatsworth Settlement **178** Triple portrait of Charles I (detail): Copyright reserved; children of Charles I (detail): Copyright reserved **179** Charles I on horseback: National Gallery, London; Henrietta Maria (detail): Copyright reserved **180** Battlefield: (Tony Evans); engraving of battle: National Army Museum;

Edgehill medal: Trustees of the British Museum (Christopher Barker) **181** Essex (detail): By kind permission of His Grace the Duke of Portland, on loan to the National Portrait Gallery; Drawing of Colours: Dr Williams Library (National Army Museum); Prince Rupert: Niedersachsisches Landesmuseum, Hanover **182** Priming flask: Cromwell Museum, Huntingdon; Battle of Naseby: Anne S. K. Browne Military Collection, Providence R.I. **183** Fairfax: The British Library (John Freeman); stained-glass figures: (C. M. Dixon); title page: Cromwell Museum, Huntingdon **184** Chair: Victoria and Albert Museum (Phoebus Picture Library); Charles I (detail): Copyright reserved; engraving of trial: Mary Evans Picture Library **185** Death warrant: House of Lords Record Office **186** Shirt; London Museum; engraving of execution: Mary Evans Picture Library **187** Funeral of Charles I: Phoebus Picture Library **188** Cromwell's hat: Cromwell Museum, Huntingdon; engraving: The British Library (John Freeman); Cromwell: National Portrait Gallery **189** And When Did You Last See Your Father?: Walker Art Gallery, Liverpool **190** All illustrations: Mary Evans Picture Library **191** Bunyan (detail), Milton (detail): National Portrait Gallery; Sin between Satan and Death by Henry Fuseli: Los Angeles County Museum of Art, gift of Mr and Mrs F. M. Nicholas, Mr and Mrs H. B. Swerdlow and Mr and Mrs W. K. Glikbarg

Later Stuarts **192/3** Painted ceiling, Greenwich: Crown copyright by permission of the Controller HMSO **194** Sea battle: Admiral Blake Museum, Bridgewater (Michael Freeman); Countess of Orleans (detail): National Portrait Gallery; John Locke (detail): National Portrait Gallery **195** News of William III's arrival: Tate Gallery, London; Britannia: Mansell Collection; William III (detail): National Portrait Gallery **196** The Compleate Gamster: Radio Times Hulton Picture Library; frost fair: London Museum (Eileen Tweedy) **197** Fox hunt: Radio Times Hulton Picture Library; Walton (detail), Killigrew (detail), Dryden (detail): National Portrait Gallery **197** Drury Lane Theatre, Davenant: Radio Times Hulton Picture Library; Coffee house: British Library (Penguin Books) **198** Boscobel House: By permission of the Department of the Environment (Keith Morris); wood panel: Victoria and Albert Museum (Eileen Tweedy); Duchess of Portsmouth (detail): National Portrait Gallery; Barbara Villiers: By kind permission of the Earl Spencer; Nell Gwynne (detail): National Portrait Gallery **199** Charles at Dover: House of Commons (Phoebus Picture Library); Charles II (detail): National Portrait Gallery **200** Eyam churchyard and register: (Keith Morris); burial of victims: Mary Evans Picture Library; plague doctor: By permission of the Wellcome Trustees **201** Charles II curing the 'King's Evil': British Library (John Freeman) **202** Fire-fighting equipment: London Museum (Eileen Tweedy); **202** Painting of the Fire of London: London Museum (Eileen Tweedy) **203** Pepys (detail): National Portrait Gallery **204** Wren (detail): National Portrait Gallery; Thames by Canaletto (detail): Copyright reserved **205** St Paul's – exterior: Expression Photo Library (Brian Shuel); St Paul's – Nave: Perfecta Publications Ltd; Gibbons carving: Feildon and Mawson (Alistair Smith) **206** Tiles: Victoria and Albert Museum (Eileen Tweedy); Edward Coleman: Mary Evans Picture Library; Titus Oates: British Library (John Freeman) **207** Shaftesbury: Victoria and Albert Museum; procession: Mansell Collection **208** Microscope, observatory: Photo Science Museum, London **209** title page: British Library, by courtesy of the Madrigal Society (John Freeman) **210** Sedgemoor battlefield: Gordon Moore; Monmouth (detail): National Portrait Gallery; battle print: Mansell Collection **211** Trial: Graves Art Gallery, Sheffield; James II (detail): National Portrait Gallery **212** Jet engine: Ronan Picture Library **213** Newton (detail): National Portrait Gallery; Woolsthorpe Manor: National Trust; telescope: The Royal Society (Eileen Tweedy) **213** Newton's notebook: Bodleian Library MS.N.C. 361 roll 2 f.45v **214** Declaration of Rights: House of Lords Record Office **214** William at Torbay (detail): Copyright reserved **215** William and Mary: Photo. Hatchette **216** Glencoe: Picturepoint Ltd; Glencoe massacre: Museum and Art Gallery, Glasgow **217** Act of Union: Mary Evans Picture Library **218** Blenheim: Barnaby's Picture Library; Marlborough: By kind permission of His Grace the Duke of Marlborough; Blenheim tapestry: By kind permission of His Grace the Duke of Marlborough **219** Queen Anne (detail): National Portrait Gallery; Sarah Churchill: By kind permission of His Grace the Duke of Marlborough

Early Georgian **220/1** St James's Park and the Mall (detail): Copyright reserved **221** St James's Park today: (Mike Coles) **222** English family drinking tea (detail): Tate Gallery, London; Dr Hoadly (detail): Tate Gallery, London; sleeping congregation: Mary Evans Picture Library **223** Jethro Tull: Royal Agricultural Society of England (Eileen Tweedy); Tull's Wheat Drill: Mary Evans Picture Library; the orrery: Derby Museum and Art Gallery **224** Beggar's Opera (detail): Tate Gallery, London; Vauxhall Gardens: Victoria and Albert Museum; hunting scene: British Library (John Freeman) **225** Acrobat, dancing bear, peasants dancing, minuet: British Library (John Freeman); mop sellers and hot pudding seller: (Michael Holford) **226** State swords: HM Tower of London, by courtesy of the Armouries; the Old Pretender (detail): National Portrait Gallery **227** Landing of the Old Pretender, George I (detail): National Portrait Gallery **228** View of Bath: British Library (John Freeman) **229** Views of Bath: (Christopher Ridley) **230** Houghton Hall: (A. F. Kersting) **231** Walpole: British Library (John Freeman); George II (detail): National Portrait Gallery **232** Hogarth, self portrait (detail): Tate Gallery, London; Marriage à la Mode (detail): Courtesy of the National Gallery, London **233** Shrimp Girl (detail): Courtesy of the National Gallery, London; Chairing the Member: Trustees of Sir John Soane's Museum **234** Monument: Picturepoint; Bonnie Prince Charlie (detail): Scottish National Portrait Gallery; Culloden (detail): Copyright reserved **235** Secret portrait: West Highland Museum (R. Matassa) **236** Johnson's *Dictionary*: Courtesy of Courage Ltd, Brewers, London; Dr Johnson (detail), Boswell (detail), Handel (detail): National Portrait Gallery; Handel's organ: Courtesy of the Thomas Coram Foundation **238** Wolfe's dressing gown: Quebec House, Westerham (Eileen Tweedy) **239** The Taking of Quebec: National Army Museum, London; Death of Wolfe: Ickworth House (National Trust); Pitt: British Library (John Freeman) **240** Stowe House: (John Bethell); the gardens of Stowe: By kind permission of the Head Master of Stowe School (Keith Morris) **241** Capability Brown (detail): National Portrait Gallery

George III **242/3** Old Customs House quay: Victoria and Albert Museum (John Webb) **244** Factory children: Mary Evans Picture Library; toll gate: British Library (John Freeman); carriage and pair: National Gallery, London **245** Gordon riots: Radio Times Hulton Picture Library; Burke (detail): National Portrait Gallery; Pitt and George III: British Library (John Freeman) **246** Robert Adam (detail): National Portrait Gallery **247** Interiors of Syon House: (Jeremy Whitaker) **248** John Wilkes: Trustees of the British Museum **249** Wilkes' entry into London: Mansell Collection; George III (detail): Royal Academy of Art (Phoebus Picture Library) **250** Worsley Canal: *Daily Telegraph* (Clive Coote); Runcorn locks: Mary Evans Picture Library; James Brindley: Collection of the City Art Gallery, Salford (Patrick Thurston); Duke of Bridgewater's aqueduct: Mansell Collection **251** Wedgwood plaque, compotier, Queen's ware tureen; Courtesy of Josiah Wedgwood and Sons Ltd **252** Cook's secret orders: Crown copyright, Public Record Office ADM 2/1332 P.165 (Mike Freeman); Cook's landing: National Gallery of Victoria (Hamlyn Picture Library) **253** Joseph Banks (detail): National Portrait Gallery; Honeysuckle, death of Cook: (Michael Holford) **254** Mr and Mrs Andrews: National Gallery, London; Countess Howe: The GLC, Trustees of the Iveagh Bequest; The Harvest Wagon: The Barber Institute of Fine Arts, University of Birmingham **255** The Haymakers: Upton House, National Trust; **255** Anatomical drawings of horses: Royal Academy of Arts **256** Musket: HM Tower of London, by courtesy of the Master of the Armouries; surrender at Yorktown: Musée de Versailles (Service Photographique des Musées Nationaux) **258** William Aiton: Crown copyright, by permission of the Controller, Royal Botanical Gardens, Kew; erica, mesembryanthemum, limodorum: Trustees of the British Museum (Natural History) **259** Joseph Priestley (detail), Erasmus Darwin (detail): National Portrait Gallery **260** The Iron Bridge: Transworld Features Syndicate Ltd; Coalbrookdale: Photo. Science Museum, London **261** Boulton and Watt's beam engine: Crown copyright, Science Museum, London; James Watt (detail): National Portrait Gallery **262** Woburn Abbey Canaletto Room: By permission of His Grace the Duke of Bedford **263** Woburn Abbey: By permission of His Grace the Duke of Bedford (Mike Freeman); Blue Drawing Room: By permission of His Grace the Duke of Bedford; Reynolds Room: By permission of His Grace the Duke of Bedford (Aspect Picture Library); Sèvres china: By permission of His Grace the Duke of Bedford; Englishmen abroad: British Library (John Freeman) **264** Satan Visiting Job with Sore Boils, Elohim Creating Adam, The Simoniac Pope: Tate Gallery, London **265** William Blake (detail), Coleridge (detail): National Portrait Gallery; Grasmere: British Tourist Authority; Wordsworth: Radio Times Hulton Picture Library **266** HMS *Victory*: Aspect Picture Library; Nelson on the *Victory*: Nelson Museum, Monmouth (Eileen Tweedy) **267** Lady Hamilton: National Maritime Museum, London (John Bulmer); Council of war: National Maritime Museum, London **268** News vendor's bill: Radio Times Hulton Picture Library; death of Nelson: National Maritime Museum, London, Greenwich Hospital Collection **269** Patch boxes, pottery group: National Maritime Museum, London (Eileen Tweedy) **270** Corunna medal: National Army Museum; Sir John Moore (detail): National Portrait Gallery; Retreat to Corunna: British Library (John Webb) **271** Rifle brigade: National Army Museum; George III (detail): Copyright reserved

Regency **272/3** Covent Garden hustings (detail): Reproduced by gracious permission of Her Majesty Queen Elizabeth II **273** Covent Garden today: (Mike Coles) **274** Death of Perceval: Mary Evans Picture Library; Peterloo, freeborn Englishman: British Library (John Freeman) **275** Policeman: British Library (John Freeman); Cato Street Conspiracy: Mansell Collection; Duke of Wellington: Mary Evans Picture Library **276** Duck shooting, prize fight, country fair: British Library (John Freeman); the waltz: Mary Evans Picture Library **277** Fencers, Harriette Wilson, whist players, Westminster rat pit: British Library (John Freeman); Kean as Richard III: Victoria and Albert Museum; Beau Brummel: Mary Evans Picture Library **278** Furniture and clock from Brighton Pavilion: Royal Pavilion, Brighton; banquet, cross section of the Pavilion: British Library (John Freeman) **279** View of the Pavilion: (Keith Morris) **280** Wellington's field set, Wellington (detail): Wellington Museum, Apsley House (Eileen Tweedy); Napoleon: Bibliothèque Nationale, Paris **281** Battle of Waterloo (detail): Wellington Museum, Apsley House (Eileen Tweedy) **282** Flight of Napoleon, Last Stand of the Imperial Guard: National Army Museum **283** Soldiers: National Army Museum; The Man Wot Drives . . .: British Library (John Freeman) **284** The Ranger's House: (John Couzins) **285** The Trial of Queen Caroline (detail): National Portrait Gallery; The Kettle and the Pot: British Library (John Freeman); Prince Regent: National Portrait Gallery **286** Shelley (detail), Keats (detail), Byron (detail): National Portrait Gallery; Fournier – Funeral of Shelley: Walker Art Gallery, Liverpool **287** Faraday in his Laboratory: Royal Institution, London (Eileen Tweedy) **288** The Rocket: Science Museum, London, Crown copyright; George Stephenson: Mary Evans Picture Library **289** Goods train: Science Museum, London (Eileen Tweedy); Trevithick's railroad and advertisement: Photo. Science Museum, London **290** Reform jug: Courtesy of J. & J. May Ltd (Eileen Tweedy) **291** Reformed House of Commons (detail): National Portrait Gallery; voters: Mary Evans Picture Library; William IV: British Library (Eileen Tweedy) **292** Constable – Study for the Leaping Horse: Victoria and Albert Museum; Constable – Seascape study: Royal Academy of Arts (Phaidon Ltd); Constable – The Haywain: Trustees of the National Gallery, London **293** Turner – Petworth House, Turner – The Shipwreck: Tate Gallery, London; Turner – Rain, Steam and Speed: Trustees of the National Gallery, London

Victoria **294/5** Victoria and family (detail): Copyright reserved **296** Wheat field: Mary Evans Picture Library; traction engine: Radio Times Hulton Picture Library; shop: Mary Evans Picture Library; Sainsbury's: Courtesy of J. Sainsbury Ltd **297** Dame school: Mary Evans Picture Library; council school: Mansell Collection; stage coach: Mary Evans Picture Library; steam engine: Science Museum, London, Crown copyright **298** Proclamation jug: Courtesy of J. & J. May Ltd (Eileen Tweedy); Coronation of Victoria (detail): Copyright Reserved **299** Queen Victoria (detail): National Portrait Gallery; Victoria's desk at Osborne: Erich Lessing (Magnum) from the John Hillelson Agency **300** SS *Great Britain*: (Malcolm Aird); Launch of the SS *Great Britain*, SS *Great Western*: City Art Gallery, Bristol **301** SS *Great Eastern*: Radio Times Hulton Picture Library; I. K. Brunel: Brunel University Library; railway engine: Mansell Collection **302** Souvenirs of the Great Exhibition: By courtesy of the Victoria and Albert Museum (Eileen Tweedy); navvies: Radio Times Hulton Picture Library **303** Opening of the Great Exhibition (detail), Machinery Hall (detail): Reproduced by gracious permission of Her Majesty Queen Elizabeth II **304** Millais – Ophelia: Tate Gallery, London; Millais: Academy Editions; Holman Hunt – Christ in the House of His Parents: Tate Gallery, London **305** Ford Maddox Brown – The Last of England: Tate Gallery, London; Elizabeth Siddal: Ashmolean Museum, Oxford; Jane Morris: Academy Editions; Ford Maddox Brown (detail): National Portrait Gallery; Dante's Dream: Walker Art Gallery, Liverpool; Hireling Shepherd: City Art Gallery, Manchester; Rossetti, Holman Hunt: Academy Editions **306** Bugle: Museum of the 17th/21st Lancers, Belvoir (Eileen Tweedy); Council of War, Men of the 47th Foot: National Army Museum; Charge of the Light Brigade: (Eileen Tweedy) **307** W. H. Russell, Florence Nightingale: Radio Times Hulton Picture Library **308** Charles Dickens: Radio Times Hulton Picture Library **309** Cooling graveyard, Forge at Chalk: (John Bulmer); The Brontë Sisters (detail): National Portrait Gallery **310** Paper cartridge: Pattern Room, Royal Small Arms Factory, Enfield; Sir Henry Havelock, Sir Colin Campbell: Mansell Collection; Charge of the Queen's Bays: By permission of the Colonel, 1st The Queen's Dragoon Guards **311** Lucknow memorial, Medical Group No. 1, Maxim gun: National Army Museum **312** Houses of Parliament: (Brian Shuel); Pugin (detail), Barrie (detail): National Portrait Gallery **313** House of Lords: (Perfecta Press); Gladstone and Disraeli plates: (Eileen Tweedy) **314** The *Beagle*, Charles Darwin: Down House (Royal College of Surgeons) **315** Darwin's finches: Trustees of the British Museum (Natural History); T. H. Huxley, Bishop Wilberforce: Radio Times Hulton Picture Library **316** Livingstone's sextant: Royal Geographical Society; Stanley, Livingstone: Livingstone Memorial, Blantyre; the meeting: Mary Evans Picture Library **317** Tippu Tip, African Slave: United Society for the Propagation of the Gospel; slave chain: Royal Geographical Society **318** Victorian souvenirs: (Eileen Tweedy); Jubilee procession: Guildhall Art Gallery, London **319** Naval review at Spithead: National Maritime Museum, London **320** Mafeking siege money: National Army Museum; scout camp, Mafeking night: Radio Times Hulton Picture Library **321** Baden-Powell march: National Army Museum; Boer soldiers, Boer families: Radio Times Hulton Picture Library

Twentieth century **322/3** Production platform: Shell; miners: National Coal Board **324** Newsboy: Radio Times Hulton Picture Library; *Titanic*: Popperfoto Ltd; British Empire Exhibition poster: Lords Gallery; Allied leaders handkerchief: Leslie L. Hook (Eileen Tweedy) **325** Mosley: Keystone Press Agency; Neville Chamberlain, Royal Family: Popperfoto Ltd **326** Bicycle poster: Lords Gallery; Marie Lloyd poster: Victoria and Albert Museum; Vesta Tilley: Jasmine Spencer **326** Edwardian melodrama advertisement: The Mander and Mitchenson Theatre Collection; Gaiety Girl poster: Lords Gallery **327** 'Hello Rag Time' programme cover: The Mander and Mitchenson Theatre Collection; Edward VII in a Daimler: Montague Motor Museum; Egyptian Hall poster: London Museum; Cricket team: Radio Times Hulton Picture Library; Flying at Hendon poster: London Transport; Henley Regatta **328** Radio Times Hulton Picture Library Elgar: Mary Evans Picture Library; Lady Elgar, Elgar's house, still life: (John Bulmer) **329** Nucleus disintegrator: Cavendish Laboratory, Cambridge (Michael St Maur Shiel); Rutherford (detail): National Portrait Gallery **330** Page from Scott's journal: By kind permission of Sir Peter Scott and the Trustees of the British Museum (Popperfoto); Cape Evans, Camp on King Edward VII Plateau: Popperfoto Ltd **331** Group: Popperfoto Ltd; King Edward VII: Keystone Press Agency **332** Suffragette badges: London Museum (Eileen Tweedy); Votes for Women poster: Mary Evans Picture Library; arrest of Mrs Pankhurst: Radio Times Hulton Picture Library **333** Pankhursts in Holloway: Radio Times Hulton Picture Library; Coronation souvenir poster: Jasmine Spencer **334** 'Scrap of Paper' poster: Imperial War Museum (Eileen Tweedy); French, von Klück: Radio Times Hulton Picture Library **334** Mons retreat: Robert Hunt Library **335** German prisoners: Robert Hunt Library; King's message: Jasmine Spencer; recruiting office: Radio Times Hulton Picture Library; George V and the Kaiser: Popperfoto Ltd **336** Still life: Imperial War Museum (Michael Freeman); Haig: Radio Times Hulton Picture Library; troops: Imperial War Museum (Camera Press) **337** Field dressing station: Popperfoto Ltd; tank: RAC Tank Museum; ammunitions factory: Imperial War Museum (Camera Press) **338** Sassoon: Radio Times Hulton Picture Library; Owen: *Journey from Obscurity, Wilfred Owen 1893–1918* by Harold Owen, published by Oxford University Press (National Portrait Gallery); Brooke: Radio Times Hulton Picture Library **339** Menin Road: Imperial War Museum; La Mitrailleuse: Tate Gallery, London (John Webb); A Battery Shelled: Imperial War Museum (Eileen Tweedy) **340** Cornwell relics: Imperial War Museum (Eileen Tweedy); Jellicoe: Radio Times Hulton Picture Library; Beatty: Robert Hunt Library; *Seydlitz* scuttled: Imperial War Museum (Camera Press) **341** U-boat poster: Imperial War Museum (Eileen Tweedy) **342** Poster: Imperial War Museum (Eileen Tweedy); gas victims: Imperial War Museum (Camera Press); Germans surrendering: Robert Hunt Library; front page of the *Daily Chronicle*: John Frost Historical Newspaper Service; ration book: Imperial War Museum (Eileen Tweedy) **344** Newspapers: John Frost Historical Newspaper Service; undergraduates unloading milk: Rado Times Hulton Picture Library **345** Food convoy, sailors at power station: Radio Times Hulton Picture Library; poster: Labour Party **346** Abdication document: Radio Times Hulton Picture Library; Prince of Wales in 1919: Popperfoto Ltd **347** Prince of Wales hunting: Popperfoto Ltd; Edward VIII in Wales and George VI: Popperfoto Ltd; wedding: Radio Times Hulton Picture Library **348** Spitfire: RAF Museum, Hendon (Perfecta Publications Ltd); waiting pilots: Popperfoto Ltd; scramble: Imperial War Museum (Camera Press) **349** Operations room, Spitfires: Imperial War Museum (Camera Press); preparing bullets: Popperfoto Ltd **350** Bomber over London: Imperial War Museum (Camera Press); rescue workers: Keystone Press Agency; bomb damage, London: Popperfoto Ltd; Churchill in Manchester: Keystone Press Agency **351** bomb damage – Coventry, Air-raid Wardens: Keystone Press Agency; Churchill poster: Imperial War Museum (A. C. Cooper Ltd) **352** Medal: Spinks Ltd (Eileen Tweedy); Montgomery, Rommel: Popperfoto Ltd; action at El Alamein: Popperfoto Ltd; prisoners: Keystone Press Agency **353** Sinking of the *Bismarck*: Associated Press; Admiral Tovey: Keystone Press Agency **354** HMS *Belfast*: (Michael Freeman); Allied Commanders: Imperial War Museum (Camera Press); armada, commandos, V-2 rocket: Imperial War Museum (Camera Press); flag: Jasmine Spencer **356** Front page of the *News Chronicle*: John Frost Historical Newspaper Service; Members of the Expedition, Hillary and Tensing, Base Camp: Royal Geographical Society **357** Porters, Tensing on the summit: Royal Geographical Society; Her Majesty the Queen in Canberra: Popperfoto Ltd **358** Royal Family: Fox/Keystone; Marathon: All Sport (Mike Powell); Daley Thompson: All Sport (Tony Duffy); Mini: Syndication International **359** Twiggy: Syndication International; Beatles: EMI; Carnival: Spooner/Gummer (Arkell); Lord Olivier: Granada Television; Benjamin Britten: Popperfoto; Torvill and Dean: All Sport (Tony Duffy)

Gazetteer **360** Castle: British Travel Authority; **362** Abbotsford: Mary Evans Picture Library; Sir Walter Scott (detail): National Portrait Gallery; Robert Burns: Trustees of the Burns Memorial, Alloway **363** Stone of Destiny (both pictures): Keystone Press Agency **364** George Eliot (detail): National Portrait Gallery; football match: Mary Evans Picture Library; **365** George Bernard Shaw (detail): National Portrait Gallery; Shaw's Corner: A. F. Kersting **366** Balmoral 1896: Radio Times Hulton Picture Library; Banbury Cross: Mary Evans Picture Library **367** Rudyard Kipling: Radio Times Hulton Picture Library; Beau Nash: Bath Municipal Libraries, Victoria Art Gallery; **368** Berkeley Castle: British Tourist Authority; Baldwin: Popperfoto Ltd; Sir Richard Grenville (detail): National Portrait Gallery **369** Neville Chamberlain: Popperfoto Ltd; Churchill: Mansell Collection **370** Delius: Mansell Collection; Highland Games: Mary

Evans Picture Library **371** Gravestone: City Museum, Bristol **372** Catharine of Aragon (detail): National Portrait Gallery **373** Lady Nelson: Radio Times Hulton Picture Library; Arnold Bennett (detail): National Portrait Gallery **374** Investiture of Edward VIII: Mary Evans Picture Library; Black Prince: Mansell Collection **375** Robert Ferrar: Radio Times Hulton Picture Library **376** Stringfellow aeroplanes: Crown copyright, Science Museum, London; Churchill: Radio Times Hulton Picture Library; Marconi: Marconi Ltd **377** Lawrence of Arabia: Radio Times Hulton Picture Library **378** Coldstream Guards: Radio Times Hulton Picture Library; Ruskin: Mary Evans Picture Library **379** Coventry: Fox Photos Ltd **380** George Stephenson (detail): National Portrait Gallery **381** Captain Webb: Mary Evans Picture Library; Captain Webb matches: Bryant & May Ltd; Bothwell, Viscount Dundee: Radio Times Hulton Picture Library; Thomas Carlyle: Mary Evans Picture Library **384** George IV: Radio Times Hulton Picture Library; Resurrectionists: Mansell Collection **385** R. L. Stevenson, Stevenson's home: Mansell Collection **386** Farnborough: Illustrated Newspapers Group; Tennyson: Mansell Collection **387** Trial of Mary, Queen of Scots: Trustees of the British Library **388** Pocahontas: Mary Evans Picture Library **389** Captain Kidd: Radio Times Hulton Picture Library; batsman: Mary Evans Picture Library **390** Hawarden: Mansell Collection **391** Sir Robert Walpole (detail): National Portrait Gallery; Crómwell: Radio Times Hulton Picture Library **392** Jarrow marchers: Radio Times Hulton Picture Library **393** George Romney (detail): National Portrait Gallery **394** Fox Talbot (both): Photo. Science Museum, London **396** Lloyd George: Radio Times Hulton Picture Library **397** Buckingham Palace (both): Radio Times Hulton Picture Library **398** Rossetti: from *The Poet's Corner* by Max Beerbohm, published by William Heinemann (Mansell Collection); Mrs Siddons: Royal Shakespeare Theatre, Stratford-upon-Avon; Garrick, Kean, Macready: The Mander and Mitchenson Theatre Collection **399** Northcliffe: Mary Evans Picture Library; *Daily Mail*: John Frost Historical Newspaper Service **400** Freud: Associated Press; Karl Marx: Mansell Collection; Marx's tomb: Camera Press (Peter Mitchell); Lenin: Mansell Collection **401** Collins Music Hall: The Mander and Mitchenson Theatre Collection; Marie Lloyd: Popperfoto Ltd; Little Tich, The Royal Albert Hall: Mary Evans Picture Library **402** Elizabeth Barrett Browning: Radio Times Hulton Picture Library: Robert Browning: Mary Evans Picture Library; Queen Charlotte's Ball, deb's parade: Radio Times Hulton Picture Library **403** King's Cross 1861, Jonathan Wild: Mary Evans Picture Library **404** Bomb damage in St Paul's; Fox Photos Ltd; press cuttings: *Daily Express*; Attlee: Keystone Press Agency **406** Mary Shelley (detail): National Portrait Gallery; Marston Moor: National Army Museum; Thomas Cook & Son trade mark: Mansell Collection **407** Rolls: Radio Times Hulton Picture Library **409** Nonsuch: Radio Times Hulton Picture Library **411** Royal Family at Osborne: Radio Times Hulton Picture Library **412** Sir Philip Sidney: Radio Times Hulton Picture Library **413** The Young Pretender: Radio Times Hulton Picture Library **414** Lord Palmerston: Mary Evans Picture Library **415** Henry James: Radio Times Hulton Picture Library; Football at Rugby: Illustrated Newspapers Group **416** Edward VII: Illustrated Newspapers Group **417** John Paul Jones: Mansell Collection; Gilbert White: Popperfoto Ltd **418** Richard Parker: Mansell Collection; Charles II: Mary Evans Picture Library **421** Tay Bridge: Mansell Collection; Tichborne claimant: Mary Evans Picture Library **422** Turpin: Radio Times Hulton Picture Library; Warwick: BPC

The publishers also acknowledge their indebtedness to the following books and journals which were consulted for reference:

Abbeys, Castles, and Ancient Halls of England and Wales by John Timbs and Alexander Gunn (Frederick Warne); *Age by Age: Landmarks of British Archaeology* by Ronald Jessup (Michael Joseph); *The Age of Elegance* by Arthur Bryant (Penguin); *Alfred the Great* by Eleanor Shipley Duckett (University of Chicago Press); *Alfred The Great* by H. R. Loyn (Oxford); *Alfred The Great and His England* by Eleanor Shipley Duckett (Collins); *Anglo-Saxon Architecture* by H. M. and J. Taylor (Cambridge); *The Anglo-Saxon Chronicle* edited by Dorothy Whitelock (Eyre and Spottiswoode); *Anglo-Saxon England and the Norman Conquest* by H. R. Loyn (Longman); *Anglo-Saxon Saints and Scholars* by Eleanor Shipley Duckett (The Macmillan Company); *The Anglo-Saxons* by David M. Wilson (Thames and Hudson); *Anne Boleyn* by Hester W. Chapman (Jonathan Cape); *The Archaeology of Roman Britain* by R. H. Collingwood & Sir Ian Archibald Richmond (Methuen); *Art in Britain Under The Romans* by J. M. C. Toynbee (Oxford); *The Ascent of Man* by J. Bronowski (BBC); *Auchinleck* by John Connell (Cassell); *August 1914* by Barbara Tuchman (Constable); *The Battles of Wales* by O. M. Morgan (Salisbury Hughes); *Bede's Ecclesiastical History of the English People* edited by Bertram Colgrave and R. A. B. Mynors (Oxford); *Blue Guide to Wales* edited by Stuart Rossiter (Ernest Benn); *The Book of the City* edited by Ian Norrie (High Hill Books); *Britain, Rome's Most Northerly Province* by G. M. Durant (G. Bell); *Britain and her Army* by Correlli Barnett (Allen Lane); *Britain and Ireland in Early Christian Times AD 400–800* by Charles Thomas (Thames and Hudson); *Britain in the Roman Empire* by Joan Liversidge (Routledge); *British Battle Series* by Katherine Tomasson and Francis Buist (Pan Books); *British Battlefields* series by Philip Warner (Osprey); *Britannia* by Sheppard Frere (Routledge); *The Bronze Age Round Barrow in Britain* by Paul Ashbee (Phoenix House); *Brunel and His World* by John Pudney (Thames and Hudson); *The Buildings of England* series edited by Sir Nikolaus Pevsner (Penguin); *Caesar* by Irwin Isenberg (Cassell); *Captain Cook, His Artists, His Voyages* (*Sydney Daily Telegraph*); *Captain Cook, the Seamen's Seaman* by Alan Milliers (Penguin); *Captain Cook and the South Pacific* by Oliver Warner (Cassell); *Castles of England* by Garry Hogg (David and Charles); *The Castles of England* by Frederick Wilkinson (George Philip); *The Castles of Scotland* by Susan Ross (George Philip); *The Castles of Wales* by Alan Reid (George Philip); *Celtic Britain* by Nora K. Chadwick (Thames and Hudson); *The Celts* by Nora K. Chadwick (Penguin); *Chambers Biographical Dictionary* edited by J. O. Thorne (W. and R. Chambers); *Charles Edward Stuart* by David Daiches (Thames and Hudson); *Charles II* by Hesketh Pearson (Heinemann); *Civilisation* by Kenneth Clark (BBC/John Murray); *The Collapse of British Power* by Correlli Barnett (Eyre Methuen); *The Coming of Christianity to Anglo-Saxon England* by Henry Mayr-Harbing (Batsford); *The Companion Guide to Kent and Sussex* by Keith Spence (Collins); *A Concise History of England* by F. E. Halliday (Thames and Hudson); *A Concise History of Scotland* by Fitzroy Maclean (Thames and Hudson); *Conquest of Gaul by Julius Caesar* edited by S. A. Handford (Penguin); *Costume: An Illustrated Survey from Ancient Times to the Twentieth Century* by Margot Lister (Barrie and Jenkins); *Costumes of Everyday Life* by Margot Lister (Barrie and Jenkins); *The County Books* series edited by Brian Vesey Fitzgerald (Robert Hale); *The Court at Windsor* by Christopher Hibbert (Longman); *Cricket: A History* by Rowland Brown (Eyre and Spottiswoode); *Cromwell, Our Chief of Men* by Antonia Fraser (Weidenfeld and Nicolson); *The Crystal Palace* by Patrick Beaver (Hugh Evelyn); *The Dark Ages* edited by David Talbot Rice (Thames and Hudson); *D-Day, Spearhead of Invasion* by R. W. Thompson (Pan Ballantine); *Defeat Into Victory* by Sir William Slim (Cassell); *The Deluge: British Society and the First World War* by Arthur Marwick (Bodley Head); *The Desert Generals* by Correlli Barnett (William Kimber); *The Dictionary of National Biography* (Oxford); *Discovering London* by Norman Hillson (Herbert Jenkins); *Douglas Haig: The Educated Soldier* by John Terraine (Hutchinson); *Drake* by Ernle Bradford (Hodder and Stoughton); *The Edwardians* by J. B. Priestley (Heinemann); *El Alamein* by David Carver (Batsford); *The Elizabethan Image* by Roy Strong (Tate Gallery Publications); *England in the Nineteenth Century* by David Thomson (Penguin); *England in the Reign of Charles II* by David Ogg (Oxford); *The English* by J. B. Priestley (Heinemann); *English Cathedrals* by Peter Meyer (Thames and Hudson); *English Costume from the 2nd Century BC to 1952* by D. Yarwood (Batsford); *English Furniture AD 43–1950* by E. T. Joy (Batsford); *English Furniture of the 18th Century* by David Nickerson (Weidenfeld and Nicolson); *English Historical Documents c. 500–1042* edited by Dorothy Whitelock (Eyre and Spottiswoode); *English History*, A Survey by Sir George Clark; *English Life* series edited by Peter Quennell (Batsford/Putnam); *English Social History* by G. M. Trevelyan (Longman); *The Escape of Charles II* by Richard Ollard (Hodder and Stoughton); *Excavations at Clickhimin, Shetland* by J. R. C. Hamilton (Edinburgh: HMSO); *Field Guide to Archaeology in Britain* by Eric S. Wood (Collins); *The First Battle of Britain 1917–18* by Raymond H. Fredette (Cassell); *Fishbourne: A Roman Palace and Its Garden* by Barry Cunliffe (Thames and Hudson); *Forts and Castles* by Terence Wise (Almark); *George IV, Prince of Wales* by Christopher Hibbert (Longman); *George IV, Regent and King* by Christopher Hibbert (Allen Lane); *Glencoe* by John Prebble (Penguin); *Gloriana, The Years of Elizabeth I* by Mary M. Luke (Gollancz); *The Grand Tour* by Christopher Hibbert (Spring Books); *The Great Invasion* by Leonard Cottrell (Evans Bros.); *The Great War 1914–1918* by John Terraine (Hutchinson); *The Greater Anglo-Saxon Churches* by E. A. Fisher (Faber); *Greater London* by Christopher Trent (Phoenix House); *A Guide to the Prehistoric and Roman Monuments in England and Wales* by Jacquetta Hawkes (Sphere); *Hanover to Windsor* by Roger Fulford (Batsford); *The Herberts of Wilton* by Tresham Lever (John Murray); *History of England* by Sir Keith Feiling (Macmillan); *History of England* by Thomas Babington Macaulay (J. M. Dent); *History of England* by G. M. Trevelyan (Longman); *A History of Scotland* by Rosalind Mitchinson (Methuen); *History of the Second World War* by B. H. Liddell-Hart (Cassell); *A History of Wales* by J. E. Lloyd (Longman); *A History of Warfare* by Field Marshal Viscount Montgomery of Alamein (Collins); *The Home Fronts 1914–1918* by John Williams (Constable); *How They Lived (Vol. I)* Compiler: W. O. Hassall (Blackwell); *How They Lived (Vol. II)* Compilers: M. Harrison and O. M. Royston (Blackwell); *How They Lived (Vol. III)* Compiler: A. Briggs (Blackwell); *The Ice Age* by Björn Kurtén (Hart-Davis); *The Ice Age in Britain* by B. W. Sparks and R. G. West (Methuen); *An Illustrated Cultural History of England* by F. E. Halliday (Thames and Hudson); *An Inventory of the Historical Monuments in the City of York (Vol. I, Eboracum, Roman York)* (Royal Commission on Ancient and Historical Monuments of England); *Iron Age Communities in Britain* by Barry Cunliffe (Routledge); *Isambard Kingdom Brunel* by L. T. C. Rolt (Penguin); Jackdaw Publications (Founded and Distributed by Jonathan Cape Limited); *James VI & I* by D. H. Wilson (Cape); *Julius Caesar* by Michael Grant (Weidenfeld and Nicolson); *King Arthur in Legend and History* by Richard Barber (Boydell Press); *King Edgar* by Helen Panter (Morgan Books); *King John* by W. L. Warren (Penguin); *Kings and Queens of England* series, General Editor Antonia Fraser (Weidenfeld and Nicolson); *The King's Arcadia: Inigo Jones and The Stuart Court* by John Harris, Stephen Orgel and Roy Strong (Arts Council); *The King's Peace* by C. V. Wedgwood (Collins/Fontana); *The King's War* by C. V. Wedgwood (Collins/Fontana); *Liaison 1914* by Sir Edward Spears (Eyre and Spottiswoode); *The Life of Shakespeare* by F. E. Halliday (Duckworth); *Literature and Western Man* by J. B. Priestley (Heinemann); *Living History* by Alan Sorrell (Batsford); *London* by David Piper (Thames and Hudson); *London, A Pictorial History* by John Hayes (Batsford); *London, The Biography of a City* by Christopher Hibbert (Longman); *London Growing* by Michael Harrison (Hutchinson); *London on the Thames* by Blake Erlich (Cassell); *The Lowlands* by Ian Finlay (Batsford); *Maiden Castle, Dorset* by R. E. M. Wheeler (The Society of Antiquaries); *Making of a Nation 1689–1789* by A. J. Patrick (Penguin); *The Making of Early England* by D. P. Kirby (Batsford); *Mayfair, a Town within London* by Reginald Colby (*Country Life*); *The Medieval Castle* by Philip Warner (Arthur Barker); *Men and Places* by J. H. Plumb (Penguin); *Mons: The Retreat to Victory* by John Terraine (Batsford); *Montgomery as Military Commander* by Ronald Lewin (Cassell); *The Mystery of Stonehenge* by Franklyn M. Branley (David and Charles); *The Narrow Margin* by Derek Wood and Derek Dempster (Hutchinson); *Nelson* by Arthur Bryant (Collins/Fontana); *Nelson and His World* by Tom Pocock (Thames and Hudson); *Nelson and the Age of Fighting Sail* by the Editors of *Horizon Magazine* (Cassell); *The Norman Achievement* by David C. Douglas (Collins/Fontana); *Northumberland and Durham* by Iris Wedgwood (Faber); *The North-West Frontier of Rome* by David Divine (Macdonald); *Old English Towns* by F. R. Banks (Batsford); *Orkney* by Patrick Bailey (David and Charles); *Oxford* by Ralph Durand (Oxford); *The Oxford Companion to the Theatre* edited by Phyllis Hartnoll (Oxford); *Oxford History of England* (XV Volumes) edited by Sir George Clark (Oxford); *Pagan Celtic Britain* by Anne Ross (Routledge); *The Pelican History of Art* by Sir John Summerson (Penguin); *The Pelican History of England* series (Penguin); *A Place in History* by Paul Johnson (Weidenfeld and Nicolson); *The Prince of Pleasure and His Regency* by J. B. Priestley (Heinemann); *The Private Papers of Douglas Haig* edited by Robert Blake (Eyre and Spottiswoode); *The Purnell History of the 20th Century* A. J. P. Taylor, Editor-in-Chief (BPC); *Queen Elizabeth I* by J. E. Neale (Cape); *The Quest for Arthur's Britain* edited by Geoffrey Ashe (Pall Mall Press/Paladin); *R.A.F. Biggin Hill* by Graham Wallace (Putnam); *The Rebellion of Boudicca* by Donald R. Dudley and Graham Webster (Routledge); *Richborough Excavations* edited by Barry Cunliffe (Society of Antiquaries); *The River Dart* by Ruth Manning-Sanders (Westaway Books); *Robert, Earl of Essex, an Elizabethan Icarus* by Robert Lacey (Weidenfeld and Nicolson); *Roman Archaeology and Art* by Sir Ian Richmond (Faber); *Roman Britain* by Aileen Fox and Alan Sorrell (Lutterworth); *Roman Britain* by I. A. Richmond (Jonathan Cape); *Roman Britain and Early England 55 BC–AD 871* by P. Hunter Blair (Nelson); *The Roman Conquest of Britain (43–57)* by D. R. Dudley and Graham Webster (Batsford); *The Roman Imperial Army of the 1st and 2nd Centuries AD* by Graham Webster (A. and C. Black); *Roman Roads in Britain* by Ivan D. Margary (John Baker); *Rommel as Military Commander* by Ronald Lewin (Batsford); *The Rommel Papers* edited by B. H. Liddell-Hart (Collins); *Royal Dukes* by Roger Fulford (Collins); *Royal Homes* by Neville Williams (Lutterworth); *Saxon England* by John Hamilton and Alan Sorrell (Lutterworth); *Scotland* by Gordon Donaldson (Oliver and Boyd); *Scottish Revolution 1637–1644* by David Stevenson (David and Charles); *The Second World War* by Winston Churchill (Cassell); *Shakespeare, The Poet and His Background* by Peter Quennell (Weidenfeld and Nicolson); *Shakespeare's England* by Levi Fox (Wayland); *Shakespeare's England* by the Editors of *Horizon Magazine* (Cassell); *The Shape of History* by Donald Turnbull (Macmillan); *The Shell Book of Offa's Dyke Path* by Frank Noble (Queen Anne Press); *Shetland* by J. R. Nicolson (David and Charles); *A Short History of English Literature* by Gilbert Phelps (Folio Society); *A Short History of the Second World War* by Basil Collier (Collins); *Sir Walter Raleigh* by Robert Lacey (Weidenfeld and Nicolson); *The Somme* by A. H. Farrar-Hockley (Batsford); *The Spanish Armada* by Jay Williams (Cassell); *Sport in Society* by P. C. McIntosh (C. A. Watts); *Steel Bonnets* by George MacDonald Fraser (Barrie and Jenkins); *Steinberg's Dictionary of British History* (Arnold); *The Stuarts* by J. P. Kenyon (Collins/Fontana); *Sutton Hoo* by Charles Green (Merlin Press); *The Sutton Hoo Ship Burial* by R. L. S. Bruce-Mitford (British Museum); *The Swordbearers* by Correlli Barnett (Eyre and Spottiswoode); *Tacitus and Germania* translated by H. Mattingley (Penguin); *They Saw It Happen (1689–1897)* edited by T. Charles Edwards and Brian Richardson (Blackwell); *Tourist's England* by Arthur Grand (Frank Graham); *The Tower of London in the History of the Nation* by A. L. Rowse (Weidenfeld and Nicolson); *A Traveller's Guide to Battlefields of Europe Volume I* edited by D. Chandler (Hugh Evelyn); *A Traveller's Guide to Literary Europe Volume II* edited by Margaret Crosland (Hugh Evelyn); *The Trial of Charles I* by C. V. Wedgwood (Collins/Fontana); *Van Dyck: Charles I on Horseback* by Roy Strong (Allen Lane); *Victoria R.I.* by Elizabeth Longford (Weidenfeld and Nicolson); *Victorian Cities* by Asa Briggs (Penguin); *The Victorian Scene 1837–1901* by Nicholas Bentley (Weidenfeld and Nicolson); *Wales* by Gilbert Stone (George Harrap); *The War for America* by Piers Mackesy (Longman); *Wedgwood Portrait Medallions* by Robin Reilly (National Portrait Gallery); *Wellington's Peninsular Victories* by Michael Glover (Pan Books); *Welsh Border Country* by P. T. Jones (Batsford); *The West Country* by S. H. Burton (Robert Hale); *Where They Lived in London* by Maurice Rickards (David and Charles); *Who's Who in History* series, General Editor C. R. N. Routh (Blackwell); *William and Mary* by Henry and Barbara van der Zee (Macmillan); *Windsor Castle in the History of the Nation* by A. L. Rowse (Weidenfeld and Nicolson); *The Works in Architecture of Robert and James Adam* by John Swarbrick (Alec Tiranti); *The World of Charles Dickens* by Angus Wilson (Penguin); *Wren* by Margaret Whinney (Thames and Hudson)

The publishers wish to acknowledge their indebtedness to the following for permission to use quotations:

Richard Barber and The Boydell Press Ltd for an extract from *King Arthur in Legend and History* (1973) by Richard Barber; Eyre and Spottiswoode Ltd for an extract from *The Anglo-Saxon Chronicle*, a revised translation edited by Dorothy Whitelock with David C. Douglas and Susie I. Tucker; Eyre and Spottiswoode Ltd for extracts from *English Historical Documents c. 500—1042* edited by Dorothy Whitelock; Faber & Faber Ltd and G. T. Sassoon for the extract from 'Counter Attack' in *The Collected Poems of Siegfried Sassoon*; The Estate of H. Mattingley (1948 and 1970) and Penguin Books Ltd for the extracts from *Tacitus and Germania* by Tacitus, translated by H. Mattingley; The Executors of the Estate of Harold Owen and Chatto & Windus for extracts from 'Anthem for Doomed Youth', 'Strange Meeting' and a quotation from the draft preface to Wilfred Owen's planned volume of poems, taken from *The Collected Poems of Wilfred Owen* edited by C. Day Lewis, 1963; The Pall Mall Press Ltd for an extract from *The Quest for Arthur's Britain* by Geoffrey Ashe; Penguin Books Ltd and Nevill Coghill for lines from *The Canterbury Tales* by Geoffrey Chaucer, translated by Nevill Coghill (Penguin Classics, Revised Edition 1960) © Nevill Coghill, 1951, 1958, 1960; Penguin Books Ltd for extracts from *Conquest of Gaul* by Julius Caesar, translated by S. A. Handford; Sidgwick & Jackson Ltd for lines from 'The Soldier' in *The Complete Poems of Rupert Brooke*; John Terraine for the quotation from *General Jack's Diary* by Brigadier General James Lochhead Jack, edited by John Terraine (Eyre and Spottiswoode, 1964)

Contributors The publishers gratefully acknowledge the assistance of the following contributors: Will Allan; Anne Angus; Dulcie Ashdown; Adrian Brink; Anthony Cheetham; John O. E. Clark; Gila Curtis; Diana de Deney; David Hunn; W. F. Inglis; Anne Kings; Patricia Ledward; David Levy; Maurice Rickards; Simon Rigge; Basil Skinner; Keith Spence; Judith Taylor; Margaret Willes

Artists Victor Ambrus; Gary Hinks

Photographers Malcolm Aird; Michael Coles; John Couzins; Mike Freeman; Alain Le Garsmeur; Keith Morris; Chris Ridley; Mike Taylor; Eileen Tweedy

Printing and Binding by Jarrold & Sons Ltd, Norwich

40/051–2

Published by The Reader's Digest Association Limited, 25 Berkeley Square, London W1X 6AB